*To our parents, grandparents, aunts, uncles, and cousins
—to our loved ones and our friends who have inspired and
supported us throughout our lives—for giving us the
examples of integrity and caring that we have always tried
to follow, our deepest thanks*

Todd and Jeff


*To my wife, Randye, for her love and support*

Jeff

## SOURCES OF INCOME

Motion Pictures
Television
Ringtones
Sampling
Home Video/DVD
Greeting Cards
Sheet Music/Folios
Dolls, toys, Music Boxes, General Boxes
Interactive Games
CD-ROM/Multi-media Audio Visual Configurations
Special Products Albums
Streaming
Foreign Countries
Performances
Advertising
Lyric Reprints
Karaoke
Theme Parks
Compilation Albums
Record Sales
Trailers
Limited Edition Collectibles
Downloads
Broadway/Off Broadway/The Road

# Contents

INTRODUCTION    xix

1.  Music, Money, Songwriting, and Music
    Publishing                                              1

Music Publishers and What They Do    2
  *Singles, Albums, CDs, and Cassettes  3  / Demos   4 /*
  *Proper Administration   4  /  Television and Movie Music   5  /*
  *Commercials   5  /  Foreign Promotion and Collection of*
  *Royalties   5  /  The Publisher, Writer/Performer, and Record*
  *Contracts   6  /  Infringement Actions   6  / Home Video   6*
The Inner Workings of a Music Publisher    6
  *Business and Legal Affairs Department   7  / Copyright   7 /*
  *Foreign   7 / Royalty   8  / Promotion   8  / Creative   8  /*
  *Computer   8  / Chief Executive   9*
The Acquisition of Rights by a Publisher    9
  *Individual Song and Exclusive Agreements   9  /*
  *Administration Agreement   10  / Foreign*
  *Subpublishing Agreement   10*
The Songwriter–Music Publisher Relationship    11
Publishing Contracts    11
  *The Individual Song Contract   12   / The Exclusive*
  *Songwriter's Contract   13*

Important Provisions of Songwriter–Publisher Contracts   13
  *Sale of the Musical Composition   14   / Return of Songs
  to the Writer   14   / The Term   14   / Rights Granted to
  the Publisher   15   / Exclusivity   15   / Compensation
  16   / Sharing of Advances   16   / Minimum Song
  Delivery   17   / Advances   17   / Writing with Other
  Songwriters   19   / Motion Picture and Television Theme
  Exclusions   19   / First-Use Mechanical Licenses   20   /
  Restrictions on Promotion   21   / Altering of Compositions   22   /
  Ownership and Promotion of Recordings   23   / Foreign
  Subpublisher Fees   23   / Audits   24   / Infringement Claims   25   /
  Writer-Performer Development Deals   26*
Sources of Income for the Music Publisher and Songwriter   28
  *Performance Right Payments   28   / CD, Record, and
  Tape Sales (Mechanical Royalties)   29   / Television
  Series   31   / Motion Pictures   32   / Home Video/DVDs   33
  / Commercials   34   / Broadway Musicals   35   /
  Instrumental CDs/Records of Popular
  Songs/Sing-Alongs/Karaoke   36   / Video Jukeboxes   36
  / Lyric Reprints in Novels or Nonfiction Books   36   /
  Lyric Reprints in Magazines   38   / Monthly Song Lyric
  and Sheet Music Magazines   38   / Public Service
  Announcements   38   / Recordings of Hit Songs with
  Changed Lyrics   39   / Medleys   39   / Promotional
  Videos   40   / Greeting Cards   41   / Computer and
  Board Trivia Games   42   / Television Commercials for
  Motion Pictures   42   / Home Video (Television
  Programs)   43   / Home Video (Recording Artists)   43
  / Foreign Theatrical Royalties (Motion Pictures)   44   /
  Dolls and Toys   44   / Television Programs and Motion
  Pictures Based on Songs   44   / Books Based on Motion
  Pictures (Lyric Reprints)   45   / Books about a Lyricist   45   /
  Novelty Albums   46   / Lyrics on Albums, Cassettes, and CD
  Packages   46   / Sheet Music and Folios   47   / Television and
  Motion Picture Background Scores   47   / Lyrics and Music on Soda
  Cans   47   / Lyrics on T-Shirts and Posters   48   / Audio Recordings
  of Books   48   / Special Products Albums   48   / Television Sale Only
  Albums   49   / Record Clubs   49   / Key Outlet Marketing Albums   49   /
  Limited Edition Collectibles   50   / Musical Telephones   50   /
  Singing Fish   51   / Theme Parks   51   / Ringtones   51   / Music Boxes
  52   / Internet   52   / Changing Mechanical Rates   52*
Conclusion   52

## 2.  Music, Money, Copublishing, and Administration   53

Standard Terms of a Copublishing Agreement   55
  *Sharing of Income   55   / Compositions Covered by the*

*Agreement 56 / Transfer of Copyright and Other Rights
57 / Term of Agreement 57 / Ownership of Songs
after the Contract Has Ended 57 / Advances 57 /
Nonrecoupable Payments 59 / Costs of Demos 59 /
Additional Costs 59 / Payment of Royalties to Songwriters 60 /
Sharing of Income between the Two Publishers 60 /
Administration Charges 61 / The Writer's Performance
Right Income 61 / The Publisher's Performance Right Income 61 /
Reversions and Direct Collection of Income 61 / Royalty
Distributions to the Writer's Company 62*

Administration Agreements 62
*Fees Charged for Administrative Services 63 / Dura-
tion 63 / Territory 63 / Royalty Statements 64 /
Royalty Payment Dates 64 / Cover Records and New
Uses 64 / Monies Earned during the Term 65 /
Advances 65 / Pros and cons of Administration
Agreements 65 / Choosing the Right Administrator 66*

## 3. Music, Money, and the Recording Artist      67

Inside the Business 69
The Most Important Points in Every Recording Contract 69
The Term 70
Artist Royalty Clauses 71
*Recording Artist Royalties 72 / Retail Price Base 72 /
Wholesale Price Base 72 / Factors That Determine an
Artist's Royalty 72 / Graduated-Increase Royalty
Provisions 73 / Sales Level Increases 73 / Contract
Option Year Increases 74 / Royalties for Sales Outside
the U.S. 74 / Album Price Lines and Royalty
Rates 75 / Packaging Deductions 76 / Free Goods 78 /
The 90% Sale Provision 79 / New-Technology Royalty Rate
Reductions 79 / Cut-Outs and Surplus Copies 80 /
Royalty Payments and Accounting Statements 80*

Advances 81
Album Release Obligations 83
Record Company Expenses 85
*Videos 85 / Tour Support 87 / Promotion Ex-
penses 87 / Recording Costs 88*

The Artist's Obligations 90
*The Minimum Recording Obligation 90 / Satisfaction
of an Artist's Delivery Commitment 91 / "Greatest
Hits" Albums 91 / Recording Sessions and Studios
92 / Album Artwork 92 / Warranties and
Indemnities 93 / Sideman Provisions 95 /
Re-Recording Restrictions 95 / Solo Albums 96 /
Provisions for New Band 97 / Recording and Delivery of
Albums 98 / Delivery of the Final Master Recording 98 /*

*Ownership of the Recordings*   99
Motion Picture, Television, and Commercial Uses   101
Shipping and Return Policies   102
*Returned Recordings and the Artist's Royalties*   102
Insurance Policies   104
Confidentiality Clauses   104
Artist–Production Company Agreements   104
*Flow-Through Clauses*   105
Controlled-Composition Clauses   106
*Mechanical Rates   106  / Sales Plateau Increases   106 /
Increased Royalties for Later Albums   107  / Canadian
Sales   109  / "Lock In" Rate Date   109  / "Greatest
Hits" Albums   110  / Maximum Royalty Cap   111  /
Singles and EPs   113  / One-Use-Only Mechanical
Royalties   113  / Midpriced, Budget, and Record Club
Reduced Royalties   114  / Increased Royalty Rates for
Compositions That Are Published by the Record Company
114  / Changing Mechanical Rates   114*
Copyrighted Arrangements of Compositions in the Public
Domain   115
*New Artist Pricing   116  / Contract Development   116*
Internet   116

4.   Music, Money, and Television                          118

The Television Industry   118
*The Making of a TV Program   119  / The Market   120*
Types of Television Music and How Music Is Used   122
The Television Music Budget   122
Television Underscore   123
The Television Underscore Contract   124
*Composer Services   125  / Starting and Completion
Dates   125  / Composing Fees   126  / Screen Credit
129  / Exclusivity of Composer's Services   129  /
Ownership of the Copyright   129  / Music Publishing
129  / Membership in a Performing Right Society   130
/ Suspensions and Terminations   131  / Disposition of
the Score   132  / Transportation and Expenses   133  /
Share of Advance Payments   133  / Warranties   133  /
Assignments   133  / Royalty Payments   134  /
Theatrical Version Release   134*
Television Synchronization Rights (Getting Songs into Series, Specials,
and Made-for-TV Movies)   134
*The Importance of Hit Songs   134  / Negotiating the
Television License for a Song   137  / Fees Charged   138 /
Hit Songs Used as Television Show Themes   145*

Life after a Song Gets into a Television Program (Where the Real
   Money Is Made)  155
   *Option Fees  156  / Video Cassettes, DVDs and Discs  157  /
   Hit Singles from Television Programs  160  / The
   Television Series Soundtrack Album  162  / Television
   Commercials Promoting the Program  162  / Sheet
   Music Folios  163  / Royalties from Motion Picture
   Theaters  163  / Television Broadcasts of the Series, Special,
   Made-for-TV Movie, or Miniseries  163  / Television Songs
   in Commercials  163  / Television Songs in Other Television
   Programs  164  / Television Songs Used in Motion Pictures  164  /
   Conclusion  164*

## 5.  Music, Money, and Motion Pictures  167

Overview  167
   *The Movie Industry  167  / The Making of a Film  169
   / The Market  169*
Types of Motion Picture Music and How Music Is Used  170
The Film Music Budget  170
Use of Pre-Existing Hit Songs in Films  171
   *How Much to Charge for a Song  173  / Fees Paid for Existing
   Songs  175  / Opening and Closing Credits  175  / Multiple
   Uses of a Song 176  / Lyric Changes  176  / Duration of
   License  177 / Rights Granted to the Film Producer  177  /
   Territory  178  / Limited Theatrical Distribution  178  /
   Soundtrack Album Guarantees  178  / Motion Picture Producer
   Cut-Ins  179  / First-Use Restrictions  180  / Trailers and
   Advertisements  181  / Deferred Payments/Indie Films 181  /
   Home Video Advances  182  / Restrictions on the Use of Songs
   in Other Films  182  / Exclusive Holds  182  / Reductions of
   Fees Due to the Use of Many Hit Records  183  / A Publisher
   Having More Than One Song in a Film  184  / Student-Produced
   Films  184  / Rescoring and Replacing Songs in a Film
   Prior to Release  185  / Promotional Television Programs  185
   / Nonprofit Films and Free Use of Music  185  / Screen Credit  186
   / Music Cue Sheets  186  / Getting Hit Songs into Films  187  /
   Producers and the Selecting of Songs  187  / Recap  189*
The Song Written for a Motion Picture  189
   *Breaking into the Business  190  / Song for Film  191  / "Song
   Written for a Film"  191*
Life after the Motion Picture Release (Where the Real Money
   Is Made)  197
   *Home Video Licensing  197  / Hit Singles from Motion
   Pictures  201  / Soundtrack Album  202  / Television
   Commercials Promoting the Film  203  / Sheet Music
   Folios  204  / Motion Picture Songs in Commercials  204  /
   Royalties from Motion Picture Theaters  204  / Television*

*Broadcasts of the Motion Picture* 205 / *Film Songs Used in Television Programs* 205 / *Film Songs Used in Other Motion Pictures* 206 / *Miscellaneous Income* 206
The Motion Picture Background Music Score 206
*History of the Field* 207 / *The Feature Film Background Score Contract* 207
Sources of Income: The Background Scorer 217
*Composing, Arranging, and Conducting Fee* 217 / *Foreign Theatrical and Other Performance Royalties* 218 / *U.S. Cable, Network, and Local Television Performances* 220 / *Soundtrack Albums* 221
Conclusion 222

6.  Music, Money, and Commercials                        223

The Advertising Industry and How It Works 224
*The Advertising Agency and Its Use of Music* 225 / *The Importance of the Advertising Agency* 226 / *The Jingle* 226 / *Creation of a Jingle and the Monies That Can Be Earned* 227 / *The Independent Writer* 227 / *The Jingle Production Company* 227 / *The Writer as Employee of an Advertising Agency* 227 / *Hit Songs Used In Commercials* 228 / *Permission to Use a Hit Song In a Commercial* 228 / *Advantages and Disadvantages of a Hit Song Being Used in a Commercial (From a Publisher's and Writer's Point of View)* 229
Jingles (Songs Written for Commercials) 230
*The Jingle Writer and the Advertising Agency* 230 / *The Agency and the Production Company* 230
Negotiating with an Advertising Agency for a Hit Song 231
*Parties to the Agreement* 232 / *Ownership* 232 / *Duration of License* 232 / *Exclusivity versus Nonexclusivity* 233 / *Number of Commercials* 233 / *Payment* 233 / *Options* 233 / *Territory* 234 / *Media* 235 / *Foreign Countries* 235 / *Restrictions* 235 / *Restrictions on First Broadcast Use by Another Product* 236 / *Lyric Changes or Instrumental Uses* 236 / *Performance Rights* 236
Radio and Television Royalties for Advertising Music 237

7.  Music, Money, and Performances                        238

The Performing Right 238
The Organizations and How to Join 240
*ASCAP* 240 / *BMI* 241
Types of License Agreements 242
Writer and Publisher Contracts and Termination Dates 243

Considerations in Making a Decision   244
ASCAP and BMI Income and Distributions   244
Components of ASCAP and BMI Income   245
   *Domestic   246   / Foreign   246   / Special Distribu-*
   *tions   246   / Interim Fees   247*
Payment Dates and Methods of Payment   248
   *ASCAP   248   / BMI   250*
ASCAP and BMI Payment Philosophy and Rules   250
   *ASCAP   250   / BMI   252*
Payment Changes   253
Co-Written Compositions   254
Services Provided   255
ASCAP Payments and Payment Rules   255
   *Types of Performances and Their Values   255   /*
   *Weights   256   / Payment Formulas / Weights into*
   *Dollars   260   / Radio   261   / Network Television*
   *262   / Network Payment Formulas   263   / Local*
   *Television   264   / Cable   265   / Music and Lyrics in*
   *Commercials   266   / Payments   267   / Live*
   *Performances   268   / Per Program Distributions   268   /*
   *Internet 268*
The BMI Payment Schedule   268
   *Radio   269   / The 1977 Song Bonus   270   / 1987 and 1998*
   *Payment Schedules   271   / BMI Radio Payments   274*
   */ Voluntary Quarterly Payments   275   / Survey of*
   *Performances   277   / Television   277   / Types of*
   *Performance   277   / Network Television   278   /*
   *Payment Schedule Rates   278   / Local Television   280*
   */ Cable   281   / Music and Lyrics in Commercials   281*
   */ Live Performance Payments/Internet   282*
SESAC   282
   *Payments   282   / Contracts   283*
Chart Songs—What They Earn   283
Future Changes   285

**8.   Music, Money, and Broadway**                    **286**

An Overview of the Broadway Musical   286
   *Broadway and Road Performances   287   / Broadway*
   *Musicals   287   / The Broadway Composer and Lyricist*
   *288   / Sources of Income for the Broadway Composer*
   *and Lyricist   288*
Rights and Royalties of the Broadway Show Writer: The Dramatists
   Guild Contract   289
   *Monies Paid to the Composer and Lyricist Prior to the*
   *Actual Production of the Broadway Musical (Option*
   *Payments)   289   / Advance Payments   290   /*

Pre-Broadway Performances   291   / The Broad-
way Opening   291   / Broadway Writer Royalties
292   / Royalty Pools   292
Weekly Costs of a Broadway Musical   293
The Weekly Breakeven Point   293
Road Performances during or after the Broadway Run   293
Weekly Costs of a Show on the Road   294
Adjustments in a Writer's Royalties (Dramatists Guild
Contracts)   296
The New York Run (Minimum Weekly Guarantee)   296
/ Touring Shows (Minimum Weekly Guarantee)   297
Broadway Shows Produced under Non-Dramatists Guild
Contracts   297
Fixed-Dollar Royalty Shows   297   /
Percentage-Of-Receipts Royalty   298   / Touring Shows
with Guarantees   298
What the Producer Must Do to Ensure Rights to a Share of
Subsidiary Income from the Broadway Show   299
Producer's Share of   300   / Producer's Right to Subsidiary
Income under non-Dramatists Guild Contracts   300
Life after Broadway (Where the Real Money Is Made)   302
Hit Singles   302   / Broadway Show Music in
Commercials   304   / Television Commercials Promoting
a Musical   305   / Television Performances of Songs in
the Play   305   / Television Performances of the Play   305   /
The Cast Album   305   / Motion Picture Soundtrack
Albums   306   / Successful Cover Records   306   /
Sheet Music Folios   307   / Royalties from Motion Picture
Theaters   307   / Broadway Songs Used in Television   307   /
Broadway Songs Used in Motion Pictures   307   /
The Broadway Musical as a Motion Picture   308   /
Home Video/DVD   309   / Noncast Albums   309   /
Catalogue Musicals   309

9.   Music, Money, and Foreign Countries                    310

Overview   310
The Role of the Subpublisher   311
Administration vs. Promotion   311   / Worldwide
Representation vs. Territory-by-Territory Agreements   312
The Subpublishing Agreement   313
Term   313   / Royalty Percentages   313   / Local Cover
Recordings   314   / Increased Fees for Cover Records
(Mechanical vs. Performance Income)   314   / Print
315   / Compositions Controlled by the Agreement   315
/ Advances   317   / How Advances Are Paid   317   /

*Information That Must Be Supplied to the Foreign Representative 318 / At-Source Royalty Payments 319 / Rights Granted to the Foreign Representative 320 / Rights Reserved by the U.S. Publisher 322 / Royalty Payment Dates and Audit Rights 322 / Retention Rights 322*

Foreign Performing Rights Societies 324
  *Organization and Distribution Rules 324*
Mechanical Royalties 326 / Ringtones 327

## 10. Music, Money, and the Buying and Selling of Songs

**328**

Overview 329
  *Purchase of Assets 329 / The Purchase Price 330 / Calculation of Net Income (Cash vs. Accrual Basis) 330 / Salaries and Other Costs of Doing Business 332 / Purchase Price Multiples 332*
The Prospectus: Its Form and Content 333
  *Business Summary 333 / Financial Information 333 / Listing of Top-Earning Compositions 334 / Net Income and Earnings History Charts 334 / Current Contracts 335 / Foreign Subpublishing Agreements 336 / Future Commitments 337*
The Letter of Intent/Short-Form Commitment-to-Sell Agreement 338
  *Description of Assets Being Sold 338 / Earnings History 338 / Purchase Price 338 / Warranties 339 / Subpublishing Agreements 340 / Income Cutoff Date 340 / Definitive Closing Date 340*
Investigating the Assets Being Acquired 341
  *Financial Due Diligence 341 / Legal Due Diligence 344*
The Formal Purchase Agreement 345
The Aftermath of the Acquisition Agreement 349
Mergers 350
Securitization 350
Conclusion 350

## 11. Music, Money, and Copyright

**351**

Exclusive Rights of Copyright 352
Works Made for Hire 353
Compulsory Licenses 353
The Audio Home Recording Act of 1992 355
Copyright Royalty Tribunal/CARP 355

Copyright Notice   356
Fees and Forms   356
Duration of Copyright   356
Revision of Copyright Renewal Procedures   358
   *Renewal Claimants   359*
Termination Rights   359
   *Termination of the Extended Copyright Renewal Term
360   / When the Termination Notice Must Be Sent   360
/ What the Termination Notice Must Contain   360   /
Service of the Notice   361   / Persons Entitled to
Terminate the Extended Renewal Term   361   /
Termination of Agreements Made During or After 1978
361   / When the Termination Notice Must Be Sent   361*
Sound Recordings   362
Infringement of Copyright   362
International Copyright Protection   363
Completing the PA Copyright Form   364
Digital Performance Right in Sound Recordings Act/Digital Millennium
Copyright Act   365
Termination Rights Under the 1998 Term Extension Act   366
Conclusion   366

## 12. Music, Money, Lawyers, Managers, and Agents

Lawyers and Their Role   367
   *Lawyers' Fees   368*
Managers and Their Role   371
   *Manager's Contracts   372   / Manager's Fees   373*
Agents   373

## 13. Putting It All Together

Mechanical Royalties   375
Recording Artist Royalties   377
U.S. Performance Royalties   377
Commercial Use   377
Motion Picture Use   379
Television Series Use   379
Foreign Mechanicals and Performances   380
The Broadway Musical   380
The Motion Picture Background Score   381
Additional Income-Producing Areas   381

## 14. Breaking into the Business

Co-Writing Songs with Writers with Publishing Deals   383
Being in a Performing Group   384
Submitting CDs and Tapes to Music Publishers   384
Demo Recordings   385
Songwriter Conferences   386
Showcases   386
Attorneys   386
Record Producers   387
Managers   388
Agents   388
Music Videos   388
Cable Television   389
ASCAP and BMI   389
Paying to Get Your Songs Published   389
Finding the Right Publisher   390
Different Types of Publishers   391
Film and Television   391
Demo Reviews in Magazines   393
Music Web Sites   393

15. Music, Money, and Sampling                                                   394
Overview   394
Format of the Sample Agreement   398
  *Copyright Registration   398   / Administration of the
  New Composition   398   / Collection of Monies/Payments
  of Songwriter Royalties   399   / Additional Sampling   399*
Recap   400

16. Music, Money, Co-Ventures, and Joint Ventures   401
Types of Joint Venture/Co-Venture Agreements   402
  *Term   402   / Co-Publishing   402   / Administration   402   /
  Advances   403   / Advances to the Co-Venture Partner   403   /
  Scope of the Agreement   404   / Songwriting Services of the
  Co-Venturer   404   / Sharing of Income   404   / Deals that
  Extend Past the Term of the Co-Venture Agreement   404   /
  Guaranteed Funding   405   / Carry Forward Advances   406   /
  Exercise of Options for Songwriter Agreements   406*

17. Music, Money, and the Internet                                               408
Main Issues   408
The Laws   409
Rights   409
  *Two Copyrights   409   / The Song   410   /
  The Recordings   410   / Synchronization Royalties   411*

ASCAP, BMI, and SESAC Internet Licenses   411
Downloads and Online Subscription Services   412
  *Pre-Loaded Music Files   412   /  Digital Downloads   413*
  */  Limited Downloads   413  /  On-Demand Streaming   414*
  */  License Requests  414  /  Royalty Reporting information   414*
Ringtone/Cell Phone Licenses   414
Promotional Streaming Licenses   418
Video Game Licenses   420
Digital Jukeboxes   422
Record Company Contracts   423
  *Royalty Calculations   423   /  Recording Artist Royalties for*
  *Download Master Recordings   423  /  Escalating Royalty*
  *Clauses   425  /  Term/Release Obligations/Advances   426  /*
  *New Pricing Approaches   427*
Music Publishing Contracts   428
  *Commercial/Release Internet   428*
Web Site Ownership   429
Deductions   430
Record Company/Traditional Versus Internet   430
Future   430

## 18. Guide to Music Industry Organizations     431

## 19. Sample Contracts     441

## Index     455

# Introduction

Experience + Knowledge + Talent + Representation + Luck = Success

From platinum records to blockbuster movies, from hit TV shows to smash Broadway musicals, millions dream of attaining glamour and wealth through music. From one-hit wonders to lifetime stars to those that make an everyday living from music to those who never give up even though the chances of making it are difficult, music is a way of life as well as livelihood for millions and an integral part of the life of many billions.

Dollars. Hundreds of dollars. Thousands of dollars. Millions of dollars. Hundreds of millions of dollars. Billions of dollars. This is the kind of money that an individual, a group, a company or a worldwide conglomerate can make in the worldwide music business. The numbers depend on creativity, luck, being in the right place at the right time, being associated with the right people and the right organizations, making the right decisions, and most of all, knowing how the business works and where the money comes from in every area of the music and entertainment field.

This book provides the basic information that the superstar, the novice, the composer, the lyricist, the businessperson, the professional, the aspiring musician, writer or artist must know to have a shot. How to make it —How much you make — How to keep the money you make — and How to continue to be successful and make a living in a world of changing tastes, short attention spans, rapidly changing technology and complex contracts. It covers in detail the money-generating facets of the music field that you need to know about, showing how things work on a day-to-day basis, who makes the decisions, and how deals are negotiated. It tells you through actual examples and real conversations what to look out for, what to ask for, and how to get it.

*Music, Money, and Success* is written for professionals and newcomers alike, be they on the creative or the business side of music. It is intended for songwriters, composers, lyricists, publishers, accountants, financial planners, agents, managers, lawyers, advertising agencies, record companies, Web site operators, motion picture and television studios and production companies, educators, banking and investment institutions, multi-national conglomerates and individually-owned businesses both in the United States and in other countries. Topics covered, in order, include:

- Songwriting and publishing
- Copublishing and administration
- Records
- Performances
- Movies
- Television
- Commercials
- Broadway
- Foreign rights and income
- Buying and selling songs
- Managers, lawyers, and agents
- Copyright
- Putting it all together
- Breaking into the songwriting business
- Sampling
- Joint Ventures
- Internet
- Music industry organizations

In recent years, the world of music has changed dramatically, and it continues to change on a daily basis. *Music, Money, and Success* has been written to make those changes understandable, as well as to clarify the basic rules that apply to everyone. Many of the concepts, approaches, analyses, and dollar figures set forth throughout this book are based on the experiences of the authors. As no two situations are alike and as laws, treaties, court decisions, license agreements, new technology, business practices, and contract and law interpretations change, current advice should always be sought from knowledgeable professionals for any situation.

Our gratitude goes to all the songwriters, composers, lyricists, artists, producers, and business people that we have dealt with over the past decades, as all of their experiences in this industry, both good and bad, have very much to do with the reasons this book was written. Particular thanks go to Michael Gorfaine, Richard Perna, and John Bettis for their willingness to share their insights, experience, and knowledge. Thanks are also due to Leeds Levy, the Dramatists Guild, Dennis McCarthy, Bob Hunka, Theodore Kaplan, Esq., Gaylon Horton, Paul Sherman, Esq., Tom Chase, Ervin Brabec, and Ralph Murphy for their help. Finally, a thank-you to the many knowledgeable people that we have dealt with and worked with throughout the years in this industry, as well as all the individuals who have helped us to complete this book.

# 1

# Music, Money, Songwriting, and Music Publishing

As NEW TECHNOLOGY continues to widen the boundaries of the entertainment industry and create new vehicles of reaching people around the globe, the need for product to take advantage of these opportunities has taken on tremendous proportions. With hundreds of television production companies churning out thousands of series episodes and specials, over 500 motion pictures being produced every year in the United States alone, satellite television, the Internet, billions of dollars of prerecorded records, tapes, and CDs being sold annually, colorization of old television series and movies, the emergence of digital recordings and downloads, advertisers using hit songs to sell their products, Broadway and road shows opening their curtains to over $1.3 billion yearly, cable and wireless technology taking over the world, the growth of pay-per-view programming and the success of pay television channels, the introduction of fiber optics and interactive media, VCRs, DVDs, computers, game consoles, and digital technology having become a staple of every home, and the emergence of high-definition television as reality—with all these developments music has reasserted its place as a cornerstone of the ever-expanding and enormously profitable business of entertainment. In this world of multinational conglomerates, well-financed entrepreneurs, and million-dollar deals stand the songwriter and the music publisher—suppliers of one of the principal elements that keep entertainment programming exciting and interesting . . . music.

Why has the creation and ownership of songs become so valuable? Why has music publishing become the darling of the investment community and the new gold rush of the century? To appreciate fully the increasing value of music operations, you need to know how the business of publishing operates, how songs are licensed, and how the money is made. This chapter reviews the myriad income-producing areas open to the songwriter, the types of contract songwriters sign, and the types of protections and guarantees that writers should look for when negotiating their agreements with a publisher.

Many different organizations in the music industry perform essential services for the songwriter or writer/performer. Some, like ASCAP and BMI, license radio and television stations and collect monies for performances of a writer's songs. Others, such as record companies, make possible the worldwide dissemination of a writer's music through the distribution, sale, and promotion of records, CDs, and tapes. And still others, such as the Harry Fox Agency, provide licensing services for songs used on records and tapes or as downloads. In this panoply of service organizations, the music publisher reigns as one of the most important. For most songwriters, the publisher represents the first step in his or her career, a step that can easily mean the difference between success or failure . . . between making it or putting your songs back in a drawer forever.

---

## MUSIC PUBLISHERS AND WHAT THEY DO

To many outside and within the entertainment industry, the function of a music publisher is vague and nebulous. In fact, the only knowledge that many people have of the term "publisher" is that it appears on the records, tapes, CDs, and sheet music they own. To enhance understanding of the role of the music publisher (which is, in effect, that of an agent, manager, lawyer, and business advisor to the songwriter and his or her original creations), the following represents a brief summary of some of the music publisher's responsibilities:

Copyrighting musical compositions in the United States and making sure that the songs it represents are also protected in foreign countries

Securing recording, television, stage, and motion picture uses of songs

Arranging for the manufacture and distribution of sheet music, folios, songwriter compilations, and other music-oriented books

Securing uses of songs in television and radio commercials

Suing infringers of musical compositions and negotiating settlements, when appropriate

Properly registering songs with the Harry Fox Agency, ASCAP, BMI, SESAC, and all other representatives and collection agents so that royalties can be

# Music, Money, and Success

## The Insider's Guide to Making Money in the Music Industry

**fourth edition**

JEFFREY BRABEC

TODD BRABEC

SCHIRMER TRADE BOOKS
NEW YORK/LONDON/PARIS/SYDNEY/MADRID/COPENHAGEN/TOKYO/BERLIN

Schirmer Trade Books
A Division of Music Sales Corporation, New York

*Exclusive Distributors:*
**Music Sales Corporation**
257 Park Avenue South, New York, NY 10010 USA
**Music Sales Limited**
8/9 Frith Street, London W1D 3JB England
**Music Sales Pty. Limited**
120 Rothschild Street, Rosebery, Sydney, NSW 2018, Australia

Order Number: SCH 10146
International Standard Book Number: 0.8256.7306.2
Library of Congress Catalog Card Number: 93-23969

For more information including new articles, book updates and additions, dollar figure changes and author speaking engagements, visit us on the Web at www.musicandmoney.com

printing number
      1  2  3  4  5  6  7  8  9  10

Printed in the United States of America by
Vicks Lithograph and Printing Corporation

**Library of Congress Cataloging-in-Publication Data**
Brabec, Jeffrey.
   Music, money and success: the insider's guide to making money in the music industry
  / Jeffrey Brabec, Todd Brabec. — 4th ed.
     p.    cm.
   Includes index.
   ISBN 0-8256-7306-2 (pbk. ; alk. paper)
    1. Music trade—Vocational guidance.  2. Music—Economic aspects.  I. Brabec, Todd.
II. Title.
ML3790.B72 2004
780'.68—dc22
                 2004009644

collected for record, tape, download, and CD sales as well as for radio, television, and Internet performances

Staying abreast of new developments and formulating relevant policies and procedures so that songs may earn maximum compensation

Promoting the creation of new songs by helping to support and develop promising writers

Negotiating fees and issuing appropriate licenses for all uses of music

Making sure that payments from licensees (record companies, video distributors, television and film producers) are paid on time and accurately

Providing information to representatives in foreign territories so that those representatives remain aware of current developments with respect to a publisher's catalog

Giving potential users prompt and correct information on songs being considered for use so that decisions can be made quickly

Promoting legislation affecting the music and entertainment industries and the protection of the rights of creators

Promoting interest in songs and their writers through special projects such as commemorative stamps, anniversary albums, single-writer folios, and compilation hit promotional albums for radio stations, producers, recording artists, film producers, television companies, video game producers, web sites, video distributors, and all other users of music

Keeping track of motion pictures, television shows, commercials, and video projects in preproduction, production, or postproduction so that compatible songs can be submitted to producers for possible inclusion

Communicating daily with representatives in foreign countries to ensure that the U.S. publisher has up-to-date knowledge of current developments in foreign territories and that the foreign representatives have an understanding of what is happening in the United States

## Singles, Albums, CDs, and Cassettes

One of the primary roles of the publisher is to secure commercially released recordings, CDs, and tapes of the songs it controls. The publisher must have an effective staff of professional managers (those who actually promote the songs) who not only know what artists are recording and the type of material needed for a particular session, but who also have a good working relationship with record company A&R executives, producers, recording artists, and managers. Considering that most singles and albums never achieve enough sales to recoup their costs of production, the chances of a song's becoming successful are slim enough. Without a record, however, the chances are virtually nonexistent. Exceptions aside (for example, songs written specifically for motion pictures, Broadway musicals, television series, or commercials), the real success and earnings of a song are contingent on its becoming a hit record or being included on a chart album or performed on a popular web site.

After a song has been initially recorded and released, the publisher will try to secure commitments from other recording artists or producers to include the composition on future albums or singles. To accomplish this, the publisher may re-demo the song with a different arrangement to adapt it for promotion in markets other than that in which it had its initial success (for example, changing the sound from rock 'n' roll to country). Another reason for creating a different version of a hit song is that certain records become the definitive version, and it may be difficult to get a recording by another artist if people feel that the best version has already been done.

The test of a good publisher is not necessarily how many records by other artists it can secure during or immediately after a particular song is on the charts (although that is extremely important), but also the number of records it can secure during the many years following a song's initial chart activity. It is not unusual for a strong publisher to get hundreds of separate recordings of a good song. Continual song promotion represents one of the real services of a music publisher.

## Demonstration Records, CDs and Tapes

Another important function of the music publisher is the financing and production of "demo recordings" of a writer's new compositions. In the music industry, these recordings or digital files are a necessity to securing a commitment to record a song. These demos can range from a simple vocal with piano or guitar to elaborate productions, with the latter becoming more and more prevalent. The costs of making demos (recording session time, musicians, singers, copyists, and duplication) are normally paid by the music publisher and, in many cases, recouped from the song's future earnings.

## Proper Administration

Another necessary and important service provided by the publisher is that of proper administration of musical compositions: registering copyrights, filing necessary information to mechanical and performing rights organizations, auditing record companies and other licensees, bookkeeping, negotiating licenses, and collecting monies due. Considering the complexity of the music industry, the hundreds of thousands of music users throughout the world, the lack of detail on many royalty statements from licensees, and the amounts of money involved ($500,000 to $1 million is not unusual for a worldwide hit song), this service is vital.

## Television and Movie Music

Another important area of concentration is the promotion of songs for television series, made-for-TV movies, and theatrical motion pictures. Standard and contemporary songs are a mainstay of these media, and whether the song is used as a theme, background music, or actually sung or performed on camera, the writer's and publisher's earnings can be substantial.

For example, a song used in a motion picture earns an initial synchronization fee for its inclusion in the film. If the motion picture is shown in a foreign country, the song will earn performance royalties. Since many films have soundtrack albums and hit singles, additional royalties will be generated by record, tape, and CD sales, as well as from radio and television performances of the songs on the soundtrack. When the motion picture is finally broadcast on one of the television networks as the "Movie of the Week" or on one of the pay television services (e.g., HBO, Showtime, the Movie Channel), additional royalties will be distributed by ASCAP and BMI. Since virtually all films are released on video, extra monies will be earned from video sales. And after its initial network or pay television broadcast, a movie may be shown for years on local off-the-air or cable television stations as well as web sites throughout the world, with additional royalties being generated.

## Commercials

An important activity for the publisher is the promotion of songs for use as part of advertising campaigns. There has been a growing tendency on the part of advertising agencies to use well-known songs (standards, Broadway music, classic rock, contemporary hits) as important parts of their promotional messages. The initial and option fees paid for the use of such songs range from hundreds of dollars to over $1 million.

## Foreign Promotion and Collection of Royalties

For most songs written by U.S. writers, the foreign market does not represent a major source of income unless the song has been recorded by a recording artist who is successful outside the United States, is in a television series shown on foreign television, is in a motion picture that becomes a hit overseas, is on a worldwide subscription service, or has attained the status of a standard. When the U.S. publisher and its foreign representatives have a good relationship and communicate effectively, songs can be successfully promoted in foreign territories and generate sizable income—a consideration that should be foremost in making any foreign representation deal.

## The Publisher, Writer/Performer, and Record Contracts

During the past decade, many publishers have taken on the new responsibility of securing recording contracts for their songwriters through record production affiliates. In many cases, the publisher may be responsible for producing the actual finished recording, or something very close to it. In others, the publisher finances an elaborate demo featuring a number of its writer/performer's songs so that a record company can hear the commercial potential of the writer as a recording artist, sign him or her to a contract, finance master recordings, and distribute the finished product. Because more and more recording artists write and record their own material, publishers find diminishing opportunities to place songs with such artists. By not only signing a writer/artist or writer/producer to create songs but also trying to negotiate an artist contract or production agreement, a publisher works to ensure a guaranteed outlet and commitment for commercial release of the artist's (and publisher's) songs.

### Infringement Actions

An important responsibility of the publisher is protecting its copyrights and enforcing the exclusive rights that it has been granted by the songwriter and the copyright laws. Considering the number of actual and potential users of songs throughout the world (record companies, film producers, television companies, video distributors, book publishers, sheet music firms, Web sites, magazines, video and audio sing-along booths, jukebox operators, restaurants, retail stores, theatrical productions), this responsibility is both far-reaching and difficult. The good publisher will spend a great deal of time and money to ensure that its songs are not used without permission and compensation.

### Home Video

An increasingly important area is that of the inclusion of songs in home videos, whether they be of recording artists, "how to" subjects, television series, exercise programs, sports promos, "the making of" programs, or motion pictures. With hundreds of millions of VCRs and DVD players and game consoles throughout the world, home video represents a significant source of income, and music publishers work hard on song promotion and licensing in this continually expanding area.

---

## *THE INNER WORKINGS OF A MUSIC PUBLISHER*

Most publishing companies are divided into a number of separate but interrelated departments, all of which are important to the company's success. Each plays an integral part in the success or failure of the operation.

## Business and Legal Affairs Department

Business Affairs (which in many companies also serves as the legal department, since most business affairs executives are attorneys) is responsible for negotiating, drafting, and approving all contractual agreements entered into by the company. In addition, if any other department requires advice on how to approach a particular situation or problem, the business affairs executive is the one who will be called on to assist because of his or her experience and knowledge of how the industry works. Since most other departments report to it or are required to "clear" their activities through it, Business Affairs can also play a major role in promoting the catalog through its relationship with the licensing personnel at record companies, motion picture and television producers, and advertising agencies, as well as formulating recommendations on how a firm should deal with the issues related to changing technology, current legal decisions, congressional trends, and the licensing of newly created uses of music.

Depending on the size of the music publisher, mechanical licensing (the use of songs on records, tapes, and CDs) and synchronization licensing (the use of songs in television programs, commercials, home video, and motion pictures) may be separate departments or may be centered in or under the auspices of the Business Affairs Department. Included in the responsibilities of these departments are the negotiation of fees for the use of songs, as well as following up on all music licenses that have or are about to expire.

## Copyright Department

The Copyright Department is responsible for the proper registration of compositions with the U.S. Copyright Office in Washington, D.C., the providing of correct copyright notices for all print and record usages, the registration of songs with ASCAP and BMI to ensure that radio and television broadcasts of songs are monitored, the filing of copyright renewals, and a panoply of other responsibilities all related to the protection of musical compositions in a company's catalog.

## Foreign Department

The Foreign Department is responsible for notifying a company's representatives throughout the world of new record releases, motion picture and television uses, the signings of new writers or recording artists, ownership percentages of songs controlled, and the acquisition of catalogs, as well as answering any inquiries received from foreign territories concerning the compositions in the catalog.

## Royalty Department

The Royalty Department is responsible for checking the royalty statements that come in from music users, making sure that the proper amounts are being remitted, crediting all monies to the proper songs, ensuring that all writers and other income participants are paid correctly, and following up with any company that has either not paid or paid incorrectly.

## Promotion Department

The Promotion Department's role is to secure trade paper articles about the company, its new signings, chart activity, special promotions, and any other facet of the company that might be newsworthy. In some companies, this department has the responsibility of promoting the catalog by designing and preparing promotional record, tape, and CD packages, songbooks, and other items for distribution to recording artists, television and motion picture producers, ad agencies, and record producers.

## Creative Department

The Creative Department's role is to listen to new material, make recommendations on what writers to sign, help writers with the structure of their songs, and promote or "run with" songs to record producers, recording artists, motion picture companies, and television producers. Many of these individuals are also familiar with the ins and outs of recording studios and produce or help produce many of the demo sessions for new songs. Many of the experienced ones are also able to produce "master quality" demos for selling writer/performers to record companies as artists.

## Computer Department

Because of the complexity of the entertainment industry and the increasing demand to stay competitive and provide myriad services to potential music users, many companies have in-house computer personnel who design and provide programs for all departments. Some major publishers not only have programs to ensure proper royalty accountings but also have programs that generate song reports by recording artist (e.g., all songs in the catalog recorded by Frank Sinatra), by type of music (e.g., jazz instrumental), by song (e.g., all records of a particular song with the initial release date and identity of the recording artist), and by income (e.g., gross and net income on an annual or 6-month basis). Some of the larger publishers, which have affiliates around the world, achieve instantaneous global communication by means of computer link-ups that provide daily, up-to-date sharing of information. For example, information about newly created songs (songwriter identity, ASCAP or BMI membership, percentage of control, exploitation restrictions such as no commercials without consent, territory controlled, etc.) may be transmitted around the world not only for registration with each foreign affiliate but also for automatic registration with foreign performance societies.

## Chief Executive

The president or chief executive officer brings in many of the deals, determines what acquisitions should be made, and provides much of the direction, insight, and motivation that make every successful company work. In some cases, the CEO's role is that of an overseer charting the direction of a firm and its overall activities; in others, it is a role of intimate involvement with the functioning of virtually every department on a daily basis. In almost all cases, the reputation, integrity, foresight, experience, and drive of the chief executive sets the tone for the entire company as well as the image of the company worldwide.

---

## *THE ACQUISITION OF RIGHTS BY A PUBLISHER*

The rights to musical compositions are acquired by music publishers by means of a number of different agreements. Later in this book we examine each kind of agreement in detail. For now, a brief overview can give a general impression of how publishers assume ownership or control of musical compositions.

### Individual Song and Exclusive Agreements

The most common songwriter–publisher agreements are the individual song agreement and the exclusive agreement. Under the individual song agreement, a writer transfers the copyright to 1 composition or a selected number of identified compositions to a publisher and, in return, receives a portion of the income earned from uses of that composition or compositions. Under the exclusive agreement, the songwriter agrees to assign all compositions written during a specified term (for example, 2 years from January 1), once again, with the guarantee of a share of the income generated and usually a proviso for weekly or monthly recoupable advance payments. Included in the rights granted to the music publisher are:

> The right to reproduce the compositions mechanically (license songs for use on singles, albums, audio cassettes, downloads, and CDs)
> The right to synchronize the compositions (license songs for use in motion pictures, television productions, and other audiovisual works)

The right to perform the compositions (license the broadcast and other performance of songs)

The right to print the compositions (license songs or their lyrics for sheet music, folios, magazines, and books)

The right to represent and license the compositions in all new media created by present or future technology

As part of these agreements, some successful writers are able to negotiate publishing or participation agreements with their music publishers. Under the copublishing agreement, the songwriter co-owns the copyright in his or her songs (usually through a wholly owned company) and receives a portion of the publisher's share of income in addition to the songwriter's share. Under the participation agreement, the writer shares in the publisher's income similar to the copublishing arrangement but does not become a co-owner of the copyright.

Publishers also receive rights in compositions through the following types of agreements. None of these actually transfers copyright ownership; instead, they transfer the rights to control and administer the compositions for a specified period of time.

## Administration Agreement

Under an administration agreement, the publisher receives the right to administer a composition or group of compositions (i.e., licensing the use of songs in recordings, tapes, CDs, television series, motion pictures, commercials, subscription services, and video productions and collect royalties from all music users) for a specified period of time. In return for its services, the publisher usually receives an "administration fee" of from 15% to 25% of all income earned during the term of the agreement.

## Foreign Subpublishing Agreement

The foreign subpublishing agreement is similar to an administration agreement. The only difference is that the compositions being represented have been written by songwriters from another country. For example, if a U.S. publisher wants to have a publisher in England represent its catalog in the United Kingdom, or if a publisher in France wants its catalog represented in the United States by an American publisher, the agreement is referred to as a subpublishing agreement. As with the administration agreement, representation is limited to a specified duration (usually not less than 3 years), and the fees retained by the foreign subpublisher for its services are negotiable within certain limits.

# THE SONGWRITER-MUSIC PUBLISHER RELATIONSHIP

One of the most important decisions that a composer or lyricist will make concerns the choice of a music publisher and the type of contract signed. If the writer makes the right choice, the chances for success in an extremely competitive, complex, and difficult business are increased immeasurably. If the wrong choice is made or the wrong contract signed, the writer may never recover financially or creatively. Also, if the publisher with whom the writer signs does not have the capabilities to promote a writer's compositions effectively, the chances of ever becoming successful, even under a good contract, are minimal.

One must remember that any contractual relationship entered into is for the long term, regardless of whether the publishing contract applies to 1 song or to all songs composed by a writer during a specified period of time. This is so because under almost all publishing contracts, the copyright ownership to the writer's songs is transferred to the music publisher. Under the provisions of the 1976 U.S. Copyright Law, the music publisher owns the copyright to most songs written after 1977 for a minimum of 35 years and, in many cases, retains such ownership for the full period of copyright protection.

Because of the length of this contractual relationship, the songwriter and his or her representative must be aware of what is a good contract and what is not, as well as what is a fair contract and what is not. Considering that the writer will have to live with the terms of the original publishing contract for many years, one should take into account the present as well as the future when negotiating its terms.

# PUBLISHING CONTRACTS

There is no such thing as a standard writer-publisher contract. Each publishing company normally has its own particular contract drawn up by its legal staff to reflect its own particular way of doing business and its own particular view of its relationship with its writers. Although many uniform provisions or procedures will be included in almost every agreement, what is standard for one company is not always standard for another.

We will first explain the provisions that are included in almost every publishing contract. After reviewing the most important of these provisions and their meaning, we will then explain the different types of clauses that may be negotiated (depending on the writer's bargaining power), the varied sources of income of the songwriter, and how much money can be earned.

Of the 2 basic types of contract that a writer signs with a music publisher, the first, and most common, is the individual song contract. The second, reserved more for writers who have a successful track record, definite or possible recording commitments, or potential in which the publisher believes, is the exclusive writer's contract.

## The Individual Song Contract

Under the terms of the individual song contract, the writer assigns to the publisher the copyright to 1 or more specified songs. For most new writers, at least those without any previous success or future recording commitments, the sale or transfer of the copyright will be for a minimal amount of money, many times for the standard contractual price of $1 or a small advance of from $250 to $750.

Because the individual song contract applies only to the song or songs specifically mentioned in the agreement, the writer can go to a number of different publishers with other songs and give each one only those songs that it is really interested in promoting. A number of successful writers who do not have an exclusive writing arrangement with any single publisher have songs published by a number of different companies. When a writer signs an individual song contract, the writer always retains the option to place other material with other publishers. In addition, by transferring the ownership of only certain selected songs to a publisher, the writer is also assured that the songs transferred are the ones that the publisher is really interested in promoting.

Most legitimate music publishers, because of their integrity and the large costs involved in doing their job, will not sign a writer if they do not feel that the songs being assigned are promotable. They may eventually discover that, after signing a writer and trying to promote the songs, they were mistaken about the songs' commercial potential, but they will not sign a writer just for the sake of a signing. To be signed by a major full-service publishing company (whether large or small) is therefore a good indicator that the writer's songs have definite commercial potential. Of course, many things can happen after a writer has signed with a company (change of personnel, the company being sold, change in musical tastes, etc.), which can diffuse the initial enthusiasm and faith in a writer's material, but such things can happen in any business. Such are the chances that must be taken for success.

Some music publishers will sign a writer knowing that they do not have the necessary capabilities to promote the writer's songs effectively. Unfortunately, too many writers are so happy that a publisher is interested in their songs that they will sign virtually anything and with anyone, without even checking into the reputation and professional capabilities of the company. It is rare that such a situation works out, and it is advisable that every writer, before signing with a publisher, at least look into the publisher's reputation and its ability to promote its material. Sometimes it might be better to receive a rejection from a legitimate publisher than to sign with a company that is not equipped to furnish the professional services required for a song to be placed with a recording artist or otherwise effectively promoted.

## The Exclusive Songwriter's Contract

The other principal type of publishing contract that a writer may sign is an exclusive agreement with 1 publisher for all songs written during a specified period of time. The term of the agreement can range from 1 year to 7 years, with provisions for weekly or monthly advances whether or not the writer's songs are being recorded or performed. The publisher has the right to publish and own all compositions written by the writer during the term of the contract.

One further point, which we will discuss at greater length later, is that all weekly or monthly payments made to the writer are treated as advances, recoupable from the future royalties of the writer. For example, if a writer is being paid $600 per week in advances, $31,200 will have been advanced in the first contract year. These monies will be deducted from any royalties that become due from record sales, sheet music, commercials, home video, television and motion picture synchronization fees, as well as from any other source of income that the publisher controls.

One of the real values of such an exclusive relationship with a publisher—and there are many—is that the writer is guaranteed a steady income, much like a salary, to meet the normal, day-to-day financial needs and living expenses while pursuing a career. In addition, since monies from record sales and performances take from 7 months to more than 2 years to reach the writer, the weekly or monthly advance payments (sometimes referred to as a "writer's draw") can lend a great deal of financial and emotional security while the writer is waiting for royalties to be collected and processed. The writer is usually given the right to use a company's recording studios to make demos and collaborate and share song ideas with other writers on a daily basis, two factors that cannot be overemphasized in the development of a career.

## *IMPORTANT PROVISIONS OF SONGWRITER-PUBLISHER CONTRACTS*

Even though the publishing contract used by one company is rarely the same as that used by another, certain important terms and provisions are in almost every contract, whether it is 1 page or 50 pages in length. The following section discusses and explains some of the most important of these standard provisions so that when a company shows interest and offers you a contract, you'll know what to expect.

## Sale of the Musical Composition

In virtually every publishing contract, the songwriter (composer or lyricist) sells his or her musical composition to the music publisher. This sale includes the copyright as well as all other equitable and legal rights in the composition. In most cases, the sale is unqualified and unconditional, regardless of whether the publisher is able to secure a recording or other commercial use of the song.

Because the sale is unconditional, it is vitally important that the writer or writer's representative know the company with which he or she is negotiating and have full confidence in the company's enthusiasm in the material and professional capabilities to promote and administer the songs effectively. Too many writers sign with the first company that expresses even a slight interest in the writer or the writer's songs. And too many times, after nothing tangible has happened, the writer has nothing to show except the loss of the publishing rights in his or her material. True, the writer can always try to get a recording on the song, but the writer has lost a good deal of bargaining power by having the ownership and right to publish the song already committed to a third party.

## Return of Songs to the Writer

Some publishers will return songs to the writer if they feel that the compositions are not worthy of further promotion. This is not the general rule, however, since the publisher often has expended monies for a studio demo and incurred additional expenses in protecting and commercially promoting the songs. In such cases, the chances of a writer getting a song back (unless he or she is willing to reimburse the publisher for its expenditures) are minimal. After all, the publisher may still have hope that, in some way, it will not only recoup at least part of the costs but also succeed in making the song a hit. And without the right to publish the songs, there is no possibility for any future recoupment or promotion.

The prevalent practice in the industry with respect to writers who are not recording artists is for the music publisher to retain ownership of all songs transferred to it by the writer. If a writer is a recording artist with a guaranteed contract with a major record label, however, reversion clauses are many times negotiated so that the music publisher may own the songs only for a specified period of time. Occasionally, these clauses prohibit reversion if the publisher has not recouped its advances or restrict reversion only to compositions that have not been commercially exploited by the publisher (e.g., not used in a television program or motion picture, not released on a CD, etc.).

## The Term

The term of an exclusive agreement is usually for an initial period of 1 year with up to 6 additional option years at the election of the music publisher. In most cases, the options are automatic unless the publisher notifies the writer to the contrary before the end of the current year. A variation, if the writer is a recording artist, is for the term to be coextensive with the artist's current agreement with a record company or, if the publisher is trying to secure such a contract for the writer/performer, coextensive with the agreement that is finally signed.

## Rights Granted to the Publisher

In addition to copyright ownership of the composition, the writer transfers the following rights to the publisher:

The right to license performances on radio, television, the Internet, or other media (with these rights normally assigned to either ASCAP or BMI for representation and collection of royalties)

The right to make arrangements of the composition and translations for exploitation in non-English-speaking territories

The right to dramatize the title, music, and lyric plot of the composition for use in motion pictures or television programs

The right to license the composition for records, tapes, CDs, downloads, video cassettes, streaming, and DVDs

The right to license uses of the composition in motion pictures, television programs, live theatrical stage productions, and commercials

The right to print the composition for use in sheet music, books, magazines, and folios and license others to do so

The right to license the title of the composition as the title of a motion picture, television series, or episode in a series

The right to exercise any and all other rights in the composition that may then or in the future exist

The right to negotiate licenses for the use of compositions in both current and future technology

## Exclusivity

Under the exclusive songwriter's agreement, all songs written by a writer during the term of the contract are owned by the music publisher. On rare occasions, exceptions are made; for instance, songs written specifically for motion pictures may be excluded from the agreement, since motion picture companies normally demand copyright ownership when they hire a writer to compose film music or songs. Even then, the writer is normally required to use his or her best efforts to retain all or a portion of copyright ownership for the publisher, and only if those efforts are unsuccessful will the exclusion apply.

## Compensation

The writer will be paid the following royalties for uses of his or her musical compositions:

*Sheet Music.* 5¢ to 15¢ for individual pieces of single-song sheet music sold in the United States and Canada (with some contracts guaranteeing the songwriter 50% of the publisher's receipts from such uses).

*Folios.* From 10% to 15% of the wholesale selling price of each folio or songbook sold in the United States and Canada. Since there are a number of songs in any folio, this 10% to 15% royalty will be shared on a pro-rata basis with all other royalty-bearing songs in the folio. In addition, if a folio is designed exclusively around the songs of a particular writer or writing team, an additional 2% to 5% is usually added. As with sheet music, some writers receive 50% of the publisher's income from songs used in folios or songbooks and an additional percentage from personality folios.

*CDs, Tapes, Records, Downloads, and Home Video.* 50% of the earnings received by the publisher for sales in the United States.

*Television and Motion Picture Synchronization Rights.* 50% of all monies received by the publisher from licensing songs for use in theatrical films and television programs.

*Commercials.* 50% of all sums received by the publisher for the licensing of songs for use in radio, television, Internet, and print ads.

*Foreign Exploitation.* 50% of all monies received in the United States that are earned in countries outside the United States from records, tapes, CDs, downloads, home video, sheet music, television, and motion picture rights, commercials, and all other sources of income, excepting the publisher's share of performance royalties.

*Performances.* Since ASCAP, BMI, and SESAC pay the songwriter and publisher directly and separately for radio, television, and other types of performance of songs, the writer (unless a copublishing or participation agreement has been signed) will not share in the royalties received by the publisher. In the event that a publisher does receive the songwriter's share of performance income (e.g., if it licenses performances directly to a music user rather than use the services of ASCAP, BMI, or SESAC), the writer will be paid 50% of those fees.

## Sharing of Advances

On occasion, the songwriter will share an advance paid to a publisher by a music user if the advance relates exclusively to the writer's song or songs. In most instances, however, advances are paid on the basis of an entire catalog and will not be shared with the songwriter, since it is virtually impossible to determine a proper division of such an advance. For example, if a record company wants to do a compilation video of hit songs by a writer/performer and pays the publisher an advance attributable to an identifiable number of titles, the writer of those songs will normally receive a proportionate share of the advance. But if a print company pays an advance to secure the right to print sheet music and folios of all present or future songs in a publisher's entire catalog, the songwriters will not share in such "catalog advance" monies, since it does not relate to specifically identified titles.

## Minimum Song Delivery Requirement

In many agreements, especially if weekly or monthly advances are being paid, the writer may be required to create a certain number of songs during each period of the contract. In most cases, the requirement is on a yearly basis (e.g., 15 wholly written songs per year, or 20 co-written songs in which the writer has at least a 50% interest, or enough portions of newly written compositions to add up to the equivalent of 10 wholly written songs), but can be on a monthly or quarterly basis depending on the amount of advances being given, the publisher's policy, and the reputation of the writer.

Such clauses are a necessary incentive for some writers and also provide a safety valve for the publisher if a writer is not actively writing songs, since if the minimum commitment is not met, the publisher will have the right not only to suspend all advance payments but also extend the current period (year or quarter) of the contract until the minimum delivery commitment is fulfilled. Many writers may be reticent to agree to such a clause, as they feel that the creative process does not work on a scheduled basis. The minimum commitment required by the publisher is normally a reasonable one, though, and most professional writers exceed the requirement.

If the writer is a recording artist as well, the minimum delivery commitment may relate to commercially released recordings of his or her songs. The provision will function as outlined above with the only exception being that a song is not considered delivered to the music publisher until it is commercially released on an album or single. For example, a sample clause may provide that if 10 newly recorded songs are not released in the United States during any 1 year of the agreement by the writer as a recording artist or producer, the current 1-year period of the contract will be extended until such occurs. If such an extension occurs, all dates at which the publisher can exercise any option rights for additional periods will be moved back accordingly and, in most cases, no further advances will be due the writer during his extension/suspension period.

## Advances

If the music publisher is granted the exclusive rights to all songs created by a writer during a specified period of time, advances are usually paid to the writer on a weekly, monthly, or yearly basis. These monies are always recoupable by the publisher from future royalties due the writer for uses of his or her songs. For example, if a writer has been advanced $30,000 during the first year of an agreement and earns $45,000 in royalties, the publisher will recoup its $30,000 and give the writer the excess ($15,000). The publisher will normally not begin to recoup a writer's advances (even if the writer is immediately successful) until the second or third year of the agreement, since earnings normally take from 5 months to over 2 years to be distributed by the various collection organizations, performance right societies, and foreign subpublishers.

There are many variations on how advances are computed, such as advances based on the achievement of certain earnings plateaus (e.g., an additional $10,000 if a song has earned $20,000 in gross royalties), songs reaching the charts or certain positions thereon (e.g., $10,000 if Top 50, another $10,000 if Top 10, and an additional $15,000 if #1), the publisher achieving recoupment of all past advances or a percentage thereof (e.g., $25,000 if the publisher has recouped all prior writer advances or an additional $20,000 when the publisher has recouped 75% of all advances given to the writer). Each agreement will have its own particular variations dependent on the needs, expectations, and bargaining power of both parties.

A number of agreements also use what is known as a "minimum/maximum" advance formula to compute annual advances after the initial period of the term expires. Under this type of clause, the amount of the advance payable to the songwriter during each option year is based on a percentage of the monies earned in the prior year, but with a "floor" and a "ceiling" provided for regardless of the amount of earnings. For example, a publisher might offer a songwriter an advance of $50,000 for the first year, with option year advances being based on 75% of the prior year's earnings with the following minimums and maximums:

|            | *Minimum* | *Maximum* |
|------------|-----------|-----------|
| 1st Option | $50,000   | $100,000  |
| 2nd Option | $60,000   | $125,000  |
| 3rd Option | $75,000   | $150,000  |

A number of variations determine how advances are paid to a songwriter. The total advance for a particular year may be paid at the commencement of that year (e.g., $50,000 on signing, $60,000 on commencement of the first option year, $75,000 on commencement of the second option year, etc.), on a quarterly basis, in 12 equal monthly installments (e.g., $48,000 per year payable in 12 monthly installments of $4,000 each), or on a weekly basis.

## Writing with Other Songwriters

Since many writers collaborate with writers who are not subject to an exclusive agreement or who control their own publishing, the publisher will request that its songwriter use his or her best efforts (or, at a minimum, his or her reasonable efforts) to secure the co-writer's share for the publisher. This provision is hard to police or control, since it is difficult to determine whether best or reasonable efforts have been expended. In addition, the legitimate publisher recognizes that collaboration not only is a fact of life in today's music business but also may be a necessary and valuable part of a writer's success. Absent fraud or bad faith on the part of the writer, therefore, this provision is usually not strictly enforced.

Certain publishers may dissuade their songwriters from collaborating with other writers who either are not affiliated with that publisher or will not assign their share of a new composition to the publisher. This attitude, however, represents an antiquated view not only of how the creative process works but also of how the music industry functions, and it has become less and less of a factor in both the writing process and contract negotiations. In fact, most signed contracts only require the songwriter to use reasonable efforts either to try to secure the publishing for the co-writer's share of any collaboration, or at least to inform the other writer that he or she has an exclusive agreement with a particular publisher.

## Motion Picture and Television Theme Exclusions

Under virtually all exclusive songwriter agreements, the music publisher has the ownership (or co-ownership) rights to all musical compositions written during the term of the agreement. But certain songwriters, in addition to writing hit songs, also have a successful track record of writing songs for motion pictures and television series. Since film producers and television companies usually demand that they own or co-own the copyright to any composition written specifically for one of their projects where a writing fee is paid, a number of writers will try to exclude such "written on assignment" compositions from their songwriter agreements, the rationale being that the exposure of such songs in films and television series will enhance the reputation of the writer and the other compositions that he or she may write. The writer may also argue that the publisher has no right to cut off a source of income that the writer has counted on for many years, since if the publisher demands ownership of such songs, the film and television companies will cease doing business with that writer.

Once again, the resolution of these issues depends on the respective bargaining power of the publisher and writer, with final settlement usually taking one of the following forms:

The publisher retains ownership of all compositions written during the term of the agreement with any "on assignment" song requests being considered on a case-by-case basis.

The writer is able to compose a specified number of songs directly for a film or television project during any 1 year of the term, provided that such activities do not take a substantial amount of time and do not interfere with his or her songwriting services.

The writer is allowed to write for such projects provided they are for a fee rather than on a "spec" (or speculation) basis and the writer uses his or her best efforts to retain a portion of the copyright ownership for the music publisher.

If a writer is allowed to write for such projects, the music publisher will often demand that all or a portion of the composing fee paid by the film producer or television company be paid to the publisher (especially where there are outstanding unrecouped advances to the writer) or, in the alternative, have the writer sign a letter of authorization that ensures that the film or television company will send all songwriter monies earned from the composition (soundtrack album and single mechanical royalties, print income, etc.) directly to the music publisher for distribution or recoupment of advances. These same considerations and approaches also apply if the writer has a past track record of writing commercial jingles for advertising agencies and wishes to continue such pursuits during the term of the exclusive songwriter's agreement.

If a writer has written a composition prior to signing with a publisher and has secured its use in a motion picture or television series, the synchronization or composing fee paid for the song is usually excluded from the publisher's rights even if the preexisting composition is brought into the deal by the writer. In these cases, however, any monies earned from the song after the release of the film or broadcast of the series (performance royalties, soundtrack album sales, cover versions, etc.) are collected by the publisher.

## First-Use Mechanical Licenses

Under the U.S. Copyright Law, the songwriter and his or her music publisher have approval rights over the first recorded and released version of a newly written composition (i.e., a "first use" license). After a composition has been released to the general public on a CD, tape, or record, any other recording artist has the right to record and release that composition, subject only to the payment of mechanical royalties to the writer and music publisher. If a writer is a recording artist, he or she will many times restrict the publisher from granting such first-use licenses on any self-written compositions to other recording artists until a decision has been made whether or not a particular song will be recorded by that writer. In effect, the writer/performer is claiming the sole right to decide whether to record a song on his or her own album, and the publisher may not promote or license the song to anyone else prior to either the writer/artist's CD being released or the writer/artist's decision not to put the song on the album. Since writer/artists need the best songs possible for their own albums, such restrictions are very understandable, and most music publishers will agree to them.

There are many variations in the resolution of these types of negotiations, with some publishers giving the writer/artist total approval rights over which songs are to be restricted and others limiting the number of songs that may be "held" during any one period by the writer/artist. The following is just one example of such a provision:

> Publisher further agrees that, in the event Writer notifies it that Writer requests that a "first use" mechanical license not be issued for a specified Composition, Publisher shall consult with Writer on such request; it being agreed that Publisher shall have the final decision as to whether such a license shall or shall not be issued. Notwithstanding anything to the contrary contained above, in the event that Writer had entered into a recording artist agreement with a Major Record Company and Writer requests that Publisher not issue a first-use mechanical license to a third party for a Composition being recorded pursuant to said recording artist agreement, Publisher agrees to comply with such request provided Writer has given written notice of such to Publisher, that no more than five (5) such Compositions are so restricted at any one time (unless all such Compositions are to be embodied on one (1) Album in which case up to eleven (11) such Compositions may be restricted) and that such restriction shall not apply to any commitments made by Publisher prior to its receipt of said written notice from Writer. It is further agreed that such a "first mechanical license" restriction shall not be effective for a period in excess of nine (9) months from the date of Writer's notice.

## Restrictions on Promotion in Certain Areas

In any negotiation with a songwriter, the music publisher will try to secure as many rights as possible without any restrictions so that it will be able to channel its promotion efforts in a wide range of income-producing areas. For example, it may promote songs not only to recording artists and record producers but also to film and television companies, advertising agencies, video manufacturers, karaoke firms, video jukebox distributors, print dealers, and so on. The songwriter, however, may have concerns, either creative or political, as to how his or her songs are used, and many times will try to restrict the publisher's promotion efforts and ability to grant licenses for certain types of uses. These negotiations usually revolve around the use of songs in commercials, political (or "special interest") radio and television campaigns, and X-rated motion pictures, but can also extend to any use in a motion picture, television series, or other audiovisual project that may be seen or heard by the public. Because many writers value the integrity of their songs and have concerns about how and in what context they might be used, the negotiations on these issues can become quite heated and, in some cases, can make or break a deal.

Recognizing that commercials can have the potential of denigrating a song by identifying it with a consumer product, especially when the lyrics are changed, many publishers will give approval rights, or at least consultation rights, to the songwriter, who thus can express his or her objections. Others will ask the writer to list the types of product of concern (alcohol, tobacco, hygiene, bathroom, etc.) and agree that songs will not be licensed for use with such identified "objectionable products" without the writer's consent. Other publishers will demand that such decisions are within their exclusive province and provide for no restrictions on licensing. In film and television the issues are a bit more difficult, because restrictions in promotion and licensing in those media are the lifeblood of many publishers' activities. Because uses in movies and TV rarely hurt songs and have the potential of generating enormous amounts of income, to say nothing of the large media exposure they generate, music publishers try to limit any writer approvals in this area. As for use in X-rated and sometimes NC-17 films, however, writer approval rights are many times accepted by the publisher.

If approvals are given to the writer, the time fuse for the writer to say either yes or no is usually a short one, such as 3 to 5 days. Quick answers to producers, especially in the making of television series, where scripts are being rewritten and scenes taped on a daily basis, are essential for getting songs into such projects. Writer approval clauses usually provide that if a writer does not respond within the negotiated time frame, the use is deemed approved and the publisher may negotiate the license.

## Altering of Compositions

In many agreements, the publisher has the right to make changes in a writer's songs if, in its good-faith judgment, such changes are justified for the successful promotion of the songs. Even though such unilateral alterations rarely occur, songwriters usually try to limit the type of change that can be made without their consent or, as an alternative, be provided with the right to make the changes themselves before someone else is given the opportunity. If a composition is an instrumental, the composer may also secure the right to select the lyricist if a publisher wishes to have words written or the right to approve or disapprove the final lyrics. A contract may also include restrictions on any reduction in writer royalties to the original writer caused by the addition of a new songwriter to the song; many agreements guarantee that the original writer's share will not be reduced past a certain point.

With respect to translations of the English lyrics to a song for foreign versions, the local performance societies in each country outside the United States have rules that cover the percentage of royalties that any translator may receive for a contribution, and the original writer must adhere to those rules. Before any foreign-language version is written, however, it is imperative for the original songwriter and music publisher to ensure by agreement that the non-English-language writer receive a share of the royalties only on the non-English-language version, and not on all versions of the song.

As for changes in the melody of a song or its overall nature, the music publisher virtually always has the right to make different musical arrangements for promotion purposes, but usually is restricted from changing or altering the substance of the composition. This is a very gray area, since determining what is and what is not a substantive change can be difficult; contract language should be specific.

## Ownership and Promotion of Demo Recordings

Under most songwriter agreements, when a writer produces a demo session for new songs, the music publisher owns not only the compositions performed at the session but also the actual performance. Occasionally, since many of these demo sessions result in "close to master quality" recordings, the publisher may be able to promote these demo recordings for use in television programs and motion pictures—and collect the synchronization and video fees negotiated for their use.

Some songwriters, especially if they are recording artists or potential recording artists, will try to restrict the publisher from exploiting these demos when the writer is also a performer at the session. Where a record agreement already exists, such promotion by the music publisher will always be subject to the rights of the writer/artist's record company. If the writer is not a performer, or is a performer without a record deal, many of a publisher's activities in promoting demos may be consummated only with the approval of the writer. Alternatively, the contract might list certain specified prohibitions (e.g., licensing to an X-rated film or to a commercial product campaign), with all other exploitation considered acceptable. A songwriter who is able to negotiate co-ownership of the demo performances—usually accomplished by the writer's paying directly for a portion of the costs of the recording session—may also take a cut of any license fees generated by uses of the demo.

## Foreign Subpublisher Fees

Because licensing the use of compositions in countries outside the United States is so complex, virtually all music publishers use local publishers in foreign countries to represent their catalogs. Since these foreign publishers (referred to as "subpublishers") render all the normal publishing services (protection of songs pursuant to local laws, registration of compositions with performance and mechanical societies, negotiation of licenses, collection of royalties, auditing of music users, promotion of cover records, preparation of royalty statements), they charge from 5% to 25% for their efforts. Because these fees are deducted from the gross income earned in any foreign territory before monies are remitted to the United States, they effectively reduce an American publisher's income, and thus a songwriter's income, which is a percentage of the publisher's.

Many songwriters try to minimize subpublishers' fees to no more than an agreed-upon percentage of foreign-generated income. For example, if a writer negotiates a "not in excess of 20% foreign retention" percentage and $10,000 is earned in England, the British publisher will not be able to take more than $2,000 for its services, with the remaining $8,000 being sent to the United States. Occasionally, if the songwriter has substantial bargaining power or if the U.S. publisher uses affiliates (as opposed to independent third parties) in foreign territories, an "at source" agreement may be negotiated, which provides that the songwriter's share of income will be computed "at the source" of the income rather than after the subpublisher has deducted its fees. For example, if a writer is to receive 50% of monies earned on an "at source" basis and $10,000 is earned from CD sales in England, the writer would be entitled to a $5,000 share of foreign income (rather than 50% of $8,000, as in a non-source or "receipts" agreement). Since foreign subpublishers do provide services and have their own operating costs, many U.S. publishers will reject these "at source" provisions because the subpublisher's fees will be deducted entirely from the publisher's share of income.

It should be noted that the songwriter's share of foreign performance income is collected not by the subpublisher but by the local performance societies, who remit these royalties directly to ASCAP, BMI, or SESAC in the United States for distribution to the songwriter. Therefore, subpublisher fees are never deducted from the songwriter's share of performance income, as that money flows (after deduction of performance society fees) directly to the songwriter.

## Audits

Some of the most important clauses in a songwriter's agreement are those that outline the songwriter's rights to inspect the books of the publisher if the writer feels that he or she is not being accounted to correctly. Although these rights are rarely exercised, most lawyers, when negotiating such clauses, put a great deal of time and effort into ensuring that the writer may audit a publisher's records. A songwriter's representative usually asks that the writer has at least 2 or 3 years to make an objection to any royalty statement. Audits are usually limited to 1 per year with a proviso that at least 30 days' written notice be given so the books and records can be organized. Occasionally the publisher will also be able to postpone an audit date for 30 to 60 days. Some negotiations result in provisions that guarantee that the publisher will pay for all reasonable costs of any audit that proves that the writer has been underpaid by a certain percentage (e.g., if there was an underpayment error of 15% or more) or a certain dollar amount (e.g., if there is an error in excess of $5,000).

## Infringement Claims

The infringement clause addresses what happens if someone claims that a songwriter's composition infringes on another writer's composition. Most contracts provide that the writer will compensate the publisher for any costs expended in defending or settling a claim in addition to any monies or profits that must be paid as a result of the infringement litigation or any settlements designed to resolve the claim. For example, if a third party files an infringement claim against a composition that cost $50,000 in legal fees and court costs and an actual judgment is rendered for another $100,000, the writer will be obligated to reimburse the music publisher for the full $150,000. This is true under most agreements even if the claim is defended successfully or is dismissed without merit, because the writer has agreed to indemnify his or her publisher against claims regardless of whether or not infringement is proven.

Even though most writers never have to face an infringement claim, their lawyers do spend a great deal of time on these clauses, since if a claim is made, the results can be financially devastating to a songwriter regardless of how successful he or she may be. The writer is virtually always entitled to hire his or her own legal counsel to assist in defending and protecting the writer's interests. Because the stakes in winning or losing can be extremely high, with lawyer's costs alone ranging from $25,000 to $150,000, the publisher normally retains the right to control the conduct and strategy of the defense—although in most cases, suggestions and input from both the publisher's and writer's lawyers will be shared, because everyone is really on the same side.

Since not all infringement claims have merit, some attorneys are able to negotiate a clause that provides that the writer is liable to the publisher only if the litigation results in a nonappealable judgment against the publisher or a settlement is reached with the songwriter's approval. Another alternative is to provide that the songwriter will have to reimburse the publisher only a portion of the legal costs if no infringement is found or if the third party withdraws its claim. The value of these alternative approaches for the songwriter is that he or she will not be liable for money spent to defend claims that never should have been made. Since many of these claims (whether valid or not) result in settlements prior to actual litigation, some writers negotiate clauses that guarantee that the writer must approve any settlement payment over a certain amount (e.g., $5,000), a provision that at least gives the songwriter some control over how the music publisher deals with a claim when it is received.

Since these claims can result in expensive judgments, most agreements give the publisher the right to withhold from the writer's royalties the amount of money that may have to be paid out if the claim is successful. For example, if another writer or publisher is suing for $200,000 plus a transfer of the entire copyright, the music publisher being sued will hold at least $200,000 in royalty income due the writer (plus an additional amount to cover expected legal fees) to ensure that if the case is lost or there is a large settlement, the money will be in house, ready for payment. The writer, on the other hand, will try to limit the withholding only to monies generated by the song in question and not the earnings due from other compositions in his or her catalog. The writer will also try to limit the time during which the publisher can withhold royalties (e.g., "if a suit is not instituted within 1 year from the date of the claim, all monies will be released") or provide that if the writer gives the publisher a surety bond that has sufficient collateral attached to it, all "held monies" will be distributed. Getting one of these protective clauses into the songwriter's agreement, however, depends on each party's relative bargaining strength, as well as the experience of the negotiators and whether the songwriter's lawyer has been able to negotiate such a provision in a previous agreement with the publisher.

## Writer–Performer Development Deals

Because so many recording artists write their own songs, the opportunities for music publishers to place songs on new albums have been somewhat diminished. This lack of access to many of the current writer/recording artists has encouraged a number of music publishers to go into the business of developing new writer/performers into recording artists. If a writer/performer is able to secure a recording agreement, most if not all of the songs on his or her albums will be written by the writer/artist and hence owned and controlled by the publisher.

Most of these development deals begin with one of the publisher's A&R staff hearing a young band in a local club, hearing a tape, or getting a referral from a music attorney, manager, agent, or writer signed to the company. If the publisher feels that the members of the group have potential both as writers and as performing artists, a development deal will be offered. Under this type of agreement, the publisher usually guarantees that it will finance the production of a certain number of demos so that the group can be presented to record company executives and A&R representatives. The term of these agreements is usually from 6 to 18 months, with further rights based on whether the publisher is able to secure a recording agreement for the group within the development period. For example, a contract might provide that the publisher will have 1 year to get a group a record contract, and if that happens, the publisher can extend its rights to the group's songs during the full term of the record agreement.

There are a large number of variations in these artist development deals, but most provide for the following:

A set period for the publisher to secure the writer/performer a record deal (1 year, 18 months, etc.).

A guarantee that a specified number of new songs featuring the writer/ performer will be produced in a professional recording studio.

- A guarantee that these sessions will take place within a specified period of time after the signing of the development agreement (2 months, 6 months, etc.).
- A guarantee that a minimum amount of money will be expended by the music publisher for the recording sessions ($600.00 per song, $1,000.00 per song, etc.).
- Advances to the writer/performer during the term of the development deal ($2,000 per month, $3,500 per month, etc.).
- A minimum number of newly written compositions to be delivered by the songwriter/performer during the artist development term (10 new compositions, 12 new compositions of which writer has at least a 50% interest, etc.).
- Options on the part of the publisher to extend the development aspects of the agreement if it fails to secure a record deal within the allotted time (e.g., "in the event that the publisher does not secure a record agreement within 1 year from the signing of the development deal, it shall have 1 option to extend the term of the agreement for an additional 6 months provided it pays the songwriter/performer additional advances" or "if a record deal is not signed within 9 months after the publisher has completed the required number of showcase recordings but negotiations have commenced with an interested record company, the term of the development deal will be extended until the negotiations either result in a recording artist agreement being signed or such negotiations cease because terms cannot be agreed upon or the record company loses interest").
- A guarantee that if a record deal is secured through the efforts of the music publisher, the songwriter–publisher aspects of the development deal will continue through the entire term of the record agreement negotiated on behalf of the writer/performer. Occasionally there will also be a guarantee that, if a record deal is secured and the record company drops the writer/artist or fails to exercise any option for additional albums, the publisher will have the right to secure another artist agreement with a different label.
- A guaranteed minimum recording-artist royalty, recording fund, album guarantee, and advance structure if a recording agreement is secured. For example, a sample clause might read:

The music publisher shall have the right to negotiate and commit the songwriter/performer to a recording contract if the following minimum terms are contained in the recording artist agreement:

1. *Album Guarantees.* A minimum of 1 CD containing at least 10 compositions will be recorded during each contract period.
2. *Royalties.* A minimum of 10% retail royalty will be paid to the writer as a recording artist for each album sold.
3. *Advances.* The writer/artist will receive an advance of at least $50,000 per year or per album from the record company.

4. *Recording fund.* The record company will expend a minimum of $100,000 in record-
   ing costs for the initial album produced and at least $150,000 for each additional
   album produced.
5. *Release guarantees.* A minimum of 1 CD containing at least 10 compositions will be
   commercially released to the general public in the United States during each 18-
   month period of the recording agreement.

Under these types of minimum-guarantee development agreements, if the
music publisher is able to negotiate substantive terms less favorable than those
guaranteed (e.g., in the above example, a $75,000 recording fund versus the
guaranteed $100,000, an 8% royalty versus the guaranteed 10%, advances of
$25,000 per album versus $50,000), the writer/performer may, in many cases,
reject the recording agreement. In the event that the major substantive terms
conform with the minimums specified in the development deal, however, the
publisher can commit the writer/performer to the record contract.

Record agreements are not that easy to come by, and they are becoming
more and more difficult to negotiate. The publisher will try to guarantee as few
major areas as possible in the development deal, since "getting a record deal" is
the most important goal. The writer/performer's lawyer, on the other hand, will
try to secure as many minimum guarantees as possible to prevent the music
publisher from committing the writer/performer to a bad record agreement.
The reality of these situations is usually that both parties need each other's
resources to secure the interest of a record company: the publisher provides
financing, direction, and connections, and the writer/performer provides the
raw creative talent that will hopefully ensure a marketable product. Because of
that mutual need, the negotiations of development deals are usually handled
very quickly and reasonably, with only a minimum of the posturing and veiled
or unveiled threats that sometimes characterize other types of agreements.

## SOURCES OF INCOME FOR THE MUSIC PUBLISHER AND SONGWRITER

The financial value of a songwriter's and music publisher's catalog is based
on the quality of the songs, the frequency and nature of their use, and how they
are licensed. The following section reviews many of the varied sources from
which songwriters and publishers receive income.

### Performance Right Payments

One of the largest continuing sources of royalty income for writers and
publishers is the performance right payments from ASCAP, BMI, and SESAC, as
well as from affiliated performance societies in foreign countries. ASCAP, an
association of writers and publishers founded in 1914, and BMI, a broadcaster-

owned corporation organized in 1939, negotiate license fee agreements with the users of music—radio and television stations, cable stations, Web sites, concert halls, wired music services such as Muzak, etc. The agreements give the user the right to perform the music and lyrics of any member of these organizations. The license fees collected by ASCAP and BMI (over $1.2 billion in 2003) are then distributed to the writers and publishers whose works are thus performed. (Chapter 7 discusses these activities in greater detail.) This "performance right" is one of the most important rights of the U.S. Copyright Law as well as the copyright laws of most foreign countries. It is based on the concept that a writer's creation is property and that a user must acquire a license in order to perform a copyrighted musical work.

The primary types of music use that generate ASCAP and BMI performance royalties are feature performances (a visual vocal or instrumental on television, a radio performance, etc.); background music on television series, specials, movies of the week, and feature films; theme songs to television series; advertising jingles; production company and network logos; and copyrighted arrangements of public domain compositions (a new arrangement of a song no longer under copyright). Each type of music use has its own relative value—features are worth more than themes, themes are paid higher than background music, etc. In addition, both ASCAP and BMI have different payment formula schedules, thereby producing different payments for the same type of music use depending on whether you are a member of ASCAP or an affiliate of BMI. Further, these payment and distribution schedules can frequently change, sometimes without notice to writers and publishers.

As for the $270 million coming in each year from foreign performances of U.S. writers' and publishers' works, both ASCAP and BMI have agreements with most of the foreign performing right societies of the world whereby money collected in the foreign marketplace is forwarded to ASCAP and BMI for distribution to their writer and publisher members. Most of the money distributed in the United States is "writer money," as most U.S. publishers collect their foreign performance monies directly from the foreign society through local subpublishers. The foreign performing right societies generating the most income for U.S. writers and publishers are those located in England (PRS), France (SACEM), Canada (SOCAN), Germany (GEMA), Italy (SIAE), Japan (JASRAC), and Australia (APRA).

## CD, Record, and Tape Sales (Mechanical Royalties)

One of the major sources of income for the songwriter and music publisher is the "mechanical" royalties due from the sale of records, tapes, and CDs. With the revision of the 1909 U.S. Copyright Law effective January 1, 1978, a Copyright Royalty Tribunal (which no longer exists) was established whose role is to monitor the mechanical royalties paid to songwriters and music publishers. Rate adjustments were provided for in the legislation based on the U.S. Consumer Price Index.The statutory mechanical royalty payable to songwriters and music publishers was increased from 2¢ to 2.75¢ per song and then, through a series of escalations, to 5¢ in 1986, 5.25¢ in 1988, 5.7¢ in 1990, 6.25¢ in 1992, 6.6¢ in 1994, 6.95¢ in 1996, 7.1¢ in 1998, 7.55¢ in 2000, 8¢ in 2002, and 8.5¢ in 2004. (There is also a durational formula based on 1.65¢ per minute of playing time, but we will concentrate here only on the 8.5¢ rate.) Under the mechanical rate in effect in 2004–05, a million-selling single would be worth a total of $85,000 per song in combined royalties to the publisher and writer, instead of the $20,000 that would have been earned prior to 1978.As for album, tape, and CD sales, the above royalties would be multiplied by the number of songs on the album, tape, or CD. For example, if 10 songs were included on a CD and each received a 8.5¢ royalty, a total of 85¢ in mechanical royalties would be generated from the sale of each album. If the CD sells between 1 million and 10 million copies, the aggregate writer and publisher royalties for the album would range from $850,000 to $8,500,000.

It should be mentioned that the per song statutory mechanical royalty can be reduced under certain circumstances (for example, if the writer is the recording artist or if the record is sold as a midline, record club, television-only, compilation, or budget album) so that the royalty figures can be less than those mentioned above. Such "reduced rates" are voluntary, however, and occur only if the publisher agrees or if the songwriter is a recording artist and has no choice but to accept lower royalties.

Many recording artist and producer agreements contain language that provides that if the recording artist or producer has written or co-written a song, has ownership or control of a song, or has any interest in any composition on the album, tape, CD, or single, the mechanical royalty rate payable by the record company is reduced. Such compositions are referred to as "controlled compositions." Many contracts attempt to establish a 75% rate (e.g., 6.375¢ in 2004–05) for all controlled compositions computed at the rate at the time a record is produced, the date of the recording contract with the artist, the date that a particular album commences recording, or the date the recording is originally released (regardless of whether the same recording is released again at a later date in another album). Other times, the record company will establish a maximum aggregate mechanical penny royalty limit for an album (for example, 64¢ per album). Under these clauses, the artist or producer guarantees that he or she will secure reduced mechanical rates on all songs on the album so that the maximum penny rate payable by the record company to music publishers and songwriters for all songs is not exceeded. If this maximum aggregate album royalty rate is surpassed, the difference is normally deducted from the artist's or producer's record, songwriter, and publishing royalties (or the per-song royalty rates for the writer/artist or writer/producer will be reduced proportionately). These clauses also usually apply to Canadian royalties.

For example, if a writer/performer has a 10 song x 6.375¢ maximum royalty rate on his or her album (i.e., 63.75¢) and, instead of writing all 10 songs, writes only 8 and records 2 songs written by outside writers who demand the 8.5¢ statutory 2004–05 rate per song, mechanical royalties would look as follow:

| | |
|---|---|
| 63.75¢ | Album royalty maximum |
| −17¢ | (2 outside songs at 8.5¢ each) |
| 46.75¢ | |
| ÷8 | Number of artist written songs |
| 5.84¢ | Per-song royalty to writer/artist and publisher |

As you can see, the writer/artist's mechanical royalty has been reduced to 5.84¢ per song from 6.37¢ per song because of the inclusion of two outside-written songs on the album. As the writer/artist records more outside written songs, the artist's per-song royalties for the artist's own works will be further reduced. In fact, in some cases, where the writer/artist has recorded a substantial number of other writers' songs, the writer/artist has been put in a position of receiving no royalties for his or her own songs, since the aggregate album royalty maximum has been paid out to outside songwriters and publishers. There have also been instances where the writer/artist's mechanical royalties have been in the minus column for every album sold because of the operation of these controlled-composition clauses. Many of these clauses also provide that the writer/artist will receive a mechanical royalty for only one use of his or her song regardless of the number of versions contained on the album, cassette, CD, or single.

On the other hand, some record companies will give the writer/artist a full statutory mechanical rate (as opposed to the reduced controlled-composition rate) if the writer/artist assigns a portion of his or her publishing to the record company's publishing company. Such an arrangement ensures that the writer/artist will receive full mechanical royalties and, in most cases, will guarantee the writer additional advance income, since publishing contracts invariably provide for either yearly or per-album songwriter advances.

## Television Series

When a producer wants to use an existing song in a television program, weekly series, special, miniseries, or made-for-TV movie, permission must, with few exceptions, be secured from the music publisher of the song. In this regard, the producer of the show will decide on how the song is to be used (background vocal or instrumental, sung by a character on camera, over the opening or ending credits) and the medium over which the program will be broadcast (free television, pay television, basic cable). The producer or its "music clearance" representative will then contact the publisher of the composition, describe how the song will be used, ask for a specified period of time to use the song in the program, negotiate a fee, and then sign what is known as a

| Program | Song |
|---|---|
| *CSI* | "Who Are You" (The Who's recording used as the theme to this series about crime scene investigation) |
| *The Sopranos* | "Woke Up This Morning" (A3 recording used as the theme to this HBO series about the Mob) |
| *Frasier* | "You Can't Take That Away From Me" (background while Niles and Daphne dance at a party on the eve of Daphne's wedding to Donny) |

"synchronization license." Since home video has become an important ancillary market for television programming, negotiations will usually take place for that medium as well. Considering that some television programs are also released in movie theaters in foreign countries, the producer may also request such rights and negotiate additional fees for such non-television uses. And since many television programs are eventually broadcast in media other than that on which they were initially aired (e.g., a pay television program being broadcast on free over-the-air stations), a producer may also request prices for a wide range of additional options. Synchronization fees for a worldwide 5-year free television license range from $1,500 to over $3,000, with fees varying for pay and cable television use and for other media such as home video and foreign theatrical.

## Motion Pictures

When a motion picture producer wants to use an existing song in a theatrically released film, it must negotiate with the music publisher for use of the composition. Once an agreement is reached, the producer will sign a synchronization license, which will give it the right to distribute the film to movie

| Film | Songs |
|---|---|
| *Chicago* | "All That Jazz" |
| *Moulin Rouge* | "Lady Marmalade" |
| *Cast Away* | "Light My Fire" |
| *The Full Monty* | "Flashdance (What a Feeling)" |
| *The Bodyguard* | "I Will Always Love You" |
| *Catch Me If You Can* | "The Look of Love" |

theaters, sell it to television, and use the song in "in context" television promos and theatrical previews. The amount of the motion picture synchronization fee depends on a number of factors, including how the song is used; the overall budget for the film and the music budget; the stature of song being used; the actual timing of the song as used in the film; whether there are multiple uses; the term of the license; the territory of the license; and whether there is a guarantee that the song will be used on a soundtrack album or released as a single.

The synchronization fees charged by music publishers are usually between $15,000 and $60,000. In addition, record companies normally charge between $15,000 and $60,000 for the use of master recordings (i.e., the original hit recording) in a motion picture, but, depending on the stature of the artist, the licensing policy of the record company and the nature of the recording being used, these fees can be greater or less than the range referred to above. On occasion, a music publisher will reduce the synchronization fee for a song if the producer guarantees that the song will be on a soundtrack album released by a major label. For example, a publisher might charge $25,000 for use of the song in a film but give the producer a $22,000 alternative quote if the song makes the soundtrack album. Considering the phenomenal success of some motion picture soundtracks and the royalties they can generate, such a reduction in the synch fee may substantially benefit the publisher and the songwriter in the long run. The "alternative quote" arrangement also helps the motion picture producer (especially where a film has a great number of outside songs), as its up-front costs are reduced.

Some film producers will occasionally want to include a preexisting song in a motion picture only if the music publisher guarantees that the film company will share in the earnings from all or selected subsidiary markets (e.g., soundtrack album sales, single sales, downloads, ASCAP or BMI radio, television and web performances, foreign theatrical royalties). Other producers will try to secure a portion of the copyright ownership to the song. Most publishers will refuse such conditions, but sometimes arrangements are made on a short-term basis to ensure that the song gets into the film (e.g., the producer may receive 25% of the mechanical royalties from the soundtrack or single released from the soundtrack for 5 years from its release date).

## Home Video/DVDs

Since the home video market has become enormous in almost every country in the world, the sale of videos represents a significant source of revenue for the music publisher and songwriter. Home video licensing is normally handled in one of three ways:

1. A per-video royalty: Under this approach, the royalty paid is based on a set rate (usually from 8¢ to 15¢ per song) for each video sold. For example, if

100,000 videos are sold and a particular song has a 8¢ royalty, the payment will be $8,000.00.

2. A one-time buy-out: Many video distributors demand that publishers accept a one-time buy-out fee for all video rights regardless of how many videos might be sold—a fact of life in today's market that must be faced and negotiated accordingly.

3. A rollover advance: Under this formula, the producer or video distributor pays a certain advance for a specified number of videos, with additional predetermined sums paid as additional sales plateaus are achieved—for example, $8,000 for the first 100,000 units and an additional $8,000 for each additional 100,000 units sold.

## Commercials

An extremely valuable source of income for the songwriter and music publisher is the use of songs in radio and television commercials for consumer products. The fees paid by advertising agencies and their clients for commercials can be substantial (e.g., from $75,000 to $750,000 per year for successful songs), depending on whether it is a radio or television commercial, a national or limited-territory campaign, whether there are options for other countries of the world, if the original lyrics are being changed or new lyrics added, and whether all advertising rather than only product category exclusivity is being requested by the agency. On occasion, an advertising agency will ask for a non-broadcast test period during which it will test the commercial in shopping malls, interagency screenings, and the like to see if the pairing of the song and the product is effective. Fees for this off-air testing range from $1,000 to $10,000, and the term is normally from 2 to 4 months. Other times, an agency will request a limited-broadcast test period, during which a commercial will actually be aired in a specified regional market (for example, television in Florida only for 2 months, or a 3-month test in cities that contain not more than 10% of the total U.S. population). Fees for this type of regional-broadcast test period normally range from $5,000 to $45,000, depending on the duration of the test

| Song Title | Product | Genre |
|---|---|---|
| "Fly Like An Eagle" | U.S. Postal Service | Classic Rock |
| "Dancing Queen" | Visa | Pop Classic |
| "Start Me Up" | Microsoft | Classic Rock |
| "I Dream of Jeannie" | Tropicana | TV Theme |
| "I Will Always Love You" | Verizon | Pop Classic |
| "Close to You" | Hertz | Pop Classic |
| "I Feel Pretty" | Canon | Broadway |
| "Pink Panther" | Heineken | Movie Theme |
| "Rhapsody in Blue" | United Airlines | Standard |

period, the importance of the song, the product being advertised, and whether there has been a lyric change.

Certain major advertisers may request total exclusivity from a publisher, but the fees for this type of grant are substantial for a recent hit song or well-known standard (from $250,000 to over $1,000,000), since the song is effectively being taken out of the marketplace. Most commercial licensing agreements provide for restrictions only on licensing for competing or similar products. For example, a beer commercial may restrict the writer or publisher from licensing the same song for another alcoholic beverage commercial, but will allow licensing for use in a food or automobile advertising campaign. In addition to the fees paid by the agency or client for the use of a song, the writer and publisher may be eligible to receive radio and television broadcast royalties from ASCAP or BMI provided that the performance rights have been reserved, the amount of royalties being dependent on whether the song is a past or present hit, the amount of music used, whether the lyrics have been changed, whether the commercial has a national market versus a limited territorial exposure campaign, and whether the media buy schedules (i.e., the actual broadcast dates) can be obtained from the agency or broadcasting stations.

## Broadway Musicals

One of the most lucrative markets for a song is its use in a Broadway show, since if the play is a hit, the income from live theatrical performances, soundtrack albums, singles, motion picture rights, touring productions, video, sheet music, and stock and amateur production rights can mean hundreds of thousands of dollars for the songwriter and music publisher. However, considering that the vast majority of musicals presented on Broadway lose most if not all of the money invested and that getting a song into a Broadway play is extremely difficult, this is an area with which most songwriters and publishers, unless they are involved with songs actually created for the play, will have little or no contact. With the success of shows such as *Mamma Mia!, The Lion King, Movin' On, Beauty and the Beast, 42nd Street, Tommy,* and *Smokey Joe's Cafe,* all of which used preexisting songs, the field has opened up somewhat for writers and publishers, but in most cases, the access still is just not there.

Music royalties for the Broadway run and first-class national touring productions usually range between a 1.5% and 4% pro rata share of the box office receipts if a percentage royalty is negotiated (which can mean from $200,000 to over $10,000,000 per year for all songs in a hit show), or a fixed dollar amount per week (from $250 to over $750 regardless of the success of the play) if a non-percentage royalty is agreed to.

## Instrumental CDs/Records of Popular Songs/Sing-Alongs/Karaoke

Certain companies specialize in selling instrumental versions of hit songs accompanied by printed lyrics or lead sheets, so that amateur singers can add their own voices. Some sell equipment (microphones, players with recording, dubbing, and playback capabilities, etc.) to enhance the quality and facilitate the use of such instrumental recordings. Royalties payable to writers and publishers in this area are normally: (1) the statutory mechanical royalty rate per song per version for each tape distributed; and (2) from 4¢ to over 8¢ for each lyric sheet of the song included with a tape or CD. A number of firms also market video versions of the sing-along concept with the lyrics and music contained on a laser disc, DVD, or video cassette. Royalties paid for such uses are sometimes calculated on the wholesale price of each disc, with all songs sharing the aggregate royalty on a pro rata basis. It is more common, however, for a writer and publisher to charge a set penny royalty (e.g., from 12¢ to 14¢ per song for each sing-along DVD or tape distributed). In addition, there is usually a one-time fee given to each publisher of between $300 and $350 for the right to include the song in the video—sometimes referred to as a "fixation fee." The licenses in this area normally last for 7 to 10 years but can be longer and are usually for the world (or the world excluding Japan). It is also common to receive an up-front advance for the initial 5,000 to 7,500 copies distributed (e.g., $600 to $900 if you are licensing at a 12¢ rate, or $700 to $1,050 at a 14¢ rate).

## Video Jukeboxes

Even though the popularity of the video jukebox is greater in Europe, there is a small but growing market in the United States. The video used on such machines is normally a promotional video produced by the record company for its artist, and the royalties to the music publisher are one-time $25 fixation or synchronization fee for use of the song in video jukeboxes, plus 10¢ per month per song for each individual video jukebox containing the song. Another formula used is 3¢ per play. The duration of these agreements is normally 1 year, but can be longer if agreed to by the parties.

## Lyric Reprints in Novels or Nonfiction Books

Another source of income for the songwriter and music publisher is the use of song lyrics in nonfiction books or novels. All fees are dependent on the number of lines being used, the context in which the song is used; the importance of the song; the number of other song lyrics used in the book; whether hardcover, paperback, or both are included in the request; the total budget for such clearances; the territory in which the book will be distributed; and whether

| *Book* | *Song Lyrics* |
|---|---|
| *Mystic River* (Dennis Lehane) | "Pirates" (Ricki Lee Jones) |
| *The Beach House* (James Patterson) | "Memory Hotel" "Statesboro Blues" |
| *Hearts in Atlantis* (Stephen King) | "Black Slacks," "Tallahasee Lassie" |
| *Personal Injuries* (Scott Turow) | "Yesterday," "A Bushel and a Peck" |

*The Silence of the Lambs*
(Thomas Harris)

*Scene*

James Gumb, the psychopathic killer whose murders cause the psychological struggle between FBI agent Clarice Starling and the incarcerated Dr. Hannibal "The Cannibal" Lector, sings the lyrics to Fats Waller's "Cash Your Trash" while in the shower.

English or both English and foreign translation versions are being requested. Normal fees for hardcover books are between $100 and $1,200, with additional fees normally required for paperback and book club editions. In addition, information on the plot of the book, the publisher, and the context in which a lyric is to be used is normally requested by the music publisher prior to approval and a price quotation being given.

One example of such book use is Joseph Wambaugh's best-selling novel *The Secrets of Harry Bright* (William Morrow and Company, Inc.) which contained portions of the lyrics to 12 songs, including "One for My Baby," "I Believe," "Ain't She Sweet," "Strangers in the Night," "Once in a Lifetime," "Hound Dog," "I'll Be Seeing You," and "Make Believe." Another example is Nancy Sinatra's *Frank Sinatra, My Father,* which was published by Doubleday & Company and contained portions of the lyrics to many of the songs that the singer made famous. A third illustration is Chief Justice William Rehnquist's *The Supreme Court: How It Was, How It Is* (William Morrow and Company, Inc.), which used a portion of the lyrics to the standard "The Last Time I Saw Paris."

As in the case of all lyric reprints of copyrighted songs, inclusion of the correct copyright notice is required either on the page containing the lyric or in a separate section devoted to copyright acknowledgments, normally located at the beginning of the book.

## Lyric Reprints in Magazines

Another source of income is the negotiated fee for the use of song lyrics in weekly and monthly magazines. Fees for such magazines range from $50 to $450 for one issue, but can be more depending on the stature of the composition, the weekly or monthly circulation, and whether it is a special issue (e.g., $550 or more for Valentine's Day or Christmas issues) or supplement. One example of such a magazine use was *New Woman's* Valentine's Day article entitled "Love Songs," which reprinted the lyrics to, among other songs, "My Funny Valentine," "Just in Time," "The Way You Look Tonight," and "Killing Me Softly with His Song." Another illustration of such a use was *Seventeen* magazine's use of the lyrics to the Jerome Kern and Oscar Hammerstein II classic "All the Things You Are" in an article entitled "How to Write a Love Letter." As with novels and nonfiction books, the music publisher will always require that correct copyright notice be printed with the lyrics.

## Monthly Song Lyric and Sheet Music Magazines

For lyric magazines the normal fees paid to music publishers are between $50 and $500 per issue, with additional monies sometimes due if a particular song becomes a Top 10 or 20 Pop Hit (e.g., an extra $50 if a song reaches #20 on the Billboard Top 100 Pop Single chart). For sheet music magazines, the per-song royalty can be a pro rata share of 12½% of the subscription price of each issue, with advances usually based on the number of yearly subscribers (which in some cases can be as many as 150,000 copies). For example, if the yearly subscription price is $14 for 9 issues, the per-issue royalty base price would be $1.55 (or $14.00 divided by 9). It is somewhat standard that no deduction be made for postage and handling, as these are costs absorbed by the magazine's publisher. It is also customary for price reductions to occur for multiple-year subscriptions, and the base royalty for each such issue will normally be reduced accordingly. It is also common for free copies of each magazine to be given to the music publisher and that an additional 2% to 4% of each issue be printed as royalty-free, not-for-sale promotional copies, which may be used for advertising purposes. Set per-composition dollar fee licensing (as with lyric magazines) is also common in this area.

## Public Service Announcements

Permission for the use of a song in public service announcements is occasionally given for either no charge or a nominal administration fee of from $100 to $500 for a limited period of time. The television spot for U.S. Safety Belts that featured Barbara Mandrell's recording of "Sleeping Single in a Double Bed" and the Department of Transportation's "Don't Drink and Drive" announcement using Michael Jackson's hit song "Beat It" are two examples of licensed song use for public service announcements.

## Recordings of Hit Songs with Changed Lyrics

On occasion, publishers will receive a request from a recording artist or producer to change the lyrics to a well-known song so that it can be recorded and released under a new or similar title. Most of these revised versions are not successful, but a few, such as Al Yankovic's "Eat It" (based on Michael Jackson's "Beat It") and Cheech and Chong's "Born in East L.A." (based on Bruce Springsteen's "Born in the U.S.A.") became successful hit records in their own right.

Assuming the music publisher approves the use, the licensing can be handled in a number of ways. Considering that the success of the new version is normally dependent on the popularity and recognizability of the original hit song, some publishers will require that the copyright and publishing rights to the new lyric (and the new song) be owned by them, with the new lyricist receiving no credit or royalties for the lyric. Other publishers will allow the writer of the new lyrics to receive writer's credit as well as a share of the mechanical and performance royalties. In such a case, the royalties due the writer of the original hit song would be reduced for sales and performances of the new revised version, since an additional writer would be sharing in the earnings. In some cases, the music publisher will also give up a portion of the copyright ownership in the new song so that the royalties due not only to the original writer but also to the publisher will be reduced in the same ratio.

As a practical matter, most publishers will refuse any request to change the lyrics of a well-known song. A further complicating factor is that many writer-publisher contracts provide that the original songwriter has approval rights over any changes in English lyrics. In such a case, permissions have to be secured from both the music publisher and the songwriter.

## Medleys

Every few years, a single or album containing a medley of prior hits becomes successful. An example of such a record was the album *Stars on Long Play*, which contained shortened versions of 29 Beatles compositions strung together, with individual song uses ranging between an 8-second use for "Nowhere Man" to a 46-second use for "Day Tripper." The flip side contained an additional three medleys with a total of 24 previous hit songs ranging from Little Richard's "Slippin' and Slidin'," "Jenny, Jenny", and "Lucille" to "Venus," "Bird Dog," "Runaway," and "At the Hop."

Since this type of album uses a large number of songs with all uses being between 8 and 50 seconds, the mechanical licensing is normally handled in a different manner than the usual album or single, where each song might receive a statutory royalty rate. For a medley, each song is usually licensed on a pro rata basis according to the number of songs contained in the medley of which it is a part or its duration compared to other uses on the album. On occasion, a minimum or "floor" royalty (e.g., 3¢) may be guaranteed for each song regardless of its duration or the number of songs on the album. For example, if a medley album contains 30 songs and all are licensed at 8.5¢, the total mechanical royalties due on the album would be $2.55. Because this aggregate royalty is normally prohibitive to the record company releasing the album, many publishers agree on a formula that computes the normal statutory royalties due on one 10- to 15-song album (between 85¢ and $1.27 in 2004–05) and provides that all songs will share in that aggregate royalty either equally or based on their relative durations. In the case of singles, each song in each medley (1 on each side) will normally share in either the 8.5¢ that would be due if the medley were treated as 1 song or 17¢ if the record company will pay a 2-song royalty. In such a case, each of the 5 songs used in the 1-song royalty scenario would receive approximately 1.7¢, unless a minimum guarantee (e.g., 3¢) was agreed to.

Many publishers will give a reduced rate only if they are given a "most favored nations" clause in the license. This clause guarantees that if another publisher or song receives a better rate, they will also get the benefit of such a rate. For example, if one publisher agrees to a 3¢ royalty with a "most favored nations" clause and another publisher's song receives 4¢ from the record company, the first publisher's royalty will be automatically raised to 4¢. The same concept can also apply to all terms of a license if so negotiated by the parties.

A common variation of the medley situation occurs when an original song is recorded that uses a portion of an existing song. In such a case, the two songs can either share all monies earned from the new version equally or, depending on the duration of the use, divide such monies on an agreed-upon percentage basis. There have also been instances where the owners of the preexisting hit song have received a full statutory mechanical royalty as if theirs were the only song on the single.

For a record producer, it is advisable that reduced-royalty arrangements for all songs be made prior to the recording and distribution of the CD or cassette containing a medley. If a producer waits until the recording is completed to "clear" reduced rates from writers and publishers, he or she may be obligated to pay a full statutory mechanical royalty for each song recorded, regardless of whether a use is 5 seconds or 40 seconds.

## Promotional Videos

All record companies need the right to release a video of their recording artists for MTV, VH1, and similar channels, as such exposure is essential for success in today's market. Because these videos are a necessary promotion vehicle and extremely expensive to produce (with costs from $50,000 to over

$750,000), some publishers will give a free license for this type of use provided that the record company does not receive any fees or payments for use of the clips. Other publishers, however, negotiate a flat up-front fee, usually from $100 to $250. The terms of these licenses range from 18 months to life of copyright, and the territory of use is almost always the world. In cases where the music publisher will give only a short-term license (e.g., 18 months to 2 years), the record company will many times negotiate for guaranteed options to extend the agreement for an identical period of time, usually at a set or negotiated fee. If a recording artist is the writer of a composition, however, the recording artist agreement will normally provide that the record company has the right to use the composition in a promotional video for no fee. For example, a clause found in many recording artist agreements reads:

> Artist grants to the record company an irrevocable license, under copyright, to reproduce each Controlled Composition in motion pictures and other audiovisual works ("pictures"), and to distribute and to perform those pictures throughout the world for the purpose of promoting Audio Recordings, and to authorize others to do so, without payment.

Once the artist's video leaves MTV and similar promotion areas and is sold for home use to the general public, however, the publisher and record company usually do negotiate a royalty structure for such uses. The fees charged depend on the policies of the companies involved and usually encompass a set penny rate for each song, a pro rata percentage of the wholesale price of the video, or a percentage of the net profits of each video manufactured and sold.

## Greeting Cards

The greeting card market can, for certain compositions, be a surprisingly valuable source of income. In this area, the major companies prefer to enter into exclusive agreements for the right to use the title or a portion of the lyrics of a song for use on the face of the card, as the inside message, or both. The duration of these agreements are from 1 to 3 years, and the rights granted can be for the United States, the United States and Canada, or the world. In addition, the music publisher is usually given the right to approve a reasonable facsimile of how the lyrics will be used and how the card will look prior to its manufacture, sale, or distribution. The music publisher will also require that the appropriate copyright notice be contained on the card itself, normally on the back of the card.

A variety of royalty formulas apply here, with one of the more prevalent being a percentage of the wholesale price of each card, less trade discounts. Assuming that 100,000 cards are sold in a 3-month period at a wholesale price of 40¢ and with a lyric royalty of 5%, the calculations would look as follows:

|          |          |                          |
|---------:|---------:|--------------------------|
|          | 100,000  | Cards sold               |
| x        | $.40     | Wholesale unit value     |
| $ 40,000 |          | Aggregate wholesale value |
| x        | 5 %      | Royalty %                |
| $ 2,000  |          | Gross song royalty       |
| –        | 1.8 %    | Trade discount           |
| $ 1,964  |          | Net song royalty         |

Certain card manufacturers prefer a 1-time payment (rather than a percentage per card royalty), and the fees in this area range from $100 to over $2,000 for a 1-year period for a specified number of cards (e.g., $500 for the right to print up to 4,000 greeting cards). If the music is also used in a greeting card or used by itself without the lyrics, the card company will pay a mechanical royalty or a percentage thereof for each card manufactured and sold.

## Computer and Board Trivia Games

A number of game manufacturers use a few seconds of well-known songs as part of their question-and-answer trivia games. Since the music of these songs is played, such uses are many times treated like a mechanical royalty, with the exception that each song licensed for the game will sometimes receive a reduced statutory-rate fee or a penny rate because of the short use (in most cases, from 5 to 10 seconds). Rates in this field are usually for 4¢ to 12¢ per composition depending on duration, importance of the song, and the number of songs used in the game. Sometimes an advance will be paid on a specified number of games (e.g., on 5,000 games), with a "most favored nations" clause provided. If advances are given, they are usually of the "rollover" type, which guarantees that the writer and the publisher will receive a set advance each time a certain sales plateau is reached (e.g., $200 for each 10,000 games sold, with the initial $200 payable upon the signing of the agreement and $200 each time a 10,000-unit sales plateau is reached). Royalty buy-outs are also common.

## Television Commercials for Motion Pictures

If a song is used in a motion picture, the right of a motion picture producer to use clips from the film in television advertisements and theatrical previews is almost always granted by the music publisher in its synchronization license. In the event that a song is used out of context in the commercial, an additional fee is normally negotiated. Although it is not common, occasionally a producer will use a song that is not contained in the film as part of its television advertising, preview teaser, or trailer campaign for the motion picture. In such a case, the producer will contact the music publisher and negotiate a fee for television commercial and/or theatrical trailer/teaser use only (usually from $12,000 to over $95,000).

## Home Video (Television Programs)

Whether the television program is an old collector's item series, a successful miniseries, a hit weekly program, a "best of" collection containing highlights of many shows, a variety special, or a behind-the-scenes look at the making of a show, there is a growing market for video versions of television programming. Since the units sold in this area do not reach the large numbers that a major motion picture video might generate, however, licensing is sometimes handled on a shorter-term basis (e.g., 7 to 15 years rather than life of copyright) and on a royalty percentage basis rather than a perpetual 1-time buy-out, as is prevalent in the motion picture industry. In addition, advances are also normally much smaller (e.g., a 5,000- to 10,000-unit advance being common). Per-video royalties are usually based on either a penny rate (e.g., 8¢ to 15¢ per song) or on a percentage of the wholesale price. The percentage is shared on a pro rata basis according to either the number of songs on the video or each song's duration in relation to the total running time of the entire program or the aggregate timing of all music on the video.

The major television production companies demand that the music publisher and songwriter accept a one-time buy-out payment for all videos manufactured and distributed regardless of the actual number that may eventually be sold. Such demands originally started with network television hit series but have now been extended to other series, made-for-TV movies, miniseries, and specials and are a fact of life that must be dealt with if you want your songs used in television programs. Fees in this area normally range between $6,000 to $11,000 depending on whether the song is used as background music or sung by a character in the program, its importance to the story line, whether there are multiple uses, whether it is used over the opening or closing credits, and the projected success of the video in the marketplace.

## Home Video (Recording Artists)

As in television program video licensing, some licenses are buy-outs, but many provide for song royalties to be based on either a pro rata percentage of the wholesale price or a set per-song amount (8¢ to 15¢) for each video sold. Depending on the video appeal and marketability of a particular recording artist as well as the producer's video policy, it is not uncommon for a music publisher to receive an advance based on from 5,000 to 25,000 units. If a writer is the recording artist, the recording contract will dictate the video payment formula, which normally ranges from 0% to as much as 50% of the record company's receipts (less a distribution charge, shipping, and tape duplication costs, as well as union payments) or, in the alternative, a percentage of the wholesale price of each video sold or set penny rate. When the writer is the recording artist, the record company may also have the right to recoup from 50% to 100% of the costs of producing the video from these royalties.

## Foreign Theatrical Royalties (Motion Pictures)

In most countries outside the United States, motion picture theaters are required to pay performance royalties for music used in theatrically distributed films (in many cases, 1% of the box office). These fees are collected by the local performance right society in each country, which in turn remits the writer's share of such monies directly to ASCAP or BMI in the United States, which then pays the royalties to the writer. (The music publisher normally allows its representative in each foreign territory to collect its share for remittance to the United States.) Because of the worldwide appeal of many U.S.-produced motion pictures, it is not unusual for successful films to generate between $50,000 and $300,000 in total foreign theater performance royalties.

## Dolls and Toys

Many dolls and other toys use music or tapes or microchips. Formulas in this area are many times based on the statutory mechanical per-song royalty rate, with some based on the timing of each song in relationship to other songs, a pro rata equal share for each song used in the medley, specified reduced statutory rates (e.g., 7¢ per song), full statutory royalties, or higher negotiated rates. The need of the producer to use a particular song that might be identifiable with a particular doll (e.g., an Elvis Presley doll using "Hound Dog" or "Love Me Tender") will dictate the royalty rate which is ultimately accepted. Another emerging market for song use is the area of "interactive toys" that talk to children as well as move their mouths and roll their eyes as they sing famous songs. Although these dolls carry a high retail price, they can sell in the millions each year, and depending on the royalty rate charged, writers and publishers can earn over $50,000 per year on a successful interactive doll.

## Television Programs and Motion Pictures Based on Songs

On occasion, a television or film producer will use the title and story line of a song as the basis for either a made-for-TV movie, a television series, or a theatrical feature film. The usual negotiation in this area includes:

Option payments to maintain exclusivity while a script is being developed or financing is being secured (usually from 5% to 10% of the actual acquisition figure, with a portion of such payments sometimes deducted from the final payment)

A final purchase price, which is usually due at the end of the option period, upon commencement of production, or upon actual first telecast or release

A percentage of the producer's net profits

A percentage of all merchandising rights derived from the television show or film (with a restriction on the producer's sharing in any preexisting merchandising contracts to merchandising unrelated to the television show or film)

The right to participate in sequels or spin-offs

Separate synchronization fees for the use of the song in the television program or motion picture

Possible music consultancy or music supervision during the production of the project

Possible composing fees for the creation of additional songs for the project

Approval or consultancy rights on the script

There are no hard and fast rules in this area, however, as everything depends on the importance of the song and its title to the project, the budget for the program or film, the license fees received from the network in the case of a television vehicle, the current popularity and topicality of the song, and the bargaining power and knowledge of the negotiating parties.

## Books Based on Motion Pictures (Lyric Reprints)

On occasion, a screenplay or book based on a popular motion picture will be published after the film's release. If a character in the film has sung a song in a particular scene, the book publisher will request permission to include the composition in the printed edition. The fees for such uses are similar to those for novel reprints and usually range from $100 to over $1,500 for hardcover rights, with similar amounts due for paperback and book club editions. The music publisher will require that correct copyright notice be given in the book for each song used and will usually request 1 or 2 complimentary books for its files.

One example of such a screenplay is Woody Allen's *Hannah and Her Sisters,* published by Random House, which uses portions of the lyrics to the standards "I'm Old Fashioned" (Jerome Kern and Johnny Mercer), "The Way You Look Tonight" (Kern and Dorothy Fields) and "Bewitched" (Rodgers and Hart), among others. Another example is *The Wizard of Oz: The Screenplay* by Noel Langley, Florence Ryerson, and Edgar Allan Woolf, which contains the lyrics to, among others, E. Y. Harburg and Harold Arlen's "Over the Rainbow," "Ding Dong! The Witch Is Dead," "We're Off to See the Wizard," and "If I Only Had a Brain (If I Only Had a Heart) (If I Only Had the Nerve)."

## Books about a Lyricist

A book publisher will sometimes put together a comprehensive reproduction of all the lyrics by a legendary writer, such as Cole Porter, Oscar Hammerstein II, or Lorenz Hart. Since many of these books are "coffee table" size, cost from

$30 to $50, and sometimes contain 150 to 200 lyrics, the typical licensing formula provides for a set fee per song or an equal sharing by all songs of either a percentage of the wholesale price or a share of the author's book royalty. For example, one such book, which contained commentary about the lyricist as well as reprints of his more famous lyrics, had all music publishers and songwriters sharing 20% of the book writer's royalty. Since the writer's hardcover royalty was 10%, all songs contained in the book shared a 2% retail price royalty (or 20% of 10%). Thus, if the book had a retail selling price of $40, all songs would share in the 80¢ per book royalty. Simple mathematics indicate that most of these projects are not large income-producing items by themselves, but they often have the potential of re-exposing compositions to the heads of record, motion picture, television, and advertising companies and thus generating new uses. These books therefore can be extremely important promotional vehicles, and music publishers should negotiate their royalties accordingly.

## Novelty Albums

Novelty and nostalgia albums occasionally become real money-makers for the music publisher and songwriter. One such example is Tee Vee Tunes' *Television's Greatest Hits* double album, which contains shortened versions of 65 famous television themes (sometimes including the voice over announcer) from the 1950s and 1960s, including *The Lone Ranger, Perry Mason, Leave It to Beaver,* and *Star Trek.* As in any such project, you never really know whether such an album will be successful or not but, in the case of *Television's Greatest Hits,* the results were astonishing: the album made the *Billboard* Top Pop Album chart, selling over 200,000 copies in the United States. In addition, the "Jetson's Theme" single made the pop charts, and a number of forgotten themes from old television series were reintroduced to a brand-new audience.

As for the business and licensing aspects of such a project, music publishers usually work with the producer and often accept a reduced mechanical royalty (e.g., 50% to 75% of the statutory rate) because of the large number of compositions contained on such an album, because virtually all uses are between 30 and 90 seconds, and because this type of album is, from an economic standpoint, impossible to produce if a statutory-rate payment must be paid for each composition used.

## Lyrics on Albums, Cassettes, and CD Packages

Unlike other areas, where fees are usually charged by music publishers for the reprinting of lyrics to a song, it is standard industry practice not to charge record companies for the use of lyrics on album packaging or inserts included with tapes, CDs, or albums. In effect, publishers treat such requests as promotional in nature and do not require any payments. When record companies do ask for permission, however, it should be made clear that proper copyright notice be contained on the lyric sheet.

## Sheet Music and Folios

*Best of Motown, Best of Nashville, Movie Songs of the 90s, The Best Christmas Songs Ever*—these are but some of the many folios released each year. At one time, the sale of sheet music was a major source of income for the music publisher, but with the increasing monies that can be earned from the sale of records, cassettes, and CDs, the use of songs in commercials, the synchronization fees from motion picture and television uses, and the performance royalties received from ASCAP, BMI and their foreign affiliates, this area has for many songs become a secondary income-producing source. It remains a valuable area, though, as it can provide a steady stream of good income for some songs and, for others, a substantial infusion of royalties. For example, successful songs may be distributed in a multitude of arrangements for piano solo, piano duet, guitar, concert band, jazz ensemble, vocal solo, choral arrangement, electronic piano, organ solo, and as part of a "best of" or "songs from a motion picture" series. In addition, sheet music may also be printed in non-music-oriented books such as Merv Griffin's "Jeopardy Theme," which appears in Alex Trebek and Peter Barsocchini's *The Jeopardy! Book.*

## Television and Motion Picture Background Scores

A substantial source of income for certain writers and publishers is the earnings generated by background music scores to television series and motion pictures. Although this is a very specialized field normally requiring substantial musical training in composition and orchestration, the field has opened up to many writers initially identified solely as "pop writers" (Stewart Copeland ·of the Police, Tangerine Dream, Jay Gruska, Danny Elfman of Oingo Boingo, Randy Newman, Ry Cooder, et al.). Most composers in this field are not signed specifically to 1 publisher and normally assign the copyright (or a portion thereof) to whatever film studio or production company is making the film. The publishing and songwriter revenue emanating from background scores includes royalties paid by network, local, public, basic cable, and pay television, as well as by movie theaters outside the United States.

## Lyrics and Music on Soda Cans

A somewhat rare but extremely valuable source of income can be the use of lyrics or music to a song on soda cans or other consumer product packaging. Such uses usually occur as part of a limited or seasonal campaign and are licensed on a 1-time fee use (much like a television commercial where there is unlimited broadcast rights during a specified period of time), rather than a per-can royalty basis. One such promotion was the use by Pepsi Cola of the lyrics and music to "Winter Wonderland." On the Pepsi cans themselves, which were colored a deep blue with white silvery snowflakes, the sheet music was also displayed in white and silver. The names of the writers, Felix Bernard and Dick Smith, were featured near the top of the can, and the copyright notice was displayed near the bottom.

## Lyrics on T-Shirts and Posters

The T-shirt business can be a substantial source of income for certain compositions with popular lyrics or specific lyric lines. Licenses in this area normally provide royalties on a per T-shirt sold basis, with royalties calculated on an agreed-upon penny rate, a percentage of the wholesale price, or a percentage of the suggested retail list price of the shirt. For example, a 12½% to 20% wholesale royalty is not unusual. It is common for an advance to be given and a proviso included that an appropriate copyright notice for the song be printed somewhere on the T-shirt. Occasionally, the music publisher may request that a sample T-shirt be provided so that it can view the finished product before approving and finalizing the transaction. Posters are handled in much the same way.

## Audio Recordings of Books

Since a large number of popular novels and other books are being transferred to audio tapes and CDs for listening in autos or at home, the lyrics to songs used in the print edition of the book are many times contained on the tape or CD. In these cases, the licensing is usually handled as if a song is being used on a recording artist's CD or tape, as publishers view this type of exploitation as an extension of the "mechanical" right. Since a full use of any song is rare in any book, music publishers and tape distributors normally agree on a reduced mechanical license rate for every recording manufactured and distributed.

## Special Products Albums

A continuing and valuable income source for well-known songs is their inclusion on the various albums, CDs, and tapes released by the Special Products divisions of the major record companies. Most of these albums are compilations of various songs and recording artists that fit into a special theme. For example, the project themes can be the "best" hits from the 1980s, the "greatest" movie or television themes, the "best of" Elvis Presley, Fats Domino, or the Platters, and any number of Reader's Digest packages.

These "special products" albums usually contain a large number of songs controlled by several music publishers and, unless they feature only one recording artist, usually contain a large number of master recordings owned by various record companies. Because of the great number of royalty-bearing compositions on these albums, the record company will normally ask each music publisher to give a reduced mechanical rate for every song used. In most cases, a 75% statutory rate is agreed to by publishers, but rates can be as high as 100% and as low as 50% depending on the value of the particular song to the project and the negotiating stances of the other publishers who control songs on the album. It is somewhat standard when these requests are received to ask for a "most favored nations" clause in one's acceptance of a reduced mechanical rate so that if another publisher gets a higher royalty, a publisher granting a lower rate will be guaranteed the same rate. Occasionally, such a clause will relate to all songs on the album with the exception of one or two songs which demand a statutory royalty. It is also common to receive an advance on a certain number of future sales (e.g., for the first 50,000 units sold) and, in some cases, a minimum guarantee (e.g., a guaranteed sale of 25,000 units).

## Television Sale Only Albums

Another variation of the "special products" album is those compilation CDs and tapes that are sold by mail order solely through television advertising. Occasionally the recording artist appears in these commercials (if a particular artist is being featured), and there is always a "crawl" showing the titles of many of the songs on the album being advertised. As in special products licensing, mechanical rates are many times negotiated on the basis of 75% of the statutory rate per song. Most publishers will also give a free synchronization license for the television marketer to use the song as part of the commercial. Although many people fail to realize the value of these television mail order packages, they can sell in the hundreds of thousands and generate substantial royalties.

## Record Clubs

Record club uses represent a real money-making proposition for many writers and publishers. These are the clubs that sign up members through mail campaigns, usually with a "4 albums for the price of 1 album" incentive offer. Mechanical royalties are usually negotiated in the range 75% of the statutory rate. It is also advisable to make sure in the license that royalties will be paid on CDs and tapes that are not sold but given away as incentives for new club members.

## Key Outlet Marketing Albums

Another source of mechanical income is the use of compositions on albums sponsored by a commercial product and sold as part of a marketing plan for a company's retail customers. One example of this type of album is a compilation entitled Pour It On which was put together and sold by Starbucks. The album included recordings by Judy Garland, Sarah Vaughn, Nancy Wilson and Chet Baker and sold at Starbucks locations. Compositions used on these special marketing albums are many times licensed at a reduced statutory rate (75%) and it is standard for the publisher to secure an advance on a certain number of units upon signing of the license agreement (e.g., an advance on from 20,000 to over 100,000 units). On occasion, an advance is only given to those publishers who accept a reduced statutory rate with the publishers not accepting the reduced rate royalty receiving royalties on actual sales only without the up front signing advance.

## Limited Edition Collectibles

The commemorative plate, rendering, statue, sculpture or other collectible (such as a hand painted porcelain egg) represent a growing market and opportunity for songwriters and music publishers since many of these items include a digital music or musical voice chip which allows the buyer to play a particular song which in some way relates to the subject matter of the collectible. The price of these collectibles range from $50 to over $200 and, when music is used, the collectible usually relates in some manner to a particular solo performer or group (e.g., Elvis Presley, Frank Sinatra, the Beatles, etc.) or to a motion picture which has a well known musical theme or song score (e.g., The Wizard Of Oz). Some examples of this genre are a crystal domed porcelain sculpture of the Beatles that plays "Sgt. Pepper's Lonely Hearts Club Band," Frank Sinatra hand painted dolls containing excerpts of the singer performing "Witchcraft" and "My Way," a porcelain clear domed sculpture of Marilyn Monroe that contains a digital sound chip of the actress singing "Diamonds Are A Girl's Best Friend", a crystal-clear domed structure of Elvis Presley with Graceland in the background that plays "Love Me Tender", a Dorothy from The Wizzard Of Oz musical portrait doll that features an excerpt from Judy Garland's classic version of "Over The Rainbow" and an heirloom collector plate featuring Patsy Cline singing her hit "Crazy."

When a music publisher licenses a composition to the company producing the collectible, the term of rights is usually for a limited period, (e.g., for 7 years) or for a set period with an option (e.g., 4 years with an option on the part of the collectible company to extend the term of the license for an additional 3 years). The per collectible royalty is sometimes based on the U.S. statutory rate, but many times the contract provides for a higher negotiated rate for sales in the United States with a larger royalty for sales in countries outside the United States since the mechanical rate in foreign countries is usually higher than that in the United States. One can also negotiate a graduated rate in the United States to reflect increases in the statutory rate or upon commencement of the option period.

## Musical Telephones

There are a number of special telephones on the market which play your favorite song in place of the normal ring when someone calls. One such example is a singing Elvis Presley telephone which has a replica of Elvis in a gold lamé suit holding a guitar on the base of the telephone. When the phone rings, the replica begins to dance while the song "Hound Dog" is heard. There is also a demo button which you can push to see and hear the performance without waiting for someone to call. Another example is an Elvis phone which plays "Jailhouse Rock". Since this type of use is an audio reproduction, licensing may be handled on the basis of the statutory mechanical rate per telephone but such rates are usually negotiated higher (e.g. 50¢ or more).

## Singing Fish

Another interesting use of music is in connection with the man made fish that turns its head and sings a well known song. One example is a big mouth bass mounted on a wall plaque which sings such compositions as the Bobby Mc Ferrin written "Don't Worry, Be Happy" and the more appropriate "Take Me To The River". There are a number of variations in this area but most are currently battery operated which can be activated either by a motion sensor or by a manually operated push button. Licenses are many times issued at the statutory mechanical or higher negotiated rate for the territory of the United States with increased rates for a worldwide license.

## Theme Parks

Another source of income is the licensing of musical compositions for their use in theme parks such as Disneyland, Disneyworld, and Universal Studios. The licenses in this area are usually for the life of copyright of the composition and encompass either one particular attraction at one identified theme park (e.g., The Country Bear Jamboree at Disneyland or the Back to the Future attraction at Universal) or specified theme attractions at parks around the world. Fees in this area usually range from $5,000 to $15,000 depending on the duration of the license, the rights being granted and the number of theme parks that are being permitted to use the composition.

## Ringtones

The use of the melodies of hit songs as ringtones for cell phones is an increasing source of revenue. License terms vary with formulas in the United States ranging from 10% to 16.15% of the actual retail selling price to the consumer for the completed transmission, download, upload or other delivery of the recording (or revenue earned) with either a guarantee that the consumer price on which the royalty percentage is based will not be lower than a certain amount (e.g., 99¢), that the ringtone will sell within a certain price range (e.g., between $1.00 and $3.00) or that a minimum royalty (e.g., the statutory mechanical rate or other negotiated rate such as 10¢) will be paid regardless of the percentage formula calculation. A one-time per song upload fee of from $25 to $50 may be paid. The contract will usually provide that the ringtone use will not exceed 30 to 45 seconds. The territory will be for the United States unless additional countries are agreed to.

## Music Boxes

A number of music box manufacturers, in addition to using public domain compositions, also use copyrighted songs in their product line. These uses usually concentrate on songs whose melodies are very well known or have a seasonal message, such as "White Christmas" or "I'll Be Home for Christmas." These uses are many times treated as a mechanical license, with the fee per box being either a full statutory or greater rate for the U.S. if there is a merchandising right included or, if the license is for the world, a higher negotiated rate.

## The Internet

A major source of publisher revenue in the future will be the mechanical and performance payments for downloads of music, streaming audio, subscription royalties, ringtones, the synchronization fees for audio visual and commercial uses as well as the negotiated or statutory fees for any protected uses on the net.

## Changing Mechanical Rates

United States statutory mechanical rates change every two years. In 2002–03, the rate was 8¢ per song or 1.55¢ per minute. In 2004–05, the rate is 8.5¢ per song or 1.65¢ per minute; and in 2006–07, 9.1¢ per song or 1.75¢ per minute, whichever is larger.

---

## *CONCLUSION*

The world of songwriting and music publishing is not really all that mysterious. Just as every other business has its particular rules, special ways of conducting business, idiosyncrasies, and unique revenue-producing areas, so too does songwriting and music publishing. This onetime business of pennies, piano rolls, and sheet music has been transformed by the technology of the communications industry into a multibillion-dollar worldwide industry and one of the crucial centerpieces of entertainment programming. It is a difficult field to succeed in and a difficult field to remain successful in. But even though it is based on creativity, it is a business like any other business, and knowledge of its inner workings is one of the real keys for a lasting and productive career.

# 2

# Music, Money, Copublishing, and Administration

$M$OST AGREEMENTS between songwriters and music publishers take either of the two basic forms discussed in the previous chapter, the individual song agreement or the exclusive agreement. Two other types are worthy of discussion, however, and these form the subject of the present chapter. Both types, the copublishing agreement and the administration agreement, are many times available only to established, successful songwriters. Moreover, both types concern a writer who has formed his or her own small publishing company but wishes to make use of the greater financial, administrative, and promotional resources of a major music publisher.

The copublishing agreement is one of the most significant contractual arrangements in the music industry. It gives the songwriter a share of certain rights and income that he or she would not be entitled to under the normal writer–publisher contract. As we have seen previously, industry practice is for the writer to sign with a publisher on a song-by-song basis or on an exclusive basis for all musical compositions written during a specified period of time. Under the terms of such contracts, the writer transfers the copyright of a song or songs to the publisher and is paid 50% of all earnings received by the

*53*

publisher from those songs. Under the terms of the copublishing agreement, however, the writer sells and transfers only a portion of the copyright and retains the other portion for his or her own publishing company. More importantly, the songwriter receives not only his or her standard 50% share of all earnings but also a portion of the 50% that normally is reserved to the music publisher. As a general rule, the copublishing arrangement is usually available primarily to writers who have a successful track record of past hits, writer/performers who have the potential of securing a record deal, or writers who have a current recording artist contract and who have the bargaining power to negotiate such an agreement with a music publisher.

The music-publishing business is highly competitive, and if a particular writer is in demand or has written songs that a publisher feels have the probability of being hits, the publisher may agree to enter into a copublishing agreement as an inducement for the writer to sign. Obviously, if a publisher realizes that the only way to sign a particular writer is to give him or her part of the future income usually reserved solely to the publisher, it usually will do it. Such a decision represents a sound business decision: if the writer's songs do fulfill their commercial potential, both the established publisher and the writer will gain substantially.

Five basic sets of circumstances lend themselves to the signing of a copublishing agreement. The first is where the writer has had a number of hits while signed as an exclusive writer to a publisher and the contract is approaching its expiration date. Considering the writer's past success, the current publisher (or another competing publisher) might offer a copublishing arrangement for all future compositions as an inducement to re-sign or sign as an exclusive writer.

Another situation that often occurs is where the successful writer already has his or her own publishing company and a major publishing company wants to sign the writer and control his or her material. Under such circumstances, the major company will normally agree to a copublishing arrangement in order to get the right to publish a part of the songwriter's past and future compositions.

A third situation is where a recording artist has written his or her own material and has a recording contract with a major label. In such a case, a publisher will virtually always be willing to enter into a copublishing agreement with the writer/recording artist, since the publisher knows that the recording artist will release self-written material and there will be guaranteed commercial exposure of the songs.

A fourth common situation is where a writer has signed a single-song contract and the song becomes a major hit. Such a writer, because of this success, will have the necessary bargaining power to negotiate not only an exclusive songwriter's agreement but also a copublishing agreement with a major publisher for all future songs.

Finally, a major publisher may offer a writer a copublishing contract in lieu of high advances to keep the costs of signing the writer at a moderate level. In these instances, the songwriter trades the immediate financial benefit of higher advances for a share of the publisher's income. If the songs are successful, that agreement can mean substantially increased future royalties, which can more than compensate the writer in the long run.

## STANDARD TERMS OF A COPUBLISHING AGREEMENT

A number of variations on the copublishing agreement may be negotiated. The basic terms are fairly standard, however. The following section describes both the usual provisions and the principal variations that may be encountered by the writer or the writer's representative in negotiating a copublishing agreement.

### Sharing of Income

The first important aspect of the copublishing agreement is how the various parties to the agreement share the income that is earned from CD and tape sales, downloads, videos, performances, motion picture and television synchronization rights, commercials, streaming, and all other sources of revenue generated by a writer's songs. The most common sharing of income arrangement in this area is known as the "50/50" split." This equal sharing of income (50% to the writer's company and 50% to the major company) refers only to those monies that represent the music publisher's share of earnings. It does not relate to the writer's share, since the songwriter will still receive his or her songwriter's royalties regardless of the terms of the copublishing agreement.

A simple diagram comparing the standard writer–publisher contract and the copublishing agreement can best explain this sharing of income between the writer's publishing company and the major publishing company. Under the standard music industry publishing contract, the writer generally receives 50% of the net income earned from uses of his or her songs, and the publisher receives the other 50%. For example, if a total of $100,000 is received by the music publisher from the sale of CDs, downloads or audio cassettes, the publisher would be entitled to retain $50,000 and the writer would receive $50,000.

Under the copublishing agreement, however, the writer receives not only his or her 50% share of songwriter income but also receives a share of the publisher's share. If we keep our previous example of $100,000 received by the publisher from CD, download, and tape sales and assume a 50/50 copublishing arrangement, the income would be shared as set forth on the next page:

As can be seen, the songwriter receives 50% of all monies received, with his or her publishing company and the major publisher sharing the remainder equally. In effect, the writer and his company receive 75% of all monies earned, and the major "copublisher" receives the remaining 25%. To illustrate the ar

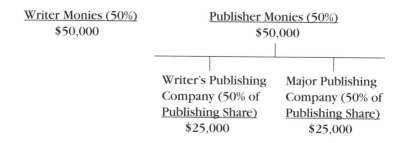

rangement once again through the use of actual dollar figures, the sharing of income looks as follows:

Writer:
$50,000.00     Writer's 50% share
+$25,000.00    Writer's 50% share of publishing
$75,000.00     Total earnings for the writer

Major Co-Publisher:
$25,000     Copublisher's 50% share of publishing
           monies

The basic 50/50 copublishing agreement is not the only type of royalty split encountered in the music industry. Another type of copublishing agreement provides for a 75/25 split of publishing income between the writer's company and the major publisher. Under such an arrangement, the writer will receive his or her full writer's share of income (50% of all monies that are earned) as well as an additional 25% of the publisher's share of monies earned (25% of the remaining 50% of all income). Assuming our $100,000 example, the writer's company would receive 25% of the $50,000 publisher's share ($12,500) and the major co-publisher would receive the other 75% ($37,500). Under this arrangement, the writer and his or her publishing company would receive an aggregate total of $62,500 of the $100,000 earned and the major publisher would receive the remaining $37,500.

## Compositions Covered by the Agreement

The agreement will normally cover all future compositions created by the writer during the term of the copublishing agreement as well as, in some cases, all past songs written by the writer and owned by the writer's publishing company. Furthermore, many agreements specify that the contract covers all compositions by other writers that are acquired, owned, or controlled by the writer's publishing company during the term of the agreement.

## Transfer of Copyright and Other Rights

Under the usual 50/50 split agreement, the writer's publishing company will transfer 50% of the copyright ownership of all compositions to the major publisher. In addition, the writer's company will also normally give the major publisher all administration rights, including the right to license the use of the musical compositions throughout the world and the right to collect any monies that may be earned by the compositions. As with songwriter agreements, the copublishing agreement may also contain certain restrictions (e.g., no commercial uses without consent) or exclusions (e.g., motion picture or television dramatization rights with respect to the story line of the song).

## Term of Agreement

The initial duration of the agreement can vary, but the usual arrangement is for an initial contract term of 1 or 2 years, with a number of successive options on the part of the major publisher to extend the agreement for additional 1-year periods. The first period of the term may be for 1 year with 3 successive 1-year options; 2 years with two 1-year option periods; 6 years with no option periods; or any other variation that may be negotiated. Other agreements may be tied to the release of a minimum product commitment (e.g., for 3 years or the release in the United States of 24 songs on a major record label, whichever is later) or the recoupment of all advances paid under the agreement.

Options to extend the agreement are of basically two types: the automatically renewable type and the type that has to be acted on by the major company for it to be effective. The former (or automatically exercised option) needs no affirmative action on the part of anyone for the contract to be extended; the option is automatically exercised at the end of the original term or the preceding option period unless there is notice to the contrary. The second type of option clause needs some type of affirmative action by the established company for it to be effective: in most cases, written notice given to the writer's company prior to the end of the current period.

## Ownership of Songs after the Contract Has Ended

Unless there are provisions to the contrary, and subject to any copyright reversion laws, all songs that are subject to the copublishing agreement will remain jointly owned by the writer's company and the major company for the life of copyright of the compositions.

## Advances

*Signing Advances.*   Depending, of course, on the reputation of the writer, the existence of any recording artist commitments, the quantity and quality of the songs controlled by the agreement, and the inclusion of any preexisting hit songs, the major publisher may make substantial monetary payments to the writer or the writer's publishing company at the time the copublishing agreement is signed. These payments are treated as advances recoupable from any future royalties that may become due to either the writer or the writer's publishing company. To put it simply, all royalties that become payable to the writer or his or her company under the agreement will be used to reimburse the financing publisher for the monies advanced at the time the contract is signed. For example, if $175,000 is given to the writer at the signing of the contract, then the first $175,000 in royalties due the writer or the writer's publishing company will be used to recoup the advance given. Until that happens, the writer and his or her company will not receive any royalties, although earnings statements with the current recoupment status will be sent.

*Option Year Advances.*   In addition to advances given upon signing, the major company usually pays an advance whenever it exercises an option to extend the duration of the agreement. Such advances can be paid either in a single lump sum at the start of an option period or in several monthly or quarterly payments during each option year of the contract. For example, there might be a payment of $60,000 upon commencement of each option period, or the same $60,000 could be paid out in $5,000 equal monthly installments. If the agreement is for more than 1 year (e.g., a firm 3-year deal) but there are no options, the agreement is often structured so that advances are either paid at the start of each 1-year period of the term, upon recoupment of advances or upon any number of variables negotiated by the parties.

*Advances Based on the Release of Commercial Recordings.*   If the writer is a recording artist, the copublishing agreement may guarantee a specified advance if an album containing songs written and recorded by the writer is released during each year of the agreement. The amount of this type of advance varies, dependent on the writer/artist's commercial success and appeal, the number of songs by the writer that are contained on the album, the reputation of the label releasing the CD or tape, where the release occurs, how high it gets on the trade paper charts, and whether or not past advances have been either totally or substantially recouped.

The rationale behind record release advances is that a music publisher stands to make a substantial amount of money from a hit single or chart album by an artist performing self-written songs. If the writer is already a successful recording artist, the chances of recouping such an advance are good. Also, a hit record receives plenty of airplay, which in turn can influence other recording artists to re-record ("cover") some of the songs and encourage film and television producers as well as advertising agencies to use the songs in their projects—occurrences that will bring the publisher additional income.

## Nonrecoupable Payments

On occasion, a major publisher will give the writer payments that will not be recoupable from future royalties. Such payments are treated by the publisher as acquisition costs; the publisher is in effect buying the rights being transferred. This type of arrangement is not the norm, but it can occur when dealing with major recording artists who write their own songs. The payments are usually made upon the commercial release of an album containing a certain minimum percentage of songs written by the writer/artist, but are sometimes made at the commencement of the copublishing agreement as a further inducement for the writer to sign the contract—especially when preexisting songs are being brought into the agreement.

## Costs of Demonstration Records

One of the necessary costs of doing business as a publisher are those incurred in the making of demo recordings that can be played for record company A&R executives, recording artists, or others who are responsible for listening to and selecting material for singles or albums. The costs of such demo sessions are usually 50% to 100% chargeable to the songwriter, recoupable from royalties due the songwriter, or recoupable from the gross income (or net income, in certain cases) prior to distribution of income under the agreement. Since in the copublishing arrangement the writer's company is also the publisher of any compositions that are produced at a demo session, the costs of such sessions are many times divided between the major company and the writer's company according to each party's percentage of copyright ownership, with the writer's company's contribution normally being recovered from future earnings of the songs rather than paid up front.

A number of agreements also include a maximum cost allowable for the making of such demo CDs. For example, it might be written into the contract that the total costs of any demo session shall not exceed a certain amount of money per song. The limit can be put at a dollar figure depending on and the type of demo to be made and the current rate of making such CDs in professional recording studios. Such a limit on spending will protect the writer against large expenditures that were not anticipated at the time the agreement was originally signed. Since the publisher is not in the business of spending money needlessly, however—especially since all costs are initially paid by it—such restrictions are normally counterproductive. The writer is never required to put up any money for the demo recording session, since any cost that may be attributable to the writer for the session will be deducted from future royalties.

## Additional Costs

Other costs of doing business are usually shared by the major publisher and the writer's company by means of a deduction-from-earnings approach. These costs include copyright fees, lead sheet preparation fees, and the purchase and distribution of promotional records. Once again, a portion of these amounts are deducted from future royalties due the writer's company (and those of the writer, if provided for in the songwriter's contract) and are not paid by the writer's company when the costs are actually incurred. Normal overhead costs such as rent, electricity, telephones, and such are not charged to the writer's company.

## Payment of Royalties to Songwriters

The major publisher initially collects all monies earned by the compositions (excluding the songwriter's share of performance income) and distributes the writer's 50% share of income directly to the writer. On occasion, the major publisher will pay such monies directly to the writer's company, which will then be responsible for paying the writer his or her share of songwriter royalties.

## Sharing of Income between the Two Publishers

Under the terms of most copublishing agreements, the major publisher will pay the writer's company a percentage of all earnings that are received, minus the following deductions: all songwriter royalties; costs of printing, arranging, and editing printed editions of the songs; all fees of the Harry Fox Agency, Inc., or other collection agencies; administrative charges of foreign collection agencies or foreign subpublishers; and certain agreed-upon administrative, promotion, and copyright fees. For example, the following clause, in one variation or another, is found in virtually all copublishing agreements:

> Publisher shall pay to Co-Publisher fifty percent (50%) of the net income actually received in the United States by Publisher or credited to Publisher's account against a prior advance from the exploitation of the Compositions. "Net income," as used herein, shall mean the gross receipts derived by Publisher from the exploitation of Compositions, less the following:
>
> a. Royalties and other sums which are paid by Publisher to the author and composer of the Compositions.
> b. Actual and reasonable collection or other fees customarily and actually charged by the Harry Fox Agency, Inc., the Canadian Musical Reproduction Rights Agency, Ltd. (CMRRA), and any other industry-wide collection agent which may be used by Publisher and, if applicable, subpublishers which may be used by Publisher.
> c. Administrative and exploitation expenses of Publisher with respect to the Compositions, including: (i) out-of-pocket copyright registration fees and costs, (ii) the costs of transcribing lead sheets, and (iii) the costs of producing demonstration records, to the extent not recouped pursuant to the terms of the Songwriter's Agreement.
> d. The costs of printing and distribution of the Compositions provided Publisher actually incurs such costs.

## Administration Charges

Some major publishers will occasionally deduct an additional 10% to 15% administration charge on either all gross income or the publisher's share of income (i.e., gross monies less writer's royalties) derived from the songs covered by the agreement to cover general administrative and promotion costs. This administration charge may also be used to cover such costs as copyright fees and the preparation of lead sheets, if recoupment of such costs is not provided for in another part of the contract.

## The Writer's Performance Right Income

One major exception to the rule that all monies due the songwriter are collected by the publisher occurs in the area of performance right income, since all monies earned from the performances of a writer's songs on radio and television stations are sent directly to the songwriter by either ASCAP, BMI, SESAC, or their foreign affiliated societies. These monies will not be collected by the publisher unless there is an express agreement to the contrary (e.g., a clause that allows the publisher to recoup an advance from the songwriter's share of performance income and the assignment of such royalties or letter of direction to pay is permitted under ASCAP, BMI, or SESAC rules) or the music publisher has licensed such rights directly to a broadcasting station or producer.

## The Publisher's Performance Right Income

There are two separate ways of sharing the publisher's performance right income from ASCAP or BMI. Under the first and more standard type of agreement, ASCAP or BMI pays the major publisher all the publisher's performance royalties, and the major publisher will then pay the writer's company its share. Under the second type of arrangement, ASCAP or BMI pays the writer's company as well as the major publisher directly and simultaneously. The latter type of arrangement is not that common and will virtually never occur while the major publisher has unrecouped advances to the writer or the writer's publishing company on its balance sheet.

## Reversions and Direct Collection of Income

Most copublishing agreements last for the life of copyright of the compositions controlled by the agreement. Occasionally, especially where the writer is a successful recording artist with bargaining strength, the compositions may revert to the songwriter's publishing company after a number of years or after all advances have been recouped. Additionally, some agreements provide that, even though the song ownership rights do not revert, the songwriter's publishing company will be entitled, at some specified time in the future, to collect its share of all royalties (including songwriter monies) directly from any users or music industry collection organizations. The writer's company may also be allowed to administer, control, and issue licenses for its share of each composition, with the major publisher licensing only its respective share. For example, under such a reversion of administration rights, a film producer who wants to use a song in a motion picture will request a license and fee quote from both the major publisher and the writer's company, and if the song is used, both companies will issue the license and be paid directly.

## Royalty Distributions to the Writer's Company

Under most copublishing agreements, the major publisher will pay the writer's company within 45, 60, or 90 days following each semiannual accounting period. This normally occurs between August 15 and September 30 for all monies received during the previous January 1 through June 30 period and between February 15 and March 31 for all monies that are received during the previous July 1 through December 31 period.

## Recap

The copublishing agreement is an excellent way for a songwriter to realize income over and above the normal 50% writer's share of royalties. Yet such an arrangement may not be available for most songwriters during the early part of their careers and, for many, during any part of their careers. It is available to songwriters who have had commercial success either as a writer or as a writer/ recording artist and to writers who have a recording commitment or are about to sign with a record company. The music business has been changing in this area, however, with more and more songwriters being able to retain a portion of their publishing income. For this reason, the copublishing agreement is taking on an ever-increasing role in a writer's maximizing his or her present and long-term income.

---

# ADMINISTRATION AGREEMENTS

Since the music and entertainment businesses are extremely complex, it is in many cases extremely wise for a writer to find a full-service major music publisher to handle the everyday administrative duties involved in protecting and promoting his or her songs as well as licensing, collecting, auditing, and processing the income those songs generate. One of the main differences between the copublishing agreement and the administration agreement is that the songwriter (through a publishing company that he or she owns) retains full copyright ownership of all songs. In addition, since the fees charged by the major publisher doing the administrative work are usually not large, the writer will normally be entitled to retain between 80% to 90% of all monies earned. This arrangement is usually reserved for established songwriters who have formed their own publishing companies and are not currently under a copublishing agreement with another publisher.

## Fees Charged for Administrative Services

Depending on the bargaining power of the writer and the services being offered by the administrating publisher, the fees charged are between 10% and 25% of all income collected. However, if the writer is a successful recording artist who automatically generates substantial income or the administered catalog is a motion picture or television company with guaranteed performance income, the fees charged for administration may be as low as 7% of the publisher's share of income, depending on the services being provided. For example, if the writer is looking only for the proper registration of songs with performance and mechanical rights organizations, the filing of copyright applications, and the dissemination of necessary information to ensure the proper collection of royalties, he or she should negotiate for lower fees. And since the administrating publisher usually pays royalties on a semiannual basis, if the catalog is generating substantial earnings, the interest on the monies being held can certainly cover a large number of costs and ensure a profit. But if the services needed include not only the above but also promotion, the recording of new demo records and tapes, the drafting of songwriter agreements, the negotiation of licenses, the securing of new usages, issuance of separate royalty statements to songwriters, and counseling as to worldwide trends or developments in the music and entertainment industries, higher fees can certainly be justified.

## Duration

As there is no transfer of copyright ownership in an administration agreement, the duration is always for a specified number of years, normally with all rights (other than collection of monies earned during the contract period) reverting to the writer's company at the end of the term. In most cases, the duration of administration arrangements is between 3 and 7 years, but depending on the needs of the parties and whether advances have been recouped, the term can be shorter or longer.

## Territory

There are many variations in the territory covered by an agreement, since this area, once again, is totally negotiable. For example, most agreements cover the United States or the United States and Canada, but an agreement can entail the world or selected countries throughout the world (e.g., all English-speaking territories). If the territory encompasses countries outside the United States, there may be an administration fee (usually 10% to 25%) deducted in the foreign country and, in many cases, an additional percentage fee charged on the foreign monies received and processed by the administrating publisher in the United States. Such a fee is justifiable if the U.S. publisher is performing a real service (for example, servicing foreign countries with cue sheets and perfor- mance and record information, organizing the catalog for proper representa- tion, drafting songwriter and other related agreements, issuing licenses, or pre- paring royalty statements). If the U.S. publisher is performing little or no real function, however, the fees charged on foreign-generated earnings may be mini- mal or there may be no fee at all.

## Royalty Statements

Depending on the nature of the agreement and the fees being charged, the administering publisher may either prepare and send statements specifying the gross income for each song (which would necessitate writer statements being prepared by the administered company) or compute and prepare both writer and publisher statements for all compositions that earned money. Obviously, since the latter alternative is more costly and time consuming, the administra- tion fees charged are normally higher.

## Royalty Payment Dates

As with the copublishing agreement, accounting statements and royalty checks are issued twice per year within 45 days to 3 months after each 6-month period. For example, monies received by the administrator during January through June of any year would be distributed between August 15 and October 1 of that year.

## Cover Records and New Uses

If a major reason for entering an administration agreement is the use of the established publisher's creative and promotion staff, many contracts provide incentives if a new recording or motion picture/television use is secured. For example, the writer may agree to increase the fee retained by the administrat- ing publisher from 20% to between 25% and 40% if the major publisher's staff is responsible for convincing a recording artist to release a new version of a song. If that new version reaches the charts as the "A" side of a single, the percentage may be further increased, and if it achieves the Top 10 or Top 5, yet a further increase might be provided. There are innumerable variations in this area, including transfer of a portion of the copyright ownership to a song and extension of the term of the agreement. Such an approach can give the admin- istrating publisher the necessary incentive to expend its total promotion efforts on behalf of the administered compositions.

## Monies Earned during the Term

Since receipt of royalties for CD, download, and tape sales, radio and television performances, and other uses can take from 6 months to over 2 years from the date that a royalty-generating use of a song occurs, many publishers provide that they will be entitled to collect all monies earned during the term of the administration period regardless of whether those monies are received after the expiration date of the agreement. These provisions, in effect, guarantee that the administrator will get its fee on all sales, performances, or other uses that occur during the period it has rights to the compositions. On the flip side of the coin, the writer will try to limit the time period that the administrator is entitled to collect. If the concept is acceptable, this issue is usually settled by allowing the administrating publisher to accrued income collection rights for 9 to 18 months after the term of the agreement has expired.

## Advances

As with the copublishing agreement, advances are many times given to songwriters and their publishing companies, all of which are recoupable from their share of the income generated during the term of the agreement.

## Pros and Cons of Administration Agreements

Songwriters who own the publishing rights to their songs can gain some real benefits by allowing a full-service publisher to handle all the business and promotion aspects of their catalogs. But considering the demands on both time and personnel (registering copyrights; registering with ASCAP, BMI, or the Harry Fox Agency; negotiating and issuing licenses; drafting agreements; preparing royalty statements; filing infringement suits or negotiating settlements; promoting of songs for television, motion pictures, and commercials; paying for demo sessions; notifying foreign countries; organizing a catalog), some publishers are not that interested in certain administration deals. Obviously, if a substantial amount of work is going to be done and all songs will be lost in 3 to 5 years, many publishers feel that it is just not worth the trouble, especially since time and effort are being taken away from handling the songs that they own for the life of copyright. Additionally, the profit margins on many of these agreements are so small that they are not worth entering into.

On the other hand, if an administered catalog is earning substantial monies (e.g., a hit recording artist's songs or a motion picture or television catalog), the administration fee as well as the interest earned on the monies generated might be well worth the efforts expended regardless of the limited duration of representation. In addition, if an administering publisher is weak in one area of music (e.g., rock, soul, or country), it may enter into such an agreement just to get a foothold in that area. There are also some catalogs that are so prestigious by their very nature that many publishers will accept a short-term administration relationship because being associated with such a catalog will enhance their reputation and, more than likely, generate additional business from other sources.

## Choosing the Right Administrator

Since an administration agreement, by its very nature, is usually not a commitment for an extended period of time, many writers do not undertake the necessary research to find out which publisher is best suited for their needs. After all, many feel that if they make a mistake, it can always be rectified by going to an experienced publisher when the current agreement ends. But a great deal of damage can be done in a very short period of time and a substantial amount of money lost by being with the wrong administrator—whether it be a publisher, lawyer, manager, or other representative. A writer must be aware that 2 or 3 years can, in the wrong hands, create a lifetime of problems and that any decision should be made only after extensive research on the reputation, personnel, and capabilities of the company being chosen to act as administrator, regardless of the amount of up-front advance money that may be offered to secure the deal.

# Music, Money, and the Recording Artist

The Phone Call from the Record Company

RECORD COMPANY EXECUTIVE: Hello, this is the Vice President of Business and Legal Affairs for _____ Records. As you know, our A&R people are very interested in signing your client to a recording artist agreement. Before I send you a summary deal memo of our proposal, I'd like to go over the main points of the offer so we know whether or not we have a deal.

ATTORNEY: That sounds good to me. The more issues and areas we can define and agree to before you draft a deal memo, the better for everyone.

RECORD COMPANY EXECUTIVE: We'd like to sign the artist for 1 album, and we need to have options for 6 more albums after the first. We'd also like to have the right to issue a "greatest hits" album over and above the option albums. The royalty rate will be 15% of retail for albums and 14% for singles. We'll pay on 90% of all recordings sold and will reduce the artist royalties by 50% for sales outside the United States. There'll be a guarantee that one video will be produced per album, the cost of which will be cross-collateralized with both the artist's audiovisual royalties and audio, CD, and tape income. We'll advance your client $150,000 on signing the agreement, with an escalating advance payable for each new album that is recorded and released. The amount of each option album advance will be based on 66⅔% of the earnings from the most recent past album. As your client is a songwriter, there will also be a 75%-of-statutory mechanical rate, with a 10-song cap payable as songwriter and publisher royalties for sales of each album released, and with a 2-song cap on singles. The mechanical rate will be the one in effect when the artist starts to record the album. Those are the basic terms. What do you think?

ATTORNEY: I'll discuss the offer with my client and will get back to you with our counterproposal. I do want you to know that, in its present form, the proposal is unacceptable. However, if we can get a 16% album rate on 100% sales without producer royalty deductions, with percentage escalators based on the achievement of sales plateaus as well as option years, increased royalties in at least the major foreign territories, a release guarantee for each album in not only the United States and Canada but also in the United Kingdom, an understanding that only 50% of the video costs will be recouped from the artist's audio recording royalties, guaranteed tour support, minimum guarantees as to album advances regardless of the earnings from the most recently released album, either a 12-times-statutory mechanical rate cap or, in the alternative, a 13-song-times-75% rate cap for albums, no packaging deduction for downloads or other digital distributions and an effective mechanical rate determined by the U.S. release date of each album, we'll at least have something to talk about.

One of the most complex and important relationships in the music industry is that between the recording artist and the record company. It is a contractual relationship that controls virtually every aspect of a performer's career, from how much he or she makes to whether or not there is even a chance of becoming the next Madonna, Backstreet Boys, Britney Spears, Enrique Iglesias, U-2, Shania Twain, Elvis Presley, Dr. Dre, Lauryn Hill, Eminem or Garth Brooks.

The cornerstone of this part of the entertainment industry is the record contract; a 25- to 100-page legal document prepared by high-priced lawyers designed to do one thing and one thing alone: protect the record company at all costs. For the average person, it is virtually impossible to understand. In many instances, even attorneys who are not versed in the jargon and hidden meanings of this specialized area find themselves negotiating what seems to be a good contract only to discover, after their client reaches the top of the charts and is considered the industry's next superstar, that the contract is a total disaster. For example, it is not unusual for 2 recording artists to sign contracts at identical royalty rates with the same company and have their actual earnings for the sale of the same number of tapes, CDs, downloads, and videos be totally different because of the interaction of the other provisions negotiated. It is also not unusual for 2 performers to sell 1 million CDs of an album and reach #1 on the charts, with one receiving a royalty check for $2 million and the other $1.20 (or even worse, a debit balance statement of minus $200,000).

## INSIDE THE BUSINESS

In a world where Rolls-Royces, airplanes, yachts, art masterpieces, and million-dollar estates are bought on whims, and where 1 word in a 50,000-word agreement can mean the difference between success or failure and ultimate financial security or bankruptcy, it is absolutely essential that the performer and his or her representatives understand not only the basic provisions of the recording contract but also what the document actually means in terms of "real" money. With this in mind, the present chapter outlines the most important provisions of the record contract and explains the hidden meanings, pitfalls, and industry practices that really determine the amount of money you earn from the sale of CDs, tapes, digital downloads, streams, and videos, as well as whether you really have a chance as a recording artist. In addition, many of the important variations that can be negotiated (both from the artist's and the record company's point of view) are explained, so that when a record company says it's interested, you'll know what to do.

## THE MOST IMPORTANT POINTS IN EVERY RECORDING CONTRACT

Before signing a record contract, every performer must know the answers to the following questions, since they will have a substantial effect on not only the direction of his or her career and the amount of money that is earned but also whether or not the artist will ever be on the charts or receive a Grammy.

1. *Time Limit:* How long will the contract last?
2. *Options:* How many times may the contract be renewed, for how long, and by whom?
3. *Recordings and Releases:* How many sides will a performer record, and does the record company have to release the finished recordings commercially?
4. *Royalty Clauses:* How much money does an artist receive from the sale of singles, albums, cassettes, CDs, downloads, and videos?
5. *Reduced Royalty Clauses:* How much does an artist receive for sales in foreign countries, record club or television album collections, radio station promotional copies, and low-priced budget albums and new technology?
6. *Record Company Deductions from a Performer's Royalties:* What expenses do record companies deduct from a performer's earnings?
7. *Escalating Royalty Clauses:* Are there ways to guarantee that as an artist becomes more successful, royalties will be automatically increased?

8. *Costs of Packaging a CD, Tape, or Other Recording:* How much money do record companies deduct from an artist's royalties for the cost of album covers, special inserts, download services, and tape, CD, minidisc (MD), or video containers?

9. *Free or Discount Recordings:* How many recordings can a company give away for free or at a discount without paying royalties to the artist?

10. *Returns and Reserve Accounts:* Since an artist is not paid for tapes, CDs, and other recordings that are returned for credit, how much money can be withheld from royalties in anticipation of such returns?

11. *Advances:* When do record companies give cash advances to artists? What criteria do they use?

12. *The Recording Artist as a Songwriter:* Do record companies pay lower songwriter royalties to artists who perform their own songs? Can a million-seller or successful "best hits" album mean financial disaster to a writer/performer if other songwriters on the album don't agree to reduce their writer and publisher royalties?

---

## THE TERM

The term of the recording agreement is usually structured around either the artist's recording and the delivery of a long-playing album or the record company's commercial release of the album. For example, a representative contract will state that the initial period of the recording artist agreement will commence on the date that the contract is signed and will expire 6 months after the commercial release in the United States of the initial album recorded under the agreement. Another alternative is for the initial period of the term to last until 9 months after the artist has delivered his or her minimum delivery obligation (e.g., enough individual master recordings to constitute 1 long-playing album of at least 35 minutes of playing time), regardless of whether or not such recorded material has been released. Variations in this area depend on the policies of the record company involved and the negotiating strength of the artist but most provisions calculate the term on a certain time period after either the artist has recorded and delivered the album to the record company or commercial release of the recording. Occasionally, depending on the artist and the expectations of the record company, the initial period may cover only a single or an EP, with options for long-playing albums; but that is all subject to negotiation.

In addition to the initial period, which usually covers the artist's first album, the record company will always have a number of options to extend the recording agreement for additional periods and additional albums. Most recording agreements will give the record company the right to exercise from 4 to 9 separate options, each of which will control a newly recorded separate album. For example, a sample clause might read:

Artist grants to the record company six (6) separate and consecutive options to extend the term of the recording artist agreement. The record company may exercise those options by sending the artist notice at any time prior to the expiration of the then current contract period of the term. If such notice is sent, the agreement shall be extended for an additional option period. If such notice is not sent, the recording agreement shall terminate at the end of the current contract period of the term.

Since there have been instances where a record company has mistakenly not sent the requisite option pickup notice and has, because of such failure, lost the recording services of an artist that it wanted to keep, some recording agreements provide that even if notice is not sent, the record company will still have the right to the artist's services unless the artist sends a termination notice and the record company does not formally exercise its option to renew the agreement within a certain number of days after it receives the notice.

On occasion the term of the recording agreement is based entirely on the recording and release of a specified number of albums and does not include options. For example, an agreement might state that the term of the recording agreement shall expire upon either the delivery or commercial release of the fourth album recorded under the artist agreement. Another alternative is for the term to be for a set number of albums, with options for additional recorded product (e.g., 2 albums firm, with options on the part of the record company for 4 newly recorded additional albums).

## *ARTIST ROYALTY CLAUSES*

The Artist shall be paid a royalty of 15% of the applicable suggested retail list price in respect of all long-playing albums manufactured and sold for which payment has been received.

The royalty clauses represent some of the most important parts of any recording contract, because these provisions determine how much money an artist will receive from the sale of records, tapes, CDs, downloads, other audio recordings, and videos. The figures used in almost all contracts are expressed in terms of percentages rather than in actual dollar figures and are usually based on either the suggested retail list price or wholesale price of each recording or tape, depending on the business practices of the particular record company. The royalty percentage provisions cannot be treated in isolation from the rest of the contract, but must be read in conjunction with a number of other clauses that effectively reduce the base on which the royalty percentages are computed. For example, if a 20% artist royalty read in conjunction with all other contract provisions and reductions such as producer royalties, packaging costs, free goods, and new technology deductions actually equals 12%, ecstasy may turn to depression when the first royalty statement is received.

## Recording Artist Royalties

The royalty that an artist receives for the sale of CDs, tapes, and other configurations ranges from a low of 7% to a high of 25%. New artists usually receive a 10% to 12% royalty, whereas very successful artists receive from 17% to 25% of the retail selling price of each CD, tape, or other recording sold.

## Retail Price Base

The artist royalty percentage is usually based on the suggested retail list price of each recording that is sold. For example, if an album sold for $18 and the artist had a 10% royalty, the artist would theoretically receive $1.80 from the sale of one CD or tape. As will be seen in subsequent sections, other contract clauses will reduce that amount in practice.

## Wholesale Price Base

A number of major companies use the record's wholesale price as the base on which artist royalties are computed. Since the wholesale price is roughly one half the amount of the suggested retail list price of a CD or tape, the artist should (if the company pays on the wholesale price) receive twice the royalty that would be received if the record company used a retail price base. For example, a 15% retail royalty would normally be the equivalent of a 30% wholesale royalty.

## Factors That Determine an Artist's Royalty

The royalty percentage is completely negotiable, but as already indicated, the standard figure for new artists is between 10% and 12%. In this regard, the following chart summarizes some of the main factors considered by a record company when deciding how much it will pay the artist. The factors listed in the chart represent only some of the basic considerations weighed by the record company in its determination of how much it will pay a particular artist. High royalty percentages for well-known artists can easily be justified, since the company is almost assured of recouping its costs and making a substantial profit. Newer groups, however, do not have a guaranteed audience and rarely sell enough records to recoup even the recording costs of their first or second album, to say nothing of the substantial costs involved in the pressing, packaging, advertising, and promotion of each release. Therefore, until a record act establishes a certain guaranteed sales level and consumer acceptance base, its artist royalty will usually remain low. If the A&R staff at the label really believe in the artist and feel that the artist has the potential of becoming a superstar, higher royalties can and have been negotiated.

| *Low Percentages* | *High Percentages* |
|---|---|
| New group | History of sales |
| Unknown national reputation | Artist celebrity status with broad market appeal |
| Inexperienced in live performances | Good live performances |
| Unknown manager | Experienced record attorney |
| | Bidding war |
| | Good video act |

## Graduated-Increase Royalty Provisions

A number of recording artists, recognizing that their initial royalty percentages may be low, negotiate escalating royalty clauses that increase their royalties proportionate to their success in selling albums. Such "sales success" clauses are not necessarily used only in new artist agreements; they also appear in the contracts of more established artists. In addition, if the artist contract is renewed by the record label for additional option years, it is often agreed that the performer's royalty percentage will be increased during each successive option year.

## Sales Level Increases

| *Example:* | *Number of Albums Sold* | *Artist Royalty* |
|---|---|---|
| | 1 to 249,999 | 10% |
| | 250,000 to 499,999 | 11% |
| | 500,000 to 749,999 | 12% |
| | 750,000 and over | 13% |

Graduated royalty percentages normally become operative when the recording artist achieves certain stated sales level plateaus. For example, if an artist has album sales over 250,000 units, the artist royalty might be increased. If sales reach the 500,000 level, there may be a further increase in the artist royalty. And if the 750,000 or 1 million sales marks are passed, there may be additional increases. Such escalating royalty percentages normally apply only to the number of recordings sold in excess of the stipulated sales plateaus. For example, if an artist's royalty is increased from 10% to 11% at 250,000 copies, the 11% increased rate will apply only to albums sold after the initial 250,000. In addition, these escalating royalty rates usually apply only to album sales as well as to non-reduced-royalty sales (i.e., top line, full-priced product versus record club, midpriced, or budget albums). Occasionally, graduated royalty provisions are written into contracts that apply to the sale of singles, but the plateaus that must be reached for increases are usually higher than in the album agreements (e.g., increases at 750,000 or 1 million).

In this example, as an artist sells more albums, the album sale royalty is progressively increased. If sales are only 100,000 albums, the royalty is 10%. But if sales achieve the 250,000 mark, the artist receives an 11% royalty on every sale over 250,000 up to 499,999, where the next increase becomes operative. The escalating royalties apply only to sales that occur after a certain sales plateau has been reached. The higher royalty is virtually never retroactive to sales achieved before a plateau is achieved.

## Contract Option Year Increases

Another variation on the theme of escalating royalty provisions is to increase the artist's royalty percentage when the record company picks up an option for another year. A number of recording agreements provide that the artist will receive a certain royalty for the first 2 contract periods and an increased royalty if the company extends the contract for additional option years (e.g., 12% for the initial period and first option period, 13% for the second option period, 14% for the third option period, and 16% for any subsequent option period). Under these type of option year increase provisions, the new increased royalty percentage will apply only to those albums or singles recorded during the particular option year and will not be retroactive to albums or other configurations recorded and released during prior years, when a lower royalty rate was in effect.

## Royalties for Sales Outside the United States

Most record contracts contain provisions that reduce the artist royalty for sales of recordings outside the United States. The actual rates many times are dependent on whether or not the U.S. company has an affiliate in the foreign country or licenses the manufacture, distribution, and sale of its recordings through a third-party record label in the territory. A sample artist royalty schedule for foreign sales might grant 85% of the U.S. rate for Canadian sales; 75% of the U.S. rate for United Kingdom, the EU, Japan, and Australia sales; and 66²⁄₃% of the U.S. rate for all sales in the remainder of the world. Depending on the record company, the reductions in artist royalties for nondomestic sales may be expressed in actual royalty percentages rather than as percentages of the U.S. rate. For example, a representative foreign royalty clause for an artist receiving an 18% U.S. royalty might list a 16% royalty for Canada, a 14% royalty for the United Kingdom, and a 12% royalty for all other territories.

Some record companies will agree to increased royalties for the artist in the event that certain aggregate sales plateaus are achieved in a combination of certain specified foreign territories. For example, a record company may agree that in the event that either 500,000, 750,000 or 1 million full-priced albums are sold in a specified group of identified foreign territories (e.g., United Kingdom, Australia, Japan, France, Germany, and Canada), the artist royalty on all sales after the plateau has been reached in those territories shall be increased by 1% or 2%.

## Album Price Lines and Royalty Rates

Record companies sell recordings under a number of different suggested retail price points depending on the status of the artist, the nature of the product recorded, and the length of time a particular album has been in commercial release. It is important to know the various designations used and corresponding retail price ranges, since an artist's royalty will usually be different depending on the price line under which an album is sold. For example, almost all record labels have what is known as the "top line," "full-priced line" or "highest-price line," which relates to that company's prime artists and releases. As the name designates, albums in this category have a suggested retail list price at the top of the price guidelines (e.g., from $12.98 to $18.98 for CDs depending on the record company). Most companies also have a midpriced line, which usually carries a suggested list price range of between 20% to 40% lower than the price of the top line product. Many companies also have a new or developing artist line which is less than full price. Companies also have a budget line, which usually covers albums in the lowest suggested list price range.

*Midline and Budget Line Royalty Rates.* The highest artist royalty rate is applied to the so-called top line product, with reduced rates usually applicable to midline and budget albums. In most agreements, the record company will pay the artist a 75% rate on midprice recordings and from 50% to 66⅔% for budget albums. For example, if an artist negotiated a 15% album royalty in the recording agreement and an album was sold as part of the midpriced line, the artist royalty would be 11.25% (i.e., 15% x 75% = 11.25%). If the suggested list of the same album was eventually reduced for sale as part of the record company's budget line, the artist royalty for such budget sales would normally range from 10% to 7.5% (i.e., 15% x 66⅔% = 10% or 15% x 50% = 7.5%).

*Other Reduced-Royalty Albums.* In addition to midline or budget albums, there are a number of other recordings on which the record company will reduce the artist's royalty due to the nature of the product being sold and the type of distribution outlet handling the sale. The recording contract should contain specific provisions dealing with these reduced royalty rate albums.

*Mail Order and Television-Only Packages.* The mail order business has become an important profit center for many record companies, as it is not unusual to sell a million albums through television-only advertising. For example, the "Best of . . ." television albums have proven that this area can be a lucrative source of income, even though the profit margin on each album is much smaller than for sales at the normal retail level. The standard clause for such mail order or television-only albums provides for an artist to receive one half of the top line royalty rate based on either the net sales of such records or the suggested retail price of such albums. For example, if a record company markets such a television album and the artist has a 15% royalty percentage for normal retail sales, that artist will receive a 7.5% royalty for the television record sales (or one half the normal royalty). If, on the other hand, an artist is one of a number of artists on one of these albums, the artist would receive the applicable one-half royalty based on the number of that particular artist's performances on the album in relation to the total number of performances from all artists contained on that album.

*Record Club Albums.* In most recording agreements, the artist will receive from 50% to 66⅔% of his or her normal top line royalty for recordings sold through record clubs. For example, if an artist has a 15% royalty rate, the rate for record club sales would normally range from 7.5% to 10% depending on the applicable percentage reduction contained in the artist agreement. In the event that the record company owns the record club or the record club is an affiliate of the record company for which the artist records, the royalty rate able to be negotiated by the artist is many times higher than if the record club is an unaffiliated third party with no connection with the artist's record label.

## Packaging Deductions

One of the single largest items deducted from an artist's royalty base before computation of the actual per-album royalty is the cost of the covers, sleeves, and containers in which the recording is packaged. These packaging deductions (also known as "container deductions" or "container charges"), are always expressed in percentage terms rather than actual dollar-and-cents figures. The percentage ranges from 15% to 25%, varying from company to company depending on the type of configuration being sold. On rare occasions, a certain configuration will not have any packaging deduction (e.g., a single packaged in plain whole stock paper). Because of their impact on an artist's royalties, packaging deductions should be a major consideration when negotiating the artist's royalty computation provisions of any recording agreement. For example, it is more than possible for an artist with a high royalty rate and a high packaging deduction percentage to make less in royalties than an artist at another record label who has a lower rate but also a lower deduction.

*Actual Packaging Percentages.*    Packaging deductions usually range from 10% to 20% for vinyl records, 20% to 25% for analog cassettes, and 25% for CDs and other nonanalog configurations, including new technology distributions. The actual percentage is usually based on and deducted from the suggested retail list price of the particular recorded configuration that is sold. Other variations may specify the type of price point and definition on which the container deduction is applied (e.g., the actual selling price, the list category price, the advertised price, the constructed price), but for the purposes of this discussion, we'll focus on the suggested retail list price calculation.

*Operation of the Packaging Deduction.*    To illustrate how the packaging deduction works and how it affects the royalties paid to the recording artist, Table 3.1 sets forth the calculations under the scenario of an artist having a 20% royalty with a 25% suggested list price packaging deduction and selling 1 million full-priced CDs.

The same formulas can be used for each type of configuration (e.g., analog cassette, vinyl, digital cassette) that is sold, the only differences being the suggested list price of the specific audio format and the container deduction percentage applicable to that type of configuration. For example, if the con-

TABLE **3.1**   Packaging Deduction on a Million-Selling Album

Without Packaging Deduction

| | | |
|---|---|---|
| $ | 18.98 | Suggested list price |
| | x20% | Artist royalty |
| $ | 3.79 | Artist royalty |
| | x1,000,000 | CDs sold |
| $ | 3,790,000 | Actual royalty |

With Packaging Deduction

| | | |
|---|---|---|
| $ | 18.98 | Suggested list price |
| | x25% | Packaging deduction % |
| | 4.74 | Actual deduction |
| $ | 18.98 | Suggested list price |
| – | $4.74 | Packaging deduction |
| $ | 14.24 | Reduced royalty base |
| $ | 14.24 | Reduced royalty base |
| | x20% | Artist royalty % |
| $ | 2.84 | Artist royalty |
| | x1,000,000 | CDs sold |
| $ | 2,840,000 | Actual royalty |

figuration is an analog cassette or reduced-price CD and the artist has a 20% packaging deduction and 20% royalty rate in his or her agreement, the same formula would be used as in Table 3.1, but with different figures inserted into the suggested list price and packaging deduction percentage lines.

| | |
|---|---|
| $ 12.98 | Suggested list price |
| x20% | Packaging deduction % |
| $ 2.59 | Actual deduction |

| | |
|---|---|
| $ 12.98 | Suggested list price |
| – $2.59 | Packaging deduction |
| $ 10.39 | Reduced royalty base |

| | |
|---|---|
| $ 10.39 | Reduced royalty base |
| x20% | Artist royalty % |
| $ 2.07 | Artist royalty |

## Free Goods

In addition to not receiving royalties on recordings that are returned for credits, the artist will also not be paid on recordings that are given away for free as part of merchandising or discount programs. For example, the record company may, rather than putting a discount on recordings that are shipped to its retail customers to make them cheaper and more attractive to purchase, give the retailer or wholesaler a number of free or bonus recordings instead—a strategy that in effect discounts all recordings purchased. To illustrate, rather than discounting the per-unit price of every 100 albums ordered by a retailer, the record company may only invoice the customer for 80 or 85 albums, with the remainder being distributed as "free" or "bonus" recordings.

Since this type of marketing and sales incentive plan is extremely common and the principle of nonpayment on such free recordings is well established, most artists try to negotiate a limitation on such giveaways. Some clauses will limit such free goods to the "standard merchandising program" guidelines set by the record company for the majority of artists signed to the label. Under this type of provision, the record company will often specify its current policy (e.g., 15% on albums, 20% on singles) so that all parties know what is being agreed to. Other protective clauses will set an actual percentage limit, which cannot be exceeded without the consent of the recording artist. For example, the record company may agree that no more than 15% of all albums distributed will be treated as free or bonus recordings. Additionally, if an album is a major hit, the artist may be able to negotiate a lower percentage for that particular album.

This type of free-goods limitation also comes into play with respect to re- cordings that are sold through record clubs—especially when new record club customers sign up and receive a number of albums either for free or for a few pennies. Obviously, the availability of well-known albums by well-known artists for rock bottom prices represent a real incentive tool for record clubs to secure additional memberships, and because of this, most artists will try to limit the number of albums that can be used in such programs. In most cases, such protective clauses provide for a specified percentage limitation with respect to such non-royalty-bearing free goods. For example, the artist may demand that not less than 50% of the albums distributed through a record club be royalty-bearing albums, whether or not they have been used as part of a membership drive.

## The 90% Sale Provision

Certain record companies structure their artist agreements to provide that royalties will be paid on only 90% of recordings that are actually sold. For example, if an artist had a 20% album royalty and the record label sold 1 million full-priced CDs and tapes, the artist would receive a royalty on only 900,000 units. Some artists are able to secure a higher royalty rate when signing with a "90% of sales" label because of the differential between an actual sales royalty base versus a 90% sales royalty base, but this is a subject left to bargaining power and negotiating strategy.

## New-Technology Royalty Rate Reductions

Most recording agreements will provide for a reduced royalty rate on new-technology recordings, which can include digital distribution. For example, when the minidisc was introduced in the early 1990s, most record contracts entered into immediately prior to or during that time structured the artist royalty rates for the new configuration as a percentage of the normal top line royalty rate. For example, a sample clause might state that the artist royalty rate for albums sold in the new technology format would be from 80% to 90% of the otherwise applicable rate. Under such a new-technology reduced-royalty provision, if an artist received an 18% royalty on top line CDs, the artist rate on albums sold in the new format would range from 14.4% to 16.2% (i.e., 80% x 18% = 14.4%, and 90% x 18% = 16.2%).

To prevent the artist's royalty from staying at the reduced new-technology level long past the time when the new configuration has become an accepted format, many artists will either negotiate a cutoff date for the reduced rate (e.g., 5 years after the introduction of the new format to the general public) or include a proviso that the lower rate will end if the record company starts to give other artists higher rates. If the cutoff date approach is selected, many of the clauses will contain language that provides for good-faith negotiations between the artist and the record company to arrive at a mutually agreeable rate, with the negotiations usually taking into account not only the industry practices at the time of the cutoff date but also what other artists of comparable stature are receiving. Many contracts treat downloads as new technology.

## Cut-Outs and Surplus Copies

All record company contracts have provisions that stipulate that once a particular album is either deleted from the catalog and sold as discontinued merchandise (a "cutout") or is sold as scrap, surplus, or excess inventory at less than from one third to one half of the record company's subdistributor price, no royalties will be paid. The same nonroyalty payment provisions also apply to recordings distributed to reviewers for critiques and to radio stations for airplay. Many artists are able to negotiate a time limit prior to which the record company may not sell a particular recording as a cutout (e.g., no album may be sold as a cutout until 2 years after the initial release of the recording). And in some cases, the artist is even given the first opportunity to purchase all of the cutout recordings at the cutout price.

## Royalty Payments and Accounting Statements

Royalty payments and statements to artists are made twice per year, usually in May for the 6-month period from September through February and in November for the 6-month period from March through August. Certain record companies set the semiannual periods two months earlier. As with most royalty accounting clauses, the contract will provide that each payment be accompanied by a royalty statement, with some contracts providing that a statement need not be sent if royalties have not been earned, charges have not accrued, or the artist does not specifically request one. During the active term of the recording artist agreement (while the artist is recording new albums for the label as opposed to the period after the artist has fulfilled the entire album delivery commitment), however, statements are normally sent even though no sales have occurred.

Many agreements provide for specific time limits during which the artist may object to a royalty statement, audit the record company, or sue the record company for either nonpayment or incorrect payment of royalties. For example, some agreements provide that a royalty statement is binding on the recording artist unless the artist objects to the statement in writing within 1 to 3 years after the statement has been either sent by the record company or received by the recording artist. Many contracts that provide for the time limit to commence on the receipt of the statement will also provide that a royalty statement will be deemed to have been received by the artist from 30 to 90 days after the statement has been mailed.

The artist who wishes to audit will usually have to first object to a statement within certain time periods and then, if the artist intends to hire an accounting firm or other representative to conduct the audit, give advance notice to the record company, usually at least 30 days before the artist's auditors intend to commence their audit. The record company usually has the right to postpone the audit at least once by giving notice to the artist within a specified number of days prior to the audit commencement date. For example, a sample provision might give the record company the right to postpone an audit for 1 to 2 months provided that it gives the artist notice at least 10 to 20 days prior to the scheduled commencement date. There also may be limitations on the amount of time that the audit may last (e.g., if the audit is not completed within 2 months from commencement, the record company may have the right to end the audit period upon notice to the artist), provided that the record company has been cooperative with the auditors.

There are usually restrictions on what the auditors can examine (e.g., manufacturing records or other records that do not relate to actual sales reports or other distributions of the artist's recordings are normally unavailable), when they can examine the records (e.g., only during regular business hours), who the auditors can be (e.g., certified public accountants from a firm that is not currently examining the record company's books), and where the audit is to take place (e.g., only at the record company's regular place of business).

## ADVANCES

In virtually every recording agreement, the record label will guarantee the artist a series of advance payments throughout the term of the contract. There is usually an advance to the artist upon the signing of the record agreement, with additional advances payable on the occurrence of a number of various events, such as commencement of recording of an album, completion of the recording of an album along with its delivery to and acceptance by the record company, commercial release of an album, and commencement of an option period. Additionally, advances may be due the artist if certain sales plateaus are achieved during a certain period of time after the release of an album in the United States (e.g., $50,000 if album sales reach 1 million units within 18 months after release) or if the actual recording costs are less than those allocated by the record company for the completion of a particular album (e.g., the artist receiving the difference between the $150,000 spent in recording an album and the $200,000 in costs budgeted for the album). Table 3.2 illustrates the artist's advances under a recording agreement that has a 1-album guarantee plus options for 5 additional albums.

A common advance formula that is used in many recording agreements to calculate the monies due the artist for option albums is one that is known as either the "minimum/maximum" formula or the "floor/ceiling" formula. Under this type of provision, the record company will compute its actual advance for an option album based on a percentage of the earnings generated by the most

TABLE **3.2**   Recording Agreement Advances to Artist

Initial Period:

$200,000 upon signing (to cover the initial album recorded under the agreement)

Option Periods:
$225,000 for the second album
$250,000 for the third album
$275,000 for the fourth album
$300,000 for the fifth album

Payment of Option Album Advances:
10% upon commencement of the option period
10% upon commencement of recording of the option album
20% upon delivery to and acceptance by the record company of the completed option album
60% within 10 days following U.S. release of the option album

recently released prior album, the percentage usually being from 50% to 75%. There will also be a "minimum" or "floor" to prevent the advance from being less than a certain figure and a "maximum" or "ceiling" to prevent the advance payable to the artist from exceeding a certain dollar amount. In many cases, the earnings used in the computation will be limited to full-priced sales in the United States and Canada and further limited to a specified period after the commercial release of the particular album being used in the calculation (e.g., 12 months to 18 months after the release date of the most recent album).

A sample "floor and ceiling" advance clause might read:

With respect to the second through sixth option albums, the advance payable to the artist will be 75% of the royalties earned by the artist from sales of full-priced albums during the 12-month period following release in the United States of the prior album with the following floor and ceiling amounts:

| Album | Floor | Ceiling |
|-------|-------|---------|
| 2nd   | $150,000 | $250,000 |
| 3rd   | $175,000 | $275,000 |
| 4th   | $200,000 | $300,000 |
| 5th   | $225,000 | $350,000 |
| 6th   | $250,000 | $400,000 |

The advance provisions of a recording artist contract are subject to countless variations, depending on a number of factors including but not limited to the past success of the artist, the desire of the record company to sign the artist, the projected sales base throughout the world, the percentage being used in a minimum/maximum formula, and the expertise and experience not only of the artist's representatives but also of the record company's business affairs and legal departments. Regardless of the amount of the advances being paid, how the computation is structured, and the actual timing of payments to the artist, it must be remembered that these monies are advances; by their very nature they are totally recoupable and deductible from the future earnings of the recording artist. They are, in effect, a prepayment of royalties that may or may not be actually earned. For example, if an artist receives a $100,000 advance and eventually earns $150,000 from sales of albums, a check would be remitted for $50,000. If the artist only earned $40,000 from album sales, however, no monies would be forthcoming because there still would be a debit balance of $60,000 in the artist's account. In addition, once multiple album advances have accumulated without substantial earnings, it is more than possible for an artist to have a hit record and not receive a royalty check or even clear the negative balance in his or her account.

## ALBUM RELEASE OBLIGATIONS

One of the most important guarantees that any artist can secure is the guarantee that the record company will release the recorded album to the general public in the United States. In most cases, if a record company spends the requisite $60,000 to $500,000 to record an album, it will release it, since without such a release, the project will become a total write-off. However, it is not that uncommon for a record company to lose faith in an artist (perhaps because the finished recording does not meet the company's expectations, there are financial problems at the company, the company has been sold, or the A&R executives who were behind the act have left the company) and shelve an entire album without releasing it. The adage about "not throwing good money after bad" does come into account in such situations, as record companies do cut their losses occasionally even if it means taking a total loss on the project. This is especially true if the record company feels that it will have to expend in promotion, advertising, marketing, and video production monies at least as much as it has spent in recording the album and in advances to the artist. After all, if the record company has paid the artist $75,000 in advances for the album, spent $200,000 to record the album, and is looking at future expenses of $75,000 for a video and an additional $200,000 in manufacturing, promotion, trade advertising, and marketing costs, it is no wonder that certain albums are pulled from the release schedule if the faith of the company's creative, business, and financial executives is not there. The reality of the situation is that sometimes it is better to retreat and fight another day, a conclusion that might be disastrous for an artist's career but that might make perfect sense to the record company.

If an artist can negotiate a release guarantee, it is to his or her benefit. A sample guaranteed release clause might read:

Record Company agrees to release each album recorded pursuant to the product commitment provisions of the recording agreement through normal retail channels in the United States within 4 months after delivery of each such album to the record company.

Since Canada is an important market closely related in geographic location and musical tastes to the United States, this territory may also be included in the release guarantee.

In addition to the United States and Canada, there are a number of other important territories for which artists try to negotiate guaranteed release schedules of their albums. For example, the United Kingdom, Australia, Germany, Japan, France, Benelux (Holland and Belgium), Italy, and the Scandinavian countries can all be important album sale territories and, depending on an artist's bargaining power and international sales base, such guarantees can be vital to an act's chances of succeeding overseas. If such nondomestic release guarantees can be secured, the release date obligation is usually within 1 to 3 months after the U.S. release date. Additionally, certain major recording artists are able to secure guaranteed release commitments in many of the so-called minor territories as well as those countries that represent major sales territories.

Now that the release guarantee concept has been discussed, the realities of the record industry must be introduced into the equation. Even though an artist has a guaranteed release clause in the recording agreement, other provisions in the agreement will almost always modify this obligation. For example, some agreements may provide that if an album is not released within a certain period of time (e.g., 30 to 90 days after the so-called guaranteed release date), the artist can send the record company notice that the release commitment obligation has been breached. If such notice is sent, the record company usually has from 60 to 120 days to release the album. If it does, the breach will be deemed to have been cured and the artist will have received what was denied—the commercial release of the album. If the release does not occur within the extra time period, however, the artist may have a number of different options ranging from termination of the recording agreement to being able to license the release of the album to another record company. In most cases, if the third-party licensing remedy is taken, the artist can require his or her recording company to enter into an agreement with another record company selected by the artist but usually within certain agreed-upon business and legal parameters (e.g., that the royalty will be within certain percentages guidelines, that all union fees will be paid, that audit rights are provided for). In most cases, when the artist is allowed to license a release in a territory, the monies will be paid to the record company for distribution as if the album were released under the original contract.

## *RECORD COMPANY EXPENSES*

### Videos

Since videos can in many cases be as important to a performer's career as audio recordings, this entire area is of benchmark importance to both the performer and the record company. Additionally, since the sums of money that can be expended in the planning and production of audiovisual performances are enormous and the chance for recoupment of expenditures a very speculative proposition, the provisions relating to the making of videos represent one of the most contentious areas in any recording agreement negotiation.

In most contracts, the record company not only will have the option to decide how many videos it will produce on a particular artist but will also have the final decision as to how much money will be spent. During the negotiations and depending on one's bargaining power, however, a number of inroads can usually be made that will guarantee at least certain commitments from the record company. For example, a minimum amount of money may be guaranteed to be expended on each video produced (e.g., the record company will allocate a production budget of not less than $75,000), and a minimum number of videos produced for every album the artist records. There may be additional commitments for single releases, such as the record company guaranteeing a video for each single that is released or a guarantee of further videos if a single reaches the Top 25.

As for the choice of concept, script, story board, the composition being recorded, choreography, director, producer, production personnel, and other creative and business aspects of the video, control over these items depends once again on the track record and bargaining power of the recording artist. If there is little bargaining power, the record company will normally exercise total control over all of these aspects, usually after consultation with the recording artist. If the performer is somewhat successful, the creative aspects will be many times handled on a mutual approval basis, whereby both the record company and the artist have to agree on the concept, planning, and production of the video, with the record company usually having the final decision in the event of a dispute or disagreement. And if the artist is an extremely successful superstar, most if not all of the creative and business issues will be within the hands of the performer, with possibly some consultation or limited approval rights held by the record company, especially with respect to actual costs exceeding budgeted amounts. For example, in a superstar's contract, the concept, planning, story line, script, shooting dates, and location are determined by the writer/artist. The selection of the composition being used in the video, however, will almost always be a mutual decision between the record company and the recording artist. Additionally, in a superstar contract there will always be a minimum amount of money guaranteed for each video—a minimum that, in most respects, is usually in excess of the entire advance and recording budgets for most performers. For example, it is not unusual for "deemed approval" per-composition video budgets for superstars to be in the $400,000 to $750,000 range.

*Recoupment of Video Costs.* Since the monies expended on an artist's video are virtually always treated as additional advances recoupable from the artist's royalties, there are a number of ways that recoupment is handled by the record company. The preferable approach for the recording artist is for the expenses of videos to be recouped only from the income generated by the video. Since most videos are "promotion only" vehicles and do not generate any income in and of themselves for the record company, most record company contracts provide that the company can use monies received from other areas to recoup the costs expended on videos. Initially, the production cost of each video (which usually includes flat-fee payments to music publishers and unreimbursed duplication and delivery expenses in addition to all the costs related to the planning and making of the video, but usually excludes overhead costs and service costs of the employees of the respective record company) is charged to what is usually referred to as the recording artist's video account. In most contracts, however, the record company can transfer from 100% to 50% of the video account to the recording artist's audio account so that the record company will be able to use monies due the artist for the sale of CDs and cassettes ("audio account royalties") for reimbursement of the monies expended for the production of videos.

Since the monies spent on videos can range from $50,000 to over $750,000, the negotiations relating to how the record company can get its money back can be very intense. Large recoupable items such as videos can easily wipe out a record company's profit margin or an artist's entire royalty account. Occasionally, recording artists are able to get the record company to agree that the audio account and the video account will not be cross-collateralized, but in most cases, at least a portion of the video account expenses will be recoupable from the recording artist's CD, download, and audio tape royalties. Certain writer/performers are able to exclude songwriter and publisher mechanical royalties from the recoupment equation, but many contracts provide that mechanical royalties can also be used by the record company to recoup all or a portion of the video costs.

*Video Royalties.* Since many recording artists' videos are released for sale to the general public (as opposed to serving as "promotion only" vehicles and sent to MTV, VH-1, etc.), it is important for every writer/artist to negotiate a royalty structure in the recording agreement that will cover videos sold on the commercial market. Certain record companies, at least with respect to new and unproven artists, do not pay royalties on videos that are sold at the retail level. Most companies, however, will negotiate and provide for a royalty (either on a to-be-negotiated good-faith basis or actual set penny or percentage royalty basis) in the recording artist agreement.

Depending on the policy of the record company involved, a number of different formulas can be used to determine how much a recording artist/ writer gets paid for the sale of videos, whether they be single-composition, promotion-only videos or, more likely, multicomposition video projects. Some record companies will pay the artist a percentage of the wholesale price of the videos; others will pay on the basis of net receipts received by the record company; some will pay on the basis of a percentage of the list price; and others will pay a set penny rate. In addition, if a writer/artist is a superstar, the record company will more than likely provide in the agreement that if other artists signed to the label receive higher royalty rates than those negotiated in the current agreement, the superstar will automatically get the benefit of such higher royalty rates (i.e., a "most favored nations" clause).

## Tour Support

If the recording artist is an accomplished live performer or if the record company desires that a new group go on the road to establish an audience and sales base, the record company will many times provide a certain amount of money in tour support. Occasionally, a lump sum may be guaranteed (e.g., $100,000 for a 3-month U.S. tour) or a certain amount of money allocated to each live performance (e.g., $4,000 per performance), with certain limitations on the maximum amount of money it will be obligated to pay (e.g., $2,500 per performance but not in excess of $30,000 during the entire length of the tour). In most cases, a record company executive must approve a written tour budget confirming the concert dates and itemizing how the money is to be used—a safeguard that record companies do not want to give up. The monies expended in this area are normally treated as additional advances to the recording artist and are recoupable from any royalties due the artist under the recording contract. On occasion, mechanical income due the performer is excluded from the recoupment formula, but this is a matter always left to negotiation.

## Promotion Expenses

Since independent promotion can be an important aspect of establishing an artist or making a particular recording a hit, record company contracts will usually provide that all or a portion of third-party promotion expenses will be treated as additional advances to the recording artist recoupable from royalties due under the recording agreement. Such costs are usually 100% recoupable with respect to newer and less powerful artists and 50% recoupable for more established artists. The record company will often agree to consult with the performer as to the actual promotion and marketing plans designed for a single or album but almost always will have the right to make the final decision.

In recent years music publishers have tended to contribute guaranteed monies to their writer/recording artists for promoting their albums and singles, over and above monies expended by the performer's record company. Occasionally, such guarantees are part of the music publishing contract (e.g., the music publisher committing a minimum of $25,000 in independent promotion and marketing for each album released); at other times, they represent voluntary decisions on the part of the publisher either of its own volition or at the request of the writer/performer's management, attorney, or record company. Sometimes the record company may be able to commit only a certain amount of promotion money for a newer artist, and the monies expended by the writer/artist's music publisher can make the difference in pushing the writer/performer or recording over the top. Most promotion-related monies paid out by music publishers are, as in record contracts, treated as additional advances that are recoverable from publishing royalties due the songwriter/performer from sales of CDs, downloads, and tapes, film and television synchronization uses, publishing performance monies, print licensing, and other income-generating sources controlled by the publishing agreement.

## Recording Costs

Depending on the stature of the artist and the type of contractual relationship entered into between the record label and the performer (e.g., artist signing directly to the record company, artist being signed through a production company, artist signed through a third party by means of an inducement letter), the costs of recording an album is paid directly by the record company, by the artist, or by the artist's production company.

If the artist is signed directly to the label and does not have an established sales base, is recording a first or second album, or has not had great success, the record company will control the purse strings and retain control of all payments relative to the recording and delivery of the album. If the artist is established and has prior experience in the financial aspects of recording albums, however, the record company will many times provide the artist or the production company with an album fund from which all recording costs will be taken. This fund, which usually takes the form of an up-front advance (e.g., $250,000 payable 30 days prior to the commencement of recording) but which can be structured on a reimbursement basis, enables the artist or production company to pay all recording costs. In most cases, if the artist's expenses do not exceed the recording fund (e.g., if the artist spends $175,000 out of a $250,000 recording fund), the amount left over is kept by the artist and treated as an additional advance recoupable from the artist's royalties.

The costs of recording an album, single, EP, or any other recorded configuration designed for commercial release are always treated as advances to the recording artist and recoupable from royalties due that artist. Such costs are recoupable not only from royalties derived from the album for which they were incurred but also from royalties due the artist from all other recordings produced during the term of the agreement. In other words, recording costs are cumulative during the term of the recording contract, and the record company will be able to recoup royalties due from any recording released during the agreement to cover any recording costs expended during the agreement. For example, if the costs of the initial album were $100,000 and the artist earned $50,000 in royalties, there would be a debit balance of $50,000 in the artist's account. If the costs of the second album were $125,000 and the artist earned $150,000 in royalties from that album, no royalties would be distributed, because there still would be a recording costs debit balance of $25,000 from both albums, even though royalties earned from the second album exceeded the recording costs for that particular album (e.g., $100,000 + $125,000 = $225,000 in recording costs, less $50,000 and $150,000 in royalties = $200,000 in earnings, resulting in a $25,000 deficit for the two albums). It is more than possible, therefore, that an artist can have 3 unsuccessful albums and a major hit on the fourth album and still receive no royalties because of the overall debit balance incurred from the unrecouped recording costs of the initial 3 albums.

Recording costs under most agreements include all direct costs relating to the making of the audio recording. They include all costs for arrangements, orchestration, and copying; all union scale payments to the recording artists and all others who perform on the recording, in addition to all payroll taxes or other taxes required to be paid on such earnings; all instrument rental, cartage, hall rental, studio, and engineering charges; mastering, remastering, mixing, and remixing fees; recording costs; transportation, hotel, per diems, and living expenses; all costs related to delivery to the record company of the fully edited master recordings; all monies that may be due from any collective bargaining agreements based on union scale payments; any payments made or required to be made for "sample" clearances of other compositions or recorded performances owned by third-party writers, music publishers, record companies, producers, or artists; and any advance payments, fees, or royalties payable to personnel and companies rendering services with respect to the recording of the compositions on the album.

The record company expects that the artist will stay within the recording budget. In the event that costs exceed the maximum budget amount, the record company will usually take responsibility for payment of any such overage expenses, usually after notice to the artist. If the record company does assume responsibility for such over-budget items, it will normally either deduct the overage from any future advances due the artist or recoup the money from recording artist royalties and, in many cases, writer and publisher mechanical royalties.

# THE ARTIST'S OBLIGATIONS

## The Minimum Recording Obligation

The minimum recording obligation (sometimes referred to as the "minimum delivery obligation") refers to the number of individual master recordings that the artist will record during each contract period of the term of the recording agreement. For example, a contract may state that during each period of the term the artist shall record enough songs to constitute one long-playing album of at least 35 minutes in duration. In some cases, the record contract will refer to the number of individual sides; in other cases, the contract may refer to a minimum number of individual sides plus any additional recordings deemed necessary by the record company for satisfactory completion of the album (e.g., 10 recorded sides plus up to an additional 5 sides at the record company's discretion).

Under all recording agreements, the current period of the term will be extended until the artist actually delivers to the record company the minimum recording obligation. For example, if an agreement states that the artist will deliver to the label a minimum of 12 newly recorded sides within 6 months from the commencement date of the contract, with the same guarantee applicable to each exercised option period, the agreement will always have a provision that extends the current period of the term for a certain period of time after actual delivery, to cover the eventuality that an artist might take longer than expected in the studio and deliver the requisite recordings after the contract deadline. Since timely delivery of recordings according to the schedule outlined in the recording agreement is vitally important to the record company and can be considered a serious breach by the artist, the record label will, if there is a substantial delay, many times be able to demand reimbursement of all monies paid to the artist that are related to the sides being recorded, suspend the agreement, or even terminate the agreement.

On occasion, a record company will not allow a recording artist to go into the studio to record the minimum recording obligation. This can occur for a number of different reasons, with some of the primary ones being loss of faith in the artist, the departure of the A&R executives who signed the act, a change in musical tastes at the label or by the general public, financial difficulties at the label, and negative attitude or discipline problems with the artist. When this occurs, the record label is usually obligated only to pay the artist the union scale payments that would have been due had the artist been allowed to go into the studio and record the minimum recording obligation for that period— a provision that is referred to as the "pay or play" clause.

In the event that the record company elects to go this route and does not allow the artist to record the minimum delivery obligation, the artist will often have the right to terminate the agreement so negotiations can commence with other labels. In most cases the artist must send the record company written notice demanding that it allow the artist to record sufficient master sides to fulfill the minimum recording obligation within a specified period of time (e.g., within 60 days after receipt of the notice). If the record company does not allow the artist to commence recording within that time period, the term of the recording agreement will be deemed to have been terminated at the end of the period.

## Satisfaction of an Artist's Delivery Commitment

In many contracts, clauses define what can or cannot be recorded by an artist to fulfill his or her album delivery commitment. Some companies will structure the record agreement so that an artist can record only in a certain designated style or styles for an album to count toward the delivery commitment. For example, a sample clause might provide that the artist's performances will be in the rock, pop, metal, or rap genre for them to be acceptable. Or a provision might have the artist guaranteeing that the style of any new recordings will be similar to the performances contained on previously released albums. Obviously, this type of clause can lead to major disputes between the performer and record company, as most artists have a tendency to grow in their musical tastes or change their style of performance to place themselves in the midst of a popular new musical trend. Consequently, the wording of such clauses is important to each side of the negotiating table, especially when millions of dollars in recording costs, video costs, promotion commitments, marketing expenditures, and album advances are at stake.

Other restrictions in this area include re-recordings of material previously released, live performances, instrumental recordings (where the artist is a vocalist), and special themed albums (e.g., a Christmas album). Having such restrictions in an artist's contract does not necessarily mean that a performer may not record such compositions, as such recordings may be made with the approval of the record company. Whether or not such approval is given, however, depends on the relationship of the company and the artist, whether there has been past financial success and the nature of the album.

## "Greatest Hits" Albums

Virtually all record contracts give the record company the right to compile and release a "greatest hits" album. For most recording artists, such a right is never exercised, because only a select number of artists ever have enough hits to justify the release of such a recording. Occasionally, the sides to be included on a "greatest hits" package must be approved by the performer; the agreement usually contains certain provisos of what type of compositions are automatically deemed approved. For example, a sample clause may provide that the "A" side of any single that reached the Top 40 is deemed approved by the artist; such a proviso ensures that all hits will be put in the "greatest hits" album regardless of how the artist feels about certain compositions artistically. Should there be disputes over which recordings to include on the album, some contracts provide that the artist and the record company may each select a certain number (e.g., the record company selects 60% of the album and the artist 40%).

In certain instances, the record company may ask the artist to record new songs for inclusion on the "greatest hits" package. Sometimes these new recordings are mere "filler"; other times, the record company hopes that one of the new recordings will become a hit single and further enhance the album's sales. The bargaining power of the parties when negotiating the record contract will determine how such newly recorded material will be approved. In any event, along with such a "new recordings" clause will always be a parallel provision that mandates that such new recordings must be delivered to the record company within a certain number of days after a formal request is made (e.g., within 60 to 180 days after a request)—a clause designed to ensure that the scheduled release of the "greatest hits" album will not be delayed because new material scheduled for inclusion on the album has not been delivered.

## Recording Sessions and Studios

In many cases, the studio to be used for recording an album is chosen by the record company after consultation with the recording artist. Established performers, however, are able to select the recording studio (provided it meets certain technological specifications) after consultation with the record company. The same principles and considerations also apply to the selection of recording personnel, arrangers, and other creative personnel at the recording sessions.

## Album Artwork

In the case of new or less-established artists, the record company will usually have final approval rights over artwork, as it will want to reserve the right to determine how a particular artist is presented and marketed. This right will always encompass photographs, photographic settings, and likenesses, since the matter of establishing the right image for an artist is of utmost importance to the record company, whose vision and checkbook is definitely at risk. In many cases, the budget for the album artwork is totally discretionary with the record company; in other cases, specific provisions are made in the record agreement guaranteeing certain minimum artwork expenditures. In the case of well-established artists, the record company will many times leave the album artwork totally up to the recording artist—subject, of course, to certain reviews by its legal department to prevent potential litigation on issues ranging from right of privacy, libel, copyright infringement, criminal law, and civil rights.

The record company will many times, in the case of well-established acts, provide not only a specific approved budget for album artwork but also give the artist the right to prepare all the materials for delivery to the record company. A sample clause might read that the artist will be given an agreed-upon amount of money (e.g., $35,000) and, in return, present color-corrected negatives, camera-ready artwork, and proofs that will provide the record company with sufficient materials to prepare the album cover and inserts for the upcoming release. Additionally, the record company will usually demand that all liner notes and other credits be supplied by the artist simultaneously with the delivery to it of the album artwork.

Budgets for album artwork can range from $10,000 to over $100,000, depending on the elaborateness of the project. In cases where the artist has been given the responsibility of providing all artwork elements, if the costs exceed the approved budget, the excess is many times treated as an additional advance to the artist, recoupable from recording artist royalties or, if the artist is also a songwriter, from the songwriter and publisher royalties due the performer for sales of the album. How the record company is reimbursed for excess artwork expenditures is a matter of negotiation, though, with the outcome, as usual, dependent on the bargaining power of the parties.

## Warranties and Indemnities

Some of the most important clauses in any recording artist agreement are those dealing with the warranties and indemnities made by the artist, whether as a performer or a songwriter. The initial warranties relate to the right of the recording artist to enter into the agreement and fulfill its obligations. Secondly, the artist usually warrants that his or her recorded performances will not violate or infringe upon the rights of any third parties. Additionally, the artist represents that no other person or company has any rights that will in any way interfere with the services being provided under the recording agreement. If the artist is a songwriter, the warranties will also run to the originality of the compositions that are created under the agreement and embodied on the albums released by the record company. The warranty sections of the recording agreement are always accompanied by the indemnity sections, provisions that dictate what happens either when a claim is made that a warranty has been breached or when a breach of warranties has been proven through a court judgment or settlement.

Some of the major arguments between opposing lawyers occur when the warranty and indemnity provisions are negotiated; the issue of who is ultimately responsible for payment of the expenses related to a claim can have monumental financial implications. Considering that the legal fees expended even in infringement cases that are won by the artist and record company can easily exceed $400,000, these provisions are hard fought, especially by experienced attorneys who have seen profits from a hit record fly out the window from even a "crackpot" claim.

Many record contract indemnity clauses provide that the artist will hold the record company harmless from any loss or damages (including attorneys' fees) that are related to any claim or action that is inconsistent with the warranties made by the recording artist. Under such provisions, the artist is held responsible for reimbursement of all the record company's expenses in defending itself and the artist against a claim from a third party, whether or not the artist has actually breached his or her warranties under the agreement. For example, if another record company sues the artist's current record company, alleging that the artist is still under contract to it (a breach of representation by the artist, if proven), the artist would be responsible for all monies expended in defending the action, since this would be a claim inconsistent with the artist's representation that he or she was free and clear to sign a new recording agreement. It doesn't matter who wins the litigation; all that is needed to trigger indemnification by the artist under such a clause is for a claim to be received, since whether or not a claim is proven to be true is immaterial to the issue of who has the responsibility for the fees expended in defending the claim.

Because of the financial implications inherent in such clauses, the artist's lawyer will try to negotiate provisions that base indemnification by the artist only on claims that actually result in a judgment against the artist and record company. Such a proviso insulates the artist from paying out monies in instances where the artist has not in fact breached any warranties, since it distinguishes financial responsibility for the defense of claims alleging that a breach has occurred but that are never proven, and claims that actually result in a judicial finding or settlement establishing that a breach by the artist has occurred.

An additional issue that always comes up in the negotiations concerns what the record company can do when a claim is received. In virtually all instances, the record company will be able to hold an amount of royalties due the artist that is consistent with the amount of money that might be lost if the claim against the company and artist is successful. For example, if the record company determines that $150,000 might be lost if a suit is lost, it will have the right to withhold $150,000 of an artist's royalties to cover such a possibility. On occasion, the record company may also be able to withhold the payment of future advances to an artist (e.g., an upcoming album advance), but such remedies are always a matter of negotiation.

Since the record company will always have the right to withhold a portion of the artist's royalties in the event of a claim, the attorney for the artist will usually request that the monies being withheld be placed in an interest-bearing account (sometimes segregated from the record company's other funds) so that the artist will, if the monies are eventually released, receive the benefit of the interest that would have been made had the monies been paid and placed in the artist's bank account. Record companies will many times also agree to release the monies being held if litigation is not commenced within a certain period of time (e.g., if a suit is not filed within 1 to 2 years from the date that the claim letter was received), if the litigation is dismissed or claim withdrawn, or if the artist is able to post a bond with collateral securing the recovery of the monies being released.

The record company will almost always have the right to select the law firm that will control the defense on its behalf. In most cases, the artist will be able to retain independent personal legal counsel, provided that such counsel will not be able to interfere with the conduct and direction of the defense. The artist's lawyer, however, will usually be able to advise as to strategy and provide input to the legal staff retained by the record company.

## Sideman Provisions

In many recording agreements, the record company will allow its artist to perform as a backup musician or "sideman" on the commercially released recordings of other recording artists. Such clauses are usually a courtesy to the artist, a goodwill gesture that represents an exception to the contract's "exclusivity of recording services" provisions. If the record company agrees to such a clause, the artist's ability to perform as a sideman is usually conditioned upon the other record company's not being able to feature the photo or likeness of the sideman artist on the album cover or in any advertisements or promotions of the album. Additionally, there are always guarantees that a courtesy credit on the album liner notes will be given to the sideman's record company, that any credit for the sideman will not be larger than the credit afforded other sidemen, that any credit for the sideman will only be as a sideman, and that the recording sessions using the artist as a sideman will not interfere with the requirements of the artist's primary agreement.

## Re-Recording Restrictions

If a recording artist changes record labels or is dropped from one label and signs with another, there are always certain restrictions placed on the artist by his or her previous company as to what songs can be recorded for the new record company. Almost all contracts prohibit the artist from re-recording any selection for the new company that had been recorded while under contract with his or her former record company. These re-recording restrictions are not open-ended in duration, however; they always contain stated time limitations after which restrictions no longer apply. Many contracts take the approach of prohibiting any re-recording of past material for the later of (1) from 5 years after a particular recorded performance has been delivered to or released by the record company, or (2) 3 years after the expiration of the artist's featured recording contract. Under such a proviso, if an artist recorded and delivered a composition in December 2003 and the artist's contract with the record company lasted for 2 more albums until November 2007, that artist would not be able to re-record that same composition for another record company until

November 2010, 3 years after the contract ended (i.e., not December 2008, which is 5 years after the song was delivered).

Other record companies have longer re-recording restrictions. For example, some companies prohibit the artist from re-recording for 5 years after the expiration of the contract. Occasionally these restrictions apply not only to the recording services of the artist as a featured performer but are extended to the services of the artist as a producer. For example, if an artist is also known as a producer for other acts, a restriction in the contract might prevent the artist from producing another artist who is re-recording a composition previously recorded by the producer/artist. If such a clause is contained in the recording agreement, the restricted period is usually shorter than that imposed on the artist for re-recording as a featured performer.

## Solo Albums (For Members of a Group)

The individual members of a group may have plans for eventual solo careers or at least for recording solo albums. Provided that the desire for a solo album does not interfere with the group's recording and touring schedules and the record company's album release and promotion and marketing plans, contracts often allow the various members of the group to make solo recordings.

In most cases, a member of a group must give the record company written notice before beginning a solo project. If the record company consents, and provided there is no conflict with any plans it has for the group, the company usually has the right to control and release the solo album if it so desires. In some cases a specific advance is payable if the record company picks up such an option (e.g., $75,000 to the individual artist, one third of which is payable upon commencement of recording, one third upon acceptance of the solo album by the record company, and one third upon release of the solo album in the United States). In other cases, a good-faith negotiation clause may give the record company the exclusive right to negotiate with the solo artist as to the terms of an agreement (e.g., advance, recording budget, royalties) for a period of time (usually from 30 to 90 days) or the right to match an offer from a third-party record company. In the latter instance, the individual artist will be obligated to supply the record company with all substantive terms of the bona fide third-party offer, and the record company will usually have from 15 to 60 days to match the offer. If the offer is not matched, the solo artist will be free to enter into the proposed third-party agreement. But if the terms of the agreement eventually negotiated by the solo artist with a third party are less favorable to the artist than as originally presented to and rejected by the group's record company, that company will usually get another opportunity to match the final offer.

## Provisions for New Band Members and Departing Band Members

The record company will always demand that any new member of a contracted group ratify and sign the existing recording agreement before becoming part of the group. This is true whether the new performer is replacing a member of the group who has left or is being added to the group without any current member leaving. The ratification form that is signed by the new member can take a number of different forms, but usually will provide that the new member has read all the provisions of the recording agreement, has received independent legal advice from outside counsel, and agrees to be bound by all the terms and conditions of the recording agreement as if the new member were an original signatory to the agreement. The effective date of the new member's acceptance of the contract is usually the earlier of the date of his or her signing of the ratification agreement or the new member's actual rendering of services to the group.

In the case of a band member's leaving the group, the recording agreement will always provide that the leaving member must send written notice to the record company. Within a certain number of days after receiving the notice, the record company will usually have the right to elect a number of different options relating to not only the leaving member of the group but also the remaining members of the group. These options include the right to terminate the recording agreement with the group, the right to require the remaining members of the group to provide a substitute performer for the leaving member, and the right to have the remaining members perform as a self-contained act without replacing the leaving member.

The record company will also have the right to negotiate with each performer of the group with respect to the signing of a new recording agreement. For example, the company may have the right to acquire the individual services of any member of the group by sending that member notice of such within 30 to 90 days after a leaving member has given notice. In many cases, if the record company elects to sign an individual remaining member or a leaving member, a provision will bind the parties to good-faith negotiations concerning the terms of the new agreement. If within a certain time period (e.g., 60 days or 90 days) negotiations do not result in an agreement, the artist will normally be able to negotiate with other record companies, with the proviso that the current record company will have a certain number of days (usually 30 to 45) to match any offer from another record company. In other cases, the record company, if it so chooses, will elect to have the leaving member sign an identical contract to the one that he or she signed as a group member, the term of which usually consists of the remaining balance of the group contract.

In addition, some record companies will require any leaving member to go into the studio to record a number of demonstration recordings pursuant to either a budget approved by the record company or one that is mutually approved by the artist and label within certain previously negotiated guidelines. The record company will then usually have a specified number of days after it receives the finished demo recordings to decide whether or not it wants to exercise its right to sign the leaving member as an exclusive recording artist. Under this type of provision, the record company is giving itself the opportunity to listen to what the leaving member can do as an individual artist and make a decision only after it is able to review newly recorded performances.

### Recording and Delivery of Albums

Virtually all contracts provide for a specified outside date by which the initial album must be delivered to the record company. For example, if an artist agreement commences on January 1, the contract may provide that commencement of recording will start no later than March 1 and that completion of the album be satisfied not later than July 1. Other agreements may not refer to a commencement of recording date but only refer to a guaranteed completion and delivery date for each album. For example, a delivery provision may provide that the initial album be delivered within 90 to 180 days after the recording agreement is signed and that each option album be delivered within 90 to 180 days after commencement of each option period of the term. Some agreements compute delivery dates for option albums from the delivery or release of the previous album (e.g., each subsequent album being delivered no earlier than 9 months nor later than 18 months after delivery of the prior album or no earlier than 6 months nor later than 12 months after the U.S. release of the prior album).

When an artist changes record labels, restrictions in that artist's contract with the old label may restrict the timing of album releases by the new label. For example, the new record company may not be able to release a newly recorded album until a specified number of months after the old record company has released (or, per contract, should have released) the last album recorded under its agreement with the artist. These restrictive clauses can also be tied to the delivery of an album (e.g., the artist agreeing not to have an album released by the new record company until 6 months after the delivery of the last product commitment album to the old record company).

### Delivery of the Final Master Recording

In cases where the recording artist is responsible for all aspects of the recording project or in instances where the artist is being furnished by a production company that is acting as producer of the album, the record company will normally require that the producer/artist furnish the record company with all consents and clearances necessary for the release of the completed album and its cover and liner notes, correct writer and publisher information on all compositions recorded, timely submission of all musicians union contracts and W-4s, clearance of any sampled recordings or musical compositions, and mechanical licenses for compositions that are not written by the artist or controlled by a company owned or controlled by the artist or producer.

Most record companies will, once the album is completed, require that the artist or producer deliver two DATs of the master recording. Occasionally, the record company will also require an additional reference lacquer. In many contracts, the record company will have a specified number of days from its receipt of the master tape of the album to approve or disapprove of the completed recording. For example, a sample acceptance clause may state that if the record company does not notify the artist/producer that a particular album is unacceptable within 20 days of receipt, that album shall be deemed to have been accepted. In some cases, there may be a warranty that all outtakes will also be delivered to the record company, but such a requirement is always subject to negotiation and agreement by the parties. Additionally, record companies will usually agree not to release any outtakes without the permission of the recording artist.

Considering the amount of time, effort, and money involved with the recording of an album, the issue of "what is or is not acceptable" is of paramount importance not only to the record company but to the artist as well. After all, the record company may easily have a commitment of from $200,000 to over $3 million on the line and will therefore demand as much perfection as possible in the final master recording, in terms of both technical competence and creative expression. The artist, on the other hand, will try to limit the record company's approval rights to the technical acceptability of the album (a domain of engineers and experts involved in the "sound" aspects of recording) and not to the artistic expression or creative direction taken by the performer on a particular recording. Established recording artists usually succeed in securing language that guarantees acceptance by the record company as long as the master recording is technically satisfactory for commercial release to the general public and the compositions have not been previously recorded by the artist, provided that the style of such performances is not adverse to the past performances of the artist. Less-established artists and new performers must accept language that usually gives the record company more leeway in accepting or rejecting an album (e.g., the record company may require that the performances be of a contemporary nature, etc.), language that can many times enable the record company to become involved in the creative focus and expression of the recorded project. The record company will almost always have the right to require the artist to re-record any master that is deemed to be unacceptable.

## Ownership of the Recordings

Unless the contract contains other provisions, the artist agreement will usually state that the record label is the copyright owner of the performances recorded during the term of the recording agreement. In many cases, the ownership will be termed a "work made for hire" under the U.S. Copyright Act, and, if upheld, there may be no reversion of rights to the recording artist or record producer. The general grant-of-rights clause of the recording agreement gives the record company the right, among other things, to manufacture and distribute audio and audiovisual recordings of the performances of the artist under the record company's trade name, to perform such recordings, and to package and exploit such recordings, all such rights being subject to the other terms of the agreement, including those provisions that guarantee royalty payments for most types of commercial exploitation. Depending on one's bargaining power, a number of restrictions can be negotiated by the artist (e.g., initial release of any recording to be on the record company's "top line" label, no inclusion of a master on "compilation" or "television only" albums until a certain amount of time has elapsed after the initial release of the recording, approval over certain motion picture or advertising commercial uses), but in most cases, the record company will have fairly unrestricted rights to exploit the master recordings in the manner that it sees fit to promote the artist.

In cases where the artist is able to cause a reversion of ownership of his or her recorded performances contractually via negotiation (an occurrence that usually happens only with the biggest superstars or in the case of a licensing of preexisting masters agreement), that right is often subject to the record company's having recouped all advances paid to or on behalf of the artist. Such reversion provisions normally refer to a grant of rights that will last for a certain number of years after the expiration of the term of the recording artist agreement, with an automatic extension of time if the record company is still in an unrecouped position at the time of the agreed-upon reversion date. For example, a sample clause might read:

> All rights in and to the recordings shall revert to the recording artist 15 years after the expiration of the term of the recording agreement, said agreement to expire upon the commercial release in the United States of the fifth album recorded during the term of the record contract. Notwithstanding the above, however, in the event that the record company has not recouped all of the advances previously paid to the artist (e.g., signing advance, commencement of option advances, album delivery and acceptance advances, commercial release advances, etc.) or paid to others on behalf of the artist (e.g., audio and audio visual recording costs, per diems to performers, musician union fees, etc.), the rights to the master recordings shall remain with the record company until either all such advances and direct costs are recouped or until the artist repays the record company the total outstanding unrecouped advance balance related not only to the most recent album but all albums recorded under the artist agreement.

In the event that such a "repayment of any outstanding advance balance" provision is included in a recording agreement, the effective reversion date will usually be the last day of either the calendar quarter or semiannual calendar period during which the repayment by the artist is made. For example, if the artist repays the unrecouped advance balance on July 14 of a particular year and there is an "end of the semiannual calendar period" reversion date, the transfer of ownership of the recordings to the artist would not occur until December 31 of that year. If an "end of the calendar quarter" reversion date had been used in the above scenario, the reversion date would be the end of September.

## MOTION PICTURE, TELEVISION, AND COMMERCIAL USES

Considering that the use of a master recording in a motion picture can generate from $15,000 to over $60,000 in licensing fees, the use of a master recording in a television series from $1,500 to over $12,000, and the use of a master recording in a national television consumer product commercial from $75,000 to over $750,000, income from these sources can have a substantial impact not only on the record company's bottom line but on the artist's earnings as well. In addition to the licensing fee received by the record company, these uses can also open up a number of other opportunities, such as being included on a soundtrack album or being introduced to a new audience by means of increased exposure to the general public, all of which will usually have the potential of positively affecting sales and other uses of the recording.

Most recording agreements will provide that the artist will receive 50% of the net license fee received by the record company for the motion picture, television, or commercial use. As to the definition of what is "net" in a licensing situation, duplication costs, out-of-pocket charges, and all third-party payment obligations such as union payments and, if applicable, songwriter and publisher royalties will be deducted from the gross monies received to arrive at the net. For example, if a master recording is licensed for use in a motion picture at a fee of $30,000 and it costs the record company $1,500 in duplication costs and union fees, the net licensing fee would be $28,500 (i.e., $30,000 – $1,500 = $28,500). Under the 50% sharing formula, the record company would retain $14,250 with the remaining $14,250 being paid to the recording artist. In the event that the artist is in an unrecouped advance position, the monies will be used by the record company to reduce the outstanding negative advance balance. Streaming income is many times shared this way.

In many recording agreements, the record company will have sole discretion in deciding whether to license a certain master recording for use in a particular motion picture, television series, or commercial. Depending on the artist's bargaining power, stature, and quality of legal representation, the negotiations may result in the record company's having to secure the approval of the artist before entering into any such licensing agreements. Unless one is a superstar, it is not common for an artist to have total approval over all film and television uses, as most record companies try to retain as much discretionary power in this area as possible. On the other hand, a large number of artists are able to secure consent rights over the use of their recorded performances in certain types of motion pictures (e.g., X-rated theatrical films) and consumer product commercials, especially with respect to certain types of products, such as alcohol or hygiene products.

## *SHIPPING AND RETURN POLICIES*

Record companies normally extend to their distributors, rack jobbers, and other customers the privilege of returning all unsold tapes and CDs for credit. Considering that the vast majority of albums do not recover their costs, this "return privilege" can become a major problem to the record company. In addition, if a record company has a policy of consistently overpressing and shipping more albums than can realistically be sold, this problem can be further aggravated. For example, in the case of a company that overships, the artist may be initially ecstatic about the number of records out in the market. What the artist does not realize, however, is that out of a shipment of 200,000 CDs, 50,000 might be bought by the general public, with 150,000 returned as unsold goods. Fortunately, most record companies adopt a more judicious approach in the pressing and shipping of recordings, especially in the case of new artists without any established sales pattern or base. With these companies, the return rate is usually lower than that of a company that overships just for the sake of having large numbers of recordings in the stores. But even in the case of companies with more selective and modest shipping policies, the number of CDs, tapes, and other recordings that might be returned can still be substantial.

### Returned Recordings and the Artist's Royalties

In every recording contract the artist and the record company agree that royalties will be paid only on recordings that are actually sold or distributed to the general public, not on records that are manufactured and shipped but eventually returned. For example, if 500,000 albums are shipped and only 300,000 are actually sold at the retail level, with the remainder being returned for credit, the artist will be paid on the 300,000 exclusively. If for some reason a performer is overpaid because the record company's accounts indicated more sales than eventually occurred, the record company will always have the right to deduct such "excess royalties" from future sales due the artist and, in some cases, demand immediate reimbursement.

*Reserve Funds and Anticipated Returns.*   Recognizing that there are always going to be returns (regardless of the artist) and that unsold recordings may continue to come back for years after the initial release date of an album, single, or EP, record companies normally withhold a certain percentage of an artist's royalties in anticipation of such returns. These withheld royalties are referred to as "reserves" and are designed to ensure that the record company will not overpay an artist based on the initial sales figures from its distributors instead of actual sales to the general public. For example, if a record company ships 600,000 albums to its distributors, who then sell those albums to a number of retail stores, the initial sales figures to the record company will indicate that all 600,000 records have been sold. Let us also assume that during the following 12 to 18 months 300,000 of those albums are returned to the company for credit since they could not be sold. If the record company had based its royalty computations on the original sales figures from its distributors, it would have already remitted royalties to the recording artist on a full 600,000 albums sold, resulting in an overpayment on 300,000 albums—a costly mistake for artists making $1 to $2 per album.

*Reserve Fund Holdback Percentages.*   Under the reserve clause provisions, therefore, the record company is allowed to hold back a certain percentage of the artist's royalties to protect itself against large numbers of returns. In effect, the company is paying only on recordings that it feels have actually been sold to the public and not those that it anticipates will be returned for credit. There are rarely any stated limits as to how much the record company is thus allowed to hold back. Each company has a different policy, usually with lower percentages for established artists and higher percentages for newer groups. Some companies even hold as much as 50% of an artist's royalties pending a final accounting as to how many records have actually been sold. The vast majority of companies, however, have lower reserve percentages, which range from 20% to 40% depending on the past track record of the artist. Different configurations may have different reserve percentages because of the history of returns for that particular type of recording. For example, the reserve percentage on a long-playing album may be 25% to 30%, but on singles and EPs the reserve may be 30% to 40%.

*Liquidating the Reserve Fund.*   The reserve fund can pose real problems for many recording artists, since it substantially reduces the artist's initial royalty payments and postpones the date when he or she will finally be paid all royalties due. In addition, if a company's reserve percentage is much higher than the actual number of returns (for example, a 50% royalty holdback where only 25% of the CDs and tapes are actually returned), the artist might be penalized unjustifiably. Since most reserve clauses are open ended, many artists try to negotiate a limit on the amount of time that a record company can withhold such reserved royalties. For example, some agreements guarantee that the company will liquidate the reserve within a "reasonable amount of time." Other contracts are more specific and put an actual time limit of from 12 to 24 months for a complete accounting of any monies being held in anticipation of returns. Still others will actually recite the record company's current reserve policy (for example,"no withholding in excess of 35% of all recordings sold and paid for") or, in the alternative, provide a returns history for a particular recorded configuration at the artist's request so that all parties know what to expect. And others will base the reserve for a particular album on the actual return percentage of the prior album plus an additional "safety net" percentage (e.g., 30% + 5% = 35% reserve). Many record companies will also have a provision in their contracts that if they become aware of any facts concerning the artist that might indicate that returns on a particular album in excess of the contractual limitations may occur, a larger reserve may be put into effect for that album.

## INSURANCE POLICIES

Since the record company is making a substantial investment in a recording artist, the record contract will usually have a clause that permits the label to purchase insurance covering the performer's life or any disability suffered due to illness or accident. The record company will be the beneficiary under the policy and will pay the premiums. In the event that the record company elects to take out insurance, the artist will agree to be available for any medical examination that is required for the issuance of such a policy.

## CONFIDENTIALITY CLAUSES

The record contract may limit both the artist and the record label from disclosing the major negotiated provisions to the press or the general public. Such a clause enables the record company to protect information about what it gave to one artist from the legal and business representatives of other artists who may already be signed or who will be signed in the future. There are exceptions to the disclosure rules (e.g., disclosure of information being allowable to legal, financial, and investment advisors of the artist, to governmental agencies, etc.), and occasionally the record company and artist will agree to consult with each other over a mutually agreed-upon press release about the signing or renegotiation of a recording agreement. In most cases, the record company will have the right to issue the press release and the "final say" as to its wording.

## ARTIST–PRODUCTION COMPANY AGREEMENTS

It is common in the recording industry for the artist to be signed to a production company, which in turn signs with the record company as the provider of the performing services of the artist. This arrangement is extremely prevalent in the case of superstars and established artists, especially when these performers not only produce or coproduce their own recordings but take on the responsibility of many of the creative and business aspects surrounding the conception, creation, recording, and delivery of their albums.

The production company will always warrant that it has a binding agreement with the performer that guarantees that the artist not only is required to perform exclusively for the production company but also will comply with all the terms of the record company–production company agreement. The record contract will further provide that if the production company does not fulfill its obligations or enforce its rights with respect to the recording artist, then the record company will have the right either to fulfill an obligation or to remedy a default on the part of the production company. For example, if the production company defaults on a royalty payment to the artist, the record company may step in to assure proper payment to the artist. The record label will demand to see a copy of the contract between the artist and the service or production company, and will secure guarantees that no revisions or modifications will be made in the production company–artist agreement without the approval of the label.

## Flow-Through Clauses

Because of the enormous investment on the part of the record company in the recording, distribution, manufacturing, promotion, and marketing of albums (to say nothing of the monies expended to sign the artist and secure the rights), the record label will always demand that the artist sign a "flow-through clause" that will guarantee that, if the production company furnishing the services of the artist defaults on its obligations, the artist will fulfill his or her obligations directly to the record company. Under this type of arrangement, the record company effectively protects its investment and rights to the artist's services, since the artist is in reality agreeing to be obligated directly to the record company.

The record company will use its flow-through rights to the artist in a number of situations, the most common of which are the liquidation or dissolution of the production company, a bankruptcy or insolvency filing, an assignment of rights for the benefit of creditors, a failure by the production company to fulfill its obligations under the recording contract, or a breach by the production company of a term of its contract with the recording artist that jeopardizes the record company's rights.

## CONTROLLED-COMPOSITION CLAUSES

One of the most important areas in any recording artist agreement negotiation is that related to how the performer gets paid for self-written compositions ("controlled compositions" in industry lingo) on an album, EP, or single released by the record company. A controlled composition is defined in a number of ways depending on the record company, but it always includes musical compositions written by the performer and musical compositions that are either owned or controlled by the performer's publishing company. These provisions (known as "controlled-composition clauses") tend to be as hotly negotiated as any clause in the contract (including artist royalty rates, advances, video budgets, and deductions), since they can and do have a major impact on how much money a performer can make as a songwriter and, in many cases, how much money the performer will not make because he or she wrote a song.

### Mechanical Rates

Most record companies will try to reduce the amount of mechanical royalties (i.e., songwriter and music publisher royalties due for the sale of recordings) that they have to pay to their songwriter/recording artists. For example, most record companies will pay the writer/performer only 75% of the statutory mechanical rate per musical composition written by the artist for each CD, tape, or record sold in the United States.

To illustrate, the mechanical royalty computations for 1 copy of a 10-song album would look as follows:

| | |
|---:|:---|
| 8.5¢ | Statutory rate (2004–05) |
| x 75% | Controlled rate |
| 6.375¢ | Per-song royalties |
| x 10 | Songs on album |
| 63.75¢ | Aggregate mechanical royalties |

Under the above scenario, if 1 million albums are sold in the United States, the record company would pay $637,500 in mechanical royalties, rather than the statutory $850,000.

### Sales Plateau Increases

Occasionally, these controlled composition rates can be increased based on a recording artist's success in the marketplace (e.g., an album or single achieving certain predetermined sales levels), but such increases are always subject to negotiation and are rarely given voluntarily. To illustrate, if the writer/performer has to accept a 75% rate on all self-written compositions, some agreements will provide for the record company to pay a 75% rate for sales of each album up to

500,000 units, increase the royalty to 82.5% or 85% for sales between 500,001 and 1 million, and further increase the mechanical royalty rate to full statutory or 100% for all albums sold after 1 million.

A sample sales incentive/royalty increase clause may read as follows:

> With respect to the writer/performer's self-written compositions that appear on any album recorded hereunder, the controlled composition royalty rate shall be increased from 75% to 82.5% for all full-priced sales in excess of 500,000 but not in excess of 1,000,000. For full-priced sales in excess of 1,000,000 but not in excess of 1,500,000 units, the 82.5% rate shall be increased to 90%. For full-priced sales in excess of 1,500,000 but not in excess of 2,000,000 units, the 90% royalty rate shall be increased to 97.5%. And for full-priced sales in excess of 2,000,000 units, the mechanical royalty shall be 100% of the minimum statutory rate.

To see how such graduated mechanical royalty increases affect a writer/performer's income, Table 3.3 (using the above record contract clause) shows how the songwriter and music publisher monies are computed and what can be lost or gained by having or not having one of these sales incentive clauses in a recording artist agreement. Considering that an additional $616,240 can be made or lost by the writer/recording artist under the scenario in Table 3.3, "increased mechanical rates based on sales plateaus" clauses can be very important to a performer's financial stability.

## Increased Royalties for Later Albums

If a writer/performer has to accept a 75% mechanical rate in the recording artist agreement, it is often possible to negotiate a higher rate for subsequent albums. For example, if a writer/performer has signed a 7-album recording

TABLE **3.3**  Sales Plateau Increases for Recording Artist Royalties

Assuming a recording artist/writer sells 4 million albums in the Unites States and has written all 10 songs on the album, the royalty calculations with and without a sales incentive provision for an increased mechanical rate would be as follows:

A. Without a sales incentive provision

| | |
|---|---|
| Albums sold | 4,000,000 |
| 2004–05 statutory royalty rate | x .085 |
| Per-song royalty | $ 340,000 |
| Controlled rate (% of statutory) | x 75% |
| Per-song controlled royalty | $ 255,000 |
| Songs on album | x 10 |
| Total writer and publisher royalty | $2,550,000      *(cont'd.)* |

TABLE **3.3** (*CONT'D*)
B. WITH A SALES INCENTIVE PROVISION

| Sales level | 1–500,000 | 500,001–1,000,000 | 1,000,001–1,500,000 | 1,500,000–2,000,000 | 2,000,001–4,000,000 | 1–4,000,000 (total) |
|---|---|---|---|---|---|---|
| Albums sold | 500,000 | 500,000 | 500,000 | 500,000 | 2,000,000 | 4,000,000 |
| 2004–05 statutory rate | x .085 | x .085 | x .085 | x .085 | x .085 | |
| Per-song royalty | $42,500 | $42,500 | $42,500 | $42,500 | $170,000 | |
| Controlled rate (% of statutory) | x 75% | x 82.5% | x 90% | x 97.5% | x 100% | |
| Per-song controlled royalty | $31,875 | $35,062 | $38,250 | $41,437 | $170,000 | |
| Songs on album | x 10 | x 10 | x 10 | x 10 | x 10 | |
| Total royalty | $318,750 | $350,620 | $382,500 | $414,370 | $1,700,000 | $3,166,240 |

agreement with a record company (e.g., 1 album plus options for 6 more), the mechanical rate might be increased from 75% to 82.5% or 85% for compositions on the fourth and fifth albums or even to 100% on the sixth and seventh albums. Variations in this area depend on one's bargaining power and the experience of one's representatives. All are based on the principle that if a writer/artist has recorded more than 3 or 4 albums for the same record company, the albums must be fairly successful and thus be generating profits for all parties. That being so, the writer/recording artist should not be penalized for being a songwriter. A sample clause might read:

> Notwithstanding the 75% Controlled Composition statutory rate provisions of this Agreement, it is agreed that all musical compositions written by the writer/artist which are embodied on the fourth and fifth albums recorded hereunder will be paid at 85% of the statutory rate. For musical compositions written by the writer–artist that are embodied on the sixth and seventh albums, payment of mechanical royalties for musical compositions written by the writer/artist shall be paid at 100% of the statutory rate.

## Canadian Sales

In addition to covering sales in the United States, the controlled-composition reduced-royalty rate provisions of the recording agreement also apply to sales of albums and singles in Canada. The clauses relating to Canada usually provide that the 75% rate will be based on the compulsory mechanical rate established under the Canadian copyright law or, in the event that the law does not provide for one, on the rate established by the major record companies and major music publishers. On occasion, the clause will mention an actual penny royalty (e.g., 7¢) that would become effective if either of the other two alternatives do not exist.

## "Lock In" Rate Date

Since the compulsory statutory mechanical rate has gradually increased over the past years, most record company contracts will provide that the royalty rate for a particular composition on a particular album or single will be frozen at the rate in effect on a particular negotiated date. In this way, the record company's mechanical royalty costs for songs written by its writer/artists will be fixed and will not be subject to increase if the compulsory statutory rate goes up at some time in the future.

For example, some contracts provide that the rate will be that in effect when the recording of an album commences; others calculate the effective date as the year in which the album is released; others use the year in which the record contract is signed; and still others fix the mechanical rate as of the date that an album is delivered to the record company. Sometimes the contract will provide that the earlier of either the actual delivery of an album or the date on which the album should have been delivered is the date that should apply. Occasionally, the controlled rate will be based on the statutory royalty rate in effect on the date of manufacture of a particular album, but this is not common.

To illustrate how one of these clauses works and how it can affect a performer's income, let us assume that a writer/artist has a mechanical royalty "lock in" date of when the album is delivered to the record company. In our example, the album was recorded in late 2003 and delivered to the record company on December 20 of that same year. Since the statutory mechanical rate in 2003 was 8¢ per composition, the writer/artist's mechanical rate would be fixed at 75% of 8 cents (i.e., 6¢). The album is released in the United States in June 2004 and sells 1 million copies. On January 1, 2004, the statutory mechanical rate was increased to 8.5¢ per composition. Because the writer/artist's royalty rate was fixed in comparison to the statutory rate in effect during 2003, however, the writer/artist would not get the benefit of the new increased rate even though all of the actual album sales occurred during 2004-05. The difference (with the 2003-based calculations on the left and the 2004-05 calculations on the right) would be calculated as follows:

| | | |
|---|---|---|
| 8¢ | Statutory rate | 8.5¢ |
| x 75% | Artist rate | x 75% |
| 6¢ | Royalty per song | 6.375¢ |
| x 10 | Songs on album | x 10 |
| .60¢ | Album royalties | 63.75¢ |
| x1,000,000 | Sales | x 1,000,000 |
| $600,000.00 | Total | $637,500.00 |

| | |
|---|---|
| $637,500.00 | 2004-05 rate |
| -$600,000.00 | 2003 rate |
| $37,500.00 | Difference |

As one can see, the results of the negotiations as to when a mechanical rate is "locked in" or fixed can be crucial to the amount of money a writer/artist makes from sales of albums or singles.

## "Greatest Hits" Albums

One area where a writer/artist can often negotiate an exception to the lock-in rate date provisions of the recording agreement has to do with "greatest hits" packages. Since "greatest hits" albums take recorded performances from a number of different albums (with many of the compositions being paid at differing mechanical rates because the albums were released during a wide span of years), some artists are able to get the record company to agree that the mechanical rate payable for all self-written compositions on such an album will be that in effect when the "greatest hits" album is released to the general public in the United States. For example, if a number of the compositions were being paid at 75% of a 6.25¢ rate because they were initially contained on albums that were recorded in 1993 when the statutory rate was 6.25¢, the mechanical payments for these compositions for sales of a "greatest hits" album released in 2004 or 2005 (when the statutory rate had increased to 8.5¢) would be calculated on the 2004–05 rate rather than the lower 1993 rate.

## Maximum Royalty Cap

In addition to the controlled-composition rate and the lock-in date for a particular album, the other important clause in the record company's controlled-composition provisions is that which determines the maximum amount of mechanical royalties a record company is willing to pay on a particular album. Here a writer/performer's lawyer must be not only a proficient negotiator of the legal aspects of an agreement but also an accountant and mathematician, since all these clauses work in concert with each other and cannot be considered independently of one another. If they are dealt with in isolation, financial disasters can, have, and will continue to happen.

The way these clauses usually work is that the record company dictates that no more than 10 times the controlled artist/writer rate of 75% times statutory will be payable in mechanical royalties on any 1 album regardless of how many compositions are on the album or when sales actually occur. A sample clause might look as follows:

> Notwithstanding anything to the contrary contained in this Agreement, with respect to net sales of albums in the United States and Canada, the maximum aggregate mechanical copyright royalty rate payable by the record company in respect of any particular album (excluding multiple albums), regardless of the number of selections embodied therein or the playing time thereof, shall be ten (10) times the Controlled Composition rate (hereinafter the "Maximum Aggregate Album Rate").

To understand how this type of clause works in a recording agreement, we will first illustrate what the cap means in dollar-and-cents terms. The record company is taking the position that it will not pay more than 63.75¢ per album in mechanical royalties for sales in the United States. The calculation is as follows:

| | |
|---|---|
| 8.5¢ | 2004–05 statutory rate |
| x 75% | Controlled rate |
| 6.375¢ | Per-song royalty |
| x 10 | Maximum songs per album |
| 63.75¢ | Maximum album royalties |

If the writer/artist records 12 or even 14 compositions on the album, the maximum album cap will still be 60.75¢, the same as for 10 songs.

In the case of the writer/artist recording only self-written compositions, the royalty calculation is a straightforward procedure. The tricky part occurs when the writer/artist writes a portion of the album and elects to include compositions by other songwriters. Even though choosing the best songs for an album (whether or not they are created by the writer/artist) is a justifiable and commendable aesthetic decision, it can have a disastrous effect on the writer/artist's songwriting income.

For example, if the writer/artist records 12 compositions for an album, 5 of which are self-written and 7 of which are by outside songwriters, the writer/artist might receive only a minuscule mechanical royalty for each self-written song because of the mechanical payments made for the outside songs. If we make the assumption that the music publishers of the 7 outside songs all demand a 100% statutory mechanical rate (i.e., 8.5¢ per song in 2004-05), the record company will be obligated to pay 59.5¢ in mechanical royalties for all the outside songs each time an album is sold. Since the maximum amount of aggregate royalties that the record company has agreed to pay per album is 63.75¢, there remains 4.25¢ that can be paid to the writer/artist for the 5 self-written compositions, which means that the writer/artist will be receiving only .85¢ per composition each time an album is sold.

|  |  |
|---:|:---|
| 63.75¢ | Royalty cap per album |
| −59.50¢ | Outside songs royalties |
| 4.25¢ | Remaining royalties |
| ÷ 5 | Writer/artist songs |
| 0.85¢ | Per-song royalties |

If the album sold 1 million copies in the United States, the writer/artist would receive $8,500 in mechanical royalties per song—a far cry from the $85,000 earned by each outside song licensed at the statutory rate. Because of the inequities involved in how these maximum royalty rate caps operate on the writer/performer's mechanical income, it is not unusual for a writer/artist to try to convince the writers and publishers of the outside songs to accept a 75% rate so that all songs will receive the same royalties per album sold. Depending on the relationships between the various parties, sometimes this is accepted by the writers and publishers of the outside songs and sometimes it is not. Occasionally, a writer/artist may not record an outside composition unless an agreement is reached for a reduced rate, a position which sometimes succeeds in getting acceptance of the reduced rate and sometimes doesn't.

Even worse, some situations can put the writer/artist in the unenviable position of owing the record company money each time an album is sold. As absurd as it may seem, this is not an uncommon occurrence in the case of writer/artists who do not write all the songs on their albums. Clauses in virtually every recording artist agreement provide that in the event that the mechanical royalty cap for a particular recording is exceeded, the excess can be deducted from the writer/performer's recording artist royalties.

For example, if an album contains 9 songs by outside songwriters and 1 song by the recording artist, and all of the outside songs are licensed at the statutory rate of 8.5¢ per composition, the record company will be obligated to pay 76.5¢ in mechanical royalties to the publishers of the 9 outside songs (i.e., 8.5 x 9 = 76.5). If the recording artist's contract specifies a 63.75¢ mechanical royalties cap, the record company is paying over 12¢ in excess of the maximum that it agreed to pay, and will take that overage from any recording artist royalties due the writer/performer.

A modification that has been negotiated in this area is to have the royalty cap per album calculated on a rate of either 12 times 75% of the statutory rate or 10 times the statutory rate (rather than 10 times 75% of statutory)—or, in the case of CDs, which contain more compositions than cassettes, 12 to 13 times the statutory rate. This type of revision gives the writer/artist more leeway to pick outside songs without being financially penalized for such a decision.

## Singles and EPs

With respect to other audio configurations which are released to the general public, the royalty cap is usually 2 times 75% of statutory for 7-inch singles, 3 times 75% of statutory for 12-inch singles, and 6 times 75% of statutory for EPs. If a writer/performer is an established recording artist, it is possible to negotiate caps based on the statutory rate rather than 75% of the statutory rate. For example, many established artists are able to secure a 51¢ royalty cap on a 6-song EP (8.5¢ x 6 songs = 51¢) rather than the 38.25¢ cap (8.5¢ x 75% = 6.375¢ x 6 songs = 38.25¢) that is usual for newer artists.

## One-Use-Only Mechanical Royalties

Many record contracts provide that only one mechanical royalty will be payable per composition, regardless of how many times that composition appears on the album or single. For example, if the same composition is repeated a number of times with different mixes, the record company will usually pay mechanical royalties only for the first use of the composition on a particular recording, with the other uses being deemed non-royalty-generating uses. To illustrate, if a recording company put two versions of the same song on a single in 2004–05 and the song was licensed at the statutory rate, the record company would pay only 8.5¢ per unit sold, not 17¢. It is possible to negotiate better terms (e.g., payment for up to two uses of the same composition), but it is very difficult to receive mechanical royalties from the record company on a per-use basis for unlimited uses of a composition on an album, single, or EP.

## Midpriced, Budget, and Record Club Reduced Royalties

In addition to the 75% or other reduced-rate clauses that affect a writer/artist's mechanical royalties, virtually all record contracts will further reduce the mechanical rate when the artist's albums are sold as part of its midprice or budget lines or if the album is sold through a record club. In most cases, rates for this type of sale are calculated at from 75% to 50% of the controlled composition rate. For example, if a writer/artist receives 75% of the statutory rate for compositions on full-priced product (6.375¢ in 2004–05), the mechanical rate per composition for midpriced, budget, and record club sales might be 75% of the 75% rate (i.e., 75% x 8.5 = 6.375 x 75% = 4.76¢). Many of the very successful writer/recording artists are able to raise some of these rates (e.g., 80% to 90% for midpriced albums, etc.), but all recording artist agreements contain some form of reductions for lower-priced products.

## Increased Royalty Rates for Compositions That Are Published by the Record Company

A number of record companies guarantee a full statutory mechanical rate to writer/performers who allow the record company's music publishing firm to own or co-own the compositions. Restrictions attached to this guarantee may include an aggregate royalty cap of from 10 to 13 times the statutory rate for each album, a limitation of one royalty payment per composition despite the number of times a composition appears on the album, a minimum statutory-rate calculation versus a durational statutory-rate formula, and a proviso that the 100% statutory rate applies only to top line, full-priced product. Even with these restrictions, receiving a full statutory royalty rather than a reduced-rate royalty can mean a substantial amount of extra money for the writer/performer. If the record company is able to guarantee a full statutory rate, this many times will mean the difference in choosing one publisher over another, especially if the advances, royalty splits, and other terms being offered by competing publishers are close.

## Changing Mechanical Rates

The statutory mechanical rate has changed over the years and will continue to change every two years through 2007 based upon a negotiated agreement between writers, publishers and record companies. For that reason, the dollar figures in the examples in this book need to be periodically re-computed. The formulas by which such figures are arrived at remain valid, and all the reader has to do to calculate up-to-date figures is to use the procedures set forth and insert the new statutory rate in the place of the 2004–05 statutory mechanical rate we've used. For example, if the current statutory rate is 9.1¢, the reader should substitute 9.1¢ for 8.5¢ in the calculations, and the results will be valid.

Since statutory mechanical rates are subject to change, it is possible for a writer/artist to have complied with the maximum album cap at the time a particular recording is released but be penalized for recording outside compositions at some time in the future depending on how those outside compositions are licensed. For example, if a writer/artist had a 10-times-statutory album cap for a recording released in 2004 or 2005, 85¢ would be the allowable maximum for that album. If the album contained 7 compositions written by the artist and 3 outside compositions, each would receive 8.5¢ for every album sold. In the event that the statutory rate is increased to 9.1 cents (as in 2006), the 3 outside compositions would begin to generate 27.3¢ in aggregate royalties for album sales (rather than 25.5¢), leaving 57.7¢ to be shared by the 7 artist-written compositions (instead of the 59.5¢ previously paid).

The reason that such a changing statutory rate is able to reduce the monies earned by the artist-written compositions is explained by the way outside compositions are usually licensed. Most music publishers license their compositions on what is known as a "floating statutory rate," which enables the rate to fluctuate depending on the current rate in effect when the recording is manufactured and distributed rather than the rate in effect at the time when the initial recording was either manufactured or distributed. How an outside composition is initially licensed can therefore affect a writer/artist's earning capacity on any album recorded during the term of the recording agreement. A recording artist must accept the reality that, depending on the terms of his or her controlled-composition clause and how such provisions interrelate with the maximum album cap limitations, royalties for artist-written compositions can decrease due to increases in the statutory rate for outside songs.

---

## COPYRIGHTED ARRANGEMENTS OF COMPOSITIONS IN THE PUBLIC DOMAIN

A number of limitations are placed on recording artists who record a song that is in the public domain (a song no longer protected by copyright). A number of record companies refuse to pay any writer or publisher mechanical royalties for public domain compositions. Other companies pay a flat 50% or 75%-royalty rate. Another approach, accepted by most record companies, provides that the company will pay the recording artist/arranger on the basis of the percentage that ASCAP or BMI pays the writer/artist for the performances of the copyrighted arrangement. ASCAP and BMI will treat an arranger as a writer and pay royalties according to the amount of new material that has been added to the original public domain composition. For instance, a PRO could credit and pay a new song based on a public domain composition at 10% up to 100% (rather than 0% for a public domain non-copyrighted arrangement) based on the significance of the changes.

## New Artist /Developing Artist Pricing

A number of record companies will further reduce the mechanical royalties due to the new artist-writer when they sell the album at a lower list price than that of albums by more established artists. For example, the contract may provide that if the list price of the album by the new artist is between 80% and 66.66% of the top-line suggested retail price of a particular album, the mechanical rate for controlled compositions might be 75% of the already reduced controlled rate. And if the actual retail list is less than 66.66% of the top-line suggested retail list, the new controlled rate could be reduced to 50% of the applicable mechanical rate. Many companies will limit the number of albums sold under this pricing structure (for example, the initial 100,000 units) or will put a time limit on the reduced pricing policy.

## New Contract Developments

Because of significant controversy over certain "standard" record contract clauses as well as the emergence of viable digital distribution of music models, the basic record company contract is in the process of revision for artists. Among the changes being discussed and, in some cases, implemented are the following:

- Maximum 4 album commitment (rather than 6 or 7 common in many agreements).
- One royalty rate for all territories (rather than reduced %s for foreign country sales) and for all formats (CDs, tape, vinyl, etc.).
- Artist royalty base calculations to be based on the published price to the dealer (wholesale price/PPD) less discounts rather than the suggested retail price (SRLP) less container deductions.
- The elimination of the "New Media Royalty deduction" for downloads and Internet sales.
- Elimination of packaging/container deductions for downloads.
- Elimination of escalating royalty rates based on reaching certain sales plateaus.
- The higher album royalty rate to be applied to downloads of individual tracks rather than the lower single royalty rate.
- A review of what recording costs should not be recoupable from artist's royalties.
- The sharing of some types of income on a 50/50 net basis.
- Elimination of free goods in the digital area.
- The 75% artist royalty for "new technology formats" to be increased to 100% when such format exceeds 20% of United States Recording Music Revenues.

- Reasonable audit costs and interest up to a specific figure to be reimbursed to artist if an audit uncovers under payment of royalties over a certain dollar amount or percentage figure (e.g. 10%).
- Reporting of royalties on a monthly basis rather than twice a year.
- Continuing advances to an artist over the contract term to maintain the record company ownership of the sound recording copyright.

- Cross-collateralization of all or part of an artist's non-recording revenue as part of the record deal. These could take the form of a joint venture between the artist and the record company whereby the record company shares in many areas of the artist's career rather than just record sales and master use licenses. The non-recording revenue areas covered could include a share of merchandising, sponsorships, live performance fees, tours, songwriting and music publishing royalties, brand associations, media rights and book projects, among others. The size of record company advances, non-recoupable payments and the revenue split between the artist and the company would be among the factors determining the feasibility or desirability of these type of deals.

## INTERNET

The emergence of the Internet and other new technologies in the distribution of music have changed the way record companies and artists negotiate some of the standard record contract clauses. Some of the main issues involve Web site ownership, the whole area of deductions (packaging, etc.), the calculation of royalties for downloads, sales outside "normal retail channels," performance right payments for artists for digital audio transmissions and many others. These issues are covered in the chapter entitled "The Internet."

# 4

# Music, Money, and Television

Each YEAR, well over 4,000 individual series episodes are produced for the ABC, CBS, and NBC television networks, the Fox, UPN, and WB networks, first-run syndication, pay television, cable services, and PBS. In addition, many movies of the week, miniseries, and one-time specials add to the annual total of television production. This multibillion-dollar business is a lucrative field for composers, theme writers, songwriters, and music publishers. Whether it is a brand-new network or local television series, a series that has been running for years, or a series that was a hit years ago and runs forever in local television, cable, and foreign syndications, the composer and songwriter royalties from a single series can represent a substantial annuity for life.

## THE TELEVISION INDUSTRY

The producers of television shows include most of the same studio production companies and independents that are involved in the feature film area, plus many more. With over 1,000 commercial television stations operating in the United States, thousands of broadcast outlets outside the United States, and the presence of many cable systems and services (HBO, Cinemax, the Movie

Channel, USA Network, etc.), this field generates total annual revenues of many billions of dollars in the United States alone. And with technology expanding the broadcast spectrum at an increasing rate each year in addition to the increasing proliferation of broadcast stations in the foreign marketplace, the demand for product for these stations to air continues at an all-time high.

Despite the increasing need for programming, production companies are dealing with an initial loss on every show produced. Production costs for an individual episode can range from $750,000 to $1 million for ½-hour network shows and from $1 million to over $2 million for 1-hour shows. Renegotiations add even more costs. As the network license fees normally cover between 60% to 80% of these per-episode production costs, production companies must look to future local television syndication, cable and foreign television sales, DVD and home video, and in certain cases, foreign theatrical distribution merely to recoup their initial production investment, much less to make a profit.

## The Making of a Television Program

Practically all television programs are produced by either major production companies affiliated with a studio (Paramount, Warner Bros., Disney, 20th-Century Fox, Sony/Columbia, DreamWorks, MGM, etc.), independent television production companies, production arms of the various television networks or a combination of each. Because the production costs of a weekly series are high, and the back-end royalties of success so great, the networks many times negotiate ownership stakes in weekly series .

For network shows, the first step is usually the production company's "pitching" a script or an idea to the network with the network assuming the costs of a final script if there is interest. If the script is accepted as a possible series, the network and the production company negotiate a fee for the making of a pilot episode. If the pilot goes to series, a per-episode license fee is negotiated, which the network will pay the production company for each episode. The production company will use these license fees to defray part of the costs of production of each episode, with the remaining costs of production borne by the production company. Many of the larger production studios have put under contract a number of successful writers and writer/producers who develop most of the new programming ideas for the studios. Studios are also oftentimes informed as to the type of programming that the network may want for the new season. In those instances, the in-house writers come up with ideas and write the treatments, and the studio pitches it to the network.

With the cost factor of production for network television of prime import to both the television studios as well as the networks, the old days of unlimited money spent for an unlimited number of new season pilots is over. The number of new full-scale pilots has been reduced in recent years, with some studios approaching the networks with short "presentation" films of a prospective new series rather than a full-length pilot. If the network shows interest, it might either order 1 additional full-length episode or pay a certain amount of financing dollars to finish the "presentation" episode. Live "showcases" of new series ideas are also being tried in an effort to cut the costs of producing a pilot.

## The Market

For many years the primary initial market for any series was the ABC, CBS, and NBC television networks. In the 1980s a major change occurred whereby many shows started to be produced for initial airings on individual local television stations rather than on the networks. The success of this concept of the "first-run syndication" of shows (e.g., *Star Trek: The Next Generation* and *The Simpsons*) drastically changed the viewing habits of many households in addition to eroding the network share of viewing. Also, new "networks" were formed (Fox, UPN, WB). The emergence and success of cable and pay cable also created opportunities for the production of original programming for these areas. What once was a straightforward progression of an initial network run plus subsequent sales to specific other types of users has now become somewhat fractured.

The changes affecting where shows are initially aired and where they are sold next has created serious income flow complications for many television composers, since what once was a steady royalty stream from a progression of sales to specific types of broadcasters has now become more tenuous. For clarity, we will first discuss the normal progression of sales that a television series goes through, along with the possible royalty that a composer receives in each medium. We will then look at some of the changes that have taken place in that normal progression and see how those changes have affected a writer's royalty income.

When a show is produced for network television, the network has a license to air each show twice (the initial broadcast plus a repeat) and sometimes has the option to run the show out of the primetime hours (e.g., late at night or during the day) for additional fees. Assuming the show is successful enough to stay on the air, 22 (or fewer) original episodes will be produced and aired during the first season, with some or all of the shows repeated once. An additional 22 new episodes will be produced for each subsequent network season, and the show will cease production once it is finally either canceled by the network or, in some cases, voluntarily closes down. Simultaneously with (or soon after) the network run, the show is sold to foreign television markets. When the show has aired on network television for at least 3 to 4 years (66 or 88 episodes), the show will be syndicated (licensed) to local television stations for either once-a-week airings or "stripping" (broadcast 5 days a week). Because of the need for programming, recent years have sometimes seen series going to syndication with only a season's worth of episodes.

Based on the above scenario, the composer's performance royalties for a show that averaged 10 minutes of background music per episode might look like the following:

| | |
|---|---|
| Network season 1 (44 airings): | $ 68,200 |
| Network season 2 (44 airings): | $ 68,200 |
| Network season 3 (44 airings): | $ 68,200 |
| Network season 4 (44 airings): | $ 68,200 |
| Network season 5 (44 airings): | $ 68,200 |
| Foreign royalties per year: | $120,000 |
| First-year syndication: | $ 45,000 |
| "Strip" syndication: | $170,000 |

In this example, the composer would be receiving close to $70,000 a year for as long as the show aired on network in addition to receiving foreign country royalties approximately 1½ years after the foreign performances took place. Once the show is canceled by the network (in this case after 5 seasons), the writer would start to receive U.S. local television royalties for as long as the series continues to run in syndication, which for many shows means decades. For successful series, syndication many times begins during the network run; the writer may simultaneously be receiving network as well as local television royalties on a performance statement.

In recent years, due to the depressed market prices for local television off-network series as well as the increasing ownership interest by major production companies in the cable area, many network shows are being initially sold to the basic cable services (USA Network, Lifetime, the Family Channel, etc.) rather than local over-the-air television syndication. Since the performance license fees paid by cable services to ASCAP and BMI at this time are significantly lower than those paid by local television stations, many composers have experienced a serious drop in their royalties once a show leaves the networks and bypasses the local television market. In this situation, the composer's network and foreign earnings will be similar to the first example, but the cable earnings might be in the range of $5,000 to $40,000 a year rather than the local television annual earnings of $100,000 or more for a heavily syndicated "strip" show.

Two other markets for television series involve the licensing of the series to pay cable as well as to DVD and home video rentals or sales. Pay cable generates performance royalties for the composer, whereas the home video market rarely does. Many composer contracts, when dealing with home video, provide no additional compensation for these uses and are many times worded as a buy-out or included in the "all in" initial composing fee. The DVD market is becoming a major income source for "old" TV series where entire seasons or the "best of" become million sellers. For many "reality" TV shows, where there are no repeats or syndication possibilities, DVD releases are the next step.

## *TYPES OF TELEVISION MUSIC AND HOW MUSIC IS USED*

The television field, by its very nature, provides composers and songwriters with a broad spectrum of music uses: the series theme song (e.g., James Newton Howard's theme to *ER;* Mike Post's theme to *NYPD Blue*); the underscore (e.g., Dennis McCarthy's episodic scores for *Star Trek: The Next Generation* and *Star Trek: Voyager;* Alf Clausen's scores to *The Simpsons*; the song written for a specific scene in a television show; the use of a preexisting song in a television show (any hit song used in *Friends* or the hit songs sung by the characters in the *Ally McBeal* series); the hit song used as a theme for a series (The Who's "Who Are You" for *CSI: Crime Scene Investigation*; Sammy Cahn's 1955 "Love And Marriage" for *Married . . . With Children*); the network and production company logo; promo music for upcoming or current shows; and the commercial jingle. Each of these types of music may be heard continually throughout the broadcast day of any television station. Moreover, each type generates not only a different initial writing fee (or synchronization fee if it is a preexisting piece of music) but also very different amounts of performance royalties from ASCAP, BMI, SESAC, and foreign performing rights societies.

## *THE TELEVISION MUSIC BUDGET*

One rule of thumb used by some studios and production companies to estimate and arrive at the music budgets for series as well as movies of the week is to allocate $20,000 to $25,000 per hour for all music-related costs. If a show is a 1-hour series or a 2-hour movie of the week, the initial rough music budget would be $20,000 to $25,000 for the series episode and $40,000 to $50,000 for the movie of the week. For a miniseries, the per-hour budget would probably be projected somewhat higher. The budgeted music costs include the composer's creative fee, studio rental time, tape, engineers, musicians, instrument cartage and rentals, music licensing fees, and miscellaneous other music-related costs.

After the initial allocation figure, the actual costs of each project are discussed and calculated more accurately. Some factors that affect the cost are the size of the orchestra that is to record the work, the amount of music to be composed, and the number of preexisting songs that are to be licensed. If a large orchestra is needed and 2 or 3 hit songs are used in the show, the costs of musicians, studio time, and synchronization fees could substantially raise the $25,000 per hour figure. On the other hand, if very little music is needed for the show and no outside songs are being licensed, the music costs could be substantially less than the initially allocated $20,000 to $25,000 rule of thumb. For example, a first-season ½-hour show containing only 2 to 3 minutes of music might be completed with a $3,000 to $7,500 composer "package deal."

Another common budgeting approach involves preparing an initial generic budget from a "read through" of a script. The music supervisor looks at a show and determines whether it needs a full orchestral score or suits itself to an electronic or small-ensemble score. One then determines whether "outside" songs as well as master recordings are necessary. After completing all of the cost estimates, there is a discussion with the producer to see if the figure allocated for music fits into the total budget and to find out if the producer is in agreement with the necessity of all the items included.

One factor that affects the budgets of shows that have been on the air for 3 or 4 years is a change in the way production companies negotiate the terms of the synchronization licenses for outside songs. For shows still in their initial seasons, producers many times negotiate 5-year free television synchronization licenses for between $1,500 to over $3,000 per song. When shows go into their third or fourth seasons, a number of production companies negotiate "all media, in perpetuity, worldwide" synchronization licenses for outside songs at substantially increased fees ($6,000 to over $12,000, for instance). Although this total buy-out approach increases the music budget for shows in the third or fourth season, it is necessary, as the company now knows that it has enough episodes to go into syndication and prefers not to renegotiate 5-year licenses each time they become due. In some cases, this occurs in the first year. For any long-term project (e.g., movies of the week and miniseries), most studios automatically request "worldwide in perpetuity or life of copyright" licenses, since this type of television release almost always has promise of a home video release, a foreign television release, and a possible foreign theatrical release. Although the synchronization costs will be initially higher, money and time will usually be saved by the production company in the future by paying for long-term licenses up front. These life-of-copyright licenses are many times handled on an option basis with respect to each different medium.

## *TELEVISION UNDERSCORE*

The great majority of the music heard on television, whether it be an episodic 1-hour or ½-hour show, a movie of the week, or a miniseries, is the background score. This is the music underneath action or romance scenes and in portrayals of emotion. It is the music that accompanies, enhances, and explains much of the visual elements of television. Its writers are often composers with extensive symphonic training, since the field many times requires writing for and conducting full orchestras. But for many shows, this type of experience is not necessary, as the "feel" of the show may not lend itself to full scoring.

Although television composers may have differing styles, they all agree on the type of show for which they would like to score: a successful series. To be the primary background composer of a long-running series such as *ER, CSI, The X-Files, Law & Order, Star Trek, Cheers, Dallas, M\*A\*S\*H, Murder, She Wrote,* or *Fantasy Island* represents not only very steady work but also substantial domestic and foreign royalties long after the series is canceled.

An extra benefit of being the initial score composer on a series is that most television theme songs are composed by background composers. Many theme songs are written as part of the initial background composing contract that a composer signs, and many others are written by composers who have had past successes with themes whether or not they are the primary composer for a new show. Whereas the score needs to be composed anew for each separate episode of a series, the theme needs to be written only once, and the performance royalties for this 1-time composition can sometimes be more substantial than the underscore composer performance royalties.

*History of the Field.*   Underscore has been an integral part of television shows ever since the dawn of television in the 1940s. What started as live performances of program orchestras supplemented with the use of some "canned" music has evolved into episodic scores many times worthy of feature films, despite lower television music budgets and the extreme time constraints placed on both composing and recording.

The history of television music has been determined much by the public taste for either 1-hour dramatic shows or ½-hour situation comedies ("sitcoms"). During the years when dramatic and action shows are prevalent, the background scorer is able to develop composition to a much greater extent than in sitcom eras, when the use of a background score is usually at a minimum. The introduction of the synthesizer also changed the world of television composing, as it allowed individuals to create extensive timbral and textural variety with 1 instrument. Anyone who watches any evening of television will experience the three types of television background scores: the large orchestral score of 10 to 25 minutes in an hour series, the small-ensemble score of 1½ to 3 minutes for sitcoms, and the electronic music score used in both types of programs.

## THE TELEVISION UNDERSCORE CONTRACT

Most terms in contracts for television music are fairly standard, with the primary differences being whether the composing agreement covers the series pilot, a series pilot plus a commitment for all subsequent episodes, a single show within a running series, or multiple episodes of the same series. Other factors include the stature of the composer, the power of the composer's agent or a "package deal" where the composer bears most of the costs related to the production of the music.

The basic areas covered in every television series underscore contract are the type of services to be performed by the composer, the compensation for those services, the type and placement of on-screen credit, the length of the agreement, the delivery requirements, the ownership of the copyright, and whether the composer or the production company will bear most of the costs of producing the music.

## Composer Services

The standard agreement will provide that the television underscore composer is hired to compose, arrange, orchestrate, record, and produce original music for use in an episode of the television series. The composer shall deliver to the producer a master tape of the score in addition to lead sheets, audio cassette copies, and session contracts no later than the date specified by the producer. The composer must also consult with the producer of the show as to the music and must comply with the recommendations, directions, and requests of the producer in all areas, including those regarding artistic taste and judgment. In addition, the composer is required to make any changes, modifications, or additions to the score when requested to do so by the producer. Many of these contracts also contain an all-purpose clause stating that the composer is to "perform all services and duties customarily performed in this field by a composer, scorer, conductor, arranger, and orchestrator."

## Starting and Completion Dates

With time being very much of the essence in the television industry, starting and completion dates must be strictly adhered to. It is not uncommon for a writer to compose, score, and record an episode in 5 to 7 days (2 or 3 days is sometimes necessary), with dubbing of the music taking place a day later and actual television broadcast occurring within a week after the dubbing. Many series allocate more time for this process, but the nature of the business requires the ability to produce on a moment's notice.

A typical scenario after a composer is hired is for the composer, the music editor, and the show's producer or director to come together for a viewing of a work tape of the program. This is the "spotting" session. At certain points, the tape of the show will be stopped to discuss where the music should begin and end as well as the style or "feel" of the music. After all of the ideas are discussed, the tape progresses to the place for the next music cue. At the end of this session, the composer goes home and makes his or her own notes. Four to five days later the music editor will send to the composer a complete list of the music cues broken down as to the timing and so on. The composer then writes the score over the next 5 to 7 days and shows up at the recording session, where copied parts are given to the musicians. The score is then recorded while viewing the episode on a large screen or video monitor. During some sessions, practically no changes are made by the producer and the score is "perfect" as is. At other sessions, many changes have to be made on the spot with the "studio and musician cost clock" running. Experienced and able composers can write 2 minutes of score and orchestration in a day. In the recording session, it is normal to record approximately 4 minutes of music per hour. For movies of the week, 3 weeks of composing time is considered realistic. The proliferation of home studios has changed the economics and composing time for series.

## Composing Fees

The composing fees paid to television background scorers are unlike those paid to film composers both in terms of the initial writing fee as well as the range of composing fees separating the "top end" composer from the "bottom end" composer. A very good film composer can command a 6-figure composing fee, whereas even the most successful television composer receives far less even when composing for the top money-makers: the 2-hour movie of the week or the miniseries. Although music fees do vary in television based on the stature of the composer and other factors, they tend to be fairly close.

Nonpackage composing fees for episodic series range from $3,500 to more than $7,000 for a 1-hour dramatic series and $1,500 to $3,500 for a ½-hour series. These fees vary based on the amount of music the episode needs, the type of orchestration necessary, and the music budget. The state of the national economy and of the television industry also plays a major role in the amount a composer is paid.

As for package deals, there was a time when $20,000 to $25,000 represented a reasonable range for these "all in" arrangements. The range has decreased somewhat in recent years, and some are now in the high 4-figure range. In these situations, the writer must be exceptionally careful to determine what music costs he or she is undertaking and what costs are excluded from the deal and borne by the producer. For example, someone who agrees to a $10,000 to $15,000 package deal for the music in a 1-hour show and intends to hire musicians and do a professional job will almost always suffer a personal loss. For that reason, many of the lower-fee "package" deals can be made profitable only by using a home studio.

A composer who undertakes a package deal needs not only to exclude certain items from the deal (costs of singers and lyricists, synchronization rights, etc.) but also to be able to "control" a hands-on producer or director who either has difficulty in explaining what he or she wants or constantly changes his or her mind. When possible, a composer should always try to show a producer in advance what he or she is doing, an approach that helps slow the ticking of the financial clock at the session. A composer should also know the studio where the score is being recorded and be assured of a good technical staff and professional engineers.

Two of the most common composer exclusions to a package involve the amount of music and the size of the orchestra. As for the music, a cap should be placed on the maximum number of minutes needed, with additional compensation provided for in the event that additional music is required. As for the orchestra, the composer should be responsible only for what was originally contracted, with the producer being responsible for paying any additional musicians called in at the session.

The following clauses provide a feel for the types of arrangements as well as dollar amounts that composers receive for episodic television scores:

*E X A M P L E 1.* A guaranteed network television 13-episode series
    (1) $3,750 for the pilot
    (2) $2,500 for each of the next 12 episodes, provided that the composer's services are required.
    (3) $2,500 for each episode aired during the second half of the television season in which the composer has written the music

Assuming that the show is picked up for an entire first season of 22 episodes and the composer scores all 22 episodes, total composer compensation would be $56,250.

*E X A M P L E 2.* Individual episode of a network primetime series.
    (1) $2,500 upon completion of all of the composer's services.

*E X A M P L E 3.* A package agreement for a network series
    (1) $12,000 for each episode for which the writer composes the music during the initial network season of the series
    (2) $13,500 for each episode of the second network season for which the writer composes the music
    (3) Fees paid 50% at commencement and 50% on completion

In Example 3, the composer, not the studio, has undertaken most of the costs of the music budget for the series (a package deal), and although the fees are significantly greater than the straight composing deals of Examples 1 and 2, the composer's costs in producing the music can be very high. In Example 4, most of the music production costs are again borne by the composer.

*E X A M P L E 4.* A package agreement for a series
    (1) $25,000 for the initial episode
    (2) $25,000 for each episode of the initial network season
    (3) $27,500 for each episode that the composer scores during the second

network season

Although the figures in this example are higher than those in Example 3, the difference could be due to the relative stature of each composer, the amount of music to be composed, the number of musicians hired, or the inclusion of additional music production costs.

The most sought-after type of contract is the network pilot and series contract, as it ensures that a composer will score not only the pilot episode but also all or many of the series episodes. If the show becomes a hit, the writer can earn hundreds of thousands of dollars a year in domestic and foreign performance monies in addition to the composing fees generated by each new episode.

The producer hires the composer to compose, orchestrate, and conduct for the first 13 episodes of the series, with an option on the composer's services for any episodes produced for the second half of the initial television season on the same terms and conditions as the first 13 episodes. The producer's notice to pick up the option on the composer's services must be given to the composer, in writing, within 10 business days of the show's producer being given an unconditional network commitment for the production of additional shows. The composer compensation is as follows:

*E X A M P L E 5.*  A network pilot and series contract
    (1) $3,750 for the pilot episode
    (2) $2,500 for each of the next 12 episodes that the composer's services are required
    (3) $2,500 for each new episode scored by the composer and aired during the second half of the television season

In example 5, the composer would receive a total of $56,250 in composing fees, assuming the composer wrote the music for all 22 episodes of the network season ($3,750 for the pilot, $30,000 for episodes 2 through 13, and $22,500 for the final 9 episodes). Normally, there is no minimum number of episodes referred to for the second half of the season, as the show could be canceled anytime during this period.

*E X A M P L E 6.*  A pilot and series "package deal" contract
    (1) $17,500 for the pilot
    (2) $15,000 for each subsequent episode of the series
    (3) $20,000 for each episode aired during the series' second season

Another variation of the package deal might read $14,000 for each episode of the first season, with an increase to $16,000 per episode for the second season.

In recent years, many of the "full series" contracts have come to be handled as a continuing sequence of options on the producer's part, whereby the composer is paid an amount for each episode for which he or she "renders and completes" services, and continues to receive the contract money each time the producer exercises its option for the composer's services for each subsequent series episode.

## Screen Credit

The composer's screen credit for episodic television will be in either the show's opening or closing credits. The type and placement of the composer credit is a negotiable item. The following are sample clauses:

1. "Composer shall receive credit in the form of MUSIC BY (*name of composer*) in the opening titles on a separate card."
2. "Composer shall receive credit on a separate card in the closing titles in the form of MUSIC BY (*name of composer*)."
3. "Composer shall receive credit of MUSIC BY in such place and size as Producer may elect."

## Exclusivity of Composer's Services

Although many television music contracts merely state that the composer must perform all of the services required according to the production schedule and the producer's direction and instructions, some contracts directly specify the exclusive nature of the agreement:

1. "Though the composer's services are on a nonexclusive basis (the composer can work on other projects during the term of this agreement), this project is to be considered as "first priority."
2. "Composer agrees not to render services of a similar nature to anyone unless the producer's specific written consent is received."

## Ownership of the Copyright

Practically all television background composing contracts fall under the rubric of "employee for hire" or "work made for hire," under which the producer becomes the author and copyright owner of the work. The grant-of-rights clause that the composer signs is normally similar to those contained in feature film composing contracts, in that the producer becomes the owner of "all now or hereafter existing rights of every kind and character whatsoever throughout the world, whether or not such rights are known, recognized, or contemplated." The term "producer" in this context normally means the studio or production company making the television series.

## Music Publishing

The standard contractual arrangement in the television industry gives all of the music publishing rights to the producer by means of the employee-for-hire contract. As the owner of the copyright and all of the rights that flow from that ownership, the producer is not only allowed to collect income generated by the musical work from most sources but also is able to license to others all of the rights of copyright, rights that can generate millions of dollars of royalty income.

Occasionally, writers with substantial past success may be able to negotiate some retention of partial publishing rights to their work. In doing so, though, the up-front composing payment may be reduced as part of the negotiation with the production company. Other times, a writer may keep all or a portion of the publishing if the production company is a small one or one not knowledgeable about the "value" of owning music copyrights. Those situations, however, are the exception rather than the rule.

## Membership in a Performing Right Society

"The composer must be a member in good standing of a performing right society as well as any other applicable labor organization, guild, or union that may have jurisdiction" or "composer's public performance royalties throughout the world are to be paid directly to Composer from Composer's own affiliated performing right society" are variations of the standard clause whereby composers are assured of receiving the writer's share of performance royalties whenever the series is broadcast anywhere throughout the world. This clause is essential to any contract, as the U.S. and worldwide performance royalties represent, for most composers, their main source of composing income. The following example of the possible composer earnings from a successful show should help put the importance of this clause into perspective:

*E X A M P L E.*  A composer has 15 minutes of background music in each of 66 episodes (3 seasons) of a 1-hour primetime network television series. All 66 episodes are repeated once (132 airings), and the show is sold to foreign countries and eventually widely syndicated on U.S. local television stations. Possible composer royalties might be as follows:

| | |
|---|---|
| U.S. network television airings: | $316,000 |
| Foreign television performances: | $196,000 |
| Initial-year U.S. local television performances: | $110,000 |
| Total performance right income: | $622,000 |

Although the performance rights clause was a fairly standard one during the 1960s and 1970s, attempts to modify and condition the clause emerged in the 1980s. The modifications in these contracts involved primarily the instances where the producer could license a show's music directly to a user, thereby bypassing the performing right organizations completely.

Although composers have had for decades the right to license their music directly to a user, the new wording of these clauses became a concern, since most did not provide any specific amount to be paid to a composer when a show was broadcast, nor did these provisions make any specific mention of the all-important principle of continuing writer royalties for the life of copyright based on continuing performances of the work.

Two variations on this clause follow:

1. "In the event that the society does not license the performing rights in the background score, the producer may license the score directly and negotiate a reasonable fee according to industry standards and shall divide such negotiated fee between writer and producer."
2. "In the event that a broadcasting station does not have a blanket nondramatic performing right license with ASCAP or BMI and the station's agreement with the producer states that a license must be provided, then the producer may license the score directly. Once the license is issued, the producer has to negotiate with the writer in good faith as to what the fee should be. If no agreement can be reached, the negotiation will go to arbitration."

As new variations on the standard clause continue to be introduced during the negotiations, many writers and their representatives have expressed concerns that not only are many of the clauses vague as to what the performance fees would be but many also seem to provide for a 1-time-only fee with no reference to any entitlement right to continuing writer royalties when the show is rebroadcast.

One variation of this clause actually spells out the factors that should be taken into account in negotiating the direct license fee, with the listed considerations being the amount and type of music use, the status of the composer, and other "relevant factors of custom and practice in the industry." Although this type of contract actually has a list of items to be considered in negotiating a fee, some of the items listed continue to be very vague.

A major concern of many composers with these clauses is the effect that they could have on a composer's foreign royalties. The foreign television market is now larger than the U.S. market, and this profitable source of composer royalties may be given up entirely if a composer agrees to some of these clauses. The best advice to give on handling this type of clause is to talk to one's lawyer or representative so that he or she can advise as to both the short-term and long-term ramifications of signing such a document and negotiate accordingly.

## Suspensions and Terminations

Suspensions come into play when either the writer cannot perform his or her services or the production company has to put a halt to production for any of various reasons. The key triggering terms of "disability," "default," and "force majeure" are covered in the section on feature film contracts in Chapter 5, and those same definitions apply to the television world.

In the event that any disability, default, or force majeure occurs during the term of the agreement, the composer's services are suspended for the period of the occurrence. If the suspension is due to composer disability or default (e.g., the composer's mental or physical inability to compose or the composer's failure, refusal, or neglect to compose), no compensation is paid to the composer and, in many cases, the composer is prevented from working for anyone else. If the suspension occurs owing to a force majeure (e.g., the production of the show has to cease due to labor disputes, fire, an act of God, or war), the composer is normally allowed to work for others as long as he or she is able to resume work immediately on the original production when it again commences. If the force majeure situation continues for a certain amount of time (5 weeks, for example), the composer can terminate the agreement, with payment due for all of the composer's work completed prior to the force majeure. The producer can also terminate the composer if the composer suffers an illness or incapacity (disability) continuing over a stated amount of business days or a force majeure situation lasting more than a set number of weeks. In such a situation the producer is obligated for all composer payments due up to the time of the suspension. If the composer's default results in termination, the producer is under no obligation to the composer for any payments due prior to the default situation.

Some contracts provide for the absolute right of the producer to terminate a composer's services. These provisions normally refer to the producer's "sole discretion" and provide for composer termination at a stated period of time (3 weeks, for instance) after receipt by the composer of the producer's termination notice. Some contracts even provide for a similar composer right to terminate the contract with the producer.

## Disposition of the Score

As with feature films, the producer has no obligation to use the background score in the program or to exercise any of the rights granted to it under the agreement. If the producer does not like the score for any reason and decides not to use it, the producer can do so, with the only obligation to the composer being the payment of all of the compensation provided for in the contract. A corollary to this clause is the provision whereby the composer waives "moral rights," with the producer retaining the right to rearrange, edit, cut, and add to the score any time the producer may so choose. Though this is not a heavily negotiated clause, composers should be aware that an occasional practice in certain countries is to replace the U.S. composer's original episode score with a local composer's score when the show is aired in that country. Such a replacement score, if used with permission, can have a profound effect on a composer's foreign earnings, and negotiations should bear in mind this possibility.

## Transportation and Expenses

Since most television scoring and recording occurs in the cities where the main production facilities are (Los Angeles and New York), most television composer contracts do not provide for transportation and living expenses. Owing to the increasing production and studio costs in those cities, though, a trend has arisen toward producing shows and occasionally scoring and recording the music elsewhere (e.g., Vancouver or Toronto). In instances where the composer is required to score and record the music away from his or her home base, business or first-class transportation, hotel, and meals are contractually provided for.

## Share of Advance Payments

Most contracts state that the composer will not share in any advance or guarantee payments for the music that the producer may receive from making a subpublishing, licensing, or other collection type of agreement. For example, if the producer of a television show makes an agreement with another publisher for representation in a specific territory and receives an advance against future royalties generated in that territory, the composer will usually not share in the advance but will receive composer royalties as they are earned.

## Warranties and Indemnifications

The composer represents that he or she is free to enter into the agreement, that the music will be totally original to the composer, that the music does not infringe upon any other copyrighted composition, and that no rights in the music have been previously conveyed by the composer to any other party. The composer also agrees to indemnify the producer "from and against any liability, loss, claims, costs, and expenses arising from" the material that the composer has provided for the show. If a claim does arise and the producer takes on the responsibility to defend it, the composer will usually be liable for many of the costs expended in fighting the claim or litigation as well as the amount of any adverse judgment in the case.

## Assignments

The producer usually has the right to assign or license the rights to the agreement to any other party.

## Royalty Payments

Most background music agreements contain an attachment or exhibit that specifies the various types of royalties that will be paid should the music be exploited beyond the broadcasting medium. (These royalty figures are covered in depth later in this chapter.) A typical exhibit would cover the composer's share of earnings derived from licenses covering the sale of piano copies, sheet music, portfolios, band arrangements, mechanical rights, synchronization rights, and foreign uses. Soundtrack album royalties would also be specified.

## Theatrical Version Release

A fairly common clause in 2-hour television movie as well as television miniseries contracts is the theatrical version clause, which provides additional composer compensation if the movie or miniseries is released outside of the United States as a theatrical (movie theater) release. Though there will be a definition of what actually constitutes a "theatrical release," a sample clause might provide for an additional one-time composer payment of $15,000 if the movie is released in two or more international territories. The amount of this additional compensation is an item subject to negotiation. Some of the factors taken into account include the amount of the original composing fee as well as whether or not the movie or miniseries was a "package" deal.

---

# TELEVISION SYNCHRONIZATION RIGHTS (GETTING SONGS INTO SERIES, SPECIALS, AND MADE-FOR-TV MOVIES)

## The Importance of Hit Songs

In contemporary television, music has taken on a significant role in the success or failure of a series, miniseries, special, or made-for-TV movie. Because of this significance, producers and their music supervisors put a special emphasis on selecting hit songs or recognizable standards that are right for a particular scene or project. One has only to watch reruns of *Happy Days, M\*A\*S\*H, Cheers, Friends, The Simpsons,* or *Saturday Night Live* to realize the impact of well-known songs in helping a show succeed (see Table 4.1 for examples). Granted, the premise, writing, and acting all have to be there for a program to make it, but if a television program has these basics, good music can add that final touch to the elusive formula of what makes a hit.

TABLE 4.1   Hit Song Used in Television Series

| Song | Series | Use |
|---|---|---|
| "Con Te Partiro" (Andrea Boccelli) | *The Sopranos* | Background to Tony Soprano talking to his wife on the phone and also during a barbecue at the Soprano's house. |
| "Footloose" | *Will & Grace* | Background while Kevin Bacon and Will do their version of the classic film song. |
| "Your Song" | *The Simpsons* | Elton John sings for Apu and his wife in the back of Kwik E Mart on Valentine's Day. |
| "My Way" | *Sabrina the Teenage Witch* | Sung to the Sex Pistols recording by a vampire driving a car. |
| "Begin the Beguine" and "Night and Day" | *Friends* | Played on a stereo while Joey is taking dance lessons with the superintendent on the roof of the building. |
| "Who'll Stop the Rain" | *Cold Case* | Background while a killer and his brother are taken from a car into the police station in the rain. |
| "Leader of the Pack" | *American Dreams* | Sung by Hilary Duff as the lead singer of the Shangri-Las on American Bandstand. |
| "Hot, Hot, Hot" | *Everybody Loves Raymond* | Background as Raymond talks to a woman at his highschool reunion. |

## The Phone Call from the TV Producer

*Setting:*

Office of the Vice President of Business Affairs for a major music publisher.

*The Phone Call:*

MUSIC SUPERVISOR: Hi, this is the music supervisor from (Name of Television Series). We'd like to use the song (Name of Composition) in a scene for an episode in which two of the characters find themselves in a singles bar.

PUBLISHER: How would you like to use the song and what rights do you need?

MUSIC SUPERVISOR: The use will be a 2-minute background vocal, as we'll be using (Name of Performer)'s record on a jukebox. There is a possibility that one of the characters may also sing a few lines either while the record is being played or a couple of scenes later. For your information, I'm getting a fee quote from (Name of Record Company) so we can use the master recording with his actual performance. For the use, we'll need a worldwide price quote for the following media:

1. A 5-year free television license
2. An option for a 5-year renewal
3. An option for a life-of-copyright free television license
4. Options for a pay television license for both 5 years and for life of copyright as well as an airline option
5. An option for all television rights for life of copyright
6. An option for a home video buy-out
7. An option for theatrical use outside the United States
8. An option to use the song in television promos for the series

PUBLISHER: That's quite a laundry list. When do you need the quotes?

MUSIC SUPERVISOR: Well, we're really under the gun. The scenes are being filmed tomorrow and I need your confirmation whether we can use the song and how much it will cost almost immediately, so we can know whether we'll have to go with another song.

PUBLISHER: Okay. Let's go through the list: $2,500 for the 5-year free TV license and $3,000 for the 5-year renewal. Life-of-copyright free television will cost $5,000. Pay TV for 5 years will be $3,500 and for life of copyright $6,000. All television life-of-copyright will be $11,000. Home video will be $10,000. Foreign theatrical will be $9,000. Airlines will be $3,000. And out-of-contact television promos will be an extra $2,000 per week.

MUSIC SUPERVISOR: Thanks. A couple of the fees seem a bit high, but between you and me, they all fit in with our budget. I'll send you a letter confirming our understanding and, if the song is used, I'll request a license.

With over 100 television companies in the United States and usually over 400 series, specials, and made-for-TV movies actually in production at any given time, the previous call occurs over 100 times a day virtually 365 days every year. It is a call that can take on many variations and consist of many twists. It is a call that everyone hopes for. It is a call that can produce hundreds of thousands of dollars in future income. It is a call that requires an immediate answer. And it is a call that you had better be ready to take. With 4,000,000 viewers watching even the lowest-rated network series and over 100,000,000 tuned into the best, television can be the answer to a songwriter's prayer. Because of its importance, this chapter reveals what you need to know about getting your songs on television and making the right deal.

## Negotiating the Television License for a Song

When a producer wants to use an existing musical composition in a television program, weekly series, special, miniseries, or made-for-TV movie, permission must, with few exceptions, be secured from the music publisher who owns the song. The producer or music supervisor of the show will decide what song he or she wants to use in the program and the scene in which it will appear, how the song will be used (e.g., background vocal or instrumental, sung by a character on camera, over the opening or ending credits), and the media needed (e.g., free television, pay television, subscription television, pay-per-view, or basic cable). The producer or its "music clearance" representative will then contact the owner of the composition, describe the context of the program and particular scene in which the song will be used; ask for a specified period of time to use the song in the program (usually from 3 years to life of copyright), negotiate a fee, and then sign what is known in the television business as a "synchronization license."

In many cases, the "synch license" is signed after the first broadcast of the program, but the negotiations and securing of permission to use a song virtually always occur prior to the inclusion of the song in the program or, at the latest, prior to the initial broadcast date. Some series and made-for-TV movies have quite a bit of lead time before their actual air date, and then the song permission negotiations take place at a reasonable pace. Most television programs secure price quotations from music publishers for the use of songs either during the scriptwriting stages of a project or immediately after a final script for an episode has been approved. Many weekly series and some miniseries and specials, however, clear music while scenes are being shot or, because of impromptu ad-libs during taping, last-minute additions, or editing delays, a few days prior to actual broadcast and sometimes even after the airing.

On occasion, the producer may also want to alter the original lyrics of a song to make a scene work better or add a laugh, and such a request will always be a part of the initial negotiations. Since home video has become an important ancillary market for television programming, negotiations (many times on an option basis) will take place for home use as well. Considering that some television programs (normally miniseries, made-for-TV movies, and 2-hour episodes of certain series) are also released as films to motion picture theaters in countries outside the United States, the producer may also request rights and negotiate additional fees for such nontelevision uses. And since many television programs are eventually broadcast in media other than that on which they were initially aired (e.g., a series originally made for and broadcast on pay television being subsequently shown in the free over-the-air syndication market), a producer may also request option prices for a wide range of additional media such as pay television for the world outside the United States, public broadcasting stations, nonpay cable in the United States and Canada, and pay cable in certain foreign countries, as well as any number of variations and combinations of these.

## *Actual Fees Charged for Songs Used in Television Programming*

Free Television (ABC, CBS, NBC, Fox, WB, UPN, Independent Local Stations, and Syndication). The standard synchronization fees charged by music publishers usually range from $1,500 to over $3,000 for the use of a song in a television series for unlimited television distribution of the program for 5 to 6 years throughout the world. For example, when you hear a well-known song in the background on virtually any network series, you can assume that the use of the song cost the producer from $1,500 to over $3,000 for a 5-year free television license. Certain producers occasionally request that the term of such licenses be for longer periods (for example, 10 to 15 years at either double or triple the aforementioned rates or guaranteed options after expiration of the initial license period at specifically agreed-upon or "to be negotiated in good faith" fees). And others sometimes request life-of-copyright synch licenses for songs used in certain hit series, with fees ranging from $6,000 to over $10,000 depending on a number of factors, including the music budget for the program, whether the song is a well-known standard or current hit as opposed to a new song in need of exposure, the song's importance to the series episode and the particular scene in which it is performed, how many times it is used in the program, the manner of the use (e.g., background music from a jukebox or sung by a character on camera), and the song's remaining copyright life.

Under a free television synchronization license, the music publisher gives a series producer the right to include a musical composition in a particular television program and to sell that program to any station in the world without any further payment. For example, the series can be sold to a television network for early-morning, primetime or late-night airing and unlimited repeats, to syndication, or on a station-by-station basis during the term of the license, with the only conditions being that the television stations showing the series do not charge their viewers a fee to watch the program and that they have a valid performance license, which permits them to broadcast the music contained in the episode or series.

In addition to the length of the term of the license, the actual timing of the song's use is also important in negotiating a fee. For example, if the duration of the song used in the program is less than a full or substantial usage (30 seconds or less), then the fees charged by many publishers are reduced. But if the song is a recognizable hit or standard and the use is important to the context of a particular scene (such as a main character singing the song on camera or a background mood use that is essential to the plot of the episode or series), there is usually no reduction in the synchronization fee even if only 15 to 30 seconds are actually used. One example of a show that usually merits reduced synchronization fees is *Jeopardy!*, since only 10 to 30 seconds of a hit song are usually broadcast as part of one of the audio question-and-answer categories. As an illustration, the famous Jerome Kern–Oscar Hammerstein II standard "Ol' Man River" from *Showboat* was performed for a few seconds as a musical clue in the "Famous Rivers" category. The answer of the Mississippi was correctly given, the song was mentioned by Alex Trebek, and the copyright owner received important exposure from this brief but widely watched use. Another example from the same show was the use of the theme from the motion picture *Jaws* as a clue to the category of "Scary Movies." Alex Trebek asked, "What monster would you expect to meet after you've heard this music?," the *Jaws* theme was played, the answer of a great white shark was correctly given, and the game moved on to a new category.

The synchronization fees to use master recordings (the original hit record of a song such as Whitney Houston's "I Will Always Love You" or Stevie Wonder's "I Just Called to Say I Love You") are normally more costly, depending on the type of license request, with such monies paid to the record company that owns the rights to the single or album cut being used. The reason that such "master fees" are usually more expensive than those charged for the song itself is that there are no performance royalties paid to the record companies or performers for the broadcast of recordings in the United States. The existence of such broadcast performance royalties for songwriters and music publishers, which continue as long as a particular television program is broadcast, enable music publishers to keep their synchronization fees at a low or moderate level. Record companies, however, do not receive any such royalties based on how many times a program is broadcast; therefore, they usually charge more for the use of a master recording because their only income will be the 1-time payment for the synchronization license.

PAY OR SUBSCRIPTION TELEVISION (HBO, CINEMAX, THE DISNEY CHANNEL, SHOWTIME). The prevalent fees charged by music publishers under a 5-year license for the use of a song in a program on pay television range from $2,500 to over $3,500 but, as with network or syndicated programs, can be increased or decreased depending on the length of the use, the stature of the song, whether it is background music or sung on camera, its importance to the plot of the show, and whether it is used more than once in a given episode. The territory for such licenses used to be the United States and Canada, but with the emergence of pay and cable television in most foreign countries, producers are more and more frequently requesting worldwide rights. For many programs, the term of the synchronization license is from 3 to 5 years but can be shorter or longer depending on the popularity of the program and distribution needs of the producer. For example, some producers ask for only 2 to 3 years, as they may feel that the pay television life of the project may be short. Others request terms of from 5 to 15 years, and many request life-of-copyright licenses, with fees raised accordingly.

There is a growing trend for producers to request guaranteed options at set fees or at "good faith negotiation" prices to ensure that if a program continues to be broadcast after the initial license term has expired, the procedures for renewing the license will be predetermined. For example, a 25% increase may be negotiated for each successive renewal period, or there might be an actual dollar schedule for all possible option periods in the initial contract (e.g., $2,500 for the first 5 years, $3,000 for the second 5 years, $3,500 for the tenth through fifteenth years, etc.) to prevent any chance of a misunderstanding between the publisher and producer as to the music cost of a show's future distribution. Obviously, these guaranteed option clauses are extremely important to a television producer, as they assure that any song put in a series will remain in that series regardless of any future changes in the copyright ownership of the composition (e.g., the song reverting to the writer) or the personnel at the music publishing company that gave the initial permission—an important guarantee if the program is a hit. After all, it could get very expensive if a major star in an episode of a hit series sang a song on camera and there was no guarantee that the song could be used in repeats of that series after the 5- or 10-year term of the initial synchronization license expired. Because of this, many of the major television producers license all outside songs for the entire term of copyright of the particular composition rather than dealing with option agreements—a much more expensive approach, but one that guarantees that a song will not have to be taken out of the program at some future date.

Basic Cable Television. Many television programs appear only on basic cable, the type of nonpay system that many viewers use to get better reception, pick up distant signals, or receive programming not available from the over-the-air free television stations. The synchronization fees charged by music publishers for the use of songs in programs distributed via basic cable are in the range of those charged for free television. Depending on the actual number of subscribers for a particular system, however (for example, an area where only 1 million households receive cable), fees can be lower. Many times, basic cable is included in the free television or pay cable price quote.

Educational And Public Broadcasting Television (PBS). Because of the noncommercial, listener-supported nature of public television and the lack of substantial government funding for its programming, the following "reduced" synchronization fees have been established by the various interested parties for music used in PBS-distributed shows:

*Programs First Broadcast from 2003 to 2007:*

3-year license for the use of a song in a program
$112.40 per feature performance
$56.81 per background performance
$33.75 per minute for a concert usage
$56.81 per theme (single program or first series program)
$23.06 per theme (other series program)

The music publishers who belong to the Harry Fox Agency receive the benefits of this formula under their blanket agreement with the agency. Under procedures worked out between the Public Broadcasting Service and the Harry Fox Agency, PBS will send the Fox Agency copies of all music cue sheets for shows broadcast on its affiliated stations. Fox Agency personnel then review the cue sheets, identify the songs controlled by its publisher members and how they are used, bill PBS for the appropriate fees, and then distribute the monies to the publishers of the songs used. For example, if a song was sung by an actor on camera ("featured use") in a PBS program in 2003 through 2007, the fee would be $112.40. If a song was used as background music, the fee would be $56.81. And if a song was used as a theme for a series, the synch fees charged the producer would be $56.81 for the first program and $23.06 for each subsequent episode. As with all television synch fees, the publisher of the song would pay the songwriter a minimum of ½ of the monies received.

Additionally, if the program is still being broadcast on PBS stations after the initial 3-year license has expired, a further payment of 25% of the original fees will be paid by the show's producer for an additional 1-year license, a 50% payment for another 3-year license, with 25% payments due for each succeeding 3-year period during which the show is aired. Rather than paying fees every 3 years, producers also have the option of paying an additional 100% fee prior to the end of the initial 3-year period. If this payment is made, the producer will be entitled to use the song in that program indefinitely.

ALL TELEVISION MEDIA. Rather than request separate licenses for free television, cable television, and pay television, a number of producers will ask for an "all television" synchronization license, usually for the life of copyright of the composition being used. Pursuant to the terms of such a license, the producer is able to distribute the program via any television medium without having to resecure permission from the music publisher. Since this type of license is all-encompassing, fees are fairly expensive and range from $7,500 to over $12,000.

*Short-Term Free TV Licenses.*    Many times, producers of late-night network, local, or syndicated programs being broadcast on nonpay television stations will request licenses for periods of less than the standard 5 years. Some examples are certain music-oriented programs, which usually ask for 1 to 3 years with options, since their programs concentrate on current hits with the options designed primarily for "greatest hits" or anniversary shows; topical programs that are not likely to be rerun after 3 years; repeats of the *Tonight Show, Letterman,* and *Saturday Night Live;* and game shows such as *Jeopardy!* that occasionally use hit songs in their question-and-answer categories and usually request short-term licenses for either the United States and Canada or (depending on their distribution plans) the world. The synchronization fees charged by publishers are normally reduced for such "lesser term" licenses.

*Multiple Uses of a Song in a Show.*   In many cases, a song will be used a number of times during a made-for-TV movie, miniseries, special, or series episode. For example, it may be used as background music to a scene and also sung on camera by one of the characters, used as background music in a number of different scenes, used as the theme in addition to background mood music, or used once in a scene and also under the closing credits. The initial fee quotation should take into account that a song is used more than once, and the price is almost always increased accordingly even though the actual cumulative duration of the use may be less than a full version (e.g., 3 background uses of 10, 25, and 40 seconds or a nightclub performer singing partial versions of the same song in two different scenes of the same episode). In most instances when a television producer requests a song, he or she will specify that there will be more than one use, and a publisher will be able to quote a fee that reflects such multiple uses. Portions of the script or scene descriptions will also be provided on request. Because of the time constraints involved in shooting network television series, continuing script revisions, and the likelihood that changes will be made while a scene is being shot, the experienced publisher will check the actual music cue sheets (or watch the program) to make sure that the song was used in accordance with original request from the producer.

A number of approaches are used to price multiple uses of a song in an episode, with some publishers charging what 1 full use of 3 minutes would have cost (regardless of the number of shortened versions, as long as the 3-minute total is not exceeded), but most charging extra for additional uses regardless of the aggregate timing (e.g., $10,000 for all television for the first use and between $1000 to over $3,000 for each additional use). As in other areas, however, each licensing negotiation is somewhat different from the others that have preceded it, and each must be dealt with on a case-by-case basis after weighing all the factors involved in the particular request.

*Additional Payment Formulas for Television (When There Are Numerous Songs Used in a Show).*   Certain television programs such as specials or anniversary shows use large amounts of existing songs. If these shows were to be licensed at the free television 5-year rate of $1,500 to $3,000 per song, the costs would be prohibitive. For example, many of these shows use clips of 5 to 15 seconds of each song, and if 50 such uses occurred, the producer would have to spend between $60,000 and $125,000 for the music synchronization rights alone—a figure that doesn't take into account the additional fees paid to a composer for new music written specifically for the show, option fees for different media, or payments made to record companies for the use of master recordings. Since such an aggregate music budget is in almost all cases unaffordable, music publishers will normally agree to reduce their fees and negotiate a payment formula based on the duration of each performance and how such timing fits into certain negotiated categories (e.g., less than 10 seconds, between 1 and 2 minutes, or in excess of 1 minute). For example:

| Timing (Seconds) | Points | Synch Fee For Each Song |
|---|---|---|
| 1 to 30 | 1 | $400 |
| 31 to 60 | 2 | $500 |
| 61 to 120 | 3 | $600 |
| over 120 | 4 | $750 |

*Foreign Theatrical Distribution of U.S.-Produced Television Programming.* For most television shows (because of their ½-hour or 1-hour duration and subject matter), the possibility of release as a motion picture in countries outside the United States is nil. Capsulized versions of miniseries are sometimes released for foreign theatrical distribution, however. In addition, some of the major television producers are increasingly securing options from music publishers to cover possible foreign theater release for 2-hour made-for-TV movies and series episodes (usually as part of a 2- or 3-episode combination). The fees charged for this type of license are normally between $5,000 and $8,000 but can be more depending on, among other factors, whether there are multiple uses throughout the miniseries or television movie. The term of such foreign theatrical release licenses are for the life of the copyright of a song (like the standard motion picture synchronization license) rather than the 5- to 15-year television license requested by many producers.

*Television Performance Royalties (ASCAP and BMI).* One of the reasons why synchronization fees are low is the future income that can be generated from broadcast of a series or program on television stations in the United States, Canada, and other countries around the world. This entire area is a complex one, but the next page examples should give the reader a basic grasp of the type of money that songwriters and music publishers earn from ASCAP and BMI when music is broadcast on a primetime network television series.

*Promotional Spots for Television Programs.* Occasionally, television producers will ask for the use of a song in a television advertising campaign.

| How Music Is Used | *Combined Royalties to the Writer and Publisher for 1 Primetime Network Television Broadcast* |
|---|---|
| Sung on Camera | $3,000 |
| Background to a Scene (3 minutes) | $1,200 |
| Theme of Program | $1,300 |

designed to promote an upcoming series or bring attention to an important event in a current program. The licenses for such uses are normally very limited and the synchronization monies paid to the music publisher and songwriter are usually between $1,500 and $4,000 per week. In addition to the synchronization fees, these uses can also be very valuable in terms of reexposure of the song to millions of viewers as well as in performance income. Consequently, many publishers license these uses at prices that are very affordable to the producers or television stations requesting permission.

An example of a network television promo is:

| *Song* | *Program* | *Use* |
|---|---|---|
| "YMCA" | *ABC Television* | Network promo announcing the new Friday night lineup of shows/"YMCA" changed to "TGIF." |

*Songs Used as Episode Title of Television Series and as Theme or Background Music.* On occasion, a television series producer will want to use the title of a famous song as the title of a particular series episode and also employ the song in various scenes for dramatic effect. In such cases, the music publisher must find out whether the series episode is a dramatization of the story of the song or if the producer just wants to use the title and song because it helps the mood of an already written script. The series *Jake and the Fat Man* was famous for its use of standards as both the title of each episode and as background either at the start or throughout the episode. In almost all cases, the title and song were used only for dramatic effect and because they fit into the plot of the episode. In such cases, the fees charged are normally between 50% to 200% above those quoted for the use of a song in a television show but can be more, depending on the stature of the composition being used, the uniqueness of its title and whether it has ever been used before in such a manner.

## *Hit Songs Used as Television Show Themes*

| Show | Theme |
|------|-------|
| *CSI/CSI: Miami* | "Who Are You" |
| *CSI: Miami* | "Won't Get Fooled Again " |
| *Providence* | "In My Life" |
| *Las Vegas* | "A Little Less Conversation" |
| *Married ... With Children* | "Love and Marriage" |

Rather than hiring a composer to write a theme song for a new television series, many producers will use a well-known song as the show's opening and closing theme. This is also true for revival series where the new producers do not have the rights to the theme song used in the original series. When presented with such a request, a music publisher may take one of a number of different approaches to handle the licensing, the most prevalent being a per-show fee for each series episode. For example, synch payments of from $1,800 to over $3,000 per episode for a 5-year license are not uncommon, with additional fees charged for "bumpers" (the 5- to 10-second intros to commercial breaks). It is also becoming more common for a life-of-copyright license to be negotiated for use of the song in the series, with the fees ranging from $7,500 to $12,000 per episode. Each case, however, must be treated on its own merits recognizing the stature of the song being requested (e.g., current hit, well-known standard, or prior hit in need of new exposure), the budget for the series, the policies of the production company producing the show, the performance monies that will be earned from ASCAP or BMI, and the possibility of a television series soundtrack album or hit single coming from the program.

*Music Clearance (Getting Permission to Use Songs in Television Series).* Most television producers do not have the resources to find out who owns the rights to the vast number of musical compositions that they may want to use in their productions. Because the job of tracking down rights can be monumental (close to 10 million songs are registered with ASCAP and BMI alone) and has been made even more difficult because of the reversion laws in many countries and an emerging trend toward 2 or more copyright owners of a single song, producers who do not have the finances for in-house staffs rely on a number of independent service organizations to assist them in their investigation, negotiation, and clearance of rights to use existing songs in television series. Granted, producers can contact ASCAP, BMI, and the Harry Fox Agency for information on the ownership of selected compositions, but producers then have to follow up and negotiate licenses, a process than can be expensive and time consuming. Consequently, a large number of them use independent "clearance" organizations to fulfill this need. The following section discusses a number of alternative ways of finding out who owns a song.

INDEPENDENT MUSIC CLEARINGHOUSES. A number of independent agencies represent certain television producers who do not have in-house researcher/negotiators. These agencies' sole purpose is to find out who owns a song, explain how a song is to be used, and request (and many times negotiate) fee quotes for television synch licenses. The fees for such research, negotiation, and licensing services are paid by the television producer on a per-show, per-song, or flat-fee series basis.

IN-HOUSE TELEVISION PRODUCTION STAFFS. Many producers have personnel on staff to "clear" (i.e., get permission for a negotiated fee) preexisting outside music that will be used in a television program. For example, Twentieth Century-Fox Television, Warner Bros. TV, Columbia Pictures, Paramount TV, and Universal all have in-house music clearance departments, which negotiate the terms of synchronization licenses for outside music used in their series.

THE HARRY FOX AGENCY. At one time, many producers employed the services of the Harry Fox Agency, Inc., in New York for music clearance. This agency (which has information on a vast number of songs and would also research ownership rights when necessary) would contact its publisher members for permission and secure a "price quote," which was then forwarded to the television producer. A commission of between 4% and 5% was charged for a worldwide synchronization license secured through this service, which included the preparation and issuance of licenses. This commission was deducted from the license fee. In 2002, this service was discontinued.

LAW FIRMS. On occasion, synch requests will be handled by attorneys or paralegals. Some of the major entertainment law firms now have separate departments (usually composed of paralegals) dealing with this area for the firm's television producer clients. At one time, the licensing of music for television was a fairly straightforward and uncomplicated business. In recent years, however, because of the many reversion laws in countries such as England, Australia, and Canada, the need for a producer to secure options to extend its rights into new media, the potential inclusion of broadcast rights as part of the negotiation of the synchronization license, the somewhat complex determinations involved in the issue of who really owns the rights to license the extra years of U.S. copyright protection added to all songs written prior to 1978, the ramifications of the *Rear Window* case, and the increasing trend of having 2 to 10 separate publisher owners of a song (many of which have no knowledge of the music industry), the business of licensing hit songs and famous standards has become extremely complex. Consequently, the trend to use law firms and specialized clearance agencies to negotiate synchronization rights will more than likely continue to grow.

ASCAP AND BMI. Both ASCAP and BMI have "index" or repertory information departments, which assist producers trying to locate the owner or owners of a song. These performing rights organizations have information on virtually every song that has ever been performed and are many times the first stop for producers or music clearance services. ASCAP and BMI do not assist in any negotiations, though, and are purely a resource point for finding out who owns a particular song. Both organizations also have repertory Web sites.

THE COPYRIGHT OFFICE. If all else fails, a producer can request the U.S. Copyright Office to do a search of its registrations to find the current copyright owner of a song. This service, effective July 1, 2002, costs $75 an hour, cannot be done on a moment's notice without an extra fee being charged, and is usually employed only as a last resort.

*Sharing of Payments.*    Pursuant to all so-called standard songwriter agreements, where the publisher owns 100% of the copyright, the writer (or writers, if applicable) receives 50% of any synchronization fees and the music publisher will retain the remaining 50%. The writer who has a copublishing agreement with the music publisher will also receive a share of the income traditionally retained by the publisher. In almost all cases, the music publisher is the one who is paid the entire television synch fee, with the songwriter receiving his or her portion of the monies on the accounting dates specified in the songwriter's agreement with the publisher.

*The Performance Right.*    A synchronization license historically has not included permission to broadcast the composition on television. It is purely a license that gives a producer the right to include a musical composition in a film or taped program. A producer will normally have to rely on a television station's performance license with ASCAP, BMI, and SESAC for the right to broadcast the program or series. Most television synchronization licenses provide that the program or series can be broadcast only over stations that have valid performance licenses with ASCAP, BMI, SESAC, the music publisher, or its duly authorized representative.

In the past few years, some producers have requested performance fee quotes (usually a 1-time payment versus ASCAP and BMI's per-broadcast royalty procedures) to cover the possibility that a broadcaster may not have a valid performance license or that ASCAP and BMI might, at some time in the future, be prevented by law from licensing music broadcast on television. Publishers and songwriters (because of their nonexclusive agreements with ASCAP and BMI) have the right to make such arrangements and, at times, issue such performance licenses to television producers. This complex area has been troubled by a great deal of past litigation between the broadcasters and ASCAP and BMI, as well as legislative efforts that would have eliminated continuing payments to writers and publishers of music used on television. It is imperative that one knows the ins and outs of the performance rights business and the monies that can be earned or lost before negotiating such a license.

*Television License Renewals.*    As previously indicated, many television producers initially request a 5-year world television license for first-run series because this will usually give them sufficient time to see if a show is a hit or has a chance for syndication. Once the 5-year period has expired, the producer must renegotiate another license with the publisher for a further period if the series is still being broadcast in any country of the world. Because of the enormous failure rate of most television series, most licenses are never renewed. For successful syndicated series, however, producers do negotiate license renewals. The same is true for primetime network series that are airing simultaneously in local syndication, for hit series that have been running for at least 5 years, and for series that become popular in foreign countries.

In the case of popular series that are broadcast through syndication, the requested renewal term is many times from 10 to 15 years. The per-song synchronization fees payable to the music publisher range from $3,000 to over $5,000 for a 10-year free television license and $4,500 to over $7,500 for 15 years. There has also been a recent trend for the producers of extremely successful older syndicated series to request life-of-copyright renewal licenses so that they won't have to contact the publisher every 5, 10, or 15 years for additional renewal licenses. For most songs, such a request could mean a 30-, 40-, 50-, or 60-year license; therefore, the fees charged are substantial, ranging from $7,500 to over $12,000.

For this reason, the well-organized publisher will have an extensive "tickler" system (in many cases, completely computerized) that will bring up reminders that a television synchronization license for a specific program is about to expire so that a renewal notice can be sent to the producer and negotiations commenced. For example, if the initial synchronization license is for 5 years commencing January 15, 2004, a notice will be sent to the television producer in September 2008 reminding it that the license will expire on January 14, 2009, and that a new license will be needed if the program is still being broadcast after that date. In some cases, reminder letters are automatically generated by computers without anyone at a publishing company having to draft a notice or look up a file. Even though some of the larger television producers do keep track of when their synchronization licenses expire and either call or send out notices, a good publisher will not count on a producer's voluntary notification that a new license is needed.

*Blanket Synch Agreements for Old Programs.*     Occasionally a television producer will plan to redistribute a number of old series or specials to the syndication market but, because of the weakness of the programs due to age, subject matter, or noncolorization, will want reductions in the normal fees charged for music rights. In such cases, the producer will many times go directly to music publishers with a fee formula covering all songs owned by a particular publisher regardless of the show. Such an approach not only reduces a producer's actual cost of licensing songs but also lessens its music clearance costs, since individual negotiations do not have to take place for each song.

*Why Synchronization Fees Are Low.*   You might think it strange that music publishers who control major contemporary hit songs as well as time-tested standards might allow a television producer to use a composition in a series or special for only $1,500 to over $3,000 for a 5- to 6-year period. The answer is very simple. The use of a song on television leads to performance (broadcast) income, home video monies, and in many cases, reexposure of a song to millions of people, including motion picture producers, record producers, recording artists, advertising agencies, and other potential users of music.

As for performance income, many series continue to be broadcast for decades after their network run not only in the United States but in foreign countries as well. And since ASCAP, BMI, and their affiliated societies in countries outside the United States collect money from television stations that broadcast the shows and distribute royalties to the writers and publishers of the music used in those programs, the performance royalties can be substantial for songs used in popular series. As for video income, more and more television series (or certain selected episodes or specials) are being released to home video, with the royalties or 1-time buy-out monies being in many cases very lucrative. As for reexposure of a song, many fine compositions need new life breathed into them, and a television series can be the perfect vehicle for reintroducing a good song to millions of viewers (including people who choose the music used in motion pictures, commercials, and other television series). In addition, television can generate increased interest in newer songs, as in the case of "I'll Be There For You" from the *Friends* television series, and "Smuggler's Blues," which was the centerpiece for a *Miami Vice* episode and a hit record because of it.

Because television is such a powerful medium, with millions of people watching even the lowest-rated shows (for example, one A. C. Nielsen Co. national rating point represents 1,245,000 homes in a total U.S. television universe of 124,500,000 homes), and one that will be in existence for years to come, it is extremely important to get songs into series at prices that are not only fair to the writer and publisher but also affordable to producers who normally deficit finance the network run at losses from $100,000 to over $1,000,000 per episode. The long-term royalties that result from having a song in a hit series can mean a guaranteed annual annuity for the publisher and writer as well as his or her family and heirs.

*Music Cue Sheets and Their Importance.*   After a television program has been produced and there is a final edited broadcast version, the producer will prepare what is known as a "music cue sheet," which lists all the music used in the show, including how each song was used, its timing in seconds, and the identity of the writers and publishers as well as their performance rights affiliation. Since ASCAP and BMI use the music cue sheets for each episode of a series to determine how music was used, who owns the music, and how royalty payments should be made, it is essential that the writer and publisher secure a copy for review. Mistakes on cue sheets as to timing, whether a song is background music or sung by an actor on camera, and writer and publisher identification and performance rights affiliation are not unusual, and it is vital to correct any inaccuracies before the cue sheet is sent out by the producer. On rare occasions, a song may even be left off the cue sheet altogether. Since a good publisher will forward all cue sheets of television shows to its foreign representatives (who then register them with their local performing right society to ensure that royalty payments are made for foreign broadcasts of the programs), a correct cue sheet takes on added importance—especially since most foreign societies will not distribute royalties without proper ownership information, but will instead put the royalties in a suspense account or, in the worst-case scenario, distribute your money to someone else.

A final reason why it is important to have copies of cue sheets is that they indicate the original broadcast date of an episode, a fact that can be used to check whether or not the performance has been logged by ASCAP or BMI. For example, if you know that the initial broadcast of a show containing your song was on ABC on January 14, you can look at the ASCAP or BMI royalty statement for the January through March quarterly period of that year to see if the network television performance showed up. If the use did not appear on your royalty statement or the performance was not credited properly (for example, if monies were paid for a background instrumental use rather than a more profitable "on-camera song sung by an actor or singer"), you can contact the show's producer and ASCAP or BMI to rectify the mistake and make sure that you receive your correct royalties.

Music cue sheets take a number of different formats, depending on the company preparing the cue sheet, with some indicating who sang the song, others giving brief scene descriptions, and some reflecting the mood of a scene. All, however, give the identity of the television network broadcasting the series, the first air date, the title of the compositions, how the music was used (background vocal, visual instrumental, etc.), the timing of the use, the number of uses during the episode, and complete writer and publisher information for each composition use in the particular episode including performance rights affiliation for each songwriter, composer, lyricist, and publisher.

*Television Programs Produced in Foreign Countries.*   If a television program or series is produced in a territory outside the United States by a foreign producer, the music publisher's representative in that country usually has the right to grant a worldwide synchronization license for a U.S. composition. For example, if a series is produced in England, one's subpublisher in the United Kingdom will be able to grant the local producer the right to use a song in a particular episode in every country of the world. In such a case, if the series is broadcast in the United States (as many British series are), the U.S. publisher will not be able to charge an additional synchronization fee for the use of the program. Even though an additional fee is not paid for distributing a series outside the territory in which it was produced, all synchronization licenses guarantee that the U.S. publisher and songwriter will be entitled to the performance royalties generated by the broadcast of the foreign-originated program on television stations in the United States—a provision that can mean thousands of dollars to the U.S. writer and publisher. For example, if the BBC or Granada Television in England produces a program using an American song and that series is broadcast in the United States, the U.S. writer and publisher will not be able to charge an additional synch fee (as this was done by their representative in England), but they will receive royalties from ASCAP or BMI when the program is shown. Since ASCAP and BMI also have contractual relations with performance societies around the world, broadcast royalties will also be collected for the U.S. writer and publisher in virtually all major foreign countries.

*Motion Pictures Shown on Television.*   When a theatrically released motion picture is finally broadcast on television, no additional synch fee is paid to the music publisher and songwriter, since these rights are always included in the overall fee initially paid by the film's producer when it secures the right to use the song in the motion picture. The music publisher and songwriter will receive performance royalties through ASCAP and BMI (or their foreign affiliates) for such television broadcasts, however. That guarantee can mean thousands of dollars each year if the film is a television favorite.

*The Importance of Network Series That Are Guaranteed for Syndication.*   When a series airs on network television during its first or second year, all that a music publisher and songwriter can usually hope for, other than the initial synchronization fee, is the ASCAP or BMI performance income for the initial broadcast and possibly 1 repeat. And with the high failure rate of network series (most programs never reach the minimum episode mark at which a program may be considered commercially viable for weekly syndication by local TV stations), that is normally all you will get.

When a series is in its third, fourth, or fifth year of first-run production and a producer wants your song for a particular episode, however, a whole new set of negotiating considerations come into play. First of all, you know that the series has been popular enough to interest syndicators and has enough taped or filmed episodes in the can to play on a 5-day-per-week basis across the country. Sometimes a syndication deal has already been negotiated with stations around the country (as in the cases of *Law & Order, Married . . . With Children,* and *Cheers,* which were being aired simultaneously on the networks and in syndication), a factor that guarantees additional performance money long after the series has left network television. Additionally, if you are giving the producer only a 5-year synch license for the program, you can virtually count on receiving another synch fee in 5 years for repeats of the series on local television. Many publishers consequently put extra effort into getting their songs into successful, guaranteed-syndication network series, as the monetary returns (e.g., synch fees every 5 or 10 years in many cases and years of performance royalties for television broadcasts) can easily mean tens of thousands of dollars in future income. In fact, because of the built-in future income guarantees of a hit series, fees are sometimes even reduced by publishers to give the producer or music supervisor an extra added incentive to use a particular song in a scene.

*The Importance of Written Confirmation.*  Since requests for songs are often made over the telephone, with the producer or its representative and the music publisher taking notes on the particulars of the conversation and agreement, it is vital to summarize the terms and send them to the other party as soon as possible after the phone call. By following such an approach, both parties will know if there is a misunderstanding within a couple of days, which is usually ample time to work out an agreement prior to a song's actually being put in an episode. If an episode has a short time fuse (e.g., a scene being shot that day or the next morning), the producer will normally fax the publisher a confirmation letter asking for a countersigned copy or corrections by return.

At one time, these confirmation letters were very short and simple (e.g., $2,500 to use "Title of Song" in "Title of Series" as a background instrumental for 2 minutes for a period of 5 years from the initial network broadcast of the episode). In this day of expanding markets and media, however, the telephone conversations are becoming more complicated, making confirmation letters an absolute necessity. For example, if you give a price for the use of a song in a network television series and option prices for both domestic and foreign home video, pay TV, cable TV, educational stations, foreign broadcast, airlines, promotional uses, Web site, and foreign theaters, all commencing on different dates, both parties had better be sure that they understood the conversation.

It is also imperative that if there is a mistake or a point that needs to be clarified in these confirmation letters, the clarification should be done by phone and in writing immediately by letter, fax, or e-mail. Nothing should be taken for granted. If you find yourself thinking, "Well, that's not exactly what I meant but it's fairly close," or, "I'll fix the mistake later," correct the misunderstanding or clarify the choice of words at once. Doing so will save a lot of hard feelings and ill will in the future, to say nothing of preventing litigation because a so-called minor issue all of a sudden becomes a major one after the television program has been aired or used in another entertainment medium.

*Getting Hit Songs into Television Programs.*  Music publishers play an important role in convincing television producers and their music supervisors to use past hit songs in their programs. The good ones vigorously promote their catalogs with sampler albums, full-version CD packages, catalog lists, and songbooks. Many publishing companies have film and television departments whose sole purpose is to secure uses in these areas. Because of the increasing use of past hit recordings in television shows, record companies can also be invaluable when they push the use of their recordings (and consequently the song and writer) with producers. Good working relationships with and proximity to the Los Angeles-based television company music department heads and music supervisors (because of their knowledge and instincts of what is right for a scene and what makes a successful soundtrack album) as well as independent music consultants is extremely important. Music clearance companies can also play a role, as some of these firms have expanded into the field of music consultancy. Web sites can also be important.

It is also vital to know what the needs are for series in production. Contact with producers or music supervisors to suggest ideas can help, as television companies appreciate constructive promotion. In this regard, never use the shotgun approach of suggesting every song in one's catalog for a particular series (unless you are sending a hit sampler album); good relationships and respect come from selectivity and good judgment in your submissions. For example, if a series has a 1970s setting and the producer is looking for period songs, it would be unprofessional and unproductive to submit 1980s or 1990s material. Depending on the project, however, there may be scenes that call for pre-1970s songs (for example, a flashback or a scene that might have some "oldies" on a record player or jukebox), and 1950s submissions would then be acceptable and many times appreciated.

Many music publishers are also able to secure a plot outline or script of a made-for-TV movie or miniseries from the producer or music supervisor (either during the preproduction or actual shooting stage) and thus give specific suggestions for the use of compositions as either background music or visual vocals for use in individual scenes. Such an opportunity gives the inside track to any music publisher with a variety of songs in its catalog.

*Producers and the Selecting of Songs.* Prior to making the final choice of which songs will actually be used in a television program, some producers select a large number of possible songs and secure fee quotations from various music publishers. As in the motion picture field, the rationale behind such a "laundry list" approach is to ensure that a producer will have an extensive list of songs in various price ranges to choose from, with the final decision many times being made on budgetary rather than creative considerations. For example, if a producer, director, or music supervisor has a specific song in mind for a particular scene but the fees quoted by the music publisher are too expensive for the music budget of the series, it is sound business practice to have commitments on a number of alternate, less-costly songs. If the song is being used as a visual vocal (i.e., being sung on camera by one of the characters in the film), however, the producer obviously does not have the luxury of waiting until postproduction to make a decision as it must be made prior to the scene being rehearsed and shot. For visual vocals, the producer will usually secure price quotes for only a few compositions and make its decision quickly.

In this regard, most of the major television production companies know which publishers are flexible in their pricing policies and easy to work with. Many television producers and their music supervisors also have a good knowledge of the types of songs certain publishers control, as many of the large producers have extensive music libraries and reference materials, which they review when making selections. The music publishers who continue to be successful in the promotion of songs for use on television, however, are those who promote their catalogs day in and day out, since the constant personnel changes at many television production companies make it vital continually to let people know what you have. Good working relationships with the people at the various production studios cannot be overemphasized; this is the factor, provided, you have the songs to license, that many times gets your songs on television and gives you the edge over other companies.

*Blanket Synch Agreements for Current Series.*   One of the methods used by many of the larger music publishers to secure more uses of their songs in television series is to enter into blanket agreements with producers whereby their entire catalog is offered up front at set rates, with certain monetary incentives built in if the producer uses a specified number of songs during any 1-year period. For example, a publisher may guarantee a producer that all songs chosen for a particular series will be licensed at a certain mutually agreed-upon rate (e.g., $2,500 for a 5-year free television license) until such time that the series has used 8 compositions during a year. For all compositions used in excess of the 8-song minimum, the fee might be lowered (e.g., $2,000 for a 5-year license). Under such an arrangement, the producer is provided some incentive for using a certain publisher's catalog, as it knows that if enough songs are used, the overall price will be reduced. There are a number of variations in this area; the above example illustrates only one of the ways that publishers deal with producers to promote their catalogs.

*Precleared Compositions.*   Another method of promotion used by music publishers is to provide a series producer and music supervisor with a list of songs that can be used without any problems. Because many compositions may be somewhat difficult to clear for television use (because the songwriters or their estates have approval rights over television uses, reversions have occurred, there are potential renewal problems, or a large number of copyright owner/music publishers control a song and all have to be consulted), producers will many times discourage the use of such songs in favor of songs on which they can receive immediate permission upon their request. Consequently, if a producer has been provided with an extensive list of "precleared/no problem" songs, a preference is many times given to such songs, if only because of the immediacy of the approval process—an important factor in a business that, unlike the choosing of songs for motion pictures, is under substantial time restraints to get quick and definitive answers.

*The Experience Factor.* Because of the time pressures placed on producers and music supervisors of most weekly television series, there does many times exist a preference to deal with music publishers who have experience in negotiating television synchronization agreements. Since nothing is more frustrating than to be discussing a television license with someone who has no experience or no real knowledge of the contractual status of a song in a catalog or is uncooperative, producers have a tendency to deal with people who know the rules and are flexible and competent enough quickly to find a way to arrive at license terms that are fair and equitable to all parties concerned. Having experience, understanding, and flexibility in the music licensing department, therefore, is an essential element in successfully placing songs in television programming, an element whose importance cannot be overemphasized.

## LIFE AFTER A SONG GETS INTO A TELEVISION PROGRAM (WHERE THE REAL MONEY IS MADE)

For many songs used on television, the real money comes from sources other than the fee paid for their inclusion in the television program (see Table 4.2 for the possible royalties of a song in a television program). Granted, that initial payment can be substantial; still, the major royalties for many television

TABLE **4.2** Television Song Royalties

| | |
|---|---|
| $   7,500 | Synchronization option fees |
| 8,500 | Home video buy-out fee |
| 800,000 | U.S. radio and television performance royalties for a hit single |
| 85,000 | "A" side of a single (U.S. CD/tape sales, 1 million copies) |
| 85,000 | U.S. album sales (1 million copies) |
| 10,000 | Sheet music and folios |
| 23,000 | Television broadcasts of the program on pay, subscription, network, and syndicated television |
| 200,000 | Commercial |
| 26,000 | Motion picture use |
| 53,500 | Foreign "A" side single CD/tape sales |
| 85,000 | Foreign album sales |
| 575,000 | Foreign radio and television performance royalties for a hit single |
| 20,000 | Miscellaneous royalties including Internet |
| $1,978,500 | Total writer and publisher royalties |

songs will come from the sale of tapes and CDs (if the song hits the Top 40), radio and television performances, commercials, uses in other television shows and motion pictures, soundtrack album sales, downloads, streaming, sheet music and folios, television broadcasts throughout the world, cover recordings, home videos, and the Emmy Awards show. Because of the importance of this "after television synch license" income and what it means to the song, its creator, and the music publisher, the following sections review the major revenue producing areas and the type of money that television songs can earn.

## Option Fees

As previously indicated, many television producers will request only a 5-year worldwide free television license (sometimes the request is for 6 years) when they initially contact a music publisher for the use of a song. Options will usually be built into the initial request (e.g., an option for an additional 5 years or for successive 5-year periods, an option to distribute the program to basic cable and to pay television, an option for home video use, an option for out-of-context promo uses, an option for foreign theatrical release), but in many instances, the music publisher and writer will receive only the initial synchronization fee for free television.

At such time that the producer is able to distribute the program in areas other than on free television, the appropriate option will be exercised and additional monies will be paid to the music publisher. For example, if the program or series episode is initially licensed only for free over-the-air television and the producer enters into a distribution agreement for the series with the Arts and Entertainment Cable Network (a basic cable service), an additional fee will be paid to the music publisher for this additional medium. If the series is eventually distributed to the home video market, another fee will be paid. And if the program is distributed to any other area not covered by the initial synchronization fee, additional monies will be paid.

To illustrate, a representative scenario of how these options work for a program that starts on pay television might look as follows:

In 2004 a song is licensed for use in a television series episode on a 5-year pay television basis for $3,500. The agreement includes options: (1) to extend the term for 2 additional 5-year periods on free television and basic cable for $2,800 and $3,300 respectively; (2) to release the episode on home video cassettes and DVDs for an $8,000 buy-out; (3) to extend the pay television term for $4,000; (4) to use the song in out-of-context promos for $2,000; and (5) to release the program in foreign movie theaters for $7,000.

If the program continued to air on pay television through 2010, was distributed to the home video market in 2007, was shown on free television and basic cable in 2011, and was theatrically distributed in foreign countries in 2006, the following fees (all resulting from the initial license) would be paid to the music publisher:

| Year | Medium | Amount |
|------|--------|--------|
| 2004 | Pay Television | $ 3,500 |
| 2004 | Promo Use | 2,000 |
| 2006 | Foreign Theatrical | 7,000 |
| 2007 | Home Video Release | 8,000 |
| 2009 | Pay Television Renewal | 4,000 |
| 2011 | Free Television | 2,800 |
| 2016 | Free Television Renewal | 3,300 |
| | | $30,600 |

As one can see, if all the various options normally included in a television synchronization license are exercised by a producer, the monies can be substantial and stretch out over a long period of time. Because of that ultimate dollar total, many producers will initially bite the bullet (or at least provide an option to do such) and license a song for a 1-time fee either for "all television for the life of copyright" or on a "broad rights" motion picture-type basis, which will include all rights including video. Either type of license can usually be secured for a price that will be cheaper in the long run. With the option type of license, moreover, the options are usually not open ended, but have to be exercised by the television producer within a specified period of time (e.g., within 24 months from the initial broadcast date of the television program).

## Video Cassettes, DVDs and Discs

The market for home video distribution of television programming is growing, whether the program is an old collector's item, a successful miniseries, a bit weekly series, a "best of" collection containing highlights of many shows, a variety special, or a behind-the-scenes look at the making of a show. As with television synchronization, there are a number of things that you have to know before negotiating a license agreement for the use of your song on a video cassette, laser disc, DVD or other home use technology. Much of it has to do with your experience in dealing with this field on a day-to-day basis, as you eventually learn how far you can negotiate with each individual company and where you should draw the line. For those who don't have the necessary experience, however, the following section explains the most important principles that underlie every request.

*Duration of the Home Video License.*   Since the units sold in this area do not reach the large numbers that a major motion picture might receive (40,000 to 100,000 for a successful television series vs. 400,000 to over 20 million units for a successful film) and do not have the lasting shelf life of theatrical releases, the licensing may occasionally be done on a shorter-term basis (e.g., 7 to 15 years rather than life of copyright) and on a per-unit royalty basis rather than the 1-time buy-out fee common in the motion picture industry. The producer of an extremely successful network television series, however, will commonly demand "life of copyright" or "in perpetuity" agreements, with a 1-time up-front payment to cover all home video sales regardless of how many are actually sold. When faced with a life-of-copyright agreement, always remember that you may be granting a license for over 100 years, since the U.S. Copyright Law protects new songs for 70 years past the songwriter's death. Unfortunately, most times the fee will be dictated by how much the television producer can afford to pay for music in a particular series episode. Still, you should always bear in mind the long-term nature of what you are negotiating and do your best to make sure that the eventual price is as fair as possible.

*Video Royalty Rates for Songs.*   Following are the most prevalent of the different video approaches used by television producers in this area.

VIDEO BUY-OUTS. All of the well-financed Hollywood television producers and most of the major independents who regularly produce series programming demand 1-time worldwide buy-outs on home video rights for television series. If a publisher elects to give a worldwide buy-out on video cassettes, DVDs and discs, the fees charged many times range from $5,000 to over $10,000 for a life-of-copyright home video buy-out of a song.

PENNY RATE PER SONG FOR EACH VIDEO SOLD. Some independent television producers still accept the per-unit penny rate formula for songs used in television programs, since the up-front costs to get the program into the home video market will be sizably reduced if payments are restricted to actual sales. For example, many small producers can't afford to buy out a song for $5,000 to $10,000 when there are no guaranteed sales and instead prefer a simple royalty based on actual sales figures payable every 3 or 6 months. If a penny rate is used, a royalty of between 8¢ and 15¢ per song is not uncommon, with additional monies due for multiple uses or if a song is used as the theme of the program. These per-unit royalty formulas are becoming extinct, however, and have already become a thing of the past for songs used in all major contemporary television series.

ROLL-OVER ADVANCES. Many of the smaller producers who license on a "penny rate per video sold" basis prefer what is known as a "rollover advance" home video license because it alleviates quarterly or 6-month accounting obligations. Under such an approach, the publisher receives an agreed-upon advance that covers a set number of videos at the time the agreement is signed (e.g., $900 for the first 10,000 units sold). Then, as each 10,000-unit sales plateau is reached, an additional $900 is paid in advances for the next 10,000-unit block of sales.

PERCENTAGE OF THE WHOLESALE PRICE. Video royalties may be based on 4% to 10% of the wholesale price and shared on a pro rata basis according to the number of songs on the cassette or disc, each song's duration compared to the aggregate timing of all music on the video, or each song's duration in relation to the total running time of the entire program (music and nonmusic portions combined). For example, if 10 songs are used on a video that has a wholesale price of $10 and each music publisher agrees to a 6% pro rata royalty formula, the per-song royalties will be 6¢ (6% of $10 = 60¢ divided equally among the 10 songs). Occasionally, a minimum per-song royalty (or "floor") is also negotiated by the publisher so that the actual music royalties received cannot fall below a certain amount. For example, a song might be licensed under a 6% wholesale royalty formula, but in no event may the actual royalty be lower than 5¢ per video.

*Royalties Based on Timing.*   When a home video of a television series contains a large number of compositions, the video royalty formula many times used by the show's producer is one based on the timing of each song. Under such a formula, a song that is used for only 10 seconds will receive less royalties than a song that is performed for 2 minutes. All compositions are allocated points based on how much of a composition is used, with each point equating to a monetary royalty. For example:

| *Timing Points* | *Points (Royalties)* |
| --- | --- |
| Under 30 seconds | 1 (4¢) |
| 31 to 60 seconds | 2 (6¢) |
| 61 to 120 seconds | 3 (7¢) |
| Over 2 minutes | 4 (8¢) |

*Advances.*   In cases where a video buy-out is not demanded, many producers will guarantee the music publisher an advance based on from 5,000 to 20,000 units (e.g., $500 to $2,000 at a 10¢ rate), which will be paid upon signing the agreement or upon the release of the video. The amount of any advance, however, will depend on the producer's initial sales projections, the popularity of the show, whether or not there may be sales in countries outside the United States, whether foreign rights can be secured, the duration of the use, and the producer's music budget. Advances can therefore be lower or higher than the range stated above, as each situation is different.

*Territory.*   With more and more series becoming popular in foreign countries, there is a growing trend among television producers to request worldwide licenses with royalty payments made to the U.S. publisher at an agreed-upon penny rate or buy-out fee rather than the established royalty rates in each foreign territory. Because of the differing fee structures in most foreign countries, producers avoid "territory by territory" royalty arrangements and in virtually all cases will not use a song if they can't get a worldwide license at a set fee.

*Deleting Songs from Consideration for a Television Series Because of Home Video Policies.*   As in the motion picture industry, if a television producer has a "video buy-out or nothing" policy and a music publisher or writer does not agree to license on such a basis, the song will usually not be used, even though it may be perfect for a particular series episode, and another song will be substituted. Here the importance of knowing what is going on in the television and video industry cannot be overemphasized. If a writer or publisher negotiates with a producer without having a grasp of what is currently happening in the field (or at a particular production company) and of the options available, he or she can forget about getting songs in videos of television shows.

*Deleting Songs from Videos of a Television Series.*   A producer's "video buy-out only" policy may not only apply to the initial consideration of whether a song will be used in a series but also extend to the inclusion or deletion of a song in the home video version. For example, if a producer cannot negotiate a video buy-out with the music publisher of a song used in a broadcast episode, it may take the song out of the home video version of the series. On occasion, if a song was not originally cleared for home video use (i.e., the original synch license was for television use only), the producer may not even contact a publisher to negotiate a fee but will simply insert new music into the home video version. Since video rights are nowadays almost always negotiated simultaneously with the synchronization license, the deletion of a song from the home video version commonly occurs only with respect to older programs. It also occurs with new series because of budget reasons.

## Hit Singles from Television Programs

Even though television songs do not become hits with the frequency of motion picture songs, the hit single nevertheless represents an important source of income for the composer, lyricist, and publisher of television songs.

| *Hit Song* | *Television Series* |
| --- | --- |
| "I'll Be There For You" | *Friends* |
| "The X-Files Theme" | *The X-Files* |
| "Twin Peaks" | *Twin Peaks* |
| "Moonlighting" | *Moonlighting* |
| "Miami Vice Theme" | *Miami Vice* |
| "Welcome Back" | *Welcome Back, Kotter* |
| "Peter Gunn Theme" | *Peter Gunn* |
| "Happy Days" | *Happy Days* |
| "Hill Street Blues" | *Hill Street Blues* |

*Mechanical Royalties.* The writer's music publisher (usually the television company, when the song is written specifically for the series) will normally license a television song to a record company for the statutory mechanical royalty for every record, tape, and CD sold. For example, if 1 million singles of a song are sold in the United States, the mechanical royalties to the writer would, under the 2004–05 statutory rate of 8.5¢ per song, be $42,500, with the same amount being paid to the music publisher. In addition, if the million-selling single contains an additional song from the television program, another $85,000 in aggregate writer/publisher royalties will be due, unless a lesser rate was agreed to by the music publisher. And if the song is covered by other recording artists on albums, singles, or CDs, the mechanical income from the sales of those other versions can add up to hundreds of thousands of dollars long after the song's initial popularity.

*ASCAP and BMI Royalties.* In most cases, the principal immediate source of a writer's and publisher's income from a hit single comes from the royalties earned for radio and television performances of the song. Depending on a number of factors including the amount of airplay a song has received, the types of stations on which it is broadcast, its eligibility for award or bonus payments, the writer and publisher performance royalties normally range from $400,000 to $600,000 for a Top 10 song and can run as high as $1,000,000 for a #1 across-the-board hit. In addition, there are also increased royalties from ASCAP for hit songs as well as for songs that have been past hits and that are used as background or theme music on radio or television shows, and extra bonus payments from both ASCAP and BMI for performances of songs that have attained (and continue to maintain) certain performance levels.

If a song from a television program becomes a standard, is recorded by many different artists, or is used by television and motion picture producers in other films or series, it has the potential of generating hundreds of thousands of dollars in performance income for years after the initial television broadcast. For example, it is not unusual for a popular song to earn from $25,000 to $100,000 per year in "catalog" performance royalties after its initial chart activity as a hit single.

*Foreign Performance Royalties.* Foreign radio and television songwriter and publisher earnings represent the least-understood area of music and lyrics income, even though for many writers and publishers it is their main source of royalty income. One need only to look at the amount of American music on the foreign pop charts as well as the television series aired in England, Canada, Australia, France, Germany, Italy, and Japan, among others, to appreciate the importance of the foreign marketplace as a substantial and continuing source of royalty income. Pursuant to agreements that ASCAP and BMI have with over 80 foreign performing right societies throughout the world, those foreign societies license performances of U.S. writers' and publishers' works, collect the money, and forward it to ASCAP and BMI, who in turn pay the appropriate members. For songwriters with a song in a television series, the areas that can generate foreign performance royalties include radio, television, cable, wired music, and live performance.

## The Television Series Soundtrack Album

*Friends:* The Rembrandts' "I'll Be There For You" (TV version), Hootie & the Blowfish's "I Go Blind," Toad the Wet Sprocket's "Good Intentions," Lou Reed's "You'll Know You Were Loved," k.d. lang's "Sexuality," Barenaked Ladies' "Shoe Box," R.E.M.'s "It's a Free World Baby," Pretenders' "Angel of the Morning," and Joni Mitchell's "Big Yellow Taxi."

*The Sopranos:* A3's "Woke Up This Morning," Frank Sinatra's "It Was A Very Good Year," Cream's "I Feel Free," Bruce Springsteen's "State Trooper," Elvis Costello's "Complicated Shadows," and Bo Diddley's "I'm A Man."

Because of the international appeal of many American-produced television programs and their music, soundtracks have the potential of being a significant source of revenue for television companies, record companies, recording artists, and the writers and publishers of songs in television series.

As with singles, the composer and the lyricist through their music publisher will normally license the U.S. mechanical rights to their songs for the statutory rate per song. Since some television series soundtracks sell well over 1 million copies (as in the case of *Miami Vice* and *Moonlighting*), the aggregate royalties can exceed $850,000 from the United States alone. And because some television soundtrack albums do very well outside the United States, the foreign market can be another gold mine for writers and publishers.

## Television Commercials Promoting the Program

Virtually all series, made-for-TV movies, miniseries, and specials use commercials to advertise the broadcast date of the program. On occasion, payments are made for the use of songs in those commercials, but normally these rights are given as part of the license to include the song in the program. For example, the television producer usually gets the right to include the "in context" use of the song in any television commercials. If, however, the song is being used other than as it is used in the program (for example, being used as thematic background throughout the commercial and over a number of scenes), additional fees are usually negotiated. Occasionally, a television producer will also use a song that is not in the television program as part of the advertising campaign. In these cases, additional fees will be charged.

## Sheet Music Folios

Songbooks that contain classic television songs such as the themes from *I Love Lucy, The Brady Bunch, Cheers, Happy Days, Gilligan's Island, Friends,* and *All in the Family* generate good sales. The standard royalties for such folios are between 10% and 15% of the retail selling price, with all copyrighted compositions sharing equally in the aggregate amount.

## Royalties from Motion Picture Theaters (When a Television Program Is Released as a Motion Picture)

Occasionally, U.S. television programming (usually made-for-TV movies or capsulized versions of miniseries) is released in the foreign theatrical marketplace. In most countries outside the United States, motion picture theaters are required to pay royalties to the local performing right society for the music used in films.

## Television Broadcasts of the Series, Special, Made-for-TV Movie, or Miniseries

Whether or not a television program has a theatrical exhibition and home video release, it will usually continue its life after its first broadcast throughout the world on subscription or pay television, basic cable, and over-the-air free television stations. In the United States, ASCAP and BMI monitor such broadcasts and distribute royalties to the writers and publishers of songs contained in the programs actually broadcast. Through their arrangements with affiliated performance societies around the world, broadcast royalties are collected in virtually all territories outside the United States for television showings of programs. Because of the continuing need for programming to fill the schedules of television stations, recognized series remain a valuable source to fill air time and attract viewers. And for programs that consistently earn high ratings, the performance royalties from television broadcasts throughout the world can represent a lifetime annuity for the writers and publishers of the songs contained in them.

## Television Songs in Commercials

Another source of income for the television song is its use in radio or television commercials advertising consumer products. The fees for such commercial use can be substantial (e.g., from $75,000 to over $750,000 per year for successful songs), depending on whether it is a radio or television commercial, a national or limited-territory campaign, whether there are options for use in foreign countries, if the original lyrics are being changed or new lyrics added to an instrumental hit, and whether total advertising versus product category exclusivity is being requested by the agency. Some examples of television songs used in consumer product advertising include the *Bonanza* theme for Taco Bell, the *Cheers* theme for UPS, the Love Boat theme for Princess Cruise Lines, the Peter Gunn theme for Kibbles 'n' Bits and for Ford trucks, the *Alfred Hitchcock Presents* theme for Energizer batteries, and the *I Dream of Jeannie* theme for Lexus and Tropicana.

## Television Songs Used in Other Television Programs

The use of well-known television themes as either background music or visual vocals in other series can be extremely valuable in terms of both performance income and reexposure of songs to millions of people. (Some examples of such uses are set forth in Table 4.3.)

Since most television producers pay between from $1,500 to over $3,000 to use one of these songs in a television series under a 5-year free television license, with additional monies paid for themes, multiple uses, or if the song is used as the title of an episode in addition to background music, the writers and publishers can, unless a life-of-copyright license is agreed to for a $7,500 to over $12,000 all television fee, expect to receive synch fees every 5 years if the series is successful and goes into syndication. And with more and more network series requesting options for additional media (pay or subscription television, cable, foreign theatrical release, home video), extra monies may be forthcoming as the programs are purchased by different suppliers. Since ASCAP and BMI pay royalties for television broadcasts, as do their affiliated societies in foreign countries, substantial performance monies can also be earned by the writer and publisher for years after the program has been initially aired.

## Television Songs Used in Motion Pictures

Another lucrative source of income is the inclusion of television songs in motion pictures as theme, background (often from a TV set within a scene), or visual vocal. (Table 4.4 provides some examples of this type of use.) Because of the various royalty-generating media involved in motion pictures (home video, cable broadcast, soundtrack album, etc.), this area can mean hundreds of thousands of dollars in long-term income to the writer and music publisher.

## Conclusion

As one can see, having a song in a television series, made-for-TV movie, special, or miniseries can open up an unlimited number of opportunities and prove to be a lifetime annuity for writers and music publishers. From hit records, commercials, and videos to motion pictures, foreign theater performances, other television shows, and option fees, the financial life of the television song can last well beyond the initial broadcast.

TABLE **4.3** Television Songs Used in Other Programs

| Song | Original Television Program | Other Television Program |
| --- | --- | --- |
| "I Dream of Jeannie" | *I Dream of Jeannie* | *American Dreams* (played during a scene which has the old series on a television set) |
| "American Bandstand Theme" | *American Bandstand* | *American Idol* (the superstar hopefuls sing together) |
| "The Dick Van Dyke Show Theme" | *The Dick Van Dyke Show* | *Spin City* (black and white scene ala the old television series) |
| "Happy Days Theme" | *Happy Days* | *Friends* (as Phoebe is about to have triplets, the doctor who is a fan of the Fonz, turns on *Happy Days* on the TV in the delivery room) |
| "Secret Agent Man Theme" | *Secret Agent* | *Ally McBeal* (in the background as the lawyers investigate a female mud wrestling club) |
| "I'll Be There for You" | *Friends* | *MTV Celebrity Deathmatch* (played while female stars from *Friends* battle in the ring) |
| "The Andy Griffith Show Theme" | *The Andy Griffith Show* | *The Simpsons* (whistled in the background to a scene in which Charles Bronson plays Andy) |
| "Movin' On Up" | *The Jeffersons* | *The Sopranos* (on TV set when Chris puts on the TV with a remote while he is frustrated with his acting) |

TABLE **4.4** Television Songs Used in Motion Pictures

| Song | Initial Television Program | Motion Picture |
|---|---|---|
| "Gilligan's Island Theme" | *Gilligan's Island* | *Blair Witch Project* (sung around the campfire at night in the woods near Burkittsville, MD, by one of the 3 documentary filmakers) |
| "Mission: Impossible Theme" | *Mission: Impossible* | *M:I-2* (Mission: Impossible 2) (over the closing credits and while Tom Cruise waits for his men to arrive by helicopter) |
| "Music from Father Knows Best" | *Father Knows Best* | *Girl, Interrupted* (on television set in the mental hospital) |
| "Movin' On Up" | *The Jeffersons* | *Basic Instinct* (on a television set while Dr. Beth Garner admits to Detective Nick Curran [Michael Douglas] that his file was given to Internal Affairs) |
| "Star Trek Theme" | *Star Trek* | *Wayne's World* (Dana Carvey whistles while looking at the stars) |
| "Bonanza Theme" | *Bonanza* | *City Slickers* (sung/ hummed by Billy Crystal and his two buddies as they ride into the ranch after successfully bringing the herd of cattle in by themselves |
| "ER Theme"/ "Seinfeld Theme"/ "Dallas Theme"/ | *ER/ Seinfeld/ Dallas* | *Contact* (during the initial scene as the camera races through time and space) |

# 5

# Music, Money, and Motion Pictures

EACH YEAR, the major Hollywood studios and hundreds of independent film production companies release from 450 to 500 feature films for U.S. theatrical distribution. Outside the United States, thousands of additional films are produced and released by foreign companies. Practically all of these films use music as an integral and necessary part of the production (see Table 5.1 for examples). And for the writers of this music, a single song or a background score can generate a lifetime of substantial earnings.

## *OVERVIEW*

### The Movie Industry

Most feature films are produced either by the major studios (DreamWorks, Universal, Sony/Columbia/Tri-Star, Walt Disney/Buena Vista, Paramount, 20th Century Fox, Warner Bros., and MGM) or by the hundreds of U.S. and foreign independent production companies. The independents range from major companies just below the rank of the well-financed all-purpose studios to medium and small continuing companies and to firms who fold up their tents after just

1 production. Although the feature film industry was once primarily the domain of U.S. companies, the industry has significantly changed in recent years with the acquisition of major U.S. studios by foreign companies (Matsushita of Japan bought MCA/Universal in 1990 and sold it to Seagram of Canada in 1995 with a sale to Vivendi of France in 2000 and to GE (NBC) in 2003; Sony of Japan purchased Columbia in 1989; News Corporation of Australia acquired 20th Century-Fox in 1985) as well as the increasing number of joint ventures between U.S. and foreign companies, partnerships between film companies and nonfilm entities, and partial ownerships through public stock acquisitions.

Filmmaking costs have skyrocketed in recent years. The average cost to produce, market, and advertise a film in 2002 was $90 million, versus a 1980 figure of $16 million. Out of necessity, films are now financed in a variety of complex ways including major studio backing, joint ventures, outside private

TABLE **5.1**   Scores and Songs in Films

| *Music* | *Film* | *Scene* |
|---|---|---|
| "Theme from *Jaws*" (classic John Williams background score) | *Jaws* | The fin of a great white shark cuts through the water while bathers play at the beach in the #1 film of 1975. |
| "My Heart Will Go On" (song written for the film by scorer James Horner and songwriter Will Jennings) | *Titanic* | The #1 box office movie of all time with this #1 song featured in the closing credits. |
| "Suicide Is Painless" (the Johnny Mandel theme from *M\*A\*S\*H* later used as the theme to one of the most successful television series of all time) | *M\*A\*S\*H* | Used throughout the film. |
| *Psycho* (Bernard Hermann's chilling and unforgettable score) | *Psycho* | The shower scene. |

or public investors, limited partnerships, and presales of ancillary and distribution rights. Regardless of how a film is financed, though, all parties involved normally have a good idea of the principal revenue-producing areas from which their investment will be recouped and, they hope, a profit made. They usually are also familiar with the various stages of production that ultimately lead to the release of a finished motion picture.

Though the stakes are high, the returns for a blockbuster hit can be monumental. In 1976 only 1 film had generated over $100 million in U.S. and Canadian box office receipts; by 2002, over 200 films had reached the $100 million mark. Considering also that foreign markets can equal or surpass the U.S. and Canadian gross (the 1997 film *Titanic* grossed over $1.8 billion worldwide with *Harry Potter, The Lord of the Rings: Two Towers, The Lord of the Rings: The Return of the King, Star Wars: Episode 1,* and *Jurassic Park* all over $900,000,000), the profit potential for a hit can be astronomical despite the high cost of producing a film and the odds against box office success.

The same factors that affect the film producer also affect the composer and songwriter, as a film's budget determines the amount of the initial writing fee (whether it be a background score or a song), and the success of the film in various types of markets determines the total amount of short- and long-term earnings the writer and music publisher receive.

## The Making of a Film

The film producer (studio or production company) acquires a property (a book, short story, or play; an outline of an idea; a developed treatment of a story) and orders a script to be written. Based on the script, the producer determines what the production will cost and then negotiates for particular actors, a director, and other personnel; chooses locations to shoot; secures financing for specific budgets; and orders completion of a final script. Principal photography—the actual shooting of the movie—commences next. The final element is postproduction: background music and songs, editing, sound effects, and so on. When postproduction is completed, prints of the film are made and the movie is ready for distribution to U.S. and foreign theaters.

## The Market

The initial market for any film is exhibition in U.S. and foreign motion picture theaters. Films are then released as video cassettes and DVDs for purchase and rental, to video on demand services with subsequent sales to pay-per-view, to pay cable services (HBO, Showtime, the Movie Channel), to the television networks, to local television stations or basic nonpay cable services (USA Network, Lifetime), and to foreign television and cable stations. Soundtrack albums and singles are often released, with many of them becoming major chart hits, in turn creating additional income from such ancillary sources as ASCAP, BMI, and foreign performance income, mechanical royalties from tape and CD sales, and commercial advertising fees.

## TYPES OF MOTION PICTURE MUSIC AND HOW MUSIC IS USED

Three types of music are primary to any film: (1) the underscore (e.g., Howard Shore's scores to The Lord of the Rings trilogy or James Horner's score to *Titanic*); (2) the song written for a film (e.g., Eminem, Luis Resto, and Jeff Bass' "Lose Yourself" for *8 Mile* and Diane Warren's "I Don't Want to Miss a Thing" for *Armageddon*; and (3) the previously existing song or song and record (e.g., Dolly Parton's 1974 song "I Will Always Love You" for the 1992 film *The Bodyguard* and Alex North and Hy Zaret's 1955 song "Unchained Melody" from the 1955 film *Unchained* for the 1990 film *Ghost*).

The background score is the music you hear under the dialogue, in chase scenes, in romantic settings, and throughout the picture. It creates or sets the mood, underscores the action, and is the primary music in practically all films. Songs, on the other hand, can be used as visual vocals (a character singing on camera), as visual instrumentals (an orchestra playing on camera), as background music (Burt Bacharach and Hal David's "Raindrops Keep Fallin' on My Head" as Paul Newman and Katherine Ross ride a bicycle in *Butch Cassidy and the Sundance Kid*), or as the opening or closing theme to the film (Alan and Marilyn Bergman and Marvin Hamlisch's "The Way We Were" for *The Way We Were* and ZZ Top's "Doubleback" for *Back to the Future III*).

The way that each of these three types of music is used within a film is important, as the particular usage not only determines the initial writing or synchronization fee but also affects the lifetime writer and publisher earnings that result from the composition's use.

## THE FILM MUSIC BUDGET

A starting point for any discussion of film music is the music budget. Though in years past the music budget was usually a specific percentage of the total cost of the picture, recent years have shown that no formula is typical and that the music budget really depends on what role music plays in the film and what price the producer is willing to pay to achieve what he or she wants the music to accomplish. Certain films contain only a background score, whereas others combine a background score with new songs and preexisting songs as well, frequently using the original recordings of those songs. For major studios, total budgets can range from $150,000 to over $1 million depending on the stature of the background composer, the type of score required (large orchestra, synthesizer, etc.), the number of preexisting and new songs being used, and the commitment that the producer or director has with respect to the role and purpose that music plays in the overall product. As in life, if you want the best, you pay accordingly.

## USE OF PRE-EXISTING HIT SONGS IN FILMS

As you can see from Table 5.2, many successful motion pictures use hit songs to create a period flavor, establish a mood, give an actor a chance to sing, make people laugh, make people cry, elicit emotions, and create interest in the movie through successful soundtrack albums and hit singles. A film producer who wants to use an existing song in a motion picture must secure the permission of the music publisher to use the composition in the film. Once an agreement is reached as to a fee, the producer will sign what is known as a "synchronization" or "broad rights" license, which will give the studio the right to distribute the film theatrically, sell it to television, use the song in motion picture theater trailers or television and radio promos, and sell videos.

### The Phone Call from the Film Company

*Setting:*

The office of the vice president of business affairs at a major music publishing company.

*The Phone Call:*

MUSIC CLEARANCE SUPERVISOR:  Hi, this is the music clearance supervisor on a film that is going into postproduction.

PUBLISHER:  Hi, how can I help?

MUSIC CLEARANCE SUPERVISOR:  As you know, we're finishing up our film and need some additional music for certain scenes. We've already shot the footage of scenes where songs are sung by the actors, but we have some important scenes which need music behind them. For your information, the film is about (description of plot).

PUBLISHER:  Do you have any songs in mind?

MUSIC CLEARANCE SUPERVISOR:  Yes, I'd like to use (name of recording artist)'s version of (name of composition). Here's a brief description of the use, and I'll send over the script pages if you need them. I've also contacted the record company that owns the master recording, and it looks like we'll be able to get permission.

TABLE 5.2  Pre-existing Hit Songs in Films

| *Song* | *Motion Picture* | *Use* |
|---|---|---|
| "London Calling" | *Die Another Day* | Background while James Bond sits in first class on a flight to London |
| "Light My Fire" | *Cast Away* | Sung by Tom Hanks when he finally succeeds in starting a fire on the beach of the deserted island |
| "Yo Ho (A Pirate's Life" For Me)" | *Pirates of the Caribbean* | Johnny Depp sings the Disney park ride theme song |
| "Unchained Melody" (Righteous Brothers recording) | *Ghost* | Background vocals (from jukebox as Patrick Swayze and Demi Moore talk and then embrace/ Swayze enters Whoopi Goldberg's body and touches Moore for the first time since his death); background instrumental (at the end of the film as Swayze leaves for the last time) |
| "Hungry Heart" (Bruce Springsteen) | *The Perfect Storm* | On the jukebox in the Crow's Nest bar while George Clooney and his crew drink prior to their final voyage |

PUBLISHER:  What kind of rights do you need?

MUSIC CLEARANCE SUPERVISOR:  We'd like to get worldwide synch rights including theatrical release, television broadcast, use of the song in trailers and promos, Web site use, and home video rights.

PUBLISHER:  Before I give a price quote, I'd like to make sure that we receive a royalty for every video sold.

MUSIC CLEARANCE SUPERVISOR:  Like the other major studios, we need a 1-time buy-out price for all videos sold.

PUBLISHER:  In that case, the total fee for all rights will be $35,000. I hope that fits into your budget, as I think the use will help the song.

MUSIC CLEARANCE SUPERVISOR: I'll check the remaining budget, but I think the price will be acceptable.

PUBLISHER: That's good. Also, is there a chance that the composition could get on the soundtrack album? Maybe I could lower my price if we could get a guarantee.

MUSIC CLEARANCE SUPERVISOR: I'll check to see if a soundtrack is being contemplated and get back to you.

### *Another Call:*

HEAD OF MUSIC AFFAIRS: Hi, this is the head of music affairs at a major studio. The director and music supervisor of (Name of Actor) new film have heard your song and would like to use it in a scene that is being shot next week. The song will be played from a CD player in (Name of Actress) apartment during a party when they first meet and begin to fall in love. It might be played for about a minute, but it could be longer depending on the final cut.

If the scene works, we might also reprise the song sporadically throughout the film and possibly use it over the opening or closing credits or both. There is also a good chance for a soundtrack album and an "A" side single release.

Because time is short, we need separate price quotes for use of the song for:

1. A 60-second or less 1-time use
2. A more-than-60-second 1-time use
3. Up to 5 uses of various lengths
4. Over opening and/or closing credits

Since you could also make quite a bit of extra money if a soundtrack album is released and if your song is released as an "A" side single, we'd like to see if you can reduce your synchronization fee in the event that these possibilities occur.

For your information, we need all the "standard broad rights," including:

1. Worldwide synchronization
2. Worldwide free, pay, cable, and subscription television
3. In-context and out-of-context television advertising and film trailer use, including promos on other film videos plus Web site use
4. Performance rights for U.S. theater distribution
5. Theater distribution outside the United States
6. Video cassette, DVD and videodisc rights on a nonroyalty 1-time buy-out basis
7. All future technology rights whether now known or not

We also need to have you agree to a reduced CD mechanical royalty if your song makes the soundtrack album, and I'd like a separate price if we decide to use the title of the song as the title of the motion picture.

I'd like to get back to the director almost immediately, so I'd appreciate it if you could give me the price quotes right away. For your information, we are considering a number of other potential songs for the same scene, so I need your fees to be competitive.

Unlike the television industry, where over 400 series, specials, and made-for-TV movies may be in production during any given week, only about 500 U.S.-produced English-language motion pictures are released each year. And since the majority of music in each film is original and written by a background composer, the competition to get existing songs into motion pictures is intense. Because of the larger monies involved and the possibility of getting a hit single or being put on a multimillion-selling soundtrack album, the ability to handle a call from a film producer intelligently is the key to success. Because of the importance of what you say during that conversation, how quickly you respond, and how well you are able to "read" the other person, the following pages will reveal what you need to know about getting your songs into movies and making the right deal. There is nothing worse than to see a film open to rave reviews with a hit soundtrack and an Oscar nomination and know that your song could have been in it . . . but wasn't.

## Determining How Much to Charge for a Song

When the call comes in from the music supervisor of a motion picture and you are trying to decide how much to charge for the use of a song, a number of factors must be considered, including:

How the song is used (vocal performance by an actor on camera, instrumental background, vocal background, visual performance by a band in the background of a scene, theme, under the opening and/or closing credits)

The overall budget for the film, as well as the music budget

The stature of the song being used (current hit, new song, famous standard, rock 'n' roll classic)

The duration of the use and whether there are multiple uses of the song

The term of the license (2 years, 10 years, life of copyright, perpetual)

The territory of the license (the world, universe, specific foreign countries)

Whether there is a guarantee that the song will be used on the film's soundtrack album and the stature of the recording artist and power of the record company releasing the album

Whether there is a change in the original lyrics

Whether deferred payments are being offered if a film breaks even or makes a profit

Whether the producer requests an exclusive hold on the song or places restrictions on its use in other motion pictures

Whether the producer also wants to use the hit recording of a song, rather than re-recording a new version for use in the film

Whether the motion picture is a dramatization of the events described in the song

Whether the motion picture uses the song as its musical theme as well as its title

Whether the motion picture is over budget at the time a song is requested

Whether a number of songs from the same publisher are contained in the film

Whether the film producer wants a share of the publishing income or a co-ownership interest in the song

## Actual Fees Paid for Existing Songs

The synchronization fees charged by music publishers are usually between $15,000 and $60,000 (with the majority being between $20,000 and $45,000), but can be lower if the music budget is small or higher if the song is used several times in the motion picture (e.g., sung by one of the actors and also used as background music as a reoccurring theme), if the use is under the opening or closing credits, if the song is a major hit, or if it is vital to the plot or particular scene of the motion picture. There are no hard and fast rules in this area, and anyone who advises that there are lacks experience. The fees are negotiated in the context of each individual film; the same song may be licensed at different rates for different projects. It's not a guessing game, though. By carefully considering the myriad factors discussed here, you will be able to say to yourself, "I did the best that I could under the circumstances."

It should also be mentioned that record companies normally charge between $15,000 and $70,000 for the use of existing master recordings in a motion picture, but depending on the stature of the artist, the length of the use, the music budget, and how the recording is being used, these fees can be greater or less.

## Opening and Closing Credits

Because the songs used over the opening credits of a motion picture many times reflect the theme or ambiance of the film, they are many times more important to the film than other songs used for background. The same is often true for use of a song over the end credits, although it is becoming more common for songs to be run during the closing credits in order to complete the requirements for a soundtrack album. The fees charged by publishers are almost always higher than other uses of music in a film and usually range from between $30,000 to $65,000 for synchronization and video rights, but each negotiation and final price depends upon many of the factors mentioned earlier (e.g., budget of the film, music budget, importance of the song, whether there are replacement songs available, etc.). If the title of one of these opening-credit songs is also used as the title of the film (but the film's plot is not based on the story line of the song) the fees are increased further (e.g., from $75,000 to over $500,000).

## Multiple Uses of a Song

If a producer uses a song more than once in a motion picture, the fees charged by music publishers will be higher than if the song is used only once. The duration of each of the uses is also important, as four uses of less than 20 seconds each is usually less costly to a film producer than four uses of 1 minute or more. The importance of the song to the plot development or movement of the film (e.g., if it becomes a signature song for an important character or if it becomes thematic of a certain reoccurring point of the film such as the first time two lovers saw each other) can also be a factor that raises the price. Obviously, it is important to secure from the film producer an overall plot summary and specific scene descriptions when negotiating fees for multiple uses of a song in a film, as you must be aware of how the song is to be used before you can give an intelligent price quote.

## Lyric Changes

Occasionally a film producer will request permission for a lyric change in a song that will either be re-recorded for the film or sung by one of the characters in the motion picture. In most cases, the changes will be of only a few words to fit a particular point in the plot or help a scene comedically, but in some cases, substantial lyric changes will occur. When such a request is received, a music publisher should ask for a copy of the new lyrics, a plot summary of the film, and a scene description including script pages so that it knows exactly how the song will be used before making a decision. Since certain lyric changes can live with a song for a long time—especially if the film is a hit or if the song is used in trailers and television advertising for the film—it is vital to know all the particulars before approving or rejecting the use.

A publisher may have certain restrictions in its agreement with the song's writer (e.g., all changes in the English lyrics to a composition must be with the approval of the writer) that require additional consents from the songwriter or his or her estate. Because of the possible negative effects that lyric changes may have on a song, especially a standard or well-known contemporary hit, a publisher must be careful in these situations, and if approval is given, an additional fee is virtually always added to the price that would have been charged had there been no change. The scriptwriter who revised the lyrics will virtually never get credit on the song nor be entitled to receive any royalties which are generated from the revised version.

## Duration of License

The term of the license is virtually always for the entire copyright life of the song, unless the film is a documentary or other noncommercial film intended for only limited theatrical release. Many times, the producer will demand "perpetual" rights, but whether or not this language is contained in the contract, the music publisher can guarantee rights only while the song is under copyright protection (i.e., "life of copyright and any and all extensions thereof that are under the control of the publisher"). Owing to a U.S. Supreme Court decision (the so-called *Rear Window* decision), if a song written before 1978 is used in a motion picture and the writer dies prior to the vesting of the copyright renewal period of the song, his or her heirs may terminate the motion picture license during the renewal period. The results of this case have caused great concern for film companies because of the possibility that they may have to delete songs from motion pictures in the future. Most studios are deemphasizing the use of pre-1978 songs that have not yet entered their renewal period or are demanding that a writer's heirs sign the film license or a separate document stating that they agree to the terms.

## Rights Granted to the Film Producer

The motion picture synchronization fee paid to the music publisher for the use of a song includes the right to distribute the film to network, local, syndicated, pay-per-view, pay, satellite, cable, and subscription television stations; the right to show the film in motion picture theaters in the United States; and the right to include the song in trailers, previews, and advertisements of the motion picture.

U.S. television performance and broadcast rights (which are normally licensed through ASCAP and BMI) are normally excluded, but some major producers have recently tried to include such rights in the license agreement, or at least to provide for negotiation, set fees, or arbitration in the event that a broadcast station does not have an ASCAP or BMI license or if ASCAP and BMI are legally prohibited from licensing television performance rights. Foreign theatrical distribution rights (i.e., the right to show a film in motion picture theaters outside the United States) are also given to the producer, but such rights are subject to the payment of performance fees by theaters to the various performance right organizations in countries outside the United States. These societies usually collect a percentage of the box office receipts or a per-seat charge for music performance rights and then send the songwriter's share of such theater monies to ASCAP and BMI and the music publisher's share to the publisher's representative in each country. The same procedure is used for foreign writers and publishers: each foreign society around the world collects monies for films distributed in its territory and remits the income to the society that represents the songwriter and the local publisher that represents the foreign publisher (e.g., PRS in England sends money to ASCAP and BMI).

## Territory

The territory of the license is normally the universe or world, but in the case of certain television miniseries, made-for-TV movies, and weekly series that are broadcast on television in the United States and shown as a feature in foreign theaters, the territory may be for the universe or world excluding the United States. In the latter case, synch fees are usually reduced to between $4,000 and $10,000 depending on the duration of the agreement, since the large U.S. theatrical market has been excluded from the license.

## Limited Theatrical Distribution

Depending on the nature of the film (normally in the case of documentaries or art films that do not have mass market appeal), the license may be for a limited duration and apply to the distribution of a film on a limited theater engagement or "film festival" basis. In addition, the territory may also be limited to the United States or to certain specified countries such as England, Australia, and other English-speaking countries. Fees for this type of license are less than those charged for commercial theatrical features with wide distribution. In many cases, the producer will also have the option to distribute the film theatrically on a broader basis for an additional fee and put it on home video for another prenegotiated fee—important rights if a film is well received or receives an award from an important film festival competition and goes into national distribution. For example, a "film festival" license may give the producer the right within 18 months after the initial showing of the film to extend the territory and the duration of the license for an additional fee.

## Soundtrack Album Guarantees

On occasion, a music publisher will reduce the motion picture synchronization fee for a song if the producer guarantees that the song will be on a soundtrack album released by a major label. Sometimes there are even guarantees of an "A" side single release, but these usually occur only when a successful recording artist on a major label records the song for the film. In this case the publisher will many times give two price quotes: a higher figure if the song does not make the soundtrack album or if an album is not released and, because of the possibility of additional ancillary album income, a lower quote if the soundtrack provision actually takes effect. For example, if a publisher gives a $25,000 quote for the use of a song in a film, it also might agree to reduce the price to $22,000 if there is a guarantee of a nationally distributed soundtrack album and may even further reduce the fee if the song becomes an "A" side single from the album.

Considering the phenomenal success of some motion picture soundtracks and the hit singles released from the albums, such a reduction in the synch fee may pale in comparison to the mechanical royalties earned from sales of the soundtrack album and singles, not to mention radio and television performance monies received from ASCAP, BMI, and foreign societies (e.g., $500,000 to over $1,000,000 for a Top 10 worldwide pop single). Each situation must be decided on its own merits, however; many film soundtracks are not huge money-makers, and a music publisher or writer may wind up reducing the synch price to get on an album that has no single releases and only sells 10,000 copies. Still, such reduced-fee arrangements are valuable incentives to motion picture producers, as they do help reduce up-front production costs (especially where a film uses a great number of preexisting hit songs, such as *Austin Powers, Wayne's World* or *Sister Act*) and many times make the difference between a song getting into a film or being left out.

## Motion Picture Producer Cut-Ins

Some film producers occasionally try to condition the use of a song in a motion picture on a guarantee from the music publisher that the film company will co-own the copyright in the composition or share in the earnings from all or selected subsidiary revenue-generating music markets (e.g., a percentage of the monies derived from the soundtrack album or single royalties).

Most publishers refuse such conditions for preexisting compositions, but sometimes arrangements are made on a short-term basis to ensure that the song gets into the film (e.g., the producer may receive 10% of the mechanical royalties from the soundtrack album for 5 years from the release of the movie or for 10 years if a song is an "A" side single). Other publishers may give the producer a copyright interest in the song or a total monetary participation, which means that the producer will share in all income from the composition regardless of whether the income is generated by the film version of the song. Others will grant the producer a life-of-copyright participation in income generated by the song's use in the film only (e.g., a percentage of the earnings derived from the sale of soundtrack albums and singles, foreign motion picture theater royalties, television performances of the film, and radio and television performances of the song itself if it is released as an "A" side single and becomes a hit because of its inclusion in the film). Obviously, such arrangements can substantially benefit the music publisher and songwriter if the song is unknown or has a weak track record and the movie becomes a real hit. But if the song is already a hit or has an income-generating life of its own outside the film and the movie is not successful, the publisher has cut someone else in on a song's future earnings for nothing in return.

Because of the uncertainties of what makes a movie a blockbuster or a bomb as well as what most major publishers feel is an affront to the integrity of business ethics (much like a recording artist or producer cutting himself in as a co-writer or copublisher for recording a song), the proposal to allow a motion picture company to share in a preexisting song's income usually elicits a negative response from the publisher. In the event, however, that such an arrangement is made as a condition for including a song in a film, the motion picture company will never share in the initial synchronization or video buy-out fee; instead its interest will only cover income generated after the film is released.

There is a growing trend for film producers to contact songwriters who are signed to exclusive agreements with music publishers to write a song or songs for an upcoming motion picture. The request can come during the preproduction scripting stage, the actual filming, or during postproduction, when the producer is looking for songs either to fit into certain scenes or to fill out a soundtrack album. In virtually all of these cases, the songwriter (who is usually a recording artist) and his or her music publisher will give the motion picture company a 50% interest in the copyright to the newly created composition. In some cases the film company will administer the entire composition, and in others the writer's music publisher and the film company will separately administer their respective shares of the composition. In virtually all instances where the writer is a recording artist, the terms of the soundtrack album will also be negotiated, including artist/producer royalties and mechanical licensing arrangements.

In some cases, the film company will provide the writer with a demo budget so that the producer will be able to hear the newly created composition, with further payments due upon delivery of the final composition to the film company and inclusion in the motion picture. For example, the film company might pay the writer $1,500 to produce a demo recording and make an additional $10,000 payment upon completion of the composition and another $10,000 to $60,000 if the composition is actually put in the motion picture. In the event that a song does not make the final cut of the film, the motion picture producer will often have the right to use the song in another of its films, but this is a matter of negotiation. On occasion, the writer is also given the right to reacquire the composition if it is not used in the film by reimbursing the film company for the monies expended.

## First-Use Restrictions

If an outside song is chosen by a film producer and the song has not been previously recorded and released as a single or album cut, the producer will sometimes ask the music publisher not to promote or license the song to any other company until the film or the soundtrack album has been released. Some publishers will agree to this, and others (especially when a song is considered a possible hit regardless of whether it is included in the motion picture) will not.

Once again, such requests are decided on a case-by-case basis, with the publisher treating them more favorably if there has been little outside interest in the song, or if its writer is a recording artist and is performing the song in the film, or if there is a commitment that a well-known or up-and-coming artist will perform the song.

## Trailers and Advertisements

As previously indicated, the synchronization license usually grants the producer the right to use all music in the film in theatrical trailers (previews of upcoming films that are shown in movie theaters) as well as in television, Web site and radio promos. On occasion, the owner of a song used in a film will prohibit the producer from using the composition in promos (especially in cases where the publisher does not like how the song was used), but such restrictions are not the norm; especially since these rights are almost always granted before the music publisher or songwriter sees the final cut of the film. Sometimes an extra fee is charged for promos that use the song out of context (e.g., that use a song throughout the entire commercial over many scenes, as opposed to just the scene in which it actually occurs), but many times these rights are part of the overall synchronization fee charged by the music publisher.

Some producers will ask for permission to use a song in trailers and promos even though the song is not in the film. This usually occurs when a film has been fully scored but the producer needs a recognizable hit (which fits the theme or advertising campaign of the film) to attract the public's attention. Because of the importance of promos and trailers to the success of a film, the fees charged can be as much as or more than the normal synch fee, even though the use is only for promotional purposes (e.g., $12,000 to $95,000 for a life-of-copyright license).

## Deferred Payments/Indie Films

On occasion, producers of independent films, documentaries, lower-budget films (e.g., from $500,000 to $4 million), or films that have substantially exceeded their production budgets at the time music is being selected will ask a publisher to reduce its up-front synch fee for a song and, in return, guarantee an additional payment at some time in the future if the motion picture turns a profit or exceeds a certain agreed-upon gross or net dollar plateau. The experienced publisher or other representative knows that such a guarantee (considering the sometimes unorthodox accounting practices of some film companies and the unsuccessful track record of most low-budget films) is usually pie in the sky and will many times refuse such a request. However, if the publisher has a good relationship with a particular producer or director, knows how profit-and-loss accounting works in the motion picture business, believes that the company will remain in business or has an affiliation with a financially stable firm, has fairly strong audit rights, or simply believes in the project, such arrangements can be and are made.

## Home Video Advances

If the publisher is able to negotiate a per-video royalty (rather than the usual 1-time buy-out), the motion picture company will usually agree to an advance based on between 50,000 and 250,000 units for major films. Obviously, if the producer has doubts as to the potential success of a film or if the budget cannot afford large up-front home video music advances, there may be no advance or one that is in the 5,000- to 10,000-unit range. Since such advances are a convenience to a film company in that they alleviate a producer's initial accounting responsibilities and a benefit to the publisher because of the immediate "in hand" monies, they will normally be given if requested. Such advance arrangements are very rare, however, and nonexistent when dealing with a major film studio.

## Restrictions on the Use of Songs in Other Films

Occasionally, a motion picture producer will try to restrict the use of a song being licensed for other motion pictures so that the song's impact will not be diminished by its use in another movie. This usually occurs when the song has an essential role in the film (for example, as its theme or signature) or is being used as the film's title, or when major promotion monies are committed to a future soundtrack album and the producer wants the motion picture and soundtrack album audience to feel that the particular use is special to that motion picture. Additionally, most record companies will not want to commit hundreds of thousands of dollars to a song when the same song may be released by another artist or record company in competition with its soundtrack album or single. If such restrictions are agreed to by the publisher, they are normally for a period of from a few months to not more than 2 or 3 years. Sometimes the restriction will last only until the release of the motion picture—a commitment that is usually treated more favorably by the music publisher if the film receives major distribution, if there is a firm release date in the not too distant future, and if there is a guaranteed soundtrack album. In the case where a song's title is being used as the title for a film produced by a major studio with guaranteed national distribution, such restrictions, as long as they are not onerous in duration, are usually acceptable to music publishers because of the substantial monies payable in such circumstances.

## Exclusive Holds

Some film producers will request an "exclusive hold" on a song that has been used in an unreleased motion picture. In effect, they are asking the music publisher for a guarantee that it will not promote or license the composition in any medium (which usually can be limited to other motion pictures or national advertising campaigns) until the film is released and, in many cases, for a number of months or years thereafter. Such a request (or, in some instances, demand) is handled on a case-by-case basis after weighing both the benefits of getting a particular song in a motion picture and the disadvantages of putting a song on the shelf for a number of months or years. A variation of the exclusive-hold request often occurs when a producer is doing a film about a well-known performer or recording artist (e.g., a Ritchie Valens, Jim Morrison, or Janis Joplin) and wants to make sure that the music publisher of one of the performer's "signature songs" does not license the song to another film company contemplating the same type of project. In these cases, there is always a fee given to the publisher (usually in the form of an option, such as "$5,000 to $8,000 for each 6-month exclusive-hold period, with such hold period lasting for no longer than 18 months"). On occasion, a portion of these option payments is deducted from the final synch fee paid when the film is produced (e.g., "¼ of all option fee payments up to $8,000 may be deducted from the final fee payable") but in most cases they are not.

## Reduction of Fees Due to the Use of Many Hit Records

A film producer who wants to use the original hit recording of a song in a motion picture must not only negotiate a synchronization license for the song itself but also go to the record company that owns the master recording for permission to use the preexisting recorded version. Since the motion picture company must pay two separate fees in these "master plus song" licensing situations (e.g., one to the music publisher for the use of the underlying musical composition and one to the record company for the use of the existing recorded performance), it will often try to negotiate a reduction in the aggregate monies paid for both the song and the recording under the rationale that the film's music budget cannot justify such a large payment for 1 piece of music. In many cases (e.g., if the quote for the song is $30,000 and the price for the use of the master recording is $33,000, with the producer having to pay an extra $2,000 to the musicians' union musician reuse fees, for a combined total of $65,000), such a request is justifiable, since certain producers simply cannot afford such aggregate fees. In other cases, however, such a negotiating tactic by a producer is merely an attempt to get the cost of music down with little or no real justification.

Obviously, there is a fine line in determining when to hold firm and when to compromise on a fee, but the expert negotiator, because of past experience with the licensing procedures of various film companies and knowledge of how the business works and what the real music budget is for a particular film, knows when to hold the line on a fee and when to compromise. Knowing the people who you are dealing with is also extremely important, since if you know someone has been straightforward with you in the past about the real financial restrictions on a film project, that trust can make decisions easier.

Without experience, though, you will more than likely come out the loser, either because your song was not used when you refused to compromise on your fee or because you gave it away.

## A Publisher Having More Than One Song in a Film

Occasionally, because of the promotion efforts of a particular music publisher or its relationship with a motion picture producer, an up-front agreement will be made that guarantees lower synchronization fees to the producer if it uses a specified number of that publisher's songs in a film. For example, a publisher might agree to reduce its per-song fees by 10% to 30% if a producer uses more than 4 of its songs in a film or guarantee a set fee (e.g., $20,000 per song) if a certain number remain in the final version. Such arrangements can be vital to a film company's ability to secure the best possible songs for a price that is within its music budget and can also help the music publisher (and its writers) because of the guaranteed theatrical exposure of its songs. In effect, they help everyone concerned even though the immediate per-song synchronization and video fees may be somewhat reduced, since all parties gain from the immediate use and resulting ancillary uses of songs in a motion picture. Such arrangements really work only if the music publisher has a large number of well-known songs that fit the needs of a particular film. For example, if a film has a 1950s setting and you have a wealth of 1950s hits in your catalog, this type of deal can be most attractive.

## Student-Produced Films

Because student-produced films have limited chances for commercial success and small budgets, many music publishers will license their songs for substantially reduced fees. In such cases, most publishers recognize the importance of assisting young filmmakers, since they are an integral part of the future of the entertainment industry. Songs will sometimes be given to these young producers for free or for a nominal cost so that their projects will be realized and their careers advanced. Most publishers, however, will provide that if the project has any type of commercial success or secures more than just film festival or art house distribution, an additional fee or fees will be paid as certain criteria are achieved—a proviso that not only helps young producers get their projects off the ground but also ensures adequate compensation to the publisher and songwriter for their generosity if the film realizes national distribution or achieves some kind of financial success. This type of arrangement is called a "step deal."

## Rescoring and Replacing Songs in a Film Prior to Release

Especially in the case of lower- or medium-budget films, the producer will often want to replace an existing song score prior to the film's release. The reasons for such a move may be many, but they usually result from a producer's initial decision to try to get the cheapest composer possible because of initial budgetary constraints. If the score doesn't work, or if the final cut of a film convinces a producer that it has a real chance in the marketplace if it has some well-known songs, the producer may decide to try to get additional songs as replacements for the music in certain scenes. Considering that the music budget may have already been depleted, the producer will many times go to record companies or publishers with whom it has worked before and try to get permission to use certain songs and master recordings at reduced prices. The producer may also contact a music consultancy service that deals in film music licensing on a daily basis and give them the assignment. Depending on the relationship between the producer or music consultant and the record company or music publisher, reduced-rate deals are many times achieved within hours.

## Promotional Television Programs

Some film companies will film the premiere of the motion picture as well as its premiere party for promotional purposes. On occasion, a company will make a television program and distribute it to stations around the country to stimulate interest in the film. Since such promotional shows do help the motion picture and expose the songs in the film, film companies many times ask music publishers for either free or minimal-fee synchronization licenses. These requests are handled on a case-by-case basis, with many of the agreements containing "most favored nations" provisions (e.g., if one song receives a fee, all other songs will receive the same fee, or if one song gets a larger fee than any other, all songs will receive that larger fee.). In negotiating such agreements, you should remember that even though there is no or only a minimal up-front synchronization fee payable, the vehicle is really for promotional purposes only and should be dealt with in that spirit. Your position in these negotiations may also determine whether the motion picture company feels that you are a person or company that it can work with on future projects, a factor that can never be minimized.

## Nonprofit Films and Free Use of Music

On occasion, when a film is produced on behalf of a certain cause with all profits contributed to the promotion of that cause, the producer will ask music publishers and record companies for free licenses. If the project and its goals seem worthwhile, most publishers and record companies will charge either nominal fees or no fees at all. Often such agreements are on a "most favored nations" basis, which guarantees payment to all songwriters and publishers if anyone else gets paid. One example of such a project is *Good Morning America,* a documentary about the letters that Vietnam soldiers sent back to their loved ones during the war. The producer sent an explanatory letter and a script to the publishers and record companies of all the songs that had been selected for the film. Guarantees were also given that a large portion of the monies earned by the film would go to Vietnam veterans' organizations. All the music publishers and record companies gave free licenses for the music used in the documentary.

## Screen Credit

Virtually all motion picture producers will give screen credit for the use of preexisting songs in motion pictures. This credit is almost always included during the crawl at the end of the film. The publisher is seldom mentioned though the film *Chicago* provided a full-frame credit to Unichappel Music. The film producer usually affords credit only to the title of the song, the writers, and, if a preexisting master recording is used, the name of the record company and the recording artist. Additionally, if a new version is made by a recording artist for release on a soundtrack album, the credits will include such information. In a field where credit provisions are important, it is vital to provide for a correct line credit in the license itself so that the proper information on the screen is assured. Credit in advertisements for the film is almost unheard of, but does occasionally occur at the film producer's option. A good example is the listing of the #1 hit song "My Heart Will Go On" in full-page newspaper ads for the film *Titanic.*

## Music Cue Sheets and Their Importance

After a motion picture has been produced and a final version has been edited, the producer will prepare a music cue sheet that lists all the music used in the film, including how each song was used, its timing in seconds, the identity of the writers and music publishers and their performing rights affiliation, and if preexisting master recordings have been used, the identity of recording artists and record companies. Considering the amount of music used in most films, this cue sheet is usually completed within 30 days after theatrical release, but depending on the producer and available staff, it can be longer.

Some music cue sheets contain specific scene explanations and dialogue details, but most contain only chronological information on the titles, writers, publishers, performance right affiliation, master recording information, timing (20 seconds, 2 minutes, etc.) and generic usage (visual vocal, background music, etc.). At the fringe of the industry are low-budget companies that do not even bother to type a cue sheet and others that do not even know what a music cue sheet is.

Since ASCAP and BMI use these cue sheets to determine how music is used, who owns the music, and how royalty payments should be made when a film is shown on television, it is essential that the writer and publisher secure a copy and review it closely. Because a motion picture uses so much music in so many ways (visual vocals, background vocals, background instrumentals, opening and closing credits, etc.), it is not unusual for mistakes to be made on cue sheets, whether it be a false timing, a mislabeling of a song's use, or an incorrect identification of the writer and publisher. By looking over a copy of the cue sheet, the writer and publisher can correct any inaccuracies before the producer distributes the cue sheet to the performance right organizations. In addition, since cue sheets are circulated throughout the world by ASCAP and BMI and music publishers send them to their subpublishing representatives in foreign countries, who then register them with their local performance rights societies; a correct cue sheet is the key to receiving what you are due. Table 5.3 illustrates the format and the type of information that should be on a cue sheet.

## Getting Hit Songs into Films

Music publishers play an important role in convincing film producers to use past hit songs in their movies. The successful ones promote their catalogs by means of sampler albums, catalog lists, and songbooks. These samplers range from CDs containing 30- to 40-second excerpts of a publisher's main songs to massive print catalogs with accompanying full-song CDs. "Idea books" suggest certain titles for certain scenes and contain separate listings of a publisher's catalog by songwriter, recording artist, era, or genre of music.

When record companies promote the use of their recordings with producers, they also help the songwriter and publisher. Important too are good working relationships with the Los Angeles-based motion picture companies' music department heads and music supervisors, as well as independent music consultants and film agents. Web sites can also be valuable.

Whether one is a songwriter, music publisher, or record company executive, it is also vital to know what pictures are in the planning stage, in production, or in postproduction (both Hollywood Reporter and Variety keep track of productions filming in and outside the United States), since contact with producers to suggest ideas can help. Many music publishers are able to secure the script of a film from the producer or music supervisor and give specific suggestions for the use of compositions as either background music or visual vocals for use in individual scenes. Film companies appreciate constructive promotion—not the shotgun approach of suggesting every song in one's catalog for a particular film.

## Producers and the Selecting of Songs

Prior to making the final choice, many producers select a large number of possible songs and secure quotations from music publishers. Usually a list of

TABLE **5.3** Music Cue Sheet

TITLE OF FILM: _____

NAME OF COMPOSER: _____

FILM COMPANY NAME: _____

U.S. RELEASE DATE: _____

| No. | Selection | Composer | Publisher | How Used | Time |
|---|---|---|---|---|---|
| 1. | Film Company Logo | Name (ASCAP) | Film Company Publishing Co. (ASCAP) | Bkg. Inst. | :10 |
| 2. | Main Title Theme | Name (ASCAP) | Film Company Publishing Co. (ASCAP) | Bkg. Inst. (Opening Credits) | 1:40 |
| 3. | Beach Scene | Name (ASCAP) | Film Company Publishing Co. (ASCAP) | Bkg. Inst. | 2:45 |
| 4. | Existing Hit Song | Name (BMI) | Outside Publishing Co. (BMI) | Bkg. Vocal | :35 |
| 5. | City Landscape Scene | Name (ASCAP) | Film Company Publishing Co. (ASCAP) | Bkg. Inst. | 1:12 |
| 6. | Existing Hit Song | Name (ASCAP) | Outside Publishing Co. (ASCAP) | Visual Vocal | :47 |
| 7. | Existing Hit Song (Master Licensed from Warner Bros. Records) | Name (BMI) | Outside Publishing Co. (BMI) | Bkg. Vocal | 1:15 |
| 8. | Car Chase Scene | Name (ASCAP) | Film Company Publishing Co. (ASCAP) | Bkg. Inst. | 2:24 |
| 9. | Existing Hit Song (Master Licensed From MCA Records) | Name (ASCAP) | Outside Publishing Co. (ASCAP) | Bkg. Vocal (Closing Credits) | 3:30 |

only about 15 to 25 songs will be given to the people clearing (i.e., getting permission to use) the music, but many times a producer may express interest in from 30 to 50 compositions even though only 10 to 15 uses are actually needed. There have even been cases of producers getting fee quotes for up to 150 different songs for a 10- to 12-song picture. If a director or music supervisor has a specific song in mind for a particular scene but the fees quoted by the music publisher are too expensive for the music budget of the film, it is sound business practice to have commitments on a number of alternate, less costly songs. If the song is being used as a visual vocal, however, the producer does not have the luxury of waiting until postproduction for actual music selection and will usually secure price quotes for only a few preferred compositions.

Most of the major film production companies know which publishers are flexible in their pricing policies and easy to work with as well as those publishers whose licensing policies conform with those of the producer. Many film producers also have extensive music libraries and reference materials that they review when making selections. The publishers who continue to be successful in the promotion of songs for motion pictures, however, are those who continually promote their catalogs, since personnel changes at many film companies make it vital to let people know what you have. Good working relationships with the people at the various studios and having a film company know that it can work with you cannot be overemphasized, as these are frequently the factors that get your songs into films.

## Recap

Considering the ever-increasing global market for films and its importance to musical compositions, knowing how to negotiate a motion picture license is one of the cornerstone responsibilities for anyone who is responsible for ensuring that songs continue to earn money. It can be a tricky business and one filled with complexities, but it is an area that, if handled professionally and correctly, has the potential of generating enormous amounts of income and exposing songs to millions of people.

## *THE SONG WRITTEN FOR A MOTION PICTURE*

One of the most difficult types of song to write for any lyricist or composer is the song specifically written for a movie (see Table 5.4 for examples). The writers of these songs usually fall into three categories. The first is the professional songwriter living in Los Angeles or another city where films are produced. The second type is the writer/recording artist. The third type is the successful record producer who is also a writer. The difficulties of breaking into this field are greater for the nonperforming writer, who must not only

TABLE **5.4**   Song Written for a Motion Picture

| Song | Motion Picture | Writer(s) |
|---|---|---|
| "Hands That Built America" | *Gangs of New York* (2002) | U2 |
| "Into the West" | *The Lord of the Rings: The Return of the King* (2003) | Annie Lenox<br>Howard Shore<br>Frances Walsh |
| "The Way We Were" | *The Way We Were* (1973) | Alan Bergman<br>Marilyn Bergman<br>Marvin Hamlisch |
| "I Don't Want to Miss a Thing" | *Armageddon* (1998) | Diane Warren |
| "My Heart Will Go On" | *Titanic* (1997) | James Horner<br>Will Jennings |
| "When You Wish upon a Star" | *Pinocchio* (1940) | Leigh Harline<br>Ned Washington |
| "White Christmas" | *Holiday Inn* (1942) | Irving Berlin |
| "Moon River" | *Breakfast at Tiffany's* (1961) | Henry Mancini<br>Johnny Mercer |
| "Raindrops Keep Fallin' on My Head" | *Butch Cassidy and the Sundance Kid* (1969) | Burt Bacharach<br>Hal David |
| "Over the Rainbow" | *The Wizard of Oz* (1939) | Harold Arlen<br>E. Y. Harburg |

write quickly but also evoke the specific feeling that a director wants for a scene. The writer/artist, on the other hand, is many times hired for film work because of past or current record success ("name value") and less on a knowledge of the intricacies of writing for film. Emergence of successful record producer/writers into this field is due primarily to their experience and ability to select, write, and produce a hit contemporary sound.

## Breaking into the Business

With few exceptions, for songwriters to have any chance of getting into this field, they must live in an area that is a film-producing center. Otherwise, it is very difficult to build the relationships and contacts necessary for not only the first break but also continuing assignments.

John Bettis, a very successful pop, film, and television writer based in Los Angeles, got his first movie credit thanks to the efforts of his music publisher. The background composer Jerry Goldsmith (*The Omen, Star Trek: The Motion*

*Picture*) needed lyrics for a piece of source music in a *Twilight Zone* segment, and Bettis was referred to Goldsmith by his publisher. This initial contact, as well as the relationship that grew from it, resulted in Bettis's being called in on 5 films that Goldsmith later scored. One of Bettis's biggest pop hits, "Crazy for You," which was recorded by Madonna, was written for the film *Vision Quest*. In this case also, Bettis's music publisher made the initial contact with the film's music supervisor. Although most of Bettis's film song work (as well as the film song work of most other successful writers) now comes directly to Bettis or his agent from people within the film industry who are familiar with his writing skills and past film work, his publisher played an essential role in helping him break into the film business.

## The Song for Film—From Start to Finish

A successful writer (or the writer's agent) gets a call from a director or music supervisor, is told that a film is in production, and is asked whether he or she wants to write a song for the film. If the writer says yes, either a script of the movie or video of the scene is provided, or the basic story line of the film is read over the phone. If the writer is a lyricist, they will discuss who the composer of the music should be (many times it is the background scorer). The writer will then be given direction and suggestions as to the "feel" of the song as well as the emotions and thoughts needed in the lyrics and the music. The director normally already has in mind a model song, which he or she has probably "temp tracked" to the particular scene in order to simulate the type of feeling needed. The writer will then be informed of the deadline for submission and will write the song and present it in "demo form" to the director or music supervisor. At this point, it is very common for the director to ask for a rewrite or, in some cases, to reject the song. After the song is rewritten and accepted, the recording artist enters the picture. A recording session has to be booked subject to a particular artist's availability. At the session, sometimes multiple versions of the same song will be recorded to see which one fits best into the movie. The writing of the song, the presentation of the demo, the rewrites, and the recording session are all under strict time limits (sometimes as short as 1 week), as the film is usually in its final postproduction phase, with final prints of the film due for release to movie theaters on a specific date.

As opposed to the above scenario, some film producers use a cattle-call approach whereby many writers are asked to submit songs for a project. Sometimes fees are paid to the writers for their submissions; at other times song submissions are on a totally speculative basis.

## The "Song Written for a Film" Contract

When a producer hires a composer or lyricist to write a song for a film, the compensation as well as the rights of all parties are set forth in a commissioning agreement. These contracts typically state that the producer employs the composer or lyricist to write a film within a stated period of time in accordance with certain ideas and instructions supplied by the producer. A due date for a demo record is set forth in the agreement, and the producer almost always reserves the right to make any changes. Upon delivery of the song, the writer receives an initial fee (e.g., $25,000 for a song, $7,500 for the lyrics, etc.) as well as a guarantee of additional future compensation in the form of songwriter royalties, which is either in the body of the agreement or attached as a separate schedule (e.g., 50% of mechanical income earned from record, tape, and CD sales as well as download income; a set rate for sheet music; 50% of any synchronization income from the uses of the song in a television series, other motion pictures, or commercials). The writer also normally receives screen credit for the composition. In consideration for the writing fee, the writer usually grants all rights to the producer (with the exception of his or her share of royalty income) under an employee-for-hire or work-for-hire contract.

*Writer Services.* The songwriter is employed by the film producer to write a new and original song (or songs) for the motion picture entitled (Name of picture). The contract will specify whether the writer is being hired to write a complete song or to provide lyrics to new or already composed music. In some cases, the contract will be a joint agreement among the producer, the composer of the music, and a separate lyricist. The "work" shall be written in accordance with such ideas and instructions as the producer may supply to the composer and lyricist and shall be suitable, in producer's opinion, for use in the film.

*Starting and Completion Dates.* Because of the time constraints of the postproduction phase, the starting date is usually the day the contract is signed. As shown in the two examples here, the completion date may be fixed or open-ended.

*E X A M P L E 1.* "The composer shall deliver the song to the Producer in the form of a demonstration record and lead sheet on or about September 10, 2003. Producer shall have the right to require composer (or lyricist) to make any changes, modifications, additions or deletions that the Producer desires and that all such changes are to be without additional compensation to the writer." The writing time in this contract was 4 days, as the agreement was signed on September 6, 2003.

*E X A M P L E 2.* "The term of the writer's employment shall commence as of the date of the agreement (May 10, 2004) and shall continue until completion of all services required by the Producer including any services required in connection with changes or modifications during the recording and dubbing of the work." The term of this contract is open ended, as it runs from the date of the signing of the agreement through the date when the recording and dubbing are complete.

*Writing Fees.*  The amount of the fee paid to a writer depends on whether a complete song (or songs) or just lyrics are being contracted for; whether the song is to be used as the theme song, as a visual vocal, or as background; the music budget of the film; whether the film is being produced by a major studio, a large independent company, or a smaller independent; the writer's stature and past film song success; whether the writer is also the artist who will perform the song in the movie, and his or her success as a performing artist; the negotiating power of the writer's agent or representative; and the current industry practice as to the range of fees being paid to writers for film songs—the going rate.

Fees can range from $1,500 for the lyrics to one song to in excess of $300,000 for a complete song if the writer is also the performing artist. All of the fees paid are nonrecoupable (i.e., cannot be deducted from royalties) and nonreturnable (i.e., the producer cannot ask for the money back if he or she does not like the song). For a reasonably successful nonperforming writer (or writing team), the range of fees might be as follows:

$7,500 to $10,000 for a lower-budget quality film from a major studio

$12,500 to $15,000 for songs in subsequent films (assuming the first film did reasonably well)

$25,000 to over $50,000 for a song for medium- to higher-budget films (assuming the writer has had a number of previous film credits)

$50,000 to in excess of $100,000 for the theme song to a major film for an established film songwriter

Obviously, if 1 or more of the writer's past film songs has been a major hit, won an Academy Award, or been nominated for any other award (Golden Globe, Grammy), the writer's song fee for subsequent films will be positively affected.

*E X A M P L E 1.*  "In full consideration of all rights granted by writer to Producer, Producer agrees to pay to writer $25,000 payable within 10 days after the execution of the agreement" (theme song for a medium-budget major release).

*E X A M P L E 2.*  "$1,500 payable promptly following delivery of the lyrics to the Producer" (lyrics to one song for a new writer).

*E X A M P L E 3.*  "$60,000 payable at $30,000 upon the commencement of the services and an additional $30,000 upon the completion of all services" (theme song for a major film release written by established writers).

*Screen Credit.* Songwriter screen credit is a negotiable item. Some major writers and writer/artists are able to negotiate a spot in the film's opening credits. Most song credits, however, appear in the film's closing credits (the credit roll); even here some writers are able to negotiate a single-frame card credit, separate from all of the other songwriter credits.

*E X A M P L E 1.* "Writer shall receive credit in the end titles of all positive prints of the film. Credit is conditional upon the performance of all the provisions of this contract and that the song is actually used in the film as released. Credit shall not be given in any form of advertising."

*E X A M P L E 2.* "Composer shall receive appropriate credit on the screen in size, style of type, and placement in the picture as the Producer, in his sole discretion, may determine. Credit shall read "music and lyrics by (Name of writer) in connection with the song title."

*E X A M P L E 3.* "Writer is entitled to screen credit on all positive prints of the film in the closing credits on a separate card."

As an example of the type of bargaining position that some major writer/artists have as to credit, both *Saturday Night Fever* (1978) and *Young Guns II* (1990) showed a writer screen credit in the opening credits of the film. In *Saturday Night Fever* the full-frame credit read "Original Music by Barry, Robin, and Maurice Gibb" and listed the songs "How Deep Is Your Love," "Night Fever," "Staying Alive," and "More Than a Woman" as well as the recording artists, the Bee Gees. The closing credits of the film listed all of the songs again as well as any other outside songs, writers, and artists (Kool & the Gang, Rick Dees, KC and the Sunshine Band, etc.). In *Young Guns II,* a full-frame opening credit read "Songs by Jon Bon Jovi," followed by a second separate full-frame credit to the background composer, Alan Silvestri. The closing credits listed the two Bon Jovi songs, "Blaze of Glory" and "Billy Got Your Guns," as well as the publisher and record company. In *Gangs of New York* (2002), U2 received a full-frame credit for "Hands that Built America."

*Grant of Rights.* The grant of rights is of the broadest nature possible in order to allow the film producer unlimited ownership of all aspects and ingredients of the film. The following clauses indicate the broad nature of the rights that the writer gives to the film producer:

*E X A M P L E 1.* "Composition is specifically ordered or commissioned by the Producer for use as part of a motion picture entitled (*Name of Picture*) and is a 'Work Made For Hire.' Producer is the author and composer for all purposes and the owner of all right, title, and interest, throughout the world, for all purposes, without condition, restriction, or limitation subject only to royalty compensation as set forth herein."

*E X A M P L E 2.* "Producer shall own all rights of every kind in and to the results and proceeds of Artist's services hereunder, including copyright and exploitation in any and all media throughout the universe."

*E X A M P L E 3.* "The complete, unencumbered, exclusive, and worldwide rights which vest in producer hereunder shall include, but shall not be limited to, motion picture, synchronization, mechanical, performing, and dramatic rights, and all other rights of every kind, nature, and description, whether now known or hereafter to become known or come into being."

The film producer will normally retain the right to change or adapt the song as well as to add music or lyrics to it. Also, the writer normally grants the producer the right to use the writer's name, likeness, and biography in the advertising and exploitation of the film for all time.

*Songwriter Royalties.* The contract, regardless of whether it is a "work made for hire" agreement or a regular songwriter–publisher agreement, will always set forth all of the areas where the songwriter receives royalties: among others, mechanical royalties from record, tape, and CD sales; a set rate for sheet music sales; 50% of any synchronization income from the use of the song in a television series, other motion pictures, or commercials; performance royalties (ASCAP, BMI, foreign societies); and foreign royalties.

*Exclusivity.* Practically all film songwriting contracts are nonexclusive (as opposed to background scoring contracts, which are exclusive), and the writer is free to continue other projects or write for others during the term of the services agreement. This nonexclusivity is conditioned, though, by clauses stating, for instance, that the writer "will not render any outside services which would prevent the work (the film song) from being completed within the time period specified in the contract."

*Publishing.* Most contracts provide the producer with 100% of the publishing rights and income of the composition. This is particularly true if the producer is a major studio or large independent. Most film studios and movie production companies have their own publishing arms, and most songs written for a film are assigned to the studio's publishing company. Music-publishing income is part of the consideration for the writer's services fee, and it is therefore not the norm for writers in this area to retain any of their own publishing. There are writers, though, who because of their past success in film or other areas are able to share in a film song's publishing income either through a copublishing or administration agreement or through some form of participation agreement. More-established writers sometimes purposely do not raise their fees, despite the success of their film songs, in order to put themselves in a better position to negotiate some form of participation in a song's publishing income.

Writers sometimes are able to retain the publishing on songs if they are employed by a medium-size or small film production company. Many of these companies do not have music publishing companies as part of their operation, and some do not understand the short- or long-term earnings that can be generated by a film song. In those cases, it is not unusual for a writer to keep the copyright as well as the publishing income that flows from that copyright. It is not uncommon for major writer/artists to retain part of a song's publishing regardless of whether the studio is a major studio or an independent. For example, the song "(Everything I Do) I Do It for You" from *Robin Hood: Prince of Thieves* was not only the most successful movie song of 1991, it also was the year's biggest worldwide hit. The song was written by Michael Kamen (the film's background scorer), Bryan Adams (one of Canada's most successful writer/artists), and "Mutt" Lange (a successful writer and Adams's record producer). Both Adams and Lange retained their publishing in this deal.

*Originality.* The writer will always guarantee that the song is totally original for the film, is not based in whole or in part on any other composition, and does not infringe upon the copyright of any other composition or the right of any other party. A certificate of authorship will also be provided by the writer as well as any other documents that the producer requires for proof of ownership.

*Use or Nonuse of the Song.* The producer of the film will usually have no obligation whatsoever to use the song in the film or to exploit the composition in any way.

*Performance Royalties.* The writer will receive his or her writer performance right royalties directly from the society of which he or she is a member. If a situation arises where a performing right society is unable to license a user for various reasons, then the writer should try to negotiate with the producer some form of continuing royalty payment for the use of the song. Without such a "safeguard" provision, the producer may be able to license the song without compensation to the writer. The same considerations are true with respect to the publisher's share of performance income if the writer has been able to negotiate a copublishing agreement with the film producer.

# LIFE AFTER THE MOTION PICTURE RELEASE (WHERE THE REAL MONEY IS MADE)

Just as with songs used in television series, movie songs can have a substantial financial life well beyond the initial synchronization or writing fee. Table 5.5 gives examples of the dollar figures a successful movie song can earn. The following sections review the revenue-producing areas listed in the table.

## Motion Picture Home Video Licensing

Since the VCR and DVD markets are enormous throughout the world, with major motion pictures selling between 400,000 and 24 million copies, the sale of video cassettes, DVDs and videodiscs can be a major source of revenue for film companies and, depending on how a song is licensed, a potentially significant source of income for the music publisher and songwriter.

Many different negotiating approaches may be used for licensing songs for home videos, with the following being the most prevalent: a 1-time-only buy-out for all cassettes, DVDs and discs sold; a set royalty for each cassette, DVD and disc sold; a modified buy-out for a stated number of units, with additional monies for additional cassettes, DVDs and discs sold (referred to as a "rollover advance"); a "to be negotiated in the future" per-cassette, -DVD or -disc royalty fee; perpetual versus limited-term contract duration; and worldwide versus country-by-country licensing.

TABLE **5.5**   Income for a Successful Movie Song

| | |
|---|---|
| $    25,000 | Synchronization and video buy-out fee |
| 800,000 | U.S. radio and television performance royalties for a hit single |
| 85,000 | "A" side single U.S. record sales (1 million copies) |
| 170,000 | U.S. album sales (2 million copies) |
| 7,500 | Foreign theatrical performances |
| 4,000 | Academy Awards Show performance in "best song" category |
| 4,000 | Grammy Awards Show performance in "best song" category |
| 20,000 | Sheet music and folios |
| 7,000 | Initial television broadcasts of the film on pay and network television |
| 250,000 | Commercial |
| 53,500 | Foreign "A" side single records |
| 85,000 | Foreign album sales |
| 600,000 | Foreign radio and television performance royalties for a hit single |
| 15,000 | Miscellaneous royalties |
| $2,126,000 | Writer and publisher royalties |

*One-Time Buy-Out.*   All of the major motion picture companies as well as many of the smaller companies demand that the music publisher or writer accept a one-time buy-out fee for all video cassette, DVD and disc rights regardless of the actual number of units that may be sold in the future.

These buy-out fees range from $5,000 to $15,000. Many of the formulas used by motion picture companies limit the video buy-out fee to between 50% and 150% of the synchronization fee (i.e., the monies paid to include the song in the film). In most cases, however, your decision as to what to charge is going to be made on whether the film has a $4 million versus a $75 million budget, the amount of money allocated to the purchase of outside music, the type of scene using the song, whether it is sung on camera or is only background music, how badly you want the song in the film, what you project the video sales to be, whether a new recording by a well-known artist will be made, whether there is a soundtrack or "A" side single guarantee, if the song has been a recent hit or is in need of some reexposure to the public, how important the song is to the film's director or producer, the amount of monies other publishers might be quoting for use of a composition in the scene, the projected success of the picture considering the plot, stars, director, producer, etc., the reputation of the studio releasing the film, your knowledge of the industry, and your negotiating ability. Unfortunately, since these negotiations occur before a film is released and before one knows the real value of the motion picture, arriving at a dollar figure can be difficult. Moreover, the film company will always look at the overall price it is being charged for all rights it needs, and as long as the video price does not take the song out of the approved budget, the amount of money charged for home video rights need not relate to any proven formula. In virtually all cases, it is your ability to negotiate the "bundle of rights" for an acceptable price that either gets a song into a film or leaves it on the cutting room floor.

Obviously, the value of such a one-time buy-out to a publisher or songwriter is that if the video does not sell well, the monies received from the buy-out may easily exceed what would have been earned if payment was made on a per-unit sales basis. However, if the video achieves substantial sales levels throughout the world (e.g., a number of films selling from 5 to over 40 million units), the buy-out monies will probably be substantially less than would have been earned if a per-unit royalty had been negotiated. For example, an 8¢ rate on 2 million videos would result in a $160,000 per-song royalty—a far cry from the $5,000 to $15,000 average buy-out fee.

*Royalty per DVD, Cassette, or Disc.*   The royalty paid for the use of a composition may be based on either a set monetary rate (usually from 8¢ to 15¢ per song) or a percentage of the wholesale or retail price of each video, shared on a pro rata basis by all songs contained in the video. The pro rata sharing is sometimes based on the duration of each song in relation to the aggregate timing of all songs or music on the video or, alternatively, the duration of the song to the duration of the entire motion picture.

The penny per cassette, DVD, or disc approach is one of the simpler ways to deal with home video distribution, since all the motion picture company has to do is to compute the number of units sold and multiply that number by the agreed-upon per-song penny royalty. For example, if 100,000 cassettes of a film are sold and a particular song has an 8¢ royalty, the aggregate payment to the music publisher and songwriter would be $8,000. There are also no calculations necessary as to a particular song's timing compared to the timing of all other music in the film and no recalculations based on changes in the wholesale or retail prices of the video—an important factor to some companies, since a video is often released at an expensive price for the rental market and then reduced to stimulate consumer sales at retail (the "sell through" price). Such a per-video royalty is unacceptable to almost all U.S. motion picture companies, but it is one of the fairest approaches, since royalties are based on actual sales of the video.

Under the wholesale price percentage formula, all songs share in a percentage of the monies paid to the motion picture company by retailers. For example, if the royalty is 5% of the wholesale price of each video shared by all songs, the computations might look as follows:

| | |
|---|---|
| $ 30.00 | Retail price |
| $ 15.00 | Wholesale price to retailers |
| x 5% | Royalty percentage |
| $ .75 | Total music royalties shared by 10 songs on a video |
| + 10 | |
| $ .075 | Per-song royalties |

If the royalty is based on a percentage of the wholesale price, many publishers provide for a minimum or "floor" on the royalties they will receive to prevent the royalty from being less than a minimum amount (e.g., 5% of the wholesale price but in no event less than the current U.S. Copyright Law statutory mechanical rate or a set monetary amount such as 10¢ per song). With respect to motion pictures produced by U.S. film companies, such percentage royalty arrangements have virtually become extinct owing to the refusal of producers to pay on a wholesale basis or pay royalties on the actual number of videos sold.

*Modified Buy-Out or Rollover Advance.* Under the modified buy-out or rollover advance formula, the motion picture company pays a certain up-front fee for a set number of videos, with additional predetermined fees paid as additional sales plateaus are reached. For example, a producer may pay $8,000 for the first 100,000 units sold and an additional $8,000 for each additional 100,000 units. The initial fee is almost always paid when the license is signed, with subsequent fees (or advances) paid at the attainment of each sales plateau. The few film companies that will accept a rollover agreement are likely to try to limit the royalties payable to a maximum number of units (e.g., "up to 1 million cassettes with no further payments due thereafter").

*Future Negotiated Fees.*   When video cassettes first began to proliferate, many publishers and writers were unsure as to what to charge for songs used in "home use" videos. Because of this uncertainty, a number were able to provide for negotiation in good faith at some specified time in the future (when some type of standard industry practices might be established). When this approach was used, the producer usually paid an advance when the agreement was signed that would be applied against the fee eventually negotiated (e.g., $5,000 as a good-faith payment, which would be deducted from the final agreed-upon fee). Now that the one-time buy-out has established itself as an industry standard, such "future negotiation" clauses have become extinct.

*Perpetual versus Limited-Term Licensing.*   Unlike some home video licenses in other areas, the license term for theatrically released motion pictures is always for the life of copyright of the song. For that reason, the person negotiating the fee agreement must not only think about making sure the song gets into the film but also realize that what is done today represents a commitment for as long as a film is sold in the home video format.

*Worldwide versus Territorial Licensing.*   Virtually all producers demand a worldwide license, in which payments for any videos distributed are made to the U.S. publisher by the U.S. film company, with no payments or royalties made to the music publisher's representative (i.e., subpublisher) in foreign territories where the DVD, cassette, or disc may be released. For example, if a U.S. publisher of a song agrees to a worldwide buyout or an 8¢ per DVD/cassette/disc royalty, the film producer will pay the U.S. publisher all monies regardless of whether sales occur in the United States, England, Germany, Sweden, or France.

In the past, a number of publishers licensed video sales only for the United States or for the United States and Canada and demanded that video distributors pay the prevailing video rates in all other countries of sale. Under this approach, royalties or other fees are paid in each foreign territory to a writer's or publisher's representative in that territory (at the rates established by law, custom, or negotiation in such territories) rather than to the U.S. publisher. Also, many songs are controlled by a U.S. publisher in only selected territories of the world owing to reversion laws in foreign countries or the terms of the agreements with foreign representatives. In such cases, the U.S. publisher may be able to give a rate only for certain territories, while the motion picture producer has to negotiate video rights with the parties who control the song in the "noncontrolled" foreign territories. Since the video rates charged in foreign territories are not standardized, virtually all motion picture producers refuse to accept this type of agreement unless the song is so vital to the movie that it cannot be deleted or replaced by another composition.

*Elimination of Songs Because of Home Video Policies.* Because of the "video buy-out or nothing" policies of the major motion picture companies, if a publisher does not agree to a buy-out payment for home video distribution, the song will not be used even though it may be right for the movie. A film's director, writer, or music supervisor has little or no influence to change the film distributor's video policy, and if a publisher or songwriter holds out for a per-unit royalty and the motion picture company's policy is one of video buy-outs only, a replacement song will virtually always be used.

*Deleting Songs from Home Video Releases.* Even after a song has been included in the theatrically distributed version of a film, if a motion picture company cannot negotiate an acceptable video buy-out contract with a music publisher or songwriter, it may choose to take the song out of the home video version. Since video rights are now negotiated at the same time as the synchronization license, such a situation usually occurs only with older movies (where licenses did not contemplate or provide for home video) and films that have "to be negotiated in the future" home video provisions.

## Hit Singles from Motion Pictures

A significant source of income for the composer, lyricist, and publisher of movie songs is the hit single. And considering that a soundtrack album can contain 4 or 5 successful singles, the monies that can be made in this area can be extraordinary.

*Mechanical Royalties.* The song's publisher normally licenses the song to a record company for the statutory royalty for every record, tape, and CD sold. In some cases, the rate will be 75% of statutory. If the song is covered by other recording artists, the mechanical license can bring in hundreds of thousands of dollars long after the song's initial popularity. Think of the many recordings over the years of Henry Mancini's "Moon River," from Breakfast at Tiffany's.

*ASCAP and BMI Royalties.* U.S. radio and TV performances of a movie song can add hundreds of thousands of dollars of royalty income if the song becomes a hit record, becomes a standard, and is recorded over the years by many artists in addition to being used in other films or television programs. It is not unusual for such a song to earn from $20,000 to over $100,000 per year in catalog performance royalties long after the movie's release.

*Foreign Performance Royalties.* For movie songs, the foreign market can represent a substantial revenue area for writers and publishers, particularly since American product is the staple of many countries' theaters as well as radio and television programming. In 2003 well over $250 million was forwarded to ASCAP and BMI for foreign performances. For songwriters with a song in a film, the areas that can generate foreign performance royalties include radio, television, cable, wired music and live performances as well as income generated by theater performances of the film. Table 5.6 gives examples of the type of writer foreign performance royalties that can be generated during the initial year of chart activity for two successful "A" side film singles.

## The Motion Picture Soundtrack Album

When a film studio decides to release a soundtrack album, the studio (or its music representatives) will either go to its affiliated record label or to the star's label (if he or she is a recording artist) or shop the project to an interested record label. The record company will usually provide a substantial advance (e.g. $500,000) to the film studio to put the album together (negotiate licenses,

TABLE **5.6**   Hit Songs from Films: Foreign Release

| Country | Society | Song A | Song B |
| --- | --- | --- | --- |
| Australia | APRA | $ 22,040 | $32,575 |
| Austria | AKM | 6,400 | 7,425 |
| Belgium | SABAM | 6,256 | 9,245 |
| Canada | SOCAN | 20,500 | 38,000 |
| England | PRS | 52,760 | 80,000 |
| Finland | TEOSTO | 1,664 | 2,500 |
| France | SACEM | 2,060 | 35,500 |
| Germany | GEMA | 16,400 | 22,400 |
| Holland | BUMA | 17,280 | 12,432 |
| Hong Kong | CASH | 556 | 1,200 |
| Italy | SIAE | 3,260 | 18,000 |
| Japan | JASRAC | 3,366 | 12,000 |
| Norway | TONO | 1,270 | 1,850 |
| South Africa | SAMRO | 1,450 | 1,250 |
| Spain | SGAE | 2,244 | 6,780 |
| Sweden | STIM | 5,670 | 7,420 |
| Switzerland | SUISA | 2,970 | 3,200 |
| Other Countries | | 4,235 | 8,525 |
| | TOTALS: | $170,381 | $300,302 |

new song costs, masters, etc.). The agreement would grant the record company the right to manufacture, advertise, and sell the soundtrack album and singles with artist royalties (negotiated) of 16% of retail pro-rated to all artists who have masters on the album. The artists would need exclusivity waivers from their record companies to appear on the album. Single releases would be scheduled (e.g. 10 weeks prior to the film release) with the album release set for no later than 3 weeks before the picture opens. Music videos would be released with each single and they would contain actual footage from the film with the costs of the videos being shared by the studio and the record company. The type of film credit would be negotiated (usually in the closing credits) and royalty statements would be issued semi-annually. In practically all cases, the film studio would be the copyright owner (a work for hire) of the new songs and masters.

When the studio wants to use a pre-existing master recording, they would negotiate a fee (e.g. $50,000) for the non-exclusive right to use the master in the film for the worldwide period of copyright in the sound recording, as well as to reproduce the master for DVDs, videocassettes, etc. for home use sale of the film and for the soundtrack album. An album royalty and screen credit would be negotiated, as well as the right to use the artist's name for advertising and other purposes.

As to pre-existing songs as well as newly written songs, the music publisher will usually license the U.S. mechanical rights to their songs for the statutory rate of 8.5¢. If there are a large number of songs on the album, the record company may ask all song owners to agree to a maximum aggregate mechanical royalty cap on each record that would be divided equally among all songs, or a 75% statutory rate for each song.

## Television Commercials Promoting the Film

Virtually all films use television commercials to advertise the theatrical release and to increase box office receipts. Although extremely expensive (with some budgets running from ⅓ to ½ of a film's cost), this method of multimillion-dollar promotion is a necessity in today's marketplace. Payments are occasionally made for the use of songs in those commercials, but normally these rights are given without charge as part of the license to include the song in the film. The motion picture producer virtually always gets the right to include the "in context" use of the song in any trailers, television commercials, airline promos, or other advertising media. If, however, the song is being used differently than it was used in the film (for example, being used as thematic background throughout the entire commercial), additional fees are negotiated. Occasionally, a film producer will also use a song that is not in the motion picture as part of the advertising campaign for the film. In these cases, a fee of between $12,000 and over $100,000 will usually be charged. Performance monies may also be available for television motion picture promo performances.

## Sheet Music Folios

Motion picture songbooks continue to generate excellent sales, and classic movie songs such as "The Way We Were," "My Heart Will Go On," and "As Time Goes By" are contained in countless non-motion picture folios. Such theme folios generally earn royalties of between 10% and 20% of the retail selling price, with the aggregate amount divided equally among all copyrighted compositions. For example, if a particular book containing 50 songs had a retail selling price of $12.95, each song might receive 2.6¢ for each folio sold. If the folio concentrates on one film exclusively, there may be an additional royalty percentage paid (for example, an extra 5%, similar to a "personality folio" rate). Single sheet-music editions are also an important source of income and exposure for certain songs, as the number of different configurations that can be distributed by a knowledgeable print company are many and varied. For example, one print company successfully distributed an Oscar- and Grammy-winning song in versions for piano and voice, piano solo, easy piano, big-note piano, piano duet, organ solo, high voice and low voice, handbell choir, easy concert band, regular concert band, jazz ensemble, vocal solo with jazz ensemble, and chorus.

## Motion Picture Songs in Commercials

The advertising industry provides a very lucrative outlet for successful movie songs. *Casablanca*'s "As Time Goes By" (a song made famous by its inclusion in a movie) has been used in the television advertising campaigns of countless products, including Ciara Perfume, AT&T's Personal Computers, and American Express. Other film songs used in commercials include "Love Story" for GE Profile Appliances, "The Pink Panther" for Heineken, "Born Free" for Ragu Sauce, "Help" for Mercury cars, and "Ghostbusters" for Ghostbusters Cereal. If the writer and publisher license their composition through ASCAP or BMI for radio and television broadcasts of the commercial, additional royalties can be generated. And since commercials are now being included on home videos as well as in movie theaters, another lucrative area is opening up for movie songs used in commercials.

## Royalties from Motion Picture Theaters

In most countries outside the United States, motion picture theaters are required to pay royalties to the local performance rights society (GEMA in Germany, SACEM in France, PRS in England, SOCAN in Canada, APRA in Australia, JASRAC in Japan, etc.) for the music used in films. The writer's share is then distributed by the foreign society to the writer's U.S. society, which will then pay the American composers and songwriters. The publisher's share of such fees is usually sent to the publisher's local representative or subpublisher in each foreign country, who then remits the royalties (less its administrative percentage) to the American publisher. Royalties for music publishers who do not have foreign representatives are handled the same way as the writer's share of performance monies.

The fees (tariff) paid by movie theaters to foreign performing right societies are usually based either on a percentage of the theater's box office receipts (between .05% to 2%, depending on the country) or on the number of seats in the theater or the number of screenings per week as well as whether the theater is in the city or the country. Some countries also have a lumpsum minimum alternative payment to the percent tariff. In certain countries, the societies allocate shares of revenue to non-music rightsholders such as scriptwriters. Most domestically produced motion pictures do not earn a great deal of money from theaters outside the United States, but for those songs contained in motion pictures with worldwide appeal the monies can be substantial. For example, blockbuster films can generate well over $300,000 in aggregate songwriter and music publisher foreign theater royalties for all the music uses.

## Television Broadcasts of the Motion Picture

Broadcasts of the movie on subscription or pay television, basic cable, and over-the-air free television stations will generate performance royalties.

## Film Songs Used in Television Programs

Since many television series use well-known film songs either as background music or visual vocals, this area, because of the synchronization, video fees and performance royalties, can be extremely valuable for the motion picture song. Representative examples of such uses include "Moon River" (*Breakfast at Tiffany's*) sung by Peg Bundy while dancing with Al at an expensive restaurant in *Married . . . With Children;* "Footloose" (*Footloose*) played while people dance in a bar as William Shatner visits Earth as the Supreme Commander in *3rd Rock from the Sun;* the "Colonel Bogey March" (*Bridge on the River Kwai*) whistled by Magnum as he carries his kayak to the beach in *Magnum P.I.;* and "Over the Rainbow" (*The Wizard of Oz*) played at a high school reunion attended by Mulder and Scully in *The X-Files.*

## Film Songs Used in Other Motion Pictures

The inclusion of a film song in another motion picture allows that song to earn income in all the ways that apply to its original use. Some examples of motion picture songs used in other films include "Theme from A Summer Place" played in the background as Julia Roberts and George Clooney talk in a casino in *Ocean's Eleven,* "Over the Rainbow" played when Tom Hanks and Meg Ryan finally meet each other in the park at the end of *You've Got Mail;* "Alfie" played in the background while Michael Douglas and Glenn Close have a drink in *Fatal Attraction;* and "Cheek to Cheek" from *Top Hat,* which is being shown on a television set in *The Green Mile.*

## Miscellaneous Sources of Income

In addition to the areas previously mentioned, other sources of income for the motion picture song include off-Broadway, touring, and Broadway musicals such as *The Producers, The Lion King,* and *Beauty and the Beast* (for a flat weekly fee or pro rata sharing of a percentage of the weekly box office receipts); singalong tapes (usually licensed at the statutory mechanical royalty rate with additional fees for the reproduction of lyrics); lyric reprints in magazines, novels, and nonfiction books (for a flat fee); published screenplays such as Woody Allen's *Hannah and Her Sisters,* which contained portions of the songs "The Way You Look Tonight" and "Bewitched" (normally for a flat fee); video jukeboxes (a small synchronization fee and a set penny rate per month for each machine); greeting cards (on a percentage of the wholesale price, a flat fee, or a set penny rate, with additional monies due if the music is played); computer, trivia, and board games (buy-outs, negotiated royalties or a percentage of the statutory mechanical rate depending on the timing of the song); recording artist videos (for a specific penny royalty, percentage of the wholesale price, or one-time buy-out fee); and interactive singing dolls and toys (licensed at the statutory mechanical rate or a negotiated rate).

---

# *THE MOTION PICTURE BACKGROUND MUSIC SCORE*

The Hobbits journey through Middle-earth to destroy the One Ring.
A young wizard on his magical broomstick triumphs in a bewitched Quidditch match.
A great white shark slides through a seemingly peaceful, moonlit ocean.
The indestructible ocean liner collides with an iceberg.
A young boy and a small alien take off into the sky on a bicycle.

All the above scenes are good by themselves, but they have been made memorable because of the music associated with them. They are prime examples of a background music score fulfilling its purpose. Whether the score is dramatic, soothing, romantic, comedic, or foreboding, it is a part of the fabric of any motion picture.

The world of the feature film background music composer is not only one of the most creatively stimulating and financially rewarding areas of music, it is also one of the most demanding in terms of musical expertise and training, conducting experience, and discipline in the meeting of rigorous deadlines. It is also a business where multimillion-dollar investments as well as the professional lives of all those involved in a motion picture wait in hopeful expectation at the end of the filmmaking process for the magic of the musical score—the glue that holds much of the motion picture together.

## History of the Field

During the early to middle years of Hollywood (the 1930s through 1950s), the great names of orchestral scoring included Erich Korngold (*The Adventures of Robin Hood*), Franz Waxman (*Sunset Boulevard*), Max Steiner (*Gone with the Wind*), Alfred Newman (*Wuthering Heights*), Bernard Herrmann (*Citizen Kane*), Miklos Rozsa (*Ben Hur*), and Dimitri Tiomkin (*High Noon*). In addition, many of the great names of the pop and musical theater world of the time (the Gershwins, Cole Porter, Jerome Kern, Harry Warren, Johnny Mercer) were also involved with songs for film as well as background scores.

In the 1960s through the 1990s, a new era of giants emerged on the scene, including John Williams, Henry Mancini, James Horner, Alex North, Elmer Bernstein, Maurice Jarre, Jerry Goldsmith, Bill Conti, Ennio Morricone, James Newton Howard, and Howard Shore, among others. Of this new generation of composers, many were classically trained and able to conduct symphony orchestras as well as arrange and orchestrate for any type of musical instrument under the sun. Others achieved background scoring success after making the transition from the pop music world. This latter category of writers includes, among others, Randy Newman (*Monsters, Inc., Toy Story 2*), Stewart Copeland of the Police (*Wall Street, Rumblefish*), Danny Elfman of Oingo Boingo (*Batman, Spider-Man*) and Marc Shaiman (*A Few Good Men, Sleepless in Seattle*).

## The Feature Film Background Score Contract

The contract that a background scorer signs with a major studio or independent production company is standard for almost all composers in some areas yet completely negotiable in others. Three of the primary factors affecting whether a standard or nonstandard contract is finally settled upon are the stature and past success of the composer, the size of the music budget and the knowledge, power and stature of the composer's agent negotiating the deal. The following clauses form the basis of any background composer contract in the world of movies.

*Summary of Basic Provisions.* The basic areas covered in every motion picture scoring contract relate to the types of services to be performed by the composer, the length of time during which they are to be completed, the fee for those services, how that fee is to be paid, transportation and living expenses, screen as well as all types of advertising credit, the ownership of the copyright, composer and artist royalties for uses of the music outside of the film, and the handling of performing rights payments.

*Composer Services.* The background scorer is hired to compose all of the background music (and in some cases, individual songs) for the film as well as to arrange and orchestrate the score; to conduct an orchestra to record the work; to produce, supervise, and edit the recording of the score; and to deliver the final, fully edited and mixed master recording in accordance with the film's postproduction schedule. Additionally, the composer is required to consult with the producer of the film not only on the recording budget but also on the placement of the music in the motion picture and the "feel" that the music should have.

*Starting and Completion Dates.* Although the time frame allowed a composer to create the score for a film varies depending on whether the composer is involved in the film from inception (rare), involved in the film commencing with the postproduction period (the norm), or involved with the film as a replacement for another composer whose score has been thrown out by the producer at the last minute, the standard amount of time allotted composers to compose and record a full background score for a major film ranges between 4 and 10 weeks. Factors affecting the time frame include the amount of music needed as well as the complexity of the instrumentation desired. The actual duration of many contracts, however, can be significantly shorter if the picture is behind schedule, over budget, or being released sooner than the studio originally planned. Any of these factors compress all postproduction aspects of the film (composing, recording, editing, dubbing, sound effects, etc.) and can force a composer to "spot," score, and record a major motion picture in a 2- to 3-week period. These postproduction "crunches" are particularly true for summer and Christmas releases—the two times of the year when the film studios jockey for position for success in the peak ticket-buying seasons. Although the "duration of services" clause will vary based on the particular studio or production company contract being used, the following clauses are representative:

*E X A M P L E 1.* "Composer shall commence services on January 4, 2004, and complete all of the services as expeditiously as possible in accordance with the postproduction schedule of the movie." This clause is somewhat open ended, and the writer must stay aware of the film's postproduction schedule in order to write, record, and deliver the master recording on time.

*E X A M P L E 2.* "Services are to be commenced on the `spotting date' of the picture and completed within 12 consecutive weeks from that date." This contract gives the composer a definite period of time in which to write and record the score. For most writers, a definite time frame is preferable to the indefinite period of the first example.

*E X A M P L E 3.* "Services to be commenced upon the signing of the composer–production company agreement with delivery to the producer of the complete recorded score, the original manuscripts of the score, and all musical orchestrations and arrangements of the score, by no later than December 31, 2003." The time allotted to composing and recording the score in this type of contract depends on the date the contract is signed versus the "no later than" delivery date arrangement.

*E X A M P L E 4.* "Services to commence as of the August 31, 2004, signing date of this contract, with the original master recordings of the score to be delivered to Producer on or about October 2, 2004."

It is also important to include in these contracts a provision that covers the composer's compensation if the producer requires his or her services beyond the specific number of weeks set forth in the agreement. For example, a contract might specify "$10,000 a week in additional compensation."

*Composing Fees.* The composing fees paid to a feature film background composer vary considerably depending on the past success and stature of the composer; the amount of music needed in the film; the type of music required; the total budget for the film; the total music budget, including the cost for licensing preexisting outside songs or master recordings; whether the film producer is a major studio, a major independent, or a minor player in the film world; the size of the orchestra needed to record the score; whether the composer is contracting to bear all or most of the costs of music (a package) or only negotiating the composing fee; whether the film is intended for wide distribution or only a limited release; the standard fees paid by a particular studio versus the fees of other studios; and the skills of the individuals on both sides of the negotiation fence—the studio and the composer's agent. Depending on many of the above factors, composing fees can range from $20,000 for a lower-budget film to in excess of $1,000,000 for a big-budget studio release using the services of a well-known composer.

The following examples illustrate 5 variations of composer compensation:

*E X A M P L E 1.* $105,000 payable as follows:
  (1) $35,000 upon the signing of the contract or the commencement of spotting (i.e., the composer, director, producer, and music supervisor watch the film and discuss where the music should be).
  (2) $35,000 upon the commencement of the recording of the motion picture score.

(3) $35,000 upon completion of all composer services as well as timely delivery of the master recording to the producer. The master recording has to be acceptable to the producer.

*E X A M P L E 2.*   $75,000 payable as follows:
(1) $25,000 upon the commencement of the spotting of the film.
(2) $25,000 upon the commencement of the recording of the film.
(3) $25,000 upon completion of all composer services under the film score agreement.

*E X A M P L E 3.*   $175,000 payable as follows:
(1) $87,500 upon the commencement of the writing services as specified in the contract.
(2) $87,500 upon the completion of all composer services as specified in the contract.

*E X A M P L E 4.*   $300,000 payable as follows:
(1) $100,000 upon commencement of the composer's services.
(2) $100,000 upon spotting of the film.
(3) $75,000 upon commencement of the recording of the master recording.
(4) $25,000 upon completion of all composer services.

*E X A M P L E 5.*   $600,000 payable as follows:
(1) One-third (⅓) upon spotting of the picture.
(2) One-third (⅓) upon commencement of the recording of the score.
(3) One-third (⅓) upon the completion of the final sound mix of the picture.

One of the considerations that dictates the amount of the fee negotiated in the composer–studio contract is whether the composer is assuming responsibility for all costs of his or her efforts (e.g., costs of musicians, recording, copying, orchestrators, instruments and instrument rentals, cartage, payroll and payroll taxes, etc.), or is solely contracting for composing and conducting services. If one is contracting for the whole package, all items that the composer is agreeing to furnish (as well as all exclusions) should be specifically spelled out in the contract in order to prevent situations where the composer ends up losing money because of unknown (at the time of signing) or significantly higher costs of some of the undertakings. Some obvious items that should be excluded include the licensing cost of any music not written by the composer, any reuse or residual payments, and any rescoring or rerecording costs required for creative reasons after the delivery of the master recording that are outside the control of the composer. Although these "all in" package deals are not the norm in the feature film area and should not be taken by any composer inexperienced in budgets and music production costs, they are attractive to some film companies and do provide composers new to the film field with an opportunity to break into the business, in addition to providing knowledgeable scorers with an opportunity for fees not within the capacity of other scorers. A composer package of $75,000 "all in" for a lower-budget quality film may generate only a minimal profit to a composer, but it does accomplish the goal of achieving a feature film credit.

*Screen Credit.* The type and placement of screen credit for a background scorer is a negotiable item. A separate card will usually read "Music by (the composer's name)." The credit can be in the main titles and of the same size as the star, the producer, writer of the screenplay, or director, or it can be at the end of the film in a size somewhat less than the other principals. Most well-known composers are able to negotiate the inclusion of their names in all paid advertising (newspapers, magazines, etc.) as well as on soundtrack albums and all printed publications (sheet music, song folios, songbooks, etc.). Most contracts normally exclude the composer's name in all advertising of the movie on screen, radio, or television, any special advertising or award or congratulatory ads (e.g., the star gets nominated for an Academy Award and the studio takes out an ad in the *Hollywood Reporter* or *Daily Variety*), or any teaser advertising.

Somewhat related to this provision is the "name and likeness" clause, which gives the motion picture producer the right to use the composer's name, likeness, and biographical information for the advertising, exploitation, distribution, and exhibition of the film throughout the world for all time. A number of "proven success" composers are able to dictate that likenesses and biographical material must be approved by the composer before any use by the film company.

*Amount of Music.* Many contracts do not specify the total number of minutes of background score that a composer must write. These contracts assume certain durational amounts typical of feature films and leave it to the composer and producer to determine at the spotting session how much music is to be written and where it is to be placed in the picture. A sample clause might read "The Composer contracts to compose, conduct, etc. all of the original music required by the Producer." Other contracts, however, actually specify a minimum number of minutes of music to be scored. "Composer agrees that the Score shall contain a minimum of thirty (30) minutes of original music" or "the music shall be approximately sixty (60) minutes in length and shall be of a high quality and professional nature" illustrate two examples of such clauses.

Regardless of the type of "amount of music" provision in the contract, the producer ultimately decides how much music is to be used in the film. The reality is that most composers end up writing significantly more music than is actually used in the final released film.

*Exclusivity.*   Many film composer agreements state that the composer's services are exclusive to the producer or company during the entire term of the scoring agreement with others stating non-exclusive but on a first priority basis until delivery of the final print and thereafter on a non-exclusive basis.

*Transportation and Expenses.*   Most composers either live or have accommodations in the cities where the primary movie production and recording facilities are located. For certain motion pictures, though, the producer will require the composer to travel. The following examples of "transportation and expenses" clauses give a feel for what is possible in this area.

E X A M P L E 1.   "$1,500 a week while away from Los Angeles for hotel, meals, local transportation, and phone (accommodations and expenses), as well as first-class round-trip transportation for the composer and spouse."

E X A M P L E 2.   "Studio shall furnish composer reasonable living expenses while on site in the amount of $1,000 per week. Such amount is provided on a nonaccountable basis and is in lieu of company furnishing composer's meals, lodging, and other normal living expenses. For any period of less than one week, the weekly rate will be prorated."

E X A M P L E 3.   "Round-trip coach class transportation plus the cost of reasonable lodging and meals."

*Ownership of the Copyright.*   Practically all background composer agreements are employee-for-hire or work-made-for-hire agreements; that is, the musical score is created at the specific request of and under the direct supervision of the film producer. For the all-inclusive composing and services fee, the composer "grants to the producer all rights, title, and interest throughout the world in perpetuity, in and to the work and the recordings." By this grant, the producer owns the worldwide copyright for the entire term of copyright protection. Under an employee-for-hire contract, the producer (the movie studio or production company) becomes the author pursuant to the U.S. Copyright Law and the composer does not have the right to recapture the copyright at the end of the 35- to 40-year period provided for under that law. Any specific rights to the music that the composer may retain must be stated in writing and signed by all parties.

The typical grant-of-rights provision signed by composers gives the studio the exclusive right to publish the composition, to make and sell sound recordings, to execute all licenses regarding the use of the work, to change the work, to combine the work with other works, and to transmit the work by any means now available or to be available in the future. Through this grant, the studio becomes the owner of all rights of copyright and is usually free to assign or license those rights to others. This clause is normally of the broadest nature possible, and it is not unusual to see the inclusion of phrases such as "all other rights of any nature whatsoever," "perpetual and unlimited rights," or "any rights throughout the entire universe whether now or hereafter existing" in the film scoring contract.

Employee-for-hire agreements are very different from standard songwriter-publisher agreements, where the songwriter assigns the copyright to the publisher but retains the right to recapture the copyright at the end of 35 or 40 years. (During the hearings on the 1976 Copyright Act, the screen and television composer community attempted unsuccessfully to change the employee-for-hire provision to make it similar to the standard songwriter–publisher contractual relationship.)

The primary composer compensation rights, in addition to the composing and services fee, set forth in most background composer contracts include all or most of the royalties as set forth in the standard songwriter agreement including the right to receive performance royalties from domestic and foreign performing right organizations; mechanical royalties; sheet music and folio royalties; foreign royalties; and synchronization royalties.

## Membership in a Performing Right Society

The composer must be a member in good standing of a performing right society as well as any other applicable labor organization, guild, or union that may have jurisdiction.

There are more than 80 performing right societies in the world, with two of the largest, ASCAP and BMI, located in the United States (see Chapter 7). For U.S. composers, the contract will state either ASCAP or BMI, depending on the writer's organizational membership. For foreign society composers, the decision as to whether the film score is licensed in the United States by ASCAP or BMI is usually based on the composer's preference, and contracts involving foreign composers should be clear on this point. Performing right societies provide to most screen composers the bulk of their life-of-copyright income. It is vitally important that a screen composer join and maintain a membership in a performing rights society.

In recent years, the performing right clause in film and television scoring contracts has undergone some major changes due to pressure from the U.S. television networks, the local television industry, and the cable television industry. Although the clause specifically states that "the composer shall receive the writer's share of royalties for public performances of the score and musical compositions," additional provisions have been added to many film and television scoring agreements to address the scenario of what happens if "a broadcasting station (or other user) does not have a current valid license agreement with ASCAP or BMI," "if it is unlawful for the performing right society to issue a license," or "if a network, local, or cable television station requires a direct license of the public performance rights."

Many of these "what if" clauses initially left it to the producer to negotiate the performing right fees without specific compensation to the composer. More recent variations of the clause provide that the producer and composer shall negotiate "in good faith" the performance right payment in the event that licensing does not occur under the auspices of either ASCAP or BMI. The main result of many of these clauses, if they become effective, is that the composer will not receive any continuing performance royalties other than the initial composing fee as well as the possibility of some "good faith" negotiated fees in the future. If a composer is going to agree to such a clause, he or she should at least try to negotiate a fee of 50% of whatever the motion picture company negotiates plus some type of specific dollar figure as a continuing performance royalty payment for all future television and all other types of broadcast uses. As the foreign performance right area is one of the film composer's most important sources of income, any clause should also be clear as to how these royalties would be handled. Legal advice is recommended for anyone negotiating this type of clause.

*Disposition of the Score.*   The producer has no obligation to accept the finished score, to use the score in the picture, to promote or exploit it, to release it on a soundtrack album, or even to release the picture. Further, the producer may request certain changes, deletions, or additions to the finished score prior to accepting it. If these changes are requested because the composer did not consult with the producer on the score or because the score is technically deficient in any way, then the composer pays the cost of the changes. In almost all other cases, the producer pays the cost for any such requested changes.

It is rare for a producer or director to throw out a fully written score because the producer or director doesn't like it or it doesn't fit the picture, but such does occasionally happen even for major background scorers. When it does occur, the original composer may be allowed to revise the original score or come up with a new score, or the producer may hire another composer to write and record an entirely new score. Even if the initial composer's score is not used in the picture, he or she does get paid for the work that is completed. Obviously, the composer's reputation and possible future work could be jeopardized by a producer's rejection of a score, and composers usually try to accede to the producer's thoughts and ideas throughout the entire postproduction process.

*Warranties.*   The warranty clause states that the composer is free to enter into the agreement, that the music will be entirely original, that the composer's services and skills are unique and of the highest caliber, and that he or she can grant all rights in the music (including the copyright) to the film's producer. Under the re-recording restriction clause, the composer agrees not to conduct, produce recordings, or re-record the motion picture score for anyone else for a stated period of time (3 to 5 years normally) commencing from the date of the delivery of the score and master recordings to the producer. The warranty clause and re-recording clause assure the producer not only that the body of work being contracted for is free from plagiarism but also that the composer is prevented from making recordings of the score for other companies that could be in competition with the producer's recording of the score.

*Instructions and Requests of the Producer.* The composer agrees to comply with all of the producer's reasonable instructions and requests, to compose the score to the best of his or her ability, and to consult with the producer as to the style, content, and all other elements of the score. In addition, the composer agrees to meet with the producer or the producer's representatives for approval of the recording budget. All costs of the recording are the producer's responsibility and not the composer's. If the composer contracts to assume some or all costs of the recording and other music costs, the contract will specifically set forth all of the areas covered by the composer's "all in" fee.

The amount of instruction and direction given to the composer depends on the filmmaker. Some producers are "hands on" individuals who give very specific instructions as to where music should go and what it should feel like. Other producers look to the composer to capture the filmmaker's view as set forth in the discussions at the spotting session.

*Suspensions and Terminations.* The producer has the right to suspend the running of time of the composer's agreement based on disability, force majeure, or default. Although these are negotiable items and vary by contract, there are certain industry standards and definitions in effect.

DISABILITY. The composer's ability to compose or perform services is interfered with because of the composer's mental, physical, or other disability.

FORCE MAJEURE. The preparation, production, or completion of a film is interrupted owing to reasons beyond the producer's control: fire, accidents, weather, labor disputes, acts of God, laws or governmental orders, shortages or an inability to obtain materials or labor, and the death or disability of a principal member of the cast or the director are a few such reasons.

DEFAULT. The composer's failure, refusal, or neglect to compose or perform any of the duties set forth in the composer's agreement with the producer.

In order for a producer to suspend a composer, some contracts specify that written notice be given to the composer within a specified period of time (e.g., 1 week) after the reason for suspension occurs. Other contracts, however, have no specific notice requirement, and a suspension is deemed to be in effect if a default or disability continues for a certain number of days. In a force majeure situation, the producer will notify the composer of the suspension, and the contract will remain in abeyance until the production again commences. During the suspension, no fees are paid to the composer and he or she must be ready to report to work when the film resumes production. In cases of the composer's disability or default, the suspension ends at such time as the composer reports to the producer for work, provided he or she is physically able to work or has cured the default.

The producer can terminate the composer's employment for any composer default, for any composer disability that lasts for more than __ weeks, or if a force majeure lasts for __ consecutive weeks. The composer, on the other hand, can terminate the agreement if he or she receives no compensation for a consecutive period of __ weeks due to a force majeure. The composer must give written notice to the producer, and the contract is terminated unless compensation is resumed within a specified period of time.

*Morality Clause.* The composer must conduct himself in a manner consistent with public conventions and morals and shall not commit any act that would prejudice the producer or the entertainment industry. This clause, a remnant of the 1930s film industry, still remains in one form or another in many film contracts, despite its broadness and vagueness.

*Orchestration.* The costs of orchestration are either included in the "composer services" provision or excluded. If at all possible, orchestration costs should be excluded from the overall composing and conducting fee, as it is a "wild card" sum that can be a very low 4-figure number or a 5-figure surprise. For example, if a composer negotiates a $75,000 services fee and then learns at the spotting session that the producer wants a 60-piece orchestra rather than a small ensemble, the costs of arranging for an entire orchestra as well as the copying of all of the individual instrument parts can be prohibitively expensive. The best advice to any composer or representative is to keep this figure as a separately paid item and not as an open part of the services fee. For example, a clause might read that the "Producer shall hire a third party orchestrator at a rate of _____ a page."

*Infringements.* In the event that any infringement or other claim is made against the producer or the publisher in regard to the musical score, any monies payable to the composer shall be withheld until a final determination is made as to the claim. Occasionally, the monies withheld must be in an amount that is consistent with the claim (e.g., if a claim is for $10,000, the producer can withhold only up to $10,000). Sometimes a clause is negotiated to provide that if the person making the claim does not file suit within a specified period of time (e.g., 1 year) after the claim letter is received or bond posted, all monies withheld by the producer must be released to the composer.

*Notices and Governing Law.* All notices, payments, statements, or other documents are made in writing and are sent either by personal delivery, telegram, telex, telefax, or registered or certified mail. The laws of the relevant state govern the agreement, and any modifications or changes in the agreement must be in writing and signed by all the parties.

*Assignment.* The producer can assign the entire agreement, at any time, to any party. The composer, on the other hand, cannot assign or transfer any part of the agreement without the written consent of the producer. On occasion, the producer will allow the composer to assign his or her royalties (e.g., as collateral for a bank loan), but the composer is never allowed to assign the actual composing services to another party. On the other hand, the composer may request that the producer remain liable for any continuing obligations (e.g., royalty payments derived from exploitation of the score) even though the agreement has been assigned to another company—a request that is usually not accepted by the producer.

## SOURCES OF INCOME: THE BACKGROUND SCORER

The various sources of income for the composer of a background score are listed in Table 5.7.

TABLE **5.7**   Sources of Income: The Background Score

| | |
|---|---|
| $250,000 | Composing, arranging, and conducting fee |
| 200,000 | Foreign theatrical and other performance royalties for a major box office film (1st year) |
| 18,000 | Initial U.S. cable television run (multiple broadcasts) over 1 year |
| 8,500 | Network television broadcast of the film (50 minutes of music) |
| 45,000 | U.S. and foreign local television performances of the film (5-year period) |
| 42,500 | Soundtrack album (U.S. mechanical royalties for 100,000 units sold and 10 tracks) |
| $564,000 | Total composer fees and royalties |

## Composing, Arranging, and Conducting Fee

When a motion picture company commissions a background music scorer to write music for a film, factors affecting the fee paid include the overall budget of the film; the budget for all music uses (background score, new songs, preexisting songs, record company and recording artist fees); the amount of background music needed for the film; the size of the orchestra required; whether the composer is undertaking a "package deal" (the exception) or contracting only for the composing, arranging, and conducting (the norm); whether the film is produced by a major company and intended for large-scale distribution or is scheduled for only limited theatrical release; the composer's past film credits and successes; the stature and bargaining power of the composer's agent; and whether the composer is able to retain a portion of the copyright to the score and publisher's share of income for his or her own publishing company.

Although the composer's fees vary depending on many factors and can swing dramatically based on a composer's most recent film, the following represents an accurate range for many motion pictures:

1. Bottom-end low-budget features: $10,000–$50,000
2. Successful composer for a medium- to high-budget film: $75,000–$300,000
3. Top-of-the-line composer for a major film: $250,000–$1,000,000

## Foreign Theatrical and Other Performance Royalties

The fees received from foreign performing right societies constitute one of the largest sources of income for U.S. film composers (see Table 5.8 for an example of the kind of money that can be generated from a successful film). As U.S. films continue to remain the staple of foreign theaters, the total license fees collected by these societies for U.S. composers are substantial.

To appreciate the size of these performance monies and how they translate into substantial dollars for U.S. film composers, a brief analysis of the English society (PRS) should be of interest. PRS, founded in 1914 and covering the United Kingdom, and many Commonwealth countries, had total 2002 domestic and foreign revenues of £272 million (approximately $428 million U.S.) and distributed approximately £231 million, after payment of operating costs, to composers, lyricists, songwriters, and music publishers. In the United Kingdom alone, PRS collected £5,700,000 from cinemas (approximately $8,900,000 U.S.), with much of that money going to U.S. film composers through distribution from PRS to ASCAP and BMI.

To put the timing of foreign royalty distributions into perspective, Table 5.9 illustrates the U.S. payment dates from one U.S. society for the background score of a 2002 film that played in many foreign movie theaters. The U.S. distribution dates set forth in this table represent significantly quicker writer

TABLE **5.8**  The Background Composer's Foreign Performing Rights Royalties for the Initial Release Year of a Major Box Office Film

| Country | Society | Composer's Foreign Royalties |
|---|---|---|
| Australia | APRA | $ 20,000 |
| Austria | AKM | 800 |
| Belgium | SABAM | 1,250 |
| Canada | SOCAN | 4,100 |
| England | PRS | 32,500 |
| Finland | TEOSTO | 850 |
| France | SACEM | 75,125 |
| Germany | GEMA | 38,010 |
| Holland | BUMA | 800 |
| Hong Kong | CASH | 1,480 |
| Italy | SIAE | 48,265 |
| Japan | JASRAC | 3,250 |
| Norway | TONO | 1,210 |
| South Africa | SAMRO | 650 |
| Spain | SGAE | 3,950 |
| Sweden | STIM | 4,250 |
| Switzerland | SUISA | 4,100 |
| Other Countries | | 12,500 |
| TOTALS: | | $253,090 |

and publisher foreign payments than in the past. These accelerations are the result of mutual agreements between societies. Some of the delays for the U.S. distribution of this money are due to the long-term holding of the money by some foreign societies as well as the distribution dates of each foreign performing rights society to its own members and to ASCAP and BMI.

The foreign monies that can be earned by film background scorers many times surpass all of the writer income that is received from all types of U.S. performances. These monies are earned regardless of how well a film has performed at the box office in the U.S., as many a domestic box office failure has generated in excess of $100,000 in writer foreign performance royalties.

In the United States, ASCAP and BMI do not license movie theaters for the music used in films. This nonlicensing status of U.S. theaters was the result of the 1948 Alden Rochelle court decision, which ruled against ASCAP's then practice of licensing movie theaters as well as the then exclusive nature of ASCAP writer and publisher agreements. Although the decision only affected ASCAP, BMI agreed to be bound by the judgment, and henceforth no U.S. movie theater has paid performance royalties for the performance of music in films for over 5 decades, despite the Alden Rochelle licensing objections having

TABLE **5.9**   U.S. Distribution of Foreign Money for a 2002 Feature Film Released
in Many Foreign Countries

| *Country* | *U.S. Distribution Dates* |
| --- | --- |
| Argentina | February, May, August, November 2003 |
| Australia | May, November 2003 |
| Britain | August and November 2003 |
| Canada | February, May, November 2003 |
| Denmark | February, May 2004 |
| France | November 2002, February, May, November 2003 |
| Germany | February and August 2004 |
| Italy | February and August 2004 |
| Netherlands | May 2004 |
| Sweden | August 2003, November 2003 |
| Spain | May and November 2003 |
| Switzerland | February and November 2003 |

been corrected many decades ago. The nonlicensing status of the music in films when shown in movie theaters is set forth in both the ASCAP Articles of Association as well as the ASCAP Consent Decree.

## U.S. Cable, Network, and Local Television Performances

The largest source of continuing royalty income for most background composers is the quarterly performance payments received from ASCAP and BMI (see Chapter 7). Background composers can and have earned well in excess of $350,000 in television performance royalties for a single successful film over the full term of copyright. And even if a film is not a success at the box office, substantial television performance earnings are still possible, since ASCAP and BMI do not distinguish in their royalty payments between high- vs. low-budget films, box office successes vs. box office failures, initial airing vs. repeats, or brilliantly composed music vs. pedestrian scoring. A screening of the top-grossing film of all time would be paid the same as moviedom's biggest failure provided that both films were shown on the same cable, local, or network television station.

Table 5.10 estimates the performance royalties for a successful composer with multiple films in distribution both theatrically and on television. The following 2 examples of the U.S. television performance earnings for the writer and publisher of the background score for an individual film over a 10-year period should help to place this area into some perspective. Although no 2

TABLE **5.10**   U.S. Performance Royalties for a Composer with Multiple Films in Distribution

| Period | Areas | Royalties |
|---|---|---|
| Year 1 | Network TV | $  38,000 |
| | Cable/Pay TV | 22,000 |
| | Local TV | 13,000 |
| | Foreign | 179,000 |
| Total Royalties | | $ 252,000 |
| Year 2 | Network TV | $  16,000 |
| | Cable/Pay TV | 43,000 |
| | Local TV | 26,000 |
| | Foreign | 201,000 |
| Total Royalties | | $ 286,000 |
| Year 3 | Network TV | $  22,000 |
| | Cable/Pay TV | 26,000 |
| | Local TV | 9,000 |
| | Foreign | 135,000 |
| Total Royalties | | $ 192,000 |

pictures are alike in terms of the amount of music or specified distribution areas, many films do earn well in the U.S. television area.

*E X A M P L E 1.*   A medium- to low-budget action adventure film generates $40,000 in pay cable distributions and $7,500 in local television distributions.

*E X A M P L E 2.*   A big-budget film generates $45,000 in network television distributions, $52,000 in pay cable distributions, and $35,000 in local television distributions.

## Soundtrack Albums

Although quite a few background score soundtrack albums are released each year, most of them are geared to a selective audience and many of them appear on specialty labels. Therefore, the sales are usually not significant. Many of these albums are not motivated by the same considerations as those prevalent in "song" soundtrack albums; primarily, to get MTV-type airplay as well as Top 10 single chart activity to help sell the motion picture during its initial theatrical release. Some background score albums do sell very well, however, particularly if the score is to a blockbuster motion picture or if there are 1 or 2 songs on the album.

A sample soundtrack score album contract where the composer is the artist (i.e., conductor of the orchestra) might read as follows: An artist royalty of 10% of the suggested retail list price (20% of the wholesale price) for sales through normal retail channels in the U.S. less packaging deductions, applicable taxes, and artist royalties due any other participating artist on the album. A percentage will also be deducted for the actual conversion cost involved (repaying the musicians according to union regulations for using the film music on a recording, mixing costs, mastering costs, etc.). The same record company deductions, reserves against returns, exclusions, and so on, of a typical recording contract would also be included. A producer royalty (e.g. 4% of the suggested retail list price) would also be negotiated and would be pro-rated based upon the number of selections on the album by other artists and producers. If the record company decides that a live album is necessary (the music is reorchestrated, rescored, and re-recorded), the compensation to the composer/conductor would include the union scale payments for each element of the composer's work. An album credit provision would also be negotiated. A sample clause might state that the composer would receive front cover and label credit of "music composed by_____" if at least 50% of all of the total selections were composed by him. Otherwise, it would be at the producer's discretion on the back cover.

For record, CD, and tape sales, the statutory mechanical publisher and writer royalty would apply unless voluntarily reduced by the music publisher or composer; for example, a record company might demand that a maximum cap on mechanical royalties per album be agreed to as a condition of the album being recorded and released.

## CONCLUSION

Having a song in a motion picture or composing a score for a film can open up an unlimited number of opportunities and prove to be a lifetime annuity for writers and music publishers. From hit records, the Academy Awards, commercials, and million-selling videos to television themes, foreign theater performances, other motion pictures, and a Grammy, the financial life of the movie song and the motion picture background score can last well beyond the Hollywood premiere.

# 6

# Music, Money, and Commercials

TO THE SOUNDS of Led Zeppelin's "Rock and Roll," a new Cadillac passes the classic finned model on the road.

\*    \*    \*

Madonna and Missy Elliott perform "Get Into the Groove" for GAP.

\*    \*    \*

Michael McDonald sings "Ain't No Mountain High Enough" and "Ain't Nothing Like the Real Thing" for MCI while promoting his new album.

\*    \*    \*

After Barry Bonds breaks the home run record, Shaquille O'Neal of the Los Angeles Lakers celebrates the NBA Championship, John Elway wins the Super Bowl and the U.S. Women's Soccer Team wins the World Cup, they are all going to Disney World to the strains of "When You Wish Upon a Star."

\*    \*    \*

From Madonna's "Ray of Light" and the Rolling Stones' "Start Me Up" for Microsoft, "This Magic Moment" for Seagram's Coolers, "Rhapsody in Blue" for United Airlines, Bob Seger's "Like a Rock" for Chevy Trucks, Genesis' "Tonight, Tonight, Tonight" for Michelob, "Ain't Nothin' Like the Real Thing" for Burger King, "Sea of Love" for Chanel Perfume, and "Simply Irresistible" for Pepsi to "9 to 5" for Emery, "Beyond the Sea" for MCI International Calling, "When a Man Loves a Woman" for Stouffers' Lean Cuisine, "New York, New York" for Philadelphia Cream Cheese, "Rescue Me" for Pizza Hut, and "Put a Little Love In Your Heart" for GAP and "You Are My Shining Star" for Sony Handycam, music is advertising.

---

## THE ADVERTISING INDUSTRY AND HOW IT WORKS

### The Phone Call from the Advertising Agency

AGENCY:   Hi, this is Bill Smith from (name of agency) in New York. I'm calling because one of our clients would like to use a song that you publish in an upcoming advertising campaign.

PUBLISHER:   Glad to hear that. Can you give me the name of the song, the product and details of the campaign?

AGENCY:   The client is (Car Company) and the song we would like to use is (title of song). For your information, we are also going to use the (name of recording artist) record of the song during the commercial. We'd initially like to have the rights to the song for use in a 2-week test period so we can show the commercial to a selected audience in shopping malls. If the response is good, we'd like then to go ahead with a major campaign. The final campaign will be for the United States for 1 year, and we'd like to have 2 additional options to extend the license for 1 year each. The media will be free over-the-air and basic cable television. Since we might also want to expand the territory for the commercial to Canada, certain countries in Europe, and Australia, we'd also like to get separate option fee quotes for Canada, Europe, and Australia. And we'd appreciate a fee quote if we were to use the commercial throughout the world plus a quote for Web site, email, print, and on hold phone use. It's our client's policy that the song can't be licensed to another car company or to any automotive parts products during the term, and your agreement to this is essential.

PUBLISHER:   Auto commercials rarely hurt hit songs, and since there is no change of lyrics, the use seems acceptable. I would appreciate it, though, if you could send me a copy of the story board so I can get an idea of how the commercial will look. I'll then be able to give you the fee quotes that you need.

AGENCY:  I'll e-mail or fax you the story board within the hour, but I must ask you to keep the concept confidential.

PUBLISHER:  I definitely will, and I'll get back to you later today with prices.

Whether the owner of a song is the sponsor, agency, jingle writer, production company, music publisher, or rock superstar, the advertising business can be a valuable source of income for both the songwriter and publisher. Since an understanding of how music is licensed in this industry is necessary to appreciate the use of music to promote consumer products and its financial ramifications, the following sections examine many of the business and legal decisions that lead to getting songs into commercials.

## The Advertising Agency and Its Use of Music

When an advertising agency produces a commercial, it has the option to use music in a number of ways. In most cases, the advertising agency hires a composer, lyricist, or production company to create a new song specifically for the commercial (e.g., "I Won't Drift Away" for AT&T, "The Pride Is Back" for Chrysler, "This Bud's for You" for Budweiser, and "Listen to the Heartbeat" for Chevrolet).

At times, a hit song may be needed to identify an important trait of the product (such as "True Colors" for photographic film and "Everything Is Beautiful" for a shiny wood finish), convey a certain message (such as "Bargain" for Nissan, "Let's Spend the Night Together" for a hotel chain and "Stand by Me" for a credit card buyer's protection program), or create a specific mood (such as the *Love Boat* theme for a cruise line, "I'll Be Home For Christmas" for a beer, and "Walk on the Wild Side" for a motorcycle). The agency may use the melody of a popular song and create new lyrics or change the original lyrics slightly to fit the advertising message (as in "What the World Needs Now" for Dove Bars, "Shout" for Polaroid, "Love and Marriage" for Fruit and Fiber cereal, and "Duke of Earl" for Hellmann's Dijonnaise Mustard).

At other times, an instrumental version of a song will be used (e.g., "As Time Goes By" for American Express Buyer's Insurance and "Whatever Will Be, Will Be (Que Sera Sera)" for Honda) or, if the song was originally an instrumental (e.g., the *Pink Panther* theme for Owens-Corning and the *Chariots of Fire* theme for Duracell batteries), the instrumental is performed with no changes. Agencies may also use a combination of the above alternatives in a campaign for a certain product, such as the use of "Secondhand Rose" instrumentally and with new lyrics in separate AT&T commercials, and "Lean on Me" for Chevrolet trucks both instrumentally and with the original lyrics.

The client or agency may also want a hit recording used in the commercial (e.g., Elvis Presley's "A Little Bit of Conversation" for Nike and Rod Stewart's "Do Ya Think I'm Sexy" for Mercury), may want a successful recording artist to sing the new lyrics for a hit song (such as Elton John with "Sad Songs" for Sasson and Aretha Franklin with a version of "Rescue Me" for Pizza Hut), or may contract with a hit songwriter/recording artist to create and perform advertising jingles for a particular product (e.g., Pepsi with Michael Jackson). Optionally, the agency may take instrumental music from a background music library or use a work not under copyright protection (i.e., in the public domain).

## The Importance of the Advertising Agency

When an agency is hired to create a radio or television commercial, it must first decide whether the campaign demands a new song chosen or whether the use of a past or present hit song is preferable. On occasion, the client may request a certain song for its overall marketing theme. In most cases, though, the advertising agency and its creative department not only develop and sell a specific campaign but also suggest the music to be used—a responsibility whose importance cannot be overemphasized, since the choice of the right music or advertising lyric is essential to getting consumers to recall the commercial and brand name when they're choosing a product to buy.

## The Jingle

If a campaign requires new music, the advertising agency consults with its client as to its ideas concerning the theme and direction of the campaign as well as the outlines of the overall creative budget, including the music budget. The agency, if it does not have an in-house music department, then usually hires a jingle production company, which specializes in advertising music, to write a song and produce a demonstration tape tailored to the planned commercial. Such a jingle production company is normally a self-contained unit that can (through its staff writers, producers, and in some cases, ownership of recording studios) write the jingle and produce a finished demo tape. The agency and its client are then able to hear a reasonable facsimile of the commercial and, if it is what they are looking for, proceed to a finished version. If an agency has an in-house music department, with a staff of songwriters, lyric creators, and producers, it will often develop and produce many of its clients' jingles without going to third parties.

Another alternative is to contact an independent songwriter, explain the theme of the campaign, and hire the composer to write the jingle. Without his or her own production facility, however, the probability of securing the commercial assignment is slim unless the writer has a successful track record for writing hit songs or a reputation in the jingle business as a successful commercial writer. Yet another alternative is for the agency to purchase the exclusive or nonexclusive advertising use rights to a past or present hit song.

## Creation of a Jingle and the Monies That Can Be Earned

The fees payable to a writer for creative services related to the writing of a radio or television jingle can range from minimum compensation to well over $250,000; the amount being dependent on the type of campaign being planned (e.g., national, local, test), the music budget, and whether the writer is an independent contractor unaffiliated with an advertising agency or a jingle production company, is signed to a production company or owns his or her own firm, is an employee of the advertising agency, has a hit song that the agency wants to use, or is a successful writer/recording artist who will create and perform advertising music.

### The Independent Writer

When an agency contacts an independent writer, the fees for writing a jingle may range from a few hundred dollars to a few thousand dollars depending on the music budget and the extent of the campaign being planned. If the agency is dealing with a superstar such as Britney Spears, Phil Collins, Stevie Wonder, or Michael Jackson, however, the total creative fees can easily range from $250,000 to over $4 million if a multiple-year arrangement is involved.

### The Jingle Production Company

It is common for the writer to own, or be signed to, a jingle production company. In such cases, the fee paid by the advertising agency to this 1-source operation includes the monies for the creation of the jingle, the costs of the recording studio, the arranger's fee, and the salaries of the musicians and singers who perform at the session. Based on the wide range of services and expertise provided by these production companies, the amount of money paid by the agency is much greater than that paid to an individual jingle writer. For example, the value of a 30-second commercial to a production company can range from $5,000 to well over $50,000, depending on whether the commercial is to be aired in local markets or is the centerpiece of a national campaign.

### The Writer as Employee of an Advertising Agency

A number of advertising agencies have in-house writers and production staffs whose primary job is to create and produce much of the music needed for their radio and television commercials. These writers receive a salary for creating jingles and normally assign the rights to their music to the agency as part of their employment agreement. The employee/writer will normally receive no other monies for creating a jingle, with the possible exception of ASCAP or BMI performance royalties and songwriter royalties if the jingle becomes a commercially released tape or CD. Owing to the costs involved, however, very few agencies are large enough to support in-house writing and production staffs.

## Hit Songs Used in Commercials

Even though most commercials use music or songs written specifically for the advertising campaign, a trend becoming more common each year is the use of past or present hit songs to sell a product. By using a hit song, the agencies attempt to capitalize on the instant recognition of the song and the continued recall of the product because of its identification with a familiar song.

The fees paid by advertising companies for the use of popular songs in commercials can exceed $1,00,000 for a 1-year use in a national campaign, with the normal range being from $100,000 to $300,000. The amount of the fee depends on, among other considerations, the past and present popularity of the song, the type of media campaign being planned, the territory involved, the nature of the product or service being advertised, the music budget, the number of songs being used in the commercial, the past unavailability of a song for commercials, whether master recording rights (the original hit record version) are also being secured, whether total advertising exclusivity as opposed to product exclusivity is being requested (e.g., a prohibition against any other advertising use of the song vs. restrictions only for competing consumer goods), whether present or future promotion of the song might be diluted because of the commercial tie-in, the importance of the song to the message of the campaign, and whether the agency wants to alter the original lyrics.

## Permission to Use a Hit Song in a Commercial

When an advertising agency wants to use a hit song in a radio or television commercial, it will contact the music publisher of the song for permission and, if the composition is available for licensing, negotiate a fee for a specified term with options. At one time, advertising agencies could also contact the Harry Fox Agency in New York, which issued licenses for many music publishers to advertising agencies, motion picture, and television companies for the use of songs. This service is no longer available.

In most cases, an agency will use a song only for a limited campaign (normally 1 year or less), but many songs have become so vital to a product and its success that they have been used for years (e.g., "When You Wish Upon a Star" for Disneyland, "Rhapsody in Blue" for United Airlines, "Anticipation" for Heinz ketchup, "Like a Rock" for Chevy, and Henry Mancini's "The Pink Panther Theme" for Owens-Corning). By obtaining an option to continue to use the song (always at an increased fee), the agency and its client are assured that, if a campaign is successful, they can continue to use the song in the commercial for a preestablished fee, an option that may be vital if the song has become inherently identified with the product or if the campaign has been a success.

If an agency wants to secure the master recording rights to a popular song (i.e., the actual hit recording), it must contact the record company that owns those rights, as the music publisher can only grant rights to use the musical composition, not a specific recording. For example, if an advertising agency wants to use the Frank Sinatra version of "That's Life", the Led Zeppelin version of "Rock and Roll," or any other hit recording, it must conduct separate negotiations with both the record company for the existing recorded performance and the music publisher for the song contained on that recording. Because of the double negotiation and double fees inherent in this type of situation, licensing a well-known song and hit record for a single commercial can be extremely expensive (combined fees from $250,000 and to over $750,000 per year are not unusual), and this approach is normally reserved for major advertisers with large media budgets.

## Advantages and Disadvantages of a Hit Song Being Used in a Commercial (From a Publisher's and Writer's Point of View)

Some music publishers and writers feel that any identification with the selling of a consumer product can damage the future earning potential of a copyright, as it may hinder additional new recordings or other uses. Some also feel that any advertising connection is anathema to the integrity of a song. With this in mind, a number of writers and publishers deny all requests to use a song in a commercial regardless of the amount of money being offered or the product being promoted. In some cases, permission is granted but the fees quoted are extremely high to ensure that, if the song is used, a premium will have been paid by the advertising agency to compensate for such loss of projected future income. In others, the fees charged are higher than usual if the songwriter or music publisher feels that the specific product identification or terms of the agreement might adversely affect either future advertising uses by other sponsors or future promotion of the original work. Finally, in cases where the songwriter, estate, lawyer, music publisher, or other authorized representative feels that the product is not right but does not want to give a flat refusal, permission may be granted but the fees will be so large that an agency and its client will find it economically impossible to go ahead with the planned campaign.

On the other hand, many music publishers and songwriters realize that the exposure generated by a national advertising campaign will generate additional uses for a song by stimulating interest in cover records and reintroducing it to a new audience, including motion picture and television producers. A large lump sum payment to the publisher and writer for the use of a song in a commercial is also a primary consideration. If one is being offered between $150,000 and $750,000 for a 1-year use in a major campaign, it is pure fantasy to think that economics may not have some influence in the final decision. The nature of the product being advertised, how the song is used in the context of the commercial, the current annual income generated by the composition from other uses, the remaining copyright life of a composition, whether the song or its future earnings potential might be hurt by the use, whether songwriter approvals have to be secured, and the nature of any lyric changes are all considerations that can either make or break a negotiation.

---

## JINGLES (SONGS WRITTEN FOR COMMERCIALS)

### The Jingle Writer and the Advertising Agency

> You hereby grant to our client (Name of Sponsor) all the right, title, and interest through the world in and to the musical composition entitled (Title of Song) written and composed by (Writer's Name) for use in the following commercial: (Title of Commercial).

The above language is standard (in one form or another) in many jingle contracts. The writer of the music or lyrics traditionally assigns virtually all rights to the agency or sponsor. In most cases, the rights sold are all-inclusive, with the exception that some writers retain their right to receive royalties from ASCAP and BMI for performances of the commercial on radio or television and songwriter royalties if the song is recorded and released to the general public as a tape or CD or used in a film or television series.

Some of the more important rights transferred by the writer to the agency or client are:

The right to register a claim of copyright to the composition in the name of the advertising agency or client

The right to use the composition in all forms of advertising and merchandising

The right to alter, expand, adapt, and edit the composition

The right to use, publish, perform, broadcast, reproduce, and exploit the composition by any means

Considering the many possible uses of music, many writers also negotiate a songwriter's agreement that guarantees them a share of income generated by nonadvertising uses. For most jingles, however, such other uses rarely occur, and a writer's income is usually limited to the writing fee and possibly royalties from either ASCAP or BMI for broadcasts of the commercial.

### The Agency and the Production Company

Since most jingle writers are signed to commercial production companies that handle all aspects of the making of the jingle, the advertising agency will usually contract with the production company instead of with the individual writer. The contract language is similar to that used in the writer–agency jingle contract, except that the production company warrants to the agency that it, not the songwriter, owns all rights to the jingle (the writer having already assigned his or her rights in the jingle to the production company). In all contracts in which a jingle is sold to an agency, the writer and production company also agree to indemnify the agency and the client against any liability, losses, and expenses, including reasonable attorneys' fees, arising out of the use of the musical composition in the commercial. Occasionally, the indemnity is limited to the amount of money actually paid by the agency to the writer or production company.

## NEGOTIATING WITH AN ADVERTISING AGENCY FOR A HIT SONG

This will confirm our agreement pursuant to which (Publisher) grants to (Advertiser) the right, license, privilege, and authority to record, at its own expense, the copy-

TABLE 6.1   Hit Songs Used in TV Commercials

| Song Title | Product | Genre |
| --- | --- | --- |
| "Let it Snow" | Lexus | Standard |
| "Rockin' Me Baby" | Wrangler | Classic Rock |
| "That's Amore" | eBay | Standard |
| "Walkin' on the Sun" | Chevy | Rock Hit |
| "Shaft" | Burger King | Movie Theme |
| "Rock and Roll" | Cadillac | Classic Rock |
| "Taxman" | H&R Block | Classic Rock |
| "Help" | GTE | Movie Theme |
| "Tonight, Tonight" | Mountain Dew | Broadway Song |
| "I Heard It Through the Grapevine" | California Raisins | Soul Classic |
| "When You Wish Upon a Star" | Disneyland | Movie Song |
| "True Colors" | Kodak | Pop Hit |
| "Hello Dolly" | Oscar Mayer | Broadway Song |
| "Mission Impossible" | Stain Stick | TV Theme |
| "Splish Splash" | Liquid Drano | Classic Rock Standard |
| "Pink Panther" | Heineken | Movie Theme |
| "Rhapsody in Blue" | United Airlines | Standard |
| "Soak Up the Sun" | American Express | Pop Hit |
| "Blueberry Hill" | Hyundai Auto | Classic '50s Rock |
| "I'm a Soul Man" | Bic Razors | Soul Classic |
| "Leave It to Beaver" | Toyota | TV Theme |

righted musical composition entitled (the Composition) and to use recordings of the Composition in commercials (the Commercials) advertising the products and/or services of Advertiser, subject to the applicable conditions contained herein.

When an agency commissions the writing of a new song for a commercial, it usually acquires all rights in the jingle for its client. The agreement for a hit song, however, is much less encompassing, as it is purely a license that permits the agency to do certain things during a specified period of time under certain conditions, with a termination of all rights after the agreement is over. (Table 6.1 shows some hit songs used in TV commercials.) The following sections explain the more important issues that occur during such negotiations.

## Parties to the Agreement

In most cases, the advertising agency gets permission directly from the copyright owner of the hit song, which is usually the music publisher. Occasionally the songwriter or music publisher has previously signed an administration, collection, or representation agreement, whereby a larger music publisher, law firm, manager, music industry agency, or other representative has been given the authority to negotiate licenses for the commercial exploitation of a particular hit song or catalog of songs. In that case, the advertising agency will contract with the administrator who is acting on behalf of the song's original copyright owner.

## Copyright Ownership

Ownership of the existing song is never transferred to the agency, as the agreement is merely a license of certain specified rights. On the other hand, if the agency creates new lyrics for the song, the agency will usually copyright the new material for its client, and the owner of the hit song will usually have no rights to the newly created lyrics.

## Duration of License

The term of the commercial license is usually 1 year for a national campaign plus a number of options (normally 1 to 3 additional 1-year options at the election of the advertising agency). As marketing campaigns take on many variations, however, the term requested by an agency can be for a day, a week, a month, a year, multiple years, or any combination thereof. For example, a license can be for a 1-day test in 1 or 2 cities with options for up to three 1-year periods on a national basis if the test results in positive consumer reaction; it can be for 1 month, as in the case of Christmas campaigns, or for a few days or a few weeks, as with Mother's Day, Father's Day, Fourth of July, Easter, Thanksgiving Day promotions.

## Exclusivity versus Nonexclusivity

Unless total advertising exclusivity is requested, the music publisher will not be restricted from licensing the song to other advertisers during the duration of the commercial agreement. The agency contract will, however, contain language prohibiting the use of the song in connection with commercials that promote competing or related products. For example, if a song is licensed for a car commercial, the same song may not be given to another automobile maker but can be simultaneously licensed for use in a commercial promoting television sets, hamburgers, or dish detergent under a nonexclusive, noncompetitive product license. Some of these noncompetitive clauses are very broad (e.g., restricting a song used in a pie commercial from any type of food product) and some are very limited (e.g., restricting a song used in a perfume commercial from other perfume, but not from cosmetics). If the fee paid for the song is very low, there may be no restrictions at all.

If the campaign is a major one or if the identification of the hit song with the product is considered vital to the promotion, the agency may request total advertising exclusivity. Such exclusivity, however, is rare, since the additional fees payable to the music publisher and songwriter for taking the song entirely off the market are normally prohibitive. Fee quotes of from $250,000 to $600,000 are not unusual for 1 year of total exclusivity. An agency may also lose interest in a song if it discovers that the song is currently being used in another product campaign or has recently been so used.

## Number of Commercials

The agency contract will specify the number of commercials that will use the song (e.g., "one 30-second television commercial, one 15-second television commercial, and one 30-second radio commercial") or, if undetermined at the time the contract is signed, a maximum number (e.g., "one 60-second commercial with up to three 20-second edits or lifts").

## Payment of Fees

The initial fee is usually paid upon signing the agreement or within a short time, such as 10 days. Any option payments are paid upon the commencement of the option period or within a few days thereafter.

## Exercise of Options

The advertising contract will be structured so that the agency is the party that decides whether or not an option is picked up. This is accomplished by written notice prior to or by the last day of the current contract period (e.g., "in the event that the agency wants to extend the license agreement for an additional 1-year period, it must notify the music publisher of its option exercise at least 10 days prior to the expiration of the current period of the term"). If the agency does not exercise such option rights, the license agreement expires and no further use of the commercial (other than the agency's right to submit the commercial for advertising industry award shows) may be made after the current period expires.

## Territory

The territory requested for a major advertising campaign is usually the United States of America, its territories, possessions, and commonwealths, but depending on the potential consumer base for the product, Canada may also be included for an additional fee. If the product has a regional base, or the planned campaign is designed as a test, or the product is new and the campaign is in a limited introductory stage, the licensed territory may be only 1 city, 1 state, a number of cities or states, or any variation thereof. For example, the territory may only be for the city of Baltimore, for the state of Illinois, or for 1 identified shopping mall in Los Angeles. If the initial territory is limited but the product has national potential, the agency will usually require options for expanded territories. For example, a campaign may be tested in a number of geographically related cities or states (e.g., Los Angeles, San Diego, and San Francisco, or New York, New Jersey, and Pennsylvania) and, if successful, expanded into other regions (Phoenix, Seattle, and Las Vegas, or California, Washington, and Oregon). Or the territory may be defined as geographic areas covering no more than a certain percentage of the U.S. population (e.g., 10%, 20%, etc.) with options extending the commercial into areas covering a larger percentage (e.g., 30%, 50%, 100%). When a commercial finds consumer acceptance, the agency wants to be able to broadcast the commercial in areas other than those specified in the original license. Therefore, options for additional media and territories are prevalent in contracts for limited-market or test commercials.

At times, the use of a song in specific foreign countries or throughout the world will also be requested, but this usually occurs only in the case of internationally accepted products (such as Pepsi-Cola, McDonald's, Budweiser, or Coca-Cola). The addition of foreign countries is usually handled on an option basis. For example, an agency may license the hit song in the United States for 1 year with three 1-year options and also have the right to extend the use into the United Kingdom for a set fee, into all of Europe for another fee, into Japan for a separate fee, and for the entire world for yet another fee. There are usually time limits as to when these various options can be exercised by the agency, the specifics of which are subject to negotiation between the music publisher, songwriter, and advertising agency.

## Media

Television and radio are the standard media requested, but depending on the thrust of the campaign, print uses may also be included in the license. Additionally, with the advent of commercials on motion picture home videos and on the Internet, home video and Internet rights may also be negotiated. Since some agencies also use the hit song as part of their in-store promotions (reduced price CDs or giveaways), extra monies may be paid the music publisher and songwriter for such "point-of-sale non-record store outlet" promotions. For example, an agency may secure an option to distribute up to 50,000 CDs or tapes of the song used in the commercial for a 1-month period at any time during the license term for either the U.S. statutory mechanical royalty rate or, if acceptable to the writer and music publisher, a reduced mechanical rate.

When an agency asks for a license for television use, a distinction is many times drawn among free over-the-air television, basic cable, and pay cable, with separate fees usually negotiated for each category. Additionally, certain advertising uses of music may be restricted to use in shopping malls, in-house training sessions, or at sales conventions, the fees for such uses being reduced accordingly. Print and email uses may also be requested.

## Foreign Countries

Since many songs have international appeal, a substantial number of commercial requests come from advertisers in countries outside the United States. Most of these requests pertain to English-speaking territories, but Germany, France, Italy, and Japan can also generate substantial income from such uses. In such cases, the writer or publisher's representative in the foreign country (the subpublisher) will often handle the negotiations after either consulting with or getting approval from the U.S. copyright owner. On occasion, the U.S. publisher (on behalf of itself and the songwriters) will negotiate directly by means of telefax or telephone with the foreign ad agency and bypass its local subpublisher, but this approach depends on the terms and conditions of the foreign subpublication agreement that controls the song. Since the foreign subpublisher many times is more familiar with what fees the market can bear in its territory than the U.S. publisher, who may be thousands of miles away, the actual negotiations are usually best handled by the subpublisher, with either input or approval from the U.S. publisher.

## Restrictions on Songwriter/Recording Artists

When an agency pays a well-known writer/performer substantial monies for the use of a song, it may also request a prohibition on the licensing of any other song in the writer's catalog in conjunction with a competing product during the term of the commercial license agreement. Such catalog restriction clauses are not common and are totally negotiable, with any prohibition dependent on, among other things, the amount of compensation being paid, if the writer/ artist's performance is being used in the commercial, and whether the writer/ artist has control over the use of his or her songs and recordings, since in many cases a third-party music publisher controls the songs and a record company controls the recordings of the writer/artist's performances of those songs.

## Restrictions on First Broadcast Use by Another Product

Since agencies do pay substantial fees to use hit songs in commercials, a number will request that the music publisher not license the song to another advertiser for use in a commercial for a product campaign that will be broadcast in advance of the initial airing of its television or radio commercial. Such a request is understandable and may be acceptable provided that the restriction does not encompass a substantial period of time, that the fee is large enough to compensate for possible loss of other advertising income, and that the publisher is not prohibited from entering into noncompeting product license agreements during the restricted period for commercials that will be broadcast after the expiration of the nonbroadcast period.

## Lyric Changes or Instrumental Uses

If the lyrics of the hit song are to be revised by the agency to fit the theme of the commercial (e.g., "Leave It to Beaver" becoming "Leave It to Cargo" for Old Navy, "Shaft" becoming "Shaq" for Burger King, and "I'm A Soul Man" becoming "I'm A Bic Man" for Bic razors), or if entirely new lyrics are to replace the original lyrics, the exact nature of the lyric revisions or new lyrics will always be specified in the license agreement so that no misunderstanding will arise between the agency and the music publisher or songwriter as to what was intended and agreed to prior to the commercial's being on the air. If the composition is used instrumentally and without the original lyrics, or both instrumentally and with new lyrics in separate commercials, that will also be indicated in the body of the contract. Specificity in this area cannot be overemphasized for the protection of all parties to the license agreement, since the more concrete and exact a contract is, the less likely that there will be a lawsuit. It is also common for a publisher to charge more for the commercial use of a song when a lyric is changed than when it is not.

## Performance Rights

The agreement for a hit song is similar to a television synchronization license in that the advertiser/client (like the producer of a television series) is given the right to include the composition in the commercial, with the broadcast or performance of that composition being conditioned on a radio or television station's having a valid performing right license from ASCAP, BMI, or some other person, firm, corporation, or association (including the music publisher) duly empowered to grant such rights on behalf of the copyright owners.

## RADIO AND TELEVISION ROYALTIES FOR ADVERTISING MUSIC

Most music used in commercials is written specifically for the product being promoted. When the agency or sponsor has not bought out the broadcast rights for a jingle, performance royalties can be earned but are usually insignificant unless the advertising campaign lasts many years. Nonetheless, most of the large advertising agencies have had in-house music publishing divisions for many years, and there is a growing trend for even small agencies to set up music publishing companies to collect this "newly discovered" source of income.

In the case of hit songs used in commercials, however, substantial monies can be made. All that is needed is information on the advertising field, experience with ASCAP and BMI commercial payments, and reasonableness in one's negotiating position with the agency or sponsor. A single phone call, handled correctly, can result in hundreds of thousands of dollars in immediate income as well as additional dollars in performance royalties.

During a recent Christmas season all of these hit songs were being used in television ads: "Be-Bop-A-Lula" for UPS, "If I Didn't Care" for Philips lightbulbs, "Big Girls Don't Cry" for Pert Plus shampoo, "Life Is Just a Bowl of Cherries" for Playtex, "Teach Your Children" for Fruit of the Loom, "Sea of Love" for Chanel No. 5, "Mississippi Queen" for Miller Genuine Draft, "Shout" for Polaroid, "As Time Goes By" for Honda Accord, and "Strangers in the Night" for Timex watches. This world is one that anyone with a hit song should pursue.

In the commercial music performance area, a few words of caution are necessary. Extreme care is important when drawing up contracts of this kind. A badly drafted licensing agreement can prevent ASCAP or BMI from licensing the commercial. The ASCAP and BMI payment rules are very precise as to the reservation of performance rights, qualifying duration for payment, change of original lyrics, and the necessity of broadcast schedules. The payments in this area are significantly different between ASCAP and BMI, and writers or publishers must keep that in mind before counting performance money.

# 7

# Music, Money, and Performances

FOR MOST SONGWRITERS, film and TV scorers, and music publishers, the performing rights area represents their greatest source of continuing royalty income. Throughout the world, writers and publishers receive each year over $4 billion in royalties from this right of copyright, yet very few understand what the right is, where these royalties come from, who negotiates them, who collects them, how the royalties are computed, what choices can be made, how 1 organization compares with another, and how one can leave 1 organization to go to another. Considering that performance royalties continue well beyond the lives of many writers, specific and correct knowledge of this area is a necessity for anyone involved in any aspect of the music field. Though the royalty figures do vary for any given type of use based on many factors, Table 7.1 sets forth the type of monies that can be earned in this field.

## THE PERFORMING RIGHT

Despite its name, the performing right has nothing to do with artists or performers. It is a right of copyright that is set forth in the U.S. Copyright Law, as well as the laws of most countries, and that applies to the payment of license

TABLE **7.1**   Performing Right Royalties for Various Types of Uses

| Type of Performance | Writer and Publisher Royalties |
|---|---:|
| #1 *Billboard* pop song of the year | $  1,500,000 |
| 10 minutes of background music score per episode on a network television series airing for 10 years | 1,664,000 |
| Theme song for a network television series on the air for 5 years | 364,000 |
| Song performed on primetime network television | 3,600 |
| Hit song used in a commercial with a 2-year broadcast run | 300,000 |
| #1 pop shart single | 720,000 |
| #10 pop chart single | 400,000 |
| #50 pop chart single | 90,000 |
| 15 minutes of background music score on each episode of a widely syndicated local television series airing for 1 year | 240,000 |
| 1 performance of a primetime network television series theme song | 1,500 |
| A major popular song's lifetime of copyright earnings | 7,500,000 |
| Jingle performance on network television | 80 |
| Production company logo | 80 |
| Worldwide foreign performances of a Top 10 chart hit | 750,000 |
| 1 radio performance | 6¢ |
| Foreign performances of the background score from a #1 worldwide blockbuster movie | $      500,000 |

fees by music users when those users perform the copyrighted musical compositions of writers and publishers. This right recognizes that a writer's creation is intellectual property and its use requires permission as well as compensation. Performances can be songs heard on the radio or on a jukebox; background scores performed on television; or music performed live or on tape at a Las Vegas show, a major concert venue, a local rock 'n' roll or jazz club, or a symphonic concert hall. Performances can also be music channels on an airplane, music at a convention, or music on hold on a telephone. Music users (those that pay the license fees) include the major television networks, U.S. local television and radio stations, pay cable services (HBO, Showtime), basic cable (USA Network, MTV, the Nashville Network), concert halls, Web sites, the hotel industry, colleges and universities, nightclubs, bars and grills, and many others. In short, in most situations where music is played (with the exception of the home), a user is paying a license fee, an organization is collecting those fees, and writers and publishers are being paid royalties for the performances of their copyrighted works. To put the size of this field into perspective, there are many billions of worldwide licensed performances each year by many hundreds of thousands of users.

In America, this right's primary recognition came as part of the 1909 Copyright Act, with further definition under the 1976 Copyright Revision Act. The right covers the nondramatic performance of copyrighted musical works. It does not involve dramatic rights, also known as grand rights, where performances of a composition are licensed directly by the copyright owner. Dramatic, or grand rights, include works being performed in musicals (the live theater), operas, ballets, and so on. Compositions, though considered dramatic in the context of their original theater or opera setting, are generally under the nondramatic right when performed individually on radio or television. In the United States, three organizations negotiate license fee agreements with the users of music and distribute those fees back to the writers and publishers whose music and lyrics are being performed. The organizations are the American Society of Composers, Authors, and Publishers (ASCAP), Broadcast Music, Inc. (BMI), and SESAC. As 97% of the license fees in this area are either ASCAP or BMI, the primary focus of this chapter is on those two organizations.

## THE ORGANIZATIONS AND HOW TO JOIN

### ASCAP

The American Society of Composers, Authors, and Publishers is an unincorporated membership association formed in 1914 by writers (composers and lyricists) and music publishers. ASCAP's charter members included Victor Herbert, John Philip Sousa, Jerome Kern, and Irving Berlin, among others, and its total membership in its first year of operation was 170 writers and 22 publishers. The society has a board of directors of 12 writers and 12 publishers, who are elected for 2-year terms by the membership. The president of the society is a member of the board as well as chosen by the board and has traditionally been a writer member. The basic principles that govern the society are that members similarly situated must be treated alike, that revenues collected from a particular area are to be distributed to performances in that area, and that all distributions are to be made on an objective basis. ASCAP has over 170,000 writer and publisher members, and its receipts are in excess of $600 million a year.

To be eligible to join ASCAP as a full writer or publisher member, it is necessary to have either 1 commercial recording (CD, album, jingle, cassette) of a song written or published by the prospective member, commercially available printed sheet music of the composition, a program from a concert or recital hall listing the composition, or evidence of a performance of the composition in an ASCAP-licensed medium (a letter from a club, radio, or television station confirming the performance, a cue sheet from a film or television producer or a broadcasting station or a web site performance) listing the song or background score with writer and publisher information included. Writers and publishers must submit separate membership applications in order to be paid.

Once the writer or publisher meets the eligibility requirements, an application must be completed and forwarded to ASCAP for election to membership. For publisher memberships, it is also necessary to clear with ASCAP the prospective company name to make sure that the name is not currently being used by another U.S. or foreign publisher. Applying online is available.

Writer and publisher elections are held monthly, and the specific month in which one is elected determines the extent of any retroactive payments. The following 2003 election chart shows the retroactive period covered by each election:

| *Writer Elections* | *Retroactive Crediting Date* |
| --- | --- |
| January–March 2003 | April–June 2002 performances |
| April–June 2003 | July–September 2002 performances |
| July–September 2003 | October–December 2002 performances |
| October–December 2003 | January–March 2003 performances |

| *Publisher Elections* | *Retroactive Crediting Date* |
| --- | --- |
| January–March 2003 | July–September 2002 performances |
| April–June 2003 | October–December 2002 performances |
| July–September 2003 | January–March 2003 performances |
| October–December 2003 | April–June 2003 performances |

## BMI

Broadcast Music, Inc., is a corporation organized in 1939 by members of the radio broadcasting industry, with which writers and publishers affiliate. Publisher affiliation was available from inception, with writer affiliation commencing in 1950. BMI has a board of directors consisting of 13 executives associated with companies in the broadcasting field and 1 BMI employee who is the president. BMI has over 300,000 affiliates and its total receipts are over $550 million a year.

The eligibility requirements to become affiliated with BMI as a writer or publisher are basically the same as those set forth for ASCAP with the addition of affiliation available to a writer whose work is likely to be performed. Once the writer or publisher meet the eligibility requirements, an application for writer or publisher affiliation must be completed and returned to BMI. As with

ASCAP, publisher names must be cleared for use with BMI prior to the application being completed. Affiliation takes effect upon the writer or publisher signing the contract and BMI countersigning the document.

## TYPES OF LICENSE AGREEMENTS

The most common type of license agreement signed by users with ASCAP and BMI is the "blanket license." This license allows a user (a radio or television station, for instance) to perform any works in the ASCAP or BMI repertory during the term of the license for a specific negotiated fee. This unlimited access to repertory includes all of the past works of writer and publisher members or affiliates as well as the works written by such members or affiliates during the entire term of the license agreement with ASCAP or the writer and publisher affiliation agreement with BMI. The license also covers the works of writers who are members of foreign societies. The blanket license allows a user to perform the copyrighted works of writers and publishers without worrying about infringement litigation (performing copyrighted works without permission), the administrative record keeping of what is being performed, or the identity of the correct parties to be paid and what the payment is to be. Blanket licenses are negotiated agreements in which the license fee paid by the user can be, among others, a flat dollar fee, a per subscriber or gross revenue fee, a fee based on net receipts from sponsors, or on such other objective factors as the number of full-time students for universities, the seating capacity and the types of equipment used in nightclubs, and live entertainment expenditures for hotels. License agreements have a maximum term of 5 years.

A per program license is where a station pays a license fee only for each program using ASCAP or BMI music that is not otherwise licensed directly or at the source. The fee is dependent on the advertising revenues the program has generated for the station. They also pay on incidental music fee for music uses not contained in specific programs and ambient uses in local news programs. The core provisions of this license were set by the court decision in the Buffalo Broadcasting local television rate proceeding.

Two other forms of license involve the writer and publisher (the copyright owner) making an agreement directly with a user or directly with a program producer (a film or television producer, who then grants the license to a user). These latter two forms of license are permitted under the ASCAP and BMI agreements with writers and publishers, as those agreements are nonexclusive and enable a writer to license his or her works directly even though he or she is a member of ASCAP or an affiliate of BMI.

## WRITER AND PUBLISHER CONTRACTS AND TERMINATION DATES

A writer or publisher who wishes to join ASCAP or affiliate with BMI fills out an application, and signs a contract. These contracts are legally binding agreements that set forth the specific contractual obligations, duties, and remedies of all parties. Contracts change so always be aware of the most recent PRO contract.

The ASCAP agreement is the same for both writers and publishers and gives the society the right to license the nondramatic public performances of the member's works. The agreement also grants ASCAP the right to enforce and protect the rights of public performance, to prevent infringement of such works by litigation, and to have all of the rights and remedies for enforcing the copyrights as well as the right to sue under such copyrights. The agreement is subject to the provisions of ASCAP's 1950, 1960, and 2001 consent decrees with the government as well as the society's articles of association and any resolutions of the ASCAP board of directors. The agreement also states that the board of directors must consist of an equal number of writers and publishers and that the royalties distributed must be divided into 2 equal sums for division to writer and publisher members.

The duration of the current ASCAP agreement runs from January 1, 1996, with each writer or publisher having the right to terminate that agreement by giving written notice prior to October 1 of any year of the agreement. Provided notice is given, the contract is over as of December 31 of that year. These are year-to-year agreements, with the right to terminate being allowed during any year of the contract. All writer and publisher contracts are identical.

The contracts that most writers and publishers sign with BMI are the same, but provisions can be negotiated provided the writer or publisher makes such a request and has the bargaining power to effect a change. Although most initial affiliation agreements are not negotiated, many successful writers and publishers renegotiate the provisions prior to any extension of the contract.

Most BMI writer agreements are for a period of 2 years and continue thereafter for additional terms of 2 years each unless terminated by either party by registered or certified mail at least 3 months (some say 60 days) prior to the end of a term. For example, if a writer signed a BMI contract on June 30, 1993, the contract would run until June 30, 1995, and continue to renew for additional 2-year periods (June 30, 1997; June 30, 1999; June 30, 2001) unless terminated. A writer could terminate by giving registered or certified notice to BMI no sooner than 6 months prior to June 30, 1995, or any 2-year term after that and no later than 3 months (some day 60 days) prior to June 30, 1995, or any 2-year term after that.

Most BMI publisher agreements are for a period of 5 years from the date of signing and continue for additional periods of 5 years each unless terminated by either party by registered or certified mail not more than 6 months or less than 3 months prior to the end of a term. If the termination date is missed by a publisher, the contract extends for an additional 5-year period. For example, if a publisher signed a contract on June 5, 2000, and wished to terminate the contract sometime afterward, notice would have to be given no sooner than 6 months prior to June 5, 2005, and no later than 3 months prior to June 5, 2005. If these termination dates were missed, the contract would extend to June 5, 2010.

Some of the types of BMI deals negotiated by certain writers and publishers include year-to-year, 6-month, quarterly, or monthly agreements. For writers who own their own publishing companies, agreements are sometimes negotiated where the duration of the writer and publisher agreements are the same and coterminous (beginning and ending on the same days) and have the same termination notice requirements.

## CONSIDERATIONS IN MAKING A DECISION

Since all three U.S. organizations are organized differently, have entirely different payment formulas, owners, contracts, and philosophies, and collect substantially different amounts of money, the decision as to which one a writer and publisher should join or affiliate with should not be taken lightly, as millions of dollars in royalty income can be at stake if the wrong decision is made. Two of the most important considerations in this decision should be which organization will best protect your copyrights over their entire copyright life and which organization will compensate you best, both in the short term as well as the long term, for U.S. and foreign performances of your works.

The primary areas that need to be considered include the length of contract and the procedures to terminate that contract if one wants to leave; fairness and equality of treatment in the distribution of royalties; recognition of the value of all of a writer's and publisher's copyrights whether they be new or old works; procedures whereby each organization changes its payment rules; relationships with foreign societies; maximum and accurate collection of foreign income; and internal procedures for handling foreign money.

Although many writers at the start of their careers fail to appreciate the importance of this decision, it represents one of the most important ones they will ever make, as it will affect performance royalties many years after the writer has stopped writing or has died. Mistakes can be costly in this area, and it is far better to learn the basics at the start of one's career rather than midway or at the end.

## ASCAP AND BMI INCOME AND DISTRIBUTIONS

The starting point for how much an ASCAP or BMI performance is worth is the total income that comes into each organization. Table 7.2 sets forth the

TABLE **7.2**  ASCAP and BMI Receipts and Distributions

| Year | ASCAP Receipts | ASCAP Distributions to Members | Estimated BMI Receipts | Estimated BMI Distributions to Affiliates |
|------|------|------|------|------|
| 2002 | $635,055,000 | $587,266,000 | $574,000,000 | $483,000,000 |
| 2001 | 646,139,000 | 509,310,000 | 541,000,000 | 450,000,000 |
| 2000 | 577,157,000 | 480,304,000 | 501,000,000 | 417,000,000 |
| 1999 | 560,039,000 | 435,028,000 | 454,000,000 | 370,000,000 |
| 1998 | 508,348,000 | 424,480,000 | 440,000,000 | 360,000,000 |
| 1997 | 482,124,000 | 416,565,000 | 420,000,000 | 345,000,000 |
| 1996 | 482,579,000 | 397,379,000 | 390,000,000 | 320,000,000 |
| 1992 | 389,979,000 | 312,029,000 | 280,000,000 | 230,000,000 |
| 1990 | 358,083,000 | 277,465,000 | 245,000,000 | 195,000,000 |
| 1988 | 296,617,000 | 234,838,000 | 250,000,000 | 200,000,000 |
| 1986 | 252,199,000 | 197,707,000 | 190,000,000 | 160,000,000 |
| 1984 | 208,683,000 | 168,215,000 | 140,000,000 | 110,000,000 |
| 1982 | 186,974,000 | 152,340,000 | 120,000,000 | 100,000,000 |
| 1972 | 69,467,000 | 52,899,000 | 40,000,000 | 30,000,000 |

total domestic and foreign receipts of ASCAP and BMI as well as the total royalty distributions each year to writers and publishers. The table also illustrates the substantial growth of this field over the past decades. In the case of ASCAP, the figures are exact, as annual financial statements are issued to the membership. In the case of BMI, reliable estimates are given as to annual receipts and distributions, since BMI does not issue financial statements to its affiliated writers and publishers. The BMI year, as opposed to the ASCAP January-through-December year, runs from July 1 of one year through June 30 of the following year. The operating costs for ASCAP are 14-15% with BMI in the area of 16-17%. Since SESAC, the third U.S. licensing organization, is estimated to collect between $30 million and $40 million annually (approximately 3% of the ASCAP and BMI total), they have not been included in the chart.

## COMPONENTS OF ASCAP AND BMI INCOME

The primary job of ASCAP and BMI is to negotiate license fee agreements with the users of music for the nondramatic performance of copyrighted works and to pay those fees back to writers and publishers based on the performances of their songs. Knowledge of the sources making up each organization's total income is important, as it relates directly to the royalties paid for music and lyrics in any licensed area.

## Domestic

In the domestic area (U.S. users of music), the largest single source of revenue comes from television, with radio in second place and general (concert halls, nightclubs, hotels, etc.) and background music operations third. The remainder of each organization's total income comes from the symphonic and concert field and interest on investments. Using ASCAP as a guide, since it does publish financial figures, the society's 2001 total receipts figure of $646 million included $245 million from television, $182 million from radio stations, $76 million from the general licensing area, $4.4 million from the symphonic area, and $6 million from interest. To illustrate comparative growth, the 1972 ASCAP year of $69 million in receipts showed $33 million from television, $18 million from radio, $8 million from general licensing, $314,000 from the symphonic field, and $860,000 from interest.

## Foreign

In recent years, the greatest area of income growth for both ASCAP and BMI has been the foreign area. The reasons for this growth have primarily been due to the ever-increasing popularity of the U.S. repertory overseas as well as the substantial increase in the number of radio and television stations in foreign countries. Every major country of the world has a performing rights society that collects for ASCAP and BMI writers and publishers when their works are performed in the foreign territory. These societies forward those monies to ASCAP and BMI, which in turn distribute them to their members or affiliates. Through agreements with these foreign societies, ASCAP and BMI also collect for foreign writers and publishers whose works are performed in the U.S. and forward those monies to the particular society of which the foreign writer or publisher is a member.

In 2002 ASCAP received approximately $148 million from foreign societies for foreign performances of its writers' and publishers' works. BMI's 2002 foreign receipts figure is estimated at $120 million. By contrast, in 1987 ASCAP's foreign collections totaled $50 million, with BMI's at approximately $30 million. Considering that most major music publishers collect performance money directly from foreign societies through local subpublishers, most of the foreign money received and distributed by ASCAP and BMI is writer money.

## Special Distributions

An important element of the ASCAP and BMI annual income figure is whether any area (television, radio, foreign, etc.) received a "special distribution" of past monies in that year. These "special distributions" represent distributions to writers and publishers outside the regular quarterly distributions and are usually the result of a settlement or court decision regarding a user's past fees to ASCAP and BMI.

The important thing about these distributions is that they usually involve a substantial amount of additional money for performances on which ASCAP and BMI have already paid. Most writers and publishers consider this "found money" even though it may have taken years of negotiation or litigation to finalize them. It is important for every writer and publisher to stay informed of these retroactive settlements or decisions in order to ensure that they are distributed by a writer's or publisher's organization based on the specific criterion of the past performances covered by the settlement. Although this criterion may seem obvious, it has not been universally followed by some in the past. For any "special distribution," the factors that you must be aware of are the total amount of the retroactive settlement, the total amount being distributed to writers and publishers, the past performance years being paid on, and the types of performance and medium sharing in the distribution. A few examples of "special distributions" include year 2000, 2001, and 2002 ASCAP total distributions of $120 million for settlements in the cable area; 1992 ASCAP distribution of $19 million from a settlement agreement with the NBC television network for performances occurring during the years 1977-91; ASCAP distributions in 1985 and 1987 of $14 million and $43 million respectively from local television stations for the years 1979, 1980, and 1984-86; and BMI special distributions in 1985, 1986, and 1990 of local television monies for the performance years 1979-87.

As many of the license agreements being made by ASCAP and BMI concern new types of users and some involve retroactive payments for prior periods of time, writers and publishers should stay aware of all new agreements made in order to make sure that they get their fair retroactive share of any past due monies received by ASCAP or BMI from a user.

## Interim Fees

Of increasing importance to the amount of royalties being paid to writers and publishers are the situations where users and the performing rights organizations are not able to reach final agreements on what license fees should be for a particular period of time. The result of not being able to negotiate a final agreement has been that many users (the television networks, the local television industry, the pay and basic cable industry, etc.) as well as ASCAP and BMI have litigated the matter or gone to a rate court in order for third parties (judges or magistrates) to set what the fees should be in a given area. In many of these cases, the user continues to pay at the old agreement rate or pays an "interim" court-set rate pending the final outcome of the trial or hearing and all of its appeals. In interim fee cases, many years or decades can elapse before final license fees for an area are determined.

# PAYMENT DATES AND METHODS OF PAYMENT

## ASCAP

ASCAP pays its publishers for U.S. performances approximately 6 months after the end of each 3-month performance quarter, with writers being paid a few weeks later. Performance statements are issued with all payments. The following chart illustrates the payment dates for 2003 performances and can be used as a general guide to ASCAP payments.

| *Performances* | *Publisher Payment* | *Writer Payment* |
|---|---|---|
| January–March 2003 | September 2003 | October 2003 |
| April–June 2003 | December 2003 | January 2004 |
| July–September 2003 | March 2004 | April 2004 |
| October–December 2003 | June 2004 | July 2004 |

ASCAP distributes royalties for foreign performances of ASCAP writer and publisher works in February, May, August, and November of each year. Each distribution covers a specific number of countries, time periods, and areas of performance (film, radio, etc.). Performance statements listing all performed titles in each country are issued along with the payments.

ASCAP writers have the choice of receiving their quarterly royalties either on a "current performance" basis or a "4 funds" basis. The current-performance plan distributes in 1 check 100% of the monies due a writer for a 3-month performance period. For example, if a writer's radio, television and wired music performances totaled 8,000 performance credits for a quarter and the value of 1 credit for that quarter was $5.00, the writer would receive a check for $40,000. The 4-funds method of distribution, on the other hand, calculates each writer's quarterly distribution by taking into account the writer's most recent 4 quarters of credits (20% of the check), the total of all of the writer's performance credits for the last 5 years (40% of the check), the total of a writer's "recognized works" credits for the last 5 years (20% of the check) and the total of all of a writer's performance credits for the past 10 years, as well as the writer's continuous quarters of ASCAP membership up to a maximum of 168 quarters (20% of the check). In 1999, the 4 Funds Plan was replaced by the Averaged Performance Plan, a simpler and less complex system that averages the dollar value of performances over time.

It is important for every ASCAP writer to know what plan of payment he or she is on, as one's method of payment does have an effect on one's domestic royalty distributions. For example, if a writer was averaging $2,500 a quarter in royalties on the Averaged Plan, has a major chart song or becomes the composer of a network television series with many minutes of music in each episode, the short-term royalty checks for the new activity would be far less than what would have been paid if the writer were on current performance, the reason being that only 20% of each averaged check is based on a writer's most recent quarter of activity. The remaining 80% of each check involves 5- and 10-year averages of a writer's quarterly distributions. On the other hand, if an averaged writer was making in the area of $15,000 to $20,000 per quarter and had little or no current activity, the writer's distribution would still remain good for quite sometime, as 80% of that writer's payment is based on a 5- and 10-year average of his or her past performance dollar values.

The royalty calculations that determine each Averaged Performance writer's quarterly royalties have no effect on the value of royalty distributions being paid to writers on current performance. This system is merely 1 of 2 different ways that a writer chooses to receive his or her royalties.

The Averaged Performance Plan's writer's checks have three elements in their computation. Twenty percent of each check is based on the most recent performance quarter's credits times the current performance dollar point value for that quarter times 20%. For example, if a writer had 2,500 performance credits in the first quarter of the year 2000, the first computation would be as follows: 2,500 x $5.30 credit value x 20% = $2,650. Similarly, 60% of the check is based on the averaged dollars over twenty performance quarters. In this example, the computation would be 2Q1995 through 1Q2000 quarterly credits x each quarter's Current Performance credit value divided by 20 x 60%. The remaining 20% of the check is based on averaged dollars over the last forty quarters. In this example, you would take each quarter's credits for the period second quarter 1990 through first quarter 2000 and multiply them by each quarter's current performance point value, then divide by 40 and multiply by 20%. The total of all 3 computations would result in the writer's check received for the first performance quarter of the year 2000. Writers under this plan receive the same amount of royalties as would a Current Performance writer but over an extended period of time. This plan also makes it easier for writers in this system to project what their distributions will be as opposed to the 4 Funds system, as 77% of the Averaged Performance payment is based on five and ten year averages with 23% based on the most recent quarter's credits. A writer can switch from the Averaged Performance Plan to the Current Performance Plan or vice-versa by giving notice prior to October 1 of any year with the switch taking effect the first distribution of the next year (January).

Both types of writer distribution plans serve a purpose depending on a writer's long-term past and current activity, as well as the writer's financial needs both now and in the future. Most ASCAP writers once on current performance remain on current performance throughout their entire membership. Advice as to which payment plan is best for you should always be sought from knowledgeable representatives.

Publishers are paid the full value of their quarterly statement credits in 1 check. For instance, if a publisher's catalogue generated 50,000 performance credits in a quarter and the value of 1 publisher credit for that quarter was $5, the publisher's check would be for $250,000.

## BMI

BMI pays its writers and publishers for most domestic U.S. performances approximately 7 months after the end of each 3-month performance period. Performance statements are issued with each check.The following 2002 performance periods and their payment dates are representative of payments.

| *Performance Quarters* | *Writer and Publisher Payment* |
| --- | --- |
| January–March 2002 | October 2002 |
| April–June 2002 | January 2003 |
| July–September 2002 | April 2003 |
| October–December 2002 | July 2003 |

BMI makes 4 foreign performance distributions each year as part of their domestic distributions, and each covers specific countries and time periods. Performance statements are issued with each foreign distribution.

BMI writers and publishers receive in each distribution check the full value of all performances in a quarter. If a publisher receives $25,000 for the publisher share of a particular writer's works for a 3-month period, the writer also receives $25,000 in 1 check for those performances.

## *ASCAP AND BMI PAYMENT PHILOSOPHY AND RULES*

The payment philosophy and payment rules for the two main U.S. licensing organizations are entirely different for every medium licensed (radio, television, background music services, live performances, etc.) as well as for every type of performance (theme songs, underscore, feature performances, jingles, etc.). Understanding each organization's underlying philosophy and payment practices is a necessity for understanding your royalties, past, present, and future.

### ASCAP

ASCAP's philosophy and rules are set forth in 5 documents: (1) the ASCAP Weighting Rules, (2) the Weighting Formula, (3) the Writer's Distribution Formula, (4) the Publisher's Distribution Formula, and (5) the Articles of Association. The Weighting Rules outline the limits that govern ASCAP's board of directors in weighting performances. As all types of performances have different crediting weights (35%, 50%, 12%, 100%, 3%), which translate into royalties, these limits are important in defining the relationship between types of performances. The Weighting Formula contains the specific weights for each type of performance as well as other rules affecting the value of performances in any licensed area (television, radio, etc.). The Writer's Distribution Formula explains the 2 types of payment plans available to writers (current performance and averaged), and the Publisher Distribution Formula explains the publisher's method of payment. The Articles of Association describe the obligations of writer and publisher membership, the procedures used for complaints and protests, the eligibility standards for membership, the voting process used to elect the board (any member who has performance credits in the latest available survey year preceding the election gets 1 vote; additional votes are based on the number of credits each member has during that year, with a maximum of no more than 100 votes for any member), and many other items.

In general, ASCAP distributes the license fees collected from a specific area only on the performances occurring in that area. The value of a performance is determined by the amount of fees collected in that area, the amount of ASCAP performances in that area during a 3-month period, the types of performance, and the relationship of that area's license fees to the license fees of all other areas. Writer and publisher payments are made according to the results of census (100% pickup) or sample surveys of performances in each of the areas licensed; live performance license fees (nightclubs, concert halls, etc.) are distributed on the basis of actual performance information as well as on feature performances on radio and all uses on television. Pursuant to a "follow the dollar" philosophy, licensees are surveyed in proportion to their fees to ASCAP.

The values for every type of performance are set out in percentage terms in the Weighting Formula (100% of a use credit for a feature performance, 35% to 50% for theme songs, etc.). Payment formulas using these percentages arrive at the number of credits for a particular type of performance. The number of credits generated by a performance varies based on the medium in which the performance occurs (e.g., radio, television, cable), the type of performance (visual vocal, background music, theme song, jingle), and the economic significance of the station. The total of all writer or publisher credits in a quarter are then divided by the total amount of money available for distribution in that quarter to arrive at the value of 1 credit. A writer's or publisher's quarterly credits are then multiplied by that dollar value to arrive at the writer or publisher quarterly royalty check. For instance, if 6 million ASCAP writer performance credits are generated in a quarter from all feature performances, background music, theme songs, and jingles, and the writer money available for that distribution is $30 million, the value of 1 writer credit for that 3-month period will be $5.00 ($30 million divided by 6 million credits). If a writer has 20,000 credits for all of the compositions in his or her catalog, for instance, the writer check would be $100,000. The reason, incidentally, that ASCAP uses weights for different types of performances rather than specific dollar amounts on a printed schedule is that it is impossible to know in advance of each quarter precisely how many ASCAP performances there will be in that quarter or what the exact distributable income will be for that quarter.

In the radio area, all feature uses of songs (regardless of their past performance history) are treated equally when performed on the same station, with the exception that works that generate more than a certain number of radio feature credits (or another number as designated by ASCAP) in a quarter are given an extra payment. In the television area, all types of performances are given specific crediting weights, which translate into dollars. Certain songs that have a substantial history of past performances receive additional crediting (money) when they are used as background music or themes or in commercials.

Finally, ASCAP may make special monetary awards to writers and publishers for works that achieve in any performance quarter a specified level of performance credits in 1 or more designated media, as ASCAP may specify and designate from time to time. This provision, adopted in 1992, allows ASCAP more flexibility in crediting works that achieve a high level of current success. The 1992 5,000 radio feature credit award and the 1994 radio feature premium are two examples of this provision.

## BMI

The payment rules for BMI writers and publishers are set forth in the BMI Payment Schedule. New schedules are issued periodically, with each new schedule replacing the provisions of the previous schedule. The schedule lists minimum combined writer and publisher payment rates for various types of radio, network television, and local television performances ($5 per network station for a theme, $11.50 per network station for a feature performance, 12¢ and 6¢ for radio performances, 42¢ per minute of background music on a local television station, etc.) as well as all other factors affecting the value of a given type of performance in an area. As for the areas not covered by specific dollar performance payment figures (cable, PBS, etc.), general statements are given explaining the methods of distributing monies from those areas. After calculating each quarter the amounts due writers and publishers under the minimum-rate schedule and the song bonus schedule, BMI distributes any additional license fee monies in the form of voluntary payments to certain types of performances in certain areas. For many types of performances (television background music, network themes, etc.), these voluntary payments represent the majority of their income in a given quarter, and it is estimated that between 30% and 40% of the total of each BMI writer and publisher distribution is in the form of these voluntary payments.

In the radio area, BMI pays songs primarily on the basis of their cumulative performance history, their current performance activity, and the relationship of one song to another as to past activity. Bonuses of 4 times, 2½ times, 2 times, or 1½ times the minimum rates are given to songs depending on their history of performances, with other bonuses given out to certain current-activity songs (songs with 100,000 or more performances in a quarter) and other "special credit" works. The basic BMI philosophy is to pay out all of the Payment Schedule radio and television rates as well as the song bonus rates and then distribute the remaining money in the form of voluntary payments to certain types of performances in certain areas (i.e. underscore on network television).

## PAYMENT CHANGES

Both ASCAP and BMI periodically change their methods of payment, sometimes at a moment's notice. Any change can have a substantial effect on a writer's or publisher's current and future earnings. This chapter needs to be read in light of the possibility that the system and payments in effect when you joined ASCAP or became affiliated with BMI could very well be different in the days, months, or years after you join. Only with some knowledge of past payment practices and philosophies can a writer or publisher make an informed decision with respect to which organization to join or affiliate with, as well as what to anticipate for the present and the future.

With ASCAP, any change in the Weighting Rules and the Weighting Formula must be approved by the ASCAP board of directors, and all ASCAP members must be notified in advance of such a change. Prior to 2001, notification to the Justice Department and sometimes a U.S. District Court hearing were necessary, but these provisions were removed by the 2001 ASCAP Consent Decree.

The following examples illustrate the financial ramifications of payment changes. Television background music was credited by ASCAP with a 20% payment for 3 minutes of music in 1960, with subsequent changes to 25%, 27½%, 30%, 36%, 42%, and 48% in 2000. A 50% payment for 14-week primetime network television theme songs was instituted in 1983. The prior theme rate was 10%. Jingles were increased from a 1% payment in 1960 to a 3% payment in 1982. Different payments depending on time of day were put into effect in 1973 for network television performances. An increase in payment for frequently performed radio songs was introduced in 1992 and in 1994.

With BMI, all rates are subject to change at any time. Changes occur when BMI issues a new Payment Schedule. As BMI is subject to a consent decree with the government, BMI writers and publishers may object to a change by notifying the Justice Department. Arbitration is also available for many situations.

As with ASCAP, BMI's changes also have a wide-ranging effect on affiliated writer and publisher earnings. In 1977 a bonus system for songs was instituted. In 1977 "Network A" background music was increased from 12¢ per minute per station to 22¢ and increased again in 1984 to 36¢ per minute per station. In 1980 BMI began paying on commercial jingles on an experimental basis. The entire bonus system for radio songs and "million performance works" was substantially changed in the 1987 schedule.

Any change by ASCAP and BMI in their valuing of a specific type of performance has an effect on all other types of performances. If ASCAP makes a change in the percentage weight of a particular type of performance (underscore, for instance), the values of all other performances will be affected. If BMI makes a change in a Payment Schedule rate or a voluntary payment for a given type of performance, many other rates and payments will be affected.

## CO-WRITTEN COMPOSITIONS

ASCAP and BMI writers can collaborate on compositions with each other even though they are members or affiliates of different organizations. In cases where an ASCAP writer and a BMI writer co-write a song, the publishing interest of the ASCAP writer must be placed in an ASCAP publishing company and the BMI writer's publishing interest placed in a BMI publishing company. Each writer–publisher pair will receive royalty payments from its respective performing right organization. The same arrangement would occur if ASCAP or BMI writers co-wrote a song with a SESAC writer. Each publisher's share must match its writer's share. For example, if an ASCAP and BMI writer have a 75%/25% writer split on a song, the ASCAP publisher would have 75% of the publishing and the BMI publisher 25%.

## SERVICES PROVIDED

In addition to their primary role of licensing, collection, and distribution, both ASCAP and BMI provide many other services to the music industry and the public at large. Some of these additional activities include a series of band and new-writer showcases in Los Angeles, New York, Nashville, and other cities, which are heavily attended by music industry executives looking for new talent; educational and creative-writing workshops; film scoring and musical theater workshops; grant and scholarship programs for high school and college music students and others exhibiting excellence in music; book and article awards; sponsorships of regional music business conferences and songwriter associations; index departments, which provide information on the millions of songs in the ASCAP and BMI repertories and benefits such as instrument, tour, studio and health insurance. Both organizations also spend a great deal of time and effort in the legislative area, ensuring that the rights of creators are protected, represented, and expanded.

---

## *ASCAP PAYMENTS AND PAYMENT RULES*

In general, the value of every ASCAP writer and publisher performance is determined each quarter by looking at the total amount of money that is available for distribution in that quarter, the specific monies available from each licensed medium (radio, television, live performances, etc.), the total number of ASCAP performances during that 3-month period, the types of those performances (underscore, themes, visual vocals, jingles), and the areas where each type of performance occurred (pay cable, network or local television, radio, wired music, Web sites, airlines, etc.).

Each type of performance generates a certain number of performance credits, depending on the payment formula and the medium (i.e., radio) where the performance occurs. All performance credits for all writers and publishers are totaled each quarter and divided by the total amount of income available for distribution that quarter. The resulting figure is the dollar value of 1 credit. Each writer's and publisher's performance credits are then multiplied by that value to arrive at a writer's or publisher's quarterly royalty check.

For example, if during the first performance quarter of 2004 (January through March) a writer received a performance statement showing a total of 10,000 radio credits, 4,000 network television credits, 1,500 local television credits, and 500 cable credits for 7 songs, the total of this writer's quarterly credits would be 16,000. In the same 3-month period, all other ASCAP writers generated a total of 6,984,000 performance credits for their works. The total number of writer credits to be paid on in that quarter would therefore be 7 million. If $35 million was available for distribution to writers in that quarter, the value of each credit would be $5.00. The writer with 16,000 credits would receive a check for $80,000.

### Types of Performances and Their Values

The 7 basic types of performance that ASCAP pays on are feature performances, theme songs, underscore, jingles, promos, logos, and copyrighted arrangements of public domain works. Each of these types is given a specific weight, which in turn determines its value. The weights are set forth in percentage terms and are contained in the ASCAP Weighting Formula. The highest-weighted performance is a feature performance (100%); all other types of performances receive different weights relative to this 100% weight. Since how a performance is weighted is 1 of the primary factors determining its value, every writer and publisher should be familiar with all of the ASCAP performance weights. Any composition can receive any of the various percentage weights depending on how it is used. Weights can change so always be aware of what the current ASCAP percentages are. The following should be used as a reference guide to the crediting weights in effect in the year 2003.

*E x a m p l e 1.*  A writer writes a song that is recorded and performed on radio or sung on camera by an artist on a television show. This is a feature performance and receives 100% crediting. The same song is used in a product commercial and receives 5% crediting. The song is next used as background music for a made-for-TV movie and receives 16% crediting per minute of duration. Finally, the song is used as a theme song for a network primetime television series and receives 50% crediting for all airings on network as well as subsequent airings on local and cable TV. Despite the fact that the same song is being used throughout this example, the payment for that song would be different in each situation discussed as the type of use determines payment.

*E x a m p l e 2.*  An instrumental composition by a composer is used as the theme for a feature film. Because of the film's success, the composition is released as a single and becomes a #1 chart record. Years later, the composition is used in a car commercial and is also chosen as the theme for a syndicated television series. The crediting weights for this composition would be 16% per minute of duration when the movie is shown on television, 100% when the composition is performed on radio or as a visual instrumental on television, 12% when it is used in a commercial, and 50% when it is used as the theme for a television series.

## Weights

The following list of definitions and ASCAP crediting weights (in effect in 2003) covers most of the types of performance that occur on radio and television. The list is not all-inclusive or definitive, since there are crediting variations on many of the weights specified; still, the list should cover the performances of most writers and publishers.

*Feature Performance.*  "Any performance which is a principal focus of audience attention and which constitutes a musical subject matter on a radio or television program and is not a performance as a theme, jingle, background cue or bridge music."

100% crediting for a song on the radio of any duration
100% crediting for a song on television of 45 seconds or more in duration.
100% crediting for a song on television that is under 45 seconds in duration and is a "qualifying work" (20,000 past radio and TV feature performances, among other factors).

50% crediting for a song on television that has a duration of between 15 and 44 seconds and does not meet the requirements of a "qualifying work."
25% crediting for a song on television that has a duration of 14 seconds or less and does not meet the requirements of a "qualifying work."

*Themes.* "A musical work used as the identifying signature of a radio or television personality or of all or part of a radio or television program or series of programs."

35% crediting for a theme song for a radio show.
35% crediting for a theme song for a local television series.
50% crediting for a theme song for a network primetime television series.
50% crediting for the theme for a network primetime television series that aired on the network and that is subsequently syndicated to local television or pay cable stations.
50% crediting for a previously released hit song used as a theme for a television series. The percentage crediting is based on a song's past history of performances (whether it is a qualifying work).
35% crediting for a theme for a nonprimetime network series or a series originally made for local television syndication or cable
16% crediting for each minute of duration of a theme for a feature film, movie of the week, or miniseries or theme crediting if higher.

As you can see, not all themes are credited with the same percentage. Moreover, a composition used as the opening and closing theme for a series receives 1 full payment, while 2 separate compositions, 1 used as the opening theme and the other as the closing theme, each receive a full payment.

*Background Music/Underscore.* "Mood, atmosphere or thematic music performed as background to some non-musical subject matter being presented on a radio or television program."

16% crediting per minute of duration for background music to television series, specials, movies of the week, and feature films.
50% crediting for a hit song used as background music to a television program or film.
16% per minute crediting for a hit song (qualifying work) used as background music if the duration payment exceeds 50%.

(*Note:* The Court approved in 2000 authorization for ASCAP to increase underscore to 18% per minute should conditions warrant.)
Most underscore aired on television programs or films (whether the broadcast is network, local, or cable) is paid at 16% crediting per minute of duration.

For example, if the duration of the music totals 3 minutes, the percentage crediting will be 48%. Past hit songs receive the higher of 50% crediting or the duration payment of the background use.

*Advertising Music.* "Jingle shall mean an advertising, promotional or public service announcement containing musical material (with or without lyrics), where (a) the musical material was originally written for advertising, promotional or public service announcement purposes or (b) the performance is of a musical work, originally written for other purposes, with the lyrics changed for advertising, promotional or public service announcement purposes with the permission of the ASCAP member or members in interest or (c) the performance is of a musical work, originally written for other purposes, which does not have at least 150 feature performance credits recorded in the Society's survey during the five preceding fiscal survey years."

3% crediting for any work originally written for advertising purposes; for any work originally written for nonadvertising purposes that has less than 150 feature surveyed radio or TV performance credits over the previous 5 survey years; and for a hit song used in a commercial with the song's original lyrics changed.

5% crediting for a song written for nonadvertising purposes that has 150 feature surveyed radio and TV performances over the past 5 survey years.

12% crediting for a past hit song (qualifying work) used in a commercial with no change in the original lyrics. The percentage crediting is based on the song's past history of feature performances.

For any song written specifically for a commercial (a jingle), the crediting is 3%. For any song or instrumental composition not originally written for advertising purposes (an album cut, a song from a film, a series theme song, a hit song, etc.), the crediting can be 3%, 5%, or 12%, based solely on the song's history of performances. If the lyrics are changed for any nonadvertising song (e.g., a hit song with new advertising lyrics), the credit is 3%, regardless of the song's performance history.

*Copyrighted Arrangements.* "Works in the public domain for which an arrangement has been made and such arrangement has been copyrighted."

Many copyrighted arrangements receive either 2% or 10% crediting, but the credit can go as high as 35% if the song has new lyrics and up to 50% if it has both a new title and new lyrics. Certain instrumental compositions can receive 100% crediting depending on the extent of creative treatment and original musical characteristics as well as being identifiable as a set piece apart from the public domain source music. The performance royalties for these works will be paid to the new arranger and the arranger's publisher and not to the original writers or publisher of the public domain song. Increased copyrighted arrangement crediting up to 100% is made by ASCAP via submissions reciting the reasons requesting such increased crediting with a review, if requested by a member, by the ASCAP Special Classification Committee, which then makes a determination of whether increased crediting should be given to the work. Increased crediting for public domain works is also important because many record contracts pay mechanical royalties based on the crediting the work receives from ASCAP (50%, 100%, etc.).

*Qualifying Works.* A qualifying work is any composition that, because of its history of feature performances on radio and television, receives additional crediting when it is used as a theme, background, cue, or bridge music or in a commercial.

For a song to qualify for the highest qualifying work crediting status (i.e., 50%), the work must have a total of 20,000 radio and television feature performance credits since October 1, 1959, and 5,000 of those feature performance credits must have occurred within the 5 latest survey years, with no more than 1,500 credits from any 1 survey year counting toward that total, provided, however, that when a work accumulates 150,000 radio and television feature performance credits, it is a qualifying work without any other test.

50% crediting for a qualifying work used as a theme for a television series. The crediting is based on a song's past history of feature performances and applies to network, local and cable performances.

50% crediting for a qualifying work used as background music to a television series or feature film.

12% crediting for a qualifying work used in a commercial. The extent of the crediting is based on a song's history of feature performances.

3% crediting for a qualifying work used in a commercial with the original lyrics changed to fit the advertising message.

The entire concept of qualifying works is important for all songwriters and publishers, as it provides additional crediting (and money) to works with a good history of past performances when they are used as themes or background music or in commercials. Instead of receiving the regular television background crediting of 48% per 3 minutes or the regular theme crediting of 35%, these songs could receive a 50% crediting payment if they were used as a theme or as background music in a television show. Any program that uses a past hit song as its theme (e.g., *Married...With Children*) or uses past hit songs as background music (e.g., *Friends, The Simpsons, Ally McBeal*) is normally dealing with qualifying works.

## Payment Formulas/Weights into Dollars

The ASCAP percentage crediting weight for each different type of performance is one of 4 or 5 factors in the royalty formulas that ASCAP uses to arrive at the dollar value of a performance. Once the calculations for each of these formulas are completed, the resulting figure is the total number of credits for an individual performance. For example, a network television visual vocal may generate 300 credits, a theme 150 credits, a radio performance 40 credits, 20 minutes of local television background music 55 credits, and a network jingle 10 credits. The number of credits generated by a single performance depend on the medium, the type of use, the broadcasting stations' weight in terms of the size of their license fees to ASCAP, the frequency at which the station is surveyed by ASCAP, and whether the performance is a census pickup or a sample pickup. Once the credits for an individual performance are computed, those credits are then multiplied by a dollar number to arrive at the value of that performance. Credits are the figures that are reflected on all ASCAP writer and publisher statements.

For radio, local television, and cable performances, the payment formula takes into account the weight of the station airing the performance (the median station weight is 1), the use weight of the performance (e.g., theme, underscore, jingle), and the strata multiplier for the medium in which the performance occurs (i.e., the number given to each surveyed medium that relates the license fees and credits of that medium to the license fees and credits of all other surveyed media). In the case of network television performances, a hook-up weight (i.e., the number of stations carrying the broadcast) replaces the station weight number of the other formulas. Finally, a "feature multiplier" factor is added to the formulas for radio and T.V. uses. As for the concept of strata multipliers, the July through September 1999 performance period provides an example of the range of these numbers for each medium. During that quarter, the strata multipliers for network television, local television, radio, HBO, the Nashville Network, Muzak, and airlines were 240, 135, 35, 12, 27, 80, and 4, respectively.

The formula for 3 feature radio performances in 4th Q 2002 shows the different payments for various large and small stations taking into account license fees and performances processed:

| Station Weight | | Use Weight | | Strata Multiplier | | Feature Multiplier | | Total Credits |
|---|---|---|---|---|---|---|---|---|
| 1 | x | 100% | x | 31 | x | 1.088 | = | 33.73 |
| .28 | x | 100% | x | 31 | x | 1.088 | = | 9.44 |
| .06 | x | 100% | x | 31 | x | 1.088 | = | 2.02 |

During this performance quarter, the dollar value of a writer credit was $5.78 with payments being $194.96, $54.56 and $11.66, respectively.

## Radio

For many decades, the ASCAP payment system for radio performances was that all feature songs, regardless of their stature or history of performances, were paid the same if they were similarly situated. For example, if Irving Berlin's "White Christmas" or Stevie Wonder's "Superstition" and the newest ASCAP song by the newest ASCAP writer were all performed on the same radio station back to back, the crediting for each song would be the same.

*Radio Feature Premium.* Commencing with October 1, 1993 performances, ASCAP put in a change that substantially increased the radio payments for current hit songs and well as major catalogue songs (songs from the past that continue to generate good radio air play). Though the basic ASCAP philosophy remained the same, that of treating all similarly situated songs alike on radio (ASCAP's #1 song would generate the same number of performance credits as would a song by the newest ASCAP writer if both songs were performed back-to-back on the same radio station), a 3-tier extra payment radio system was put into effect whereby songs that generate over a certain number of feature radio credits in a three-month period receive additional performance credits, which translate into additional dollars. The three qualifying tiers are: 2,500–2,999 credits in a quarter; 3,000–3,999 credits in a quarter, and 4,000 or more credits in a quarter. As a song reaches each one of these tiers, additional performance credits are added to each song's total radio credits in that quarter. All of a song's credits in all medium (T.V., wired music, etc.) are then totaled and multiplied by a per credit dollar value (e.g. $5.78 per credit) to arrive at a writer or publisher royalty.

A good example of how this tier system works is by a 12-month (four quarters) writer or publisher earnings chart of a Top 5 pop hit:

| *Dollar Amount* | *Credits* | |
|---|---|---|
| $ 26,784.52 | 4,634 | (network, cable and local television) |
| $ 1,895.84 | 328 | (wired music) |
| $194,491.22 | 33,649 | (radio) |
| $ 14,698.54 | 2,543 | (general licensing) |
| $ 52.02 | 9 | (theme/background ads on radio) |
| $ 63,516.42 | 10,989 | Tier 1 |
| $ 70,065.16 | 12,122 | Tier 2 |
| $ 77,486.68 | 13,406 | Tier 3 |
| $453,990.40 | 77,680 | |

Of the total $453,990 writer share, the tier add on monies of $211,068. represented more than a 100% addition to the radio monies. ASCAP can change the tier level numbers (i.e., 2,000 instead of 2,500 credits) and they can be applied to different genres of music so always be aware of what the current tier numbers are.

*Radio Survey.* All writer and publisher payments from radio are made on the basis of a sample survey of performances of U.S. radio stations. Each time a broadcast performance is picked up in the radio survey, multipliers are included in the payment formula to blow up that performance to a figure that approximates a national census of that song's performances. All radio stations are categorized by geographic area, by type of community within that geographic area, and by the amount of revenue (license fees) that the particular station pays to ASCAP. The survey is a scientifically designed random (based on mathematical probability), stratified (licenses are classified into groups that have common characteristics), and disproportionate (depth of the sample varies with the amount of the fees paid by licensees) survey set up by independent survey experts and is constantly being reviewed as to its effectiveness. To make distributions even more precise, there are separate format surveys of Pop, Country, Urban Contemporary, Religious, Classical, Latin, Ethnic and Jazz.

## Network Television

Performances on the ABC, CBS, and NBC television networks are surveyed on a census basis (i.e., a 100% pickup). The main rules in effect at the start of 2003 that affect the value of network performances are the following:

*Time of Broadcast.* ASCAP has four time-of-day factors that affect the value of performances on television. For Monday through Sunday programs aired between 7:00 P.M. and 12:59 A.M., a 100% payment is made. For programs airing between 1:00 P.M. and 6:59 P.M., a 75% payment is made. For programs airing between 7:00 A.M. and 12:59 P.M., a 50% payment is made. For programs airing between 1:00 A.M. and 6:59 A.M., a 25% payment is made.

To figure out the value of any performance on network television, one needs to determine what the evening 100% rate is and then reduce it to a 75%, 50% or 25% payment depending on whether the composition was broadcast on an afternoon, morning or overnight show. For example, if the payment for evening background music was $170 per minute, the afternoon background rate would be $127.50 per minute (i.e., 75% of evening), with the morning payment at $85 per minute (i.e., 50% of the evening rate) and the overnight rate at $42.50— assuming, of course, that the same number of network stations were carrying each show. For PBS, 100% crediting applies to 7:00 A.M. to 1:00 A.M. and 25% crediting for 1:00 A.M. to 7:00 A.M.

*Multiple Programs.* These are programs broadcast on network television four or more times a week. Payments for certain types of performances on these shows at one time received reduced crediting. These reductions were eliminated in the year 2000 and these type of shows are treated the same as all other shows.

*Length of Performance.*   For feature performances of a song that is a qualifying work (20,000 feature performance credits, etc.), full credit is made regardless of the song's duration. A song can be 3 seconds long or 3 minutes long and still receive 100% crediting. For feature performances with a duration of from 15 to 44 seconds that are not "qualifying works," 50% of the full feature rate is paid. For features with a duration of less than 15 seconds and are not qualifying works, 25% of the full feature rate is paid. These feature performance durational cutbacks are applied after the time of day is taken into account.

There is no durational requirement for themes. A theme can be 5 seconds long or 2 minutes long, and full payment is made in either case. Background music is paid on the basis of its duration. For example, if a 1-hour program has 60 minutes of underscore, full payment will be made for all 60 minutes of music.

*Network Hook-up.*   The hook-up weight is the number of network stations carrying the broadcast. ASCAP hook-up values are in 10-station increments. A hook-up of 200 or more stations is given a weight of 1; a hook-up of 190–99 stations is given a weight of .949. If 180 to 189 stations are carrying a broadcast, the weight is .9, and so forth. The hook-up is one of the primary factors affecting the value of any network performance.

## Network Payment Formulas

As we have seen, the ASCAP formula for valuing any type of performance takes into account the weight of the broadcasting station, the use weight for the type of performance, the strata multiplier for the medium in which the performance takes place, the feature multiplier add on to all television performances, and the time of day (the when, where and how). The result of all of these factors is the total number of credits generated by a performance. Once all performance credits are determined for all performances, the total is then divided by the total amount of money available for that distribution to arrive at the value of 1 credit. All of a writer's or publisher's credits are then multiplied by that dollar credit value to arrive at a writer's or publisher's royalty check. The following are a number of examples setting forth the network payment formulas. The factors that can change are the strata multiplier, the dollar value of 1 credit, and any use weight changes. The example is a nighttime television program broadcast on 200 stations with 3 minutes of underscore, 1 theme, and 1 jingle, with a $5.30 value for 1 credit. If the network strata for a quarter was 200 or 350 (rather than the 250 in the chart), those numbers would be substituted in the following formula.

For all television uses (features, underscore, theme songs, etc.), the network

| Strata | | Use Weight | | Station Weight | | Credits | | Credit Value | | Dollar Value |
|---|---|---|---|---|---|---|---|---|---|---|
| 250 | x | .48 (underscore) | x | 1 | = | 120 | x | $5.30 | = | $636.00 |
| 250 | x | .50 (theme) | x | 1 | = | 125 | x | $5.30 | = | $662.50 |
| 250 | x | .03 (jingle) | x | 1 | = | 7.5 | x | $5.30 | = | $ 39.75 |

payment formula would also include a factor that represents that performance's pro rata share of all live performance money (the general licensing allocation). The formula for a theme in this case would be as follows:

$$250 \ \times \ 1 \ \times \ .5 \ \times \ 1.026 \ (\text{GLA}) \ = \ 128.25 \ \text{credits} \ \times \ \$5.30 \ = \ \$679.73$$

## Local Television

ASCAP conducts a census survey of performances on local television stations (a 100% pickup) of all network series (i.e., series originally on network television and now being aired on local television stations), all first-run syndicated series (e.g., *Star Trek: The Next Generation* and *The Simpsons*), and all theatrical films and made-for-TV movies. Locally originating programs (news, sports, public affairs, etc.) are surveyed on a sample basis. The value of performances on each of the census stations reflect the license fee income from that station. For example, a theme or background performance on the #1 fee-paying station would be worth more than the same performance on the #2 station.

As for the local television stations being surveyed on a sample basis, performances picked up there are worth substantially more than the census station performances, because 1 "sampled pickup" represents many other performances of the same work on other stations. One element of the payment formula for local television performances, the station weight, takes into account the license fees of a particular station as well as the frequency of the survey sampling on that station.

To illustrate how the dual census works, take an example of a former network television series being performed on 3 census stations. The series has 9 minutes of background music and separate opening and closing theme songs. The series airs once a week primetime during a 12-week quarter; all 36 performances would be logged on the 3 census (100% pickup) stations. The writer computations and royalties might look like the figures in Tables 7.3 and 7.4. In the local area, the 4-time-of-day factors applicable to network television (100%, 75%, 50%, 25%) apply to the computation of all royalties.

The composer in this case would make a total of $3,140.53 in background

Table **7.3**   Background Music Royalty on 3 Representative Television Stations

| | Census Station 1 | | Census Station 2 | | Census Station 3 | |
|---|---|---|---|---|---|---|
| Strata multiplier | | 135 | | 135 | | 135 |
| Background weight | x | .16 | x | .16 | x | .16 |
| Minutes | x | 9 | x | 9 | x | 9 |
| Census strata/station weight | x | .15 | x | .1 | x | .004 |
| Airings/pickups | x | 12 | x | 12 | x | 12 |
| Credits | | 349.9 | | 233.3 | | 9.33 |
| Value of 1 credit | x | $5.30 | x | $5.30 | x | $5.30 |
| Total | | $1,854.58 | | $1,236.49 | | $49.46 |

music payments and $2,180.84 in theme payments for the 12-week broadcast run of the program. Assuming the show aired for a full year on the same number of local television stations with the same number of pickups, the total writer payment at the end of each year would be in the area of $23,000. If the show was then widely syndicated or "stripped" (5 days a week on many stations), the writer payments could easily exceed $100,000 per year.

## Cable

ASCAP conducts a census (a 100% pickup) of performances on all general entertainment services (HBO, Showtime, the Movie Channel, Cinemax, USA Network, Lifetime, Arts & Entertainment, the Family Channel, the Nashville Network, Nickelodeon, TNT, etc.). The use weights as well as the time of day factors are the same as for all other areas of television.

Table **7.4**   Theme Music Royalty on 3 Representative Television Stations

| | Census Station 1 | | Census Station 2 | | Census Station 3 | |
|---|---|---|---|---|---|---|
| Strata multiplier | | 135 | | 135 | | 135 |
| Theme weight | x | .5 | x | .5 | x | .5 |
| Census strata/station weight | x | .15 | x | .1 | x | .004 |
| Airings/pickups | x | 12 | x | 12 | x | 12 |
| Number of themes | x | 2 | x | 2 | x | 2 |
| Credits | | 243 | | 162 | | 6.48 |
| Value of 1 credit | x | $5.30 | x | $5.30 | x | $5.30 |
| Total | | $1,287.90 | | $858.60 | | $34.34 |

The strata multipliers in the cable field were, for many years, significantly lower than those for network or local television primarily because cable license fees to ASCAP were significantly lower than those paid by the networks or by the local television industry. Consequently, the payments for most uses were lower. Due to settlements between ASCAP and the primary elements of the cable industry in 2000, 2001, and 2002 (Viacom, HBO, Turner, local originations, etc.), cable fees and distributions have significantly increased.

## Music and Lyrics in Commercials

ASCAP has been paying on commercial music since 1960. Different registration and information requirements apply for works written specifically for commercials versus hit songs used in commercials. Also, there are 3 separate payment categories for songs or music used in commercials in effect in 2002, and all payments are made quarterly as part of the regular performance statement. Finally, there is no durational requirement in order to receive payment, nor are there any payment distinctions between background uses or "sole focus of audience attention" uses in the commercial.

### *Registration and Information Requirements*

WORKS WRITTEN FOR COMMERCIALS. For works of this type, ASCAP provides a checklist that requires the names of the composer, lyricist, and music publisher, the name of the sponsor and the product being advertised, the title of the commercial, the advertising Industry Standard Coding Identification (ISCI) number of the commercial, the song title, the first air date of the commercial, the term of the agreement between the writer and publisher and the agency, and the medium in which the commercial is airing. In addition, ASCAP requires a lead sheet and lyrics of the commercial (or a cassette or CD), advertising copy if available, a copy of the contractual agreement between the writer and publisher and the sponsor or advertising agency, and an ASCAP registration card for the work. Finally, for commercials aired on the ABC, CBS, and NBC television networks, ASCAP requires the advertising agency's commercial broadcast schedule or the talent and residual report. Both of these latter items contain information regarding the specific network and program airing the commercial as well as the date of the airing. These reports are usually submitted to ASCAP by the agency, the writer, or the publisher. The payment rate for all commercial music in this category is 3%.

WORKS CREATED FOR ANOTHER PURPOSE BUT SUBSEQUENTLY LICENSED AS COMMERCIALS. For songs and instrumental compositions originally written for nonadvertising purposes, ASCAP requires the names of the writers and publishers, the name of the product and sponsor, the song title, the ISCI number, the title of the commercial, the first air date of the commercial, the term of the license agreement, the medium in which the commercial is aired, and whether the work is an instrumental, a vocal with original lyrics, or a vocal with a parody lyric (a change of the original song's lyric to fit the advertising message). For network television commercial performances, ASCAP also requires the advertising agency's report of broadcast performances or the talent and residual report.

## Payments

Effective wtih October 1, 1993, performances, ASCAP put into effect three separate payment categories for music and songs in commercials. Prior to this date, five separate categories were in effect. The crediting percentages are 3% for works written specifically for commercials or for other works (album cuts, etc.) that were not written specifically for commercials and that do not have at least 150 feature performance credits recorded in ASCAP's radio and television surveys during the five preceeding survey years. For works that were not originally written for commercials and that have at least 150 feature performance credits in radio and television over the most recent five years but that do not meet the credit test of a "qualifying work," the percentage payment is 5%. Finally, for works that are qualifying works, the percentage payment is 12%. The 12% payment applies to most hit songs as well as standards being used by advertisers in their campagins. Songs qualify under this category if they have at least 20,000 past radio and television feature credits since October 1, 1959, and have 5,000 radio television feature credits during the most recent five years toward which total not more than 1,500 credits shall be counted for any such year. Any work that has 150,000 or more radio television feature performance credits automatically qualifies for the 12% crediting and the work does not need to meet the 5,000 credit/5-year criterion applicable to most qualifying works.

In determining the actual payments for songs or music in commercials, one needs to remember that all of the rules affecting other types of performances (network time-of-day factors, etc.) also apply to commercial music. Additional provisions limit the number of royalty payments for a jingle that is performed more than once on the same station during a 2-hour period. ASCAP also employs jingle subsamples in the local television, radio, and cable area. These subsamples of performances (a percentage of the regular surveys in these areas) result in all surveyed jingle performances being given multiples in the radio area and in the local television area to arrive at the final value of a performance. The multiple in the local television area is higher than radio because local television is handled on a combination of census and sample surveys whereas the radio survey is entirely sample. The payment formulas are the same as those used for all other network, local television, and radio performances.

For major product campaigns being broadcast primarily on network and local television, commercials using a hit song with no change in the lyrics can earn in excess of $100,000 in writer and publisher earnings over the space of 1 year. For campaigns lasting many years, the amounts can be substantial.

## Live Performances

ASCAP conducts a census survey (100% pickup) of all songs performed in the top 200 grossing U.S. concert tours as well as all songs at ten major venues (Madison Square Garden, Radio City Music Hall, Hollywood Bowl, etc.). Song use information is gathered from set lists and generally is split 95% to the headliners and 5% to the opening act. The split between one headliner and two opening acts would be 90/10 and a co-headliner split would be 50/50. Tours are ranked according to revenue (the #1 tour, the 18th tour, etc.) and payments reflect the economic value of each tour. The Symphony Concert, Recital and Educational Survey covers licensed symphony orchestras and serious concert artists on a census basis as well as all works performed in licensed edcuational institutions that pay the guest artist or ensemble $1,500 or more. Other educational institution's concerts are surveyed on a sample basis. The fees from other live performances not covered by these surveys are distributed as a surrogate on the basis of all performances on television and all feature performances on radio. Writers who have performances in areas that are not surveyed can apply for financial awards under the ASCAPLu$ Awards system. Live tour payments commenced in 1993.

## Per Program Distributions

In the local television area, stations either have blanket or per program licenses with ASCAP. A station with a per-program license pays a license fee only for each program using ASCAP music in an amount dependent on that program's revenues.

Under the blanket license, local stations pay license fees without regard to the specific musical content or revenues of any particular program. Since specific license fees can be allocated to specific television programs under the per program license, ASCAP distributes the fees from each specific program to the writers and publishers with music contained in that program.

## The Internet

ASCAP Internet licenses are based upon, among other things, revenue and traffic, and they cover both individual sites, aggregators as well as other new business models. Internet distributions commenced in 1997.

---

## *THE BMI PAYMENT SCHEDULE*

BMI pays its writers and publishers according to minimum rates set forth in the BMI Payment Schedule. Between 1972 and 2003 BMI issued 9 separate payment schedules (1972, 1975, 1977, 1980, 1984, 1987, 1987 revised, 1998, and 2002), with each new schedule replacing the schedule preceding it.

Since each new schedule normally makes changes in the basic rates of the prior schedule as well as the categories for payment, every BMI writer and publisher should become familiar with these documents, as any changes made can seriously affect one's short-term and long-term earnings. BMI also makes periodic changes in a schedule while that schedule is still in effect. For instance, BMI made a major change in 1973 with respect to the eligibility for song bonus payments under the 1972 schedule, with all of the rest of the 1972 schedule staying in effect.

Using the 1998 schedule as a guide to understanding BMI payments, we see that it sets forth a number of base penny or dollar rates that BMI is obligated to pay for certain types of performances in specific media. The primary media covered by these rates are radio, network television, and local television, with the main type of performances being feature performances, theme songs, and background music. Some of the minimum writer and publisher combined performance rates set forth in the 1998 schedule include a 12¢ and 6¢ payment for radio performances, an $11.50, $9.00 and $6.00 rate per station for network television songs, a $5.00 per station payment for a network television primetime theme, and a 42¢ and 76¢ per minute payment for background music on a show broadcast on local television. BMI may from time to time voluntarily increase these payments in any given performance quarter.

## Radio

For many decades, BMI has treated certain types of radio works differently from others. The 1968 schedule paid million-performance works, movie works, and Broadway and off-Broadway works at a much higher rate than regular "popular" songs performed on radio. For example, a Broadway work earned a writer 12¢ on radio, whereas a pop song earned 2½¢. The 1972 schedule continued this philosophy, but now the higher-earning radio works of the 1968 schedule were referred to as "multiple credit works." Publishers were treated differently from writers in that a special bonus payment of 25% was made to publishers whose catalog had between 300,000 and 500,000 feature performances over the past year, and an additional 40% payment was made to those whose catalog had between 500,000 and 750,000 performances during the same time period. The writer bonus was an additional 25% or 50% payment of earnings if the writer's feature performance earnings were between $1,500 and $3,000 or above $3,000, respectively, per year for any 3 of the last 5 years. If a writer earned more than $9,000 in the last 4 quarters, an additional 50% would be added. All of these bonuses required the signing of a new 3-year writer contract.

The 1975 schedule increased the publisher special payment to an additional 50% payment for any publisher catalog receiving in excess of 500,000 feature performances over the past year. In 1977 a major change occurred in BMI's treatment of radio works. . . .a change that would affect writer and publisher payments for the next 10 years. This change was the BMI song bonus.

## The 1977 Song Bonus

The creation of the song bonus made it possible to pay songs at 1 of 5 different rates depending on each song's performance history. The categories of payment, or "plateaus," were as follows:

*No Plateau.* Any song with fewer than 25,000 feature broadcast performances (radio and local television performances) would be paid at the lowest writer or publisher rate of 6¢ on a Radio 1 station and 2½ cents on a Radio 2 station. (Radio 1 stations are in the top 25% of all radio stations, based on the size of the license fees they pay to BMI. Radio 2 stations are all those in the bottom 75%.) Most performed songs in the BMI repertory were in this class of payment.

*Plateau A.* Any song that had between 25,000 and 99,999 performances would be paid at 1½ times the base payment schedule rate. As the 1977 schedule rates were 6¢ and 2½¢, the Plateau A song payment rates were 9¢ and 3.75¢. Any song that had at least 25,000 performances would earn 9¢ and 3.75¢ for all radio performances until it reached 100,000 performances.

*Plateau B.* Any song that had between 100,000 and 499,999 performances would be paid at 2 times the base rate. Radio performances for these songs would be paid at 12¢ on a Radio 1 station and 5¢ on a Radio 2 station. As soon as a song reached 100,000 performances, each radio performance after that would be paid at double the rates for a nonplateau song.

*Plateau C.* Any song that had between 500,000 and 999,000 performances would be paid 2½ times the base radio rate: 15¢ and 6.25¢ for Radio 1 and Radio 2, respectively.

*Plateau D.* This was the "million-performance song" plateau, where any song that had accumulated 1 million prior performances would be paid at rates 3.8 times the regular radio rate: 22.8¢ and 9.5¢.

In order to maintain a high payment for the "multiple credit" works of the prior payment schedules, BMI added a provision continuing some extra crediting for show music and movie songs and termed them "special credit works." Songs in this category would be paid at Plateau B rates from their first performance and paid at Plateau C and D rates when they reached the 500,000 and 1 million performance marks.

In addition to these song plateau and multiple credit work payments, BMI also added a voluntary payment on top of these bonuses for each quarter. These voluntary payments varied by quarter and ranged between 0% and 117%.

Between 1977 and 1987 new schedules made changes in the plateau numbers (a million-performance song was increased to 4 times the rate; Plateau B levels were decreased from 100,000 to 50,000 performances; Plateau C levels were reduced from 500,000 to 300,000 performances; changes were made for movie and show music) as well as changes in the minimum radio rates (the 6¢ and 2½¢ of the 1977 schedule became 6¢ cents and 3¢ under the 1980 schedule), but the basic theory of higher rates for high-performance songs stayed in effect.

## The 1987 Payment Schedule/The 1998 Payment Schedule

Effective as of January 1, 1987, BMI issued a new payment schedule that substantially changed the philosophy and payment practices of the prior decades. Whereas writers and publishers under the pre-1987 schedules were guaranteed specific earnings once their song reached the Plateau A, B, C, or D performance level, the 1987 and 1998 schedules created a "floating" system where songs moved up or down in payment each quarter depending on a song's own performance history, the performance history of all BMI songs performed in a quarter, and the total BMI feature performances of all songs in a specific calendar quarter. Under the old system, a writer would know what plateau (and payment) his or her song would receive based solely on the song's performance history. If a song was a Plateau C song and had a total of 320,000 past performances, the writer knew that the song would be paid at Plateau C rates until the song reached performance number 1 million, at which point it would be paid at the Plateau D rate. Under the 1987 and 1998 schedules, however, a song could go up or down in the plateaus every quarter, even if its activity stayed the same. The 5 separate payment rates of the old system remained the same (base rate, 1½ times, 2 times, 2½ times, and 4 times the base rate) but the definitions of the former plateau categories changed.

As opposed to only 3 factors affecting the radio payments of pre-1987 schedules (the size of the license fees of the radio station, the song's past history of performances, and the size of the voluntary quarterly payment), the 1987 and 1998 schedules have 7 factors. They are:

1. Whether the performance was on a Radio 1 or Radio 2 station. The payment to a writer or publisher for a Radio 1 performance is 6¢, and for a Radio 2 performance, 3¢.
2. The song's total feature performance history since 1960.
3. The cumulative performance history since 1960 of each BMI song that is performed in a given quarter.
4. How a song's cumulative performance history compares to every other BMI song's history.
5. The total of all feature performances of BMI songs in a quarter.
6. The size of the BMI voluntary radio payment for that quarter.
7. The effect of a change in surveying stations and an increased multiple increased the number of performances within the BMI system at the time of

the issuance of the 1987 schedule. Basically, an approximate .6 multiple was put into the system whereby 10,000 radio performances under the old system would now be reflected as 16,000 performances under the new system. This increase for radio performances occurring after January 1, 1987, had a profound effect on all pre-1987 songs, since new songs could now in a short period of time generate an amount of performances that songs under the old schedules took years to accumulate.

Once BMI knows all of the figures in each of the above factors, the song payments are then made according to 8 separate radio bonus categories.

*Super Bonus.* "Those songs with the highest cumulative history whose current quarter's performances constitute 10% of the current quarter's radio and local television performances of all songs" are paid at 4 times the base payment schedule rate.

To determine if a song qualifies for this highest rate, you first need to know how many BMI performances occurred in a particular quarter and figure 10% of that number. For example, if there were 15 million performances, then 10% of that total would be 1.5 million performances. You then look at the BMI song with the highest performance history since 1960 and determine how many performances that song had in the quarter. If the #1 song had 6 million prior performances and had 50,000 of those performances in that quarter, then those 50,000 performances will be paid at 4 times the base rate (super bonus), and the 1.5 million 10% performance total will be reduced to 1,450,000 performances. BMI then goes to the song with the second-highest number of past performances and pays that song's current quarter performances at 4 times the base rate. If that song had 30,000 performances in the quarter, then the 1,450,000 remaining performance number would be reduced to 1,420,000. This process is continued until the 1.5 million performance pool number is depleted.

*Upper-Level Bonus.* "Those songs with the next higher cumulative history whose current quarter's performances constitute 15% of the current quarter's radio and local television performances of all songs" are paid at 2½ times the base rate.

To find out if your song qualifies for the upper-level bonus payment, you look at the 15 million total of all performances in the quarter and determine that 15% of that total would be 2,250,000 performances. At this point BMI looks at the song with the largest performance history that was just below the last song in the super bonus category, and pays all of that song's current quarter performances at 2½ times the base rate. If that song had 25,000 performances, the 2,250,000 total figure would be reduced by 25,000 and the next song with the highest cumulative history would then be paid. When the 2.25 million number is depleted, the mid-level bonus category commences.

*Midlevel Bonus.* "Those songs with the next higher cumulative history whose current quarter's performances constitute 25% of the current quarter's radio and local television performances of all songs" are paid at 2 times the base rate.

As the performance figure for the midlevel bonus is 25%, the number of performances that will be paid at 2 times the base rate in this category is 3,750,000 out of the 15 million total. Just as in the other categories, the first song to be paid is the one with the largest performance history that was just below the last song that was paid in the upper-level bonus category. For example, if the last song in the upper category had a cumulative performance history of 1,061,402 and the next song in line had 1,061,401 performances, then the first song's performances in that quarter will be paid at 2½ times the rate and the second song's quarterly performances will be paid at 2 times the base rate. Once the current quarter's 3,750,000 number is depleted, the entry level bonus commences.

*Entry Level Bonus.* "All other songs with a cumulative history of 25,000 or more performances" are paid at 1½ times the base rate.

Any song that does not qualify for the super, upper-level, or midlevel bonus but that has at least 25,000 past performances gets paid at 1½ times the base rate for all feature performances in a quarter. Writer or publisher radio payments in this category are 9¢ (Radio 1) and 4.5¢ (Radio 2). The majority of all BMI songs are in this category and the following no-bonus category.

*No Bonus.* Any song that does not have a past cumulative performance history of at least 25,000 performances and is not in any other special bonus category is paid for all performances in that quarter at the base payment rate of 6¢ for a Radio 1 performance and 3¢ for a Radio 2 performance.

*100,000-Performance Bonus.* "Any song, regardless of its prior cumulative history, which has 100,000 or more U.S. radio and local television performances in one quarter will be awarded, for all such performances in that quarter, the next higher level bonus payment than it would ordinarily be entitled to receive." (This figure was 150,000 from 1987–1998.)

This bonus provision is important for new chart songs, as all of the previously discussed bonus payment categories take into account a song's performance history, and new songs do not yet have a performance history. This "special" bonus applies to all performances in a quarter as long as the number 100,000 is reached. As most new upper-level chart songs generate 100,000 or more performances, all of these performances would most likely be paid at the midlevel bonus payment of 2 times the base rate rather than the 1½ times the rate of the entry level bonus (25,000 or more performances). As soon as the song drops below 100,000 performances (normally, once it leaves the charts), the song is paid according to the previous bonus provisions. Successful post-

1987 BMI chart songs usually receive 2 or 3 consecutive quarters of the 100,000-performance bonus and then drop to the entry level bonus payment.

### Special Credit Works

SHOW MUSIC. For decades, BMI has given extra credit to original theater works. To qualify for super bonus payment, the composition must be from an original score written for a musical comedy, revue, or operetta in a U.S. production using Equity performers. In addition, a cast album must be released, unless the song is from a production that is presented in a first-class legitimate Broadway theater.

MOVIE WORKS. A complete musical work originally written for and performed in a full-length motion picture or made-for-TV movie and released in the U.S. after October 1, 1966, is paid at no less than 2 times the base rate (1987 Schedule) as long as it has been used as a feature work or a theme and performed for at least 40 consecutive seconds. This bonus does not apply to many songs as most songs used in films are not originally written for the film. The 2003 schedule is 2.5 times the base rate if it is a 45-second featured work, a main title theme, or closing credit work.

## BMI Radio Payments

The easiest way to understand BMI's payment of radio performances is to look at 4 different types of songs and their payments under the 1998 Payment Schedule. The songs we will look at are 2 new chart songs (one that reaches 100,000 performances in a quarter and one that does not), a no-bonus song (an album cut), and a well-known 1970s pop song being paid at the midlevel bonus (2 times the base rate) because of its performance history. The minimum writer or publisher payment schedule rate is 6¢ for a Radio 1 performance and 3¢ for a Radio 2 performance, and the BMI voluntary quarterly payment in effect for this quarter is 40% on top of radio earnings.

*E X A M P L E 1.*   New chart song with 90,000 performances in a quarter, with 80,000 of those performances being Radio 2 and 10,000 being Radio 1.

The payments for this song would be 6¢ and 3¢ for the first 24,999 performances (no-bonus category), with 65,001 performances being paid at 9¢ cents and 4.5¢ (1½ times the base rate; the entry level bonus). Once those figures are arrived at, the 40% voluntary payment is added. Most of this song's performances were paid at the entry level bonus with future quarters performances most likely paid at the same rate.

*E X A M P L E 2.*   New chart song with 425,000 total performances in a quarter, with 80,000 Radio 1 performances and 345,000 Radio 2 performances.

In this example, the song exceeded 100,000 performances in a quarter and therefore qualifies for the 100,000-performance bonus, which pays at the next higher level than the song would ordinarily receive. As the song qualifies for the entry level bonus (25,000 or more performances) all performances of this song in that quarter would be paid at the midlevel rates of 12¢ (Radio 1) and 6¢ (Radio 2), plus a 40% voluntary payment. As soon as the song drops below 100,000 performances in a quarter, the song will be paid at the entry level bonus rates of 9¢ and 4.5¢.

*E X A M P L E 3.* An album cut with a history of less than 25,000 performances.

All of this song's radio performances would be paid at the minimum payment schedule rates of 6¢ and 3¢. At one time, these songs received voluntary additional payments but recent years have shown a 0% add on.

*E X A M P L E 4.* A major chart song of the early 1970s with good quarterly catalog earnings for the past 20 years.

In this example, the song's chart activity was initially paid at the 1972 schedule rates (no song or plateau bonuses). Most of its catalog years were paid at the Plateau B (2 times the base rate) and Plateau C (2½ times the base rate) bonus levels of the 1977 through 1986 BMI schedules, where the cumulative history of a song was the sole criterion for payment. Commencing with January 1, 1987, performances, the song has been paid at the 1987 and 1998 schedule provisions, where cumulative history is only one factor determining payment. Here, the song generated 30,000 radio performances in a 3-month catalog period in 1991 and earned $3,900 for the writer. The song's cumulative history (when compared to the histories of all other BMI songs) qualified it for a midlevel bonus (2 times the base rate) for that quarter, and it was paid at 12¢ and 6¢, plus the 40% voluntary payment. In the future, this song could move up to the upper-level bonus rate or drop down to the entry-level bonus rate based on its cumulative history each quarter and on the other 1987 and 1998 bonus factors previously discussed.

## Voluntary Quarterly Payments

At least since the 1960s, BMI has maintained a practice of voluntarily increasing the values of certain types of performances in certain media during each quarter. These voluntary payments are over and above the payment schedule rates, and the practice is best summarized in a 1987 schedule statement: "Because BMI operates on a non-profit basis, we distribute all available income and may from time to time, voluntarily increase royalties." These voluntary payments each quarter represent 1 of the most important aspects of the BMI payment system; in many cases, these payments can represent more than 50% of the actual payment that is received each quarter by a BMI writer or publisher. Some examples are necessary to explain this concept.

During the years 1980 through 1990, the voluntary quarterly payment for radio performances ranged from 0% over the payment schedule rate in the second quarter of 1983 to 117% over the payment schedule rate in the third quarter of 1986. The average quarterly increase over this time period was in the area of 50% for radio earnings. If a song earned $30,000 in radio payments in a quarter according to the payment schedule rates and the voluntary payment for that quarter was 60% for radio, then the actual writer or publisher payment would be $48,000 ($30,000 + 60% = $48,000). If the same song were performed in a quarter where the voluntary payment was 10%, the actual writer and publisher payment would be $33,000 ($30,000 + 10% = $33,000).

Prior to July 1, 1982, performances, the size of these voluntary payments were set forth at the end of every BMI writer and publisher quarterly statement. The following legends are 2 such examples:

> For this quarter only, TV Network A [primetime] feature rates are increased by 110%, TV Network B [afternoon and morning] by 160% and other Network TV rates by 100%. All TV local rates are increased by 200%. All Plateau earnings are increased by 20% and radio earnings by 20%. (April–June 1982 statement)
>
> For this quarter only, themes for shows broadcast on U.S. Network prime time for more than 13 weeks will be paid at $1.00 per network station. All U.S. TV theme and background performance monies have been increased by 56%. (October–December 1979 statement)

Commencing with the July through September 1982 performance statement, BMI removed the specific description of voluntary payments and replaced it with the statement that "for this quarter only, all U.S. earnings have been voluntarily increased over payment schedule rates." The system of voluntarily increasing rates each quarter has continued at BMI to the present date, but it is now more difficult for a writer or publisher to figure out what the voluntary payments are for a particular type of performance in a particular medium. For example, in the first quarter of 1984 the statement contained a legend that rates were voluntarily being increased for that quarter. The actual voluntary increases were 97% for 14-week network themes, 97% for background music, and 59% for radio performances. In the first quarter of 1986, radio performances received a 112% voluntary increase, and local and network television themes and background music received 139%. In the first quarter of 1987, the voluntary payment for radio was 63%, for local television themes and local and network background music was 153%, and for network television 14-week themes was 281%. Finally, voluntary payments can be given to some songs and not to others. In 2002, BMI began to vary the amount of these increases between songs reaching fewer than 100,000 performances, 100,00 to 149,00 performances, and 150,000 or more performances.

## Survey of Performances

BMI employs a sample survey of performances on radio stations and bases its writer and publisher distributions for radio on the results of those surveys. BMI requests from each radio station, among other things, written logs (i.e., summaries of which compositions are being broadcast) for a period and then "blows up" those logged performances by the use of a statistical multiplier to arrive at the total radio performances of a song during a 3-month period. The figure that is shown on a BMI statement in the "Total Performances" column next to a song is the figure after the multiplier has been added.

## Television

As with radio, BMI has specific payment schedule rates for certain types of performance broadcast on network or local television stations. These rates are then multiplied. . .in the case of a network performance, by the number of stations carrying the broadcast, and in the case of certain local television performances, by a statistical multiplier. Some or all of these rates, again as with radio, are then given additional voluntary payments each quarter to arrive at the final value of a performance. The voluntary payments in television are significantly greater, proportionally, than those in radio and many times represent more than 50% of the final value of many television performances. An example should help to explain this method of payment.

*E X A M P L E.* A writer has 10 minutes of background music on a primetime network show (8 p.m.) that is broadcast on 200 network-affiliated stations. The BMI rate for background music is 55¢ a minute multiplied by the number of television stations carrying the broadcast. The voluntary payment for that quarter is 50%. The writer or publisher payment would be computed as follows: 55¢ x 10 x 200 = $1100 + 50% = $1,650.

## Types of Performance

Three types of performance on network television and local television have specific payments set forth in the BMI payment schedule.

*Feature performance.* "A performance which is the focus of audience attention at the time of the broadcast."

*Theme.* "A performance of a work which is regularly associated with a television program and identifies that program to the viewer when used as the opening and/or closing theme."

*Background music.* "A performance of a work used as a dramatic underscore to a scene where the music is not the focus of audience attention yet nonetheless is used to set the mood of the scene."

## Network Television

BMI conducts a census of performances on the ABC, CBS, and NBC television networks. This complete count of all musical performances applies only to those programs and those stations on the network feed: the network's primetime schedule, afternoon "soaps," morning shows, and a good deal of the weekend programming broadcast on network affiliated stations.

The 1998 and 2003 rules that affect the value of network performances are the following:

*Time of Day rates.* Primetime (6 P.M.–10:59 P.M.); late night (11 P.M.–1:59 A.M.); overnight (2 A.M.–5:59 A.M.); morning/daytime (6 A.M.–5:59 P.M.). The 1987 schedule had only two time-of-day payment factors (7 P.M.–2 A.M. for Group A and all other times as Group B).

*Multiple programs.* These are shows broadcast more than 3 times weekly (afternoon soap operas, 5-day-a-week morning shows, etc.). Reduced rates on these shows were eliminated in 1998.

*Type of show.* Background music performed on game shows and news and public affairs programs normally receive a lesser rate than background music used on other types of show. The 1998 Schedule eliminated these.

*Duration of background music.* "Payment for background music is based on the use of music up to one-half of the length of the program. For uses in excess of one-half of the length of the program, a proportional reduction will be made for all writers and publishers." This durational limit does not apply to background music in feature films, made-for-TV movies, game shows, or news and public affairs shows. The 1998 Schedule eliminated this provision.

*Length of performance.* If a feature performance is less than 45 seconds, the payment will be made on a prorated basis to the payment for 45-second or over feature performances.

*Network hook-up.* The number of network stations carrying a program affects the value of every performance on that program. The precise number of stations carrying a program is multiplied by the payment schedule rate for a particular type of performance to arrive at the value of a performance.

## Payment Schedule Rates

Under the 1998 Schedule revised for 2003, the following primary network television (ABC, CBS, NBC) rates were in effect:

| *Types of Performances* | *Writer or Publisher Payment* |
| --- | --- |
| Feature performance (45 seconds) | $5.75 per station (primetime) |
| | $4.50 per station (late night) |
| | $2.50 per station (overnight) |
| | $3.00 per station (morning/daytime) |

The writer payment for a full feature on primetime broadcast on 200 stations would be $5.75 x 200 = $1,150, plus any voluntary payment.

| | |
| --- | --- |
| Background music | .55 per minute per station (primetime) |
| | .36 per minute per station (late night) |
| | .26 per minute per station (overnight) |
| | .30 per minute per station (morning/daytime) |

The writer payment for 10 minutes of music on a morning show on 150 stations would be .30 x 10 x 150 stations = $450, plus any voluntary payment for that quarter. The special payment of primetime background rates for all feature films and made-for-TV movies regardless of the time of day of the broadcast under the 1987 Schedule was eliminated by the 1998 Schedule.

| | |
| --- | --- |
| Television theme song | $2.50 per station (primetime) |
| | $1.66 per station (late night) |
| | $ .29 per station (overnight) |
| | $ .50 per station (morning/daytime) |

The writer payment for a theme song on a ½-hour primetime series broadcast on 190 stations would be $2.50 x 190 = $475, plus any voluntary payment for that quarter. Under the 1987 Schedule (1987–1998 performances), BMI had a ½-hour theme rate whereby an hour show was paid two theme payments, whereas a ½-hour show was paid one. This per ½-hour theme rate as well as the 14-week super theme payment have been eliminated under the 1998 Schedule. The voluntary add-on payments during the years of the 1987 Schedule (1987–1998) for network television ranged from well below a 100% add-on to close to a 300% add on. These voluntary payments are normally different for different types of performances in the same quarter. For example, underscore could be +50% with themes at +90% and features at +110%. Fox, UPN, and WB were paid at 75% of the network rates but are now paid by the individual local TV stations broadcasting the programs.

## Local Television

For local television programming, BMI employs a combination of a census survey (100% pickup) of certain types of program and a sample survey of other types of program. Any network series that goes to syndication, any series that is made for first-run local television syndication, and any feature film or television movie of the week are covered by a census survey of performances. For all original programs produced only for a particular local television station, BMI employs a sample survey of performances whereby a performance on a local station is multiplied by a statistical multiplier based on the ratio of stations logged to stations licensed.

Through the 1990s, the performance payments in this area were relatively simple, as the rate for each type of performance, subject to a time of day factor was the same whether the performance was on BMI's highest-paying license fee station or the lowest. The 1987 Schedule had no time of day factors for local television. The 1987 Schedule performance cutbacks for certain types of shows (game shows, news and public affairs programs, etc.), the provision where background music would be paid only up to ½ the length of the program and the payment of full theme rates per each ½ hour of a program were all eliminated by the 1998 payment schedule. Currently, the rates on blanket stations are weighted to reflect the license fees paid by a station or group of stations. The rates below are neither minimums (as they were under all previous schedules) or maximums, but merely starting points.

| *Type of Performance* | Writer or Publisher Payment |
|---|---|
| Feature performance (45 seconds) | $2.00  (Daypart A-4P.M.-11P.M.)<br>.75  (Daypart B-11P.M.-4P.M.) |
| Background music (per minute) | .38  (Daypart A)<br>.21  (Daypart B) |
| Theme song (per show) | .90  (Daypart A)<br>.50  (Daypart B) |

If a writer wrote the theme and 5 minutes of background music plus 1 feature performance for each episode of a network ½-hour series that subsequently was syndicated on 80 local television stations during Daypart B, the per-station payments would be as follows:

```
50¢ (theme)        x1 station    =50¢ plus any voluntary payment
21¢ (background)x5 (minutes)x1 station = $1.05 plus any voluntary payment
75¢ (feature)      x1 station    =75¢ plus any voluntary payment
```

## Cable

In the cable area (e.g. HBO, Showtime, MTV, Discovery, etc.), BMI receives its program information from cue sheets from cable networks, program producers and distributors and other data sources and pays out on a census basis. The rates are determined each quarter by applying the amount of license collected from each network against the payable performances using as a starting point the methodology and relative weightings of the Local Television Daypart A rates. Cable monies at one time were paid twice a year but since late 1991 have been paid quarterly.

## Music and Lyrics in Commercials

BMI began paying on jingles on an experimental basis in 1980. Payments were made for qualifying music that was the sole focus of audience attention for at least 15 consecutive seconds. In 1987 commercial payments became part of the official BMI Payment Schedule, with a further change occurring in 1988 when BMI agreed to make some commercial payments for music of less than 15 seconds' duration in addition to providing bonus payments for certain hit songs used in commercials. Currently, payments vary and are made only for feature performances of jingles on broadcast and cable networks, local TV and radio, and for background uses only on ABC, CBS, FOX, and NBC TV networks.

*Registration and Information Requirements.* BMI requires the submission of a completed clearance form (available from BMI) as well as an audio tape of the commercial as broadcast. The clearance form includes the writer's name, social security number, and share; the publisher and its share; a statement relating to whether the work was written for the commercial or was adapted from an existing work (and, if an existing song, listing the original title and writers); and a statement signed by the writer and publisher that the agreement between the parties does not prevent BMI from licensing the performing rights.

Additional information requested includes the title of the work; the name of the agency and product being advertised; a schedule of broadcast time listing the commercial's placement on network television, syndicated television, and local spots (all radio and some local television performances); the performance quarter in which the commercial was broadcast; the number of "media buys" in a quarter; and whether the commercial was aired on radio or television. BMI will accept copies of the advertising agencies' own media buy schedules or talent payment reports.

*Qualification for Payments.* BMI has various payment rates for music used in commercials, many of which are based on a minimum duration of 15 seconds to qualify for payment. There is no stated payment schedule rate for commercial music, nor are many of the rules affecting other types of performances (network time-of-day factors, different payments for Radio 1 and Radio 2 performances, etc.) applicable to this area. The dollar amounts for commercial payments are decided on prior to the issuance of each commercial music statement, and payment is made for all qualifying broadcast performances.

For network television commercials, if the song is a preexisting composition, is at least an entry-level bonus song (with at least 25,000 past performances), and has a duration in the commercial of 15 seconds or more that is not interrupted by voiceover, a payment is made that includes a bonus because of the song's past popularity. If the song has a change of lyrics, a smaller bonus is paid. If the work is a background use, a lower payment is made with a bonus attached. For compositions written specifically for the commercial, payments are made but do not include the bonus.

For commercials broadcast on local television, cable, syndicated television, or radio, the music has to be the sole focus of audio attention for at least 15 seconds for payment. If the song qualifies for payment under this definition, payments are made at rates substantially lower than those for network television performance. Always check with BMI as to any changes in this area.

### Live Performance Payments/Internet/Per Program

BMI distributes royalties to the works used in all dates on the 200 top grossing tours. Tour payments began in 1996.

BMI uses radio and television performances as a proxy for the distribution of much of its other live performance money. Certain licensed concerts in the symphonic world are also paid on a census basis. Internet distributions began in 1998. License fees collected from local television per-program stations are paid to writers and publishers who have works on each program and the relationship of various types of uses (feature, background, theme, etc.) determines specific royalty payments

---

## *SESAC*

SESAC is a performing right organization formed in 1930 and incorporated in 1931. In 1992 SESAC was sold to a group of investors primarily from the music business. SESAC, a small organization, does not have an open membership policy, as ASCAP and BMI do, and writers have to be invited to join. For many years SESAC also licensed the mechanical and synchronization rights of many of its writers and publishers, but ceased that service effective January 1, 1992.

### Payments

SESAC pays writers and publishers based primarily on the position a song reaches on the Adult Contemporary, Black/Urban, College Alternative, Country, and Top 40/CHR singles charts, with other payments made on the basis of nationally released and distributed album cuts in the areas of Rock, Latin, Jazz, Christian, and Inspirational. In the case of chart singles, SESAC has a formula giving a writer and publisher a specific amount when a song reaches a particular chart position, with additional amounts called "post chart payments" paid in subsequent years. Chart payments are distributed in 4 quarterly installments commencing with the calendar quarter during which a song enters the trade paper charts. The record release payments are distributed similarly. All payments are subject to change by SESAC at any time without prior notice. In the television area, SESAC makes payments based on cue sheets and also collects performance money from foreign societies. As SESAC did not have a survey of radio performances for many years, the amount of catalog earnings distributable for any particular composition was a matter of negotiation between a writer or publisher and SESAC. In 1993 SESAC announced an agreement with Broadcast Data Systems whereby Spanish-language music stations in the top markets would be surveyed by a computerized tracking system, thus providing a per use/per play. This system was later increased to cover other genres of music. SESAC distributes its money based on many factors including chart positions, releases, actual performance information as well as other business factors.

## Contracts

SESAC does have a standard writer and publisher agreement, which can be modified through negotiation. The writer and publisher contracts grant to SESAC on a nonexclusive basis the "right to perform publicly and to license to others to perform publicly, the writer's and publisher's works throughout the world." The term of the writer agreement is 3 years, with automatic renewals for 3-year periods on the same terms and conditions as the original agreement if not terminated by the writer. The publisher contract runs for a period of 3 years, with automatic renewals for additional 3-year periods if not timely terminated. Writers and publishers can terminate these agreements by giving written notice by certified mail, return receipt requested, at least 3 months but not more than 6 months prior to the expiration of the current period of the term. SESAC contracts prior to the late 1990s were 5 year publisher and 3 year writer agreements automatically renewable. Always check for contract changes.

---

## *CHART SONGS—WHAT THEY EARN FOR PERFORMANCES*

Successful single releases generate demand for an artist's album and substantial earnings for the song's writer and the publisher. Many radio programmers as well as regular television and cable programs (e.g., MTV, VH-1) concentrate on singles, and once a single is a success, it will continue to earn royalties for decades. Table 7.5 estimates the U.S. performance right earnings for a major

TABLE **7.5**   Major Pop Chart Song Earnings

| | *Radio* | *Television* | *Wired Music and Other Uses* | *Total* |
|---|---|---|---|---|
| Quarter 1 | $320,000 | $30,000 | $   600 | $350,600 |
| Quarter 2 | 140,000 | 20,000 | 2,500 | 162,500 |
| Quarter 3 | 80,000 | 20,000 | 750 | 100,750 |
| Quarter 4 | 35,000 | 8,000 | 750 | 43,750 |
| Writer/Publisher Total | $575,000 | $78,000 | $4,600 | $657,600 |

across-the-board chart song during its first 12 months of release. Table 7.6 gives an example of what the U.S. songwriter and publisher earnings might be for the same song decades later. Table 7.7 gives a breakdown of the areas that generate income for a very successful writer's total catalog of songs. The chart assumes a currently active writer with 1 Top 10 and 1 Top 20 pop chart song during the year as well as a back catalog of 10 significant chart songs. Finally, Table 7.8 gives a range of figures of the U.S. writer or publisher earnings for various chart songs during the first year of release. The figures in the tables are intended as a reference guide and not as a guarantee. Some songs will earn less than the figures stated, others more, because of the many variables affecting a particular song or writer.

The figures as set forth in these tables are intended to show the substantial sums of performance money that can be earned by chart writers and publishers. One big hit can provide literally a lifetime of earnings for the writer as well as the beneficiaries of his or her estate. The tables also illustrate why successful copyrights are so valuable to a publishing company and why the prices to buy an existing publishing operation are so high. And considering that the foreign earnings can equal or surpass the U.S. earnings, the figures of some chart songs as set forth in the tables can be doubled for a major worldwide hit.

TABLE **7.6**   Catalog Earnings for a Past Hit Song

| *Year* | *Radio* | *Television* | *Wired Music* | *Total* |
|---|---|---|---|---|
| Year 18 | $ 40,000 | $  4,000 | $  1,500 | $  45,500 |
| Year 19 | 51,000 | 4,600 | 1,300 | 56,900 |
| Year 20 | 42,500 | 3,500 | 5,200 | 51,200 |
| Year 21 | 52,800 | 6,800 | 3,200 | 62,800 |
| Year 22 | 33,000 | 3,300 | 1,200 | 37,500 |
| Writer/Publisher Total | $219,300 | $22,200 | $12,400 | $ 253,900 |

TABLE **7.7**   Major Writer Annual Catalog Earnings

|  | *Radio* | *Television* | *Wired Music* | *Total* |
|---|---|---|---|---|
| Quarter 1 | $190,000 | $ 40,000 | $ 2,700 | $232,700 |
| Quarter 2 | 115,000 | 35,000 | 3,600 | 153,600 |
| Quarter 3 | 100,000 | 12,000 | 1,900 | 113,900 |
| Quarter 4 | 140,000 | 36,000 | 2,800 | 178,800 |
| Writer/Publisher Total | $545,000 | $123,000 | $11,000 | $679,600 |

TABLE **7.8**   Chart Song Earnings by Position over 1 Year

| *Top 100* | *Adult Contemporary* | *Country* | *R&B* | *Writer or Publisher Total* | |
|---|---|---|---|---|---|
| 1 | 1 | 1 | 1 | $250,000– | $600,000 |
| 1 | 1 | – | – | 225,000– | 500,000 |
| 1 | 10 | – | – | 200,000– | 350,000 |
| 1 | – | – | – | 200,000– | 300,000 |
| 5 | – | – | – | 125,000– | 250,000 |
| 10 | – | – | – | 90,000– | 200,000 |
| 20 | – | – | – | 65,000– | 150,000 |
| 30 | – | – | – | 50,000– | 100,000 |
| 50 | – | – | – | 25,000– | 80,000 |
| 90 | – | – | – | 5,000– | 25,000 |
| – | – | 1 | – | 150,000– | 400,000 |
| – | – | 5 | – | 100,000– | 200,000 |
| – | – | 10 | – | 75,000– | 150,000 |
| – | – | 20 | – | 40,000– | 90,000 |

*NOTE:* Individual songs may earn more or less than the ranges set forth in this chart, because most charts reflect a combination of performances and record sales and not performances alone.

## FUTURE CHANGES

The performing rights area is a field which is currently undergoing many changes. It is essential that writers, publishers and representatives stay informed of all new changes (payment formulas, surveys, weights, payment schedules, methods of doing business, etc.) if they are to intelligently understand as well as make decisions in this field. As we have seen, in many cases payments can be changed at any time without notice being given to the writers and publishers who will be affected. Always check the ASCAP, BMI, and SESAC websites for up-to-date payment information (ASCAP.com, BMI.com, SESAC.com).

# 8

# Music, Money, and Broadway

**W**ITH EYE-CATCHING headlines like "Broadway Rockets to All-Time High," "*Cats* Sweet $1.2 Million," "Hairspray A Hit," "*The Lion King* Earns Over $960,000 per week in N.Y.," "*Phantom* with $16.5 Million Advance," "*South Pacific* $695 G," and "*The Producers* on Broadway grosses $1.6 million in one week," Broadway theater has always held a certain glamour and fascination for both writers and those willing to invest their money. And even though costs have increased dramatically and risks remain high (well over 50% of productions do not recoup their initial capitalization), interest remains strong.

## AN OVERVIEW OF THE BROADWAY MUSICAL

Even though the Broadway theater represents a much better than even chance for investors to lose millions of dollars (for example, *Seussical* which lost almost $10,000,000 and *Chaplin,* which closed during tryouts at a loss of $4,076,460), there is always that chance that a particular musical will be the next *My Fair Lady* or *Phantom of the Opera*. And if a show is an unqualified success (such as *The Producers,* which recouped its $10,500,000 Broadway investment in 9 months, *The Phantom of the Opera* grossing $3 billion worldwide, *Cats,* which played over 17 years on Broadway, or *A Chorus Line,* which has netted over $40 million worldwide), the financial rewards for both the investors and the writers can be monumental.

To give an idea of how much can be earned from a hit Broadway musical, the bookwriter/composer/lyricist of a hit musical can make in excess of $1 million annually from the Broadway run alone. And even if a show is not a financial success, there are innumerable sources for the composer and lyricist to earn millions of dollars during the life of their songs. For example, there are the monies from CD and tape sales of the cast album, hit singles and cover recordings, professional U.S. and foreign touring companies, revivals, stock and amateur productions, sale of the motion picture rights, radio and television performances of songs from the play, television broadcasts of the original play or its motion picture version, foreign theatrical exhibitions of the play as a movie, sheet music and Broadway folios, home video, and commercials.

## Broadway and Road Performances

During the early 1970s, the Broadway theater was in a somewhat depressed condition financially. There, of course, had been some outstanding musicals each year, such as *Grease* and *Pippin,* but the glamour and excitement had started to wear a bit thin. Beginning with the 1974-75 theatrical season, legitimate theater once again started to generate increased interest among investors as well as substantial gains in both Broadway and touring production box office receipts. Then came the 1975-76 theatrical season, which was the most successful ever with respect to combined Broadway and road gross receipts. During that period Broadway alone accounted for over $70 million, with road performances generating an additional $52 million. In fact, the combined gross for both Broadway and road totaled over $123 million, the highest amounts ever recorded in the history of the theater up to that time. During the years that followed that historic season, the grosses have, with few exceptions, continued to grow, and in the 2002-2003 season the combined figures were in excess of $1.35 billion with Broadway accounting for over $720 million and the road over $632 million.

## Broadway Musicals

Some of the greatest financial successes in the theater have been musicals. Productions such as *The Producers, Oklahoma!, The Phantom of the Opera, Cats,* and *42nd Street* are just a few of the shows that immediately come to mind.

*Costs of Financing Broadway Musicals.* The production of a Broadway musical is an extremely expensive undertaking. At one time, a show could be brought into New York for less than $300,000. During the past 20 years, however, costs have escalated drastically, and Broadway musicals now usually require from $5 million to $15 million to open in New York.

*Weekly Costs of Operating Broadway Musicals.*   Once the millions required to get a play produced have been secured from investors, the next major expense (if a play is able to stay open) is the ongoing cost of keeping a show running. From the salaries of and guarantees to actors, the producer's expenses, and the theater's percentage of box office receipts to newspaper, radio, and television advertising, to the royalties due the authors and composers and the cost of stagehands and rentals, these operating expenses easily range from $350,000 to $600,000 per week and can mean the difference between keeping a show open or closing the doors once and for all.

## The Broadway Composer and Lyricist

In this world of multimillion-dollar investments, enormous profits, and equally enormous losses, the bookwriter, composer, and lyricist of a Broadway musical can earn unbelievably large amounts of money during the New York run, as well as for many years after the final curtain goes down on Broadway. In fact, the Broadway show does not necessarily have to be successful for the songwriters to make money. In some cases (depending on the quality and appeal of the songs in the show), the composer and lyricist may receive substantial long-term royalties from exploitation of the compositions in other areas, even if the original Broadway production is not terribly successful or, in a few cases, a total failure. Although the emphasis of this chapter is on the musical aspects of the Broadway show, the authors do not mean to lessen the role or importance of the bookwriter/librettist in any manner, since without that individual's contribution the Broadway musical would not exist.

## Sources of Income for the Broadway Composer and Lyricist

Innumerable potential sources of both immediate and long-term income are available for the writers of Broadway musicals. The following list represents the most significant:

Option payments from the show's producer
The advance based on the amount of capitalization for the show
Out-of-town pre-Broadway performances
The Broadway opening and New York run
The Broadway show cast album
Hit singles and cover records
U.S. touring productions during and after the Broadway run
Radio and television performances of songs from the show
The motion picture sale: (a) The soundtrack album; (b) Television perfor-

mances of the film; and (c) Foreign performances of the film in theaters
Stock, amateur, and foreign theatrical productions
Television and radio advertising commercials using songs from the play
Television performances of the play
Advertising commercials promoting the play
The Tony Awards telecast
The Academy Awards telecast (if the play is made into a motion picture)
The Grammy Awards telecast (if songs from the play become hit records)
Home video/DVD/Pay Per View
Uses of songs from the play in motion pictures unrelated to the Broadway
    musical
Uses of songs from the play in television series

---

## RIGHTS AND ROYALTIES OF THE BROADWAY SHOW WRITER: THE DRAMATISTS GUILD CONTRACT

The Dramatists Guild's contract represents a large number of important composers and lyricists in the Broadway theater. Since the guild has always been in the forefront of protecting the rights of theater writers, its minimum compensation standards and guidelines for the participation of income by its members should be reviewed prior to negotiating any Broadway agreement. When a Broadway show is produced, the producer, bookwriter, composer, and lyricist sign what is known as the "Approved Production Contract for Musical Plays (APC)," an agreement that is certified with the signature of a representative of the Dramatists Guild, Inc. The following sections analyze and explain the various rights and royalties that are guaranteed the composer and lyricist of Broadway show music under this contract.

### Monies Paid to the Composer and Lyricist Prior to the Actual Production of the Broadway Musical (Option Payments)

When a theatrical producer becomes interested in a specific property for production on Broadway, it normally acquires an option to produce the play from the bookwriter, composer, and lyricist. This option agreement guarantees to the producer the exclusive rights to produce the play and give it an agreed-upon period of time to find interested investors and actually produce the musical. Because most Broadway productions take months, if not years, to reach the stage, the Dramatists Guild requires the producer to pay the author, composer, and lyricist of the musical certain minimum payments from the time that the agreement is signed to the point where the show is actually produced.

In this way, the writers are ensured a certain amount of income prior to the show's opening. These option payments are deductible from capitalization advance payments and, provided production costs have been recouped, from up to 50% of future royalties due the writers. It should also be stressed that the guild's compensation standards are only minimums, and depending on a writer's past success record and bargaining power, these option payments can be negotiated upward.

The option payments stipulated by the Dramatists Guild to be shared among the writers are:

*First Option Period.* $18,000 for the 12-month period after the effective date of the contract, which is payable upon signing

*Second Option Period.* $9,000 for a second 12-month option period, payable prior to the end of the first year

*Third Option Period.* $900 per month for a maximum of 12 months during the third year

## Advance Payments

In addition to the option payments, the producer will also pay to the bookwriter, composer, and lyricist the following aggregate advance payments:

2% of the capitalization of the musical, payment to be made on the first day of full-cast rehearsal but in no event later than 5 business days before the initial first-class performance (i.e., a live stage production in a regular evening bill in a first-class theater in a first-class manner with a first-class director and cast)

2% of any additional capitalization contributed to the musical, payment to the writers to be made within 10 business days after the producer has received such monies

The total sum of these two advances is reduced by 2%, and that net amount is then payable to the writers. The aggregate advance payment need not be in excess of $60,000, regardless of the amount of capitalization secured by the producer to put on the musical.

Capitalization, for purposes of the advance payment calculation, is defined as the amounts contributed by investors in order to pay production costs and obtain an ownership interest in the venture producing the musical, plus a percentage of certain loans secured by the producer but not including, among other items, security bonds and other union or theater guarantees, option payments to the writers, and certain advertising, promotional, and press-related costs. As with the option payments, these advance payments are deductible from up to 50% of future royalties due the writers of the musical once the production costs of the musical have been recouped.

## Pre-Broadway Performances

Most Broadway musicals tour a number of weeks or months prior to their New York openings. In this way, the show can be "tried out" before live audiences and any changes, new songs, replacements, or fine tuning that may be necessary can be made before the Broadway opening. In some cases, the out-of-town run results in only minor changes; in others, entire scenes and musical numbers are discarded and replaced. In some instances, the pre-Broadway run will be the end of the line for the show, since disastrous out-of-town reviews have been known to close some musicals even before the Broadway opening. The out-of-town pre-Broadway run can be as little as a few weeks (for example, 3 weeks each in Boston, Philadelphia, and Washington) or as long as 1 year.

Pursuant to the provisions of the Dramatists Guild contracts, the bookwriter, composer, and lyricist of the musical are guaranteed a set fee for the first 12 out-of-town performances and varying percentages (depending on whether or not a show has recouped its costs) of the gross weekly box office receipts for all subsequent pre-Broadway out-of-town, New York preview, and regular performances. The actual minimum aggregate royalties to be divided among the librettist, composer, and lyricist are:

*Initial 12 out-of-town performance weeks and each week of preview performances, prerecoupment:* $4,500 for each full performance week

*Thirteenth and subsequent performance weeks, prerecoupment:* 4.5% of the gross weekly box office receipts until the official press opening in New York or the end of the week during which all production costs have been recouped, whichever is earlier

*Postrecoupment performances:* 6% of the gross box office receipts starting with the week after the show has recouped its investment

## The Broadway Opening

After the out-of-town pre-Broadway run, the musical normally enters New York for previews. Once the musical opens, the writers are guaranteed a minimum royalty of 4.5% of the weekly gross box office receipts until the show's costs have been recouped, and 6% of such receipts thereafter. For example, a hit musical on Broadway will usually take in from $550,000 to $800,000 per week in ticket sales. If the writers were sharing the guild's postrecoupment minimum of 6% (2% each to the composer, lyricist, and bookwriter), the weekly writer royalties would range from $11,000 to $16,000 each. And by multiplying this figure by 52 weeks, each writer would receive from $572,000 to $832,000 in annual royalties from the Broadway run of the show alone—if they are receiving the minimum royalty set by the Dramatists Guild. Successful writers can and do negotiate better royalty arrangements because of their past history of hits and stronger bargaining power.

## Broadway Writer Royalties

To illustrate the minimum royalty provisions and what they mean in actual dollars for the composer and lyricist, let us take a play that opens on Broadway as a smash hit and runs for 4 years. The bookwriter, composer, and lyricist are each receiving the 1.5% prerecoupment and 2% postrecoupment share of the gross weekly box office receipts under their guild contract. The musical is sold out for the first year with an average $700,000 in weekly receipts, and recoupment of costs is achieved at the end of the year. In the second year, it averages $690,000; in the third, $580,000; and in its final year on Broadway, $400,000. Under this scenario, the bookwriter's, composer's, and lyricist's weekly royalties from the Broadway run of the show would be computed as follows for each writer:

*First year:*

| | |
|---|---|
| $700,000 | Average weekly gross box office receipts |
| x 1.5% | Writer royalty (prerecoupment) |
| $ 10,500 | Weekly royalty |
| x 52 | Weeks in 1 year |
| $546,000 | *Annual writer royalties* |

*Second year:*

| | |
|---|---|
| $690,000 | Average weekly gross box office receipts |
| x 2% | Writer royalty |
| $ 13,800 | Weekly royalty |
| x 52 | Weeks in 1 year |
| $717,600 | *Annual writer royalties* |

*Third year:*

| | |
|---|---|
| $580,000 | Average weekly gross box office receipts |
| x 2% | Writer royalty |
| $ 11,600 | Weekly royalty |
| x 52 | Weeks in 1 year |
| $603,200 | *Annual writer royalties* |

*Fourth year:*

| | |
|---|---|
| $400,000 | Average weekly gross box office receipts |
| x 2% | Writer royalty |
| $  8,000 | Weekly royalty |
| x 52 | Weeks in 1 year |
| $416,000 | *Annual writer royalties* |

## Royalty Pools

Another formula being used on Broadway is the Royalty Pool arrangement where all royalty participants (for example, music and lyric writers, bookwriter, director, choreographer, etc.) share in an agreed-upon percentage of the weekly operating profits of the musical with certain guaranteed minimum per point royalties. For example, if the royalty pool was 35% and the weekly operating profit was $100,000, then 35% would be shared by all royalty participants based upon their points and 65,000 would go to the show's investors (65%).

## WEEKLY COSTS OF A BROADWAY MUSICAL

With normally the only source of income being from the sale of tickets, the weekly expenses of a show can either make or break most musicals. Just a few of the continuing expenses that must be met every week are the theater's percentage of receipts, salaries of cast and stage crew, the writer and director's royalties, newspaper advertising, television commercials, the producer's fee, and office expenses. On occasion, the sale of the motion picture rights will result in a substantial influx of money to cover costs and help recoup part of the investment, but for most Broadway musicals, box office receipts either keep a show open or close it. Table 8.1 sets forth many of the weekly expense categories for a show on Broadway.

### The Weekly Breakeven Point

Broadway musicals (depending, of course, on the elaborateness of the production) normally break even at between $400,000 to $600,000 per week. If a show is running at only 50% to 60% capacity, it will probably not be recouping its investment. And in most cases, if a Broadway musical is running at a sizable loss (e.g., from $100,000 to $300,000 per week), it is normally advisable to close it and minimize the continuing weekly expenses even though this usually means losing the show's entire investment. In some cases, however, it may be advisable to keep a Broadway musical open, especially if the audience reaction and word of mouth (as opposed to the reviews) have been good, if there are hit records from the score, or if the production has been nominated for or won a Tony or New York Drama Critic's Award. If a show can be prevented from closing, it may start to generate a larger audience (especially with the use of radio and television advertising) and actually begin to recoup some of its initial investment and even make a profit.

## ROAD PERFORMANCES DURING OR AFTER THE BROADWAY RUN

Many successful shows have national touring companies that play selected cities throughout the United States and Canada during and after the Broadway run. For example, Cats opened on Broadway in October 1982 to rave reviews and capacity audiences. Three and a half years later, it was still selling out in

New York and had 2 national companies and 1 Canadian touring company playing in Los Angeles, Chicago, and Toronto; over 5 years later it was still on

TABLE **8.1**   Weekly Expenses of a Broadway Show

*EXPENSES*

*Salaries*

Cast
Chorus
Musicians and conductor
Crew
Stage manager
General manager
Press agent
Wardrobe and dressers
Extra stagehands
Equity vacation pay
Star vacation pay

*Publicity*

Television
Newspaper
Photo and signs
Printing and promotion
Press expense
Television residuals
Subway and misc. advertisements
Group sales

*Departmental*
Electrical
Props
Costume
Carpenter
Rentals

*Theater Costs*

Rent and administration
Box office and mail staff
Theater staff
Payroll taxes
Union pension and welfare
Air conditioning
Theater expenses
Tickets
Transportation

*Miscellaneous*

Office expense
Legal
Accounting
Payroll taxes
Insurance
Local taxes
League dues
Pension and welfare
Miscellaneous

*Royalty Payments*
Writers
Dirctor/choreographer
Producer's fee
Other royalty
Participants

Broadway with 2 touring companies; and over 10 years later it was grossing close to $400,000 per week on Broadway and over $500,000 on the road.

## Weekly Costs of a Show on the Road

One of the most expensive projects in the entire area of Broadway musicals is to take the show on a national tour. Because of the additional costs involved (from per diems, living expenses, travel, and cartage to print advertising, theater rentals, crew salaries, and the monumental expenses of television commercials), producers try to organize such tours for only the most successful shows. Table 8.2 illustrates the type of monies that must be spent in taking a Broadway show on the road.

TABLE **8.2**   Costs of a Broadway Show on the Road

*EXPENSES*

| | | | |
|---|---|---|---|
| 1. | *Salaries* | | |
| | Cast | $ 41,000 | |
| | Chorus | 24,000 | |
| | Cacation and sick pay | 2,400 | |
| | Stage managers | 4,900 | |
| | Company and general managers | 6,000 | |
| | Press agents | 2,500 | |
| | Wardrobe/dressers/makeup | 4,600 | |
| | Production manager and supervisors | 1,700 | |
| | Conductor | 2,500 | |
| | Music coordinator/supervisor | 1,300 | |
| | Overtime and rehearsals | 2,500 | |
| | | $ 93,400 | *Total* |
| 2. | *Royalties* | | |
| | Author(s) | $ 67,000 | |
| | Director | 24,000 | |
| | Choreographer | 6,000 | |
| | Set and costume designer | 6,000 | |
| | Lighting designer | 2,300 | |
| | Sound designer | 1,500 | |
| | | $106,800 | *Total* |
| 3. | *Producer's Fee* | $ 16,000 | *Total* |
| 4. | *Publicity* | | |
| | TV | $ 15,000 | |
| | Print advertising | 4,000 | |
| | outdoors photos and signs | 3,600 | |
| | Press agent expenses | 3,500 | |
| | | $ 26,100 | *Total* |
| 5. | *Departmental* | | |
| | Electrical and sound | $ 5,000 | |
| | Costume, hair, and makeup | 5,000 | |

|                                    |          |       |
| ---------------------------------- | -------- | ----- |
| Carpenter and props                | 2,000    |       |
| Rentals                            | 27,000   |       |

TABLE **8.2** *(cont'd.)*

*EXPENSES*

|                                         |            |       |
| --------------------------------------- | ---------- | ----- |
| Company and stage managers              | 250        |       |
| Maintenance reserve                     | 4,000      |       |
|                                         | $ 43,250   | *Total* |
| 6.    *Theater expenses*      |            |       |
| Fixed theater expenses                  | $ 20,000   |       |
| Rent and sharing terms                  | 60,000     |       |
| Theater and box office staff            | 16,500     |       |
| Stagehands                              | 32,000     |       |
| Musicians                               | 41,000     |       |
|                                         | $169,500   | *Total* |
| 7.    *Miscellaneous*         |            |       |
| Office expense                          | $   1,500  |       |
| Legal                                   | 600        |       |
| Accounting                              | 600        |       |
| Casting                                 | 600        |       |
| Payroll taxes                           | 6,000      |       |
| Union benefits                          | 6,000      |       |
| Insurance                               | 8,000      |       |
| League dues                             | 550        |       |
| Travel and living reserve               | 3,000      |       |
| Long-distance calls, photocopying       | 750        |       |
| Miscellaneous                           | 1,800      |       |
|                                         | $ 29,400   | *Total* |
| *TOTAL WEEKLY EXPENSES*                 | $484,450   |       |

## *ADJUSTMENTS IN A WRITER'S ROYALTIES (DRAMATISTS GUILD CONTRACTS)*

### The New York Run (Minimum Weekly Guarantee)

In the event that, after a musical has recouped its investment, the weekly box office receipts do not exceed 115% of the weekly breakeven point for the show, the combined aggregate writer royalties will be reduced to $3,000 per week plus 35% of the weekly profits for that week, rather than the normal 6%-of-gross royalty. If the director of the musical receives for any such week a royalty that is less than the full royalties specified in his or her contract, then the writer's percentage may be reduced on a pro rata basis from 35% to no less than 25%. If this formula of $3,000 per week plus percentage of the profits takes effect, the total royalty may not exceed the normal 6% postrecoupment amount.

### Touring Shows (Minimum Weekly Guarantee)

In the weeks before the touring costs are recouped, if the weekly box office receipts do not exceed 110% of the weekly breakeven point, the writers shall receive an aggregate $3,000 plus 25% of the weekly profits. As with the Broadway run, the total royalty shall not exceed the prerecoupment 4.5% rate. After recoupment of costs has been achieved, if the 115% weekly breakeven point is not exceeded by the box office receipts, the writers will share a guaranteed $3,000 plus 35% of the weekly profits, but shall not earn more than the equivalent of the 6% weekly postrecoupment royalty. As on Broadway, the 35% can be reduced to not less than 25% if the director is not receiving full royalties during a particular week. During any week that a musical (whether it be on Broadway or on tour) suffers a loss, the writers will share a combined $3,000 fixed royalty and will not be paid on a percentage basis.

---

## BROADWAY SHOWS PRODUCED UNDER NON-DRAMATISTS GUILD CONTRACTS

Since shows written by non-Dramatists Guild members are produced without using the guild's Approved Production Agreement, there are a number of arrangements that may be made between the parties involved in such a musical. The following section explains some of the more prevalent approaches in these agreements.

### Fixed-Dollar Royalty Shows

In a number of cases and especially where the Broadway show is using preexisting songs, the producer may try to negotiate a specified weekly dollar payment, which usually ranges from $250 to over $750 per song. Under such a fixed-payment plan, the producer does not have to deal with a percentage of the weekly box office receipts but merely pays the individual songwriters (or their estates) and music publishers a set fee every week regardless of whether the production becomes a hit or not.

Such a formula, obviously, can work to a writer's advantage if a show is unsuccessful since, depending on the guaranteed payment negotiated, the monies paid may be more than would have been earned under a percentage-of-receipts plan. If a show is a hit or even moderately successful, however, this set fee arrangement can mean the loss of thousands of dollars over the long run, especially if road or touring companies are also included in the set weekly royalty formula. For example, if a song is receiving only $100 per week and the gross box office receipts range from $350,000 to $600,000 per week, the lost income can be monumental.

These weekly guaranteed payments are normally based on an 8-performance week and will be reduced proportionately during any week in which there are fewer performances.

## Percentage-of-Receipts Royalty

Most Broadway musicals use a percentage of the weekly box office receipts in determining how much the composers and lyricists of a show will receive. In the case of songs written by a number of writers (e.g., a show with a number of preexisting compositions) each song may receive a pro rata share of the agreed-upon percentage (e.g., 15 compositions sharing 4% equally), or each song may receive a pro rata percentage dependent on its timing and use in the play (e.g., each song getting its proportionate durational share of 70 minutes of music). On the other hand, if the same writers have written all the songs in a play, those writers will receive the entire percentage. Depending on the negotiating power of the writers, these percentages usually range from 4% to 6%, with well-known Broadway musical writers receiving more. Obviously, if a show is grossing $500,000 a week, the difference between a 4% and 8% royalty ($20,000 vs. $40,000) can be substantial.

One interesting variation on the pro rata sharing of royalties by different writers formula occurred in the musical Sugar Babies, which had a lengthy run on Broadway and on the road. Twenty songs (including such standards as "Don't Blame Me," "I Can't Give You Anything but Love," and "On the Sunny Side of the Street") shared in a percentage of the box office receipts according to whether the use was music and lyrics, music only, or lyrics only. Under the formula, the total royalties due all writers and publishers were divided in half, with 50% being attributable to lyrics and 50% to music. Each song shared in 1 or both funds according to its use.

## Touring Shows with Guarantees

A fairly common variation of the percentage-of-receipts royalty occurs when a successful musical is touring the country under arrangements that guarantee the play a certain amount of money each week regardless of actual ticket sales. Under such arrangements, the producer receives a specified sum, and the theater takes anything over that amount up to a certain limit, with the producer sometimes receiving a percentage of the theater's share. Then the overage either goes to the producer or is shared by the producer and theater on a percentage basis (e.g., 60% to the producer and 40% to the theater).

If the writers are receiving their royalties based on a percentage-of-receipts formula, their royalties are based on the monies received by the producer and not those to which the theater is entitled. Suppose, for example, that the box office brings in $500,000 in 1 week. The guarantee arrangement allocates the first $250,000 per week to the producer and the next $150,000 to the theater; the remainder ($100,000) is shared, 60% to the producer and 40% to the theater. The writers' 6% royalty comes out of the producer's combined guarantee and share of the remainder:

| *Producer* | | *Theater* | |
|---|---|---|---|
| $250,000 | Guarantee | $150,000 | Guarantee |
| + 60,000 | 60% of $100,000 | + 40,000 | 40% of $100,000 |
| $310,000 | Total | $190,000 | Total |
| x 6% | Writer royalty | | |
| $18,600 | Writer royalties | | |

---

## WHAT THE PRODUCER MUST DO TO ENSURE RIGHTS TO A SHARE OF SUBSIDIARY INCOME FROM THE BROADWAY SHOW (DRAMATISTS GUILD CONTRACTS)

In order for the producer of a musical to share in the income generated from the cast album, a motion picture sale, the home video market, commercial uses (such as games, dolls, T-shirts, souvenir programs, and toys), stock performances (including university resident theaters and dinner theaters), amateur performances by nonunion actors, concert tour versions, and theatrical performances in certain foreign territories, it must present the musical in one of the following ways:

### United States

1. One of the following series of consecutive paid public first-class performances in the United States: 10 previews plus the official press opening in New York City; 5 previews plus the official press opening and 5 regular performances; 5 out-of-town and 5 preview performances plus the official press opening (provided there are not more than 42 days between the last out-of-town performance and the first preview performance); or 5 preview performances and the official press opening in New York, if the play has been produced previously by someone other than the current producer and

the show has substantially the same cast and scenic designs of the prior presentation.

2. Sixty-four paid out-of-town performances occurring within 80 days of the initial performance.

3. Sixty-four performances as outlined above in arenas or auditoriums if, because of the nature of the play, its size, or complexity of the production, playing in traditional first-class theaters would not be feasible or desirable.

*United Kingdom.*   If the play is initially produced in London, there must be 21 consecutive performances in London. If the play is initially produced outside of London, there must be 64 performances within 80 days after the first performance, with such performances taking place either totally outside London or partly outside and partly in London.

*Australia and New Zealand.*   There must be 21 consecutive first-class performances, including an official press opening.

## Producer's Share of Subsidiary Rights

If the producer has achieved the above criteria, the producer and the investors who financed the play will be allowed to share in the revenue derived from subsidiary rights according to 3 alternative formulas, as set forth in Table 8.3. Unless the producer and the writers of the musical jointly select Alternative III at the signing of the production contract, the producer can choose either Alternative I or Alternative II on or before midnight on the first day of rehearsal at which the producer requires all cast members. If the producer does not give such notice, the writers may select the plan for the producer by giving both the producer and the Dramatists Guild notice on or before midnight of the next business day following the first rehearsal date. If both the producer and the writers fail to choose an alternative, then Alternative III will automatically apply.

Since subsidiary income from a Broadway musical can be substantial, many producers keep a show open even though losses are being incurred just to make sure that they become entitled to a share of this potentially valuable future source of income.

## Producer's Right to Subsidiary Income under non-Dramatists Guild Contracts

Since writers who are not members of the Dramatists Guild do not use the guild agreement, the right of a producer to share in the many subsidiary sources of income that flow from the musical is negotiable in such cases. While many of these contracts are based on principles outlined in the Dramatists Guild Approved Production Contract, the actual terms are subject to the negotiating expertise and bargaining power of the parties.

TABLE **8.3** Three Alternative Formulas for Sharing Subsidiary Rights Revenue

| Type of Right | I | II | III |
|---|---|---|---|
| Media productions (television, sound-track albums, motion pictures, video cassettes, etc.) | 50% in perpetuity | same | 30% in perpetuity |
| Stock and ancillary performances (equity stock, resident theaters, dinner theaters, concert tour versions, opera versions, etc.) | 50% for the 1st 5 years/25% for the next 5 years | 30% for 36 years | 30% for the first 20 years/25% for the next 10 years/ 20% for the next 10 years (total of 40 years) |
| Amateur performances (English-language versions using non-professional actors) | 25% for 5 years | 0% | same as for the stock above |
| Revival performances | 20% for 40 years | same | same |
| Commercial use products (wearing apparel, toys, games, figures, dolls, souvenir books and programs, etc.) | (a) 10% of the gross retail sales of goods sold at the theater (not to exceed 50% of the producer's license fee) | same | same |
| | (b) 50% of the producer's net receipts from sales in other locations | same | same |
| | (c) Rights extend during the period in which producer retains the right to produce the play in a territory and for no more than 5 years after said rights have expired for contracts entered into prior to the expiration date | same | same |

## *LIFE AFTER BROADWAY (WHERE THE REAL MONEY IS MADE)*

For many songs from musicals, the real money comes from sources other than the Broadway run or the national and foreign touring productions. Granted, a handful of writers make millions of dollars from live theatrical performances, but the major royalties for many writers come from the sale of hit records, tapes, and CDs; downloads and streaming; radio and television performances of the songs from the show; commercials; motion pictures using Broadway songs as theme or background music; the theatrical release and television broadcasts of the motion picture; sheet music and folios; option and acquisition payments for the production of the musical as a film; television broadcasts of the show; cover recordings; home video; and the Tony Awards show. Because of the importance of this "non-live theater income" and what it means to the financial well-being of a songwriter and music publisher, the following sections review how the money is made and what you must know to make it.

### Hit Singles from Broadway Shows

One of the most lucrative sources of income for the composer and lyricist of the Broadway musical is the hit single, since #1 songs can generate in excess of $300,000 in tape and CD sale income and over $600,000 in radio and television performance royalties. In addition, because of the mass exposure that hit singles receive, a number of important areas are opened up such as commercials, movies, and television series, which can generate hundreds of thousands of dollars in short- and long-term income for the writer and music publisher.

On many singles, the recording artist is not the performer who originally sang the song in the show. One example is Stephen Sondheim's "Send in the Clowns," the 1976 Grammy Award winner from *A Little Night Music;* the 2 major recordings of that song were by Frank Sinatra and Judy Collins. Another example is "Memory," from *Cats,* which reached the charts on recordings by both Barbra Streisand and Barry Manilow. With *Funny Girl,* on the other hand, Barbra Streisand had a hit record of *People,* the song that she also performed in the show. In still other instances, hit records were made by both original cast members and other recording artists; notable examples are the hit singles from *Hair* and *Hello, Dolly!*

*Mechanical Royalties.*    The writer or his or her music publisher will normally license the Broadway song to a record company for the U.S. statutory penny royalty for every record, tape, and CD sold (8.5¢ per song in 2004–05). For example, if 1 million singles of a song are sold, the combined mechanical royalties to the writer and publisher will be $85,000. If the million-selling single contains an additional song from the Broadway show and a reduced royalty rate is not agreed to, there will be another $85,000 in aggregate royalties due the publisher and writer. In addition, if the song or songs are covered by other recording artists on albums, singles, or CDs, the sales of all other versions can result in thousands of dollars of mechanical income long after a song's initial popularity. One example of a song standing the test of time is "Ol' Man River," from Jerome Kern and Oscar Hammerstein II's *Show Boat,* which has had over 400 recordings from such diverse artists as Chet Atkins, Count Basie, Jeff Beck, Tony Bennett, Pat Boone, Dave Brubeck, Ray Charles, Cher, Sam Cooke, Floyd Cramer, Papa John Creach, Jim Croce, Bing Crosby, Sammy Davis, Jr., Tommy Dorsey, Maynard Ferguson, the Flamingos, Aretha Franklin, and Judy Garland to Stephane Grappelli, Screamin' Jay Hawkins, Al Hirt, Al Jolson, Howard Keel, Robert Merrill, Glen Miller, Oscar Peterson, Louis Prima, Lou Rawls, Della Reese, Charles Rich, the Righteous Brothers, Paul Robeson, Bobby Rydell, Frank Sinatra, the Temptations, Lawrence Welk, and Joe Williams.

*ASCAP and BMI Royalties.*   In most cases, the largest immediate source of a writer's income from a hit single comes from the royalties earned for radio and television performances of the record. Depending on a number of factors, including the amount of airplay a song receives, the types of station it is broadcast on (e.g., AM, FM, network, or local), and whether it is eligible for bonus payments, the ASCAP or BMI writer and publisher royalties can run well over $750,000 for a major hit. In addition, there are also increased royalties from ASCAP for songs that have previously been hits that are used as background or theme music on radio or television shows and bonus payments from BMI for performances of songs written specifically for Broadway musicals. And if a song from a Broadway musical becomes a standard, is recorded by many different artists, or is used by television and motion picture producers, it has the potential of generating a steady flow of performance income for years after the Broadway show has closed.

*The Song and Its Role in the Broadway Musical.*   The main purpose in writing music or lyrics for a theatrical play is not necessarily to write a chart record; it is primarily to create the best possible songs to enhance and develop the dramatic content and flow of the play itself. If a song or songs from a Broadway musical are recorded and become successful in their own right, all the better for the writers and the show from which the songs were taken. Many musicals with excellent music and lyrics, however, have not had hit singles, and it is wrong to judge the worth of a particular show by the number of successful singles that come from it. For example, *A Chorus Line,* which won almost every award possible on Broadway, did not have any songs that became commercial hit singles, yet the show was an enormous success from an artistic and— considering it has grossed over $40 million—a financial point of view.

## Broadway Show Music in Commercials

Another source of income for the Broadway song is its use in radio or television commercials advertising consumer products. Since the fees for such commercial use can be substantial (e.g., from $75,000 to over $750,000 per year for well-known songs), this area can represent a major source of potential income for the writer and his or her publisher. Some examples of Broadway show songs used in commercials are:

| Product | Song | Play |
|---|---|---|
| Mountain Dew | "Tonight, Tonight" | *West Side Story* |
| Intel and Canon | "I Feel Pretty" | *West Side Story* |
| Oscar Mayer | "Hello, Dolly!" | *Hello, Dolly!* |
| Mercury | "Ease on Down the Road" | *The Wiz* |
| Mercury Aerostar | "Age of Aquarius" | *Hair* |

## Television Commercials Promoting a Broadway Musical

Because television is such an important medium, virtually all Broadway musicals use television commercials to advertise their presence and promote ticket sales. Although extremely expensive, this method of promotion has, in many cases, had spectacular results. On occasion, payments are made for the use of songs in these commercials, but normally such rights are given without charge because of the promotional nature of the spots.

## Television Performances of Songs in the Play

Each year, the Tony Awards show is presented on network television to an audience of millions of viewers. During this annual presentation, there are 3 basic situations where Broadway show music is used and for which composers and lyricists receive ASCAP and BMI performance royalties. They are:

*Staged production number.* Actual production numbers from the shows that were nominated for Best Musical of the Year.
*Background music used while Tony winners accept their awards.* Music is ordinarily played while the award winners walk to the stage for their acceptance speeches. In addition, instrumental music is performed to introduce the celebrities who act as presenters.
*Song medleys.* During the course of the evening, there usually is a production number that contains songs from either past or current Broadway shows.

The writers of music performed on the Tony Awards show are paid by ASCAP and BMI according to the duration of music used, the number of uses during the show, the number of local television stations carrying the program, how the song is used, whether bonuses for theater works are applied, and the song's performance history.

## Television Performances of the Play

A number of Broadway musicals have been televised in their entirety, normally at the end of or after their New York run. Such televised performances represent an additional source of income for the songs used in a Broadway show, since there are up-front synchronization right payments as well as the possibility of ASCAP or BMI nondramatic performance royalties. Payments in this area are much smaller than those negotiated when a musical is produced as a theatrical feature motion picture. Because there is a possibility that a televised version of a musical might hurt the sale of motion picture rights or injure the potential box office for either the Broadway run or road performances, such television performances are not that common.

## The Broadway Show Cast Album

At one time, the Broadway cast album was a significant source of income for the writers and publishers of a musical. Such past successes as *My Fair Lady* and *The Sound Of Music* sold millions of copies worldwide, and shows such as *Hair, South Pacific, Hello, Dolly!, Jesus Christ Superstar,* and *Fiddler on the Roof* further added to the reputation of the Broadway cast album as a financial goldmine. In recent years, however, Broadway show albums have not generated the sales and enthusiasm that they had in the past. Of course, there have been a number of very successful records such as *A Chorus Line, Grease, Rent, Funny Girl, 42nd Street, Cats, Les Miserables,* and *Phantom of the Opera,* but the cast album, as a genre, has not shown the international consistency and mass appeal that were once expected of a hit Broadway musical.

*Mechanical Royalties (Audio Recording Sales).* The composer and the lyricist (many times through their music publisher) will normally license the mechanical rights to their songs in the United States for the statutory rate (8.5¢ per song or 1.65¢ per minute of playing time in 2004-05). For example, if there are 15 songs on a Broadway cast album, the record company would pay a total of $1.27 for each album sold. The computations would be:

| | |
|---|---|
| 8.5¢ | Per-song royalty |
| x 15 | Songs on the album |
| $1.27 | Royalties due per album |

This $1.27 per album would normally be shared equally by the publisher and the writers, unless the writer copublishes the songs.

Obviously, if the album has songs by a number of different writers (such as *42nd Street, Sophisticated Ladies,* and *No, No, Nanette)*, the aggregate royalties would be shared on a song-by-song basis. Moreover, if there are a large number of songs on the cast album, a record company may ask that the owners of the compositions agree to a maximum aggregate mechanical royalty cap on each record (e.g., 95¢). In addition, some producers will demand a 75%-of-statutory rate for all or selected songs on a cast album, especially if some of the songs have only partial uses, if there are more than 15 songs on the album, or if most or all of the songs are by 1 writer or group of writers.

*Record Contract Royalties.* In most cases, the producer of the Broadway musical will negotiate the record contract for the original cast album. Where the writers have the requisite bargaining power, however, they may retain the right to make the agreement themselves. Pursuant to the terms of the recording contract, the record company will usually agree to pay a royalty based on a percentage of the retail selling price of 90% to 100% of all tapes and CDs sold. This record royalty is normally shared by the writers of the show and the play's producer. All recording costs and advances are deducted from any monies due the writers and producer before any royalty payments are made by the record company. For example, if a Broadway cast album cost $400,000 to produce and a $50,000 advance is also given, no royalties will be distributed until all the recording costs and advances had been recouped by the record company.

## Motion Picture Soundtrack Albums

If a Broadway musical has been produced as a major theatrical feature film, the motion picture soundtrack album can generate substantial mechanical and performance income for the writers and publishers of the original Broadway production. For example, *Chicago* went to #2 on the charts, *Oklahoma!* was on the trade paper album charts for over 300 weeks, *The King and I* and *South Pacific* over 250 weeks, and *The Sound of Music* over 230 weeks. As with the "live" Broadway cast album, mechanical royalties may be paid either at the statutory rate or, if negotiated downward, at 75% to 85% of the statutory rate for a 12- to 13-song album. In addition to mechanical royalties, a royalty percentage (similar to that received by a recording artist) of 1% to 4% is many times negotiated for the writers and publishers of the songs contained on the album.

## Successful Cover Records

One of the best examples of the lasting popularity of some Broadway songs is Barbra Streisand's *The Broadway Album,* which contained songs spanning over 5 decades of theatrical history, from *Show Boat* (1927) to *Sunday in the*

*Park with George* (1984).The album's sales of over 3 million copies in just a few months of 1985 proved that, with the right combination, theater songs will always earn money. In 1993, Streisand did it again with her *Back to Broadway Album,* which went to #1 on the charts in its first week of release.

## Sheet Music Folios

Even though the print business has not been as profitable as it once was, Broadway-oriented theme books continue to generate good sales.The standard royalties for such folios are between 10% and 15% of the retail selling price; all copyrighted compositions normally share equally in the aggregate amount. If the folio concentrates on 1 play exclusively, an additional royalty percentage may be paid (e.g., an extra 5%, similar to a "personality folio" rate).

## Royalties from Motion Picture Theaters

In most countries outside the United States, motion picture theaters are required to pay royalties to the local performing right society for the music used in films. The writer's share of such monies is distributed by the local society to either ASCAP or BMI, which then pays the U.S. composers and lyricists. The publisher's share of such fees is normally distributed to the publisher's local foreign representative, who then remits the appropriate share to the U.S. publisher. Most countries charge theaters a percentage of the total box office receipts, but some base fees on the number of seats in each theater as well as other factors. Most domestically produced motion pictures will not earn a great deal of money from theaters outside the United States, but for those Broadway musicals that become motion pictures with worldwide appeal, the monies can be substantial. In fact, $100,000 to $300,000 in combined writer and publisher theater performance royalties are not unusual for hit films.

## Broadway Songs Used in Television Programs

Since many television programs use well-known standards either as background music or sung by a person on camera, this area can be extremely valuable for the Broadway song in terms of performance, synchronization, and home video income (e.g., $9,500 for an all-television license, $7,500 for a video license, synchronization option payments, ASCAP and BMI performance income), as well as reexposure to millions of people.

## Broadway Songs Used in Motion Pictures

Another extremely lucrative source of income is the inclusion of Broadway show songs in motion pictures as either theme, background music, or visual vocals. Because of the various royalty-generating media involved in motion pictures (e.g., the initial $15,000 to $60,000 synchronization fee, performance income from television broadcasts of the film, soundtrack album sales, royalties from theaters exhibiting the film in foreign countries, home video sales of the motion picture, and performance and mechanical royalty income from hit records taken from the show), this area can mean hundreds of thousands of dollars to the writer and music publisher.

## The Broadway Musical as a Motion Picture

Even though the heyday of the Broadway musical as a major motion picture is over, for those musicals that are transferrable to film, the profits can still be substantial. The motion picture sale can take a number of different turns and encompass a number of areas, but virtually every agreement will encompass most of the areas that follow.

*Payment for the Rights.* The motion picture company will pay a negotiated fee (e.g., from $1 million to over $10 million) for the rights to produce a motion picture based on the musical. Obviously, the final compensation is based on the success of the show on Broadway and on the road, the conviction of the producer that the show can be successfully made into a commercial film, whether the film will have international appeal, and what is given up by the writers in other areas of the agreement.

*Percentage of the Proceeds from the Film.* The producer, writers, and music publishers are many times given a percentage of the net monies earned by the motion picture after the breakeven point for the film has been reached. A number of different formulas are used in this area depending on the company producing the film, and each is extremely complicated. For example, breakeven for a film company normally includes the recoupment of a multiple of the direct costs of making the film, fixed deferred payments (as opposed to deferred income based on how well the film does), a production fee for the film's producer, overhead fees to the producer equal to a set percentage of the production costs, supervisory fees to the film company financing the production, and the bank interest on the money needed to produce the film.

*Fees for Remakes or Sequels.* The film's producer will usually be given the right to produce a remake or sequel provided a specified fee ($250,000 and above) is paid within a certain number of days after principal photography has begun. If additional compensation based on a percentage of the net earnings was received on the original film, the same formula or a percentage thereof would also be received for the remake. As for sequels, the fees paid and percentages are many times more than those that would be payable for a remake of the original film.

*Fees for Television Films or Series.* In addition to the motion picture, sequel, and remake rights, the film producer will also try to negotiate for television rights to a made-for-TV movie or series based on the play if the theatrical film is actually produced. In the event that the television version is released theatrically outside the United States, a further payment (usually the equivalent of or more than the television fee) may be due. If a television series is based on the play (including a spin-off based on characters in the play), additional fees will be due, dependent on, among other factors, the running time of the series. In addition, many contracts provide for payments of negotiated fees (sometimes based on a percentage of the initial fee) for each rerun of the program up to a certain limit.

## Home Video/DVD

Home video income meant at one time something only if the Broadway play was made into a feature film. Now, however, home video versions are being made of actual live stage musicals. As in the television series and motion picture area, there are a number of different ways to license songs for home video (e.g., the 1-time buy-out for all sales, the rollover advance or set dollar amount for a set number of units, and the per-unit royalty or penny-rate-per-song formula).

## Noncast Albums of the Broadway Musical

There has been a recent trend by record companies to produce new recordings of a show with performers who were not in the original production. This trend has not only affected older shows such as *Carousel, South Pacific,* and Showboat but has been extended to newer musicals as well. Such an approach takes the Broadway album out of the sometime limited "cast album" category and puts it into the mainstream record-buying market.

## Catalogue Musicals

A popular form of contemporary musical is the show using the individual songs of a successful writer or writer/artist with a story structured around them. Some examples are *Mamma Mia!* based on the Abba catalogue of songs, *Movin' Out* which uses Billy Joel compositions, *Smokey Joe's Café* based on the catalogue of Jerry Leiber and Mike Stoller, *Love, Janis,* an off-Broadway production based on the life of Janis Joplin, *We Will Rock You* from Queen, *Tonight's the Night* based on Rod Stewart songs, *Saturday Night Fever* from the Bee Gees, *Taboo* using Boy George compositions, and the *Boy from Oz* playing Peter Allen songs.

# 9

# Music, Money, and Foreign Countries

EVEN THOUGH at one time most U.S. writers did not earn most of their income in foreign countries, this is quickly changing. The money is there, and if one knows the market, it can be extremely important to the songwriter or writer/performer. There are many parallels to doing business in the United States, but each foreign country has its own rules and its own distinct way of licensing music, collecting royalties, and protecting copyrights. It is vital that a songwriter and his or her music publisher select the right foreign representative, since it is virtually impossible to handle and promote one's music or lyrics adequately thousands of miles away without the assistance and expertise of competent local personnel, as well as some understanding of local rules.

## OVERVIEW

In a world of fluctuating exchange rates, local music publishers sharing monies earned from songs they do not own, income being lost because local collection societies have not been given the proper information, foreign translators receiving a portion of a U.S. writer's royalties, mechanical income being based on a percentage rather than set dollar rates for record sales, 2-year delays in the transmittal of royalties, U.S. writers and publishers of songs used in films and television programs receiving nothing because music cue sheets have not been registered, motion picture theater royalties based on the number of seats or a percentage of ticket sales, and complicated formulas for keeping track of what songs are being used and how much should be paid, dealing effectively with music in countries outside the United States is not for the novice.

This chapter explains the major things that one must know when negotiating for foreign representation, including:

The role of the subpublisher and the factors that go into choosing the right one

The duration of the agreement

The information that must be supplied for effective representation

The importance of daily or weekly contact

Advances and guarantees

Cover recordings and local-language versions

CD, tape, DVD, and home video sales, television series, commercials, and motion pictures

ASCAP and BMI's relationship with foreign performance societies

Retention rights if a song is recorded by a foreign artist

Fees charged by foreign representatives for handling U.S.-originated songs and catalogs

Extensions based on nonrecoupment of advances or failure to deliver enough commercially released recordings

Keeping track of what has already happened thousands of miles away or, in the case of Australia and other countries, 1 day into the future.

---

## THE ROLE OF THE SUBPUBLISHER

The role of the foreign subpublisher is, in most respects, the same as that of a music publisher in the United States. For example, its services include protecting copyrights; registering songs with the local mechanical and performance collection societies; promoting new uses; collecting royalties; auditing royalty statements from record companies, video distributors, and other users of music; negotiating licenses; and suing infringers.

### Administration vs. Promotion

As with U.S. publishing companies, certain foreign publishers are known for their administrative abilities, others for their promotion capabilities, and still others for a combination of the two. In choosing a subpublisher, therefore, a writer or publisher has initially to decide what he or she is looking for and then select the subpublisher that best fits those needs. For example, a major writer/ recording artist with international stature may only want to make sure that monies earned from his or her self-contained recordings and performances are properly collected in each territory. In such a case, a subpublisher known for its administrative abilities would be the ideal choice, since local promotion is not an important consideration. On the other hand, if a writer or publisher is looking for cover records by local artists or local territorial exploitation of new uses, the selection may be a subpublisher noted for its strong relationships with local record, television, and film producers in its territory.

## Worldwide Representation vs. Territory-by-Territory Agreements

Another choice to be made is whether or not you want to commit your catalog to one company for the entire world (such as through an overall agreement with a company that has fully staffed offices in all major territories) or select foreign representation on a country-by-country basis depending on specific needs and expectations in each particular territory. One advantage of going with a worldwide company (besides the daily communication and transmittal of information that occurs between offices) is that, if there is a problem a few thousand miles away, one can always try to resolve it with personnel working in the company's U.S. headquarters. This immediate access by local telephone or appointment rather than dealing by means of fax, letter, or staying up half the night to talk to someone during business hours in a foreign territory can be very important.

On the other hand, there is always the fear that one's catalog might not get the personal attention that it deserves when affiliation is with a major worldwide conglomerate that owns or administers hundreds of thousands of songs. In addition, as in any multinational business, a company may have effective personnel in 1 country and an inefficient office in another country. Because of these problems, a number of writers and publishers feel that choices should be made on a territory-by-territory basis; in some cases, that means that one's foreign representatives will be a combination of worldwide U.S.-based companies and local independent firms. For example, you might have one major in certain territories, another major in others, and a number of local independents in territories where you feel you can get better service from a nonmajor. A third alternative is to allow an independent U.S. publisher with which you have a good relationship to represent your songs overseas through its subpublishers in each area of the world. Through such a relationship, a writer or publisher who does not know the foreign market can use the expertise and experience of a U.S. company to select and communicate with its own network of independent foreign affiliates.

There are no hard and fast rules in this area, as all decisions are predicated on one's knowledge (or lack thereof) of each country outside the United States.

Obviously, if you do not have a good grasp of the foreign music market, it may be safer and easier to let a U.S.-based company with offices in foreign countries represent your songs. But if you do have a knowledge of the foreign market (or don't mind taking the time or incurring the expenditure to learn), picking and choosing on a territory-by-territory basis may be advantageous depending on your specific needs in each separate territory of the world.

## *THE SUBPUBLISHING AGREEMENT*

The agreement whereby a writer, writer/performer, or U.S. music publisher grants the right to represent musical compositions in countries outside the United States is known as a "subpublishing agreement." Because of the ever-increasing importance of foreign countries to the earning power of U.S.-origi-nated compositions and the many positive and negative consequences that can occur owing to how one deals with the relationship created by this type of contract, it is a document that should not be taken lightly. With this in mind, the most important provisions of foreign subpublishing agreements are reviewed here.

### Term

Decades ago, it was not uncommon to commit an entire catalog to a foreign representative for the life of copyright of each composition controlled by the subpublishing agreement. Thus many standards are still currently controlled overseas by companies for the full term of copyright protection through agree-ments that were signed 60 or 70 years ago. The standard duration of subpublishing agreements in today's market, however, is normally from 3 to 5 years, with 3 years being the minimum accepted by many foreign royalty col-lection societies. The term of an agreement is one of the many negotiable items contained in any subpublishing agreement; variations of the term are based on the amount of advances given, retention rights for local cover recordings, the right to collect "pipeline" royalties (monies earned prior to the expiration of the term of the subpublishing agreement but not yet paid by the music user until after the end of the term), released-album guarantees, extensions if ad-vances have not been recouped, rules of local performing rights societies, suspensions due to breaches, and extensions based on the nonachievement of guaranteed earnings plateaus.

### Royalty Percentages

The compensation received by the foreign representative is always based on a percentage of the monies generated by the songs controlled by the agreement. For example, if a U.S. publisher enters into a subpublishing agreement with a foreign publisher for the territory of France, the French subpublisher would receive a percentage of the royalties earned by the compositions from CD and tape sales, television and radio broadcasts, advertising commercials, motion picture uses, and other exploitation that actually occurs in France. The standard fees fall within the 10% to 25% range, but if a writer/artist is a super-star with a worldwide audience and guaranteed international album and single releases, the fees may be as low as 5%, since the subpublisher's role is merely to administer and properly register the songs, issue licenses on the artist's record-ings, and collect monies generated by the artist. If a certain catalog is successful enough to generate uses and income by its very nature (e.g., that of a televi-sion- and movie-oriented company with successful worldwide series or films), the fees chargeable by subpublishers may be in the 10% to 15% range, since these catalogs virtually guarantee substantial television, theatrical, and soundtrack album income. If a catalog does not have such guaranteed income-producing music, however, the fees charged by a local subpublisher will usually be in the 15% to 25% range.

## Local Cover Recordings

If promotion of the U.S. catalog is one of the reasons for selecting a certain subpublisher, most agreements will provide that the subpublisher may retain a larger percentage of the income that is generated from a local recording or other use secured in the particular foreign country (a "cover record"). For example, if the fee on a CD that originated in the United States is 25%, that fee may be raised to between 30% and 40% for a single or album recorded and released by a foreign recording artist. Some agreements provide that if a local recording is secured, the subpublisher's percentage on all versions of the song contained on that cover record will be increased. Since this type of provision can be some-what unfair if the original U.S. version is a major hit, this is something that one must guard against; unless, the local version becomes a major hit in a foreign territory where the U.S. version is not generating substantial income already. If one signs with a worldwide company, it is often specified that if there are to be increased percentages for local cover records, such increases shall only apply to the territory in which the cover record is released (or becomes a hit, if appli-cable) and not to all countries controlled by the agreement.

## Increased Fees for Cover Records (Mechanical versus Performance Income)

Many of these "increased cover version percentage" clauses relate to me-chanical income only (i.e., the sale of CDs, tapes, and other audio recordings). This is a royalty-generating area that is fairly easy to monitor, since royalty statements from record labels indicate earnings by specific record number and recording artist. Some contracts, however, allow the subpublisher to take an increased fee on radio and television performance income generated by the cover version of the song as well—an inclusion that is extremely hard to monitor, since performing rights societies do not account separately for different broadcast versions of the same song. When performance income is included in the subpublisher's increased percentage on cover recordings, one formula that is used to compute the performance income due the cover record versus the original version is based on a ratio of the mechanical income derived from the cover record to that derived from the original. For example, if total mechanical royalties during a period amounted to $100,000, with the local cover record accounting for 40% of that amount, 40% of the performance income on all versions of the song would go to the cover record and 60% to noncover recordings. In such a case, if $100,000 in performance income was earned on a song and a subpublisher was entitled to retain 40% of cover record income and 25% of noncover income, its share of performance income would be computed as follows:

| *Performance Income* | *Subpublisher Fee* | *Monies to Subpublisher* | *Monies to U.S. Publisher* |
|---|---|---|---|
| $40,000 (40%) | 40% (cover record) | $16,000 | $24,000 |
| $60,000 (60%) | 25% (noncover) | $15,000 | $45,000 |

## Print

The U.S. publisher usually receives either 12.5% to 15% of the marked retail selling price on printed editions of all compositions or 50% of the subpublisher's net income. In many cases the print area is not a major source of income, but sizable monies can be earned from songwriter personality folios or specialized editions such as a folio from a hit album or theme-based packages such as a "best of Broadway" folio.

## Compositions Controlled by the Agreement

The compositions controlled by the agreement may comprise:

The entire catalog of a U.S. publisher
All songs written by a certain writer or writer/artist
Selected compositions
An individual hit song

*Entire Catalog.* In the event that an entire catalog of compositions is being represented, many agreements contain the following language:

> Publisher grants to Subpublisher the following rights in and to all the musical compositions listed on Schedule A as well as any and all musical compositions currently or hereafter owned or controlled by Publisher during the term of this Agreement

In effect, the U.S. publisher is assigning its entire catalog (including all future songs acquired during the term) to the subpublisher for representation in a specified foreign territory. In an age where publishing companies are bought and sold on an almost weekly basis, however, many publishers exclude major catalog acquisitions from the subpublishing agreement, since such large infusions of compositions (and the income generated therefrom) are usually not contemplated during the negotiations leading up to the signing of a foreign representation agreement. For example, if a U.S. company with 70,000 songs buys another publishing company with 50,000 songs, the subpublisher of the acquiring company would normally be required to renegotiate the terms of its agreement with the acquiring publisher if it wanted to represent the 50,000 songs that were bought. In most cases, however, a reasonable number of new songs are expected to be added every year to a catalog, and such compositions written in the normal course of business (e.g., by staff writers signed exclusively to the U.S. company) would normally be represented by the subpublisher at no further cost.

*Writer/Artist Compositions.* When dealing with the catalog of a writer/performer, the standard agreement will relate to all songs written by the writer/artist or all songs written by the artist that are contained on that artist's commercially released albums.

*Individual Hit Songs.* On occasion, if a song becomes a hit in the United States and there are no foreign commitments, a number of subpublishers will contact the U.S. publisher for representation of that 1 song exclusively. In virtually all such cases, advances will be paid for the rights being transferred, the amount dependent on whether the song is scheduled for release in a particular foreign territory, the past success of the recording artist in that country, the influence of the record company releasing the single or album in the foreign territory, and the adaptability of the song for local cover recordings and other local income-generating uses. If one enters into a number of these single-song deals with a number of different subpublishers for separate countries, it can get quite time consuming and burdensome trying to keep track of what each subpublisher in each foreign territory is doing with the song. It is often wise, therefore, if one has established a successful relationship with a particular foreign publishing company in the past, to use that firm for future single songs, or at least give that subpublisher the opportunity to match any advance or other terms offered by another company in the same territory.

## Advances

Since negotiation bidding in foreign countries can be very competitive depending on the catalog or songs being offered, advances are the norm if a catalog or song is likely to generate income in the subpublisher's territory. For example, monetary advances in the 6- or 7-digit range are not unusual depending on the catalog and territory involved. The amount of the advance being offered should not be the only factor considered in choosing a foreign representative, however, as the company's integrity, reputation for administration and promotion, royalty rates, retention rights, and duration of the agreement must all be factored in the "good deal" versus "bad deal" equation. Many writers or publishers will go with the offer that contains the largest up-front payment, but poor administration and inadequate promotion may ensure that the advance is the last money that will ever be seen. If a deal looks too good to be true, one should be wary; companies are not charities that give money away to worthy individuals or causes. And don't underestimate a firm just because it is in a foreign country or its representatives do not speak proper English. No subpublisher stays in business by making bad deals or losing money. In most cases, they know their market and how it works much better than you do.

## How Advances Are Paid

Depending on the type of subpublishing agreement being entered into, the advances payable to the U.S. writer or music publisher can be structured in a number of different ways, including:

A 1-time payment upon signing (e.g., $20,000 upon execution of the agreement).

Specified advances at the start of each 1-year period of the subpublishing agreement (e.g., $10,000 upon signing and $10,000 on each 1-year anniversary date of the term of the agreement).

Advances upon the release of each album featuring the writer/performer, with reductions depending on the number of songs controlled on each such album (e.g., $50,000 upon the commercial release of each album in the territory, provided the writer/artist has written or controls at least 80% of the compositions on the album). Under this type of guaranteed-percentage control clause, if the guarantee is not met, then the advance is reduced proportionately. For example, if the writer/artist guarantees that 100% of each album will be written by the artist and the subpublisher agrees to pay $100,000 for such an album, an album on which only 80% of the songs are written by the artist would receive a reduced advance of $80,000.00 ($100,000 x 80% = $80,000).

Advances upon recoupment of all or a specified percentage of the previous advance (e.g., $100,000 upon recoupment of 80% of the previous $100,000 advance).

Advances on local chart activity (e.g., $5,000 if a song reaches the Top 20 on the local trade paper charts, $10,000 if it achieves Top 10, and an additional $10,000 if the song becomes #1). Advances in this area are predicated usually on 100% control of a particular song, with pro rata reductions in the event that there are co-writers whose share is not controlled by the subpublishing agreement.

Advances based on a company's acquisition of other U.S. catalogs (e.g., a mutually agreeable advance in the event that the U.S. publisher acquires a major company for representation).

Advances based on actual earnings in the foreign territory (e.g., in the event that $50,000 is earned during the initial 1-year period of the term, an additional advance of $50,000 will be paid to the U.S. publisher).

## Information That Must Be Supplied to the Foreign Representative

Certain basics must be adhered to concerning the type of information that should be supplied to one's subpublisher to ensure that proper registration can be made, licenses issued, and monies collected for uses of the songs controlled by the subpublishing agreement. Foremost is correct information as to the title of the composition; the songwriter's identity, plus authorship percentages if there are co-writers; performance rights affiliation of the songwriters and music publishers; and the publisher's control percentages if there are more than 1 copyright owner or administrator. For example, if you are a music publisher and you own only 33⅓% of a particular song because 2 other songwriters have collaborated with your writer (both of whom are signed to different publishers), it is vital that the foreign representative be given all the facts. If the basics are not provided to one's subpublisher in a correct format, there will be no guarantee that foreign earnings will be remitted for uses outside the United States. And even if those earnings are eventually remitted after mistakes have been rectified and proper identification has occurred, delays may have sapped a good portion of the interest or other investment income that could have been achieved had the royalties been transmitted and received in a timely manner.

In addition to the creation and ownership information referred to above, the U.S. music publisher or other representative should submit the following to the foreign subpublisher:

All record and release information on the compositions so that mechanical royalties and performance royalties can be collected for the compositions that have been commercially released in the territory. This information should include the date of the recording's initial release in the United States, release information in other territories, and record label identification, as well as the title of the album, album number, configuration information, and the recording artist's identity.

Copies of recordings released on major labels that are likely to be released in foreign territories. It is advisable to send one's subpublisher at least 1 copy of each recording released in the United States that contains a composition controlled by the subpublishing agreement. Because of the expense involved, however, this many times is not done.

If the songs have appeared in any U.S.-produced television series or motion picture, copies of the music cue sheets prepared by the producer of the series or motion picture must be sent to the subpublisher for registration with the local performing rights society. If this is not done, performance royalties due from television broadcasts or motion picture theater showings are likely to be either delayed or lost forever.

Certain foreign territories need lead sheets and lyric sheets of the compositions to be able to make effective registrations with their local collection societies. If published sheet music of a composition is available, it should be sent to the foreign subpublisher.

## At-Source Royalty Payments

A number of subpublishing agreements contain what is referred to as "at source" royalty language. This means that there will be no extra charges or deductions from royalties passing from one foreign territory to another before being remitted to the United States.

An example of such language is as follows:

All royalties payable shall be based on gross income received at the source and shall not in any way be reduced by any charges including, but not limited to, any sublicensees granted by Subpublisher except only for:

(i) Those fees and commissions paid by the Subpublisher to the performing rights societies, mechanical license societies and other collection agents in the territory; and

(ii) Payments made by the Subpublisher for any "value-added" taxes and other taxes, if any, required to be deducted in the territory.

The inclusion of this language will prevent a foreign company from double deducting its fees on monies earned in portions of the territory covered. For example, if an agreement covers the separate countries of Germany, Austria, and Switzerland, with all monies remitted to the United States by the German office of a subpublisher, such language will prevent the German affiliate from deducting fees that may have already been deducted by the Austrian or Swiss affiliate that actually collected the monies. Without such an "at source" provision, the

Austrian company could take its 20% and forward 80% to the German office, which in turn might deduct an additional 20% from the 80% before remitting the remainder to the U.S. publisher. Under such a system, the U.S. publisher would receive 64% of the monies earned in Austria (e.g., $100 x 80% = $80 x 80% = $64) rather than the 80% that it should have received under an 80/20 agreement with "at source" language.

Another value of such an "at source" provision is that it will dictate the maximum terms of any agreements between U.S. companies with foreign branch offices or wholly owned affiliates in other countries and ensure that contracts between such related companies in foreign territories are at an "arm's-length" basis. For example, if one signs an 80/20 "at source" worldwide subpublishing agreement with a U.S. company that has 75/25 subpublishing agreements with its foreign affiliates, 80% of the monies earned in a foreign country would be remitted to the U.S. regardless of the foreign affiliate's entitlement to a 25% share according to its contract with the U.S.-based parent company.

## Rights Granted to the Foreign Representative

The U.S. writer or publisher will, in most cases, grant the following rights in and to the musical compositions to the subpublisher:

*Mechanical Rights.*   The right to issue mechanical licenses and collect royalties for the manufacture and distribution of records, tapes, CDs, and other audio recordings is always granted to the foreign representative. If these rights are not given to a local representative, mechanical royalties will many times be remitted by the local mechanical collection society to the Harry Fox Agency in New York for distribution to its publisher members.

*Performance Rights.*   The local foreign representative is given the right to register the songs with the performance rights society in the territory and collect the publisher's share of income earned by performances of the songs on radio and television as well as in hotels, restaurants, discos, elevators, live concerts, and motion picture theaters. The writer's share of that performance money, however, is remitted by each local society directly to ASCAP, BMI, or SESAC (depending on the writer's U.S. affiliation) and is not paid to the foreign subpublisher. ASCAP, BMI, or SESAC, in turn, will remit the songwriter monies directly to the writer in each organization's foreign royalty distributions.

If a publisher does not have a representative in a foreign territory collecting its performance income, the publisher's share of any foreign earnings is forwarded directly to ASCAP, BMI, or SESAC in the United States for distribution. A U.S. publisher that does not have a foreign representative registering songs and collecting monies in its territory, though, takes an unwise risk that all monies earned in a foreign country will be remitted to the U.S. The foreign market is complicated and intricate, and the only way for a company to ensure that monies are being handled and accounted for properly is to have someone in a foreign country looking after its affairs.

## *Audiovisual Rights*

TELEVISION AND MOTION PICTURES. The U.S. publisher normally gives the foreign representative the right to issue synchronization rights to include songs in television shows and motion pictures that originate or are filmed or produced in the specific territory controlled by the subpublisher. For example, the subpublisher in Germany usually is able to issue a synchronization license for the use of a composition in a motion picture or television program produced in Germany but will not be able to issue a license for a film or television program produced in the United States or any other country outside of Germany.

VIDEO CASSETTES AND DVDs. Whether or not to grant home video rights to the subpublisher for projects produced outside the foreign territory represented by the subpublisher but distributed within that territory is a major decision that must be faced by the U.S. publisher. As for motion pictures produced in the United States, the film producer will almost always demand that the U.S. publisher grant home video rights on a worldwide basis. Under such a grant, all monies for sales of videos in any foreign country would be paid to the U.S. publisher and not to the foreign representative in the country of sale. Because these worldwide grants are a fact of life in the U.S., video rights for motion pictures are normally excluded from the rights granted to the subpublisher. As with motion pictures, most producers of U.S. television series do not want to pay each foreign subpublisher royalties for video sales in foreign countries and demand worldwide licenses—a 1-time buy-out fee for all home video sales, a per-cassette penny royalty, or a rollover advance. The subpublisher is usually given the right to negotiate home video licenses for audiovisual projects produced in the foreign territory, at least with respect to sales in that particular territory.

RECORDING ARTIST VIDEOS. Since many of the songs on music videos are written or controlled by the recording artist, the record company will virtually always have a provision that grants it the worldwide right to manufacture and distribute short or long home video versions of the artist's performances. As for songs written by outside writers, the record company will have to negotiate a separate agreement with the publisher of each song, with, in most cases, a worldwide license granted on a per-cassette royalty or buy-out basis. As in the film area, it is rare that a subpublisher would be allowed to negotiate a separate video license for this product for sales in its territory.

COMMERCIALS. Occasionally the right to include a song as part of a commercial produced and broadcast in a foreign territory is given to the subpublisher, but many times such a right is retained by the U.S. publisher. If this right is granted to the subpublisher, it is usually conditional upon the subpublisher's receiving approval for each particular request (usually after having sent the U.S. publisher all details concerning the use including the name of the product, type of campaign, duration of license, and whether the lyrics will be changed). And even in cases where the subpublisher has total control over the granting of a commercial license, these rights will still be subject to any specific restrictions contained in the underlying songwriter's contract under which the U.S. publisher secured its rights.

PRINT. The right to include the songs in folios or to manufacture and distribute sheet music is virtually always included in the rights being granted.

## Rights Reserved by the U.S. Publisher

Depending on the bargaining power of the parties, it is not uncommon for the U.S. publisher or writer to exclude the following areas from the rights given to the foreign subpublisher:

Dramatic or literary rights (e.g., motion pictures, television shows, or books based on the story line of the song or using characters created by the writer and appearing in the song)
Commercials, political campaign uses, and endorsements
Grand rights (the right to use a song in a stage musical or live theatrical drama)
Ownership of the copyright
All other rights that are not specifically granted by the terms of the subpublishing agreement

## Royalty Payment Dates and Audit Rights

As in almost all publishing agreements, royalties will normally be accounted for twice a year, with semiannual payments and statements sent to the U.S. music publisher between 45 and 90 days after December 31 and June 30 of each year. On occasion, a subpublisher will be able to pay on a quarterly basis. The terms and conditions pertaining to audit rights are similar to those contained in U.S. publishing agreements (at least 30 days' notice, conduct of the audit being during normal business hours, restrictions on how many times one can audit, etc.).

## Retention Rights

Most foreign subpublishers will try to provide that, regardless of the termination of the agreement, they will retain some or all of the following rights for a period of time:

*Pipeline Monies.*   This right enables the subpublisher to collect monies that have been earned during the term of the agreement but not yet received at the time the agreement expires. For example, if the expiration or termination date is June 30 and a hit record comes out in May, the record sales and performance royalties will not be paid until long after the June 30 date. The subpublisher will want to collect and take its fee on all activity that occurred during its period of representation. This negotiable item is usually conceded by the U.S. publisher, especially if the subpublisher has not been able to collect monies earned prior to its representation because a prior subpublisher had similar retention rights. In addition, if large advances have been paid to the U.S. publisher, the subpublisher will many times be given the right to collect such accrued earnings if the advance has not been recouped. If, however, no advances have been paid, there may be a total cutoff of all rights upon expiration of the agreement.

If retention of such so-called pipeline monies is granted to a subpublisher, a time limit on such rights (such as 6 to 18 months) is often demanded by the U.S. publisher to prevent a pipeline collection period from being entirely open ended. Additionally, guarantees that the terminated subpublisher will not have administration rights during the collection period ensure that the new foreign representative will have all necessary rights to represent the song or songs. In another variation of the right to pipeline money, all collection rights are terminated, but the new subpublisher must pay the prior representative its contractual fee (e.g., 10% to 25%) for all such monies earned during the prior term but not paid until after expiration of the agreement. Since the new subpublisher is doing accounting and other administrative work under such a scenario but paying the full subpublisher's fee to another party, the U.S. publisher may have to give its new representative an additional percentage (e.g., 5% to 10%) as compensation, which will reduce the monies being remitted to the United States.

*Retention Rights If Advances Are Unrecouped.*   If advances paid to the U.S. publisher have not been recouped, the foreign subpublisher may have the right to extend the agreement for a specified period of time, thus giving it a better opportunity to recover its advances. It is advisable for the U.S. publisher to place a time limit on such retention of the catalog, as it would be very unwise to leave such rights open ended. If such an extension is necessary, it is preferable for the U.S. publisher to provide for an additional retention period only if the foreign representative has not recouped a specified percentage of all advances, such as 75% to 90% rather than 100% of all past advances. In addition, such recoupment and extension clauses are often based on monies earned but not yet paid prior to the termination date, as good-faith estimates can be made as to the amount of money that is in the pipeline.

*Retention Rights on Guaranteed Albums.*   If advances are paid upon the release of albums (in the case of a writer/performer), the subpublisher will normally have retention rights to the songs on any such album that is released in the last 6 months or 1 year of the agreement. Such a provision is fair, because royalties generated by the album will not be received by the subpublisher until 4 to 9 months after chart activity. Thus it is reasonable, if the subpublisher has paid an advance for it, to retain the right to receive earnings derived from its use. After all, if an album is released 1 day before the expiration of the subpublishing agreement and an advance is paid upon such release, the foreign representative will have no way to recoup its money unless the contract is extended for the songs on that album.

*Retention on Local Cover Records.* In many cases, the subpublisher will retain the right to administer a composition if a local cover record has been released during the term of the agreement. The same applies to other uses (e.g., local film and television uses) generated by the promotion efforts of the foreign subpublisher. There are many variations on this theme such as retention only if the cover record becomes a hit, reaches a certain trade paper chart position, earns in excess of a certain amount of money, or is actually secured by the subpublisher (rather than a "fall in" without any effort), with the usual retention period being from 1 to 3 years either after release of the record or the termination of the agreement.

For example, one such clause might read:

> With respect to any Composition which is embodied on an "A" side of a single cover record which attains a chart position of 40 or better in the official French singles chart during the term hereof, Subpublisher shall retain its rights to said Composition for an additional one (1) year period after expiration of the term.

---

## FOREIGN PERFORMING RIGHTS SOCIETIES

All major countries have a performing right society that licenses the copyrighted works of its own nationals as well as U.S. writers and publishers. A number of these societies also administer the right in certain other countries and territories where no local society exists. As many U.S. writers and publishers receive the majority of their income from foreign sources, Table 9.1 lists the primary societies of the world. Each of these societies has its own rules and procedures for the distribution of money to its own members as well as to foreign societies. Some of these rules are similar to those in the United States; others are very different.

### Organization and Distribution Rules

A look at 3 English-speaking societies should be of help in understanding the royalties that come to writers and publishers from foreign countries. PRS

TABLE **9.1**   Foreign Performing Right Societies (Partial List)

| | |
|---|---|
| Algeria (ONDA) | Korea (KOMCA) |
| Argentina (SADAIC) | Malaysia (MACP) |
| Australia (APRA) | Mexico (SACM) |
| Austria (AKM) | Netherlands (BUMA) |
| Belgium (SABAM) | Nigeria (MCSN) |
| Bolivia (SOBODAYCOM) | Norway (TONO) |
| Brazil (UBC/SICAM) | Paraguay (APA) |
| Bulgaria (JUSAUTOR) | Peru (APDAYC/SPAC) |
| Canada (SOCAN) | Philippines (FILSCAP) |
| China (MCSC) | Poland (ZAIKS) |
| Chile (SCD) | Portugal (SPA) |
| Costa Rica (ACAM) | Russia (RAO) |
| Czech Republic (OSA) | Singapore (COMPASS) |
| Denmark (KODA) | Slovakia (SOZA) |
| Britian (PRS) | South Africa (SAMRO) |
| Finland (TEOSTO) | South Korea (KOMCA) |
| France (SACEM) | Spain (SGAE) |
| Germany (GEMA) | Sri Lanka (SLPRS) |
| Greece (AEPI) | Sweden (STIM) |
| Hong Kong (CASH) | Switzerland (SUISA) |
| Hungary (ARTISJUS) | Trinidad & Tobago (COTT) |
| Iceland (STEF) | Turkey (MESAM) |
| India (IPRS) | Uruguay (AGADU) |
| Ireland (IMRO) | Venezuela (SACVEN) |
| Israel (ACUM) | Yugoslavia (SOKOJ) |
| Italy (SIAE) | Zimbabwe (ZIMRA) |
| Japan (JASRAC) | |

administers the right in Great Britain as well as other overseas territories, with SOCAN covering Canada and APRA covering Australia and New Zealand.

All of these societies are governed by a board of directors consisting of writers and publishers elected by the membership, and pay out all license fees collected after expenses of the operation are deducted. In all cases, separate pools of license fees are set up from each licensed area for distribution to writers and publishers who have performances in each area, with the payment split allocated 50-50. Distributions are made quarterly by SOCAN and PRS, with APRA distributing semiannually (in some cases, quarterly or monthly), and all use a combination of census and sample surveys of users for distribution purposes. All these societies make live performance (concert) and movie theater distributions.

The distribution rules for each society are precise, with no preset fees or minimum amounts in any payment formula. In the case of APRA and SOCAN, compositions generate performance credits, with PRS allocating points to performed works. For example, SOCAN gives 1 credit on television for each second of duration of feature music, with theme and dramatic music receiving a percentage of the feature credit for each second of duration. There is no payment for jingles, and a time-of-day factor (performances between 2:00 a.m. and 5:59 a.m.) reduces the credits for all works. All stations are weighted, for value purposes, in terms of their license fees to SOCAN. APRA also gives 1 full credit to feature music for each second of duration on television, with themes, background music, and commercials paid at 75%, 50%, and 7.5% of a full credit per second of duration, respectively. APRA also has time-of-day factors, with evenings (6–10:30 P.M.) at 100% crediting, mornings, afternoons, and late night at 30% (6 A.M.–6 P.M.; 10:30 P.M.–midnight), and midnight to 6:00 a.m. at 10%. PRS allocates its performance points primarily on duration with no time of day television factors. All 3 societies divide the number of credits or points in each area by the distributable income to arrive at the value of a performance.

## MECHANICAL ROYALTIES

As in the United States and Canada, mechanical royalties are payable for the distribution of audio recordings in foreign countries. As opposed to the United States and Canada, where the rate is expressed as a penny rate, the mechanical royalty provisions in other territories are usually expressed as a percentage of either the retail selling price (RSP) or the published price to the dealer (PPD). Under such formulas, all compositions on a particular album or other recording share in the aggregate royalties calculated under the percentage computation. Table 9.2 provides information on how mechanical royalties are arrived at in selected foreign territories.

TABLE **9.2**  Foreign Mechanical Royalty Rates

| *Country* | *Mechanical Rate* |
|---|---|
| United Kingdom | 8.5% PPD |
| Japan | 6.0% RSP |
| Austria, Belgium, Denmark, France, Germany Italy, Netherlands, Norway, Spain, Sweden, Switzerland | 9.009% PPD |
| Australia | 8.7% PPD |
| Canada* | 7.7¢ or 1.54¢ per minute after 5 minutes |

*rate currently in negotiation

There are mechanical right societies in virtually all territories that license recordings and collect income therefrom. Table 9.3 identifies some of those organizations and the territories of representation.

TABLE **9.3**   Foreign Mechanical Right Societies

| Society | Territory |
| --- | --- |
| AMCOS | Australia |
| SABAM | Belgium |
| CMRRA | Canada |
| SODRAC | Canada |
| NCB | Denmark, Finland, Sweden and Norway |
| GEMA | Germany |
| SDRM | France |
| JASRAC | Japan |
| SIAE | Italy |
| STEMRA | Netherlands |
| SGAE | Spain |
| SUISA | Switzerland |
| MCPS | United Kingdom |

Unlike the U.S., where the performing right society and the mechanical right society are separate entities, in many countries the performing right society is also the mechanical right society (e.g., SACEM, GEMA, etc.).

Discussions are taking place between the international mechanical rights society association BIEM and the international record industry association IFPI concerning whether mechanical royalties in Europe should be based on a percentage of the actual realized price (ARP) of recordings rather than the current published price to dealer (PPD).

## *RINGTONES*

Though the Internet is not a real source of income outside the U.S., mobile phone ringtones are. The MPRT rates charged by the societies are usually a percentage of subscriber revenue (e.g., 10%, 12%, etc.) and are split many times between performing and mechanical rights (e.g., 25% performance and 75% mechanical for downloads or two-thirds performance and one-third mechanical for streams) and in other cases licensed separately. These splits could be a guide to the future rates for regular Internet downloads and streams.

# Music, Money, and the Buying and Selling of Songs

BMG AND SONY MUSIC ANNOUNCE MERGER

WARNER MUSIC GROUP SOLD FOR $2.6 BILLION

AOL AND TIME WARNER MERGE

UNIVERSAL BUYS POLYGRAM

WARNER BROS. BUYS OUT THE 500,000-
SONG CHAPPELL MUSIC CATALOG FOR $250 MILLION

POLYGRAM ACQUIRES THE 90,000-SONG WELK, ISLAND,
DICK JAMES, AND CEDARWOOD MUSIC CATALOGS

EMI MUSIC PUBLISHING WITH ITS 300,000 COPYRIGHTS
PURCHASES THE 250,000 SBK–UNITED ARTISTS–
CBS CATALOG FOR $337 MILLION

MUSIC PUBLISHING BECOMES THE DARLING OF WALL STREET

PAUL MCCARTNEY BUYS SOME OF BROADWAY'S BEST

MICHAEL JACKSON ACQUIRES
THE BEATLES' CATALOG

As the continuing emergence of new technology enlarges the boundaries of the entertainment industry, the ownership of musical compositions has become more and more valuable not only to the major conglomerates but also to any company creating programming for the general public. Hit songs and film and television scores earn increasingly large amounts of money from their use on CDs and cassettes; in audiovisual projects such as motion pictures, television series, DVD, video cassettes, and laser discs; royalty bearing downloads; and in an unlimited number of other entertainment-related distribution vehicles—print, karaoke, interactive media, Broadway, off-Broadway, regional theater, computer games, video jukeboxes, commercials, music boxes, lyric reprints in novels and nonfiction books, and so on. With all this activity, the short-term and long-term impact resulting from the ownership of compositions on a writer's income or company's bottom line can be substantial.

This chapter reveals the inside information on how these acquisition and sale agreements are structured, how the dollar multiple used in the final purchase price of buying a song or catalog of songs is arrived at, how a presentation to a buyer should be structured, where the major danger points in any purchase-and-sale negotiations are, and what areas the buyer will look at to determine whether or not to acquire a catalog at the asking price. Whether the seller is a songwriter with 1 hit song or a publishing company with hundreds of thousands of copyrights, and whether the buyer is a publishing company, investment firm, or successful recording artist, this chapter details how the deals are made.

## OVERVIEW

When buying or selling music publishing catalogs, as in any acquisition, a number of areas must be analyzed before closing the sale. First, we will look at a few of the basic concepts.

## Purchase of Assets

In the majority of acquisitions, the buyer acquires only the assets of the seller and not the corporation or other legal entity that owns the musical compositions. The right to use the music publisher's name or names is virtually always transferred to the buyer, and the legal entity is usually retained or dissolved by the seller. In cases where that does not occur, there normally is a restriction on the use of the name by the seller for a specified period of time; for example, the selling company may agree not to use its publishing company name for 5 years from the date the compositions are sold. On occasion, the buyer will actually use the prior name as representative of the compositions being acquired (especially if there is substantial goodwill involved or the name has an established worldwide identity) through the use of a "doing business as" designation, but in most cases the former name will be retired and all songs will be transferred into the publishing affiliates of the acquiring entity.

## The Purchase Price

The actual purchase price of the acquisition is almost always based on a multiple of the average annual net earnings of the selling company over the most recent 3 to 5 fiscal or calendar years. For example, if an acquisition occurs in 2004, it would normally be based on a multiple of the net income for either the period 2001–03 or 1999–03. In many respects, taking the 5-year basis is safer for the buyer, since the longer the period considered, the less likely it is for an isolated event (such as from a 1-time chart record, audit recovery, litigation settlement, or major commercial use) to have a disproportionate effect on the overall net income. A 3-year period can be acceptable, however, if the buyer is able to discount such income fluctuations. Occasionally, a buyer may also be offered the possibility of acquiring all or a portion of the publishing rights to a catalog with a very limited or no earnings history (as in the case of a new recording artist/songwriter with a current album in the Top 10 and a #1 single); instead of using past earnings as a guideline, the buyer will have to predict future earnings on the chart activity and also project earnings on future not-yet-released albums and singles—a somewhat tricky proposition, even with experience.

## Calculation of Net Income (Cash vs. Accrual Basis)

The "net income" of a catalog (which is the basis of the purchase price computations) is virtually always defined as gross royalty income received by the selling company less all royalties payable to songwriters and other third parties. Two methods are used to calculate the net income: the cash basis and the accrual basis. Under the cash basis formula, the buyer takes the gross royalty income received by the seller during a particular period and deducts the amount of songwriter and other third-party royalties actually paid out during that period. For example, if $7 million was received in 2003 and $2,500,000 was paid to songwriters and other royalty participants in that year, the net income would be $4,500,000.

The more reliable method, however, and the one that gives the buyer a truer reflection of the worth of a publishing catalog, is the accrual basis of net income computation. Under this method, the buyer takes the gross earnings received during a year and deducts the income actually paid to songwriters and other third-party royalty participants during that year, plus royalties that will be paid out in the future from that income. For example, publishers normally pay songwriters their royalties for income received between January 1 and June 30 of each year within 45 to 90 days after June 30 (from August 15 to September 30). Royalties payable to the songwriters on income received during the July 1 through December 31 period, however, would be paid out between February 15 and March 31 of the next year. Under the cash method, the royalties payable from the July 1 through December 31 period would not be reflected in the calculation of net income for the year being considered, since they would be payable on a date outside that period. What the buyer would be getting by this method is a computation based on income received during a specified year, less the royalties payable from income received from a prior year (e.g., songwriter royalties payable from July 1 through December 31 of the previous year), plus the royalties that were actually paid out for income received during the first 6 months of the year being considered. Under the cash net income basis, the seller could have a poor income period for the final 6 months of 1 year and a very successful succeeding year, and the resulting net income for the successful year would look artificially high, because the buyer would be deducting royalties paid from a low-income period (the last 6 months of the prior year) and only 1 royalty payment from the first 6 months of the successful year. The accrual basis, by taking into account the gross income received less the royalties actually paid or due to be paid on that income, will always give a more realistic view of what a catalog is actually worth during a particular year. The 5-year net income figures may look as follows:

| Year | Gross Income | Less Royalties Paid or Due | = Net Income |
|---|---|---|---|
| 1999 | $10,000,000 | $ 4,000,000 | $ 6,000,000 |
| 2000 | 8,000,000 | 3,500,000 | 4,500,000 |
| 2001 | 11,000,000 | 5,000,000 | 6,000,000 |
| 2002 | 12,000,000 | 5,500,000 | 6,500,000 |
| 2003 | 14,000,000 | 6,000,000 | 8,000,000 |
| Totals | $55,000,000 | $24,000,000 | $31,000,000 |
| | $31,000,000 | Aggregate 5-year net income | |
| | ÷ 5 | Number of years considered | |
| | $ 6,200,000 | Average annual net income | |

## Salaries and Other Costs of Doing Business

In most cases when an acquisition is being contemplated by an existing music publisher, the costs of running the catalog (salaries of employees, rent, lease commitments on the premises, postage meters, photocopying, microfilm copying, document retrieval systems, executive contracts and golden-parachute clauses, expense accounts, copyright registration fees, demonstration recording sessions, subscriptions, etc.) are usually not considered, because most large publishers can incorporate an acquired catalog into their existing system without major cost additions. Granted, there are increased costs for the acquiring party if the catalog being bought is a large one, but with the advent of computers, and dependent on the quality and experience of the personnel currently employed by the buyer, the extra costs may not be substantial. If the acquiring company is not a functioning music publisher or if it only has a small staff, which is unable to handle a large catalog, the extra costs related to the acquisition and future management of the company (especially if the buyer wants to hire all or some of the seller's personnel and absorb the salary and social costs related thereto) are many times considered in the computation of the purchase price. Under these circumstances, the seller may reject such factors, but they are something that the buyer may consider when formulating its final offer.

## Purchase Price Multiples

Once an average annual net income figure is calculated, the buyer and seller will negotiate a multiple to be placed on such earnings to arrive at a final purchase price. For example, if a multiple of 5 were used in the above illustration, the price would be $31 million, and if a multiple of 10 were used, the acquisition would cost $62 million. In recent years, multiples have been in the 8–18 range, but can be higher or lower depending on a number of factors, including the nature of the rights being acquired, the remaining copyright life of the compositions being purchased, the costs of borrowing the money related to the acquisition, the loss of income from other investment areas in which the purchase price could have been used, anticipated return on capital, the need of the seller to dispose of its publishing assets, the value of owning musical compositions to other divisions of the buyer, whether the buyer has a network of wholly owned or affiliated publishing companies around the world into which the catalog can be integrated, the relative worth of the U.S. dollar to foreign currency (which can either lower or raise future receipts), the current state of the industry, the existence of new technologies that may enhance the use of the catalog, whether the catalog represents a broad range of musical compositions or has a concentration in only 1 type of music, whether there are other bidders, and the anticipated ability of the buyer to promote the catalog in new areas effectively, along with the additional monetary returns projected therefrom.

## *THE PROSPECTUS: ITS FORM AND CONTENT*

The prospectus is the initial document forwarded to all potential buyers when a music publishing company or catalog of songs is up for sale. The document can range in length from 3 to 5 pages for a small catalog with few compositions to a small book of 200–400 pages or more for a major publishing operation. Though varying greatly in length as well as degree of preparation and skill, the basic information contained in this document is similar for all sales, and the prospectus is normally sent only to a limited number of potential buyers—those entities that are known to be seriously interested and capable of financing the acquisition price. A confidentiality letter that mandates that any information disclosed is not be communicated to outside parties or used against the selling company is also usually sent to each prospective purchaser for signature prior to forwarding the prospectus for review.

### Business Summary

The first item in the prospectus is a brief history of the company being sold and its place within the entertainment industry. Items discussed include a company's prior acquisitions of other publishing companies, principal places of business, number of employees, and the total number of compositions (both copyrighted and uncopyrighted) controlled by the company. If the list of prospective buyers includes nonmusic entities, a brief primer on the main sources of music publishing income will also be given.

### Financial Information

Income statements are given for the most recent 3- to 5-year period. In addition, annual projections for the future are sometimes provided, especially if there are current commitments or activity that will result in substantial future monies (e.g., if a publisher has a #1 song on the charts but has not yet been paid for CD and tape sales, downloads, or radio and television performances). The income statements list the gross revenues of the company, royalty or other contractual payments to third parties, advances and other costs, overhead, and net income (referred to as the "net publisher's share"). A more detailed revenue statement of the primary revenue-producing areas of performance rights payments, mechanical income, synchronization fees, print royalties, other miscellaneous fees, and foreign collections is also provided. The detailed area analysis lists specific dollars received by generic royalty source, as well as the percentage of the company's total income provided by each song revenue area.

| *Type of Revenue* | *2003 Revenues* | *% of Total* |
|---|---|---|
| Performance rights fees | $2,814,000 | 42.0 |
| Mechanical license fees | 1,608,000 | 24.0 |
| Synchronization fees | 234,500 | 3.5 |
| Print fees | 201,000 | 3.0 |
| Other fees | 33,500 | .5 |
| Foreign earnings | 1,809,000 | 27.0 |
| Total revenues | $6,700,000 | 100.0 |

## Listing of Top-Earning Compositions

A separate chart of the publishing company's top-earning songs is always included. The chart is usually compiled either as a listing of the top 25, 50, 100, or 500 songs in the catalog or by all songs earning in excess of a certain annual amount ($25,000, for instance). These charts will usually reflect each composition's earnings over a period of years in order to give the prospective buyer an impression of how the catalog has performed over the years. These composition listings include songs, television themes, and television scores.

## Net Income and Earnings History Charts

Although gross income figures are of interest to a prospective buyer, of utmost importance are the net income amounts. It is 1 thing to know how much in gross earnings is being generated by a catalog of songs, but without knowing how much money is payable to third parties from such income (e.g., songwriter royalties), it is impossible to determine what the catalog is really

Company Compositions (January 1, 2000–December 31, 2003)

| *Title* | *Revenues* |
|---|---|
| #1 (song) | $  749,321 |
| #2 (song) | 621,483 |
| #3 (TV series) | 368,501 |
| #4 (song) | 314,238 |
| #5 (feature films) | 219,452 |
| #6 through #48 (misc.) | 1,548,000 |
| #49 (song) | 28,556 |
| #50 (TV series) | 21,750 |
| 50-Song total: | $3,871,301 |

worth in net profit terms. In effect, a buyer is not only purchasing an income stream but, more important, a stated amount of money that is left over as pure profit after all royalty participants have been paid. Because of the importance of net income as opposed to gross income, the seller will always provide the buyer with summary charts for a number of recent years detailing gross income receipts, royalties that were payable from such receipts, and net income that remained after royalties were paid.

Depending on the sophistication of the seller's books and records as well as the time and effort expended in putting together the financial aspects of the prospectus, the net income charts can be presented in a number of formats. From the buyer's perspective, the more specific the information presented, the better. For example, if the seller is able to provide annual summaries of income by source (CD and tape sales, downloads, streams, public performance income, television and motion picture synchronization income, commercial fees, sheet music and folio revenues, etc.), separated into U.S.-based and foreign-generated income less songwriter royalties paid or payable from that income and with final net income figures on each category, the buyer will have an easier time digesting the numbers and formulating its offer, thus improving the chances of the negotiations being concluded quickly. The more information that is provided by the seller at the start of negotiations, the better it will be for all parties, since the more questions that are answered during the initial stages of negotiation, the more likely it will be that the talks will proceed smoothly. It is always better to give a potential buyer exactly what it needs up front rather than to provide incomplete information that will have to be filled in at a later date—a rule of thumb that should always be borne in mind when putting together any prospectus or catalog information package for prospective purchasers. An example of a 1-year income chart is set forth in Table 10.1.

This type of net income analysis should be prepared for each 1-year period being presented by the seller to the prospective buyer. The income charts can be very specific (e.g., a listing of the names of all record companies that have paid the seller any monies, rather than just 1 line that includes all aggregate record company monies), but regardless of the amount of detail provided, the charts represent the minimum amount of information that should be provided by the selling company to the prospective purchaser.

## Current Contracts

The prospectus will include summaries of all current contracts to which the selling company is a party, including all songwriter and recording artist agreements as well as all copublishing, income participation, or administration agreements with songwriters or other publishing companies. These contract summaries can prove invaluable to the prospective buyer, as they not only contain an overview of the seller's current business activities and com-

TABLE **10.1**   2003 Income Chart/Earnings History

A.   *United States*

| Source | Gross Receipts | Royalties | New Income |
|---|---|---|---|
| (1) Mechanicals (CD and tape sales) | $2,000,000 | $1,400,000 | $ 600,000 |
| (2) Synchronization (television, motion pictures, commercials) | 700,000 | 400,000 | 300,000 |
| (3) Performances (ASCAP, BMI, SESAC) | 1,200,000 | 200,000 | 1,000,000 |
| (4) Print | 140,000 | 75,000 | 65,000 |
| | $4,040,000 | $2,075,000 | $1,965,000 |

B.   *Foreign*

| Source | Gross Receipts | Royalties | Net Income |
|---|---|---|---|
| (1) Mechanical | $ 750,000 | $ 400,000 | $ 350,000 |
| (2) Synchronization | 100,000 | 60,000 | 40,000 |
| (3) Performances | 600,000 | 100,000 | 500,000 |
| (4) Print | 20,000 | 8,000 | 12,000 |
| | $1,470,000 | $ 568,000 | $ 902,000 |

C.   *Summary*

| Source | Gross Receipts | Royalties | Net Income |
|---|---|---|---|
| (1) Mechanicals | $2,750,000 | $1,800,000 | $ 950,000 |
| (2) Synchronization | 800,000 | 460,000 | 340,000 |
| (3) Performances | 1,800,000 | 300,000 | 1,500,000 |
| (4) Print | 160,000 | 83,000 | 77,000 |
| | $5,510,000 | $2,643,000 | $2,867,000 |

mitments but also can provide clues to future but currently unrecognized revenues.

## Foreign Subpublishing Agreements

The prospectus will include a listing of all agreements the company has entered into with foreign subpublishers. Foreign revenue sources include performance fees, synchronization and mechanical fees, print payments, and all other payments due the copyright owner. Information provided for each subpublishing agreement includes the name of the subpublisher, the duration of the agreement, the territories covered by the agreement, advances (if any), royalty rates, and accountings. Any special contractual provisions are also explained. For example, a representative schedule might look as follows:

| *Subpublisher* | *Territory* | *Term* | *Retention Rights* |
|---|---|---|---|
| (Name of company) | France | 3 Years (1/1/01–12/31/03) | None |
| (Name of company) | United Kingdom | 3 Years (7/1/02–6/30/05) | If a local cover recording is secured and reaches the Top 100 on the trade paper hit singles charts, the song will be retained until 6/30/07. |
| (Name of company) | Japan | 3 Years (4/1/02–3/31/05) | None |

## Future Commitments

The prospectus will also detail future financial commitments under existing agreements that will be assumed by the buyer if the acquisition is consummated. These may be installment payments due for prior acquisitions, weekly or monthly advances due songwriters currently under contract, and any number of other obligations required pursuant to the terms of the agreements being sold. A representative schedule follows:

| *Payee* | *Type of Agreement* | *Term* | *Advances Due* |
|---|---|---|---|
| (Name of songwriter) | Exclusive songwriter | 1 year plus two 1-year options (7/15/02–7/14/03, 7/15/03–7/14/04, 7/15/04–7/14/05) | Year 1: $3,000 monthly Year 2: $3,500 monthly Year 3: $4,000 monthly |
| (Name of songwriter/recording artist) | Exclusive songwriter/copublishing | 1 album plus 3 options for 3 additional albums, commencement date 3/1/03; 1 album released | $50,000 per year plus an additional $75,000 for each album recorded by the songwriter on a major record label containing at least 10 songs written by the songwriter |

## THE LETTER OF INTENT/SHORT-FORM COMMITMENT-TO-SELL AGREEMENT

Because formal acquisition agreements are quite lengthy and very time consuming to negotiate, many prospective buyers, after having reviewed the initial prospectus but before any due diligence investigations are commenced, will request that the seller sign a binding short-form agreement that will require it to sell the catalog (and guarantee that the buyer will acquire the catalog) provided certain terms and conditions are satisfied. These short-form commitment letters (which range from 5 or 6 pages excluding exhibits to over 20 pages) are essential for the prospective buyer, who may spend tens of thousands of dollars during its investigation of the assets being acquired, to ensure that the acquisition will be consummated. These short-form letters also afford the prospective buyer certain rights either to terminate the negotiations or to reduce the purchase price if certain elements are not what they were warranted to be (e.g., if the seller has substantially overstated its income, if certain litigation matters were not disclosed in the prospectus, if the terms of various songwriter agreements were misrepresented, if future outgoing advance commitments to songwriters have been understated, if the rights to certain important compositions have been or are being lost in the near future). They can also be very important for the selling company, as they provide security that a prospective buyer will not back out of the deal if all the information contained in the prospectus is correct.

Although these short-form commitment letters vary in length and in format, the following provisions are usually contained in all such documents:

### Description of Assets Being Sold

A general statement of what is being acquired (such as "all musical compositions currently owned by _____ Music") is always included. Any exceptions to the general statement (e.g., all songs written by a certain writer, any song that has not been recorded and released, any song that has not earned any income) will also be stated. If available, a list of the compositions being acquired will be attached as an exhibit to this commitment letter.

### Earnings History

An earnings history of the catalog (containing gross receipts, royalty obligations, and net income figures) will be attached as an exhibit, and the seller will warrant that such figures accurately reflect the income received from the songs being sold during the periods reflected.

### Purchase Price

The actual purchase price payable for the catalog (e.g., $45,000,000.00, $6,500,000.00, $350,000.00) will be referred to in the short-form agreement. In most cases, the actual net earnings multiple used by the buyer to arrive at the purchase price will also be included (e.g., 8 times the average annual net earnings) so that all parties know how the purchase price is being calculated.

*Payment of the Purchase Price.* The actual method of payment will be specified, whether it is a 1-time payment or an installment sale over a period of years (e.g., the total purchase price of $4,000,000.00 being payable upon full execution of the formal purchase agreement or $2,000,000.00 payable upon signing with $500,000.00 plus interest payable upon the 1st, 2nd, 3rd and 4th one year anniversaries of the signing of the agreement). Any "hold back" amounts that can be used by the buyer to satisfy any claims that might come into after the acquisition date will also be specified. For example, the contract might state that $1 million of the $4 million purchase price might be withheld for a period of 4 years to protect the purchaser from any claims that might be lodged against any of the compositions being sold.

*Reduction or Increase in the Purchase Price.* Since a buyer's interest in and commitment to pay a certain sum for a catalog is based on how much the various songs have earned in the past, should it be discovered that the income history has been overstated, the buyer will usually provide that it can either get out of the agreement or reduce the purchase price accordingly. For example, the buyer might include a provision that if the annual net income figures have been overstated by 2% (or any other percentage), it will have the option to cease negotiations and terminate the offer. In the alternative, the buyer may elect to proceed with the agreement at the same multiple, an approach that would ensure acquisition of the catalog but at a lower price. The seller, on the other hand, might demand that if its net income figures were inadvertently understated, the purchase price should be increased, an issue which should be addressed in the short-form commitment letter and not held for future discussion during the negotiations of the long-form, formal purchase agreement.

*Minimum and Maximum Purchase Price Options.* Occasionally, a seller may demand that if the purchase price falls below a certain stated amount because of adjustments in income figures resulting from the buyer's due diligence investigations, the sale agreement may, at the seller's election, not be consummated. The buyer, on the other hand, may demand that if adjustments in the seller's favor raise the purchase price to an amount in excess of the maximum figure that the buyer is willing to pay, the buyer can cancel the agreement.

## Warranties

Included in the short-form commitment letter are a wide range of warranties and representations by the seller, including statements that it owns the rights to the compositions, that they are freely assignable to the purchaser, that they do not infringe on any other compositions, that there are no "key man" clauses in any songwriter's contract that would force the buyer to hire certain employees of the seller in order to acquire the compositions, that the summary financial figures submitted represent actual earnings and do not include advances or other nonearned income, that the seller has paid proper royalties on all income received, and that, except as disclosed in the short-form agreement, there are no existing, pending, or threatened claims against the seller or any of the compositions being sold.

## Subpublishing Agreements

Attached as an exhibit to the commitment letter is a summary of all existing foreign subpublishing agreements, including information on the territories covered, the royalty percentage retained by the foreign publisher, the term of each agreement, and retention rights, as well as whether any advances were received or are due in the future.

## Income Cutoff Date

Since it is usually somewhat impractical to determine how long the buyer's various investigations of the assets being acquired will take and the length of time that will be expended in the negotiation of the long-form formal acquisition document, a specific cutoff of income date will be contained in the short-form agreement. In effect, the parties will agree to a specific date (usually at the end of a calendar quarter or semiannual period) on or after which the buyer will be entitled to all income receivable from the catalog. Under such a provision, any monies received prior to the cutoff date will remain the seller's property (subject to the payment of royalties to songwriters and other royalty participants), and any monies received on or after the cutoff date will be the property of the buyer (again subject to the payment of all royalty obligations related thereto). A sample clause might read:

> All royalties, income, or other earnings of any nature, kind, or description in respect of the Compositions received on or after January 1, 2004, regardless of when earned, shall be the sole and absolute property of the Buyer. If any such sums are received by the Seller or any of its affiliates on or after that date, they shall transmit the same immediately upon receipt to the Buyer.

## Definitive Closing Date

To prevent negotiations, investigations, and drafting of the formal purchase agreement from continuing for an unlimited period of time, the seller and buyer will normally agree on an outside closing date, the date that the final agreement is actually signed and the catalog of songs is transferred). If negotiations are still continuing as of that date, either party may have the right to terminate the agreement. In most cases, however, this right is never exercised, as an extension of time is usually agreed to; but it does put pressure on the parties to get things done as quickly as possible.

## INVESTIGATING THE ASSETS BEING ACQUIRED

After the potential buyer has reviewed the seller's prospectus, and usually after both parties have either entered into a short-form commitment letter or the prospective purchaser has signed a confidentiality letter, the buyer will conduct both a financial audit of the income figures and a legal inquiry into the assets being acquired. This "due diligence" investigation can take only a few days with respect to smaller catalogs and up to months when the seller is transferring substantial numbers of copyrights. Since the conduct of the buyer's due diligence investigation and the nature of what it uncovers is one of the most significant aspects of any acquisition (as the findings will not only determine the final purchase price but also whether or not the acquisition is consummated), the following sections review many of the areas of discovery.

### Financial Due Diligence

After analyzing the gross and net income summary sheets provided by the seller in its prospectus, the buyer's auditors will conduct a number of examinations to test not only the validity and accuracy of the figures represented but also to determine whether the seller's books and records were kept in conformance with generally accepted accounting practices. The auditors will examine actual royalty statements received from music users such as record companies, video distributors, and print companies; remittances from performing rights societies such as ASCAP and BMI, and the royalties that the seller has distributed to songwriters in conformance with the agreements by which it (or any predecessor-in-interest) acquired ownership in the compositions. In addition, inquiries will be made to determine whether correct exchange rates were used with respect to foreign income receipts, whether monetary advances were treated as earned income, whether there exist any unrecouped balances on advances received by the seller, whether income taxes were paid, whether the seller used an accrual or cash basis in matching costs with revenues on its income schedules, whether any extraordinary 1-time payments were included, and whether any income related to periods outside the years being used as the basis of the purchase price was received during and included in the basis period figures.

With this general overview, a number of the more important areas can now be reviewed in greater detail.

*Songwriter and Other Third-Party Royalty Obligations.*   Since all musical compositions have royalty obligations related to income received for their use, a primary concentration of any audit is to make sure that all songwriters were paid their appropriate share of royalties. For example, a songwriter is normally due 50% of all monies received from the sale of records, tapes, and CDs of his or her songs; 50% of all income received by the publisher from television, motion picture, and home video uses; a set penny rate for sheet music, and a percentage of the wholesale price of folios. In addition to songwriter obligations, there may be other royalty participants such as a successful songwriter's wholly owned publishing company that shares in all income receipts, a recording artist who may share in a portion of the income from a particular composition, another publisher that may have co-ownership rights, and so on, all of which must be analyzed and checked to determine whether such parties were paid proper remittances. Obviously, if net income is based on gross earnings less all royalties due on that income and the seller has incorrectly calculated its royalty obligations, the net income must be revised to reflect those inconsistencies and the purchase price adjusted accordingly. For example, in the event that the seller lists a song as having earned $100,000 in CD/tape mechanical royalties but has paid the songwriter only $40,000 as his or her 50% share, the net income on this song would be listed in the prospectus schedule as $60,000. Because of the mistake, the buyer would reduce the $60,000 to $50,000, as the songwriter should have been paid an extra $10,000. Thus, rather than the buyer's paying a purchase price multiple on an inflated net income figure (e.g., 8 x $60,000 = $480,000), the buyer would apply its multiple on the contractually correct figure (e.g., 8 x $50,000 = $400,000).

*Extraordinary Out-of-Period Audit Recoveries.*   In the normal course of business, audit recoveries will be received from record companies and other music users on a periodic basis. Such audits are a way of life and, as received by the seller, will be also received by the buyer. Since these normal audit recoveries, which always relate to monies that should have been paid in prior periods, are standard in the publishing business, most are treated as legitimate income received during the purchase price base period. In the case of substantial recoveries that relate to a number of out-of-period years, however, deletion of such income is usually demanded by the buyer. For example, if $50,000 from an audit was received in 2003 for record sales and income that should have been remitted in 1998 (a period not part of the base years on which the acquisition multiple is being applied), the buyer would naturally object to such receipts being included in the purchase price computations or, at least, request a discounting of such larger-than-usual audit recoveries.

*Special Performance Rights Distributions.*   For many decades, both ASCAP and BMI have distributed royalties over and above their normal quarterly remittances that reflected positive adjustments in past license fees paid by certain music broadcasters. These "special distributions," normally the result of retroactive settlements with a user or favorable court decisions regarding the past fees of a user, represent monies that should have been paid in the past. Since these monies are reflected on a music publisher's income reports during the year they are received (with no reference to when they should have been received), all or a portion of such special distribution income may relate to periods prior to the years on which the purchase price multiple is being applied. Considering that some of these distributions are substantial and can dramatically alter the price being paid for a catalog, this area represents a main focus of a buyer's financial due diligence game plan.

*Advances.*   Since all music publishing acquisitions are based on earnings, the financial due diligence investigation will concentrate a portion of its inquiries in discovering whether advances were received by the seller and treated as earnings in its prospectus. In the music industry, it is fairly common for a music publisher to receive an advance from a music user or other licensee, which can be recouped from royalties earned in the future. For example, if a subpublisher in Germany wants to represent a U.S. publisher's catalog in Germany, the amount of any advance being offered may be an important part of a U.S. publisher's agreeing to such representation. The due diligence investigation is designed to uncover the existence of such advances and determine what portion of any advances were earned back during the purchase price basis periods. Obviously, if an advance of $100,000 was received in 2003 and only $29,000 was actually earned in that year, the purchaser would want to apply the price multiple only on the $29,000 in earnings and not on the full $100,000. In addition, financial due diligence will also determine what portion of any advance remains unrecouped, since the buyer will not receive any income from the party that paid the advance until full recoupment has been achieved.

*Matching Income with Royalty Obligations.*   As previously discussed in the analysis of cash versus accrual basis accounting, one of the main examinations centers on the matching of income received during a particular year with the royalty obligations that are due on that income. For example, if $40,000 was received by the seller for CD sales of a specified composition, the buyer's auditors will review the royalty provisions of the underlying songwriter's agreement, determine what percentage of receipts should have been paid to the songwriter, and then match their conclusions with the amounts that the seller actually remitted to the writer. In the event of any discrepancy, an adjustment will be made in the seller's net income figures, which will then be reflected in the purchase price computation.

## Legal Due Diligence

In conjunction with the buyer's financial specialists, the buyer's attorneys will simultaneously conduct their own due diligence investigation of the rights being acquired. Considering the complexities of the music industry, the types of agreements entered into, and the domestic and foreign laws that control the rights of the parties in this area, legal due diligence is an extremely time-consuming matter that requires sophisticated expertise and is best left to seasoned professionals. Because of the size of many of the catalogs being purchased and the impossibility of checking all agreements on each of the songs being acquired within a limited amount of time, the primary focus of efforts is normally on the compositions that earn substantial amounts of money each year (the "top earners"), with a secondary focus on songs with moderate earnings and a test-basis focus on the remaining compositions.

Included in the legal due diligence investigation are a review and analysis of the copyright registrations of each composition; the underlying terms of the agreements through which rights were initially acquired from the songwriters or other copyright owners; the completeness of all song files; securement of renewal rights; validity of chain of title to the compositions; existence of any liens or mortgages; restrictions on licensing for certain media; pending, threatened, or existing litigation; the terms and duration of all license agreements and foreign subpublishing commitments; actual and possible reversion and termination rights in and to the compositions; royalty provisions of songwriter and other third-party income participation agreements; assignability of the compositions; existence of any "key man" clauses; and a wide range of other issues all related to ownership, duration of rights, impediments, restrictions, transferability, and future promotability of the compositions being acquired.

*Copyright Protection and Musical Compositions.* The 1909 Copyright Act, the 1976 Copyright Revision Act and the 1998 Sonny Bono Copyright Act form the basis of a music publisher's ownership and control of compositions as well as the duration of that ownership. Without knowing the basics of the 1909, 1976 and 1998 laws and what effect they have on a specific catalog, a prospective buyer could easily overpay or a seller undersell in any given purchase-and-sale transaction involving musical compositions.

Copyright Considerations in a Sale. In looking at a catalog, one has initially to determine the term of copyright years remaining on any given composition in the catalog. Most of the major acquisitions concluded over the past 10 years have involved publishing companies containing a combination of old copyrights (those written prior to January 1, 1978), new copyrights (those written on or after January 1, 1978), and works for hire (primarily film and television background music scores written during both periods). The 1909, 1976 and 1998 laws treat all of these works differently as to the duration of the "copyright monopoly." Although this area is a complex one, some basic rules should be borne in mind.

WORKS WRITTEN PRIOR TO JANUARY 1, 1978. Under the 1909 law, these compositions had a U.S. copyright life of 28 years from registration or publication, plus an additional 28 years of copyright protection if a renewal was applied for on a timely basis. Under the 1976 and then the 1998 law, any work still in its first term of copyright received a renewal term of an additional 67 years rather than 28 years. For works already in their renewal term, an additional 39 years of copyright protection was added by the new laws to the 56-year duration provided by the old law—in effect, giving songs 95 years of protection in the United States.

WORKS WRITTEN COMMENCING JANUARY 1, 1978. For compositions written on or subsequent to January 1, 1978, the duration of U.S. copyright protection lasts for 70 years after the death of the composer or author of a composition, a revision that brings domestic protection in line with the laws of many foreign countries.

WORKS MADE FOR HIRE. Most motion picture and television background music scores and themes are "works made for hire" and vest the copyright in the employer rather than the creator. A written agreement between the creator and the employer specifying that the work is a work made for hire is necessary. Under the 1998 law, the term of copyright for this type of work is 120 years from the writing of the composition or 95 years from its publication, whichever terminal date is earlier. The 1909 law treated these works similarly to all other music copyrights (28-year term plus 28-year renewal), with the exception that only the employer had the right to apply for the renewal.

UNCOPYRIGHTED AND UNPUBLISHED PRE-1978 WORKS. Under the 1998 law, if a composition was written prior to 1978 but was neither published nor registered for copyright before that date, the applicable term of copyright protection became the life of the writer plus 70 years, with a guarantee of at least 45 years of protection.

COUNTRIES OUTSIDE THE UNITED STATES. Pursuant to the laws of a majority of countries throughout the world, the term of copyright lasts for the life of the writer plus a minimum of 70 years, a factor that in many cases provides for identical copyright protection for compositions written on or after January 1, 1978, in countries outside the United States and in the United States.

*Copyright Searches.* So that the buyer knows exactly what has been registered in the U.S. Copyright Office on all important compositions, it may request a search of all copyright records that will provide a listing of all registrations, renewals, songwriter and copyright-owner information, assignments, conflicting claims, identity of assignors and assignees of rights, mortgages, liens, security interest agreements, notices of use, registration corrections or amendments, and any and all other documents that have been recorded and the dates thereof. Owing to the expense of such a procedure, the search is normally done on only the top-earning compositions, with test searches performed on certain selected compositions, but depending on a buyer's concerns or the lack of complete information contained in seller's files, searches may be done on substantial numbers of compositions in the catalog. Since the documents registered in the Copyright Office are the basis of the rights being assigned to a buyer and can have profound effects not only on the duration of rights and full enjoyment of such rights but also on a purchaser's ability to receive a fair return on its investment, inquiries in this area are of the utmost importance.

*Songwriter Agreements.* A review will be made of all underlying agreements whereby the seller or any predecessor-in-interest acquired the rights to the musical compositions being sold. In this regard, particular attention will be made to the provisions detailing the nature of the rights granted, the term of such rights, whether copyright renewal has been secured, restrictions on how a publisher can exploit the compositions, royalty participation, assignability of the rights, and advances that may be due. Since innumerable variations may be contained in songwriter agreements, nothing can be taken for granted even if the seller has warranted that all agreements are "form contracts." For example, one contract may provide that any assignment of rights be conditioned on the songwriter's approval or that any sale of a composition can be made only if it is part of a sale of substantially all of a publisher's assets; another might have restrictions as to how a song can be licensed; another may call for certain reversion rights if a recording is not secured within a specified period of time; and another may provide for certain restrictions on the fees chargeable by collection agents or foreign representatives.

*Subpublishing Agreements.* Since income from territories outside the United States can be substantial, the buyer will also analyze all of the seller's commitments in foreign territories so that a determination can be made as to the availability of exploitation rights in and to the catalog overseas. For example, the buyer will produce a country-by-country schedule that includes the term of each agreement, whether there are any retention rights after expiration of the contract term, royalty percentages retained by the subpublisher, and any other clauses that may affect the rights of the buyer with respect to future exploitation of the acquired assets and the ability to change representatives in a particular territory.

*Future Obligations.* The legal due diligence inquiry will also concentrate on all existing agreements that have some form of future commitment that will be assumed by the buyer. For example, if the seller has a large number of songwriters under contract to whom weekly, monthly, or yearly advances are due, the seller needs to know the exact nature of such obligations in order to formulate effectively its acquisition price and the terms related thereto.

*Guaranteed Future Income Commitments.* Another reason for an exhaustive review of all of the seller's current agreements is to determine the nature and amount of income that may be due the seller after the acquisition has been finalized. For example, there may be guaranteed advances from foreign subpublishers, option payments due from advertising agencies for the use of songs in commercials, predetermined fees for home video releases after certain sales plateaus have been achieved, guaranteed performance income from television synchronization licenses, forthcoming tape or CD releases of songs in the catalog, motion picture and television series commitments, and any number of other income-generating guarantees including litigation that will benefit the buyer after control of the catalog has been assumed.

*Expiring Agreements, Reversions, and Terminations.* One of the most vital inquiries involved in any purchase-and-sale agreement has to do with the analysis of all agreements and related compositions that generated income during the base period years and that either terminate or expire at some time in the near future. For example, certain top-earning compositions may have created substantial earnings during the period on which the purchase multiple is being applied, but a review of the seller's rights to such compositions might reveal that a number of those compositions will be lost to the seller because of the expiration of underlying contracts (such as an administration agreement expiring 2 years after the effective acquisition date), termination rights (such as a writer or estate reclaiming the final 39 or 20 years of extended U.S. copyright or recapturing rights after 35 years), foreign reversions, failure to secure renewal rights, compositions entering the public domain, and any number of other actual or potential reasons. Obviously, if a buyer is paying a multiple of 8 or 18 on earnings during a specified period for compositions that it is going to lose, adjustments on such income (and, in some cases, total deletion) will be demanded in the final negotiations that determine the actual purchase price. One of the worst things that can happen in this entire field is for a buyer to acquire very important income-generating compositions for a substantial price and then find out that it controls the rights to those compositions for only a short period of time or, even more disastrous, that it doesn't control the rights at all. Because of the enormous amounts of money being paid for music publishing assets and the value of continued ownership of those assets after acquisition, investigations conducted in this area are the crux of any buyer's due diligence inquiries.

## THE FORMAL PURCHASE AGREEMENT

In most cases, the formal acquisition-and-sale agreement will be negotiated while the financial and legal due diligence investigations are taking place. By taking such an approach, the buyer and seller will be assured that the actual signing will occur within a reasonable time after the due diligence reports have been finalized and negotiated. In some cases, however, the formal agreement will be prepared only after the results of the inquiries have been completed and any disputes arising therefrom have been resolved. This formal document, which is rarely less than 30 pages without exhibits, and usually over 80 pages without exhibits, will recite, in expanded language, most of the elements contained in the short-form commitment letter and will also contain a number of other detailed provisions covering not only what was found in the due diligence inquiries but also additional clauses dealing with a number of possible occurrences.

Some of the major areas that are covered in virtually all music publishing acquisition-and-sale agreements are as follows:

A description of the assets being acquired.

The purchase price and how it is to be paid.

The effective closing date on which the buyer will take over the catalog.

The effective date on which the buyer will be entitled to receipt of income from the catalog.

Warranties and representations by the selling company (e.g., that the songs are original, that the songs being acquired are validly owned by the seller, that there are no infringement claims, that all songwriter agreements are in full force and effect, that none of the compositions have been lost to public domain, that the seller has not made any untruthful statements, that there are no advances or other payments due third parties except as disclosed by the seller, that all compositions will be owned for a guaranteed period of time, that no efforts have been made to accelerate the collection of income prior to the closing date, that there are no "key man" clauses in any agreement, that all tax returns have been duly filed by the seller, that there are no tax liens, security interests, or other impediments on the catalog, that the seller has not declared (nor intends to declare) bankruptcy, that there are no finder's fees payable (and, if so, such are the obligation of the seller), that all songwriter or other contractual royalties have been properly paid by the seller for all monies that it received, and that all necessary corporate, partnership, or other legal action (including consents and resolutions) have been taken to assign the assets validly to the buyer).

A specific transfer of rights, including any trademarks, in cases where the name of the seller's publishing companies are sold to the buyer. If the company names are not being sold or if there are any future restrictions on either the seller entering the music publishing business or using the former company names, such will also be provided for.

The date on which all files and other catalog information will be transferred to the buyer (usually on the closing date or within a few days afterward).

In the event that there are unrecouped songwriter advances, whether the seller or buyer will get the benefit of any earnings that will be applied to reduce the outstanding advance balances.

Formulas and procedures that may reduce the purchase price in the event that the acquisition is an installment payment purchase or if there is a holdback of part of the price to be used by the seller in the event that certain warranties and representations are breached.

A confidentiality understanding restricting the buyer and seller from disclosing to the press or other third parties (except for accountants, tax advisors, attorneys, or governmental agencies) the dollar terms and other sensitive provisions of the sale agreement.

The governing state or national law in the case of disputes or interpretation of the terms of the acquisition agreement.

## THE AFTERMATH OF THE ACQUISITION AGREEMENT

Once the acquisition has been signed by both the buyer and the seller, the initial event that occurs is the transferring of all files; accounting books; records; correspondence; outstanding advance balance lists; sheet music; demo recordings; file copy phonograph records, tapes, and CDs of released recordings; and every other item that will give the buyer complete information on the catalog of songs purchased. Occasionally, the seller will retain certain royalty information in cases where it still has to process royalties to songwriters for income received prior to the closing date, but such records will be kept by the seller only for a short period of time.

Simultaneous with the transfer of files and records, the buyer will file the assignment of copyright in and to all the compositions acquired in the U.S. Copyright Office, notify ASCAP, BMI, and SESAC in the United States of the change of ownership in performance rights, notify the Harry Fox Agency of the change of ownership of mechanical rights, notify all payors of royalties of its rights, and send all applicable claim information to its foreign subpublisher representatives so that reregistration can be effected to ensure that all monies earned outside the United States will be collected by or on behalf of the purchaser.

Additionally, the business and legal affairs, copyright, royalty, licensing, and financial departments of the buyer will go through the files and issue informative memos about the new catalog to other departments (e.g., option exercise dates for songwriter agreements; contract summaries for agreements that have not been briefed by the seller; royalty rates; unrecouped advance balances; copyright renewal dates; restrictions on licensing songs to motion pictures, television series, commercials, stage productions, or other media; advance due date schedules for active songwriters; minimum delivery obligations; infringement claims that have to be pursued; outstanding pending licenses that have to be followed up on; license requests which have to be answered) so that the new songs can be integrated into the buyer's catalog administration and management systems.

## MERGERS

There has been a recent trend for companies to merge as opposed to a company buying another company or its assets. In evaluating the worth of the companies being merged, which has a direct effect on who controls the merger and whether or not the shareholders approve, the procedures and due diligence inquiries that take place in an acquisition apply in the same manner to a merger.

## SECURITIZATION

An alternate way for writers and writer/artists to raise a large amount of cash without actually selling their songs and masters is securitization. David Bowie was one of the first to use this financing method. Securities are issued at a fixed interest rate and are backed by future royalties of a writer's or writer–artist's catalogue. In return, the writer or writer–artist receives ready access to a substantial amount of cash; in short, a loan repaid from royalties. In order to qualify for this type of financing, the catalogue must have a consistent royalty history and, if it is a small catalogue, it would usually have to be bundled with other catalogues to be eligible. Some of the upsides of this arrangement, as opposed to selling or taking a loan from a bank, are that the writer or artist retains the copyrights to the songs or masters (assuming the bondholders have been paid back at the end of the term) and has normally lower admininstration costs, certain estate planning benefits, and a non-recourse loan (one that does not require a personal or corporation guarantee). There are downsides, however, including possible loss of catalogue, a higher cost of starting up as well as others. One should investigate this thoroughly as it is definitely not for everyone. The main laws that apply are the Copyright Law and the Uniform Commercial Code.

## CONCLUSION

Whether a buyer's interest stems from the seizure of an investment opportunity, a desire to increase current market share, or a realization that its current ability to compete in a world of multinational communication conglomerates necessitates the acquisition of copyrights or additional copyrights, and whether the seller is motivated by a desire to monetarily capitalize on a valuable asset or a need for substantial cash infusion to fortify other divisions, the music publishing business represents an investment that rarely disappoints either the buyer or the seller.

# 11

# Music, Money, and Copyright

THE COPYRIGHT LAW of the United States and those of other countries form the basis of the lifetime and worldwide earnings of creative works. Though the rules in this area can be quite complex as well as technical, there are some basics that every writer, publisher, representative, record company, and user of music should be familiar with.

Once a writer creates a work, the basic questions that need to be answered are what qualifies a work for copyright protection, what formalities does one have to follow, what rights does one have, how long does one own those rights, what can one do with those rights, and what happens when someone violates those rights?

The concept that a creative work is a property right was first recognized in the United States in 1787 in Article 1, Section 8 of the U.S. Constitution. Under the article, Congress was given the power to "promote the Progress of Science and useful Arts, by securing for limited Times to Authors and Inventors the exclusive Right to their respective Writings and Discoveries." The basic ownership rights for musical compositions as well as the remedies for the infringement of those rights are set forth in the 1909 U.S. Copyright Law, 1976 Copyright Revision Act, which took effect January 1, 1978, and the 1998 Sonny Bono Copyright Term Extension Act.

In the music field, the basic types of work that are copyrightable are musical works, including any accompanying words; dramatic works, including any accompanying music; motion pictures and other audiovisual works; and sound recordings. The two primary elements that a work must have in order to enjoy statutory copyright protection is that it must be an original work of authorship and that it must be fixed in a tangible medium of expression that is now known or later developed.

---

## EXCLUSIVE RIGHTS OF COPYRIGHT

The exclusive rights that a copyright owner has in a work are:

1. "The right to reproduce the copyrighted work in copies or phonorecords." This right includes the ability to authorize copies of a work that are fixed in practically any form, including tapes, records, CDs, and sheet music.
2. "The right to prepare derivative works based upon the copyrighted work." This very important right allows a copyright owner to authorize arrangements, motion picture adaptations, abridgments, translations, sound recordings, and so on that are based on the copyrighted work.
3. "The right to distribute copies or phonorecords of the copyrighted work to the public by sale or other transfer of ownership, or by rental, lease or lending." This right gives the copyright owner initial control over the first authorized record or copy of the work. After the first "copy" is authorized, all others may record the work simply by complying with the compulsory licensing provisions of the act.
4. "The right to perform the copyrighted work publicly." Financially, this is one of copyright's most important rights, as it forms the basis of all ASCAP, BMI, SESAC licensing as well as the direct, and source licensing of users and live performance venues, among others.
5. "The right to display the copyrighted work publicly." This right authorizes individual images of a work such as projecting an image of the copyrighted work on a screen.
6. "In the case of sound recordings, to perform the copyrighted work publicly by means of a digital audio transmission."

The limitations and exemptions on these exclusive rights include "fair uses" of the work, certain reproductions by libraries and archives, certain educational uses, certain face-to-face teaching activities, performances in the course of religious services (but not if the service is broadcast to the public at large), charity and other nonprofit performances (but not if an admission is charged or there is a profit motive or anyone involved is paid a fee), performances in the home, and other uses that do not require the authorization of the copyright owner.

All of these exclusive rights are initially owned by the creator of a work, and they may be individually or totally transferred to others by a written and signed document. Any transfer should be recorded in the U.S. Copyright Office by submitting a signed document of the transfer as well as the Copyright Office recordation fee.

## WORKS MADE FOR HIRE

The "work made for hire" is a special category of copyright that affects primarily film and television background composers as well as songwriters writing songs specifically for film and television series. The duration of protection, the ownership, and the right to "recapture" a copyright are all affected if a composition or score is so categorized.

A work made for hire is defined as "a work prepared by an employee within the scope of his or her employment or a work specially ordered or commissioned for use as a contribution to a collective work, as part of a motion picture or other audiovisual work. . .if the parties expressly agree in a written instrument signed by them that the work shall be considered a work made for hire." In such a case, the employer, not the writer, becomes the "author" of the work as well as its copyright owner for the entire term of copyright.

## COMPULSORY LICENSES

A very important notion of U.S. Copyright Law is the existence of compulsory licenses. These "licenses" give certain types of users (e.g., cable systems, jukebox operators, and public broadcasters) the right to use copyrighted musical works without the permission of the copyright owner, provided they follow certain procedures and make payment of royalties. In these cases, copyright owners and users are still permitted to negotiate their own agreements if they so choose, and such agreements supersede the Copyright Arbitration Royalty Panel (CARP) rates. Absent agreements between the parties, the fees collected by the Register of Copyrights for compulsory licenses (with the exception of phonorecords) are distributed to claimants by the CARPs.

Compulsory licenses include the retransmission by cable systems of distant nonnetwork programming, the right to make recordings of copyrighted nondramatic musical works once the first authorized record is made and distributed in the United States, and the right of public broadcasters to broadcast copyrighted works. Jukebox performances, once the subject of a compulsory license, are now covered by negotiated agreements between the copyright owners and the jukebox operators. If those two parties are unable to negotiate an agreement for jukebox performances, the uses would be covered by a compulsory license and subject to CARP distribution.

Prior to January 1, 1978, jukeboxes were exempt from copyright liability. The Revision Act changed that and set fees at $8 per box in 1978 with increases to $25, $50, and $63 in 1982, 1984, and 1987. In 1990 a new 10-year agreement was reached among ASCAP, BMI, SESAC, and the AMOA (the trade association representing the jukebox industry) that provided for a 1990 rate of $275 for the first jukebox plus lesser amounts for additional boxes. A 2001–2005 agreement provided $350 for the first box plus $59 per additional box for AMOA members and $79 per additional box for non-AMOA members with a CPI increase in 2002 and beyond. Video and digital jukeboxes are not covered.

For phonorecords (CDs, records, tapes, etc.), once the copyright owner authorizes one recording that is distributed to the public in the United States, anyone else may make recordings of the composition regardless of whether they have permission from the copyright owner. The Copyright Act requires that, prior to the distribution of records, a "notice of intention to obtain compulsory license" be given to the copyright owner containing, among other things, the work being recorded, the name of the new recording artist, the names of the original writers of the work, the name and address of the person or company taking the license, and the date when the phonorecords are set to be distributed. The compulsory license applies only if the primary purpose in making the phonorecords is to distribute them to the public for private use and includes the right to make an arrangement of the work as long as it does not change the basic melody or fundamental character of the work. If the names and addresses of the copyright owner are not on file in the Copyright Office records, the notice must be filed with the Copyright Office rather than directly to the copyright owner. The act requires monthly as well as annual summary accountings to the copyright owner as well as the timely payment of statutory fees. The rates as of January 1, 2004 are 8.5¢ per composition or 1.65¢ per minute of duration, with a new rate of 9.1¢ and 1.75¢ per minute in 2006–07.

In reality, most mechanical licenses that are issued in the United States are not compulsory licenses but variations of the compulsory license, with terms that are somewhat less stringent than those dictated by the Copyright Law. For example, if a record company uses the mechanical licensing services of the Harry Fox Agency in New York, the licenses issued are modifications of the compulsory license provisions and contain terms that are acceptable to virtually all major and smaller record companies. Additionally, if the songwriter is a recording artist signed to a record company, the mechanical licensing terms will be specified in the recording agreement, and such terms will supersede the compulsory license provisions of the Copyright Law.

## *THE AUDIO HOME RECORDING ACT OF 1992*

In 1992 the Audio Home Recording Act was passed, requiring equipment, tape, and disc manufacturers of digital audio recording devices and media (recordings and blank tape) to pay royalties to creators for the loss of revenue that occurs from home taping. The royalty to be paid by the manufacturers to the Register of Copyrights is 2% of the transfer price, with a minimum royalty payment of $1 per device and a maximum royalty of $12 for certain types of devices. The royalty on blank tape and other media is 3% of the transfer price.

The act divides all of the royalties received into two funds. The Sound Recording Fund receives ⅔ of the money, with 4% of that money allocated to nonfeatured musicians (2⅝) and vocalists (1⅜) who have played on sound recordings distributed in the United States, and the remaining 96% of the fund to be distributed 40% to featured recording artists and 60% to record companies. The second fund, the Musical Works Fund, receives ⅓ of the total royalties received and is split 50% to writers and 50% to music publishers. The royalties in the Sound Recording Fund are to be distributed on the basis of record sales, with the Musical Works Fund having the option of being distributed either on performances, on record sales, or a combination of both. Royalty claims can be made to the Copyright Royalty Tribunal by agents of interested parties (e.g., ASCAP, BMI, the Harry Fox Agency, the Songwriters Guild, RIAA) or by individuals themselves. The distribution of royalties within each fund can be voluntarily agreed to by all of the interested parties within that fund, but if no agreement can be reached, the distribution goes to the Copyright Royalty Tribunal or CARP for determination as to the claimants who should receive royalties as well as the amounts to be paid to each claimant. Royalties under this new right of copyright can be claimed commencing with the last 2 months of 1992, and claims must be filed with the CRT during the first 2 months of the year in question.

## *COPYRIGHT ROYALTY TRIBUNAL/CARP*

The 1976 Copyright Act created a tribunal to determine reasonable terms and rates of royalty payments under certain sections of the new law, to adjust those rates over time, and to distribute the royalty fees that come into the Register of Copyrights under these sections. The primary royalties covered are the compulsory licensing areas of the mechanical rate, secondary transmissions by cable systems, jukebox royalties, the copyright fees to be paid by noncommercial broadcasting (PBS), and the distribution of royalties under the Audio Home Recording Act. The Copyright Royalty Tribunal receives claims to royalties and distributes those fees to copyright owners or the agents for those copyright owners. If the CRT determines that a controversy exists regarding deposited funds, it will conduct a proceeding to determine the correct distribution of royalties. All final royalty determinations by the CRT are published in the Federal Register and are appealable to the U.S. Court of Appeals. In 1993, the CRT was replaced by Copyright Arbitration Royalty Panels (CARP) consisting of three arbitrators per panel. Congress is reviewing their structure.

## COPYRIGHT NOTICE

The notice that should appear on all copies of a published musical work includes the symbol ©, "Copyright," or "Copr."; the year of the first publication of the work; and the name of the owner of the copyright. For example, "© 2004 Todd Brabec" or "Copyright 2004 Brabec Music Company." Prior to March 1, 1989, this notice was mandatory, as its omission could, and did in many cases, result in loss of copyright. Since that date, however, the placement of the notice on all copies of works first published on or after March 1, 1989 is optional, although highly recommended, particularly to combat claims of "innocent infringement" of the work by others. For unpublished works, the copyright notice is not required, but it is recommended to have it on all copies.

## FEES AND FORMS

Effective July 1, 2002, the U.S. Copyright Office fee for registering a claim to copyright is a $30, a renewal registration is $60, a supplementary registration is $100, a sound recording is $30, and the recording of a transfer of copyright ownership of 1 title is $80 per registration plus $20 for each extra 10. The Copyright Office forms applicable to music use are Form PA for all published or unpublished works, Form RE for any remaining renewal copyright claims under the 1909 law, Form CA for any supplementary information to be added to a work already copyrighted, and Form SR for sound recordings. The Copyright Office also provides free of charge many informational circulars on various aspects of copyright including international copyright, copyright basics, works made for hire, and investigating the copyright status of a work.

## DURATION OF COPYRIGHT

The number of years that copyright protection lasts for a work has been increasing steadily over the past 300 years. From 14 years of protection under the 1710 English Statute of Anne and a maximum 28-year protection under the

U.S. Act of 1790, the 1909 Copyright Law established for most works a 28-year initial term of protection with an additional 28 years if the copyright was renewed. The 1976 Copyright Revision Act increased the term of protection for most copyrights created after January 1, 1978, to the life of the author plus 50 years after the author's death. The 1998 Sonny Bono Copyright Term Extension Act increased the 50 year term to 70 years after the author's death. Therefore, in the case of a work written by 2 or more authors, the term for most copyrights is 70 years after the death of the last surviving author. Although the 1976 act continued the rule that compositions written prior to January 1, 1978, must still be renewed after 28 years to receive extended protection, a 1992 change in the law provided for an automatic renewal for works first copyrighted between January 1, 1964, and December 31, 1977. For works written on or after January 1, 1978, the concept of renewal of copyright no longer applies.

*E X A M P L E.* A song is written by 4 writers in 2004. Three of the writers die in the year 2035, and the fourth writer dies at the age of 100 in the year 2075. The copyright for this work (assuming it was a joint work and not a work made for hire) would last until the year 2145, which is 70 years after the death of the last remaining author. The publisher of this work would also have copyright protection until 2145, as the duration of copyright protection depends on the length of the author's life and not who the author has assigned or transferred the copyright to.

The rules affecting the duration of copyright protection for a work fall into a number of categories depending on when the work is written and what type of work it is. The rules in this area can be somewhat complex and technical, but the following categories of works should provide most of the basics that every writer and publisher should be aware of:

*Works Written Prior to January 1, 1978.* Total copyright protection under the 1909 Copyright Law was 56 years (28 years plus a renewal of another 28 years). In the early 1960s Congress enacted a series of laws extending the duration of copyrights in their renewal term that would have fallen into the public domain in the years 1962-77. In effect, an additional 19 years of protection was added to copyrights in their renewal term, giving them a total of 75 years of copyright protection. Works still in their initial term of copyright (the first 28 years) at the time of the effective date of the 1976 Copyright Revision Act (January 1, 1978) were given an additional 47 years of protection, provided they were renewed in the twenty-eighth year of copyright. The 1998 Act added 20 more years for a total of 95 years of protection.

*Works Written on or after January 1, 1978.* The copyright protection for these works lasts for 70 years after the death of the author. If a work was written by more than 1 author and the work is a "joint" work, the term of protection is 70 years after the death of the last remaining author.

*Works Made for Hire.*   The duration of copyright protection for works made for hire written on or after January 1, 1978, is 120 years from the writing of the composition or 95 years from its publication, whichever date is earlier. Under the 1909 law, works for hire were treated similarly to other types of musical works (28 years plus a 28-year renewal), with the exception that only the employer had the right to apply for renewal.

## REVISION OF COPYRIGHT RENEWAL PROCEDURES

On June 26, 1992, Public Law 102-307 was signed into law and drastically changed the renewal provisions of the U.S. Copyright Law with respect to musical compositions initially copyrighted between January 1, 1964, and December 31, 1977. In effect, the new law made the need for actually filing a formal renewal application to extend copyright protection for an additional 47 years optional, as it would be given automatically whether or not any affirmative action was taken.

Under the 1976 Copyright Revision Act, the copyright term in a pre-1978 musical composition mirrored the provisions of the 1909 Copyright Law in that it continued to be an initial period of 28 years. There was established, however, an additional 47-year renewal term, which would become effective only if a renewal application was filed in the U.S. Copyright Office prior to the end of the twenty-eighth year. In the event that such a renewal application was not registered, copyright protection in the musical composition was lost at the end of the twenty-eighth year. For example, a musical composition that was copyrighted in 1970 would be eligible for copyright renewal in the year 1998. Provided that the renewal registration was filed in the U.S. Copyright Office by the end of 1998, copyright protection would be extended for an additional 47 years. If timely renewal was not made in 1998, however, a loss of copyright protection would commence on the first day of 1999.

Because of innumerable instances of copyright owners inadvertently failing to register timely renewal claims and the resultant loss of protection and benefits (which, in some cases, amounted to hundreds of thousands of dollars), it was considered to be in the best interests of all parties involved to guarantee continuing protection without any formal action on the part of the songwriter, music publisher, or any other copyright owner. In effect, the new law made entitlement to an additional 47 years of protection after the initial 28 years automatic, thus guaranteeing a 75-year copyright term for 1964–77 copyrighted compositions. This was increased to 95 years by the 1998 Act.

These renewal provisions do not apply to any musical compositions written on or after January 1, 1978, since copyright protection for such compositions lasts for the life of the creator plus 70 years or, in the case of a work made for hire, the shorter of 95 years from publication or 120 years from creation. Additionally, pre-1964 compositions that had been lost owing to a failure to renew their copyrights were not affected by the new law.

Even though the filing of a formal renewal registration is now unnecessary to secure copyright protection for a full 95 years (i.e., 28 years plus 67 years), there still remain certain advantages to filing. For example, having a formal renewal registration filed in the U.S. Copyright Office will constitute prima facie evidence of the validity of not only the information contained in the renewal certificate but of the copyright itself—a factor which can be very important in a court of law in the event of a copyright dispute. If there is litigation, the burden of proof will be on the party disputing the validity of the copyright to a musical composition and not on the creator of the composition.

As for the renewal process itself, both the Form RE renewal application and the $60 filing fee must be received by the U.S. Copyright Office within 1 year prior to the expiration of the initial 28-year copyright period. The initial 28-year copyright term is computed on a calendar year basis, rather than measured from the date that a musical composition is actually copyrighted. For example, if a composition was copyrighted on June 20, 1976, the initial 28-year copyright period would expire at the end of 2004 rather than 28 years from the actual copyright registration date (i.e., June 20, 2004), and the renewal period would commence on January 1, 2005. Thus the proper period to renew such a copyright would be from January 1, 2004, through December 31, 2004 (i.e., during the 1-year period prior to the commencement of the renewal period).

## Renewal Claimants

The persons entitled to claim renewal rights in musical compositions are as follows:

The author, if living

The widow or widower of the author, or the child or children of the author, or both, if the author is deceased

The executor of the author's will if the author is deceased and there is no surviving widow, widower, or child

The next of kin of the deceased author in the event that there is no surviving widow, widower, or child and the author did not leave a will

If a writer granted the music publisher renewal rights to a composition in his or her songwriter's agreement and the writer survives into the renewal period, the music publisher to which he or she assigned the renewal rights will continue to be the copyright owner of the composition.

## *TERMINATION RIGHTS*

Under the 1976 Copyright Revision Act and the 1998 Term Extension Act, creators and their representatives were given new rights to terminate grants that were made not only on or after January 1, 1978, but also prior to that date. In effect, the act provided authors, their estates, their heirs, and other duly authorized representatives the opportunity to recapture rights in and to musical compositions provided certain formalities were complied with.

## Termination of the Extended Copyright Renewal Term

The 1976 Copyright Revision Act not only increased the duration of copyright protection from 56 years to 75 years, thus allowing the writer and publisher of musical compositions to continue for a longer period of time to benefit financially from being able to license such works, but also gave the author the right to recapture rights in the musical compositions during the extra 19-year extension period.

## When the Termination Notice Must Be Sent

In order for an author or his or her duly authorized representative to terminate a music publisher's right to continue to control a pre-1978 composition, written notice must be sent to the publisher not less than 2 years nor more than 10 years prior to the effective date of termination. In this regard, termination of the extra 19-year renewal period can take place only during the fifty-seventh through sixty-first year of copyright protection (i.e., during the initial 5 years of the 19-year extension period). In other words, termination can occur only during the 5-year period commencing with the end of the fifty-sixth year subsequent to the initial copyright date, and notice must be sent not less than 2 years before that 5-year period nor more than 10 years before the same 5-year period.

## What the Termination Notice Must Contain

The termination notice should include the following information:

The name of the musical composition
The name of at least 1 of the writers
The date of initial copyright
The original copyright registration number, if available
The date on which termination is to take effect
Identification of the agreement or grant of rights to which the termination applies (e.g., songwriter agreement between [writer name] and [publisher name] dated [day/month/year]) . . .
The name and address of the music publisher or other company whose grant is being terminated

If the writer is deceased, the notice should also contain the names of the successors to the deceased writer and their relationship to the writer. And if the termination notice relates to a contract signed by someone other than the writer, the name of the surviving person who signed the contract should be included.

## Service of the Notice

The notice must either be served by personal service or sent by first-class mail to the last known address of the original music publisher or its successor-in-interest. The terminating party should make a reasonable investigation to determine the address of the party that currently owns the composition. It is also vital to record a copy of the termination notice in the U.S. Copyright Office prior to the date on which the termination is to take effect.

## Persons Entitled to Terminate the Extended Renewal Term

The original creator, if alive, is the person who is entitled to terminate the additional 19-year period of the 47-year renewal term. If the creator is deceased, the right to terminate vests in the surviving spouse. If there are children or, in the event a child is deceased, grandchildren of such deceased child, the spouse will own a 50% interest in the termination rights and the children or grandchildren will divide the remaining 50% interest in equal shares. For example, if there is a surviving spouse and 3 children, each of the children would be entitled to ⅓ of a 50% interest. If the original creator is dead, termination can be effectuated only if those persons entitled to more than 50% of the termination interests execute the notice. Executors, trustees, etc. come next.

## Termination of Agreements Made During or After 1978

In addition to the termination procedures established with respect to the final 19 years of the extended copyright renewal period, the 1976 Copyright Revision Act also established termination procedures for compositions written on or after January 1, 1978. The act gives authors, their heirs, or duly authorized representatives the right to terminate a grant-of-rights contract effective during the thirty-sixth through fortieth year after the agreement was signed. If the grant-of-rights agreement covered publication of the work, the right to terminate can occur during the 5-year period commencing at the end of 35 years from the date that the musical composition was published or at the end of the fortieth year after the signing of the agreement, whichever occurs first.

## When the Termination Notice Must Be Sent

The termination notice must be served not less than 2 years nor more than 10 years before the effective date that is stated in the notice.

## SOUND RECORDINGS

Sound recordings are considered original works of authorship under the 1976 act and are able to be copyrighted. The copyright protects the actual sounds on the record, disc, or tape and not the physical object of the record itself. The protection for sound recordings also applies to nonmusical works. The 1976 act recognizes the "authorship" notion of performers and record producers, and sound recordings are therefore fully protected. This copyright is separate from the copyrights issued for the songs being recorded. The owner-ship of a record's copyright is many times transferred to the record company as part of the negotiated artist contract. In non-work for hire 1978 and beyond recordings, a right of termination vests 35 years after delivery of the album.

The copyright notice that should be placed on all publicly distributed records, tapes, discs, etc., consists of the symbol Ⓟ, the year of first publication of the sound recording, and the name of the owner of the copyright in the sound recording or an abbreviation by which the name is generally recognizable or known. The notice should be placed on the surface of the record or on the label or container in such way as to give reasonable notice to others of the claim of copyright. The sound recording copyright applies only to original works in a fixed form (the sounds on the discs, records, tapes, etc.) that were fixed on or after January 1, 1978 (the effective date of the 1976 act) or fixed and able to be distributed on or after February 15, 1972 (the effective date of the federal law recognizing a copyright in sound recordings).

## INFRINGEMENT OF COPYRIGHT

Copyright infringement occurs when someone violates any of the exclusive rights of the copyright owner (subject to certain exemptions and limitations) as set forth in the 1976 Copyright Revision Act. As any or all of these exclusive rights may be transferred by the copyright owner to others, normally through assignment or an exclusive license, each separate owner of an exclusive right can initiate an infringement suit, as each is entitled to all of the protection and remedies accorded to the copyright owner. Infringements in the music area come up most frequently in cases where 1 song is, or appears to be, very similar to another song or where users of music perform copyrighted composi-tions without permission. Some of the remedies for infringements include attorney's fees and court costs, the actual damages suffered, a wide range of statutory damages ($750–$150,000), criminal jail terms, profits of the infringer, and injunctions. Increased penalties and damages apply to willful infringers, with reduced damages applicable to innocent infringers.

As registration in the U.S. Copyright Office is not mandatory under the 1976 Act, the act included certain provisions regarding the filing of infringement suits that strongly encourage registration. In order for a copyright owner to file an infringement case in the federal courts, a work must have been registered for copyright. For any transfer of any of the exclusive rights of a copyright, the new owner of the right must record the transfer in the Copyright Office before initiating an action. For published works that are registered subsequent to an infringement, statutory damages and attorney's fees are not available. The same nonavailability of certain remedies applies to published works that are not registered and where the infringement occurs after publication. Statutory damages and attorney fees are available provided that the published work is registered within a 3-month grace period after it is published.

A second type of copyright infringement involves the importation into the United States, without the authority of the owner of copyright, of copies or phonorecords of a work that have been acquired outside of the United States. Exceptions to this infringement include items brought into the country for the personal use of the person bringing them in. The main thrust of the clause has to do with "pirated" recordings.

The basic issues in an infringement case involve one's ownership of a copyright and whether someone else copied that original work. As for the copying issue, the court looks at whether the defendant had access to the work in some way and whether there was a substantial similarity between the 2 works.

An argument raised in some infringement cases is that the new work is a parody of the original work, that the doctrine of "fair use" applies, and that the new work therefore does not infringe upon the old work. The 1976 act states that "notwithstanding the provisions of 106 and 106A [the sections of the law that apply to the exclusive rights that a copyright owner has in a work], the fair use of a copyrighted work, including such use by reproduction in copies or phonorecords or by any other means specified by that section, for purposes such as criticism, comment, news reporting, teaching (including multiple copies for classroom use), scholarship, or research, is not an infringement of copyright." In determining whether the use made of a work in any particular case is a fair use, the factors to be considered include the purpose and character of the use, including whether such use is of a commercial nature or is for nonprofit educational purposes; the nature of the copyrighted work; the amount and substantiality of the portion used in relation to the copyrighted work as a whole; and the effect of the use on the potential market for or value of the copyrighted work.

The decisions of different courts regarding fair use many times conflict. The specific circumstances of each case go far to determine whether something is or is not a "fair use" of another's copyrighted work.

---

## INTERNATIONAL COPYRIGHT PROTECTION

U.S. copyrighted works are, in the main, protected in most countries of the world through individual treaties between the United States and foreign countries as well as U.S. participation in the major international conventions, primarily the Universal Copyright Convention, the Berne Convention and the WIPO treaties. An important point of all of these treaties and conventions is that with certain exceptions (e.g., duration), U.S. works basically receive the same protection in a country that the country gives to its own nationals. Many of the positive changes that have occurred in U.S. copyright law over the years are the result of the U.S. having to conform its law to the copyright laws of other countries and conventions in order that U.S. copyright owners may receive adequate protection in foreign countries.

## COMPLETING THE PA COPYRIGHT FORM

The PA Form is used to copyright all unpublished and published works of the performing arts. These works include, among others, music and accompanying lyrics, dramatic works including accompanying music, motion pictures, and other audiovisual works. Accompanying the completed form must be 1 complete copy of the work (lead sheet, record, sheet music, film, tape, etc.) for an unpublished work, 2 complete copies of the best edition of the work for published works, and 1 complete copy of a contribution to a collective work, along with the fee. Once the form, deposit, and fee are received in the Copyright Office, a Certificate of Registration is issued effective as of the date all completed materials were received. The certificate is prima facie evidence of the copyright and of the facts stated therein.

Under Section 1 of the PA form, the complete title of the work must be provided. If the work is a collection of songs, the overall title of the collection should be listed. If the work has any additional titles, they must also be listed. The nature of the work must also be described, such as "music," "words and music," or "musical play." Section 2 of the form requires the full name, date of birth and death (if applicable), and nationality or domicile of each author of copyrightable material for the work being registered for copyright. By "author" is meant any person who created the work (the composer, lyricist, etc.). If the author is not identified on the copies of the work ("anonymous") or is using a fictitious name on the work ("pseudonymous"), it must be so noted on the form. Under the "Nature of Authorship" section, a brief statement of each author's contribution to the work should be given. For example, words by Joseph Walter, music by Richard Murphy, and coauthor of lyrics by Ralph Perna. If a work has more than 3 authors, Copyright Office continuation forms should be completed for the other authors.

Section 3 of the form requires the date of the creation of the work as well as the date and nation of first publication of the work, if applicable. By "creation" is meant the date that an original work is fixed in a copy or phonorecord for the first time. By "publication" is meant the distribution of copies or phonorecords of a work to the public by sale or other transfer of ownership, or by rental, lease, or lending.

Section 4 requires the names and addresses of the copyright claimant(s) as well as a brief statement of how the claimant obtained ownership of the copyright if the claimant is not the author listed in Section 2 of the form. For example, a writer is the copyright claimant once a song is fixed in a copy or on a record. If the writer assigns the copyright by contract to a publisher, the "Transfer" section would state "assignment or transfer by written contract to music publisher" and the publisher would be the copyright claimant.

Section 5 should be completed only if a previous copyright registration has been made for the same work in an unpublished form and is now being registered for its first publication or if a previous registration had someone other than the author listed as copyright claimant in Section 4 and the author is now listing the registration in his or her own name. Section 5 also covers any additions or revisions of a previously registered work. The prior copyright registration number of the work must also be listed. Section 6 concerns derivative works, compilations, and changed versions. Derivative works are works based on 1 or more preexisting works (works under copyright or in the public domain) and include motion picture versions, musical arrangements, translations, dramatizations, and so on. The new material to the original work must be briefly described in this section.

Sections 7, 8, and 9 involve deposit account (companies or individuals who have accounts with the Copyright Office), the correspondence address for any inquiries about the copyright, and rules regarding the signature of the author, the copyright claimant, the owner of any of the exclusive rights of the copyright, or a duly authorized agent. All signatures in this section must be originals.

The Copyright Office issues a Certificate of Copyright Registration as of the date when it receives the form and all necessary deposits, documents, and fees. This registration should not be confused with the copyright itself, as under the 1976 law, works are copyrighted at the time that they are created in a "fixed" form.

## *THE DIGITAL PERFORMANCE RIGHT IN SOUND RECORDINGS ACT OF 1995 (DPRSRA) AND THE DIGITAL MILLENNIUM COPYRIGHT ACT OF 1998 (DMCA)*

The 1995 DPRSRA created a public performance right for artists and record companies in certain sound recordings when they are performed by digital audio transmissions. Previously only songwriters and publishers enjoyed the performance right. This new right is a limited one and covers subscription (statutory license) and on-demand transmissions. Webcasting (audio streaming of recordings over the Internet) was included under this limited right by the 1998 DMCA. FCC licensed broadcast station web transmissions are also covered. License rates and terms are to be decided by voluntary negotiation or compulsory arbitration. The first CARP royalty decision for the fees for non-exempt subscription digital services was 6.5% of gross revenues resulting from residential services in the U.S. with 50% of the royalties going to artists (45%), non-featured musicians (2.5%) and non-featured vocalists (2.5%) with the remaining 50% going to record companies.

The 1998 DMCA implements the WIPO Copyright Treaty and the WIPO Performances and Phonograms Treaty that deal with copyright protection for works in a digital form and that require countries to give protection to foreign works no less favorable than the protection afforded to domestic works. The DMCA also creates civil and criminal penalties (up to a $1,000,000 fine and 10 years imprisonment) for the circumvention of the technological measures used by copyright owners to protect their works as well as the tampering with copyright management information (title of work, author, copyright owner, conditions or terms, etc.). Limitations on the copyright infringement liability of on-line service providers is also included with the steps set forth that OSP's must follow when they either detect or are notified of infringing transmissions. These include disconnecting repeat offenders; removing infringing material on the internet and identifying infringers to copyright owners based upon subpoenas.

## TERMINATION RIGHTS UNDER THE 1998 TERM EXTENSION ACT

This law gives most authors or successors another opportunity to terminate a transfer for the added 20 years of protection given by this Act (95 years total rather than 75). The author has the opportunity during the 5 years following the 75 years of protection to terminate such a transfer provided the work was in its renewal term at the time of the law and where the rights had previously been transferred before January 1, 1978. If the old law termination right had expired and if that termination right was never exercised, then the new termination right would be available. Any termination notice must be recorded in the U.S. Copyright Office prior to the effective date of the termination. This new right does not apply to "works for hire."

## CONCLUSION

The copyright area is a complex, technical, and changing field affected by legislation, court decisions, treaties, foreign laws, and different interpretations of all the copyright acts. Consultation with an attorney versed in copyright law is essential for any inquiry or action in this area.

# 12

# *Music, Money, Lawyers, Managers, and Agents*

CREATIVE TALENT AND SKILL are one thing; it is quite another to take that talent and skill and make them successful. That is the role of managers, lawyers, and agents. The very best ones can take you to the top both professionally and financially. The worst ones can take everything you have and leave you with nothing. Decisions and advice as to contracts, image, direction, and financial planning are some of the most important things that a creator must deal with. It is the job of these representatives to make the right decisions and do what is best to achieve the short-term and long-term goals of an artist's career.

## *LAWYERS AND THEIR ROLE*

In a world of complex deals, the role of the attorney in the careers of songwriters and recording artists has significantly increased. In fact, in many cases, it is the lawyer who, through his or her industry connections, experience, and reputation, is the person responsible for securing the initial interest from a music publisher or record company. For example, the attorney many times is the person who makes contact by sending a demo tape of compositions for review and who suggests the overall terms of an agreement if the publisher or record company shows interest. And in instances where the attorney is called upon to negotiate and finalize an agreement that has been initiated by another, the ability to close the deal expeditiously and on the best terms possible is vital.

In a world of extremely complex contracts and business relationships, where 1 word in a 100-page agreement can mean the difference between financial security or bankruptcy, selection of an attorney is one of the more important choices that has to be made. It is even more important in today's entertainment industry, where the lawyer not only has to know the legal ramifications of a particular word, sentence, clause, or paragraph in an agreement (as well as how all the parts interrelate with one another) but must also have a thorough grasp of the practical, business, and financial ramifications of what is being agreed to by the songwriter or recording artist. This dual role of attorney and business advisor cannot be overemphasized, as it represents the crux of the lawyer's role in today's industry.

## Lawyers' Fees

Lawyers' fees are structured in a number of ways in the music and entertainment industry depending on, among other things, the policies of the attorney or law firm involved, the nature of the services being rendered, whether or not the attorney secured the interest of the company desiring to sign the writer or writer/artist, whether the representation relates to the negotiation of one contract or a series of agreements, whether the attorney is handling all of a client's legal affairs or has just been retained for a single negotiation, whether the attorney is being brought in by either a client or law firm to handle only a specialized aspect of the agreement or to conduct all aspects of the particular negotiation, and whether the writer or writer/artist is a known quantity who is financially stable or is at the beginning of his or her career, with little money to spend for legal representation.

In most cases, the monetary compensation received by the lawyer is based on a set hourly rate, a retainer plus hourly rate, a flat prenegotiated dollar amount, a percentage of the advances or advances received under the agreement, a percentage of the earnings generated under the agreement, or a combination of some of the above methods.

*Hourly Rates.*    Many law firms have a policy that charges to a client are based on a set dollar figure per hour of work done. For example, in the entertainment industry, fees can easily range from $200 to $600 per hour for attorneys, with less being billed for paralegals and other assistants. Law firms also charge their clients for increments of each 1-hour period of representation on a pro rata basis. If a particular lawyer charges $300 per hour, a phone call or negotiation that lasts for 15 minutes or less will normally be billed at $75 (e.g., ¼ of $300). In addition to the attorney's individual time, much of the research is given to paralegals or first-year associates, with an appropriate reduction in the hourly rate. All actual out-of-pocket costs such as copying charges, fax bills, telephone charges, messenger bills, overnight mail charges, court filing fees, courier bills, secretarial overtime, and so on will be billed to the client, as the hourly fee does not include such costs, also known as disbursements.

Because a number of items make up the monthly bill, they are either listed separately or categorized on the client's statement. For example, specific messenger fees may be itemized on a daily basis (e.g., $8 on 6/24, 6/26, and 6/29) or may be lumped into one aggregate figure (e.g., $56 in messenger fees for the month of June). In contrast to the categorization of disbursements, however, the fees charged by individual lawyers are always listed separately. A billing might read:

| Attorney Name | Rate | Hours | Total |
|---|---|---|---|
| Primary negotiating partner | $400 | 7 | $2,800 |
| Secondary research attorney | $250 | 10.5 | $2,625 |
| Research paralegal | $100 | 6.5 | $ 650 |

Depending on the particular law firm and history with the client, the monthly bills may include very general or very specific descriptions of the services rendered during the billing period. For example, the legend on the bill can be as general as "negotiation of recording artist agreement with _____ Records" or as specific as "telephone call to _____ re: Paragraph 17.05 of the proposed recording agreement with _____ Records" or "meeting with _____ of _____ Records re warranty paragraphs." The generality and specificity of a bill depend on the business practices of the law firm and the needs of the client, and they should be discussed when entering into the attorney–client relationship so that all parties know what is to be expected of them. Law firms, however, do maintain exact records of their expenses and time and can usually give the client as much detail as desired.

*Retainers.*   Certain clients pay an overall monthly or yearly fee to a law firm, from which actual hourly charges billed during a particular year will be deducted. For example, a client may pay a law firm a guaranteed $1,000 per month, which keeps that law firm constantly available for legal advice during the year. This arrangement is similar to having someone "on call," with any actual charges incurred during a particular month or year being deducted from the prepaid retainer. This type of arrangement is common between lawyers and clients who have continuing legal needs throughout the year.

*Flat Fees.*  A fairly common arrangement when an attorney is negotiating a single agreement for a client (e.g., an exclusive songwriter's agreement, a recording artist agreement, a record producer agreement) is the flat fee. Under this type of arrangement, the lawyer tells the client in advance how much the negotiation and representation will cost regardless of the amount of time expended. For example, the attorney may quote the client a $5,000 "all in" figure, and that amount will be the final fee payable whether the attorney spends 10 hours or 50 hours in finalizing the agreement. These flat-fee arrangements many times do not include out-of-pocket disbursements such as telephone, copying, and messenger services, and this issue should be discussed with the lawyer at the time one is entering into such an arrangement.

*Percentage of Earnings.*  In addition to the hourly and flat-fee arrangements, some lawyers are also entitled to a percentage of the client's income under the agreement that is negotiated. Occasionally, these percentage arrangements apply only to the initial advance received under the agreement being negotiated (e.g., 5% of the advance due the writer upon signing of the agreement). At other times, the percentage applies only to advances that are paid during the term of the agreement. And at still other times, the percentage applies to all income generated by the agreement, regardless of whether the monies are earnings or advances or whether the monies are payable during the term of the agreement or afterward.

For example, if an attorney's percentage is 10% of the initial advance and there is a $100,000 signing advance payable to the writer or recording artist, the attorney will be entitled to $10,000 upon execution of the agreement, with no further payments due. If the attorney's percentage is based on all advances received by the writer or artist during the term of the agreement and the client is guaranteed $100,000 per year in advances over a 5-year period, then the attorney will receive $10,000 each year for 5 years (i.e., 10% of each $100,000 payment). In the case where the client and attorney agree that the attorney will be entitled to a percentage of all advances and earnings generated by the agreement regardless of when received, the attorney will receive his or her percentage of income as long as the particular songwriter or recording artist earns royalties from either all compositions written during the term of the songwriter's agreement or, if applicable, recorded during the artist agreement. For example, if a songwriter writes a hit song during the term of the agreement and it becomes a well-known standard earning $50,000 to $100,000 per year over its copyright life, the attorney who negotiated the agreement would continue to receive the agreed-upon percentage for as long as the composition earns income.

Such percentage arrangements take on many forms and do not necessarily mean that the client will not be charged an hourly fee or a flat rate for the negotiation and finalization of the particular agreement; that entitlement may be in addition to the actual legal fees charged for the services rendered. As with any representation relationship, it is advisable to clarify the financial aspects of the arrangement so that all parties realize what the potential monetary ramifications are in advance.

## MANAGERS AND THEIR ROLE

Managers take on many jobs and faces. They can range from a full-scale controller of an artist's life and a comprehensive all-service person or company acting in conjunction with an artist, to a financial adviser and money caretaker, to a minor player attending to various aspects of an artist's career. Managers are exceptionally important for most artists, as they advise them on all aspects of their career, including recording contracts, booking agents, the venues and dates they should be or are performing at, the choice of a public relations firm and program, and the entire game plan for the artist's career. They also bring in accountants and financial advisors for the handling of all of the money generated by the commercial exploitation of that artist.

The reason that most artists take on a manager is to make them successful, to handle all of their business in an orderly fashion, to respond to their needs, and to do everything possible to promote their careers. Managers look for artists that they can make successful and, of course, from whom they can derive income. Some of the qualities that an artist should look for in a manager are the ability to listen to what the artist is about and to perceive what the artist's actual talent is. The ability to communicate is also important, particularly where the artist and manager disagree as well as in the area of what needs to be done to prepare the artist for the marketplace. The manager should also be cognizant of all aspects of the business side of the entertainment industry and be able to bring in the best team possible to make the artist's career both a creative and financial success. The team includes a competent staff with not only the ability to handle all of the specific duties necessary but also good working relationships with agents, accountants, attorneys, record companies, publishers, producers, and P.R. agents, among others—all of whom will work in conjunction with the manager to further the success of the artist's career.

To be effective, managers should have a relatively small number of artists that they are handling, as each artist needs a good deal of time and attention. Managers do not have to have a major track record or large offices to succeed for an artist. Many managers have small operations with a roster of two or three artists, with some of them signed to a major or independent label and the others unsigned developing acts. Other managers may have one successful act and one new band that is being promoted for a record deal. Other managers may have no signed acts but still do a spectacular job in furthering an artist's career. And there are the major managers and management companies with numerous clients, some successful and others not, some formerly successful and others about to break big. The question whose answer all artists need to feel secure with is, "Is my manager dealing effectively with all of the parties and entities that are necessary to make me a success, and is my manager achieving the goals that have been set?"

## Manager's Contracts

Although many managers do not have written contracts with their clients but only "handshake" understandings, it is always advisable to have a written contract spelling out the aspects of the manager–client relationship. A written document is not only good during the years the relationship is working but also important for both parties at times when things are not going well or at such time as the artist takes the final step of firing the manager. One of the not uncommon situations in this industry involves new artists hiring a manager who, through a good deal of hard work, achieves success for the artist. Because of the success, the artist may look around for another manager to take him or her to the next step, be advised by others to make a change, or receive offers from other managers to make a change. With or without a contract, lawsuits may occur. But with a signed contract, all of the parties will at least know the full extent of their obligations and whether or not those obligations were fulfilled.

Most management contracts specify the income areas on which a commission will be charged. Although this is a negotiable item, many contracts specify a percentage of all income generated by the artist. One of the important items that must be resolved is whether the contract specifies a commission on the artist's gross income or net income. Gross income includes the total of all income coming in, whether or not such items as attorney fees, marketing costs, recording costs, and so on will reduce the figure. Net income is the total amount of money after certain deductions are made. Net income contracts should include a specific definition of what is and what is not included in the net figure. Obviously, it would be to an artist's financial benefit to have a net figure contract. For a manager, a gross figure contract would be more financially rewarding.

The duration of most managerial contracts is for a specific number of years (3 to 5 years), with others based on the artist's continuing involvement with a particular deal (a recording agreement, for instance) that the manager has negotiated. An agreement with a new band may be for 1 year, with 4 consecutive options on the part of the manager and a renegotiation of the entire contract after 5 years. For successful artists, the annual option to renew or terminate the management agreement might be at the election of the artist. Other contracts give both parties a mutual option to terminate. In reality, you could have a situation where a new artist is signed by a manager, becomes successful, and then demands renegotiation in the middle of the contract term. Some managers will renegotiate at that time; others will renegotiate only at the end of the 5-year contract term. Termination by the artist can result in a negotiated settlement of a single payoff, a continuing involvement by the manager in deals already set up, or a declining-percentage arrangement whereby the artist continues to pay the manager a percentage of income but reduces that percentage each year over a stated number of years.

For artists taking on a manager, it is many times good to have particular goals set forth for each option period. If the manager does not meet those goals in any option period (e.g. sign the artist to a recording deal no later than 2nd option period), then the artist is able to terminate. It is also advisable to have a "no assignment of contract" or "key man/person" clause in the agreement. The last thing an artist normally wants is for his or her contract to be assigned to a different management company or to be stuck with a management company when the person who signed them leaves. Artist consent should be required in either of these situations.

It is important that every artist–manager contract have a clause stating that "the artist has carefully reviewed all of the contract provisions with an attorney and is fully aware of all the consequences and provisions of the agreement," since if a relationship breaks down, the client may charge that the contract is unconscionable, that he or she was not represented by legal counsel (or not represented by competent counsel), that he or she was naive and taken advantage of when the contract was signed, and that the contract is therefore null and void.

## Manager's Fees

The commission that a manager normally charges runs between 10% and 25%, with 15% to 20% being the norm. Variations on these percentages usually pertain to gross or net definitions and any areas that are specifically excluded from commissions. For example, one manager may charge 20% on all income exclusive of monies received for recording costs, tour support, and the writer's performing right income, whereas another manager might charge 15% of all gross income received plus any expenses that the manager incurs that are directly related to the business of the artist's career. Most managers do take their commission on all advances, merchandising, and tour earnings; some take it also on recording costs and other items. If a manager wears many hats, as many of them do, it is important for an artist not to be charged commissions on the nonmanagerial roles of the manager. For instance, the artist should not be charged a commission fee on top of the fees that come in when the manager is acting in another role.

Also, if the artist had income from ventures or careers prior to the manager's arrival (a prior record deal, for example), compensation from those projects should be specifically excluded from gross or net compensation formulas used to calculate the manager's fees.

It's always good for all parties to remember that the music business is a tough one and managers need leeway in their efforts on behalf of an artist. They are the ones on the front line and should be given enough latitude to do their job.

## AGENTS

The primary job of an agent is to find and book work for the artist, including live performances, television shows, and movie deals. Booking agents work with promoters to figure out how to sell the dates for a particular artist, how to get guaranteed commitments for that artist, and how to advertise an artist's concert dates. A primary job of the agent is to make sure that promoters pay for all of those attending a concert and to make sure that all contracts are in order.

The fee charged by agents depends on the agent's track record and what he or she can achieve for the artist. Fees are normally between 5% and 10% of what the agent books, but can be negotiated lower for a major act.

Film and television agents, on the other hand, represent background composers, theme writers, and songwriters whose work is primarily used in the movies and on television. The role of these agents is to get their clients work and to represent them in negotiating their film and television deals.

Agent contracts vary; some agents espouse handshake deals, and others use signed contracts. The contracts in this field take many forms but normally cover only the writer's career in the film, television, and soundtrack world. The commissions usually charged are between 10% and 15% of the negotiated deal. The contract normally covers the items that are commissionable (e.g., writing fee, mechanical royalties, writer publishing income, etc.) and the areas that are not (e.g., performance right royalties, nonfilm and television projects, etc.), as well as the legitimate business expenditures to be charged to the client in furtherance of his or her career. Some contracts also contain provisions whereby the writer can terminate the agreement upon written notice if the agent does not procure a legitimate job offer within a certain period of time.

# 13

# Putting It All Together

THE 9 MILLION INCOME CHART as shown in Table 13.1 is not a dream; it represents a very real scenario for a songwriter who is able to put it all together. Since the chart reflects many of the separate income-producing areas discussed in the book, this chapter summarizes how those areas can come together to create the multimillion-dollar income that people dream of.

In the following illustration, we will assume that the songwriter has a 50/50 copublishing agreement with a music publisher (i.e., the songwriter is entitled to not only his or her full songwriter's share of income but also 50% of the income reserved for the music publisher) and is also a recording artist with a 500,000-selling single as well as a 2 million unit-selling album. The opportunities that present themselves and the monies that can be earned as a result of having a hit are not exaggerated; given the right set of circumstances and the right songs, the results shown here are real and, in some respects, even less than what can be earned.

## MECHANICAL ROYALTIES

Assuming that all CD, tape, and other audio recording sales occurred in the United States during 2004–05 and the record company had agreed to pay the songwriter and music publisher the statutory mechanical rate (rather than the more prevalent 75% controlled composition reduced rate) for each composition on the single and album, the writer and publisher royalties would be as follows:

|            |                            |
|-----------:|----------------------------|
| 500,000    | Singles sold               |
| x .085     | Statutory rate (2004–05)   |
| $ 42,500   | Writer and publisher royalties |
| x 2        | Compositions on single     |
| $ 85,000   | Total single royalties     |

|             |                         |
|------------:|-------------------------|
| 2,000,000   | Albums sold             |
| x .085      | Statutory rate          |
| $ 170,000   | Royalties for 1 song    |
| x 10        | Songs on album          |
| $1,700,000  | Total album royalties   |

TABLE **13.1**   Potential Songwriter/Publisher/Recording Artist Gross Income

|              |                                          |
|-------------:|------------------------------------------|
| $   85,000   | U.S. single sales (500,000 copies)       |
| 1,700,000    | U.S. album sales (2 million copies)      |
| 1,000,000    | U.S. radio and TV performances           |
| 57,000       | Foreign single sales                     |
| 140,000      | Foreign album sales                      |
| 575,000      | Foreign radio and TV performances        |
| 25,000       | Sheet music and folios                   |
| 175,000      | Commercial                               |
| 17,000       | Television series use and video          |
| 40,000       | Motion picture use                       |
| 4,000        | Foreign theatrical performances          |
| 468,000      | Broadway show use                        |
| 800          | Lyric reprint in a novel                 |
| 350          | Video jukebox                            |
| 475          | Karaoke                                  |
| 225,000      | Background music score fee               |
| 300,000      | Foreign score royalties                  |
| 35,000       | U.S. background score TV royalties       |
| 25,000       | Internet and miscellaneous               |
| $ 4,872,625  | Total writer and publisher royalties     |
| 20,000       | Motion Picture Master Use                |
| +4,480,000   | Recording artist royalties               |
| $ 9,372,625  | *Total gross income*                     |

If additional hit singles were taken from the album, additional royalties would be earned. But for purposes of this illustration, we'll hold the mechanical royalties due from sales to $1,785,000 in aggregate songwriter and publisher income. Since the writer would receive 75% of these monies (i.e., 50% as songwriter and 25% as copublisher) and the publisher 25%, the final sharing of earnings would be:

$1,338,750    Songwriter
$ 446,250    Publisher

---

## RECORDING ARTIST ROYALTIES

The computations in Table 13.2 assume that the writer as recording artist spent $300,000 to record the album, received a $400,000 advance from the record label for the album, had an 18% album royalty rate, 16% artist single rate, a 25% album packaging deduction and no producer royalty deduction.

---

## U.S. PERFORMANCE ROYALTIES

The "A" side single reaches #1 on the pop charts and crosses over to other trade paper charts, achieving #2 on the soul charts and #1 on the adult contemporary charts. It is one of the most heavily broadcast songs of the year and earns $500,000 in writer performance royalties. The same amount is earned as publisher royalties, which results in the following monies being remitted to the songwriter:

$ 500,000    Writer royalties
+250,000    50% copublisher royalties
$ 750,000    Total performing right domestic royalties

---

## COMMERCIAL USE

Because the song's message is positive and the melody is strong, the music publisher receives a request from a major soft drink company for use in its television and radio campaign. After 2 weeks of negotiations, an agreement is reached that will allow the advertiser to use the song for 1 year as part of its campaign in the United States on radio and television. Since the agency intends

TABLE **13.2**  Album Royalty

| | |
|---|---|
| $18 | CD retail price |
| x 25% | Packaging deduction |
| $4.50 | Dollar deduction |

| | |
|---|---|
| $18 | CD retail price |
| −4.50 | Packaging deduction |
| $13.50 | Royalty base |
| x 18% | Royalty % |
| $2.43 | Artist royalty |
| x 2,000,000 | Album sales |
| $4,860,000 | Artist royalties |

Single royalty:

| | |
|---|---|
| $4 | Single Retail Price |
| x 16% | Royalty % |
| .64 | Royalty |
| x 500,000 | Copies sold |
| $320,000 | Artist royalties |

Final Calculations:

| | |
|---|---|
| $4,860,000 | Album royalties |
| + 320,000 | Single royalties |
| $5,180,000 | Total royalties gross income |
| − 300,000 | Recordings costs |
| $4,880,000 | Net income |
| − 400,000 | Album advance |
| $4,480,000 | Final royalty check |

to re-record the composition with a slight change of lyrics to fit the theme of the commercial, the advertiser has to license only the underlying musical composition and not the hit recording, which would have necessitated a separate license from the record company that owned the master. The fee for the initial year is $175,000, with the songwriter receiving 75% (i.e., $131,250) under the terms of the copublishing agreement. Under the commercial license agreement, the advertiser also has options to extend the term of the contract for 3 additional, successive 1-year periods for increased fees of $200,000, $225,000, and $250,000 respectively. If all options are exercised, a total of $850,000 will be generated under the advertising use contract.

| | |
|---|---|
| $175,000 | 2004 fee |
| $200,000 | 2005 fee |
| $225,000 | 2006 fee |
| $250,000 | 2007 fee |
| $850,000 | Total commercial fees |

Under the writer's songwriter and copublishing agreement, 75% of the $850,000 (or $637,500) will be remitted in royalty income to the songwriter, with the music publisher retaining $212,500.

## MOTION PICTURE USE

A few months after the song reaches #1 on the charts, a motion picture producer requests the right to use the composition in a scene that has a hit song playing from a jukebox in the background while two characters discuss a bank robbery plan in a bar. For the synchronization right to include the song in the film, the buy-out grant for home video distribution, and all the other rights that normally appear in a motion picture license, the music publisher charges the film producer a fee of $40,000, 75% of which will be paid to the writer by the publisher. Since the hit record is also being used in the scene, the film producer also contacts the writer/artist's record company and, after negotiations have been concluded, agrees to pay the record company an additional $40,000 for the use of the master recording. Since the writer/performer is entitled to receive 50% of any licensing income per the terms of the recording artist agreement, $20,000 of the $40,000 fee will be the artist's share from the master recording license.

Additionally, the composition and recording are put on the film's soundtrack album, which sells 1 million copies and generates $85,000 in gross mechanical income as well as master recording license royalties for use of the artist's hit recording. When the film is shown in theaters outside the United States, performance royalties will also be generated for the songwriter and music publisher via the foreign societies affiliated with the writer's U.S. performing rights organization. And when the motion picture is broadcast on television in the United States or in foreign countries, or streamed on the Internet, additional writer/publisher performance royalties will be generated for years into the future.

## TELEVISION SERIES USE

The script for a television series calls for a nightclub performer to sing a contemporary hit song during a particular scene. The music coordinator for the series calls the publisher and requests price quotes for a worldwide, life-of-copyright, all-television media synchronization license, plus an option for a home video buy-out. The publisher negotiates a $9,500 synchronization fee with a $7,500 video buy-out option for the song's use in the television series. The songwriter, through the copublishing arrangement, receives 75% of these monies and will also receive performance royalties from either ASCAP or BMI when the series episode is actually broadcast in the United States. If the series is distributed to and broadcast in countries outside the United States, the local performing rights society will license the television performance, collect royalties, and send the writer's share to ASCAP or BMI in the United States for distribution. Since the music publisher's share of foreign performance income is usually collected by a subpublishing representative in each country, such monies are usually distributed by the local subpublisher directly to the U.S. publisher, which will in turn pay the songwriter his or her 50% copublisher interest. If there is not a subpublisher in the foreign broadcast territory, the publisher royalties will be distributed by the local society to ASCAP or BMI in the United States for distribution.

## FOREIGN MECHANICALS AND PERFORMANCES

Since the market outside the United States is, for an increasing number of songwriters, becoming more and more important, record, CD, and tape sales can easily double the income generated in the United States. Since, other than in Canada, which like the United States calculates mechanical royalties on a set penny basis, the computations depend on the country of sale, the percentage used in the particular territory, and the price basis on which the percentage is applied, computations can be somewhat complex. Suffice it to say that the monies can be substantial. Since ASCAP and BMI have relationships with the other performing rights societies around the world, performances of U.S.-originated compositions are licensed by those societies on behalf of the U.S. writers and publishers. ASCAP and BMI, in turn, provide the same service for foreign writers and music publishers when their compositions are broadcast or otherwise performed in the United States.

## THE BROADWAY MUSICAL

Although Broadway is a very specialized field, some songwriters are able to transfer their skills into that area. The songwriter in our illustration has composed the music to songs for a musical that finally secures the multimillion-dollar backing needed for a show to get to Broadway. The reviews are good, and the show grosses an average of $600,000 per week during the initial year of its Broadway run. Since the songwriter, a Dramatists Guild member, is only the composer of the songs that appear in the musical, he or she is entitled to ⅓ of the 4.5% prerecoupment gross box office receipts royalty (with the book writer and lyricist sharing the remaining 3%). Assuming the musical opens during the initial week of January, plays 52 weeks during the year, and still has not recouped its investment by December 31 of that year, the writer will receive $468,000 in royalty income for the year on Broadway.

| | |
|---|---|
| $600,000 | Weekly box office receipts |
| x 1.5% | ⅓ prerecoupment royalty |
| 9,000 | Weekly composer royalty |
| x 52 | Weeks |
| $468,000 | Annual composer royalty |

## THE MOTION PICTURE BACKGROUND SCORE

Based on the writer's success in the songwriting field as well as some prior experience and training in composing and orchestrating for film, the songwriter is hired by a motion picture producer to compose a contemporary-sounding background music score for a major studio film. The negotiated composing fee is $225,000. The film is released, becomes a worldwide hit and generates substantial performance money from all the major countries in the world. After its theatrical release, the film is aired twice on network television in the United States. Within a few years, the writer and publisher receive a total of $300,000 from foreign performing rights societies and $35,000 from a U.S. performance society for the 2 network television airings.

## ADDITIONAL INCOME-PRODUCING AREAS

In addition to the sources mentioned previously, a number of other income-generating opportunities can open up for the songwriter because of a hit song or hit record. For example, a novelist might include a portion of the lyrics to a composition in the scene of a best-selling novel; a video jukebox company may include the record company's artist video on its machines; a karaoke manufacturer may select the song for use in its product line; a "how to," exercise, or other special-interest video distributor may select the composition or hit recording for use in a home video project; a sheet music manufacturer might sell single sheets of the song and include it in a varied number of folios or other print arrangements; a telephone company may ask for a cell phone ringtone license; an interactive video manufacturer may choose the song to be featured in one of its home video programs, and a doll manufacturer may select the song as part of the doll's singing repertoire—all of which generate additional year-in and year-out income for the songwriter and music publisher. Many of these opportunities continue to occur during the copyright life of a composition (e.g., a song may be used in a number of different television programs, motion pictures, videogames, and commercials and contained on a number of different albums or single releases); with each new use, relicensing generates new revenue.

Revenues from Internet-related uses (downloads, streaming, audio visual synchronization fees, subscription services, etc.) will also be a major source of both domestic and foreign income for writers, artists, publishers and record companies.

The copyright covering the song will generate money both from the streaming of songs as well as the downloading of songs. For writers who are also recording artists, the copyright covering the recording will generate royalties both from the website's streaming of records over the Internet as well as the downloading of recordings. In some cases, a statutory license fee will apply whereas in others, a negotiated fee will be applicable.

If the writer is a non-featured musician or a non-featured vocalist on a sound recording, money may also be due from the Intellectual Property Rights Distribution Fund administered by the AFM and AFTRA under the Audio Home Recording Act of 1992 ($2\frac{5}{8}$% of the Sound Recording Fund goes to non-featured musicians with $1\frac{3}{8}$% going to non-featured vocalists) as well as the Digital Performance Royalties Fund established to collect and distribute monies pursuant to the DPRA and the DMCA (5% of the statutory/compulsory license fees for the digital broadcasting of sound recordings).

Subscription services will be a major source of income. These services include an unlimited listening of songs for a fee; a specific download fee; a limited number of burns for a fee; various price structures based on options of use (specific range of streams and downloads, both time and non-timed), and many more.

# 14

# Breaking into the Business

BEING A SONGWRITER, a recording artist, or both is similar in many respects to any other business. Talent, professionalism, commitment, persistence, connections, luck, finding the right vehicle to get people to notice you, being in the right place at the right time, knowing the behind-the-scenes realities of how things work, having the right people behind you, and being with the right company are all part of the formula for becoming successful. And even though the music and entertainment industry is one of the most unpredictable fields as to who makes it and who doesn't, it is a world that has certain rules that have to be learned as well as certain approaches and routes that have proven to increase your chances of breaking in. It is very rare indeed in this business for anyone to make it without years of working hard and making the right moves.

## CO-WRITING SONGS WITH WRITERS WITH PUBLISHING DEALS

One of the best ways for a new writer to break in is to co-write a song or songs with a writer who is currently signed exclusively to a music publisher. By getting involved with such a writer, your name and your talent will be exposed to music publishers who will promote your work because of their relationship with your co-writer. If their efforts are successful, a number of things can happen, including being offered an exclusive songwriter's contract with weekly advances; getting motion picture, television, Broadway, and commercial work; and, with luck, being in the middle of a bidding war because of your hit song.

Your co-writer's publisher will usually try to publish your share of the song since it will be spending the same amount of money and expending much of the same effort on promotion that it would were it the sole publisher of the song. In fact, some exclusively signed songwriters have provisions in their publishing contracts that obligate them to use reasonable efforts to sign any co-writer. As an independent co-writer, the decision is up to you. It may give you the opportunity of being with a good promotion- and administration-minded publisher.

## BEING IN A PERFORMING GROUP

One of the best ways to succeed in today's market is to be part of a group. Your songs will be performed before audiences, some of whom may be A&R people from publishers or record companies. And if the group is signed to a record deal, your songs will have a guaranteed outlet to the general public. Also, since many of the large music publishers are signing groups (and their writers) and financing elaborate demo sessions in the hope of negotiating a recording artist agreement with a major label, writing for a performing band increases the odds for success.

By being with a band, you will also be able to create that finished sound that is many times needed when you submit demo recordings of your songs—an advantage that many writers, unless they own sophisticated home recording equipment and have the know-how to use it, do not possess. One has to be careful, though, when using one's band on a demo being submitted to a music publisher, that the version is not so unique that the publisher will not see the value of the song itself and its potential for other artists.

## SUBMITTING CDS AND TAPES TO MUSIC PUBLISHERS

At one time, music publishers had staffs who listened to unsolicited song submissions sent in by songwriters. Even though most of the submissions were rejected, it was a viable way for a songwriter to be heard. Because of an increased number of infringement suits against publishers by writers claiming that the melodies, lyrics, or ideas of their submitted songs were used without authorization or copied by others, as well as the growing cost of "errors and omissions" insurance for publishers and record companies, most established music publishers will not accept unsolicited CDs, files, or other recordings.

Such reticence on the part of the music companies to listen to new material from unknown writers is an unfortunate development, since it reduces the chances for writers without track records to get their songs heard. However, because of the ease of filing a lawsuit (whether legitimate or not) and the substantial cost of defending against even the most outrageous claims, most companies have chosen to review songs only from people they know or who have been referred by a person or firm that they know or trust. Regardless of this trend to play it safe legally, there are still some publishers who listen to unsolicited material, and it is best to call and find out about a particular company's policy before sending your demo recording.

## *DEMO RECORDINGS*

For publishers that do review songwriter's demos, one has to remember to follow a number of important rules with respect to any submission. Of major importance is that the demo sound professional. This does not mean that one has to spend thousands of dollars in studio time and musicians, as home recordings with the right equipment can many times successfully convey what is needed. One should also not try to show off instrumental virtuosity on a CD, as the publisher is listening to the structure of the song as opposed to how a finished recording might sound. If you have an interesting arrangement or some important licks which really help sell the song, then include them on the CD. It is also absolutely essential to get into the song as quickly as possible without a long instrumental introduction, which may test the listener's patience.

A good approach is not to try to overwhelm the publisher's A&R staff with 10 or 20 songs, since most company personnel do not have the time or patience to go through the entire catalog of a writer's unpublished works. Pick 3 of your best songs (with the most commercial at the start of the CD or file), as most professional listeners will form their opinion after the initial 2 or 3 songs and, many times, after the first verse and chorus of the first composition.

As for the recording itself, make sure that the songs are listed in the proper order with timings indicated, so that if a person does not like a particular song, he or she can proceed to the next one quickly. One should also submit a typed lyric sheet for each song with the names of all co-writers, their authorship shares, whether they are affiliated with another music publisher, and whether they are a member of ASCAP, BMI, or SESAC. The writer's name and phone number should be listed, along with any worthwhile reviews or credits. If you have had songs previously recorded or used in television shows, feature films, or commercials, it is best to include that information even if the songs may be owned by another publisher. The whole point is to give a company a reason to listen, and anything you can realistically add to who you are and what you have done can only help the first impression.

## *SONGWRITER CONFERENCES*

One way to increase your exposure to the music industry and get to meet people actually in the business is to attend as many songwriter conferences as possible. Most of these 1-, 2-, or 3-day meetings have panel discussions on the various business and legal aspects of music as well as creative seminars about writing, performing, and song reviewing. Besides the educational value of such conferences, you will get a chance to talk with other writers and industry executives whose only reason for being there is to help aspiring writers or performers. In fact, many well-known executives or creators who are virtually impossible to contact under normal circumstances are easily accessible during such conferences. And since the atmosphere is usually casual and receptive to the exchange of ideas, these conferences can be the perfect place to make connections, compare notes, ask questions, get advice, and most importantly, give you a sense that you belong to an industry that many times seems only a dream.

ASCAP and BMI are instrumental in organizing, sponsoring, or lending their support to these conferences, and a call to either organization should give you a good idea of what is scheduled for your area. In addition, trade publications, the entertainment section of your local newspaper, and the various songwriter organizations throughout the country are all valuable sources of information concerning forthcoming music industry seminars.

## *SHOWCASES*

For bands and singer/songwriters, one of the best opportunities for discovery is to be asked to play in one of the major showcase events held throughout the country. Many songwriter associations and music business conferences have a series of live band and writer showcases at their annual events; as these events are attended by industry executives from many major and independent companies, the opportunity can be a good one.

ASCAP and BMI have a regular series of showcases for most types of music and performances in Los Angeles, New York, and Nashville and occasional showcases in other cities. Practically all showcase participants are chosen through the submission of tapes or through ASCAP and BMI personnel's actually seeing the band or writer perform. Some of the most successful bands in the country have been signed as new bands from these showcases.

## *ATTORNEYS*

One of the most effective ways of getting an introduction to a music publisher or record company is through entertainment lawyers, since most have connections with virtually all large music publishing and record companies. They usually have negotiated agreements with such companies on behalf of their clients, represented the company itself, or have in some respect had a relationship with the company that enables them to submit a recording occasionally. The good music attorneys also have a real knowledge of each company from top to bottom and can usually contact the right person for a particular project—an asset that can not only save time but also give the agent or writer/performer a better than even chance of being heard by the right people. In addition, whether the response is positive or negative, an answer will normally be given more quickly if a known entertainment lawyer is involved.

Submissions from a lawyer are many times looked on differently, especially if the attorney has a good reputation or other clients with the company. Sometimes the person who submits a project can matter as much as the project itself.

Since most music attorneys are fairly selective and have strong feelings about what they feel is saleable, a writer's presentation must be very strong to get an attorney involved, especially if you expect the attorney to do the initial work on a reduced rate or percentage basis prior to a deal being secured. Obviously, if you have a track record of some prior success, the entertainment lawyer may have an easier time deciding whether to represent you when there is no commitment, since a sales pitch to a record company or music publisher can be more easily presented if based on your past success and future potential. If you are an unknown quantity and not part of a performing band, however, convincing a lawyer to represent you on a speculative basis can be difficult unless your tape and songs are extremely commercial or the attorney really believes in you and is willing to take a chance.

## RECORD PRODUCERS

Since record producers are many times at the end of the process of selecting what songs are recorded by an artist and what songs are actually put on an album, having a producer listen to your songs is as good as (and sometimes better than) having the actual artist hear them. As in the case with many music publishers though, submitting a song to a producer is not an easy task. Because of the potential lawsuits that may come from listening to or having had access to submitted songs, many producers are even more careful than large publishers. Still, a number of them will talk to writers with an introduction from a lawyer or acquaintance, and persistence is vital in this area.

If a writer has done the homework (knowing who is producing what artist, what types of songs are being recorded, whether the artist did well with the last album or whether a change of direction is needed, the concept of the next album, whether the producer has a stable of writers whose songs are used or is looking for some new blood, etc.) and has a professional demo recording and good songs, getting to the right producer is a possibility.

## MANAGERS

As with entertainment lawyers, many managers have an ongoing entrée to the major music publishers and record companies. Being signed with the right manager can almost guarantee the proper exposure of your songs to those who make the real decisions in the music industry. Good managers, though, are very selective in their choice of whom they represent, since they try to keep their roster of clients small and are paid not on an hourly basis but on a percentage of the monies earned by their clients. Since managers are normally responsible for all expenses and do not make any money unless their clients have some success, their decision whether to sign a writer is based on a combination of both financial and creative factors—a combination that many times does not bode well for the newcomer.

## AGENTS

In many respects, agents fall into the same category as managers, in that they usually have good contacts with the major publishing and record companies but also receive compensation based on their clients' earnings. Consequently, most agents accept only writers, artists, or writer/performers who they feel are promotable for paying jobs and will not waste their time by signing you just for the sake of having another person under contract. An agent who sees your potential and feels a real interest in your development can be a real steppingstone to getting recognized, since agents can expand your horizons into other areas, such as writing for motion pictures and television.

Since agents are as specialized as any other professional in the entertainment industry, it is wise to contact only agents who concentrate in the field that you are pursuing or, if you are established, the area into which you want to expand. An agency that specializes in securing television and motion picture assignments for composers may not specialize in securing a live 1-week stand at a local music club. It is extremely important to find out the direction and expertise of particular agents, since contacting the wrong one without doing your homework will be a waste of time for all involved.

## MUSIC VIDEOS

Because of the widespread popularity of music videos as well as the ability to produce audiovisual performances with home equipment at reasonable prices, video presentations of a writer or writer/performer have given creators a new dimension for promoting their work. One of the values of a video is that publishers or record companies do not have to go and see a writer/performer to decide whether they are interested in pursuing a contractual relationship, as they can get a good feel by watching the video. And if there is interest after reviewing the video, they can then go see the performer in person.

A video can be especially valuable to a performer who does not live close to Los Angeles, New York, or Nashville. And since most of the major music publishers are now looking for writers whom they can develop as recording artists, a good video may not only help sell the song but also display the performance potential that many publishers are looking for. An exciting video can also provide an entrée to many of the cable television stations in your area, as most public access stations are always looking for new programming to round out their broadcast schedule.

## CABLE TELEVISION

With the emergence of public access cable channels throughout the United States, the songwriter/performer has been given an inexpensive vehicle to expose his or her music and talents to the general public and to those that make the creative business decisions that run the entertainment industry. A local station can tell you what its access rules are.

## ASCAP AND BMI

Both ASCAP and BMI can be valuable resources and referral services for new writers and artists, as both organizations have people on staff who listen to tapes, go to clubs to hear performers, and generally give advice to thousands of writers every year. On occasion, they can also provide a writer or artist with a referral to music publishers who might be looking for the type of music that the writer is writing and record companies whose focus is similar to the artists. Also, these organizations' showcase series are some of the most successful in the country.

## PAYING TO GET YOUR SONGS PUBLISHED

One of the most important things to remember is that legitimate music publishers do not charge songwriters to publish or record their songs. Many companies do recoup a certain percentage of their direct costs (such as copyright registration fees, the making of lead sheets, and the costs of a demo recording session) from a writer's future royalties, but this occurs only if a song earns money. The writer should never be asked to pay any monies up front for these services.

## FINDING THE RIGHT PUBLISHER

If a writer has friends or acquaintances in the music business, they will normally be able to give some advice as to who the good publishers are. Whether these comments are based on actual experience or "on the street" rumors or hearsay, if you trust the person you're talking to, it can be a step in increasing your information about who to contact and who to stay away from. Also, never underestimate your own intuition (especially after you have talked with various companies and their personnel); many times you are the best judge as to whether there is a rapport, good support staff, and a real commitment toward your creative direction.

Another consideration that must be addressed is the type of songs that you are writing and whether they fit into a particular publisher's current catalog. For example, if you write country music, it may not be advisable to submit your songs to a publisher who deals only in theater or motion picture music, unless it has a separate branch office in Nashville promoting country music. Conversely, if you write rock 'n' roll, a Nashville publisher may not be the right company to promote your song, unless it has a Nashville pop division as well as a staffed pop office in Los Angeles or New York. It is always helpful to look at the trade paper Hot 100 Charts, as they will give you a good idea of who the successful publishers are in your field. Many of these trade magazines also have year-end issues that list the top publishers, artists, producers, and record companies in each type of music, which is a valuable way to narrow your focus.

Even though a company may not be currently hot in a particular category of music, it may be trying to get into that field or may have a prior successful track record in that field and might be looking for new writers as opposed to buying into expensive deals with recording artists, writer/performers, or producers currently successful in that genre. Writers should always try to find out whether the company is serious in its intentions to expand its base and has the requisite staff to compete successfully in the new area before committing one's song and future.

Other important things to look for are the business, legal, and creative experience of the people working at the company, its promotion abilities, whether it has availed itself of the many advances in computer technology, the quality of its foreign representatives, whether it has in-house recording studios that can be used by songwriters, its connections with motion picture and television companies, its relationships with record producers and recording artists, whether there are any such artists or producers on staff, its success in licensing songs for commercials, and its reputation as a responsive and innovative organization.

## DIFFERENT TYPES OF PUBLISHERS

Music publishers come in many forms, shapes, and sizes, and all have particularly attractive qualities to offer to a songwriter or writer/artist. Major companies (sometimes affiliated with a record company and sometimes not) are usually full-service operations with experienced personnel in all aspects of music and business. Some of these companies are primarily interested in acquisition (buying other existing companies). These companies are bottom-line financial investment entities and may serve some writers or publishers interested in getting the highest short-term offer possible. Other companies, though major operations, try to service not only their old copyrights but also their new ones. Some of the major companies have a philosophy of buying into success and chart activity, whereas others try to develop what they have as well as what will generate their business in the future.

Most motion picture and television production companies have affiliated music publishing operations to control and administer the music used in their products. Some of these companies are among the most successful at signing and promoting new writers and artists regardless of whether their music is film or television oriented. Others are primarily collection agencies administering film and television copyrights throughout the world.

Many record producers also have their own publishing companies, either in conjunction with a major company or by themselves. A number of these companies are fully staffed organizations who sign new writers. Although very selective, these companies offer an opportunity for a writer or artist to be considered in any project the producer is involved in.

Most music publishers are what is referred to as "independent" in that they are not owned by large conglomerates, motion picture companies, television producers, or record companies. Their primary or sole source of income is from the commercial use of the songs in their catalogs, and their main thrust is the protection and promotion of the music they control without having to deal with any of the company policies that may be dictated by a firm's non-music publishing divisions. And even though these independents may not have the instant access to an affiliated motion picture, television, or record company, they can be very effective (depending on their reputation and promotion capabilities) in getting songs recorded or placed in theatrical films and television series, commercials, videos, and Broadway shows. The selling point that most of these companies use is that they represent a more hands-on and personal approach to the writer and are usually very accessible to songwriters.

## FILM AND TELEVISION

The film and television field is one of the more difficult areas to break into. Many of the composers in this field have a background of symphonic or classical training at a university or conservatory. The ability to compose and orchestrate for as well as to conduct a full orchestra are a necessity for many feature films and episodic television (1-hour drama shows, particularly). Changes in the musical tastes of producers and the public have enlarged the possibilities in this field for pop songwriters, as many shows look for a contemporary sound similar to what is being played on radio. Some of the most successful films and television series have been written by writers formerly associated with the pop field. Nevertheless, large orchestral scores remain a major part of the film and television world.

This field is particularly difficult to break into if one is not living in or near the major production cities. It is possible to get your first credits elsewhere (college films, small independent films for limited release, etc.) and then bring those credits with you to Los Angeles, New York, or any other city which has major production facilities.

Initially, every composer must compile a good demo CD or tape. These demos, usually significantly more costly than songwriter demos, must show an ability to compose creatively and to create an interesting and experienced "sound." These demos range from full-blown orchestral scores to 1-person electronic scores. Once a demo is completed, it should be forwarded to composer agents, music departments of studios and production companies, and the Los Angeles film and television departments of ASCAP and BMI. A composer's credits should also be enclosed. The likelihood of gaining entry with one of these CDs or tapes is slim, but it is worth a shot. The demo CD or tape is important as a work sample that can be given to working composers with whom you come into contact as well as anyone else you may meet in the industry.

One of the best ways of breaking into television and motion pictures is to be accepted in the ASCAP or BMI film and television composing workshops. These annual workshops are held in Los Angeles, where up-and-coming composers attend instructional sessions on the creative and business sides of film and television music and finish the course by scoring, conducting, and recording a session. These finished demo recordings can then be sent by ASCAP, BMI or the writer to music departments, agents, and well-known composers who may be in need of new composers. For talented new composers, ASCAP and BMI are both excellent referral services if one's work is top-notch.

Some of the ways in which composers have broken into television and motion pictures include:

> Composing cues for more senior or successful composers who may have a series or film and who, due to time restrictions or the amount of music involved, look for new writers to compose some of the cues, usually in the style of the principal composer. Quite a few television series, both network as well as original shows for local television, have used this approach.
> Orchestrating cues for established composers who have a specific film or

television project. Many new composers get these assignments through contact with the main composer or because they have sent demos or are known to film and television agents, production and studio music departments, independent film producers, and college and university music departments. Orchestration for these projects is one of the best learning experiences that a composer can have.

Ghostwriting for other composers. Ghostwriting involves composing a score for another composer for a series or film but not receiving any credit for the work. Although the composer does gain composing experience, the credit as well as all royalties normally go to another person or to the main composer. This is a practice not encouraged in the industry.

For songwriters, one's publisher as well as one's agent can be instrumental in gaining an entrance into the field. Although many songwriters do not have orchestral training, the proliferation of synthesized scores have put less emphasis on training and more on the contemporary sound. Some successful songwriters who have composed for major films have done so by creating basic scores and then hiring orchestrators to develop the themes and write the full film score.

The most important thing that a new composer must do is to connect with as many people as possible in the film and television community. One needs to join organizations, attend conferences, and stay up on what film and television music currently sounds like. As in most areas of the music business, a certain amount of luck and being in the right place at the right time is necessary. But you must have the skills and knowledge to take advantage of any break.

## DEMO REVIEWS IN MAGAZINES

There are a number of music-oriented magazines that review and rate demo recordings submitted by writers or writer–performers. Since many of these magazines are read by music industry and A&R executives, a favorable review can assist in securing some initial interest to at least give a writer some credibility that will help open the door.

## MUSIC WEB SITES

One of the most common ways if you are a writer–artist to have your music heard is through one of the many music-related Web sites. There are many variations in this area as to whether or not there will be any compensation for downloads, streaming or CDs sold from retail sites and, if so, how much. The submission agreements must be read carefully, but the Internet is a significant vehicle because it reaches millions of people. Creating your own Web site can be a great promotional and marketing tool as well as a way to build up a fan base both locally as well as throughout the world.

# 15

# Music, Money, and Sampling

ONE OF THE MORE significant issues in today's music industry is that of sampling. It is a term that crosses all areas of music from songs, records, films, television, theatre, commercials and beyond. There are many definitions of the word "sampling"; in briefest terms, it is when a songwriter, recording artist or record producer takes a portion of an existing song, existing recorded performance, or both and integrates it into a newly recorded performance.

## OVERVIEW

Sampling can take a number of different forms; the following are the most common:

*The Song Itself.* The recording artist or record producer uses a portion of an existing song as a bridge, insert, or portion of a new song.

*The Master Recording.* The recording artist or producer uses an instrumental portion (e.g., a guitar or bass line or full instrumental track) of an existing master recording and inserts it into a newly recorded master.

*The Master Recording and the Song.* The recording artist or producer transfers an existing master recording and vocal performance of the song directly into the newly recorded master.

In cases where the producer supervising the session, re-mixer or recording artist samples without permission from the music publisher (the owner of the underlying song sampled) or the record company (the owner of the pre-existing recorded performance sampled), the publisher and record company will contact the recording artist or record company that releases the unauthorized sampled performance and advise that such use constitutes an infringement of copyright. A demand will also be made that the infringing party cease and desist all activities related to the sample, that all product be recalled from the market and that damages and profits be paid immediately.

In these instances, the matter will either proceed to litigation or, if a settlement is negotiated, will be resolved through a continuing monetary or copyright participation on the part of the sampled publisher and/or record company or a release of claims and settlement which results in a monetary payment by the sampling party to the sampled party and, many times, an agreement that the sample will be deleted from any and all recordings made and distributed in the future.

In cases where the recording artist, producer or record company requests permission prior to the actual sampling, the applicable music publisher, record company, or both will, if the use is approved, usually negotiate a settlement of the matter. If the sample is not approved, the sample can be deleted from the recording before it is released without any harm to the recording artist, record producer and recording company. In this regard and as a piece of practical advice, if permission to utilize a portion of an existing composition or recorded performance is requested by the sampling party prior to a sample being recorded or released, the owner of the sampled composition or sampled recorded performance is more likely to view the new recording in a positive manner and be amenable to a non-litigation resolution.

If the sample is approved, resolution is handled in a number of different ways including a one-time "buy-out of all rights" fee, the payment of a percentage of income received from either the new recording or the new song, or the transfer of a portion of the copyright of the new composition (plus the income generated therefrom). As a part of any negotiations, the music publisher or record company owning the sampled composition or master recording will request a copy of the new recording for review, time the duration of the sampled section, and determine its importance to the new version. There are no hard and fast rules in this analysis and final resolution is usually based on, among other things, the bargaining power of the parties, the duration of the sample in comparison to the duration of the entire new recording (although timing may have little relevance if a key element or recognizable piece of the original composition or recording has been used), the nature of the sample (i.e., whether a core portion has been utilized or just an incidental portion), the actual sales of the new version if it has been released, whether the new version has reached the charts, and whether the sampling party requested permission prior to the commercial release of the new recording.

If the sample has been approved, negotiations can take a number of different forms. For example, the publisher can grant the owner of the new composition a worldwide license to use the sampled composition for an agreed-upon share of the mechanical royalties generated by sales of CDs, tapes and other audio configurations embodying the new composition. Under this type of arrangement, the publisher and writer of the sampled composition normally receive from 5% to 75% of the royalties generated but such percentages can be higher or lower depending on the facts of a particular case. Occasionally, these payments will be made on a so called "rollover" advance basis (e.g., $2,000 for the first 50,000 tapes or CDs sold, $2,000 for sales between 50,001 and 100,000 units, an additional $2,000 for sales between 100,001 and 150,000, etc.) or an advance against a specified number of units will be given to the publisher of the sampled composition. For example, if the sampled publisher secured a 50% interest at a statutory rate, an advance of $4,250 might be requested to cover the initial 100,000 units sold. At such time that sales reached the 100,000 level, the sampled publisher would start receiving mechanical royalties on a per unit basis for future recordings sold since the pre-payment advance had already covered all royalties that were due for the initial 100,000 in sales. On the other hand, if the recording never achieved the 100,000 sales plateau for which the advance was paid, there would be no reimbursement required since most advances, by their nature, are non-returnable unless negotiated to the contrary.

If a share of the copyright ownership is negotiated, the publisher of the new composition will transfer a portion of the copyright (e.g., usually from 5% to 75% but it can be more) to the publisher of the sampled composition. In addition, the names of the songwriters who wrote the sampled composition will be added as writers and will receive credit on all uses of the new composition. Under this type of arrangement, the publisher and writers of the sampled composition will receive a portion of all income generated by the new version whether it be from CD sales, film and television uses, commercials, print or any other commercial exploitation of the new composition. For example, if the new composition is licensed for use over the opening credits to a major motion picture, the publisher and songwriter of the sampled song would not only receive a portion of the synchronization and video buyout fee negotiated for the use but would also receive their proportionate share of all income generated from all other uses generated by the film (e.g., mechanical royalties from sales of the soundtrack album or, if applicable, soundtrack single, performance royalties for television broadcasts of the film, radio and television performances of the song from the film, foreign theatrical royalties, advertising commercial fees, sheet music and folio use, CD-ROM and interactive media, lyric reprints in novels, karaoke, streaming royalties, etc.). The screen credit for the new composition will also mention the original composition.

Even if permission for the sample is approved, restrictions may sometimes be placed on how the new composition can be used. For example, in some settlements the new composition may be restricted from being placed in a motion picture, television program or video unless the writer and publisher of the sampled composition give their approval. There also may be restrictions on the use of the new composition in commercial advertising campaigns as well as new technology uses.

Many times, the writer and publisher of the sampled composition will, in the case where the sampling writer is either a recording artist or record producer, agree to be bound by the terms of the controlled composition clause of the recording artist or record production agreement. For example, if the sampling writer-artist has agreed to a 75% mechanical rate for all CDs and tapes sold in the United States, the publisher of the sampled composition may also agree that its share of royalties will be calculated on the same reduced rate. In many cases, however, the publisher of the sampled composition will demand that its share of royalties be based on the statutory mechanical rate regardless of the reduced controlled composition rate agreed to by the recording artist or producer.

This latter arrangement is very common and can have a significant negative impact on the royalties due the writers and publishers of the non-sampled portion of the composition. For example, if a writer-artist is subject to a controlled composition clause which dictates a 75% reduced rate mechanical license for a composition (6.375¢ in 2004-05) and the publisher and writer of the sampled composition demands not only 50% of the copyright and income but also a 100% statutory rate for its share (8.5¢ x 50% = 4.25¢), there would only be slightly more than 2¢ remaining in mechanical income for the writer-artist who sampled (6.375¢ - 4.25¢ = 2.125¢). And if the publisher of the sampled composition licensed its share via a "floating" statutory rate basis (which would get the benefit of any future increases in the statutory mechanical rate), the writer-artist's mechanical income would continue to decrease as the sampled composition's mechanical rate increased. This is because the 75% controlled composition rate is "locked in" as of a set date and does not change regardless of any industry wide mechanical rate increases.

As to performance income, the performance rights organizations will follow the percentages agreed to in the sampling agreement and will remit royalties accordingly. For example, if the parties agree that the sampled composition was entitled to a 60% copyright and income share of the new composition, the performance right organizations would remit 60% of the songwriter royalties due from performances of the new composition to the writer of the sampled composition and 60% of the publisher's share of all performance royalties to the publisher of the sampled composition. The remaining 40% writer's share and corresponding publisher's share of income would be paid to the writer and publisher of the new composition. These splits are set forth in the song registrations submitted to ASCAP or BMI by the music publisher. Since worldwide radio and television performances for chart songs can range from $400,000 to over $1,000,000, the negotiations as to royalty shares between the sampled composition and the new composition can have a very significant financial effect on all of the writers and publishers involved.

In most cases, the publisher of the sampled composition will administer its own share of the new composition throughout the world with direct collection of royalties from all sources.

## FORMAT OF THE SAMPLE AGREEMENT

A sample clearance/permission agreement can take many forms but the major areas of concentration which are dealt with are:

### Copyright Registration

If a portion of the copyright in the new composition is being transferred to the music publisher of the previously existing sampled composition (an occurrence which is the norm and not an exception to the rule), the parties will provide for the registration of the new composition in the Copyright Office of the United States via a registration which reflects the mutually agreed upon ownership percentages. For example, if the ownership split is 50% to the publisher of the existing sampled composition and 50% to the publisher of the new material, such will be stated in the sample agreement. If the publisher of the new material has already registered the new composition in its own name, as assignment will be prepared to transfer the appropriate share to the publisher whose composition was sampled. The publisher of the sampled composition usually has the right to sign such an assignment on behalf of the sampling publisher as its attorney-in-fact if the sampling publisher does not do so within 10 to 20 days after request to do so by the music publisher of the composition sampled.

### Administration of the New Composition

In many cases, each of the publishers will have the right in the United States and Canada to administer and exploit the new composition as well as enter into license agreements for the new composition provided no such licenses are exclusive and no mechanical licenses are issued at less than the statutory mechanical rate (with reduced rates being permissible only for those types of sales for which music publishers customarily grant reduced rates to non-affiliated record companies).

The sampled publisher usually demands that there will be restrictions placed on certain agreed upon types of commercial exploitation of the new composition and will provide that its share of the new composition not be subject to or adversely affected by any controlled composition clause in the sampling writer-artist's or writer–producer's recording artist or producer's agreement with a record company, and that synchronization licenses, advertising commercial licenses and other such licenses only be issued jointly by the sampled publisher and sampling publisher (with approval to be withheld in either party's sole discretion). Under this common scenario, if a motion picture producer, television producer or advertising agency wants to use the new composition in either a motion picture, television series or commercial, they must go to and negotiate with both the sampled publisher and sampling publisher for the right to use the new composition. In addition, the sampled publisher and sampling publisher will agree to instruct all licensees that the licensee will remit each party's respective share of monies directly to that party and that a copy of the signed license will be sent to both the sampled publisher and the sampling publisher. For example, if the negotiation of a motion picture license fee for the new composition results in a fee of $40,000 and the agreed upon money split is on a 50%/50% basis, the film producer will send $20,000 directly to the sampled publisher and $20,000 directly to the sampling publisher.

## Collection of Monies/Payment of Songwriter Royalties

Each of the publishers (both the publisher of the sampled composition and the sampling composition) will agree to collect its share of income directly from the source including mechanical royalties, the publisher's share of performance income, synchronization fees, video royalties, print income and all other miscellaneous royalties generated by the new composition. In turn, both the sampled publisher and the sampling publisher will guarantee that each will be responsible for the payment of songwriter royalties to the respective songwriters signed to them.

On occasion, if an affiliate or subsidiary of one of the publishers is a print company, there will be a stated royalty which will be deemed to be the gross royalties payable for various print configurations. For example, all parties might agree that the royalty for each copy of regular sheet music will be 20% of the suggested retail list price, the royalty for folios or songbooks which contain the new composition and other compositions will be a pro-rata share of 12.5% of the marked retail selling price and the royalty for fake books and educational, orchestral, choral or band arrangement editions will be 10% of the marked retail selling price.

## Additional Sampling

The writer and publisher of the new material will guarantee the original songwriters and the publisher of the sampled composition that no other existing compositions have been sampled in the new composition. The sampling writer and publisher will also indemnify the sampled publisher against any claims from a third party that its composition was sampled as well and will agree that, in the event another composition was sampled and a share of the new composition has to be assigned to the publisher of the additional sample, that such share will only be deducted from the sampling publisher's share of the new composition. For example, if one sample takes 50% of the copyright and income of the new composition and it is discovered that there is an additional sampled composition contained in the new composition, the copyright and income percentage given to the publisher of the additional sample will only be deducted from what remains after the share of the other sampled composition has been deducted.

The obvious danger in these situations when there are more than one pre-existing composition sampled in the new composition is that the publishers of both sampled compositions might demand 50% of the new composition (leaving the writer and publisher of the new composition with 0%) or, even worse, a demand by each of the sampled publishers for 75% or more of the new composition (leaving the writer and publisher of the new composition with, at a minimum, a minus 50% interest and an obligation to ensure, at a minimum, a payout of 50% more than is actually earned). In these situations, the irony is that it is sometimes better to have a failure rather than a hit since as more royalty generating albums, singles and other recordings are sold, the payout to third parties gets larger and larger.

The variations in this area are innumerable and the calculations as to who owns what and who is entitled to what and where the money is going are limitless. Suffice it to say that one needs a calculator at all times when dealing with the issues involved in sampling as it is relatively easy to give away more than you get if you are the writer-artist or writer-producer doing the sampling.

## RECAP

One of the main financial and copyright dangers of sampling to the party who is doing the sampling, and this is not an exaggeration, is the possible loss of 100% of the income from the new composition as well as 100% of the copyright ownership in the material newly created by the artist-writer or producer-writer that is part of the new composition. For example, some writers and publishers of existing hit songs demand 100% of all rights in the new composition which has sampled an existing hit song. This includes the copyright, administration rights (the right to license the composition and collect all royalties), all songwriter royalties (including performance income from radio and television airplay) and all publisher royalties (including record sales, advertising commercial fees, motion picture use fees and television synchronization income). This worst case scenario for the writer-artist or writer-producer doing the sampling does occur and you have to be aware of the fact that the bargaining power in the negotiations is totally in the hands of the owner of the composition being sampled. Clearance of samples prior to a recording being released or otherwise used is vital.

# 16

# Music, Money, Co-Ventures, and Joint Ventures

ONE OF THE MORE common ways for an artist–writer, producer–writer, successful songwriter, or smaller record company to grow their publishing assets, through financing or co-financing from a third party, is to align with a major music publisher under what is known as a co-venture or joint venture publishing arrangement.

The value to the major publisher of such an agreement is that it gets the benefit of the creative expertise of the artist–writer, producer–writer, songwriter or record company in that it will be able to participate in the songwriters and songwriter performers discovered by its partner. In effect, the major publisher is hiring an additional A&R source which will enhance and complement its own creative staff and, hopefully, be introduced to opportunities that it would ordinarily not have a chance to be involved with. The value to the artist–writer, producer–writer, songwriter or record company of the arrangement is that they will have a source of financing and administrative support to take their creative dream and business plan to a level that they may not necessarily be able to do by themselves.

Under this type of agreement, the major publisher usually guarantees that it will provide a certain level of financing on an annual basis which will be used by the writer–artist or writer–producer to sign other songwriters (which, in most cases, will be writer–performers). The copyrights to the compositions will be co-owned by the co-venture parties but the major music publisher will usually administer the compositions throughout the world. The major publisher will also many times be responsible for the payment of the advances required to sign the songwriters selected by the writer–artist or writer–producer.

## TYPES OF JOINT VENTURE/CO-VENTURE AGREEMENTS

There are a number of variations in these types of joint venture/co-venture agreements and some of the major structural points follow.

### Term

The term of the agreement can be for a set number of years (for example, a firm 3 year or 5 year term) or a 1 year period with a number of option years (for example, 1 year plus two 1-year options to extend the agreement exercisable on the part of the major publisher).

### Co-Publishing

The major publisher and the writer–artist or writer–producer will co-own all compositions written by writers signed with the copyright ownership and income split usually being in equal shares. For example, if a songwriter is signed to an exclusive songwriter agreement, those compositions would be co-owned 50/50 by the major publisher and the writer–artist/writer–producer/co-venture party. If, however, the writer is signed to an exclusive songwriter/co-publishing agreement where the songwriter owns a portion of the publishing rights, the major publisher and co-venture partner would own that portion of the copyright and publishing rights which is able to be retained by the major publisher under the exclusive songwriter/co-publishing agreement. For example, if the songwriter signs a standard 50/50 co-publishing agreement and owns 50% of the copyright, the other 50% would be shared equally 25% to the major publisher and 25% to the co-venture writer–artist or writer–producer.

### Administration

During the term of the co-venture agreement, the major music publisher will be the party who performs all the administrative functions related to the songwriters signed to the co-venture. For example, the major publisher will collect all royalties earned by the compositions, issue all the licenses, audit users, litigate infringements and prepare all accounting statements being sent to the songwriters. The major publisher will also prepare all the accountings to its co-venture party covering all the monies being generated by the deals signed.

There are a number of variations which can occur once the term of the co-venture agreement has expired. One variation is for both co-venture parties to begin to administer their respective share of each composition so that both parties will begin to issue licenses and collect monies for the share that it owns. This co-administration variation many times occurs only when all advances given to the songwriters signed to the co-venture have been recouped. Another variation might provide that the major publisher will have the right to acquire the co-venture party's share at a specified time in the future calculated on an agreed upon multiple of the net earnings from all the compositions. An additional variation is for the major publisher to have the right to match any offer from a third party received by its co-venture party for the sale of its share of the compositions controlled.

## Advances

Under many of these agreements, the major publisher is the party which pays all the advances due to the writers who are signed. For example, if a songwriter agreement signed by the co-venture provides for $75,000 in advances for the initial period, the major publisher would fund the entire advance. Under some agreements, the major publisher and the co-venture partner will co-finance the advances required by the deals that are signed. For example, if the writer agreement provides for $100,000 in advances to be paid to the songwriter during the initial contract period, the major publisher and the co-venture partner may each contribute 50% each. If there is such a shared financing responsibility arrangement, the major publisher may agree to pay slightly more than its co-venture partner (for example, 60% of the advances rather than 50%) in recognition of the added value being brought to the deal by the creative expertise of its partner.

## Advances to the Co-Venture Partner

On occasion, the major publisher will pay the co-venture partner a separate advance or advances (over and above the advances it pays to the songwriters signed by the co-venture) which will be recoupable from the co-venture partner's share of the net income generated by the compositions controlled. For example, if $100,000 was earned by a composition and the songwriter was entitled to $75,000 of those monies in royalties under his or her co-publishing agreement with the co-venture, the remainder would be split between the major publisher and co-venture partner on a 50%/50% basis (i.e., $12,500 each). Under this scenario, the co-venture partner's $12,500 allocation would be used by the major publisher to recoup any separate advances given directly to the co-venture partner. For example, if the co-venture partner had been advanced

$100,000, the major publisher would apply the $12,500 against the unrecouped advance balance (thus reducing it from $100,000 to $87,500).

## Scope of the Agreement

The co-venture partner usually guarantees that the major publisher will have the right to be involved with all third party songwriters which the co-venture partner wants to sign to its publishing company. In effect, if the partner wants to sign a writer, the major music publisher will be given the opportunity to participate in the deal (and, in many cases, must participate). Exclusivity as to third party signings or at least a right of first refusal on the part of the major publisher is almost always an essential part of the agreement.

## Songwriting Services of the Co-Venturer

If the co-venture partner is a songwriter, his or her services may also be covered by the agreement but this does not have to be the case. On occasion, the co-venture partner is a songwriter who is either signed to another publisher as an exclusive songwriter (but with the ability to acquire outside songs or sign outside songwriters which will not be controlled by the exclusive songwriter agreement) or is a songwriter who controls the publishing rights to his or her own songs and does not wish to be affiliated with a major publisher for the self-written catalogue. In these cases, the co-venture arrangement may only cover the compositions written by outside songwriters who are discovered and signed by the co-venture partner.

## Sharing of Income

In many cases, the net income of the co-venture is split equally between the major publisher and the co-venture party regardless of which party funded the deal. At other times, the net income is shared proportionate to the amount of money each party has contributed to the advances paid to the songwriters signed by the co-venture. For example, if the major publisher paid 75% of all advances to songwriters and the co-venture partner paid 25%, the net income of the co-venture might be split 75% to the major publisher and 25% to the co-venture partner. In these cases, the rewards follow the risk.

## Deals that Extend Past the Term of the Co-Venture Agreement

Since the term of the co-venture between the major publisher and its co-venture partner is for a set number of years (for example, from 1 to 5 years), a number of the songwriter agreements signed by the co-venture will last beyond the expiration of the formal term of the co-venture agreement. For example, if the term of the co-venture agreement is for 3 years, a one-year plus 4 one-year option songwriter agreement signed in the third year of the co-venture will last far beyond the expiration of the co-venture term if all options are exercised. In these cases, the term of the co-venture would be extended past its termination date for that songwriter agreement only provided that both parties to the co-venture continue to exercise the various options in the songwriter agreement.

## Guaranteed Funding

In many of these agreements there is usually a guarantee by the major publisher that it will contribute a specified amount of money during the term which will finance all or a portion of the songwriter agreements signed by the co-venture. For example, there might be a guarantee that the major publisher will provide a minimum amount of advance funding on an aggregate term basis (e.g., $500,000 over a 3-year period) or on an annual basis (e.g., $150,000 per year during each year of the term of the co-venture agreement).

There will also be limits on the amount of money that the co-venture partner is entitled to commit to a particular deal. For example, the co-venture partner may be able to sign deals without the approval of the major publisher if the annual advances for such agreements are under $75,000. If an agreement with a songwriter provides for advances in excess of the $75,000 annual limit (for example, $125,000 per year), the deal could only be entered into with the approval of the major publisher.

Additionally, if the co-venture partner exceeds the annual aggregate advance fund, no further agreements may be entered into without the approval of the major publisher. For example, if the aggregate advance fund for the signing of all deals during a particular year is $150,000 and the co-venture partner is allowed to enter into $75,000 deals without the approval of the major publisher, if separate $75,000 and $50,000 songwriter agreements ($125,000 total) had already been signed during the year and the co-venture partner wanted to sign another $75,000 deal, approval would be needed since the yearly $150,000 maximum would be exceeded even though the individual songwriter agreement was not above the $75,000 limit which needed approval.

There are also certain standards that must be met for any agreement to fall under the "without approval" category. For example, the qualifications might require that the compositions be owned for life of copyright or at least have a 20 year retention term, that there be a commitment that there will be a certain number of released compositions per contract year, or that the publisher have the ability to grant television and motion picture synchronization licenses without the permission of the songwriter, among other terms. If these qualifying terms are not included in the songwriter agreement, the co-venture partner will not be able to sign the deal unless the major publisher approves the deal despite the fact that the individual agreement is under the advance limit.

These guaranteed funding provisions are also usually part of the type of co-venture agreement which provides that the co-venture partner must pay a portion of the advances due songwriters (in contrast to the co-venture arrangement which has the major publisher responsible for 100% of all advances due). For example, the major publisher may guarantee that it will be responsible for up to $210,000 per year in signing advances provided that the co-venture partner is responsible for the payment of 25% of the total advances paid to songwriters. In this case, the co-venture partner would be agreeing to pay $70,000 in advances to writers if the major publisher paid out $210,000 in advances. The schedule would look as follows:

| Year | Annual Advance Total | Major Publisher 75% | Co-Venture Partner 25% |
|------|---------------------|---------------------|------------------------|
| 1 | $280,000 | $210,000 | $70,000 |
| 2 | $280,000 | $210,000 | $70,000 |
| 3 | $280,000 | $210,000 | $70,000 |

## Carry Forward Advances

Some agreements provide that if the minimum funding guarantee is not used during any 1 year period of the co-venture term (for example, if the major publisher agreed to finance $200,000 in advances to songwriters per year but only $100,00 was actually spent due to not enough writers being signed), the difference between what was guaranteed by the major music publisher and what was actually spent will be added to the advance guarantees for the next year. Under our example, the $100,000 in potential advances which was not used during the year would be added to the $200,000 in guaranteed annual advances due for the next year (resulting in the major publisher agreeing to an annual guarantee of $300,000 for that year). On the other hand, the major publisher will want each year to be treated separately and if the co-venture partner does not find enough deals to expend the amount guaranteed during a 1-year period, the advances for the new year will not be increased because of any advance spending shortfall in the prior year.

## Exercise of Options for Songwriter Agreements

Since most of the agreements signed with songwriters have option periods, a major issue in the co-venture negotiations establishing the joint venture rights and responsibilities is which party can decide whether or not to exercise an option to extend the songwriter agreement for another contract period. Since virtually all of the songwriter agreements will provide for the payment of advances when options are exercised, this issue can have an important financial impact on the co-venture parties. In many agreements, the major music publisher will give the co-venture partner the right to determine whether an option is to be exercised, provided that the maximum advance cap is not being exceeded. In some cases, however, both co-venture parties have to agree on the decision. In those cases, if there is a disagreement between the major music publisher and the co-venture partner, the party who wants to exercise the option will be allowed to do so but the compositions written during the exercised option period (and any option periods exercised thereafter) will be totally controlled by the party who exercised the option. If this occurs, all compositions by the applicable songwriter owned by the co-venture prior to the commencement of the option period shall be controlled by the co-venture. Any compositions written during the exercised option period will be controlled by the party who exercised the option and the party who did not want to exercise the option will have no rights in future compositions.

When the term of the co-venture agreement has expired but the term of a songwriter agreement extends past the end of the co-venture term, options are usually exercised only with the mutual approval of both co-venture parties; with the proviso that if either of the parties does not want to exercise an option, that party would not have the right to participate in the compositions written commencing with the start of the option period.

In some joint venture agreements, there are options known as "puts" and "calls." A "put" entitles the party exercising the option to force the other party to buy its remaining interest at a specified price (many times a multiple of the earnings over a set number of prior years). A "call" option is when one party can request the other party to sell its share back to the party exercising the call (once again, at a pre-determined price or formula).

There are also some joint venture agreements that provide that the music publisher and songwriter share in a number of sources of income (such as touring, merchandising and recording artist related income) that are traditionally not part of the publishing deal. These type of arrangements are sometimes entered into when the music publisher has been the party who has secured the recording artist agreement for the songwriter-performer (sometimes having financed all or most of the initial album released by the record company). These partnership agreements many times guarantee the songwriter certain monies during the term of the deal (either as non-recoupable payments or advances against monies that may become due) in addition to providing that certain things will occur during the active term of the venture (for example, that 3 albums will be recorded and released within 6 years of the signing of the agreement). There are also provisions which detail how the net profits will be shared by the writer and the music publisher (for example, 50%/50%, 75%/25%), how decisions of the venture are made, who manages the assets once the term has ended and whether one of the parties has the right to buy the other party's interests once the deal is over or if someone receives an offer from a third party to buy their respective share.

# 17

# Music, Money, and the Internet

INTERNET SERVICE PROVIDERS, digital rights management, compression, downloads, wireless, streaming, subscription and non-subscription services, MP3, hyperdistribution, encryption, decryption keys, platforms, interactive music, watermarking, fingerprinting - these and many more are the new words of the music business. Music via the Internet. And though digital distribution of music is still relatively new (which means that most of the money in music will still be earned for many years in the "traditional" way), the basic rights of copyright and royalties apply in this field just as they do in the traditional world of selling and listening to music. And whether it's an audio or audiovisual work being downloaded or streamed or otherwise communicated, performance, mechanical and synchronization licenses still apply and must be negotiated or dealt with on a statutory or negotiated basis. In this new world, you have a combination of the old rates, concepts and laws applying in some cases with other areas being subject to the negotiation of completely new rates based upon new business models, laws, negotiations, court decisions and developing industry practices.

## MAIN ISSUES

Some of the primary issues raised by the Internet and the digitization of music are what rights are involved in streaming and downloading and who controls those rights; are the royalty rates to be based on the country where a composition is downloaded or in the country where the server is (the country of origin); how and by whom will royalties be collected and paid; can there be territorial licensing or must all licensing be worldwide; how are record company and publishing company contracts to be interpreted as regards the issues of deductions, advances, release requirements, reduced royalty areas, etc.; what encryption, watermarking or other technology is necessary to insure the protection of as well as the assurance of accurate payment of royalties to all rightful parties and the prevention of illegal downloading, sharing of files and piracy; interpretation of as well as litigation as regards the copyright laws of the U.S. as well as foreign countries; the possible replacement of albums by single songs thereby reducing opportunities; the status of digital lockers, subscription services and mobile music; and many more.

## THE LAWS

The primary laws governing music use on the Internet are the 1976 Copyright Law, the Audio Home Recording Act of 1992, the Digital Performance Right in Sound Recording Act of 1995 (DPRA), the Sonny Bono Term Extension Act of 1998, the 1998 Digital Millennium Copyright Act (DMCA) and the 2002 World Intellectual Property Organization treaties (WIPO). Other laws will complement and develop these, but they represent the starting point for the United States.

## RIGHTS

The basic rights covering music on the Internet are:
- Streaming: the playing of songs and recordings on websites and services. Primarily the performance right (ASCAP, BMI, SESAC, foreign societies, copyright owners, record companies, recording artist, and mechanical right societies).
- Downloads: the downloading of a digital music file which is stored for current or future use/the making of a copy of a copyrighted sound recording. Primarily, the mechanical right (music publisher, the Harry Fox Agency, foreign mechanical right societies, performing right

organizations) and the sound recording copyright (record company, artists, and others).

- Synchronization: the placing of a song into an audiovisual work that is transmitted over the Internet. For example, a hit song used as the theme to a new website series (music publishers, copyright owners).

*Two Copyrights.* When dealing with the Internet, one has to remember that one is dealing with two separate copyrights each of which generate royalties. The first copyright is the one that deals only with the musical work- the song itself. The second copyright involves the actual sound recording of the work- the instruments and voices on the recording. The musical work copyright generates money for the writer and the music publisher whereas the sound recording copyright generates money for the record company, the recording artist, non-featured vocalists, musicians and possibly producers.

*The Song.* When a song is played on a website, the site must have a performance license from ASCAP, BMI or SESAC (depending on which PRO controls the song) or obtain a direct license from the copyright owner (usually the music publisher). Without such a license and assuming no exemption, the website can be liable for copyright infringement.

When a song is "downloaded"(a copy is made or stored), a license must be acquired from the copyright owner (the publisher usually) or the owner's agency (the Harry Fox Agency). Based upon the compulsory license provisions, the royalty to be paid is the statutory rate in effect at the time of the download (i.e., 8.5 cents in 2004-2005). A Copyright Arbitration Royalty Panel or Copyright Royalty judges will be setting future download rates in this area unless a negotiated agreement is reached between all interested parties.

*The Recording.* The 1995 DPSR Act and 1998 DMCA Act created a limited public performance right in sound recordings when performed by digital audio transmission (subscription, on demand, webcasting, etc.). When a sound recording (CD, tape, record, etc.) is played over a website, different royalties and negotiations apply depending on what type of website it is. As perfect copies of a work are able to be made in the digital world, the threat of unauthorized copying from website performances resulting in lost record sales is very real.

If a website is an eligible non-subscription service where records are streamed for listeners and there is no advance notice of what is being played, the website operator is covered by a "compulsory" license and has to pay the copyright owner of the records (the record company, the artist, etc.) a negotiated fee which is arrived at between the record company and the website. If a fee cannot be negotiated, the fee will be set by a Copyright Arbitration Royalty Panel (CARP). As long as the website pays this fee, they can stream records. There are also a number of other requirements a website has to comply with in order to get this compulsory license. For instance, they cannot within a three hour period play more than three songs from a particular album, including no more than two consecutively or four songs by a particular artist including no more than three consecutively (this is referred to as the "sound recording performance complement"). Other restrictions involve archived programming, looped programming and the number of times a website can repeat programs during a certain period of time.

In early 2002, a CARP decided what the rates would be for the statutory license. These rates were rejected by the Librarian of Congress and an order was issued setting the actual rates for the period October 28, 1998 through 2002. For all eligible non-subscription services performing sound recordings publicly by means of digital audio transmission (webcasting), the fee was set at 7/100s of a cent ($0.0007 cents) per performance per listener plus 8.8 % of the performance fees due to cover the making of ephemeral copies of the recordings. These fees apply to websites and commercial broadcasters (AM or FM radio retransmissions over the Internet) as well as some non-commercial situations. A lesser rate of 2/100s of a cent ($0.0002 cents) applies to certain other non-commercial situations as well as archived programming subsequently transmitted over the Internet. Each service must pay a minimum annual fee of $500 with business establishment services paying more. In addition, the Small Webcaster Settlement Act of 2002 sets forth a different percentage of revenue/ expenses fee approach (rather than the statutory/compulsory license rate) for webcasters whose gross revenues are below a certain level and for certain non-commercial webcasters. Minimum fees for 2003 and 2004 are either $2,000 or $5,000 depending on gross revenues of under or over $50,000.

Webcasters who are eligible to operate under the terms of this statutory (compulsory) license, must file an "Initial Notice" with the Copyright Office prior to the commencement of "streaming". Royalty payments as well as statements are to be made to SoundExchange 45 days after the end of each month of webcasting.

For the years 2003 and 2004, an agreement reached between SoundExchange and webcasters allowed non-subscription webcasters to pay on a per performance or aggregate tuning hour basis ($0.000762 cents per performance or 1.17 cents per aggregate tuning hour) and offers an additional gross revenue option for subscription services (10.9% of gross revenues). This agreement did not cover non-commercial webcasters or simulcasts of over the air broadcasts.

All royalties received from a website for the compulsory license are to be paid 50% to owners of a sound recording copyright (record company or recording artist), 45% to featured recording artists, 2.5% to non-featured vocalists (AFTRA) and 2.5% to non-featured musicians (AFM). The sound recording copyright and featured artists' royalties (95% of the Fund) are distributed by SoundExchange with the AFM and AFTRA distributing the remaining 5% of the Fund to non-featured musicians and vocalists.

On the other hand, if a website streams records where the customer chooses what is to be heard (interactive) or where the website provides advance play information, or cannot comply with all of the requirements of the compulsory license, the website operator must get permission directly from the sound recording copyright owner (usually the record company) and negotiate a fee. As this type of streaming provides a good opportunity for consumers to make perfect digital copies of the recording (advance notice, etc.) and therefore reduce record sales, a voluntary (as opposed to compulsory) license and negotiation must occur. If the record company and website cannot come to an agreement on the fee, the website cannot stream the records as it would be a violation of one of the rights of copyright. All royalties received by the record company because of voluntary negotiated licenses are usually paid to recording artists based upon the specific provisions of each artist's recording agreement.

For any sites that allow digital downloads, a license must be secured from the copyright owner of the recording (usually the record company) as the right to make and distribute copies of a sound recording is not covered by any compulsory license and must be negotiated with the record company.

*Synchronization Royalties.* As in other areas, when a composition is put into an audiovisual program on the Internet (i.e., an episodic series, a movie, etc.), a synchronization license needs to be negotiated and a fee paid.

---

## *ASCAP, BMI AND SESAC INTERNET LICENSES*

ASCAP, BMI, and SESAC have licenses that authorize Internet sites and services to perform all of the works in each organization's repertory (songs, scores, etc.) regardless of the file format. These Internet licenses do not authorize the reproduction or distribution of the music or sound recordings or the public performance of the sound recordings.

ASCAP issues a non-interactive license that does not allow users to download or otherwise select particular music compositions and an interactive license for sites or services that allow users to download or otherwise select particular musical compositions. A third type of license agreement authorizes public performances of ASCAP music by way of wireless devices such as mobile telephone ringtones. Three rate schedules are available for the non-interactive and interactive licenses and fees are based upon an Internet site service's revenue or activity.

BMI's main license type is one where fees are computed on a gross revenue calculation (music is the primary feature) or a music area calculation (music is a part of the total website traffic). A Corporate Image license applies where the site's primary function is to promote the off-line business that the company is in.

SESAC has a license with fees based upon the number of monthly page requests as well as whether there is advertising on the site.

It is important to bear in mind that all of these licenses are still described as "experimental" and therefore it is important to go to each organization's website for the most up to date as well as relevant license agreement.

## DOWNLOADS AND ONLINE SUBSCRIPTION SERVICES

There are numerous legitimate digital music sites and services that provide:

- Full (permanent) downloads.
- Time-limited downloads (which time out or become inaccessible after a set period of time or when a person's subscription is not renewed or runs out).
- Use-limited downloads (which have certain restrictions attached to them including limitations on the transfer of a recording to multiple devices, limitations on the number of times you can burn a recording or limitations on the number of times you can listen to a recording).

There are other sites that only distribute full downloads and CD burns without any need for a paid subscription to use the service. There are other sites that are purely subscription based and offer only on-demand streaming of music without any download availability. And there are other online services that offer full downloads, temporary downloads, on-demand streaming and CD burns on a subscription basis.

There are numerous variations as to how these sites operate, the services they provide and how much they charged. For example, there might be a 79¢ or a 99¢ single track download cost; an $8.00 or $9.99 album download cost; an $8.95 or $9.95 per month unlimited music streaming option, pay on-demand radio service; as well as many other variations as to pricing and services offered.

Some sites offer the ability to get the lyrics to compositions; others enable the consumer to look at or download the album cover artwork; and some give in depth artist profiles.

Since every company is looking for a business model which works not only for them but for the consumer as well, variations relating to prices charged for music, restrictions imposed and services offered continue to change and evolve.

*Pre-loaded Music Files.* A number of these online music services provide the subscriber with a key (sometimes called a "decryption key") which allows the subscriber to decrypt a music file that has been pre-loaded into a computer or other digital device. These pre-loaded files which are digital files that contain a sound recording of a composition are then accessed by the consumer through the use of the decryption key which is provided once it is established that the user has the right to such access via a subscription or other license agreement.

*Digital Downloads.* Record companies in the United States have been using a notice of compulsory license when notifying music publishers of their intention to offer digital downloads of songs. In the notice, the record company names the song to be downloaded as well as the identity of the songwriters and music publishers, identifies the recording artist performing the song, gives the names of the officers and directors of the record company, and provides an expected distribution date of the digital phonograph delivery ("DPD") of the song (for example, "from time to time after January 1, 2004"). Because these requests come in the form of a compulsory license, the digital download will be licensed and paid at the statutory rate unless the music publisher approves a different rate.

The current statutory rate for full downloads of a composition is 8.5¢ or 1.65¢ per minute if the song is longer than 5 minutes.

Since record companies are able to pass along the digital mechanical licenses to online music services, these services are able to use the authority of these DPD licenses to download music. In these cases, the online music service pays royalties to the record company which owns the master recording being downloaded which, in turn, pays the Harry Fox Agency the music publishing royalties due for the composition contained on the downloaded recording. The Harry Fox Agency then pays the music publisher which then pays the songwriter according to the terms of the songwriter agreement. If the music publisher is not an affiliate of the Fox Agency, the record company will pay that publisher directly.

*Limited Downloads.* Royalty rates for time-limited, use-limited and other variations of temporary downloads are currently being negotiated by the National Music Publishers Association (NMPA), the Harry Fox Agency and the Recording Industry Of America (RIAA). Failing a negotiated agreement as to what such rates shall be and how they will be structured , the rates may be finalized by either a Copyright Royalty Arbitration Panel (CARP) proceeding or Copyright Royalty Judges.

Currently, there is a stand still agreement between the major music publishers and major record companies that allows limited downloads to be distributed and subscription services to function with the understanding that, once royalty rates are established, they will be applied retroactively to all limited downloads which occurred in the past.

*On-Demand Streaming.* On-Demand Streams are real-time digital transmissions of recordings of musical compositions which allow a person to choose when he or she wants to listen to a particular recording without having a total reproduction made on the person's computer. As with limited downloads, nego-tiations between the NMPA, Harry Fox Agency and the RIAA should determine royalty rates for on-demand streams. If a voluntary agreement is not achieved, however, rates may be set either by a CARP proceeding or Copyright Royalty Judges.

*License Requests.* License requests for limited downloads or on-demand streams are many times sent to the Harry Fox Agency in electronic form but hard copies may also be submitted. Information contained in each request includes the date of the request, the name of the recording artist, the name of the record company which produced the recording, the title of the composi-tion, other names that the composition might be known as (for example, Over The Rainbow and Somewhere Over The Rainbow), the identity of the songwriter and music publisher, the playing time of the recording, the title of the existing album if the recording has been previously licensed, the configuration (for example, time-limited download, use-limited download, on-demand stream, digi-tal phonograph delivery), royalty rate codes (for example, statutory, controlled composition, if such applies), the actual penny rate (for example, 8.5¢) and the royalty rate indicated as a percentage of the statutory rate (for example, 100%, 75%).

*Royalty Reporting Information.* The use information which is provided to the Harry Fox Agency by the various online services is substantial. Information provided includes the name of the service and identification of the specific format or medium licensed, the number of permanent downloads, on-demand streams, time-limited downloads, and use-limited downloads. Additionally, in the case of pre-loaded files, information will be provided as to the identity of the manufactures for which and product lines of electronic devices on which such files were made,. For example, the name of Gateway, Microsoft, Dell, Apple or other applicable manufacturer will actually be mentioned in the pre-loaded file royalty statement sent to the Fox Agency. Accountings are issued on a quarterly basis within 45 days after the end of each quarter.

## *RINGTONE / CELL PHONE LICENSES*

There are a number of companies which have entered the market to provide compositions for use as ringtones for cell phones. Although the contracts vary from company to company or from music publisher to music publisher (if the publisher is using its own agreement), many of the following areas will be addressed.

*Term.* The duration of the agreement will usually extend for a period of from

1 to 3 years. Occasionally there may be an automatic extension unless the music publisher gives notice prior to the expiration of the term or a good faith negotiation clause once the term is over but, in most cases, the term will end as of a set date unless the parties mutually agree to an extension.

*Territory.* Most ringtone companies will try to secure a worldwide license so that there are no territorial restrictions as to where they can provide ringtones to cell phone users. The majority of U.S. music publishers, however, limit the territory to either the United States, its territories and possessions and the Commonwealth of Puerto Rico or the United States and Canada. It should be mentioned that many publishers use the services of the Harry Fox Agency in the U.S. and CMRRA in Canada for licensing in this area (rather than license directly). In cases where the territory is limited (for example, the United States), the ringtone company will have to make arrangements in other countries (e.g., Canada, the United Kingdom, France, etc.) with the representative of the publisher in those territories if it wants to sell musical ringtones outside the original licensed territory.

*Royalties.* The royalty structure is somewhat negotiable but the current industry-wide royalty in the United States is many times the greater of 10¢ for each completed download of a composition to a cell phone or 10% of all monies earned and/or received by the ringtone company from all forms of exploitation of the composition authorized and permitted under the agreement. For example, if the ringtone was sold to the consumer for $1.99, the royalty to the songwriter/music publisher would be 19.9¢ (the higher of 10¢ or 10% of $1.99). If the ringtone cost the cell phone customer 90¢, the 10¢ minimum royalty would be paid since 10¢ is greater than the 9¢ which would be paid under the 10% of 90¢=9¢ formula.

In the case of co-written compositions where there are multiple songwriters with different publishers, the royalty will be shared on a pro-rata basis based on each company's percentage of control. For example, if there are 2 writers with 2 separate publishers each controlling 50% of the composition, the 10¢/10% royalty will be shared equally. Occasionally, higher royalties are paid for special promotions or tie-ins such as cell phones being sold with the hit song from a new motion picture included as the ringtone.

*Fixation Fees.* Many agreements provide for a one-time fee for each composition that is reproduced on the ringtone company's computer server for use as a ringtone. A standard fixation fee is $25.00 per composition (although some agreements are as high as $50.00 per composition and others have no fixation fee). In the case of compositions co-written by writers signed to different music publishers, this fee is shared proportionately based on the percentage owned by each publisher.

Many agreements, when they are initially signed, have a schedule of compositions which have been made available for ringtones. In these cases, the per composition fixation fee will be paid at the signing of the agreement. For all compositions added in the future, the fee will be paid as each composition is included in the service.

*Most Favored Nations Clauses.* Many agreements contain provisions which guarantee that if another music publisher receives a higher royalty rate or higher fixation fee, the higher royalty rate or fee will be automatically raised effective as of the date that it was given to the other publisher. For example, if a publisher is receiving a 10¢ per song ringtone download royalty and the ringtone company signs a contract with another publisher at an 11¢ rate, the 10¢ rate will be increased to 11¢ as of the effective date that the new rate is given. The same increase would occur if one publisher received a 12% royalty while others had contracts which provided for a 10% rate.

It should be mentioned that most favored nations clauses many times not only relate to the money aspects of the agreement (e.g., royalty rate, fixation fee, advances excluding overall catalogue advances) but may, if so negotiated, apply to other material terms of the agreement such as territory or duration of the term as well.

*Compositions Controlled.* Most agreements start off with a schedule of approved compositions which are actually attached to the agreement. Then as the cell phone company selects new compositions to be added to the list of available ringtones, it will contact the music publisher for approval. In some cases, the publisher will agree to respond in a set number of days or within a reasonable time after the request by the ringtone company but most agreements do not have these type of mandatory response periods.

*Advances.* Some agreements provide for an advance payable on the signing of the agreement. The amount of such payment, which will be recoupable from all royalties due in the future, is totally negotiable.

*Rights Granted By The Music Publisher.* The language varies from agreement to agreement and is sometimes very broad and other times very limited depending on the negotiations and bargaining power of the parties. Virtually all agreements (other than some short term movie or other tie-in agreements which may be exclusive) are non-exclusive so that the music publisher can grant the same rights to multiple cell phone companies. Some contracts state that the ringtone company can create monophonic or polyphonic only ringtone sound recordings of the music to the composition (sometimes called Phonic Ringtones); others state that they can create ringtone sound recordings of the compositions in Midi, Wav, Adpcm or similar downloadable and transmittable digital data formats; and others refer to excerpts of pre-existing sound recordings where the ringtone is the actual master recording featuring the artist who originally performed the song (sometimes called Pre-Recorded Ringtones or Master Clip Ringtones). There are numerous definitions and ways of describing the rights being granted and the above are just examples.

Virtually all licenses exclude print rights to the lyrics of the compositions being used. Other restrictions in the agreement include Karaoke rights, synchronization rights and the right to use the song to promote any products or services.

Additionally, the license with the music publisher for the musical composition does not include sound recording rights to masters since these rights must be secured from the record company which owns the master containing the artist's performance.

Ringtone agreements also give the company the right to distribute the composition over the Internet (or any successor global computer network) or over regional wireless transmission networks for transfer to cell phones or other individual communications devices of consumers for their personal uses.

*Performance Rights.* Many licenses provide that public performances of the compositions are subject to the ringtone company securing appropriate licenses from the applicable performance rights organization (for example, ASCAP, BMI and SESAC in the United States). This will ensure that performance royalties are paid to the songwriters and music publishers of the compositions used. If the territory includes countries outside the United States as well, the agreement is subject to the rights of and licensing by the various performance rights societies outside the United States (e.g., SOCAN in Canada, PRS in the United Kingdom, etc.). Some ringtone companies also license the performance rights directly from the music publisher and songwriter.

*Timing.* There is usually a restriction that the cell phone ringtone cannot play for more than 30 seconds with some companies requesting up to 45 seconds.

*Royalty Accountings.* Royalty statements and royalty payments are sent by the ringtone company to the music publisher within 45 days after the end of each calendar quarter. The actual statement will include all royalty bearing transactions on a country-by-country, title-by-title basis including the number of transmissions, downloads or deliveries of each composition.

Audit rights are provided so that the royalty statements and royalties can be verified by the music publisher. Some agreements provide for the audit costs to be paid by the ringtone company if the audit reveals an error of 5% or more in the royalties paid for the period being audited. If an audit uncovers monies that are due, some agreements provide for such royalties to accumulate interest at "prime rate" or some other agreed upon formula. The publisher many times has to give at least 30 days notice to the ringtone company that it intends to conduct an audit and there are usually provisos that any audit will be done during normal business hours and at the place where the company keeps its books and records.

*Other Provisions.* Many agreements provide for an obligation on the part of the ringtone company to take all reasonable action to secure and maintain protection of the compositions by encryption or otherwise in conformance with copyright laws. Many provide that compositions cannot be licensed to any party that is engaged in piracy or any unauthorized uses of musical compositions. Other contracts guarantee that no promotional use on the ringtone company's web site shall be presented as an endorsement or commercial advertisement for the ringtone service.

There are also indemnification clauses which deal with claims and breaches, notice provisions which dictate how the ringtone company and music publisher put each other on notice (mailing, faxing, emailing, etc.), governing law provisions (New York, California, etc.) and clauses which give a party a certain amount of time to cure a breach or alleged breach of its obligations or representations under the agreement (for example, a 30 day period to cure a breach or alleged breach after notice has been given by the other party).

## PROMOTIONAL STREAMING LICENSES

When a new single is released, the record company or its web licensee will many times request a promotional audio stream Internet license from the music publisher of the composition for use on the artist or record company sites. This also may apply to selected songs on the album.

*Licensed Rights:* The record company and its web licensee will receive the right to transmit the composition as a user selected audio stream via the Internet on certain approved sites as well as the right to digitally encode, reproduce, archive and make copies of the composition for the streaming purposes allowed under the license.

*License Fees:* The royalty which is paid to the music publisher (on behalf of itself and the songwriter) is many times a quarter of a cent ($0.0025) per stream. Royalties will usually be paid only if the stream is in excess of 30 seconds in duration.

*Performance Rights:* Many licenses provide that the streaming can only occur if the transmission is licensed by either ASCAP, BMI or SESAC in the United States or other applicable performance right society outside the United States. This will ensure that the songwriter and music publisher will also receive performance royalties from the streaming.

*Term:*  The term is very usually very limited in duration (e.g., 90 days).

*Restrictions:*  Many of the licenses contain the following types of limitations or restrictions:

- The audio streams can only be transmitted to the users directly from or by using a link to a web page without a charge being made to the user for accessing the stream;

- The license only applies to that version of the Composition on the master recording being licensed (not to any other version).  For example, if a Norah Jones, Eminem or David Gray master is licensed for streaming, a cover version by another recording artist of the composition could not be streamed unless a new license was secured from the music publisher.

- No downloads or electronic storage on a device or system will be available to the end user.

- The end user will not be able to alter, distort, mutilate or otherwise modify the master recording or composition.

- Nothing in the rights granted can be used to imply sponsorship or endorsement of the Website or web page or of any product or service contained on the site or page.

*Credit:*  A credit line for the composition and master recording will appear on the web page or other place where users are able to select the audio streams.  Credit guarantees usually provide for information on the following:

> Composition Title
> Songwriter
> Publisher
> Recording Artist
> Record Label

*Server Location:*  There is a specific warranty as to the location of the servers (e.g., "servers are located in the United States").

*Accountings:*  The streaming royalties are paid on a calendar year quarterly basis (i.e., ending March 31, June 30, September 30, and December 31 of each year) with payment of royalties to the music publisher made 45 days later.  Audit rights are available provided notice is given at least 30 days prior to the audit and that an audit may occur only once for a particular statement.

*Disputes:* If a dispute cannot be resolved via negotiation, some agreements provide for mandatory arbitration rather than the right to litigate but this is negotiable.

---

## VIDEO GAME LICENSES

The use of music in video games is continuing to increase and is becoming a substantial source of music publishing and songwriter income. There are a number of different ways to license music in this area depending on the success of the song being used, the type of video game, how the game is distributed and the policies of the manufacturer. Some of the major issues that will be covered in many of the licenses follow.

*Music.* There will be a description of the composition being used including information on the title, songwriter, publisher and percentage controlled. There should also be a description as to how the song is used in the game.

*Game Title.* The exact title of the game will be mentioned.

*Description Of The Configuration.* Some descriptions are very broad and others are very specific. For example, some agreements include language covering all software programs or other electronic products in any format or platform that is designed for use with computers. Others refer to any existing electronic devices as well as any which may be developed in the future. Many also indicate the type of distribution medium on which the game may be distributed. For example, the contract may actually mention DVD, CD-ROM, consoles arcades, handheld devices, magnetic diskettes and optical disks as permitted distribution media. Others will be less specific or mention the previous media but provide that distribution of the game will not be limited to only the areas mentioned.

*Online Versions.* If the game is available on-line, the agreement will have language which permits the transmission of the game over telephone lines, cable television systems, cellular telephones, satellites and wireless broadcast as well as other ways of transmission which are in existence or which may be developed in the future.

*Fees.* Some agreements provide for an actual royalty but many provide for a one-time buy-out fee per composition regardless of the number of games actually sold or how many times the game is played. Per game royalties range from 8 cents to 15 cents per composition and buyouts range from $2,500 to over $20,000. As in many other areas, royalties and fees depend upon the value of the composition, the prior history or anticipated sales of the game, bargaining power of the parties and the needs of the video game producer, music publisher and songwriter.

*Term.* Some agreements have a set term (such as 5 years, 7 years, 10 years, etc.) during which the song can be used in the video game. If there is a set term, the video manufacturer will many times have the right to sell off its inventory of games for a period of time once the term is over. Other licenses last for as long as the video game is in distribution. And others state that the term is for the life of copyright of the composition.

*Territory.* The territory of distribution is usually the world.

*Companion Products.* Many game producers receive the right to release the compositions used in the video game in companion products such as an audio CD or separate DVD release of the game. Sometimes fees are actually set in the agreement (for example, 100% or 75% reduced statutory rate for a CD) and other times there is a good faith negotiation provision as to the ultimate fee that will be charged for the applicable companion product.

*Collateral Materials.* Many agreements provide that the video distributor can use the composition in its advertising, promotional and marketing materials related to the video game. This may include in-store promotions and demonstrations, DVD trailers and even advertising over closed-network college campuses as long as the use is in-context. Such promotional usage does not include out-of-context uses or other types of advertising campaigns such as network, cable or satellite television.

*Credit.* Most contracts provide that credit for the composition be given on the inside of the video game packaging. Credit may also be placed in the manual for the game or actually in the digital format of the game. If there is a master recording also licensed, the notice will usually contain the name of the record company and the name of the recording artist in addition to the composition information.

*Other Provisions.* Notice, applicable law, audit, warranty and indemnification provisions are similar to most other license agreements.

## DIGITAL JUKEBOXES

As opposed to jukeboxes which play actual physical CDs, this system uses digital recordings which are transmitted digitally from a central database or server to the individual jukeboxes around the country.

*Grant Of Rights.* The music publisher gives the digital jukebox company the non-exclusive right to copy the compositions on the company's database and to digitally transmit them to the jukeboxes for storage on the hard drive so that they can be played when selected.

*Royalties.* The royalties that are payable are based on the number of times that a composition is actually played on each jukebox. One formula provides a payment of one-half ($^1/_2$) cent each time the song is played. This royalty is referred to as a mechanical payment and is not a performance royalty since these rights are normally reserved for licensing through the performance rights organizations. There is usually a most favored nations provision in all of these agreements which guarantee that all music publishers and songwriters will receive the same royalty. Some agreements give a most favored nations clause as to all important terms and not only the royalty rates.

*Term And Territory.* The term is many times for 1 year with the territory being either the United States or the United States and Canada.

*Excluded Rights.* All audio-visual or synchronization rights are excluded from the license. Additionally, there is a guarantee that the selection of a song by a customer will not trigger any advertising (either audio-visual or audio-only) unless the music publisher has agreed to such in advance.

*Accountings.* Payments are made within 45 days of each calendar quarter.

*Promotional Uses:* Certain performances may not be paid on if they are part of a product demonstration where no fee is being charged or if the jukebox performance is part of a limited record company promotion. If the publisher agrees to such a provision, there are usually restrictions as to the number of performances that can be deemed promotional (for example, no more than 5% of the plays of a composition can be considered promotional uses).

## *RECORD COMPANY CONTRACTS*

Most past as well as current recording contracts treat the Internet, Webcasting and digital distribution under the new media or new technology designation. This contract designation provides for reduced royalties rather than top line royalties on all applicable sales. In light of the rapid emergence of this method of distribution, this clause as well as many other recording contract clauses need to be re-examined and re-negotiated in old contracts and completely redefined in new contracts. Some of the primary provisions affecting artists, record companies as well as publishing companies are the following:

## Royalty Calculations

As we have seen in the Recording Artist section, royalty clauses are expressed in percentages (15%, 20%, etc.) and are based on the suggested retail or wholesale price of each recording or tape. These top line percentages apply to the "net sales of records through normal retail channels in the U.S." (traditional "brick and mortar stores"). Reduced royalties are paid for many other categories of sales such as midline and budget albums, mail order, television package and record club albums.

The most important rate reduction contract clause is the one applicable to "new technology" as that directly affects downloads over the Internet. A few sample clauses in this area should be illustrative of record company contracts: "With respect to net sales in a particular new medium-occurring during the "Introductory Period" (as defined in such agreement) applicable to that new media, 70% of the royalty rate applicable to the first net sale of such record through normal retail channels" or "New technology configurations shall mean records in the following configurations: mini-discs, digital compact cassettes, digital audio tapes, laser discs, CD-ROM and other records embodying, employing or otherwise utilizing any non-analog technology (whether or not presently existing or hereafter created or developed), but specifically excluding audio-only compact discs. The royalty rate for any record in a new technology configuration shall be 75% of the otherwise applicable royalty rate set forth in this agreement."

Another sample clause might read "New technology formats are paid at 75% of the otherwise applicable royalty rate until such time as the record sales revenues generated from such format in any year exceed 20% of the total United States recorded music revenues. At such time, all future royalties from such format shall be paid at 100%".

In negotiating these type of clauses, artists should negotiate a cut-off date for the reduced rate so that the reduced rate will not be in effect long past the time when the new configuration or technology becomes an accepted format or way of doing business. Contracts should specify good faith negotiations to arrive at an agreeable rate or alternatively base it on what the industry is paying other artists of similar stature. Preferably, try to define downloads as a "normal retail channel" and not a new technology subject to deduction and reduced royalties. If successful, all other contract clauses would need to be redefined as well as renegotiated.

## Recording Artist Royalties For Downloading Master Recordings

With many record companies simplifying the royalty calculations for the downloading of individual tracks from an album as well as deleting packaging, new technology and most other deductions (other than some special promotion programs) from the equation including using the higher album royalty rate for the downloading of singles, a representative example of how the recording artist is paid for permanent downloads follows.

In the example, the assumption is that the recording artist has a 17% album royalty which is based on a published price to dealer ("PPD") calculation and the record company has agreed to use the album royalty rate rather than the many times lower single's rate.

| | |
|---|---|
| Dealer Price Of Track (PPD) | $0.67 |
| Program Discounts (5%) | -$0.03 |
| | |
| Base Price For Artist Royalty | $0.64 |
| Artist Royalty Rate | x17% |
| | |
| Actual Artist Royalty | $0.11 |

It should be mentioned that the artist royalty calculations might, depending on the record company, be based on the retail price or manufacturer's suggested retail list price (for example, 99 cents or 79 cents) rather than the published price to the dealer or the wholesale price of the recording and the final royalty due the artist might change somewhat depending on what items and deductions are included in the formula being used.

Obviously, if the record company applies packaging and new technology/new media deductions in addition to single vs. album royalty rates in the calculation, the artist royalties generated by downloads may be less than previously mentioned. Each case, therefore, has to be reviewed individually as much depends on the policies of the record company distributing the master recordings.

## Escalating Royalty Clauses

Escalating royalty clauses whereby an artist negotiates higher royalties based upon success may not apply to download sales unless negotiated to the contrary under current contracts as these type of sales would be considered "reduced royalty sales" under the "new technology" as well as other contract provisions. Therefore, if a contract had a 10% royalty for the first 250,000 records sold with 11% from 250,000 to 500,000 sales and 12% from 500,000 to

750,000 sales, any portion of these sales attributable to downloads would not be counted toward the reaching of sales plateaus even if an artist had 1 million downloads on a single album. This entire area needs to be rethought and re-negotiated in light of the single-song download preference (as opposed to the downloading of entire albums.

## Term/Release Obligations/Advances

The term of the recording agreement is usually structured around either the artist's recording and the delivery of a long playing album or the record company's commercial release of the album. The record company will normally also have a number of options to extend the term of the recording agreement for additional periods and additional albums. For example, an agreement might provide that the term will last for an initial contract period during which 1 album containing the writer performer's compositions will be commercially released in the United States plus 3 additional option periods with a commitment of 1 album being released during each of such periods. Under these album based deals, the current contract period will end only after there is a commercial release of an album. In other artist/record company contracts, the recording agreement is based entirely on the recording and release of a specified number of albums and does not include options. For example, the term might provide that the agreement will expire only after the commercial release of 3 newly recorded studio albums.

There are variations on this theme in songwriter agreements which might provide that the album commitment can be fulfilled by a certain number of individual compositions being released on albums by recording artists other than the songwriter, but the norm in these type of album based agreements with a writer recording artist is to condition fulfillment of the commitment only on the release of the writer's own newly recorded albums.

There are also provisions calling for advances to the artist based upon such events as the commencement of the recording of an album, the completion of the album, the delivery and acceptance of the album by the record company, the commercial release of an album or the commencement of an option period. Also, advances many times increase for each subsequent album recorded and released under the agreement (e.g. $175,000 for the 3rd album, $200,000 for the 4th, $300,000 for the 5th album, and so forth).

All of these contract provisions would affect an artist who recorded and released an album via downloads rather than through the traditional "normal retail channels" scenario. Without specific language defining "downloads of an album" as a traditional release, more than likely none of the advances would be paid nor would album release commitments be satisfied. Of course, success of a download album combined with significant traditional sales could convince a record company to treat all such sales as fulfilling contract commitments. Success is always the best negotiator as well as re-negotiator of contract terms.

Since many agreements base advances on the commercial release of albums, singles or other recordings, one of the more significant issues that is negotiated is the definition of what constitutes a commercial release of a recording. Obviously, depending on the amount of the advance which is payable to the recording artist, this can be an extremely important issue. For example, if the record company is obligated to pay an advance of between $100,000 to over $1 million upon the commercial release of an album, the company will want an assurance that the album is actually being released on a national basis so that it has a chance to succeed. For example, there might be language mandating that the release be through normal retail distribution channels. Other language may pre-condition the release on the record company distributing the album on a national basis to prevent an advance being paid on only a regional release. Music publishers who have contracts conditional upon album releases would also be similarly affected if contracts were not clear in this area.

## New Pricing Approaches For Physical Product

In light of the many changes being brought about by the Internet, record companies are also re-examining their approach to the pricing of physical product (CDs, cassettes, etc.) sold through traditional retail and other outlets.

One approach being taken by record companies in the physical product world to make pricing more attractive to consumers is to reduce the manufacturer's suggested retail list price ("MSRP") of top line albums from prices such as $16.98, $17.98 or $18.98 to $12.98. Recording artist royalties under this approach are based on the new lower suggested retail price rather than the previous higher price. For an example, if an artist has a 15% album royalty rate, it will be based on $12.98 (with all other deductions such as packaging and free goods in many cases still applying) rather than on the higher $16.98, $17.98 or $18.98 previous top line album price. This approach enables the record company to sell the albums at a cheaper price that hopefully will generate more sales. Because the price on which the artist's royalty calculation is based has been lowered, however, the actual royalty payable to the artist is reduced.

Others have instituted "developing artist" prices for albums featuring newer performers which lower the price to the consumer and effectively reduce the base on which an artist's royalty is calculated. Still others have reduced the wholesale price of top line CDs to approximately $9.00. And others have changed from a retail or MSRP based artist royalty formula with all standard deductions included to a calculation based on the published price to dealers ("PPD") with some discounts but without packaging and other standard deductions.

Other record companies have gone from a retail-based artist royalty formula with deductions to a wholesale based price calculation without almost any of the deductions which in the past have reduced the artist's royalty base price. Under the traditional retail price approach, a packaging/container deduction and free goods deduction would reduce the base (the suggested retail list price of an album) on which the artist's royalty percentage was calculated. For example, the record company might start with a $17.98 suggested retail list price of an album and then reduce the price by 20% to 25% for a packaging/container deduction and further reduce the amount by 10% to 15% for free goods or other discounts. The recording artist's royalty (10%, 15%, etc.) would then be calculated on the reduced base price of the album.

Under the new wholesale formula, the artist's royalty would be based on the price of the album to the dealer (for example, $11.00 rather than the suggested retail list price of $17.98) without any deduction for packaging and without any deduction for free goods or other standard discounts. Depending on what the wholesale price actually is, this approach may slightly increase the artist's royalty or it may result in the same monies being earned but under a more understandable and simpler calculation.

## *MUSIC PUBLISHING CONTRACTS*

In the area of music publishing, publishing contracts may provide that there must be a specified number of albums which are actually manufactured and distributed by the record company for an album to be deemed commercially released to trigger the payment of the release advance. For example, if there is a $150,000 advance payable on release of an album in the United States, the songwriter or co-publishing agreement might contain a provision which states that in order for a release to occur, the record company must manufacture and distribute at least 20,000 units. This type of clause has nothing to do with actual sales. It only ensures that the record company is supportive of the artist enough to manufacture and distribute a reasonable number of albums. In such a scenario, if the record company only manufactured and distributed 10,000 albums, no advance would be payable by the music publisher to the writer/artist. Or, in the alternative, a reduced advance might be payable.

Many publishing agreements also condition advances on the commercial release of an album by a major record company. Depending on the definition of what a major record company is, advances may not be paid because the download company did not fit the definition. Or advances may be reduced much the same way as would happen if an album were released by an indie rather than a major.

### Commercial Release/Internet

Whether or not the availability of an album for download and/or streaming constitutes a commercial release (which triggers the payment of an advance for a new album) depends on the language of the music publishing contract. Since entire albums are available for downloading but only certain songs may actually be downloaded or streamed, there is a real issue as to whether download availability vs. the commercial release of actual physical product is acceptable to justify the payment of a publishing advance which is based on an album being released.

Most agreements do not consider the availability of an album for download on an online site a commercial release. One approach which would consider download availability to be a commercial release is if download sales represent a certain percentage of all music sales in the marketplace (for example, 25%, 40%, 50%, etc.) but this represents only one of many ideas being discussed to resolve the issue.

Considering that the ability for an album to be downloaded has nothing to do with a particular record company's enthusiasm for or promotion of an album, the amount of money it may have invested in an album, the general public's awareness or lack of awareness of the album or the fact that consumers may only be interested in downloading one or two compositions from an album (as opposed to the entire album), the amount and structure of music publishing album advances payable to songwriter, songwriter-artists, and songwriter-producers (which are usually based on all or a certain percentage of songs on an album earning royalties each time an album is sold) are definitely changing in response to the differences and economics of the online marketplace.

## *WEB SITE OWNERSHIP*

Most contracts specify that the artist owns the Web site (domain name) bearing his, her or the group name. But there are some companies who take the position that the URL (Uniform Resource Locator) is something that should be owned by the record company and not by the artist. All the rights and obligations of the record company as well as the artist should be specifically listed in the contract so there is no confusion as to what can transpire on an artist site. Some items that need to be negotiated include who has access to the e-mail list of the site and who is allowed to sell merchandise and who has the right to download from the site. Other items include the right to "link" to other sites and the right of a company to use the artist's name on other Web sites. Artist manager contracts should also be reviewed as managers, in some cases, own or co-own the name of the group.

## DEDUCTIONS

All the standard deductions (e.g., packaging, free goods) and reduced royalty provisions (e.g., foreign), should be reviewed as many of these reduced royalty provisions are questionable and do not apply in a world where no physical product is actually being sold. "Container changes" of 25% on compact discs, new technology configurations and records in all other configurations should also be reviewed as to appropriateness.

## RECORD COMPANY/TRADITIONAL VERSUS INTERNET

The Internet has created a number of new ways for an artist, particularly an unsigned one, to make money as a recording artist. Unlike the traditional record company contract, these new forms can take any number of forms including a sharing of all income from sales 50/50; a sharing of a defined net (a company's operating and other costs taken out first and then a 50/50 split); a pay for play scenario where the company provides a specific amount in lieu of mechanical and performance royalties; an exclusive deal where a portion of the advertising revenue is shared; a fee covering the creation of an artists' URL and Web pages with all sales going to the artist; a percentage of the sales revenue taken by the company with content and pricing all controlled by the artist; a weekly fee to have a band's material available for download; a sharing of monies from subscription fees based on the number of downloads; an offer to owners of masters of a higher percentage for downloads than would be made under a normal record company contract, etc. Many of the arrangements are non-exclusive or are exclusive only for a short period of time. Practically none of these arrangements transfer ownership in the master recording or the song away from the artist or writer. Because of this, if an artist or writer becomes successful from one of these type of situations, they will definitely own many more rights than they would have under a normal record company contract.

## FUTURE

This entire area is in a state of flux and change as much of it is subject to current and future legislation, court and arbitration decision and appeals, voluntary business agreements, differing interpretations of copyright and international agreements and treaties, among other factors.

# 18

# *Guide to Music Industry Organizations*

THERE are many organizations that serve the needs of various sectors of the music industry and can be of great help to professionals and newcomers alike. The following national organizations are among the most important.

## *ACADEMY OF COUNTRY MUSIC (ACM)*

The Academy of Country Music is a nonprofit organization founded in 1964 to promote and increase the market for country music, with membership open to any creative or business professional whose work is related to country music. The organization conducts seminars, charity events, and showcases, and produces the Academy of Country Music Awards show.

4100 W. Alamenda Ave.
Suite 208
Burbank, CA 91505-4151
Phone # 818-842-8400
Fax # 818-842-8535
email: info@acmcountry.com
www.acmcountry.com

## *AMERCIAN FEDERATION OF MUSICIANS (AFM)*

The American Federation of Musicians of the United States and Canada is the largest organization in the world representing professional musicians. The union negoties agreements for its musician members and provides significant benefits including health care and pensions, among other options.

New York Headquarters
1501 Broadway
Suite 600
New York, NY 10036
Phone # 212-869-1330
Fax # 212-764-6134

Canadian Office
75 The Donway West
Suite 1010
Don Mills, ON M3C 2E9
Phone # 416-391-5161
Fax: # 416-391-5165

West Coast Office
3550 Wilshire Blvd.
Suite 1900
Los Angeles, CA 90010
Phone # 213-251-4510
Fax # 213-251-4520
www.afm.org

## *AMERCIAN FEDERATION OF TELEVISION AND RADIO ARTISTS (AFTRA)*

AFTRA is a diverse union representing 80,000 U.S. actors, broadcasters, and other professionals in television, radio, sound recordings, commercials, non-broadcast/industrial programming, and new technologies such as interactive programming and CD-ROMS. AFTRA often represents recording artists in Copyright Arbitration Royalty Panel Proceedings ("CARPs").

260 Madison Ave.
New York, NY 10016-2402
Phone # 212-532-0800

5757 Wilshire Blvd.
Los Angeles, CA 90036-3687
Phone # 323-634-8100
www.aftra.org

P.O. Box 121087
1108 17th Ave. South
Nashville, TN 37212
Phone # 615-327-2944

# COUNTRY MUSIC ASSOCIATION (CMA)

The Country Music Organization, founded in 1958, is a not-for-profit trade organization with 6,000 members whose purpose is to promote country music in the United States and overseas. It produces the CMA Awards show, SRO, and the International Country Music Fan Fair, and membership is available for companies and individuals who are directly or substantially involved in the industry.

1 Music Circle South
Nashville, TN 37203
Phone # 615-244-2840
Fax # 615-726-0314
www.cmaworld.com
email: communications@cmaworld.com

# DRAMATISTS GUILD, INC.

The Dramatists Guild, founded in 1920, has a membership of 7,500 playwrights, composers, and lyricists whose works are performed on the live stage. Its members are able to utilize the protections of the Guild's various production contracts and verification of box office royalty statement procedures as well as many other services.

1501 Broadway, Suite 701
New York, NY 10036
Phone # 212-398-9366
Fax # 212-944-0420
www.dramaguild.com
email: igor@dramaguild.com

# GOSPEL MUSIC ASSOCIATION (GMA)

The Gospel Music Association was founded in 1964 and has as its purpose the promotion, encouragement, and support of all forms of gospel and religious music. It provides educational and resource materials to its members, organizes Gospel Music Week, and produces the Dove Awards.

1205 Division Street
Nashville, TN 37203
Phone # 615-242-0303
Fax # 615-254-9755
www.gospelmusic.org
email: info@gospelmusic.org

## HARRY FOX AGENCY

The Harry Fox Agency, Inc., was established in 1927 by its corporate parent, the National Music Publishers' Association, Inc., to provide an information source, clearinghouse, and monitoring service for licensing musical copyrights. The Agency represents more than 27,000 American music publishers and licenses a large percentage of the uses of music in the United States on records, tapes, CDs, the Internet, and imported phonorecords. Additionally, the Harry Fox Agency handles the collection and distribution of royalties derived from the uses of copyrighted musical compositions pursuant to the licenses issued, and the auditing of the books and records of licensees utilizing copyrighted musical compositions pursuant to the licenses issued. It also represents its publisher principals in the collection, distribution, and monitoring of royalties earned under the Audio Home Recording Act.

711 3rd Avenue
8th Floor
New York, NY 10017
Phone # 212-370-5330
Fax # 646-487-6779
email: clientrelations@harryfox.com
www.harryfox.com

## NASHVILLE SONGWRITERS ASSOCIATION INTERNATIONAL (NSAI)

NSAI is a not-for-profit trade association founded in 1967 that is dedicated to professional and aspiring songwriters in all fields of music and works to protect and further the rights of all songwriters. NSAI is one of the largest songwriter organizations in the United States, with a membership of 4,000, and concentrates in the areas of legislation, education, and recognition of the song and songwriters.

1701 West End Avenue
3rd Floor
Nashville, TN 37203
Phone # 615-256-3354/800-321-6008
Fax # 615-256-0034
email: nsai@nashvillesongwriters.com
www.nashvillesongwriters.com

# NATIONAL ACADEMY OF RECORDING ARTS & SCIENCES (NARAS)

NARAS is a not-for-profit organization formed in 1957 to represent the interests of the creative and technical people in the recording industry. It has more than 8,000 members, produces the Grammy Awards show, and is at the forefront of issues involving the recording industry and its members. The NARAS Foundation is involved in the archiving and preservation of sound recordings, Grammy in the Schools, and MusicCares. In its educational mission, NARAS provides scholarships, annual grants for research and educational projects, workshops, publications, and a career handbook.

National Office
3402 Pico Boulevard
Santa Monica, CA 90405
Phone # 310-392-3777
Fax # 310-392-2306
email: los angeles@grammy.com

L.A. Office
3402 Pico Boulevard
Santa Monica, CA 90405
Phone # 310-392-3777
Fax # 310-392-2306
email: los angeles@grammy.com

New York Chapter
156 West 56th Street
17th Floor
New York, NY 10019
Phone # 212-245-5440
Fax # 212-489-0394
email: newyork@grammy.com

Nashville Chapter
1904 Wedgewood Avenue
Nashville, TN 37212
Phone # 615-327-8030
Fax # 615-321-3101
email: nashville@grammy.com

Other Chapters: Atlanta, Chicago, Memphis, San Francisco, Seattle, Austin, Miami, Washington, D.C., Philadelphia.
www.grammy.com

# NATIONAL MUSIC PUBLISHERS ASSOCIATION (NMPA)

NMPA once known as the Music Publishers' Protective Association was founded in 1917 for the protection and advancement of the American music publishing industry. NMPA promotes legislation for increased copyright protection for musical works in the United States and throughout the world, provides comments on regulatory proposals to the respective entities promulgating them such as the Copyright Arbitration Royalty Panels and the Copyright Office, and supports legal action on various copyright and music industry issues when deemed necessary in the interests of its members. The work of NMPA is supported through commissions earned by its wholly owned subsidiary, the Harry Fox Agency, Inc.

475 Park Avenue South
29th Floor
New York, NY 10016
Phone # 646-742-1651
Fax # 646-742-1779
email: pr@nmpa.org
www.nmpa.org

# PERFORMING RIGHT ORGANIZATIONS

## ASCAP (American Society of Composers, Authors, and Publishers)

One Lincoln Plaza
New York, NY 10023
Phone # 212-621-6000
Fax # 212-724-9064
Web Address : www.ascap.com

Two Music Square West
Nashville, TN 37203
Phone # 615-742-5000
Fax # 615-742-5020

1608 N. Milwaukee
Suite 1007
Chicago, IL 60647
Phone # 773-349-4286
Fax # 773-394-5639

7920 Sunset Blvd.
3rd Floor
Los Angeles, CA 90046
Phone # 323-883-1000
Fax # 323-883-1049

PMB 400
541 Tenth Street NW
Atlanta, GA 30318-5713
Phone # 404-351-1224
Fax # 404-351-1252

420 Lincoln Road
Suite 385
Miami, FL 33139
Phone # 305-673-3446
Fax # 305-673-2446

8 Cork Street
London, W1S 3LJ England
Phone # 011-44-207-439-0909
Fax # 011-44-207-434-0073

654 Ave. Munoz Rivera
IBM Plaza Ste. 1101B
Hato Rey, Puerto Rico 00918
Phone # 787-281-0782
Fax # 787-767-2805

## *BMI (Broadcast Music, Inc.)*

320 West 57th Street
New York, NY 10019
Phone # 212-586-2000
Fax # 212-245-8986
www.bmi.com

8730 Sunset Blvd., 3rd Floor West
Los Angeles, CA 90069
Phone # 310-659-9109
Fax # 310-657-6947

10 Music Square East
Nashville, TN 37203
Phone # 615-401-2000
Fax # 615-401-2707

84 Harley House
Marylebone Road
London NW1 5HN, England
Phone # 011-44-171-486-2036
Fax # 011-44-171-224-1046

5201 Blue Lagoon Drive
Suite 310
Miami, FL 33126
Phone # 305-266-3636
Fax # 305-266-2442

3340 Peachtree Rd. NE
Suite 570
Atlanta, GA 30326
Phone # 404-261-5151
Fax # 404-816-5670

255 Ponce de Leon
East Wing, Suite A-262
Bank Trust Plaza
Hato Rey, Puerto Rico 00917
Phone # 787-754-6490

## *SESAC*

55 Music Square East
Nashville, TN 37203
Phone # 615-320-0055
Fax # 615-321-6290
www.sesac.com

152 West 57th Street
New York, NY 10019
Phone # 212-586-3450
Fax # 212-489-5699

501 Santa Monica Blvd.
Suite 450
Santa Monica, CA 90401
Phone # 310-393-9671
Fax # 310-393-6497

6 Kenrick Place
London W1H 3FF
Phone # 020-7486-9994
Fax # 020-7486-9929

# RECORDING INDUSTRY ASSOCIATION OF AMERICA (RIAA)

RIAA is a record company trade association founded in 1952 whose purpose is the improvement of the music and recording industry. Efforts focus on the areas of prevention of counterfeiting, bootlegging, and record piracy, and related problems. RIAA is also the body that certifies Gold, Platinum, Multiplatinum, and Diamond sales awards.

1330 Connecticut Avenue N.W.
Suite 300
Washington, D.C. 20036
Phone # 202-775-0101
Fax # 202-775-7253
www.riaa.org

# SOCIETY OF COMPOSERS & LYRICISTS (SCL)

The main focus of the SCL is the education, promotion, and support of film and television composers and songwriters. The SCL, founded in 1983, conducts workshops for writers and filmmakers on the creative, financial, and practical benefits of music in film. Membership is open to professionals and new writers as well as film and television business personnel.

400 South Beverly Drive
Suite 214
Beverly Hills, CA 90212
Phone # 310-281-2812
Fax # 310-990-0601
www.filmscore.org

## *SONGWRITERS GUILD OF AMERICA (SGA)*

The SGA is a voluntary association of songwriters founded in 1931 whose membership is open to published and unpublished writers and estates of deceased writers. The Guild's services include reviews of songwriter contracts, music publisher audits, group medical and life plans, catalog administration, a copyright renewal service, an estate administration service, workshops and a royalty collection plan. The Guild's popular songwriters contract sets minimum royalty rates for various uses of a song, requires publishers to return songs to writers if a recording has not been made within 12 months, provides a sliding scale of percentages for sheet music, and contains a publisher audit clause and an assignment of a song to a publisher clause that cannot exceed 40 years or 35 years from the date of first release of a recording, as well as other favorable songwriter provisions. The Guild is also active in the legislative and judicial areas. In 1999, the National Academy of Songwriters became part of SGA.

The Songwriters Guild Foundation
1560 Broadway, Room 1306
New York, NY 10036
Phone # 212-768-7902
Fax # 212-768-9048
www.songwriters.org

1222 16th Avenue South
Suite 25
Nashville, TN 37212
Phone # 615-329-1782
Fax # 615-329-2623

The Songwriters Guild of America
1500 Harbor Blvd.
Weehawken, NJ 07086
Phone # 201-867-7603
Fax # 201-867-7535
email: songnews@aol.com

6430 Sunset Boulevard
Suite 705
Hollywood, CA 90028
Phone # 323-462-1108
Fax # 323-462-5430

## *SOUNDEXCHANGE*

Independent not-for-profit performance rights organization created to collect and distribute royalties to sound recording copyright owners, featured artists and to AFTRA and AFM on behalf of background musicians and vocalists from digital audio transmissions. Previously a division of the RIAA, SoundExchange is governed by a board of artist and label representatives.

1330 Connecticut Ave. NW
Suite 330
Washington, D.C. 20036
Phone # 202-828-0120
www.soundexchange.com

## *U.S. COPYRIGHT OFFICE*

Register of Copyrights
Copyright Office
Library of Congress
101 Independence Avenue S.E.
Washington, D.C. 20559-6000
Public Information Office: 202-707-3000
Forms: 202-707-9100
Fax # 202-707-2600
www.copyright.gov

# Sample Contracts

WHEN ENTERING INTO any agreement that involves your music, it's important to consult a knowledgeable entertainment attorney. However, here is a sampling of the type of contracts that may be presented to you in conjunction with deals for motion pictures, TV, advertising, and mechanical royalties.

## *MOTION PICTURE SYNCHRONIZATION LICENSE*

Agreement dated as of between_____, Music ("Licensor"), of_____, and_____, ("Producer"), of_____.

1. The musical composition ("Composition") subject to this license is: "_____ " written by_____. Licensor owns or controls_____ percent (%) of the Composition. If Licensor owns or controls less than one hundred percent (100%) of the Composition, Producer must secure a license from the parties which own or control the remaining portion of the Composition since this license covers only that share which is owned or controlled by Licensor.

2. The motion picture ("Motion Picture") subject to this license is currently entitled "_____".

3. The number and type of uses of the Composition subject to this license are: one (1) background vocal approximately one minute fifty two seconds (1:52) in duration and one (1) background instrumental approximately forty-five (45) seconds in duration used within the body of the Motion Picture.

4. The "Territory" covered by this license is: the world.

5. In consideration of the sum of _____DOLLARS ($), to be paid by Producer to Licensor upon the execution and delivery hereof, Licensor hereby grants to Producer, its successors and assigns, the nonexclusive, limited right, license, privilege, and authority to record in any manner, medium, form or language, in each country of the territory the aforesaid type and use of the Composition in synchronism or in timed-relation in the soundtrack of the Motion Picture, but not otherwise, for exploitation in any and all media now known or hereafter devised (linear format only) and to make copies of such recordings and import said recordings and/or copies thereof into any country of the Territory, all in accordance with the terms, conditions and limitations hereinafter set forth.

6. In consideration of the fee payable to Licensor as set forth in Paragraph 5 above, Licensor hereby grants to Producer the nonexclusive, limited right and license:

    (a) To publicly perform for profit or non-profit, and authorize others so to perform the Composition in the exhibition of the Motion Picture to audiences in motion picture theatres and other places of public entertainment where motion pictures are customarily exhibited in the United States or its territories or possessions, including the right to televise the Motion Picture into such theatres and such other public places, with the understanding and upon condition that the performance of the Composition in the exhibition of the Motion Picture means of television or for any other purpose whatsoever is subject to the provisions as hereinafter provided.

(b) The right to exhibit the Motion Picture in the United Stated by means of standard or non-standard television (other than as described in paragraph 6a above) including without limitation by means of "pay television", "subscription television", "CATV" and "closed circuit into homes television", is and shall be available only under the following circumstances:

(i) The Motion Picture may be exhibited by means of television by networks, CATV, local stations, closed circuits or other television providers having valid performance licenses therefore from the American Society of Composers, Authors and Publishers ("ASCAP") or Broadcast Music Inc. ("BMI"), as the case may be;

(ii) Exhibition of the Motion Picture by means of television by networks, CATV, local stations, closed circuits or other television providers not licensed for television by ASCAP or BMI is subject to clearance of the performing right either from Licensor or ASCAP or BMI or from any other licensor acting for or on behalf of Licensor.

(c) The right to perform the Composition in the synchronization of the Motion Picture in computer-assisted media including but not limited to CD-ROM, CD-I and similar home disc systems in linear form only, subject to the terms and conditions of this agreement.

7. It is understood that clearance by performance rights societies and mechanical rights societies in any portion of the Territory that is outside of the United States shall be in accordance with the customary practices and payment of the customary fees in that portion of the Territory.

8. Licensor hereby grants to Producer, in each country of the Territory, the following nonexclusive rights:

(a) To cause and authorize the fixing of the Composition as recorded in the soundtrack of the Motion Picture on so-called "audiovisual devices" now known or hereafter devised embodying all or substantially all of the Motion Picture, including, but not limited to videodiscs and videocassettes intended primarily for home use ("Videograms"); and

(b) To manufacture and distribute Videograms to the general public for "home use" which reproduce all or substantially all of the Motion Picture embodying the fixation of the Composition.

9. This license does not authorize or permit any use of the Composition not expressly set forth herein and does not include the right to alter the fundamental character of the music of the Composition, to use the title or subtitle of the Composition as the title of any motion picture or other audio-visual work, to use the story of the Composition or to make any other use of the Composition not expressly authorized hereunder.

10. The recording and performing rights hereinabove granted include the right to use the Composition in air, screen, videogram and television trailers solely for advertising and publicizing the Motion Picture, provided that the Composition shall not be used for any such purpose other than as used in the Motion Picture (i.e., as the music for the portion or portions of the Motion Picture embodying the Composition) without a separately negotiated license from Licensor.

11. The recording and performing rights hereinabove granted to Producer shall endure for the worldwide period of all copyrights in and to the Composition, and any and all renewals or extensions thereof that Licensor may now own or control or hereafter own or control without payment by Producer of any monies or consideration other than that expressly provided herein.

12. Licensor warrants only that it has the legal right to grant this license and this license is given and accepted without other warranty or recourse. If that warranty shall be breached, in whole or in part, Licensor shall either repay to Producer the consideration theretofore paid to Licensor for this license to the extent of the part thereof, which is breached or shall hold Producer harmless only to the extent of the consideration theretofore paid to Licensor for this license. In no event shall the total liability of the Licensor hereunder or otherwise exceed the consideration received by Licensor hereunder.

13. Licensor reserves all rights not expressly granted to Producer hereunder. All rights granted hereunder are granted on a nonexclusive basis.

14. Producer agrees to furnish Licensor with a cue sheet of the Motion Picture within thirty (30) days after the first public exhibition of the Motion Picture at which admission is charged (except so-called "sneak" previews).

15. The license herein granted to Producer shall be of no force or effect unless Producer shall pay the total fee specified in Paragraph 5 hereof upon the execution hereof. Licensor shall notify Producer in writing of any such breach and Producer shall have thirty (30) days in which to cure such breach. In the event of any breach of any provision of this agreement by Producer, Licensor's sole remedy will be an action at law for damages and in no event will Licensor be entitled or seek to enjoin, interfere or inhibit the distribution, exhibition or exploitation of the motion picture.

16. This license is binding upon and shall inure to the benefit of the respective successors and/or assigns of the parties hereto, provided that Producer shall remain liable for the performance of all of the terms and conditions of this license on Producer's part to be performed.

17. Producer agrees that in the event Producer shall pay a pro rata higher fee to master owner than is payable hereunder for the Composition as licensed hereunder, this agreement shall be deemed amended to incorporate such pro rata higher fee as of the date when such higher rate is paid and continuing for the duration of the period during which such higher rate is so paid.

18. This license shall be governed by and subject to the laws of the State of_____ applicable to agreements made and to be wholly performed within the State of_____.

19. Producer shall accord a screen credit with respect to the Composition on all positive prints of the Motion Picture substantially as follows:

Written by_____

No casual or inadvertent failure to give the foregoing credit shall be deemed a breach of this license, but Producer shall use its best efforts to cure any such failure prospectively if it shall receive written notice of such failure. In no event will any such failure be the basis for injunctive relief.

IN WITNESS WHEREOF, the parties have caused the foregoing to be executed as of the date first set forth above.

By_____
LICENSOR

By_____
PRODUCER

## TELEVISION SYNCHRONIZATION LICENSE

Agreement dated as of between_____ Music ("Publisher"), of_____
and_____ (Producer"), of_____.

1. The musical composition ("Composition") for which this license is issued
   is:"_____" written by_____.

2. The individual television program ("Program") for which this license is
   issued is:"_____", Episode #_____ (Airdate: )_____.

3. The term ("Term") for which this license is issued is: For the duration of
   the worldwide original term of copyright in and to the Composition and
   any and all renewals or extensions thereof that Publisher may now own
   or control or hereafter own or control.

4. The territory ("Territory") for which this license is issued is: The World.

5. The type and number of uses of the Composition to be recorded in the
   soundtrack of the Program are only as follows: One (1) continuous background vocal use not to exceed two (2) minutes and ten seconds (2:10)
   in duration.

6. In consideration of the sum of _____ DOLLARS ($), payable upon
   execution and delivery of agreement by Producer to Publisher, Publisher
   grants to Producer, its successors and assigns the nonexclusive right, license, privilege, and authority to record the Composition in synchronism
   or in timed-relation with the Program, but not otherwise, and to make
   copies of such recordings and import said recordings and/or copies thereof
   into any country throughout the Territory all in accordance with the
   terms, conditions and limitations hereinafter set forth. Publisher further
   grants to Producer the nonexclusive right and license to publicly perform
   for profit or non-profit and authorizes others so to perform the Composition in the exhibition of the Program to audiences by means of television
   including, without limitation, by means of "free television", "pay television", "subscription television", "basic cable television", "CATV" and "closed
   circuit into homes television", in the Territory during the Term, subject to
   the following:

   (a) The Program may be exhibited by means of television stations hav-
       ing valid performance licenses therefore from the American Society
       of Composers, Authors and Publishers ("ASCAP") or Broadcast Mu-
       sic, Inc. ("BMI"), as the case may be.

(b) Exhibition of the Program by means of television stations not licensed for television by ASCAP or BMI is subject to clearance of the performing right either from Publisher of ASCAP or BMI or from any other licensor acting for or on behalf of Publisher.

7. This license herein granted is only for the use in connection with direct projection and the broadcast, transmission and exhibition of the Program by means of television and television devices therefore, methods and improvements now or hereafter developed therefore, over such television facilities as Producer may select or authorize, all only in the form, during the applicable Term and in the applicable Territory referred to in paragraphs 3 and 4 above. Producer will not authorize recordings produced pursuant to the license to be manufactured, sold, or used separately from the Program. Without limitation of the foregoing, this License does not grant to Producer and Producer shall have no rights hereunder to synchronize or reproduce the Composition as recorded in the soundtrack of the Program for theatrical use or in any audio-visual devices such as, but not limited to, videodiscs, and videocassettes except as provided in paragraph 8 hereinbelow.

8. Publisher hereby grants to Producer the following option, which may be exercised, if at all, by written notice from Producer to Publisher prior to the expiration of twenty four (24) months after the initial Airdate of the Program, accompanied by payment of the fee specified hereinbelow.

(a) For an additional payment to Publisher of_____ DOLLARS ($), Publisher hereby grants to Producer the nonexclusive right license, privilege and authority to record the composition in the soundtrack of the Program in accordance with the provisions hereof and to cause the Composition, only as recorded in the soundtrack of the Program, to be reproduced in audio-visual devices, such as videocassettes, videodiscs and similar devices ("Videograms") reproducing the Program in its entirety throughout the Territory during the Term. The rights granted in this paragraph include the right to sell, lease, license or otherwise make Videograms available to the public as a device intended primarily for "home use".

9. It is understood that clearance by performance rights societies and mechanical rights societies in any portion of the Territory outside of the United States will be in accordance with the customary practices and the payment of the customary fees in that portion of the Territory.

10. This license does not authorize or permit any use of the Composition not expressly set forth herein and does not include the right to alter the fundamental character of the music of the Composition, to use the title or

subtitle of the Composition as the title of the Program, to use the story of the Composition or to make any other uses of the Composition not expressly authorized hereunder.

11. The recording and performing rights hereinabove granted include such rights for television trailers for the advertising and exploitation of the Program only, provided that the Composition shall not be used for any such purpose other than as used in the Program (i.e. as the music for the portion or portions of the Program embodying the Composition) and shall not be used in an out-of-context manner unless an additional fee is negotiated.

12. Publisher warrants only that it has the legal right to grant this license and this license is given and accepted without any other warranty or recourse. If said warranty shall be breached in whole or in part, Publisher shall either repay to Producer the consideration theretofore paid to Publisher for this license to the extent of the part thereof which is breached or shall hold Producer harmless to the extent of the consideration theretofore paid to Publisher for this license. In no event shall the total liability of the Publisher exceed the consideration received by it hereunder.

13. Publisher reserves all rights not expressly granted to Producer hereunder. All rights granted hereunder are granted on a nonexclusive basis.

14. This license is binding upon and shall inure to the benefit to the respective successors, assigns and/or sublicensees of the parties hereto.

15. This license shall be governed by and subject to the laws of the State of_____ applicable to agreements made and wholly performed within the State of_____.

16. Producer agrees that in the event Producer shall pay a higher fee to master owner than is payable hereunder for the Composition as licensed hereunder, this agreement shall be deemed amended to incorporate such higher fee as of the date when such higher rate is paid.

IN WITNESS WHEREOF, the parties hereto have executed this Agreement as of the date first set above.

By_____
PUBLISHER

By_____
PRODUCER

## *ADVERTISING COMMERCIAL SYNCHRONIZATION LICENSE*

Agreement dated as of between_____ Music ("Publisher"), of_____ and (AGENCY/SPONSOR) (Advertising Agency"), of_____.

1. Publisher hereby grants to Advertising Agency the limited exclusive right during the "Term" (as hereinafter defined) and only in the "Territory" (as hereinafter defined) to record the "Composition" entitled "_____ " (written by_____) solely in connection with One (1) Sixty Second (:60) commercial, with various edits, lifts and versions, in a television format ("Commercial") advertising_____ (hereinafter referred to as the "Product").

   This grant shall not be deemed to include the right to make any revisions in the melody, lyrics, or other aspect of the fundamental character of the Composition.

   In addition, this grant shall be exclusively limited to (PRODUCT CAT-EGORY) and Publisher agrees not to license the Composition for use in any commercial which advertises a competing product during the Term of this License.

   This license only applies to Publisher's share of the Composition which is_____ percent (%). If Publisher does not own or control one hundred percent (100%) of the Composition, Advertising Agency agrees to secure permission to use the other portion of the Composition from the music publisher which owns or controls such portion.

2. The term of this license shall be for a test period of three (3) months ("First Test Period") commencing on and expiring on_____, as well as any other period added pursuant to Paragraph 5 of this License (the "Term").

3. Advertising Agency shall have the right to use the Composition as herein-above in Paragraph 1 in ten (10) malls in the following cities:_____ ("First Test Territory") as well as any other territory added pursuant to Paragraph 5 of this License (hereinafter collectively referred to as the "Territory").

4. In consideration of the rights granted by Publisher for the First Test Period, Advertising Agency shall pay to Publisher, upon the execution and delivery hereof, the sum of _____DOLLARS ($).

5.  Publisher hereby grants to Advertising Agency the following option(s), which option(s) may be exercised, if at all, by written notice from Advertising Agency to Publisher prior to the expiration of the First Test Period or, if applicable, the Second Test Period of this license, accompanied by payment to Publisher of the fee(s) specified herein below:

    (a)  For an additional payment to Publisher of_____DOLLARS ($), Publisher grants to Advertising Agency the right to broadcast the Commercial on free and basic cable television covering not more than   percent (%) of the United States population ("Second Test Territory") for a term of three (3) months ("Second Test Period"), commencing on and ending on.

    (b)  For an additional payment to Publisher of_____DOLLARS ($), Publisher grants to Advertising Agency the right to broadcast the Commercial on radio in the Second Test Territory during the Second Test Period.

    (c)  For an additional payment to Publisher of_____DOLLARS ($), Advertising Agency shall have the right to broadcast the Composition on free and basic cable television in the territory of the United States ("U.S. Option Territory") for a term of one (1) year ("U.S. Option Period") commencing on and ending on . It is further agreed that the Commercial may also be used on the Internet (limited to Advertising Agency and agency Websites only) and for industrial purposes, (i.e. trade shows, sales meetings, in-house promotions and presentations related specifically and exclusively to the Product), during the Term hereof.

    (d)  For an additional payment to Publisher of_____DOLLARS ($), Publisher grants to Advertising Agency the right to broadcast the Commercial on radio in the U.S. Option Territory during the U.S. Option Period.

6.  The grant of performing rights is expressly conditioned upon each television system, either directly or as an affiliate of a television network and/or radio station having theretofore obtained a valid performing rights license from said performing rights society or other association or entity having the lawful right to issue such license at the time for the performance of the Composition since such rights are specifically reserved to Publisher.

    In the event, during the Term hereof, the designated representative of Publisher shall be precluded by law or judicial ruling from issuing a performance license or for any reason shall fail, refuse or neglect to issue a performance license to any television station and/or radio station over which Advertising Agency is broadcasting or desires to broadcast the Commercial, then Publisher shall provide to each station a license sufficient to enable Advertising Agency to continue its broadcast, without interruption, of the Commercial during the Term hereof. It is further agreed that the performance fees payable by any such station to Publisher in connection with said licenses shall be in accordance with the then current ASCAP/BMI payments.

Advertising Agency agrees to provide Publisher with copies of the media buys for the Commercial so that such can be provided to the applicable performance right organization.

7. Publisher reserves unto itself all rights and uses of every kind and nature whatsoever in and to the Composition other than such limited right of recording and performance specifically licensed hereunder, whether or not now in existence, including the sole right to exercise same at any and all times and places without limitation.

8. This license does not authorize or permit any use of the Composition not expressly set forth herein. By way of clarification and not limitation thereof, Advertising Agency shall not have the right:

   (a) to broadcast or authorize the broadcast of the Commercial embodying the Composition in any theatre, auditorium, or other place to which an admission fee is charged, excluding industrial and/or trade show usage;

   (b) to use the title of the Composition as the title of the Product or Commercial;

   (c) to use the story of the Composition as the story of the Commercial;

   (d) to publish and/or print or authorize the publication and/or printing of the music and/or lyrics of the Composition; or

   (e) to make, authorize or permit any change in the music or lyrics of the Composition.

9. Advertising Agency shall deliver to Publisher one (1) copy of the final Commercial after completed.

10. Publisher warrants that (i) it has sole and exclusive rights to the Composition; (ii) it has the full legal right to grant this License; (iii) the exercise of

the rights granted herein will not infringe on the rights of any third party; (iv) in order to use the Composition in the manner contemplated by this Agreement, Advertising Agency is not required to obtain any releases or consents of any nature whatsoever from any other parties; and (v) this License is given and accepted without other warranty or recourse. Publisher's total liability for any breach of such warranty shall be limited to repaying to Advertising Agency the consideration theretofore paid under this License with respect to the Composition to the extent of such breach or to holding Advertising Agency harmless to the extent of such breach, provided that Publisher's total liability shall not exceed the consideration therefore paid under this License with respect to the Composition.

11. This License sets forth the entire agreement between Publisher and Advertising Agency with respect to the subject matter hereof. This License is binding upon and shall inure to the benefit of the respective successors and/or assigns of the parties hereto, provided that Advertising Agency shall remain secondarily liable for the performance of all of the terms and conditions of this License to be performed on Advertising Agency's part. This License may not be modified or amended except by written agreement executed by the parties hereto. This License shall be governed by and subject to the laws of the State of and applicable to agreements made and to be wholly performed within such State.

AGREED AND ACCEPTED:

By_____
PUBLISHER

By_____
ADVERTISING AGENCY

## *MECHANICAL LICENSE AGREEMENT*

To:RECORD COMPANY                                    License No.:
ADDRESS                                                       Dated:


A.TITLE:                                                          WRITER(S):


B.PUBLISHER(S) AND PAYMENT PERCENTAGE:


C.RECORD NO.:                                               TIME:

ARTIST:                                                          RELEASE DATE:

ALBUM TITLE:

ROYALTY RATE:

ADDITIONAL PROVISIONS:

You have advised us, as publisher(s) referred to in (B) above, that you wish to use the said copyrighted work(s) as set forth above under the compulsory license provision of Section 115 of the United States Copyright Act of 1976, as amended (the "Act").

Upon your so doing, you shall have all the rights which are granted to, and all the obligations which are imposed upon, users of said copyrighted work(s) under the compulsory license provision of the Act after use or permission or knowing acquiescence by us in the use of the copyrighted work(s) upon the parts of instruments serving to reproduce mechanically the copyrighted work(s) (viz: phonograph records) by another person, except that with respect to records thereof made and distributed by you:

1. You shall pay royalties and account to us, as publisher, quarterly, within forty-five days after the end of each calendar quarter, on the basis of records made, distributed and not returned;

2. For such records made and distributed, the royalty shall be the statutory rate in effect at the time the record is made and distributed except as otherwise stated in (C) supra;

3. This license covers and is limited to one (1) particular recording of the copyrighted work(s) set forth herein as performed by the artist on the record number set forth herein and this license does not supersede or in any way affect any prior license now in effect respecting recordings of said copyrighted work(s);

4. In the event you fail to account to us and pay royalties as herein provided for, we shall have the right, in addition to any other rights or remedies which we shall have in such event, to terminate this license by giving you written notice that unless the default is remedied within thirty (30) days of the receipt of such notice, this license will be automatically terminated;

5. You need not serve or file the notices required by the Act;

6. This license is limited to the territory of the United States, its territories and possessions;

7. With respect to each statement rendered by you hereunder, we shall have the right, upon thirty (30) days prior written notice to you, at our sole cost and expense, to conduct a reasonable examination during usual business hours of your books and records once per year and only once with respect to any one statement, at the place where such books and records are kept with respect to such statement, and we may designate an accountant or attorney as our representative to make such examination on our behalf.

Sincerely,
MUSIC PUBLISHER
(Federal I.D. #)

By_____
  An Authorized Signatory

ACCEPTED AND AGREED:
RECORD COMPANY

By_____
  An Authorized Signatory

# Index

Academy of Country Music (ACM), 431
accountings, 62, 64, 80-81, 418-19, 420
accrual basis financing, 330-31
acquisition agreements, 328-50
  aftermath, 349-50
  assets acquired, 329-30
  closing date, 340-41
  copyright considerations, 344-46
  current contracts, 335-36
  due diligence, 341-47
  foreign subpublishing agreements, 336-37
  formal agreement, 347-49
  future commitments, 337
  income cutoff date, 340
  investigation areas, 341-47
  letter of intent, 338-41
  net income, 330-31, 334-35
  overview, 329-33
  price multiples, 332-33
  prospectus format, 333-37
  salaries, 332
administration agreement, songwriter/publisher, 10, 53, 62-66, 398-99, 402-3
  pros and cons of, 65-66
administration fees, 61, 63, 64
advances
  in administration agreement, 65
  for Broadway musicals, 290
  in co-venture agreement, 403-4, 406
  in copublishing agreement, 57-58
  in due diligence investigations, 343
  home video, 159, 182
  Internet issues, 426-27, 429
  for recording artists, 81-83
  in ringtone licenses, 417
  sharing of, 16-17, 133
  songwriters, 17-18
  in subpublishing agreement, 317-18
  for trivia games, 42
advertising industry, 224-30. See also commercials; jingles
AFM. See American Federation of Musicians (AFM)
AFTRA. See American Federation of Television and Radio Artists (AFTRA)
agents, 374, 388
album price lines, royalties and, 75-76
album release obligations, 83-84, 98, 426-27
Alden Rochelle court decision, 219-20
alteration of compositions, 22-23, 236
"alternative quote" arrangement, 33
AMCOS, 327
American Federation of Musicians (AFM), 382, 411, 432
American Federation of Television and Radio Artists (AFTRA), 382, 411, 432
American Society of Composers, Authors, and Publishers. See ASCAP

APRA, 29, 204, 325-26
A&R staff. *See* creative department
arrangements, public domain compositions,
    115
artist-production company agreements, 104-5
artist royalty clauses, 71-81
artwork, album, 92-93
ASCAP. *See also* performing rights organizations
    addresses for, 436-37
    Articles of Association, 220
    change of ownership notification, 349
    clearance services, 146-47
    co-written compositions, 254
    crediting, 241
    foreign performance royalties, 161-62
    income and distributions, 244-45
    income sources, 245-47
    interim fees, 247
    Internet licenses, 410, 412-13
    license agreement types, 242
    membership requirements, 240-41
    motion picture song royalties, 201
    payment changes, 253-54
    payment dates and methods, 248-50
    payment rules/payments, 250-52, 255-68
    registration of songs with, 7
    role of, 2
    royalty distribution by, 5, 16, 28-29, 35,
        44, 61, 115, 151, 170, 218-19, 303,
        320-21, 355
    services, 254-55, 386, 389
    special distributions, 246-47, 343
    television license fees, 121, 177
    television royalties, 143
    television song royalties, 161
    use of music cue sheets, 149-50, 187
    writer-publisher contracts, 243-44
at-source royalty payments, 24, 319-20
attorneys. *See* lawyers
Audio Home Recording Act of 1992, 355, 382,
    409
audits, 24, 80-81, 418-19
Australia, royalties, 29, 74-75, 204, 326
Austria, royalties, 326-27
averaged performance plan, 248-49

background music, motion pictures, 47, 170,
    206-7, 391-93
    income sources, 217-22, 381
background music, television, 47, 123-24,
    253-54, 257-58, 279, 391-93
background music operations, 246
background music score contracts, motion
    picture, 207-17
    amount of music, 211-12
    assignments, 217
    completion date, 208-9
    composer services, 208

composing fees, 209-11
copyright ownership, 212-13
exclusivity clause, 212
expenses, 212
infringements, 216-17
morality clause, 216
notices and governing law, 216-17
orchestration, 216
performing right society membership,
    213-14
producer instructions and requests, 215
publishing, 212-13
score disposition, 214
screen credit, 211
starting date, 208-9
suspensions and terminations, 215-16
transportation, 212
warranties, 214-15
background music score contracts, television,
    124-34
    assignments, 133
    completion date, 125-26
    composer services, 125, 129
    composing fees, 126-29
    copyright ownership, 129
    exclusivity clause, 129
    expenses, 133
    performance rights, 130-31
    publishing, 129-30
    royalty payments, 134
    score disposition, 132-33
    screen credit, 129
    share of advance payments, 133
    starting date, 125-26
    suspensions and terminations, 131-32
    theatrical version release, 134
    transportation, 133
    warranties and indemnifications, 133
band member provisions, 97-98
basic cable. *See* cable television
Belgium, royalties, 326-27
Berlin, Irving, 240
Bernstein, Elmer, 207
Bettis, John, 190-91
blanket licenses, 148, 154
    for performances, 242, 268
BMI, 240. *See also* performing rights organiza-
    tions
    addresses for, 437
    affiliation, 241
    change of ownership notification, 349
    clearance services, 146-47
    co-written compositions, 254
    foreign performance royalties, 161-62
    income and distributions, 244-45
    income sources, 245-47
    interim fees, 247
    Internet licenses, 410, 412-13

license agreement types, 242
membership requirements, 241-42
motion picture song royalties, 201
1977 song bonus, 270-71
payment changes, 253-54
payment dates and methods, 248-50
payment rules/payments, 252-53, 268-82
registration of songs with, 7
role of, 2
royalty distribution by, 5, 16, 28-29, 35, 44, 61, 115, 151, 170, 218-19, 303, 320-21, 355
services, 254-55, 386, 389
special distributions, 246-47, 343
television license fees, 121, 177
television royalties, 143
television song royalties, 161
use of music cue sheets, 149-50, 187
writer-publisher contracts, 243-44
booking agents, 374
books
audio recordings of, 48
lyric reprints in, 36-37, 45-46, 206, 381
Bowie, David, 350
Broadcast Music Inc. *See* BMI
Broadway musicals, 286-309
catalogue musicals, 309
Dramatists Guild contract, 289-93
financing, 287-88
guarantees, 296-99
income from, 380-81
motion picture songs in, 206
non-Dramatists Guild contracts, 297-99
overview of, 286-89
producer's share of subsidiary income, 299-301
road performances, 287, 293-96
royalties for, 35, 291-92, 296-98
weekly costs, 293-97
budget record sales, 75, 114
business affairs department, publisher's, 7
buying copyrights. *See* acquisition agreements
buyout video licensing, 43, 158, 160, 198, 199-200, 201

cable television, 120-21, 139-40, 169, 220-21, 265-66
Canada
release in, 84
ringtone licenses, 416
royalties, 29, 74-75, 109, 204, 326
CARP, 353, 355-56, 366, 410-12, 414-15
carry-forward advances, 406
cash basis financing, 330-31
cast albums, Broadway, 305-6
cell phones. *See* ringtones
chief executive officer, at publishing company, 9
clearance of music, 145-47, 154, 189

closing credits, use of song in, 175-76
CMRRA, 60, 327, 416
co-venture agreements
administration, 402-3
advances, 403
agreement scope, 404
carry forward advances, 406
copublishing, 402
deals extending past term, 404-5
guaranteed funding, 405-6
options, 406-7
sharing of income, 404
songwriting services, 404
term, 402
co-ventures, 401-7
co-writing songs, 19, 383-84
collaboration, 19, 383-84
collectibles, 50
commemorative plates, 50
commercial agreements, hit songs, 34-35, 231-37
copyright ownership, 232
exclusivity *vs.* nonexclusivity, 233
first broadcast restrictions, 236
foreign countries, 235
instrumental uses, 236
license duration, 232
lyric changes, 236
media, 235
number of commercials, 233
options, 233-34
parties to, 232
payment of fees, 233
performance rights, 236-37
restrictions on writer/artists, 235-36
territory, 234
commercial agreements, jingles, 230-31
commercials, 20, 223-37. *See also* jingles
for Broadway musicals, 304
Broadway songs in, 304
foreign productions, 321-22
hit songs in, 224-26
income from, 16, 377-79
motion picture songs in, 204
for motion pictures, 42, 181, 203-4
performance right payment systems for, 266-67, 281-82
promotional restrictions for, 21-22, 23, 229-30
pros and cons of hit song use, 229-30
recording usage provisions, 101-2
song promotion for, 5
synchronization fees for, 34-35
synchronization license agreement, 449-52
for television programs, 162
television songs in, 163-64
compulsory licenses, 353-54
computer and board trivia games, 42, 206
computer department, publisher's, 8-9

conducting, 217-18, 392
conferences, for songwriters, 254, 386
confidentiality clauses, 104, 333, 349
confirmation letters, 152
Consumer Price Index, 29-30
container charges, recordings, 76-78
Conti, Bill, 207
contracts. *See also* music publishing agree-
    ments; record company agreements
  sample, 441-54
controlled-composition clauses, 30-31, 106-15
  arrangement of public domain works, 115
  budget recordings, 114
  Canadian sales, 109
  "greatest hits" albums, 110-11
  later album royalty increases, 107-9
  "lock in" rate date, 109-10
  maximum royalty cap per album, 30-31,
    111-13
  mechanical rates in, 106, 114-17
  mid-priced recordings, 114
  one-use-only payment, 113
  record club royalties, 114
  record company published songs, 114
  in ringtone licenses, 417
  sales plateau increases, 106-7
  singles and EPs, 113
Copeland, Stewart, 207
copublishing agreement, songwriter/publisher,
    10, 53-62
  administration charges, 61
  advances, 57-58
  circumstances for, 54
  compositions covered in, 56
  demo recording costs, 59
  duration of, 57
  income sharing, 60
  joint ventures, 402
  nonrecoupable payments, 59
  ownership and promotion of demo record-
    ings, 60
  performance right income, 61
  reversions and direct collection of income,
    61-62
  royalty distributions to the writer's company,
    62
  song ownership in, 57-58
  terms of, 55-62
  transfer of rights in, 57
copyright, 351-66. *See also* U.S. Copyright Law
  arbitration, 353, 355-56
  arrangements of public domain composi-
    tions, 115, 258-59
  assignment of, 349
  compulsory licenses, 353-54
  duration, 356-58
  exclusive rights, 352-53, 430
  fees, 60, 61, 356

film and television co-ownership of, 19-20
first-use provisions, 20-21
foreign registration, 9
infringement claims, 6, 25-26, 93-95, 196,
    216-17, 362-63, 395
international protection, 363-64
Internet issues, 408-12
license length, 158, 177
PA form, 364-65
performance right provisions, 29
publisher's ownership of, 11, 12, 14
registration of, 4
renewal procedures, 358-59
revisions to law, 29-31
sampling and, 395-400
searches, 345-47
songwriter's retention of, 62
termination rights, 359-61, 366
transfer of, 57
"work made for hire" provision, 100, 194-95
Copyright Arbitration Royalty Panel. *See* CARP
copyright department, publisher's, 7
copyright notice, 37, 46, 356
  on sound recordings, 362
Copyright Royalty Tribunal, 29, 355-56, 410,
    414-15
Country Music Association (CMA), 433
cover recordings, 306-7, 314-15, 324
  in administration agreement, 64-65
creative department, publisher's, 8, 26-28
cue sheets. *See* music cue sheets
cut-out recordings, 80

decryption key, 413
deferred payments, film, 181-82
delivery commitments
  record company, 98-99
  recording artists, 90-91
  songwriters, 17
demo recordings
  in copublishing agreement, 59
  publisher's role in, 4, 6, 8, 23, 26
  submission procedures, 385, 392
demo reviews in magazines, 393
Denmark, royalties, 326-27
departing band members, 97-98
developing artist pricing, 116, 427
development deals, writer-performer, 26-28
digital distribution, 79-80
digital downloads, 52, 80, 327, 409-10, 413-15
  income from, 16, 116, 382
  synchronization fees and, 428-29
digital jukeboxes, 422-23
Digital Millennium Copyright Act of 1998,
    365-66, 382, 409, 410
Digital Performance Right in Sound Recordings
    Act of 1995, 365-66, 382, 409, 410

Digital Performance Royalties Fund, 382
digital phonograph delivery, 414
DMCA. *See* Digital Millennium Copyright Act
    of 1998
dolls, 44, 206, 382
downloads. *See* digital downloads
DPD. *See* digital phonograph delivery
DPRA. *See* Digital Performance Right in Sound
    Recordings Act of 1995
Dramatists Guild, Inc., 433
Dramatists Guild contract, 289–93, 381
    Broadway opening, 291
    pre-Broadway payments, 291
    pre-production payments, 289–90
    producer's share of subsidiary income,
        299–301
    royalties, 292, 296–97
due diligence investigations, 341–47
    advances, 343
    copyright considerations, 344–46
    expiring agreements, 347
    future obligations, 346
    guaranteed income commitments, 346–47
    matching income with royalty payouts, 343
    out-of-period audit recoveries, 342
    reversions, 347
    songwriter agreements, 346
    songwriter obligations, 342
    special distributions, 342
    subpublishing agreements, 346
    terminations, 347
DVDs. *See* home video; video licensing

educational television, 140–41
Elfman, Danny, 207
encryption, 409
England. *See* United Kingdom
EPs, 113
"errors and omissions" insurance, 384
European Union, royalties, 74–75
exclusive hold, motion pictures, 182–83
exclusive rights, copyright, 352–53
exclusive songwriter agreement, 9–10, 13–28,
    180, 346

"fair use" doctrine, 352, 363
fees. *See also* synchronization fees
    administration, 61, 63, 64
    agents, 374
    "buy-out of all rights," 395
    composing, 126–29, 193, 209–11
    conducting, 217–18
    copyright, 60, 61, 356
    film composers, 193, 209–11, 217–18, 381
    jingle writer, 227
    lawyers, 368–71
    lead sheets, 60, 61
    managers, 374

performing rights organizations, 121, 177,
    247
    subpublishing, 23–24, 313–15
    television composers, 126–29
    television option, 156–57
    video, 199–200
film. *See* motion pictures
film agents, 374
financial due diligence, 341–43
first-use mechanical licenses, 20–21
first-use restrictions, commercials, 236
first-use restrictions, film, 180–81
"fixation fee," 36, 416–17
fixed-dollar musical plays, 297–98
"floor/ceiling" advance formula, 81–83
"floor" royalties, 40, 159
flow-through clauses, 105
folios, 47, 163, 204, 307, 322
    income from, 16, 381
foreign department, publisher's, 5, 7
foreign market, 5, 8–9. *See also* subpublishing
    administration fees for, 64
    advertisers, 235
    artist's royalties for, 74–75
    income from, 16, 29, 32, 246, 380
    Internet issues, 409
    for motion pictures, 169
    release agreement for, 84
    translation of song lyrics for, 22–23
foreign mechanical royalties, 326–27
foreign performing rights societies, 22, 23, 29,
    61, 170, 246, 324–25, 380
    motion picture royalties, 187, 201–2, 204–5
    television royalties, 122, 161–62
foreign subpublisher fees, 23–24
foreign subpublishing agreement. *See* subpub-
    lishing agreement
France, royalties, 29, 74–75, 204, 326
free goods, recording artists, 78–79, 116, 430

games, 42, 421–22
GEMA, 29, 204, 327
Germany, royalties, 29, 74–75, 204, 326
Gershwin, George and Ira, 207
ghostwriting scores, 393
Goldsmith, Jerry, 190–91, 207
Gospel Music Association (GMA), 433
"greatest hits" albums, 91–92, 110–11
greeting cards, 41–42, 206

Harry Fox Agency, 60, 141, 146, 228–29, 320,
    354, 355
    Internet and, 410, 414–15, 434
    role of, 2
Herbert, Victor, 240
Herrmann, Bernard, 207
hit songs
    in Broadway shows, 302–3

in commercials, 228-30, 231-37, 377-79
income from, 283-85
in motion pictures, 171-89, 201-2, 379
in television, 160-66, 379-80
holdbacks, 102-4
home studio, 126, 385
home video
    advances for, 182
    of Broadway musicals, 309
    commercials on, 235
    foreign productions, 321
    income from, 16, 381-82
    of motion pictures, 169, 197-201
    recording artist, 85-87, 206, 321, 388-89
    of recording artists, 43
    royalties on, 5, 33-34
    song promotion for, 6
    of television programs, 43, 137-38, 157-60
Horner, James, 207
Hot 100 Charts, 390
Howard, James Newton, 207

indemnities
    recording artist, 93-95
    songwriter, 25-26
    television composer, 133
individual song agreement, songwriter/pub-
        lisher, 9-10, 12
infringement. *See* copyright
insurance policies, 104
Internet, 52, 117, 268, 282, 327, 365-66, 408-30.
        *See also* digital downloads; streaming
        audio
    commercials on, 235
    downloads and subscription services,
        413-15
    income from, 382
    laws governing, 409
    music publishing agreements, 428-29
    music web sites, 393
    performing rights licenses, 412-13
    promotional streaming licenses, 419-21
    in record company contracts, 423-28
    rights, 409-12
    ringtones and, 415-19
    traditional record company *vs.*, 430
    Web site ownership, 429, 430
Italy, royalties, 29, 326-27

Japan, royalties, 29, 74-75, 204, 326
Jarre, Maurice, 207
JASRAC, 29, 204, 327
*Jeopardy!* (television show), 139
jingles, 122, 226-27, 230-31, 237, 253-54, 258.
        *See also* commercials
joint venture agreements. *See* co-venture agree-
        ments
joint ventures, 117, 401-7
jukeboxes, 353-54, 422-23. *See also* video

jukeboxes

karaoke, 36, 206, 381, 418
Kern, Jerome, 207, 240
"key man" clause, 340
key outlet marketing albums, 49-50
Korngold, Erich, 207

laserdiscs. *See* home video
law firms, 146
lawyers, 367-71, 386-87
lead sheets, 60, 61
legal affairs department, publisher's, 7
legal due diligence, 344-47
letter of intent to acquire, 338-41
license renewals, television, 147-48
limited edition collectibles, 50
limited theatrical distribution, film, 178
local cover recordings, 324
"lock in" rate date, 109-10
lyricists, Broadway, 288-89
lyrics
    changes in, 22-23, 39, 176-77, 236
    on recording packages, 46
    reprints, 36-38, 45-46, 206, 381
    on soda cans, 47-48
    on T-shirts and posters, 48

magazines, 38
mail order record sales, 76
managers, 371-74, 388
Mancini, Henry, 207
marketing albums, 49-50
master recording delivery obligations, 98-99
maximum royalty cap, 111-13
MCPS, 327
mechanical licenses
    first-use, 20-21
    Internet issues, 409-10
    for medleys, 39-40
    publisher's role in, 7
    sample agreement, 453-54
mechanical royalties, 29-31, 354, 375-77
    Broadway cast albums, 305-6
    for Broadway songs, 302-3
    cap on, 111-13
    for computer and board trivia games, 42
    controlled-composition clauses, 106-15
    foreign, 326-27
    Internet issues, 423-28
    for motion picture songs, 170, 201, 202-3
    one-use-only, 113
    rate changes in, 52, 114-17
    for record clubs, 49
    reduced rates for, 30, 106, 114, 423-28, 430
    sampling and, 397
    in subpublishing agreement, 320
    for television songs, 161

medleys, 39-40
Mercer, Johnny, 207
mergers, 350
midpriced record sales, 75, 114
minidisc (MD), 79
"minimum/maximum" advance formula, 81-83
minimum recording obligation, 90-91
minimum song delivery requirement, 17
morality clause, in motion picture contract, 216
Morricone, Ennio, 207
"most favored nations" basis, 40, 42, 49, 185, 186, 417
motion pictures, 167-222
  adaptations of Broadway musicals, 308-9
  based on songs, 44-45
  breaking into, 391-93
  Broadway songs in, 307-8
  commercials for, 42
  foreign productions, 321
  foreign theatrical royalties, 44, 167, 205
  hit songs used in, 171-89
  income from, 16, 379, 381
  industry overview, 167-70
  market for, 169-70
  music budget, 170-71
  music uses of, 170
  opening and closing credits, 175-76
  producer cut-ins, 179-80
  producer's music libraries, 189
  production companies, 169
  promotional restrictions for, 21-22, 23
  recording usage provisions, 101-2
  rescoring and replacing songs in, 185
  rights granted to film producer, 177-78
  song promotion for, 5
  songs written for, 15, 19-20, 189-96
  synchronization fees for, 32-33
  synchronization license agreement, 442-45
  television broadcast of, 151, 205
  television songs in, 164, 165-66
  use of other motion picture songs in, 206
  X-rated, 21-22, 23
MPRT rate, 327
multiple uses of songs, motion pictures, 176
multiple uses of songs, television, 142
music boxes, 52
music clearinghouses, 146
music consultancy services, 185
music cue sheets, 149-50, 186-87, 188
music industry organization directory, 431-40.
  *See also specific organizations*
music publishers. *See also* subpublishing
  acquisition of rights by, 9-10
  administrative functions of, 4
  choice of, 11, 390
  film studio ownership of, 195-96
  inner workings of, 6-9
  record production affiliates of, 6, 114

  role of, 2-6
  songwriter's relations with, 11
  submission procedures, 384-85
  types of, 391
  up-front payments, 389
music publishing agreements, 9-10, 11-28
  advances, 16-18
  altering of compositions, 22-23
  audits, 24
  co-ventures and joint ventures, 401-7
  collaboration, 19
  compensation, 16
  demo recordings, 23
  development deals, writer-performer, 26-28
  exclusive agreement, 13
  exclusivity, 15
  first-use mechanical licenses, 20-21
  foreign subpublisher fees, 23-24
  individual songs, 12
  infringement claims, 25-26
  Internet issues, 428-29
  lyricist selection rights, 22
  minimum song delivery requirement, 17
  promotional restrictions, 21-22, 23
  provisions of, 13-28
  publisher's rights, 15
  return of songs to writer, 14
  ringtones, 417-18
  sale of composition, 14
  television and film exclusions, 19-20, 129-30
  term of, 14-15
  translation of song lyrics, 22-23
music publishing income sources, 28-52, 381
  audio recordings of books, 48
  background scores, 47
  Broadway musicals, 35
  commercials, 34-35, 229-30
  dolls, 44
  folios, 47
  games, 42
  greeting cards, 41-42
  home video, 33-34, 43
  Internet, 52
  karaoke, 36
  key outlet marketing albums, 49-50
  limited edition collectibles, 50
  lyric reprints in books, 36-37, 45-46
  lyrics on recording packages, 46
  magazines, 38
  mechanical rate changes, 52
  mechanical royalties, 29-31, 179, 375-77
  medleys, 39-40
  motion picture foreign royalties, 44
  motion pictures, 32-33
  music boxes, 52
  musical telephones, 50-51
  novelty albums, 46
  performance rights, 28-29

posters, 48
promotional videos, 40-41
public service announcements, 38-39
record clubs, 49
recordings of hit songs with changed lyrics, 39
ringtones, 51-52, 417-18
sampling, 394-400
sheet music, 47
singing fish, 51
soda cans, 47-48
special products albums, 48-49
T-shirts, 48
television commercials for motion pictures, 42
television programs and films based on songs, 44-45
television-sale-only albums, 49
television series, 31-32
theme parks, 51
toys, 44
video jukeboxes, 36
musical plays. *See* Broadway musicals
musical telephones, 50-51

Nashville Songwriters Association International (NSAI), 434
National Academy of Recording Arts & Sciences (NARAS), 435
National Academy of Songwriter (NAS). *See* Songwriter's Guild of America (SGA)
National Music Publishers Association (NMPA), 414-15, 436
NCB, 327
net publisher's share, 60, 333
Netherlands, royalties, 326
new artist pricing, 116
new band members, 97-98
new technologies, 79-90, 116-17, 423-28. *See also* Internet
Newman, Alfred, 207
Newman, Randy, 207
nonprofit films, 185-86
nonrecoupable payments, 59
North, Alex, 207
Norway, royalties, 326-27
novels, lyric reprints in, 36-37
novelty albums, 46

one-use-only mechanical payment, 113
opening credits, use of song in, 175-76
operating costs, musicals, 293-96
option fees, television, 156-57
option payments, Broadway, 289-90
option year advances, 58
options, 14-15, 57, 74, 233-34
  in co-venture agreement, 406-7
orchestration, for film or television, 216, 392-93

ownership of masters, 99-101

packaging deductions, recording artists, 76-78, 430
participation agreement, songwriter/publisher, 10
pay television, 120, 139-40, 169, 220-21, 265-66
"per program" license agreement, 242, 268
percentage-of-receipts musicals, 291-92, 298-99
performing groups, 384
performing rights, 238-40
  as income source, 16, 29, 61, 161-62, 201-2, 238-85, 303, 377, 378
  Internet issues, 409-10
  promotional streaming licenses, 419
  ringtone issues, 418-19
  in subpublishing agreement, 320-21
  types of performances, 29
performing rights organizations. *See also* ASCAP; BMI; foreign performing rights societies; SESAC
  addresses for, 436-37
  choosing, 244
  commercial royalties, 236-37
  Internet issues, 409, 412-13
  membership requirements, 130-31, 213-14, 240-42
  motion picture royalties, 196, 213-14
  royalties and sampling, 397
  as source of income, 28-29
  television royalties, 121, 143, 147
pipeline monies, 322-23
"pirated" recordings, 363, 409
Porter, Cole, 207
posters, lyrics on, 48
precleared compositions, 154
printed music. *See* folios; sheet music
producer cut-ins, film, 179-80
producers, recordings, 387
production company agreements, 104-5
promotion, song, 3-5, 152-53, 184, 187
  restrictions on, 21-22
promotion department, publisher's, 8, 26-28, 152-53
promotion expenses, recording artists, 87-88
promotional spots, television, 143-44, 162
promotional videos, 40-41
prospectus for catalog sale, 333-37
PRS, 29, 204, 218, 324-26, 418
public domain compositions, arrangements of, 115
public service announcements, 38-39
public television, 140-41
publishers. *See* music publishers
purchase price multiples, 332-33

qualifying works, 259

rack jobbers, 102
radio, 235, 246, 252-53
  performance right payment systems for,
    261-62, 269-77
re-recording restrictions, 95-96
*Rear Window* decision, 146, 177
record clubs
  promotional incentives, 78-79
  royalties, 49, 76, 114
record companies
  affiliated with publishers, 6
  expenses of, 85-89
  marketing and sales incentives, 78-79
  recording costs, 88-89
  role of, 2
record company agreements, 28, 67-116
  advances, 81-83
  album artwork approval, 92-93
  album release obligations, 83-84, 426-27
  arrangements of public domain composi-
    tions, 115
  artist-production company, 104-5
  artist royalty clauses, 71-81
  artist's obligations in, 90-101
  band member provisions, 97-98
  Broadway cast albums, 306
  confidentiality clauses, 104
  "greatest hits" albums, 91-92
  important points in, 69-70
  insurance policies, 102-4
  Internet and new technologies, 117, 423-28,
    429
  minimum recording obligation, 90-91
  motion picture, television, and commercial
    usage provisions, 101-2
  new contract developments, 116-17
  re-recording restrictions, 95-96
  recording and delivery of albums, 98-99
  recording ownership, 99-101
  recording sessions and studios, 92
  shipping and return policies, 102-4
  sideman provisions, 95
  solo album provisions, 96
  term of, 70-71
  warranties and indemnities, 93-95
  Web site ownership, 429
record distributors, 102
record producers, 387
record release advances, 58
recording artists royalties. *See* royalties, recording artists
Recording Industry Association of America
  (RIAA), 355, 414-15, 438
recording studio selection, 92
recordings. *See also* soundtrack albums
  album price lines, 75-76

of Broadway musicals, 305-6, 309
copyright issues, 354, 362
importance of, 3-4
income from, 16
minimum song delivery commitment and, 17
ownership of, 99-101
recoupment of video costs, 86
release guarantees, 83-84
renewal claimants, 359
reserve funds, 102-4
restrictions, on use of songs in films, 182
retail price base, 72, 427-28
retainers, 369
retention rights, foreign, 322-24
return of composition, 14
return policies, recordings, 102-4
reversion clause, 359-61, 366
  in copublishing agreement, 61-62
  in songwriter/publisher agreement, 14
RIAA. *See* Recording Industry Association of
  America (RIAA)
ringtones, 51-52, 327, 381-82, 415-19
rollover advance formula, for videos, 158,
    199-200
royalties, recording artists
  budget sales, 75, 114
  cut-outs, 80
  factors determining, 72-73
  foreign sales, 74-75
  free goods, 78-79, 116
  graduated increase provisions, 73-74
  income amounts, 377, 378
  for Internet, 408-9, 411-12
  mail order sales, 76
  maximum royalty cap, 111-13
  midline sales, 75
  midpriced sales, 114
  new technology rate reductions, 79-80,
    423-28
  90% sale provision, 79
  option year increases, 74
  packaging deductions, 76-78, 430
  percentages, 72-73
  record club sales, 76, 78-79, 114
  reduced-royalty albums, 75, 114
  retail price base, 72, 427-28
  returned recordings, 102-4
  singles and EPs, 113
  television-only sales, 76
  videos, 86-87
  wholesale price base, 72
royalties, songwriters/composers. *See also*
  music publishing agreements; performing rights
  for Broadway musicals, 288-89, 292, 296-97,
    305-9
  for commercials, 237, 377-79

compensation percentages, 16
for digital jukeboxes, 423
foreign payments, 5, 131, 218–20
income amounts, 283–85, 375–77
from motion picture theaters, 204–5, 219–20, 307
for motion pictures, 5, 20, 195, 196, 218–20
for ringtones, 416
sampling and, 397, 399
subpublishers, 313–14
for television, 20, 122, 134, 155–56
for video games, 421–22
video rates, 158–59, 198–99
royalty department, publisher's, 8
royalty distribution schedule
in administration agreement, 64
in copublishing agreement, 62
for recording artists, 80–81
royalty panels, 355–56
royalty pools, 292–93
royalty statements, in administration agreement, 64
Rozsa, Miklos, 207

SABAM, 327
SACEM, 29, 204
sample agreement, 398–400
sampling, 394–400
screen credit, 129, 186, 194, 211
screenplays, 206
SDRM, 327
securitization, 350
SESAC, 16, 61, 240, 254, 282–83, 320, 349, 437
Internet licenses, 410, 412–13
royalty distribution by, 28
SGAE, 327
Shaiman, Marc, 207
sharing of advances, publishing, 16–17
sharing of income
in administration agreement, 63
in copublishing agreement, 55–56, 60, 147
sheet music, 47, 163, 204, 307, 322
income from, 16, 381
shipping and return policies, 102–4
Shore, Howard, 207
showcases, songwriters, 254, 386
SIAE, 29, 327
sideman provisions, 95
signing advances, 57–58
sing-alongs. *see* karaoke
singing fish, 51
Small Webcaster Settlement Act of 2002, 411
SOCAN, 29, 204, 325–26, 418
Society of Composers & Lyricists (SCL), 438
soda cans, lyrics and music on, 47–48
SODRAC, 327
solo album provisions, 96
song written for a motion picture contract,

191–96
completion date, 192–93
exclusivity, 195
grant of rights, 194–95
originality, 196
performance royalties, 196
publishing, 195–96
screen credit, 194
songwriter royalties, 195
starting date, 192–93
use or nonuse of song, 196
writer services, 192
writing fees, 193
songwriter agreements. *See* music publishing agreements
songwriter income sources. *See* music publishing income sources
Songwriters Guild of America (SGA), 355, 439
Sonny Bono Copyright Term Extension Act of 1998, 344–45, 351, 357, 359–61, 366, 409
sound recordings. *See* recordings
SoundExchange, 411, 439
soundtrack albums
for motion pictures, 5, 33, 169, 178–79, 202–3, 221–22, 306
for television, 162
Sousa, John Philip, 240
Spain, royalties, 326–27
special products albums, 48–49
"spotting" session, 125
Steiner, Max, 207
STEMRA, 327
streaming audio, 52, 365–66, 382, 409, 411–12
promotional streaming licenses, 419–21
student films, 184
subpublishing, 310–27, 340, 349
fees, 23–24, 313–15
overview of, 310–11
role of subpublisher, 311–13
subpublishing agreement, 10, 313–24, 346
advances, 317–18
at-source royalty payments, 319–20
audiovisual rights, 321–22
compositions controlled by, 315–16
information needed, 318–19
local cover recordings, 314–15
print, 315
retention rights, 322–24
rights granted, 320–22
rights reserved, 322
royalty payment dates, 322
royalty percentages, 313–14
term, 313
subscription services, 382, 413–15
subsidiary rights, Broadway musical, 299–309
SUISA, 327
surplus recordings, 80

Sweden, royalties, 326-27
Switzerland, royalties, 326-27
synchronization fees, 16, 20, 23
  for commercials, 228-29
  for Internet, 52, 428-29
  for motion pictures, 5, 32-33, 174-85
  reduced, 139, 149, 178-79, 183-84
  for ringtones, 418
  for television, 31-32, 122-23, 138-55
  for video jukeboxes, 36
synchronization licenses
  for commercials, 449-52
  free-use, 185-86
  Internet issues, 409-10, 412
  motion pictures, 171-89, 442-45
  publisher's role in, 7
  renewals, 147-48
  for television, 134-55, 446-48

T-shirts, lyrics on, 48
television, 118-66. *See also* commercials
  breaking into, 391-93
  broadcasts of Broadway musicals, 304-5
  broadcasts of motion pictures, 151, 205,
      220-21
  Broadway songs in, 307
  commercials for motion pictures, 42, 181,
      203-4
  commercials on, 235
  foreign productions, 150-51, 321
  home video distribution, 43, 157-60
  in-house production staffs, 146
  income from, 16, 246, 379-80
  industry overview, 118-21
  license renewals, 147-48
  market, 120-21
  motion picture songs in, 205-6
  music budget, 122-23
  music uses of, 122
  performance right payment systems for,
      262-66, 277-81
  production companies, 119-20
  programs based on songs, 44-45
  promotional programs for films, 185
  promotional restrictions for, 21-22, 23
  recording usage provisions, 101-2
  song promotion for, 5
  song selection process, 153-54
  songs written for, 19-20, 160-66
  soundtrack albums, 162
  synchronization fees for, 31-32, 122-23
  synchronization license agreement, 446-48
  synchronization rights, 134-55
  syndicated series, 151-52
television agents, 374
television-sale-only albums, 49, 76
term
  in administration agreement, 63, 65

advertising license, 232
  in copublishing agreement, 57
  in digital jukebox licenses, 423
  in joint venture agreements, 402
  motion picture license, 177
  in promotional streaming licenses, 420
  in publishing agreement, 14-15, 26-28
  in recording agreement, 70-71, 426
  in ringtone licenses, 415-16
  in subpublishing agreement, 313
  television synchronization license, 137-42
  in video game licenses, 422
termination rights, copyright, 359-61, 366
territory
  in administration agreement, 63-64
  in commercial agreement, 234
  in digital jukebox licenses, 423
  Internet issues, 409
  in motion picture agreement, 178
  motion picture home video, 200-201
  in recording agreement, 84
  in ringtone licenses, 416
  for subpublishing, 312-13
  in television agreement, 138-41
  television home video, 159
  in video game licenses, 422
theatrical film royalties, foreign, 44, 163, 205
theatrical version release, television program,
      134, 143, 163
theme parks, 51
theme songs, television, 144-45, 253-54, 257,
      279
Tiomkin, Dimitri, 207
Tony Awards, 304-5
tour support, 87
toys, interactive, 44, 206
trailers, film, 181

underscore. *See* background music
Uniform Commercial Code, 350
Uniform Resource Locator (URL), 429, 430
United Kingdom, royalties, 29, 74-75, 204, 218,
      326
U.S. Copyright Law, 344-45, 350, 351, 357.
      *See also* Sonny Bono Copyright Term
      Extension Act of 1998
  performing rights provisions, 238-40
U.S. Copyright Law, 1976 revision, 11, 240,
      344-45, 351, 354, 357, 358-61, 362, 409
U.S. Copyright Office, 7, 440
  clearance services, 147
  fees and forms, 356, 364-65

video approvals, 85
video cassettes. *See* home video
video costs, 85-87
video game licenses, 421-22
video jukeboxes, 36, 206, 381

video licensing, motion pictures, 197–201
video licensing, television, 157–60
video recoupment, 86
"visual instrumentals," 170
"visual vocals," 153, 170, 189

warranties
 buy and sell agreement, 339–40
 film composer, 214–15
 recording artist, 93–95
 songwriter, 25–26
 television composer, 133
Warren, Harry, 207
watermarking, 409

Waxman, Franz, 207
web sites. *See* Internet
webcasting, 365–66
wholesale price base, 72
Williams, John, 207
WIPO Copyright Treaty, 366, 409
WIPO Performances and Phonograms Treaty,
  366, 409
withholding of royalties, 25–26, 93–95
"work made for hire," 100, 129, 212–13, 353,
  358, 366
workshops, for film and television composition,
  392
workshops, songwriters, 254

# About the Authors

TODD BRABEC is Executive Vice President and Director of Membership for the American Society of Composers, Authors and Publishers (ASCAP), the world's largest performing rights organization. He is in charge of all of the Society's membership operations throughout the world including over 175,000 U.S. composers, lyricists and music publishers, hundreds of thousands of affiliated writers and publishers worldwide and oversees offices in New York, Los Angeles, Nashville, London, Miami, Chicago, Atlanta, and Puerto Rico.

JEFF BRABEC is Vice President of Business Affairs for The Chrysalis Music Group where he specializes in evaluating, analyzing, and negotiating music publishing acquisitions. He has negotiated over 1,000 movie, television, video, new technology, and advertising commercial agreements for chart writers/recording artists. Brabec is contributing editor to *Entertainment Law & Finance* magazine and has been head of business affairs for Polygram Music, the Welk Music Group, and the Arista-Interworld Music Groups, as well as a legal services attorney.

The Brabecs, winners of the Deems Taylor Award for excellence in music journalism, have had over 200 articles published, including the *NARAS Journal,* the *International Association of Entertainment Lawyers Handbook*; *Entertainment, Publishing, the Arts Handbook; Entertainment, Law and Finance* magazine; *The Hollywood Reporter; Playback* magazine; The New York Law Journal; Advertising Age; Canadian Musician; and Recording magazine.

The Brabecs are former recording artists as well as entertainment lawyers and are graduates of the New York University School of Law. They are adjunct professors at the USC Thornton School of Music/Music Industry Department where they teach the business of publishing, motion pictures, television, and recording. They both lecture extensively at universities, conventions, conferences, seminars, law firms, management firms, songwriter associations, business and law schools, and ad agencies on all aspects of the business and money side of music.

For more information on the music business as well as *Music, Money and Success* updates, join us on the Web at www.musicandmoney.com.